DALÍ & FILM

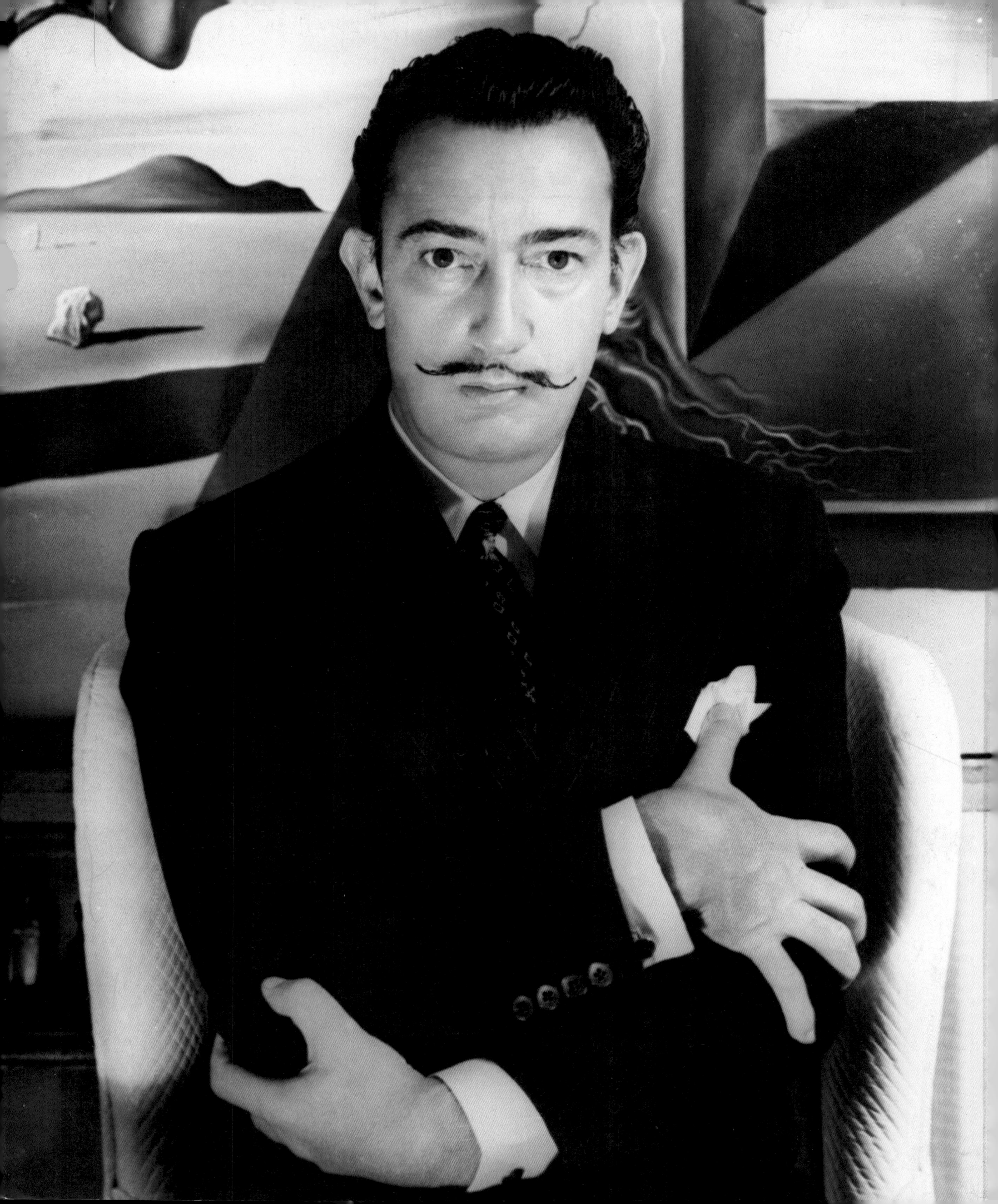

DALÍ & FILM

Edited by
Matthew Gale

Special advisors
Dawn Ades
Montse Aguer
Fèlix Fanés

Tate Publishing

First published 2007 by order of the Tate Trustees
by Tate Publishing, a division of Tate Enterprises Ltd,
Millbank, London SW1P 4RG
www.tate.org.uk/publishing

on the occasion of the exhibition
Dalí & Film
organised by Tate Modern, London,
in collaboration with Fundació Gala-Salvador Dalí,
Figueres, Spain

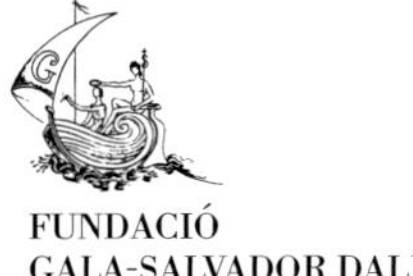

FUNDACIÓ
GALA-SALVADOR DALÍ

Tate Modern, London
1 June – 9 September 2007

Los Angeles County Museum of Art
14 October 2007 – 6 January 2008

Salvador Dalí Museum, St Petersburg, Florida
1 February – 1 June 2008

The Museum of Modern Art, New York
29 June – 15 September 2008

Exhibition at Tate Modern
With support from the Spanish Tourist Office

British Library Cataloguing in Publication Data
A catalogue record for this book is available from
the British Library

ISBN 978 1 85437 685 5 (paperback)
ISBN 978 1 85437 684 8 (hardback)

Designed by Rose
Printed in Great Britain by St Ives Westerham Press Ltd

Front cover (left): Study for the dream sequence in
Spellbound 1945 (detail, fig.106)
(right): Still from *Un Chien andalou* 1929 (detail,
fig.48a). Also reproduced on p.7
Frontispiece: Dalí on the set of *Spellbound* 1945.
Harry Ransom Humanities Research Center,
The University of Texas at Austin
Page 71: Dalí on the set of the CBS Morning Show 1956,
photographed by Philippe Halsman (detail; full image
reproduced on p.162)

Contents

Foreword by the Fundació Gala-Salvador Dalí

The aim of the Fundació Gala-Salvador Dalí is 'to promote, encourage, disseminate, enhance, protect and defend within the territory of the Spanish state and that of any other state, the artist's properties and rights of every kind; his life experience, his thoughts, his projects and ideas, and artistic, intellectual and cultural oeuvre; his memory, and universal recognition' of the contribution he made to contemporary art, culture and thought. In other words, to promote the understanding of Salvador Dalí, one of the greatest artists of recent times. The Foundation seeks to encourage scholarship, to publish essays and books and promote the dissemination of his works not only at the Dalí Theatre-Museum in Figueres but also to audiences around the world. The success of the programme of international exhibitions undertaken in recent years reflects a continuing fascination with Dalí's art in all its variety. Dalí was an artist who chose not to limit himself to a single means of expression – painting – but who consciously set about diversifying his output, working in the fields of filmmaking, illustration, engraving, sculpture, design and scenography.

Dalí's relationship with the medium of film began when he was still a child. On Sundays he would go to see films in the cinema in his native town of Figueres and he went on to play an active role in cinema through his collaboration with Luis Buñuel. And it was also with Buñuel that Dalí's forays into film came to an end. During his time in Púbol, Dalí wrote to Buñuel (c.1982–3) to suggest that they should work together again and this is how the filmmaker replied:

I received your two cables. Great idea for a film Little Demon, but I withdrew from the cinema five years ago and never go out now. A pity. Embraces – Buñuel

Dalí's relationship with film, like his relationship with other languages and forms of artistic expression, is complex and contradictory, though always demanding in terms of imagination and inventiveness. In this respect it is worth noting the interesting article, 'My Cinematographic Secrets' written by Dalí and published in *La Parisienne* on 28 February 1954, in which he states: 'If I create my film, I want to be sure that it will be, from beginning to end, a succession of wonders, because there is no point in bothering to see shows that are not sensational.' It is also interesting to note that Dalí liked to play a part both behind and in front of the camera; an outstanding example is his 'performance' in *Chaos and Creation* and the use of the camera which, as in other forms of expression, he exploits for self-promotion.

Throughout his oeuvre there are constant references and, in the case of his prolific writing, reflections, on the concept of film itself, on writing for film, on how to film; on various occasions he refers to the possibility of producing a 'tactile film' and in his autobiography *The Secret Life of Salvador Dalí* he also talks about the future of film: 'the objective visualization of virtual images that emerge from the thoughts and imagination of each individual'. These ideas will be addressed and analysed in this exhibition, both through work executed and through sketches and projects which, though uncompleted, are no less interesting.

When Vicente Todolí and Nicholas Serota approached the Foundation with the proposal to collaborate on *Dalí & Film* at Tate Modern, we welcomed the prospect of returning Dalí to Britain where he had so many friends in his lifetime – beginning with the collector Edward James in the 1930s – and where his work has always been held in high esteem. The real excitement lay in the idea of an innovative exploration of the relation between his work as a painter and his life-long love of the cinema. As the primary Centre for Dalinian Studies we have been happy to share our archives, secure loans and collaborate with the project at all levels and at all times. Thanks to this partnership, we are confident that knowledge and understanding of Dalí will be broadened. We are confident too that the exhibition will prove a revelation in London, in Los Angeles (appropriately, the home of Hollywood) in St Petersburg, Florida, and in New York. It has been a pleasure to work with the team that Tate Modern assembled and the resulting exhibition has more than fulfilled all expectations.

Montse Aguer Teixidor
Director, Centre for Dalinian Studies
Fundació Gala-Salvador Dalí

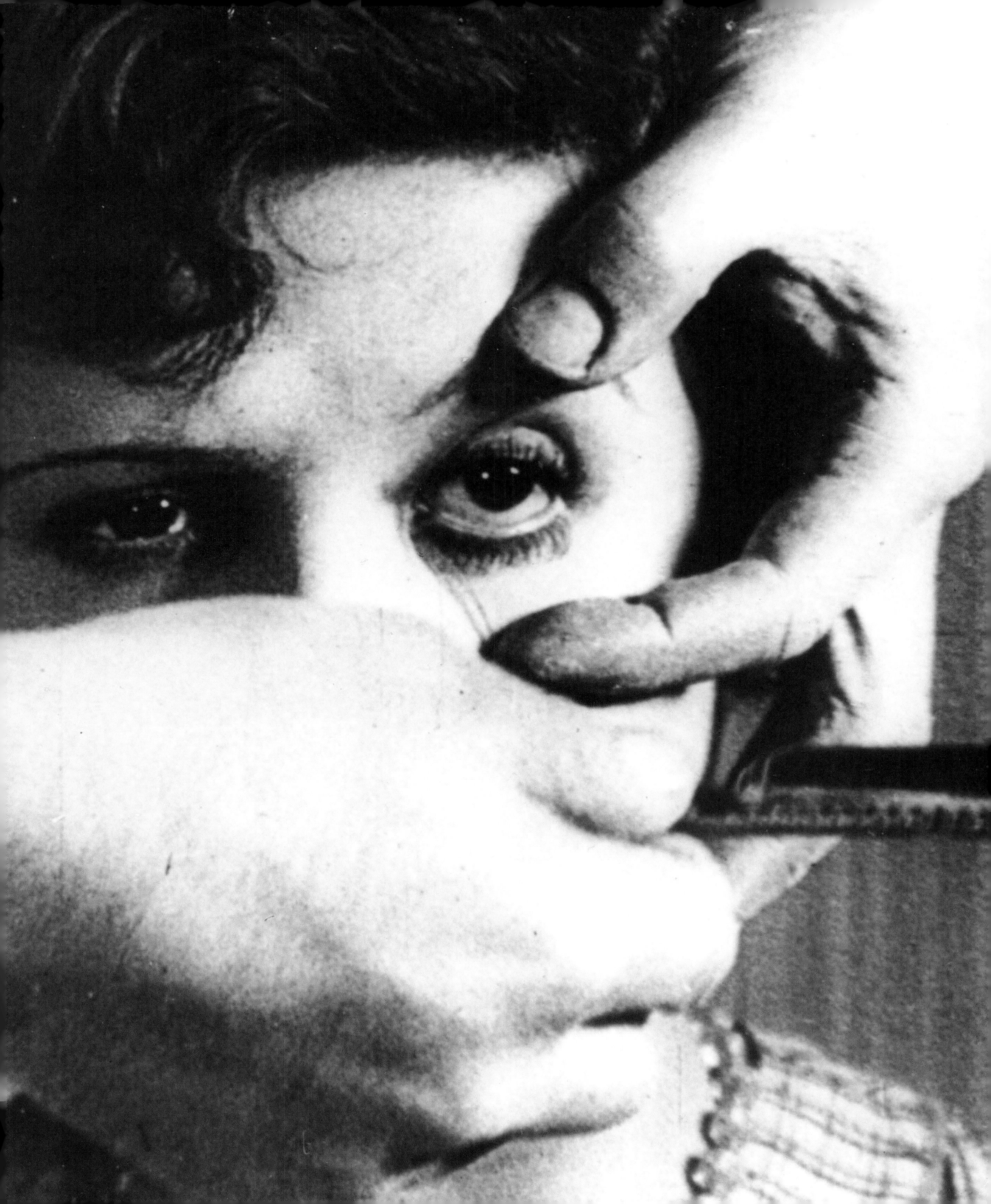

Foreword

On 1 July 1936 Salvador Dalí appeared before an audience in London to deliver a lecture entitled 'Authentic Paranoiac Phantoms'. Equipped 'to descend to the subconscious', he wore a full diving suit. The helmet was, of course, airtight. In *The Secret Life of Salvador Dalí*, he recalled the moment of realisation:

I made the most energetic gestures I could to have the helmet of my diving suit removed. Gala and Edward James ... tried to open a slit between the helmet and the suit with a billiard cue so that I would be able to breathe. Finally they brought a hammer and began to strike the bolts energetically to make them turn. At each blow I thought I would faint. The audience, for the most part, was convinced that all this was part of the show, and was loudly applauding, extremely amused at the pantomime that we were playing so realistically.[1]

Presenting himself as a Harry Houdini of the art world, Dalí's ability to attract spectacular controversy was rapidly gaining ground. He was arrested in New York three years later for deliberately breaking the shop window of his display at the Bonwit Teller store on Fifth Avenue. In the English-speaking world, at least, Dalí personified the showmanship identified with Surrealism.

Over the seventy years since his lecture at the New Burlington Galleries, the power of this self-promotion has sometimes threatened to eclipse a wider awareness of Dalí's acute intelligence, his extraordinary inventiveness and his unrivalled artistic technique. It is only relatively recently that his importance has been disentangled from this mythology. *Dalí & Film* contributes a new aspect to this reassessment by examining the internal dialogue between his work as a painter and his contribution to cinema. The imagery of his paintings is explored through time in his film projects but, equally, the spatial qualities of the cinema feed back onto the canvases.

As a child of the twentieth century, Dalí came from the first generation of artists to grow up with film and to draw upon the new medium as a natural part of their practice. It was a constant presence, constantly evolving. Louis Lumière and Georges Méliès were already establishing the new medium by the turn of the century; the first cinema was established in Figueres (showing Méliès's *A Voyage to the Moon*) in 1904, the year of Dalí's birth. A decade later the slapstick of Charlie Chaplin and Buster Keaton (who were so influential upon him) and the acrobatics of the Westerns of Tom Mix were pouring out of Hollywood for world-wide distribution.

As the exhibition and this accompanying publication lay out, Dalí's engagement with cinema was intimately allied to his career as a painter. He established his reputation in Barcelona in the 1920s through his painting, but the cross-fertilisation of imagery between different media was already apparent in his early writings. It was the potent combination of such paintings as *The First Days of Spring* and the film *Un Chien andalou*, made with Luis Buñuel, that allowed Dalí to burst upon the avant-garde in Paris in 1929. Working on paintings, scenarios and films, Dalí immersed himself within Parisian Surrealism, but there is little wonder that – on his expulsion from Surrealism in 1939 – he seized the opportunity to work in Hollywood. Varied collaborations with the Marx Brothers, Alfred Hitchcock and Walt Disney resulted, but in each project Dalí maintained his own unique vision. He balanced his pictorial practice with the potential offered by commercial studios in order to bring his ideas to larger audiences. Following this, he stepped in front of the camera in his post-war films, establishing his eccentric persona within an equally rich, if less well-known, series of projects. They confirm the continuing cross-fertilisation of ideas between different media and show how Dalí's activities relate to contemporary practice.

While the conception of *Dalí & Film* goes back many years (and there have been notable exhibitions at the Hayward Gallery in 1994 and Tate Liverpool in 1999), it is the first exhibition of Dalí's work at the Tate in London since 1980. The intervening twenty-seven years have seen the deepening of scholarship, most recently through the exhibitions in 2004 that marked the centenary of the artist's birth. Following these projects *Dalí & Film* has been welcomed with excitement and enthusiasm around the world, and I would like to thank all those – both named and anonymous – who have shown their support by lending their precious works. No exhibition is possible without this fundamental act of generosity, and this is especially true of a carefully focused project such as ours.

From its earliest stages *Dalí & Film* has benefited from the collaboration of the Fundació Gala-Salvador Dalí in Figueres, as the leading centre for Dalinian studies. We are most grateful for the openness with which the initial idea was welcomed in Figueres, and I would like to thank Ramon Boixadós, the Foundation's President, and Antoni Pitxot, Director of the Teatre-Museu Dalí, whose help has been most valuable.

The common denominators between our project and the exhibitions of 2004 have been Professor Dawn Ades and Professor Fèlix Fanés, the two leading scholars on the artist and his times, and Montse Aguer, Director of the Centre d'Estudis Dalinians. It is a measure of their dedication and knowledge that all three agreed to help us to formulate our exhibition when theirs were still underway. They were joined by Tate curators Matthew Gale (editor of this volume) and Helen Sainsbury, who have seen the project to fruition with the assistance of Cedar Lewisohn. It has been my pleasure to offer guidance at all stages to a project very close to my own interests.

I should like to add my own thanks to those expressed in the acknowledgements to all those who have offered their advice, knowledge and support. In London we have benefited from the generous advice of His Excellency the Spanish Ambassador, Carlos Miranda, and of Fernando Lanzas, the Commercial and Economic Councillor. We are also grateful for the support of Ignacio Vasallo, Director of the Spanish Tourist Office, of Miguel Angel Cusí, Director of the Catalan Tourist Board, and of José García-Velasco, President of the Sociedad Estatal de Conmemoraciones Culturales.

The catalogue, like the exhibition that it accompanies, draws widely on recent scholarship and new research. The opening essays set the scene. In her text Dawn Ades addresses the fundamental question of why Dalí turned to film at such an early stage and maintained his interest throughout his career. Fèlix Fanés traces in detail the connections to be drawn between the Dalí's 'anti-artistic' theories of the 1920s and his continuing dedication to painting in the context of the cinematic. In the third essay, Matthew Gale explores the wider context in which Dalí, Buñuel and other avant-garde filmmakers worked and measured their work. The body of the catalogue is made up of texts on individual projects contributed by the curators and by some of the leading scholars of the artist and his context: Sara Cochran, Ilene

Susan Fort, William Jeffett, Elliott H. King, Agustín Sánchez Vidal and Michael R. Taylor. In viewing Dalí's paintings through the spectrum of his film projects, the publication offers an unrivalled assessment of his career from this perspective.

Dalí & Film is distinguished in its singular focus. Its purpose is to bring together two well-known aspects of the artist's activity in a new way that is mutually revealing. In so doing the familiar is immediately seen differently, and the unfamiliar recognised as part of a wider trajectory. The integration of these different types of works make apparent continuities and richness. Dalí did not distinguish between the exploration of ideas or obsessions in one medium or another. Instead he shifted from work to work in a voracious process of auto-cannibalism. One result of *Dalí & Film* is to allow us all a glimpse of the incredible fertility of his imagination.

Vicente Todolí
Director, Tate Modern

1
Salvador Dalí, *The Secret Life of Salvador Dalí*, trans. Haakon M. Chevalier, New York 1942, London 1948, p.345.

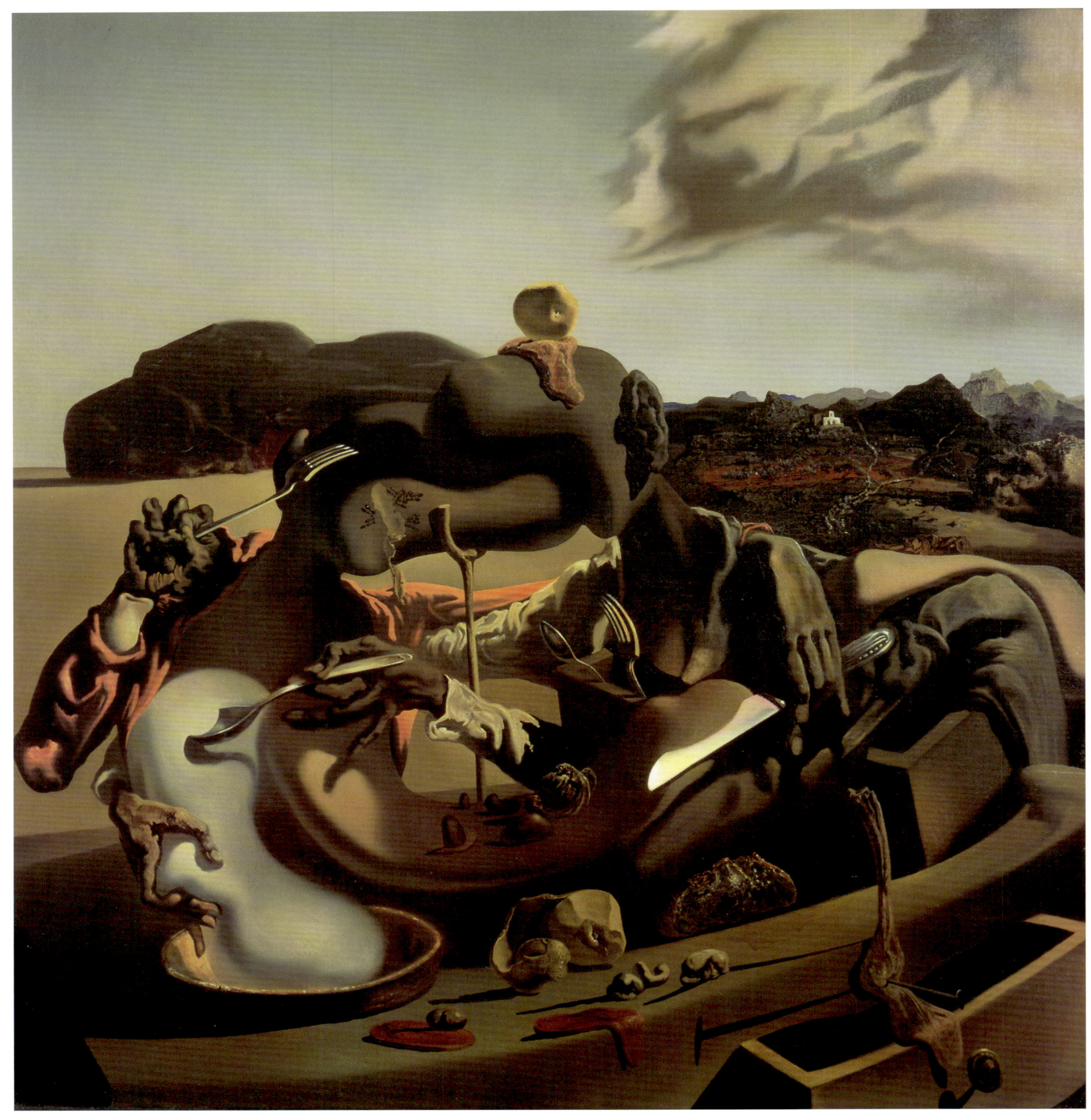

10
Autumnal Cannibalism 1936
Oil on canvas 65.1 x 65.1 cm
Tate. Purchased 1975

Acknowledgements

Salvador Dalí made images with a cool precision that belies their subversive intent. Propriety, family, convention, are all swept aside in a welter of disturbing exposures: from compliant nudes and distended appendages, to the bitter humiliation of father-figures, Dalí did not shrink from making manifest his obsessions. He drew from this deep well of desires over more than six decades, and constantly replenished it through unexpected stimuli: from photographs and architecture, to technology and unproven theories, but, most potent of all, the total immersion that came with cinema.

It has been a pleasure and a privilege to work on this major project with Dawn Ades (Professor of the History and Theory of Art, University of Essex), Montse Aguer (Director of the Centre for Dalinian Studies, Fundació Gala-Salvador Dalí, Figueres), Fèlix Fanés (Professor of the History of Art, Universitat Autònoma de Barcelona) and Helen Sainsbury (Curator, Tate Modern). Each has brought different insights to the exhibition and to this volume, and the result is the richer for that collaboration. In formulating *Dalí & Film* we have been continually fortunate in finding enthusiasm in those whom we have approached for loans. For the most part particular juxtapositions were necessary in order to capture the interconnection between Dalí's manifold activities, and we are extremely grateful for the generosity of the lenders, both private collectors and museum colleagues, without whose under–standing and commitment the exhibition would not have been possible.

The organisation of *Dalí & Film* has necessarily reflected Dalí's own passage from Spain into France, and then on to the United States. In Figueres the proposal was greeted with enthusiastic support at the Fundació Gala-Salvador Dalí. We would like to thank especially Dr Ramon Boixadós Malé, President of the Foundation, and Antoni Pitxot Soler, Director of the Teatre-Museu Dalí. We are extremely grateful for the vital impetus that they provided, and the resulting collaboration has been underpinned by the commitment of major loans from the Foundation's rich holdings and by crucial access to their extraordinary archive. We should also like to thank Joan Manuel Sevillano Campalans (the Foundation's Executive Manager) and his staff. Montse Aguer, who has been a constant source of information and advice, together with her colleagues at the Centre for Dalinian Studies have offered help and expertise with a heartening warmth.

Like Dalí, our investigations reached to all corners of Spain. We would like to acknowledge the vital help offered at various stages by the following: in Barcelona, Mariona Bruzzo Llaberia, Head of Film Archive at the Filmoteca de Catalunya, Sergi Aguilar, Director of Fundació Josep Suñol, and Teresa Ocaña i Gomà, Director of the Museu Nacional d'Art de Catalunya and her colleagues Eduard Carbonell i Estellés, General Director, Cristina Mendoza, Chief Curator, and María Jesús Cabedo in the Exhibitions Department; in Cadaqués, Pere Vehí; in La Coruña, Teresa Porto Pedrido, Director of Fundacíon Caixa Galicia; in Madrid, Juan Abelló; also in Madrid Jose María Prado, Director and Javier Herrera, Director de la Biblioteca, Archivo Gráfico y Fototeca, at the Filmoteca Española, Laura García-Lorca, President of the Fundación Federico García Lorca and Rosa María Illán; Ana Martinez de Aguilar, Director of the Museo Nacional Centro de Arte Reina Sofía and her staff; Guillermo Solana, Chief Curator at the Museo Thyssen-Bornemisza.

The international acceptance of Dalí came in Paris and, through Surrealism, then leached out internationally. We would like to thank: Tanja Kerbaum, Westdeutscher Rundfunk, Cologne, Richard Calvocoressi, former Director of the Scottish National Gallery of Modern Art in Edinburgh and his colleagues; Hans-Henrik Halfmann at Polyphon Film- und Fernseh GmbH, Hamburg; Derek Hill, London; Eric Liknaitzky, Contemporary Films, London; Christine Whitehouse, British Film Institute, London; Chrysanthi Kotrouzinis, Chief Curator of the Langen Foundation, Neuss; Alfred Pacquement, Director of the Centre Pompidou, Paris and his colleagues; the Galerie Natalie Seroussi, Paris, and Horacio Amigorena, Paris; Sjarel Ex, Director of the Museum Boijmans Van Beuningen in Rotterdam; Philip Rylands, Director of the Peggy Guggenheim Collection, Venice.

Dalí fashioned his conquest of the New World with care and secured some of his most loyal supporters there. This enthusiasm has been mirrored in the support offered in major loans by the following: Louis Grachos, Director, and Laura Fleishmann, Senior Registrar, Albright Knox Art Gallery, Buffalo; Baker Bloodworth, Vice President, Production The Walt Disney Company, Burbank and his colleagues Lella F. Smith, and Tim Cambell, former Senior Manager, Animation Research Library, Walt Disney Feature Animation; Kristen McCormick, Walt Disney Animation Research Library at Glendale; Andrea Chain, Paralegal, Buena Vista Television, Burbank; Susan J. Bandes, Director of the Kresge Art Museum, Michigan State University, East Lansing and Rachel Vargas, Registrar; Willard Holmes, Director, Wadsworth Atheneum, Hartford together with Senior Curator Eric Zafran and Associate Registrar, Mary Herbert-Busick; Josef Helfenstein, Director, The Menil Collection, Houston and his staff; Lisa Dennison, Director, Solomon R. Guggenheim Museum, New York; Philippe de Montebello, Director, Metropolitan Museum of Art, New York together with Gary Tinterow, Englehard Curator in Charge of the Department of Nineteenth-Century, Modern and Contemporary Art, and Ida Baboul, Research Associate; Glenn D. Lowry, Director, The Museum of Modern Art, New York and John Elderfield, The Marie-Josée and Henry Kravis Chief Curator, Department of Painting and Sculpture, and their colleagues; Pierre Théberge, O.C., C.Q., Director, National Gallery of Canada, Ottawa; Anne d'Harnoncourt, Director, Philadelphia Museum of Art and Innis Howe Shoemaker, The Audrey and William H. Helfand Senior Curator of Prints, Drawing and Photographs; Thomas Sokolowski, Director, The Andy Warhol Museum, Pittsburgh and Geralyn Huxley, Curator of Film and Video; Neal Benezra, Director, San Francisco Museum of Modern Art; David L. Prince, Curator, Syracuse University Art Collection; and for their exceptional generosity and help Hank Hine, Director and the Trustees and staff of the Salvador Dalí Museum, St Petersburg.

One of the benefits of working on a great exhibition when it tours to other institutions is the close contact with colleagues and it has been a great pleasure to work with those at the Los Angeles County Museum of Art, the Salvador Dalí Museum, St Petersburg and the Museum of Modern Art in New York who have been intimately involved in receiving the exhibition in the United States.

At LACMA it has been a pleasure to start the project with Bruce Robertson, former Deputy Director of Art Programs and Chief Curator, Center for American Art, and Irene Martín, Assistant Director, Exhibition Programs, and to work closely with Ilene Susan Fort, The Gail and John Liebes Curator of American Art, and Sara Cochran, Assistant Curator, Modern Art. They and their colleagues have masterminded the arrival of *Dalí & Film* in America with an attention to detail that the painter would have admired. In their various capacities, not least their command of the US Federal Government Indemnity Scheme, we should like to thank: Ian Birnie, Head of Film Programs; Stephanie Dyas, Director, Government and Foundation Relations; Carol S. Eliel, Curator of Modern and Contemporary Art, Roz Leader, Research Assistant; Sarah Minnaert, Financial Analyst, Exhibition Programs; Renée Montgomery, Assistant Director, Collections Management and Information; Alexandra Moran, Assistant Registrar; Devi Noor, Curatorial Administrator; Nancy Sutherland, Balch Research Library; VanAn Tranchi, Senior Grant Writer. Special thanks are due to Blake Koh of Sotheby's for his time and effort. In St Petersburg, the centre of Dalinian activities in the USA, we have been in regular contact with Hank Hine, Director, and his colleagues who helped in many capacities to bring new aspects to the project. We should thank Joan Kropf, Curator of the Collection, William Jeffett, Curator of Exhibitions, Peter Tush, Curator of Education, and Assistant Curator Dirk Armstrong. At The Museum of Modern Art, *Dalí & Film* has been welcomed by Glenn Lowry, Director, and John Elderfield, The Marie-Josée and Henry Kravis Chief Curator, Department of Painting and Sculpture, and it has been a pleasure to work with Jennifer Russell, Senior Deputy Director for Exhibitions, Collections and Programs, Jodi Hauptman, Associate Curator, Department of Drawings and Anne Morra, Assistant Curator in the Department of Film.

The catalogue has benefited from new research and thinking by all the authors which will extend beyond the exhibition. It has been a pleasure to share in this adventure with colleagues who have been generous with their knowledge at all times. In particular Elliott H. King's research in support of the catalogue, in addition to his contribution, has been most valuable. Advice and help of different sorts has also come from: Ned Comstock, The Cinema-Television Library, University of Southern California; Dennis Copeland, Monterey Public Library; Catherine

Forni, Geneva; Paul Hammond; Neal Hotelling, Pebble Beach Company; David Lomas; Ulla and Heiner Pietzsch, Berlin; Conchita Romero, Madrid; James Roundell, London; Valerie Smith, Queens Museum of Art; Maria Wainscoat, Monterey.

Despite his busy schedule Vicente Todolí has been intimately involved with the exhibition from its inception. At Tate Modern *Dalí & Film* would not have been possible without Helen Sainsbury's admirable calm. We have also been helped at every stage by a core team of Cedar Lewisohn, Assistant Curator and Inspire Fellow, who has provided essential support, Stephen Dunn, Registrar and Stephen Mellor, Co-ordinator Exhibitions and Displays. Stuart Comer, a constant source of help, has conceived the film programme that runs alongside the exhibition. At various moments we benefited from the help and advice of Jane Burton, Jennifer Mundy, Sophie Oliver, Nicholas Serota, Patricia Smithen, Sheena Wagstaff, and colleagues too numerous to mention in Art Handling, Communications, Conservation, Development, Exhibitions and Displays, Front of House, Press Office, and Registrars. The present volume has been masterminded at Tate Publishing by Judith Severne, Project Editor, with her usual combination of calm and attention to detail, and is indebted to colleagues there including Sarah Brown, Senior Production Controller, and Beth Thomas who replaced Alessandra Serri on picture research, as well as the skillful copy editing of Melissa Larner. First Edition Translations Ltd coordinated the elegant translations by Alayne Pullen. Advice and help of many different sorts has come from Roger Thorp, Publishing Director, James Attlee, Sales and Rights Director, and Celia Clear, Chief Executive, Tate Enterprises. The sensitivity to the project shown by Simon Elliott and Terry Stephens at Rose Design is evident in the beautifully designed catalogue.

Such a project would undoubtedly have been much the poorer without the expertise and professionalism of many others. They are too numerous to name, but each effort has been very much appreciated.

Matthew Gale

Why Film?

Dawn Ades

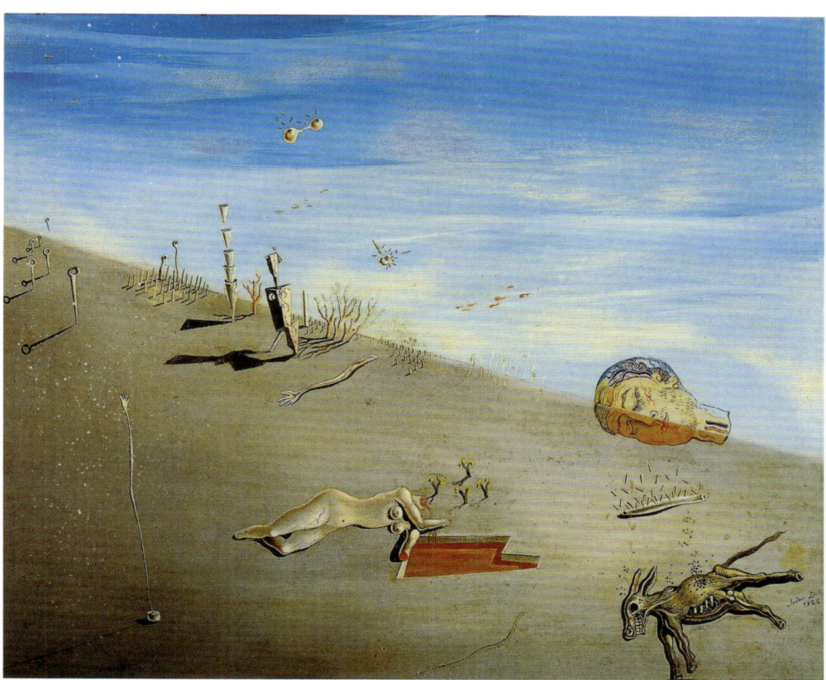

Salvador Dalí grew up during the great age of the silent film, when even small towns had at least one cinema and cine-clubs abounded. Film absorbed the old optical amusements of the nineteenth century and changed dramatically in Dalí's lifetime, with the advent of sound and of colour, animation, experiments with stereoscopic film (the Todd-AO high-definition format, for example), wraparound sound, television and video. He kept pace with the technological advances, was closely involved in one of the earliest European talkies, and made arguably the first artist's video.[1] He never gave up the struggle to work in film, proposing documentaries, sketching out scenarios, contributing to Hollywood movies, enthusiastically exploring animation, and treading an ambiguous line between directing and starring in cinematic adventures of many kinds. The story of his affair with film is in some ways one of disappointments, over-ridden by endless optimism.

Dalí knew, however, from a very early age, that he wanted to be a painter. As a child, the images of the great painters of the past were as real to him as his actual surroundings, and as an adolescent he lived for the summers in Cadaqués, where his indulgent family rented a studio and he could devote himself to painting. We know this from his own diaries of the time because even then, despite his absolute commitment to pigments and canvas, he also loved writing.[2] Indeed, he wrote almost as obsessively as he painted. Film, the 'Seventh Art', as it was regularly called in *La Gaceta Literaria* in the 1920s, occupies a very interesting position for

Dalí in relation to image and text. Though potentially antagonistic to painting, film was a medium in which he could draw both on his visual and his verbal skills in the service of his imagination, and there is a constant triangulation formed by the flow of film, painting and text.

Was there, for Dalí, a special appeal in film? Was it an alternative to his paintings, adaptable to certain effects beyond the reach of the canvas? Was it an extension of the pictorial image, or rather of his writings? Or was it just one of the many media that he utilised to give expression to ideas that had their own dynamic?

Reviewing Dalí's multifarious cinematic projects, it is curious how few saw the light of the screen. Following the great, if controversial, successes of the collaborations with Luis Buñuel – *Un Chien andalou* (An Andalusian Dog, 1929) and *L'Age d'or* (The Golden Age, 1930) – only the dream sequence of Alfred Hitchcock's *Spellbound* 1945, the video *Chaos and Creation* (directed by Philippe Halsman, 1960), the television film *Impressions de la Haute Mongolie – Hommage à Raymond Roussel* (Impressions of Upper Mongolia – Homage to Raymond Roussel, 1975) and the autobiographical *L'Autoportrait mou de Salvador Dalí* (Soft Self-Portrait of Salvador Dalí, 1967), directed by Jean-Christophe Averty, were realised in his lifetime. The only scenario, apart from *Un Chien andalou* and *L'Age d'or*, published in full at the time was *Babaouo*, in 1932. The footage shot for a major film, *L'Histoire prodigieuse de la dentellière et du rhinocéros*

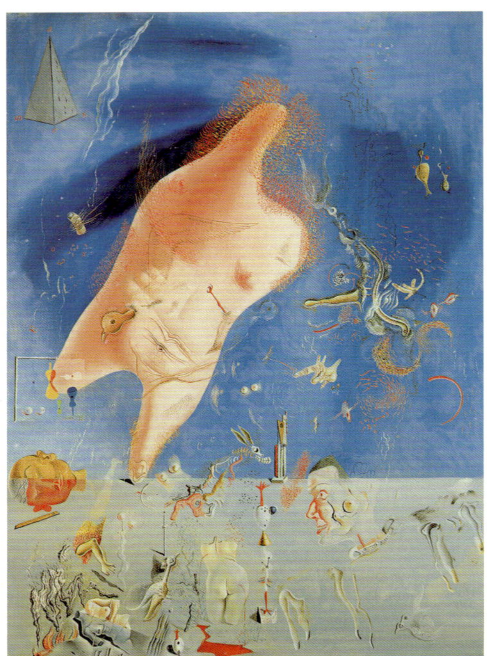

(The Prodigious Adventure of the Lacemaker and the Rhinoceros), remained unedited at his death, as did the animation for the Disney film *Destino* 1946. But many scenarios, fragmentary sketches and ideas for films lurk among Dalí's manuscripts, eleven of the most complete of which have now been translated into Spanish in the *Obra Completa* (Complete Works).[3] These, along with his writings about as well as for film, numerous cinematic and television projects that range from collaborations with the New York avant-garde to the NODO news films in Franco's Spain, testify to his unbroken desire to work in this medium.

How, then, to account for the disparity between idea and realisation? The only two fully realised films in which Dalí had a major role were *Un Chien andalou* and *L'Age d'or*, both undeniable masterpieces. The absence of a Buñuel in Dalí's subsequent projects was clearly fundamental, and there was also an increasing gap between Dalí's notion of cinema's potential to be the bearer of his ideas and the actual demands of the industry. The place of film in his thinking about art altered over time. Having enthusiastically embraced film and photography in 1927, he eventually voiced his disillusionment in the face of the massive increase in the complexity of production: 'I don't believe that cinema can ever become an artistic form. It is a secondary form because too many people are involved in its creation. The only true means of producing a work of art is painting, in which only the eye and the point of the brush are employed.'[4]

Film and photography were initially key weapons in his polemic against the old, picturesque and 'artistic', and his fervent support of modernity. This is clear from the declarations in the *Manifest groc* of 1928:

THERE IS the cinema
THERE ARE stadia, boxing, rugby, tennis
and a thousand other sports
THERE IS the popular music of today:
jazz and modern dance …

THERE ARE art exhibitions of modern artists
THERE ARE moreover, great engineering
and some magnificent ocean liners …

THERE IS the gramophone, which is
a little machine
THERE IS the camera, which is another
little machine …

WE DENOUNCE young people who seek
to repeat painting of the past
WE DENOUNCE old, authentic architecture
WE DENOUNCE decorative art, unless it is
standardized.[5]

Dalí's theoretical texts between 1927 and 1929 about film and photography distinguish firmly between 'artistic' and 'anti-artistic' film, the latter, encompassing Mack Sennett and comics like Buster Keaton, the only kind he approves. 'The anti-artistic film … reveals … the entirely new poetic emotion of all the most humble and immediate facts, which were impossible to imagine or foresee before cinema'.[6] While not necessarily directly challenging painting, the camera reveals a different reality. 'The world of cinema and the world of painting are very different; clearly, the possibilities of photography and cinema are to be found in that unlimited imagination which is born of things themselves.'[7] In practice, Dalí continued to experiment with painting, and his article 'Film-arte, film anti-artistico' (Art Film, Antiartistic Film, 1927; see pp.72–4) was accompanied by an illustration of a recent painting, *Honey Is Sweeter than Blood* 1927 (see fig.2), and a drawing of a head, both with the caption 'Cinematismo de Dalí' (Dalí's Cinematism). He considered his paintings 'anti-artistic', like the films he admired, and it was only in 1929 that he threatened to abandon painting, choosing to illustrate the final issue of the journal *L'Amic de les Arts* only with photographs.

There are two dimensions to Dalí's theories on film and cinema. First, the simple insistence on 'things themselves', on the world of facts presented by the camera. In Dalí's own work, it was his poems and poetic texts that respond most directly to this limitless arena, and which mediate between film and painting. He questioned the traditional poetic use of image and metaphor as being anecdotal and soluble like a riddle, and prefers the pure enumeration of facts. Lists, and the profusion of 'small things', as Haim Finkelstein has argued, were the common ground in Dalí's paintings and his poetry at this time.[8] In 'Poem: to Lydia of Cadaqués', Dalí lists a succession of disparate objects: 'Near the cold boulder there lies an eyelash / A torn piece of flesh signalling bad weather.'[9] The accumulation of details and their scattering in an indeterminate space recalls paintings such as *Cenicitas (Little Ashes)* 1928 (fig.3) and *Honey Is Sweeter than Blood*.

The second dimension to the new reality revealed for Dalí by film and photography concerns its imaginative possibilities, which are still rooted in fact. Film and photography have introduced a new way of looking:

Knowing how to look is a way of inventing … The camera has immediate practical possibilities, for new themes where painting necessarily remains only in the experience and understanding. Photography glides with continual imagination over new events, which in the pictorial realm have only possibilities for being signs.[10]

The objectivity of the lens *is* contemporary poetry: it is the 'Glass of real poetry'.[11]

First poet of all PICASSO
There are no poets who write
The best paint or make film. Buster,
Harry Langdon.[12]

This 'photographic imagination' owes much to technical possibilities, such as the close-up and

Below:
4
Abstract Composition 1928
Oil on canvas 148 x 198 cm
Museo Nacional Centro de
Arte Reina Sofía, Madrid

Right:
5
Untitled 1928
Oil on canvas with collage
148 x 198 cm
Museo Nacional Centro de
Arte Reina Sofía, Madrid

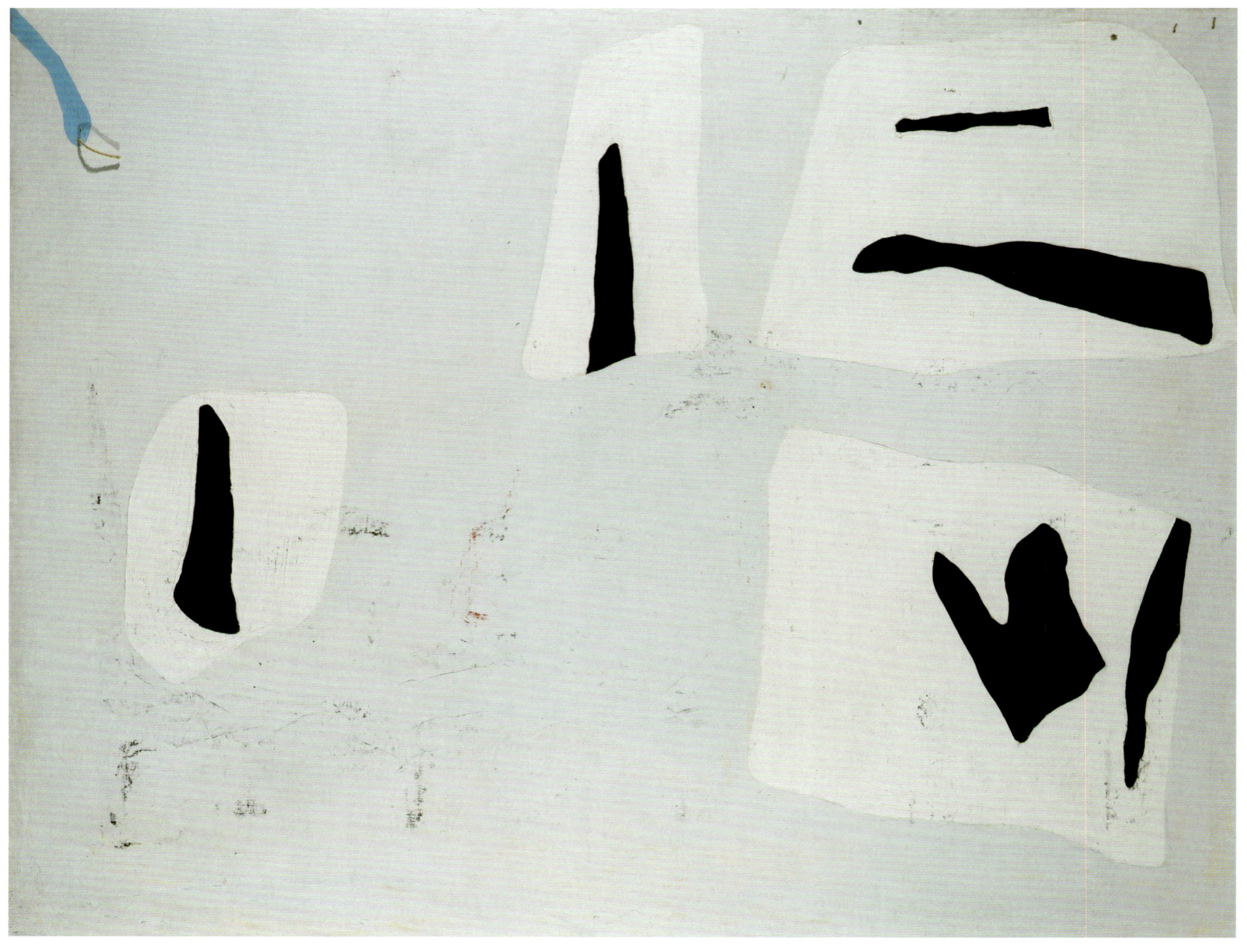

slow motion. The poetic magic of the 'film-fact' comes from its ability to transform the reality we see before our eyes. Seizing on László Moholy-Nagy's notion, in his influential Bauhaus book *Malerei Fotografie Film* (*Painting Photography Film*) 1925, that the camera is an extension of 'our optical instrument, the eye',[13] Dalí emphasised its transformative powers: 'A lump of sugar on the screen can *become* larger than an infinite perspective of gigantic buildings.'[14] One of the photographs in the last issue of *L'Amic de les Arts* was filched by Dalí from *Painting Photography Film*, a close-up of the eye of a marabou (mistitled by Dalí 'Ull d'elefant' – elephant's eye.) The inventive visuality of the close-up was explored in *Un Chien andalou*, for instance in the sequence magnifying the death's head hawk moth. It was an image that endured: one of the most striking passages in his late film *L'Histoire prodigieuse … is the attempt to film gooseflesh close-up on a female breast.

In his text 'Photography, Pure Creation of the Mind', Dalí contrasts painting more brutally with photography and film. 'The photographic crystal can caress the cold delicacy of white lavatories, follow the sleepy slowness of aquaria … In painting on the other hand, if you want to paint a jellyfish, it is absolutely necessary to depict a guitar or a harlequin playing the clarinet.'[15] Perhaps in the reference to aquaria he has in mind the extraordinary films of Jean Painlevé, where extreme close-ups of a shrimp, for example, render it completely unrecognisable and virtually abstract.[16] Dalí's point seems to be that to rival the 'photographic marvellous', which resides in the fact, painting can only resort to fantasy, symbol and substitution.

Despite the superiority, in his own arguments, of the camera, Dalí was not prepared to abandon painting. Recognition that cinematic effects were beyond the reach of painting did not stop him experimenting, and in pictures like *Honey Is Sweeter Than Blood* and especially *Cenicitas*. In the latter, he represents the metamorphosis of forms; towering over the scattered fragments of bodies (torso and breasts painted with photographic realism) and 'little things' is a large pink shape that emerges from a curved guitar-torso and seems to be in the process of mutating. The swirling blue sky of *Apparatus and Hand* 1927 (fig.18), together with the floating objects, convey, if only distantly, an urge for mobility. After this brief tussle with the 'cinematic', Dalí came into line with contemporary Surrealist/modernist modes, introduced real materials such as sand or a piece of cork into his works, and then launched into the extraordinary 'anti-paintings' of 1928, which seemed to retreat as far as possible from the 'photographic fact' (figs.4, 5). It is possible that he came to regard these large, sometimes almost blank canvases, as failed experiments since he thrust them away in the corner of his studio. Although the influence of Joan Miró and Hans Arp is evident in the amorphous shapes, they could also be an attempt to represent forms of plant and animal life as

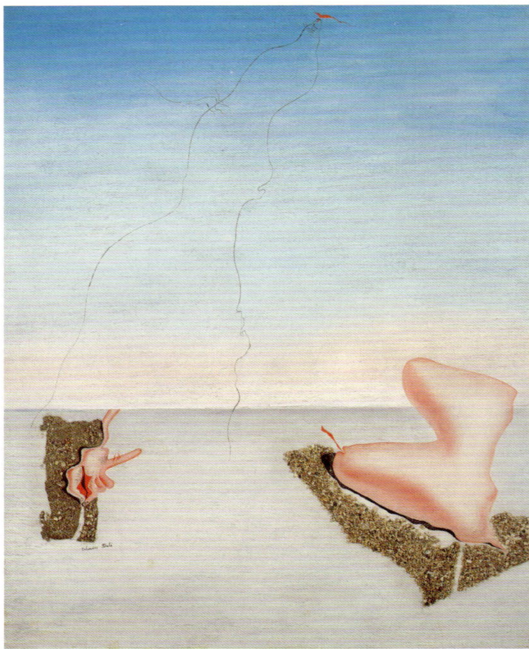

revealed by microscopic lens, slow motion or close-ups. Dalí was himself a passionate observer of nature, studying the creatures in the shallows and rocks around Cadaqués, and his forms have a curious resemblance to the 'plant-animals' of the botanist Frederick Keeble.[17] The exaggerated blobs, spidery and crab-like marks, elongated forms like late-evening shadows are also often highly sexualised body fragments. On some of these canvases Dalí stuck sand, feathers or wire, material supplements to the spare abstracted shapes – which, often thickly painted, give the illusion of being pasted paper.

The abrupt change that his paintings then underwent marks a watershed in his career, coinciding with the culmination of his intense theoretical interest in film in his collaboration with Buñuel on the script and direction of *Un Chien andalou* in early 1929. Simultaneously, he wrote a remarkable series of short 'Documentary' texts, which he sent from Paris to the Catalan newspaper *La Publicitat*, and returned to a visually realist mode of painting, distinct from the 1927–8 paintings and clearly a response to his experience of film-making with Buñuel.[18]

In the 'Documentary' texts, he further developed his ideas about the factual, now fully under the aegis of Surrealism. In the first of these, after announcing that Benjamin Péret (the poet whom he most admired) was to make a documentary film in Brazil, Dalí explained that, contrary to popular opinion, there was nothing antagonistic between rigorously objective documentary and Surrealist texts, which:

coincide from the outset in their essentially anti-artistic and more particularly anti-literary process … The documentary notes things said of the objective world anti-literarily. In parallel fashion the Surrealist text transcribes with the same rigour and as anti-literarily as documentary, the REAL free functioning of thought, of events which occur in reality in our mind, thanks to psychic automatism and to other passive states (inspiration).[19]

Promising not to write another line of theory and denouncing 'description' as 'immoral next to the marvellous means of photography and cinema', Dalí devoted himself to documenting facts. In a 20 cm square (like a film frame or photographic plate), drawn in the wet sand of the Luxembourg Gardens, he saw in succession: 'the heel of a man's shoe, the tip of a woman's shoe … the shadow of a wisp of smoke … a plant fibre flying slowly … two simultaneous drops of liquid, yet another drop of liquid, a small submarine pulled by a string, a fallen linden leaf'.[20] Prefacing this (and breaking his promise not to theorise) was a comment on recent research about the synchronicity of diverse phenomena; 'a lion's yawn, a bud opening on an acacia branch, a passer's-by steps, an ostrich's tracks, an insect's flight, the submersion of a jellyfish' share an algebraic proportion that established 'a certain rhythmic relation to which everything is subject'.[21]

This rhythmic relation fascinated Dalí, and he returned to the idea in later scenarios; however, when he asked Buñuel what value the latter placed on 'scenario, star, editing, rhythm, photo, lighting', Buñuel said he gave absolute importance to photography and editing, but as for rhythm, 'I don't know what that is'.[22] Although in Dalí's 1929 'Documentary' the synchronicity between these phenomena was to do with movement, formal rhythms – such as that noted by the naturalist D'Arcy Thompson in *On Growth and Form* 1912 – continued to fascinate him.[23] The equiangular or logarithmic spiral, which as Thompson notes is a mathematical law of growth manifest in horns, the florets of a sunflower, the Nautilus shell, was the morphological link between various objects in Dalí's later work that seem quite disconnected. The rhinoceros horn was one of these, and the origin of *L'Histoire prodigieuse …* lay in his 'discovery' of the same shape in Vermeer's *The Lacemaker*.

Film and photography entered the avant-garde consciousness in the 1920s. Despite Dalí's denunciation of what he called 'artistic film', *Un Chien andalou* and his own ideas about photography and film, which centre on the capacity of the lens, of close-up and slow motion to make the 'photographic *donnée*' strange, as well as the 'gags' of comedy, owe a great deal to the experimental pioneers like Walter Ruttman, Dziga Vertov and Moholy-Nagy. There are echoes of Ruttman's *Berlin: Symphony of a City* 1927, for instance, or Sergei Eisenstein's *October* 1927, in *Un Chien andalou*.

In his painting *The First Days of Spring* (fig.7), which inaugurates his 'return to the image' in 1929, Dalí translated his ideas about the 'document' into a variety of modes of visual recording: actual photographs, including himself as a little boy, stencils, a ready-made coloured print of a scene on board an ocean liner. Here, and even more strikingly in succeeding paintings from 1929 like *The Lugubrious Game* and *The Accommodations of Desire* (figs.8, 35), paint and photograph, or collage, are indistinguishable from one another. Sometimes, as in *Lugubrious Game*, the photographs are unrecognisable close-ups of natural objects. In the lower left of *The First Days of Spring*, the scandalous scene of a masturbating man beside a woman with flayed face buzzing with flies appears superimposed on the illustration of deck jollities, as though it is a zoom-in on a couple from that scene. Separate pictorial incidents are scattered over the surface, and though they broadly adhere to a scale determined by the non-cinematic principle of perspective (its exaggerated return here perhaps a reassertion of an especially painterly technique), their relationship follows a rhythm similar to montage sequences in *Un Chien andalou*. In *The Accommodations of Desire*, the successive images of the lion's head, hair and ants imposed on the pebbles on the beach quote part of one such sequence: 'Close up of the hand full of ants crawling out of a black hole in the palm … Dissolve to the hairs on the armpit of a young woman … Dissolve to the undulating spines of a sea-urchin. Dissolve to the head of a girl seen directly from above.'[24] Such chains of images are themselves related to descriptions of the shifting perception of an object in the prose piece 'My girlfriend and the beach': 'the new-born baby was no other than my girlfriend's pink breast … it was not her breast either: it was little pieces of cigarette paper'.[25] They also contributed to the development of one of Dalí's key concepts, the 'paranoiac-critical method'.

While Dalí's notion of critical paranoia was to be one of the most significant mechanisms linking his painting to film, there are other aspects to his work of the 1930s that have a complex relationship with film. Awareness of its power to create and manipulate another reality in time is countered by an exaggerated emphasis on the particular qualities of the static pictorial image. The re-assertion of perspective, for example, was not a return to pre-Cubist realism but, in a manner not unlike Marcel Duchamp's 'rehabilitation' of perspective in *The Large Glass* 1915–23, unmasked its artificiality while capitalising on its illusions. Sometimes Dalí used incompatible perspectives, as Giorgio de Chirico had done, and often exaggerated the effect of perspective on landscapes, buildings and objects, with forms dizzily receding. In *The First Days of Spring*, dramatic central receding lines mark the steps of a giant platform; they also resemble railway lines or even the rails of a tracking camera.

Often, perspective, which traditionally functioned to centre and harmonise a composition, was used to precisely the opposite purpose. In *Vertigo* 1930 (private collection) and *The Bleeding Roses* 1930 (fig.9), the sharp side of the building, visible at the very edge of the canvas, drops terrifyingly into empty space. Suspense and sensations of awe or fear, at which film is so adept, are conjured here through the manipulation of painting techniques. The impression of vast spaces and great hollow depths is emphasised by the use of shadows and violent differences in the relative size of objects. Perspective was drawn into the personal drama of such images as *The Font* 1930 (fig.74), or the paintings related to the 'Angelus' series, in which figures and objects are represented in miniature or loom as enormous, so that scale is disrupted and irrational (fig.132). Dalí also used the trope of the screen to reflect on the relationship between film and painting. Several paintings of the early 1930s feature a suspended sheet, which functions as screen and shield. Sometimes, as in *The Old Age of William Tell* 1931 (fig.10), shadows from an unseen form are cast on the screen. It is plausible that he was making a reference to the scene in Raymond Roussel's book *Impressions d'Afrique* (Impressions of Africa, 1910), where a lost character is made to appear by virtue of a moving shadow cast on a white cloth, one of many games between illusion and reality in the play. In Dalí's paintings, typically, associations multiply and the sheet becomes shroud or toga, hiding the body in formless drapes recalling the standing figure in the boat in Arnold Böcklin's painting *Isle of the Dead* 1883.

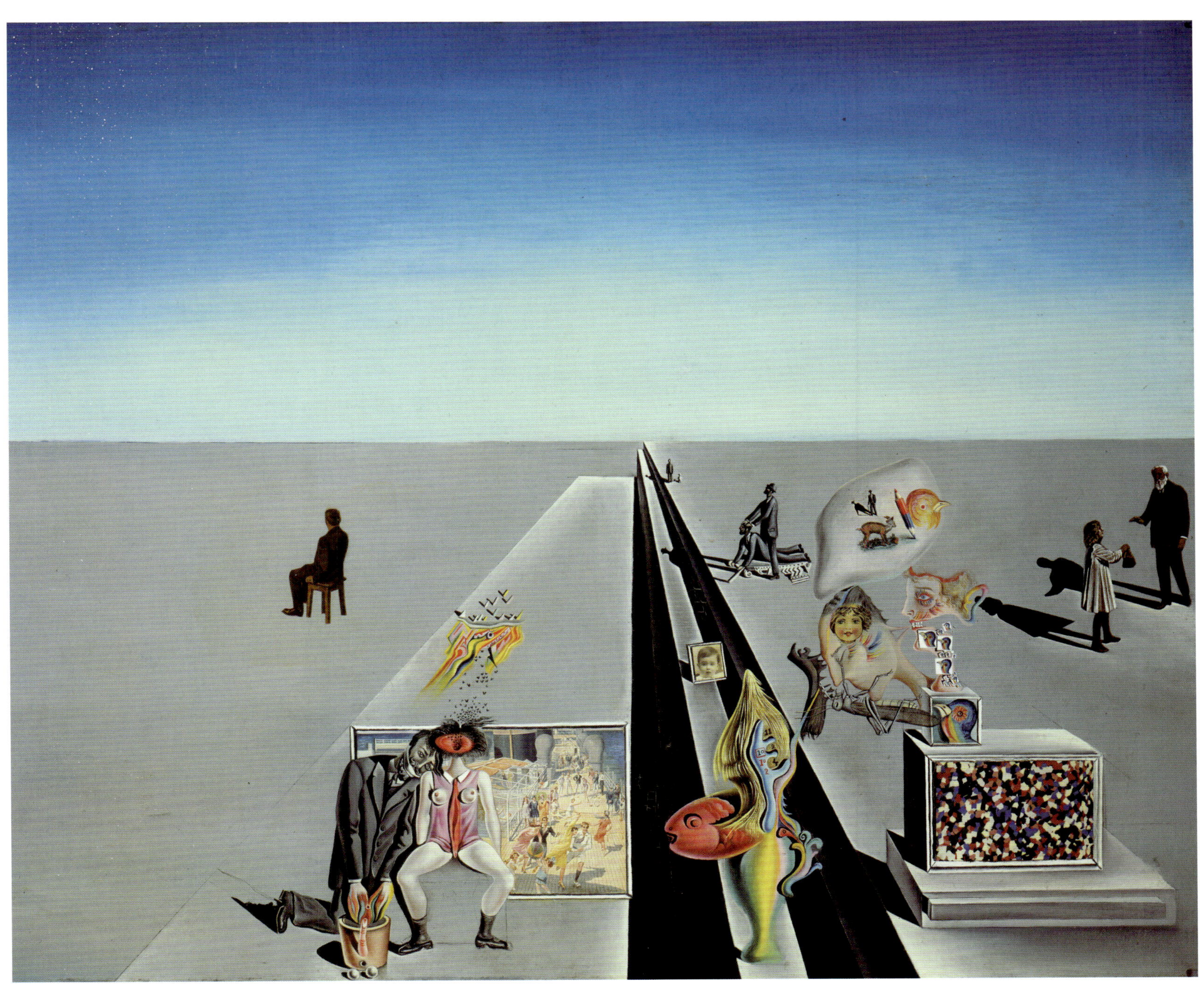

7
The First Days of Spring 1929
Oil and collage on panel
50.2 x 65.1 cm
Salvador Dalí Museum,
St Petersburg, Florida

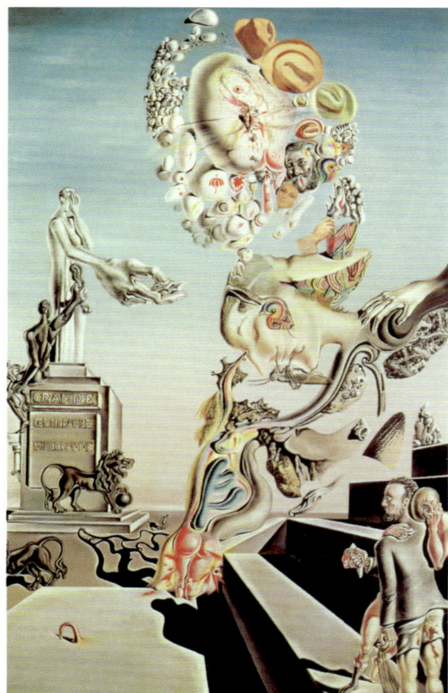

Dalí's concept of the paranoiac mechanism, 'from which is born the image of multiple figuration',[26] was to have a long and profound impact on his paintings, writings and his involvement in film. It was based, not on the common understanding of paranoia as persecution complex, but on an idea widespread in the literature of psychology and psychoanalysis at the time of a mental condition in which the subject interprets his or her surroundings according to an over-riding obsession, in a 'delirium of interpretation' that creates an alternative virtual 'reality'. This delirium was not arbitrary but, according to Dalí's associate Jacques Lacan, rooted in unconscious and suppressed emotions or desires, hence for Dalí potentially a 'document' for interpretation.[27] Critical paranoia was a rich source for Dalí, the inspiration for one of his most powerful texts, *The Tragic Myth of Millet's Angelus* c.1933[28] and for a series of paintings with multiple readings like *The Endless Enigma* 1938 (Museo Nacional, Centro de Arte Reina Sofía, Madrid). The moving image was potentially a particularly apt medium; he described the scenario *La Carretilla de carne* (The Wheelbarrow of Flesh, 1948–52) as 'the first paranoiac film', and *Destino* was almost entirely planned around this visual device.[29]

Dalí did not at first exploit film's potential in this context. In his documentary on Surrealism (*Cinq Minutes à propos de surréalisme*) he proposes mobile graphics to illustrate his paranoiac method.[30] A sequence of six drawings based on his painting *Invisible Woman, Horse, Lion* 1930 (figs.62, 63), are disposed horizontally in two columns to show the successive readings of the woman as horse and then as lion. However, what he is concerned with is the 'delirious interpretation' of the single configuration: the odalisque is at the same time horse and lion. The paranoiac reading is not a progressive transformation from a to c; the odalisque becomes horse, reappears and becomes lion. Cinematic movement can therefore demonstrate the mechanism diagrammatically but is not, at this point anyway, a substitute for the pictorial image. The reversible switch, the 'duck-rabbit' effect, in which alternative readings oscillate but are not simultaneous, as in some of Dalí's most perfected paranoiac images such as *Apparition of a Face and Fruit Dish on a Beach* 1938 (Wadsworth Atheneum, Hartford, Conn.), inheres in the static configuration of the painting.[31]

Although there is a link with the transformative imagery of earlier paintings and sequences in *Un Chien andalou*, film was not at this point for Dalí the inevitable destination of his 'critical paranoia'. The nightmare sequence that he devised for the film *Moontide* would have included a startling instance of a 'paranoiac' double image fully conceived for film, rather than the reversible pictorial image, with the needle-threatened eye becoming at the last moment the globe of the sun,[32] and *Destino* is a brilliant fusion of classic cartoon animation and Dalí's 'double images'. However, it was in *Impressions de la Haute*

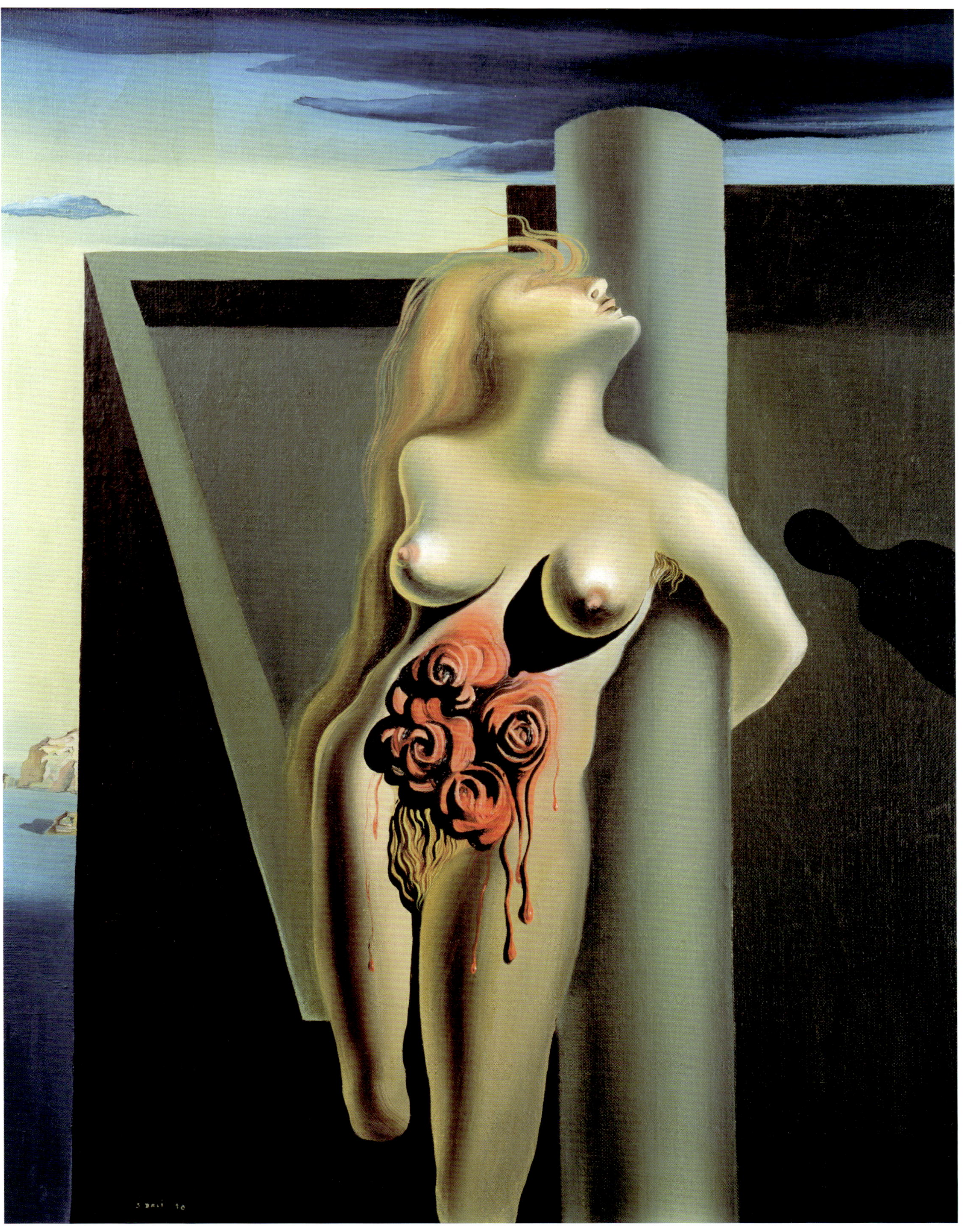

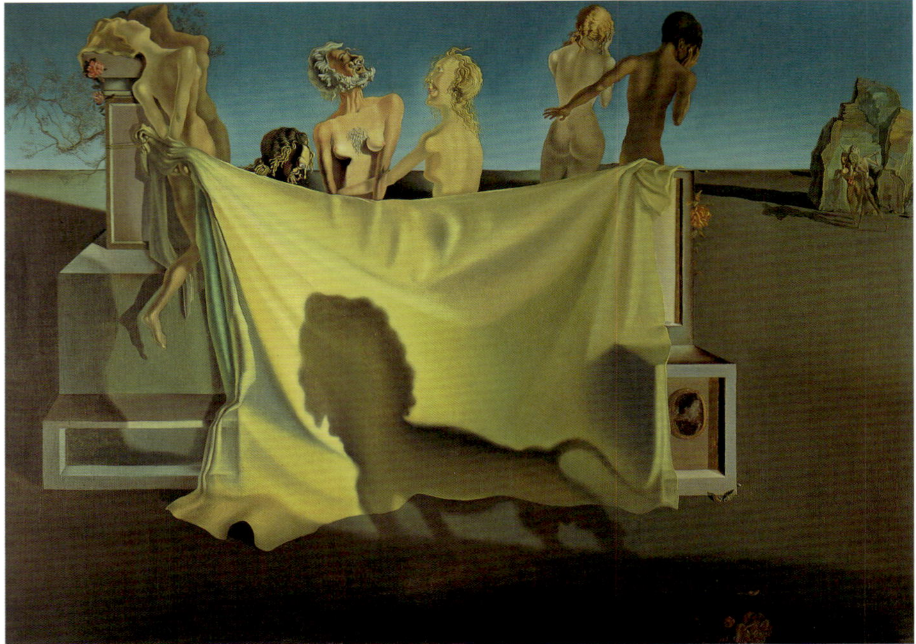

Mongolie that Dalí found an original cinematic outlet for 'delirious interpretation'. This film made for television united his long-term interest in close-up – to which he had also returned in *L'Histoire prodigieuse …* – with imaginary readings-in on a grand scale. Landscapes, animated scenes, figures and heads emerge into focus and mutate out of colourful, formless mass not unlike an unusually abstract 'impressionist' landscape. It is revealed at the end that all has been constructed from the close-up filming of the metallic band round a biro, the band pitted and stained, apparently, with uric acid.[33]

Dalí's film projects, which exist in various states from full scenarios to scattered notes, addressed pretty well every potential function of the medium, including documentary, epic and the 'impossible' scenario. The latter, of which Benjamin Péret's 'Pulchérie veut une auto' (Bonny wants a car) 1923 is a fine extended example, is closely related to the animated cartoon. 'Pulchérie veut une auto' flies off from comic-film gags into an extraordinary fairy tale of extreme and hilarious violence.[34] As in animated cartoons, figures suffer appalling accidents or die and come blithely back to life; objects and limbs mutate and transform, all effects that were unrealisable in the physical medium of cinema proper, where even the most inventive tricks and stunt comedians 'could not fully dissolve … into the celluloid world'.[35] Some scenes in *Babaouo* resemble the

'impossible' scenario, such as the horrific accident after which Babaouo, blind, gropes for his beloved Mathilde. Touching a cushion, he thinks he has found her body, and kisses her 'head and hair', which is only the loose insides of the cushion. Crying 'You are alive!' he embraces the embers of the cushion, which is now on fire. Horribly burned, he throws it away screaming 'Shit!'[36]

Cartoons signalled a new direction for experimental artists and filmmakers in the 1920s, and many avant-garde film projects combine forms of graphic animation with photographic montage. How far Dalí was aware in the 1920s of early animated cartoons like *Felix the Cat* is unclear. The plasmic, stretching and convulsing line of cartoon drawing, form changing into formlessness and back again in the twinkling of an eye, might have melded with his passion for Art Nouveau or Catalan Modernista architecture to inform his melting shapes. Certainly Eisenstein, whose own drawings were 'pseudo-pods of the primal plasma-amoeba', thought that the drawings in Mickey Mouse films shared this quality with both Picasso and Dalí.[37] Later object-constructions by Dalí like *Babaouo* 1932 or *The Little Theatre* 1934 (figs.72, 76) have another possible connection with the process of cartoon animation, in that the former used cut-out layers of celluloid to give the impression of depth in a landscape.[38] Dalí's dioramas similarly mimic three-dimensionality through two-dimensional layers of glass screens.

From 1930 on, many of Dalí's scripts aspired to be full-scale films, but apart from *Babaouo, Giraffes on Horseback Salad* 1937 and *La Carretilla de carne*, often remain an unfinished mixture of ideas for a plot and isolated, but often fully conceived, scenes. These scenes or episodes were invested with a special emotional power for Dalí; minutely imagined and described events with an emphasis on actions, their closest ties are with important texts like the 1931 'Rêverie'.[39]

La Chèvre sanitaire (The Hygienic Goat, c.1930–1), 'a talking film', undated and never made, reveals this mechanism well. It is an attempt to develop the theme of the 'documentary' *Contre la famille* (Against the Family, 1932) into a narrative film. There is no coherent and consistent storyline, but rather, general directions about themes and the effects that Dalí wanted to obtain – the gratuitous, sensations of vacuity and absence, the systematic use 'of elements that would be in sterile disaccord with the action and the scenery'. The script veers between abstract and general ideas, very concrete images (such as a decapitated chicken running about) and specific vividly imagined settings (a large deserted square under a twilight sky, a huge modernist house). It was to be a Surrealist film, with 'dreams and hypnagogic images', the intervention of 'chance of a surrealist order', the imagination and 'mental reality' co-existing with sensorial reality.[40] The most vividly imagined passages in the scenario are the minutely choreographed situations in which the protagonists come together in a dramatised encounter. At the heart of his film is a situation that is recognisably the same as that depicted in paintings and drawings of 1929–30, notably *The Invisible Man* (1930 fig.21) and *The Butterfly Hunt* (private collection, Paris).[41] This is a scene figuring a family grouped with intense concentration round something invisible in the painting but revealed in the drawing as a butterfly net. There is a paradoxical impression of secretive desires and open if deviant sexuality. That it evokes for Dalí the female sex and the womb (which he claimed to remember as glutinous, blood-red and formless) is suggested by a note in *Contre la famille*: '*Prologue scene of the butterfly hunt / Intrauterine dreams … the birth trauma of Otto Rank*'.[42] The way in which Dalí imagines and describes the scene recalls his erotic 'Rêverie', and through this situation he is similarly able to indulge his fantasies. Central to his pictorial images and also to this scene in the scenario is the figure of the father, although he is not implied in the three amorous 'themes' of the narrative. The film starts with birdsong and laughter. The camera draws back and reveals the mother who cries out and catches a butterfly. The father arrives and takes her tenderly by the shoulders:

with an expression of compassion and a certain inevitability (the Initiation Sacrifice, introduce the concept in the spoken part). Then the children arrive, and after them the aunt. The sister places herself by her

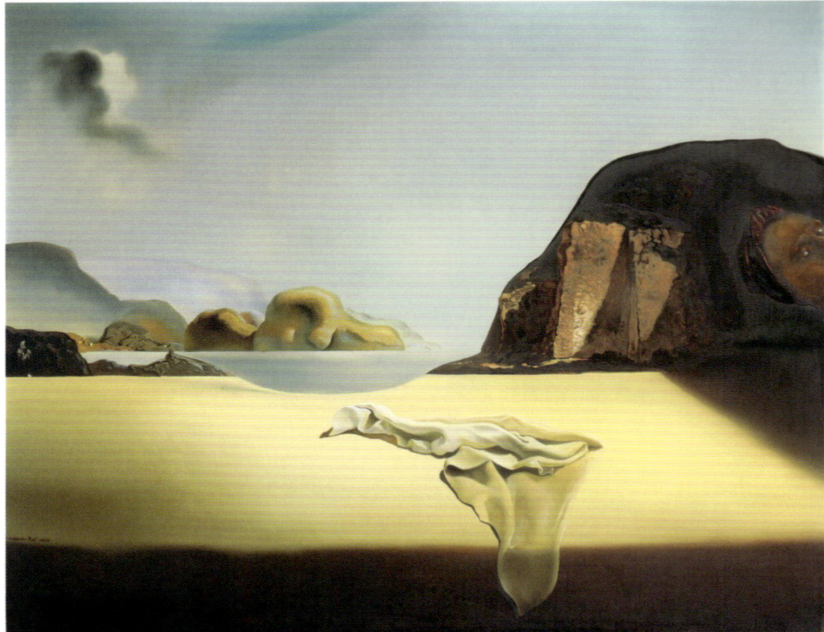

11
*The Transparent Simulacrum of
the Feigned Image* 1938
Oil on canvas 73.5 x 92 cm
Albright-Knox Art Gallery,
Buffalo, New York. Bequest of
A. Conger Goodyear, 1966

*mother so that the butterfly net held by the mother is
exactly at the height of her stomach. When the group is
formed, there is the sensation of a very grave and
solemn moment … The mother very slowly introduces
her hand into the net. The aunt bites her lips … the
father shows the whites of his eyes as if in a convulsion
… The brother watches the scene with avid curiosity.
The girl directs a look of reproach at the wife. When the
mother's hand slowly reaches the bottom of the net,
which is exactly at the height of the sister's sex, the latter
gives a penetrating, animal shriek.*[43]

The drama does not unfold as a story, though
it has temporal narrative elements, but is
encapsulated in a situation. This is why the
reverie, dream or nightmare is Dalí's most
effective cinematic model, in which, to follow
Freud's ideas, people, objects or settings can be
invested with multiple and even contradictory
affects. Such episodes in the scenario, while
echoed in figure groups in the paintings, include
motions or sounds unavailable in the static
media of canvas or paper and are agencies of
erotic suspense. The father's eyes roll into his
head like those of Modot in *L'Age d'or*, the
tension rises as the mother reaches into the net,
the girl screams, and so on. At the same time,
these filmic descriptions offer insights into the
psychological dramas underlying the imagery of
paintings like *The Lugubrious Game, The Old Age
of William Tell* or *The Birth of Liquid Desires* 1932
(Peggy Guggenheim Collection, Venice). There

is a connection between Dalí's inclination for
a single, psychologically loaded incident, the
dream narrative and his own preferred 'reverie'.
It is not so much that they resemble the episodic
cinema of his youth, but that as nuclei for an
accumulation of associations to be revealed or
hinted at, rather than as stages in a narrative, they
use suspense and deferral within a self-contained
event as an erotic device.

One can assume that Dalí envisaged
close-ups, montage and intercutting in *La Chèvre
sanitaire* as in *Un Chien andalou*, but he rarely
includes camera directions in his scenarios. His
approach to visualising the material as film is quite
different from that of Federico García Lorca.
Although the poet had less experience with
cinema, he created the film script *Trip to the Moon*
while he was in New York in 1929–30. Lorca had
watched a short 35 mm film called *777*, by the
Mexican graphic artist Emilio Amero, 'an abstract
thing about shop machines'. The two started
discussing contemporary movies, such as
'Salvador Dalí's surrealistic *Le Chien Andalou.*
Lorca saw the possibilities of doing a film of the
order of *777* with the direct use of motion … The
film was completely plastic, completely visual, and
in it Lorca tried to describe portions of New York
life as he saw it.'[44] *Trip to the Moon* is numbered
shot-by-shot, with detailed camera directions:

*51. In the street the man with the veins appears,
    lying with his arms outstretched.*

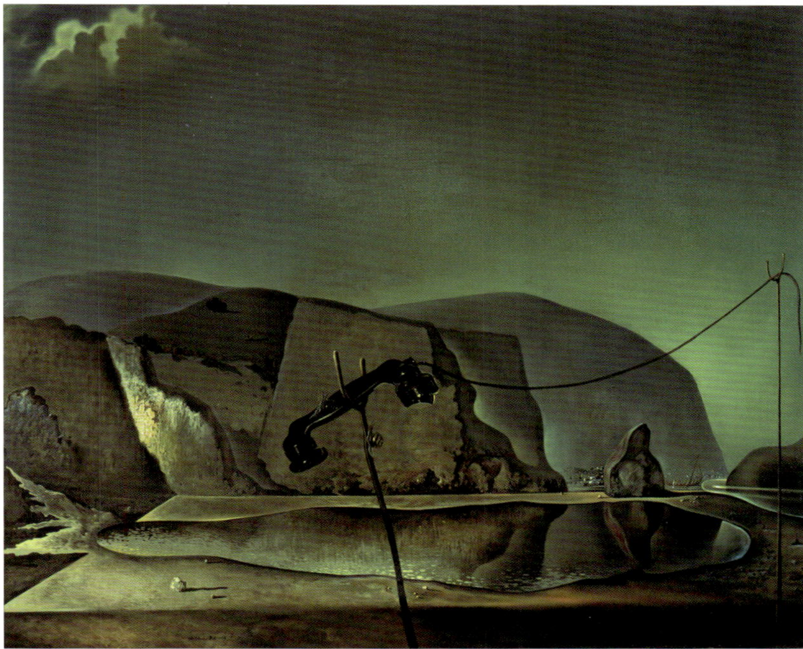

It is in the genre of the short 'surrealist-experimental' and 'impossible' films, and would have been a mixture of graphics and montage, but is effectively a shooting script, fully visualised. Lorca's script interweaves death and love through momentary and disconnected shots; it is film as ephemeral and fleeting. Dalí, on the other hand, prolongs suggestive encounters or actions to build up erotic suspense.

Dalí's writings – scenarios, novel, theoretical texts, autobiography – develop a kind of modern, personal *ut pictura poesis*, a set of narratives from which breath-taking moments can be individually extracted for pictorial images or cinematic incidents. Just as Dalí constructed his personal mythologies, such as that of the vengeful patriarch, in the guise of William Tell, Abraham, Saturn and God the Father, or its maternal variant in *The Tragic Myth of Millet's Angelus*, so he began in his paintings, instinctively it seems, to adopt the classical solution to the depiction of a grand myth – the choice of the key moment at which the preceding and subsequent elements of the story are encapsulated.

Dalí's paintings in the post-war period have a paradoxical relationship to tradition and modernity, with epic historical works that deliberately reference Velázquez, Zurbaran and many others on one hand, and on the other works positioned ambiguously vis-à-vis contemporary art like Pop and Op. Similarly, his film projects range from Hollywood bio-pics to collaborations with Andy Warhol and Jonas Mekas. Preserved among his manuscripts are plans for a film on the Spanish hero of the fifteenth-century wars of Independence (and subject of a play by Pierre Corneille), *Le Cid*, and for 'Une Vie de Goya' (A Life of Goya). The latter consists of a single page designed to resemble film credits:

scenario and artistic direction by Salvador Dalí
first colour film directed by a great painter[46]

Dalí's idea (how far this ever reached those named is unknown) was for Jean Renoir to direct it, for Charles Laughton to play Goya and Bette Davis the Duchess of Alba. As with so many of his projects, lack of funding probably scuppered his hopes. Although technologically advanced projects like the video *Chaos and Creation* were intended to mock modernist abstraction, and he often emphasised the value of the naked eye and the brush, the documentary potentialities of film continued to attract him, not least as a supplement to his status as painter and genius. He envisaged a film of his autobiography *The Secret Life of Salvador Dalí*, which was published in New York in 1942:

This was to be '"a double parallel biography" – that of DALÍ, and that of the eminent philosopher SIGMUND FREUD. The latter, with the magic of his genius – like a modern Faustus – influences and determines, from afar, the eclosion of a half-mad individual, lost in the obscurity of a tiny Spanish town.' A curious aspect of Dalí's plans was to use anamorphosis, a form of perspectival distension that rendered the image unreadable when viewed from the front. The distortion could be corrected by looking at the picture from an oblique angle. 'Dalí has conceived an original idea whereby most of the scenes will be shown on the screen in an "oblique" fashion.'[47] Presumably, the viewer would still watch the screen head on, and thus be faced with a distorted image. The idea was perhaps, as with the seventeenth-century artists who used anamorphosis to indicate a metaphysical reality beyond the apparent world, to suggest what is hidden beyond daily reality, the arena of dreams and paranoia. Dalí here transposes to film, or at least its projection, a technique to which he had recourse, or whose effects he mimics, in paintings like *Diurnal Fantasies* 1932 (Morse Charitable Trust on loan to the Salvador Dalí Museum, St Petersburg, Fl.) or *The Enigma of William Tell* 1933 (Moderna Museet, Stockholm).

Dalí frequently used film to document his exploits. Although there are fragments in *L'Histoire prodigieuse…* showing him copying *The Lacemaker*, he failed to persuade Jack Warner to make a documentary of himself painting. In 1948, he wrote to Warner (whose portrait he painted in 1951; fig.139), suggesting a short documentary to coincide with the publication of his book *50 Secrets of Magic Craftsmanship*:

Very dear friend, I have never wanted to take advantage of our great friendship for projects that might seem more or less problematic, but now and to mark the completion of my book … I have recognised the truly sensational cultural and pedagogic possibilities of realising a short documentary on the subject, with myself as protagonist … This film on my technique of painting would be historic in the history of cinema and of painting … Only the cinema can analyse efficiently each of the painter's movements and offer the spectator the development of the successive stages of the painting just as it would for those of a living organism in growth.[48]

This documentary, which would indeed have been invaluable, and would have stood beside the famous films of Picasso and Pollock in action, was never made. Film was to remain for Dalí an endlessly alluring but elusive medium, whose potential from his own changing perspective was tantalisingly appropriate to his ideas, but whose increasingly complex modes of production often placed their realisation beyond his reach.

Notes

1
See, for instance, Dawn Ades (ed.), *Dalí's Optical Illusions*, New Haven and London 2000, and Fèlix Fanés, *Dalí: Cultura de Masas*, exh. cat., CaixaForum, Barcelona, Museo Nacional Centro de Arte Reina Sofía, Salvador Dalí Museum, St Petersburg (Florida) and (as *It's All Dalí*), Museum Boijmans Van Beuningen, Rotterdam 2004–5.

2
Dalí, *Un diari, 1919–1920: Les meves impressions i records intims*, ed. Fèlix Fanés, Barcelona 1994.

3
Dalí, *Obra Completa, vol.III: Poesia, Prosa, Teatro y Cine*, intro. and notes Agustín Sánchez Vidal, Barcelona 2004.

4
Quoted by James Bigwood, 'Cinquante ans de cinema dalinien', in *Salvador Dalí*, exh. cat., Centre Pompidou, Paris 1979, p.353.

5
Dalí, Lluís Montanyà, Sebastià Gasch, *Manifest Groc* (Yellow Manifesto, or Catalan Anti-Artistic Manifesto), Barcelona, March 1928, trans. in *Salvador Dalí: The Early Years*, exh. cat., Hayward Gallery, London 1994, pp.221–2.

6
'Film arte, film anti-artístico', *La Gaceta Literaria*, Madrid, 15 Dec. 1927, p.8. See full translation republished in this volume from Haim Finkelstein (ed.), *The Collected Writings of Salvador Dalí*, Cambridge 1998.

7
Ibid.

8
Finkelstein 1998, p.16.

9
'Poema: a la Lydia de Cadaqués', *La Gaceta Literaria*, 15 Feb. 1928, trans. in ibid., p.27.

10
'La fotografía, pura creacio de l'esperít' *L'Amic de les arts*, Sitges, 30 Sept. 1927, pp.90–1, trans. as 'Photography, Pure Creation of the Mind', in *Salvador Dalí: Early Years*, p.216.

11
Ibid.

12
Dalí, letter to Federico García Lorca, 15 Jan. 1928, published in *Poesía*, 14 April 1987, p.85, and trans., Christopher Maurer, *Sebastian's Arrows: Letter and Mementos of Salvador Dalí and Federico García Lorca*, Chicago 2004, p.96.

13
László Moholy-Nagy, *Painting Photography Film* (1925), 1st English ed., London 1969, p.28.

14
Dalí, 'Film-arte, film anti-artistico'. See translation in this volume.

15
Dalí, 'Photography, Pure Creation of the Mind', p.216.

16
Jean Painlevé, *Crabes et crevettes* … For his interest in scientific films see also Dalí's 'Cinema', *L'Amic de les Arts*, no.23, 31 March 1928, p.175, republished in Salvador Dalí, *L'Alliberament dels dits: Obra catalana completa*, ed. Fèlix Fanés, Barcelona 1995, pp.89–91.

17
Frederick Keeble, *Plant-Animals: A Study in Symbiosis*, Cambridge 1910.

18
See Jordana Mendelson, 'From the Banal to the Extraordinary: Dalí's Anti-artistic Documentaries', in Hank Hine, William Jeffett and Kelly Reynolds (eds.), *Persistence and Memory: New Critical Perspectives on Dalí at the Centennial*, St Petersburg, Florida and Milan 2004, for a discussion of the different critical uses of 'documentary' in the Catalan avant-garde.

19
'Documental – Paris 1929 – 1', *La Publicicat*, 26 April 1929, trans. in *Oui: Salvador Dalí – The Paranoid-Critical Revolution Writings 1927–33*, ed. Robert Descharnes, trans. Yvonne Shafir, Boston 1998, p.93.

20
'Documental – Paris 1929 – 6', *La Publicicat*, 28 June 1929, ibid., p.106.

21
Ibid.

22
'Luis Buñuel', interview with Dalí, *L'Amic de les arts*, 31 March 1929, trans. in Descharnes 1998, p.88.

23
See D'Arcy Thompson, *On Growth and Form* (1912), new abridged ed., Cambridge 1961, pp.172 et seq.

24
Un Chien andalou scenario. *La Révolution Surréaliste*, no.12, 15 Dec. 1929, p.35.

25
'La meva amiga i la platja', from 'Dues Proses', *L'Amic de les arts*, 30 Nov. 1927, p.104, trans. in *Salvador Dalí: Early Years*, p.218.

26
'L'âne pourri', *La Femme visible*, Paris 1930 and *Le Surréalisme au service de la revolution*, no.1, Paris, July 1930, trans. in Finkelstein 1998, p.224.

27
See Robert Lubar, 'Dalí's ParaNONia', in Hine, Jeffett and Reynolds 2004, pp.123–9; David Lomas, *The Haunted Self*, New Haven and London 2000.

28
The Tragic Myth of Millet's Angelus was not published until 1963, but Dalí was certainly working on it in 1932–3 and the completed text, edited (by Breton) for publication, exists in the Fundació Gala-Salvador Dalí, Figueres. The reasons for its non-publication at the time are unknown. The text was mislaid when Dalí and Gala fled Paris in 1939, and only recovered in 1962.

29
On these projects see the texts by Agustín Sánchez Vidal and Fèlix Fanés in this volume.

30
See my text on this project in this volume.

31
The 'duck-rabbit' effect was popularised by E.H. Gombrich, *Art and Illusion: A Study in the Psychology of Pictorial Representation*, Oxford 1960, p.4, drawing upon Norma V. Scheideman, *Experiments in General Psychology*, enlarged ed., Chicago 1930, p.67.

32
See Ilene Susan Fort's text in this volume.

33
See Elliott King's 'Crazy Movies that Disappear' in this volume.

34
Benjamin Péret, 'Pulchérie veut une auto: FILM', *Littérature*, no.10, May 1923, trans. 'Bonny Wants a Car', in Dawn Ades (ed.), *The Dada Reader: A Critical Anthology*, London 2006, pp.226–31.

35
Esther Leslie, *Hollywood Flatlands: Animation, Critical Theory and the Avant-garde*, London 2002, p.15.

36
Dalí, *Babaouo, Scenario inédit, précédé d'un abrégé d'un histoire critique du cinéma, et suivi de Guillaume Tell ballet portugais*, Paris 1932; see William Jeffett's text in this volume.

37
Leslie 2002, p.223.

38
See *Il etait du fois: Walt Disney*, Paris and Montreal 2006, pp.134–5.

39
'Rêverie', *Le Surréalisme au service de la revolution*, no.4, Paris, 1931, trans. 'Daydream', Finkelstein 1998, p.150. This uninhibited tale of Dalí's masturbatory fantasies drew a severe reprimand from the PCF (the French Communist Party).

40
As 'La Cabra Sanitaria' (The Hygienic Goat), *Obra Completa*, vol.III, 2004, p.1085. Dalí explains the phrase 'the hygienic goat' in terms of his idea of the gratuitous (see Sánchez Vidal's text in this volume). The 'hygienic goat' thus had absolutely no connection, conscious or unconscious, with what it designated (though one might speculate that it could be the opposite to 'the rotting donkey', just as the painting title *The Invisible Man* is to the book *The Visible Woman*, and moreover contains notions of objectivity, sterilisation and precision, which for Dalí opposed the sentimental, emotional, putrid and picturesque).

41
'La Chèvre sanitaire' shares its title with the second part of his book *La Femme visible* 1930 (the Visible woman), where the drawing is reproduced.

42
'Contra la familia' (Against the Family), *Obra Completa*, vol.III, 2004, p.1079.

43
'La Cabra Sanitaria', *Obra Completa*, vol.III, 2004, pp.1095–6.

44
Richard Diers, 'A Filmscript by Lorca', *Windmill*, Oklahoma, spring 1963, p.27.

45
Federico García Lorca, 'Trip to the Moon', trans. Bernice G. Duncan, ibid., pp.31–7.

46
'Une vie de Goya', unpublished ms., n.d., Fundació Gala-Salvador Dalí.

47
'Samuel Godwyn presents The Secret Life of Salvador Dalí …', unpublished typescript in English, n.d., Fundació Gala-Salvador Dalí.

48
Letter to Jack Warner, unpublished ms., Fundació Gala-Salvador Dalí.

Film as Metaphor
Fèlix Fanés

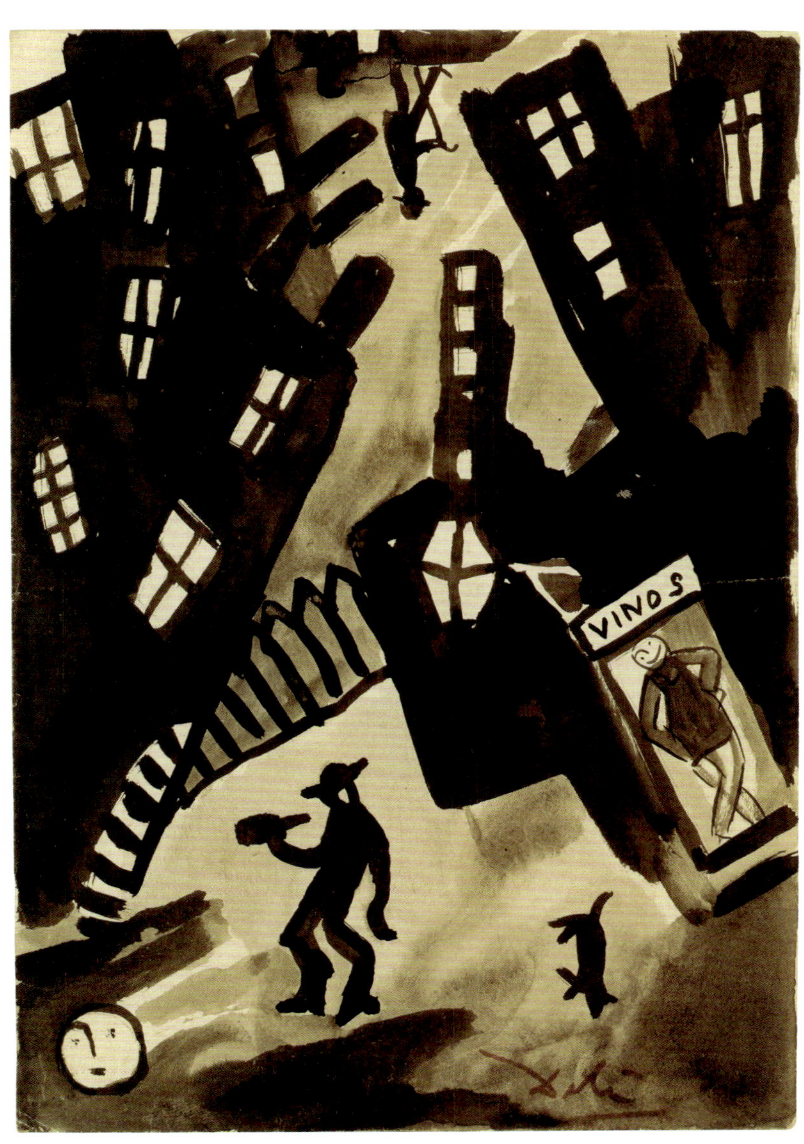

13
Madrid Suburb c.1922–3
Wash on paper 20.8 x 15 cm
Fundació Gala-Salvador Dalí,
Figueres

The mechanical eye[1]

During the 1920s and 1930s, the German philosopher Siegfried Krakauer classified mass-produced culture as 'superficial', while his colleague Walter Benjamin described those who viewed it as 'distracted'.[2] These adjectives were not used in an entirely negative sense, but rather described a new type of cultural consumption aimed at an audience that had made the transition from individual to collective. For Dalí, the surface, even epidermal, nature of the new media, and the type of audience they created, provided a foundation for an original aesthetics that he termed 'anti-art'. 'I am superficial,' he wrote in 1927, 'and the outside of things is what delights me, for in the last analysis the outside of thing is the objective.'[3] The connection between mass production and objectivity is one of the bases of Dalí's thinking at that time. From among the various forms of technical reproduction available, he chose film as a model for illustrating the new requirements of modern visuality. Rather than an instrument at the service of a straightforward realism, he saw the cine camera as an objective device guaranteeing a direct approach to a complex and fragmentary reality.

Dalí's first critical reference to film is found in a letter of November 1926 addressed to the critic Sebastià Gasch. The latter had compared Dalí's painting to jazz. 'I found your article in *La Gaseta de les Arts* extremely interesting', wrote Dalí, 'because it relates my painting to one of my strongest predilections: jazz – this marvellously

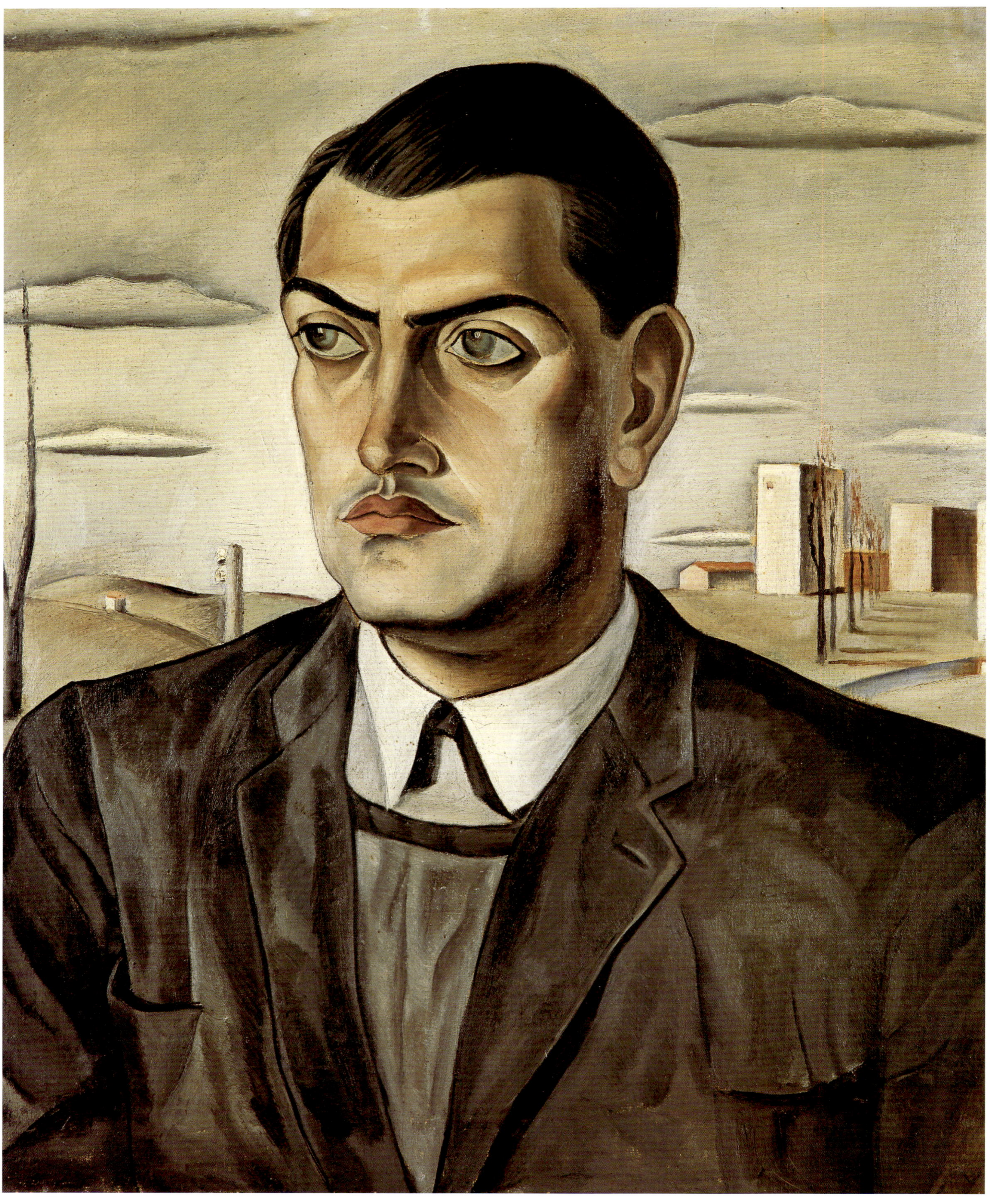

anti-artistic music'. And he continued, '"Artistic" is a horrible word which serves only to identify things completely devoid of art. Artistic diversion, artistic photography, artistic advertising. Horror! Horror! We are all in agreement about the purely industrial object, dancing and poetry, the quintessence of Buster Keaton's hat.'[4]

Initially, Dalí took the same interest in film as he did in the other products of mass society. Films fulfilled a similar function to that of industrial objects and dancing: they were manifestations of the banality of the modern world that the painter contrasted with the older forms of culture that still existed, despite the economic and political transformations that rendered them outmoded. In his essay 'Sant Sebastià' (Saint Sebastian), Dalí unambiguously contrasted the existence of 'transcendental artists' with the reality of a world in which everything is seen 'sharply' and 'with clarity', populated by ocean liners, mannequins, dancers of the *black-bottom*, *Charleston* and blues, the 'nickel-plated headlamps of an Issota Fraschini' automobile, Fox newsreels, along with Josephine Baker, Tom Mix, Adolphe Menjou and Buster Keaton.[5]

Despite the parallel between the concept of anti-art and a nihilism rooted in Dadaism, Dalí allied his enthusiasm for standardised objects to the magazine *L'Esprit nouveau*. He observed that 'Le Corbusier … tried, on a thousand occasions … to make us see the simple and moving beauty of the miraculous mechanical and industrial world that, newly born, is perfect and pure as a flower'.[6] From the pages of this magazine, Dalí adopted the hymn to the machine and praise for the industrial object as the fruit of a process of improvement that Le Corbusier had applied to architecture when he had proposed the mass-produced construction of houses in the same way as cars. However, Dalí did not confine himself to the special iconography allied to *L'Esprit nouveau* (objects in the case of Le Corbusier and Amedée Ozenfant; machines and robotic beings in that of Fernand Léger). Rather, he applied a mechanical and objective vision to established genres such as portraiture and still life. His automation is found in the way he chose to look at things, by making use of the 'anaesthetised look of the clearest eye, without eyelashes, of Zeiss' (i.e. the lens of a photographic or cine camera) rather than in any pictorial subject matter.[7] This meant a direct system of representation, devoid of intellectualism or any temptation to subjectivity or mystic transcendence. Like *L'Esprit nouveau*, he identified modernity with tradition (a living form of tradition, at least). But instead of choosing the classical world of Greece, he settled on the work of Jan Vermeer, in whom he discovered a form of painting close to the instrumental vision of the camera.

Just as Dalí rejected the laws and forms of idealist art, so he also addressed the need for a new audience, which he contrasted with the old one (bourgeois, cultivated, potbellied) that had sustained the high and refined culture. Unlike a poem by Paul Valéry or an Impressionist painting – which required some cultural knowledge in order to be understood – the work produced under this new way of seeing was accessible even to 'children and savages'. Therefore, 'modern man, half child, half savage, lover of sport, cinema, motoring and dancing' could also gain pleasure from viewing it.[8] The result was an art in which 'there is nothing to understand', just as there was nothing to understand in a comedy film.[9]

Dalí's painting of this period adhered to these principles, as can be seen in *Girl from Figueres* 1926 (fig.16), in which these approaches can be detected. The starting point was Vermeer's *The Lacemaker*. The canvas was executed in the sharp, cold, limpid manner advocated by the aesthetics of *L'Esprit nouveau*, and, against the landscape background, a Ford publicity sign can be seen as a tribute to advertising and to the technological modernisation of work emanating from American Fordism and Taylorism.

In his pursuit of objectivist painting, the metaphor of film took on increasing significance for Dalí. Immediately after executing the two important oil paintings *Apparatus and Hand* 1927 (fig.18) and *Honey Is Sweeter than Blood* 1927 (see fig.2), Dalí published 'Film-arte, film anti-artístico', his first article devoted exclusively to film. In this he identified the essence of his aesthetic project with film by defining the anti-artistic director as a creator who:

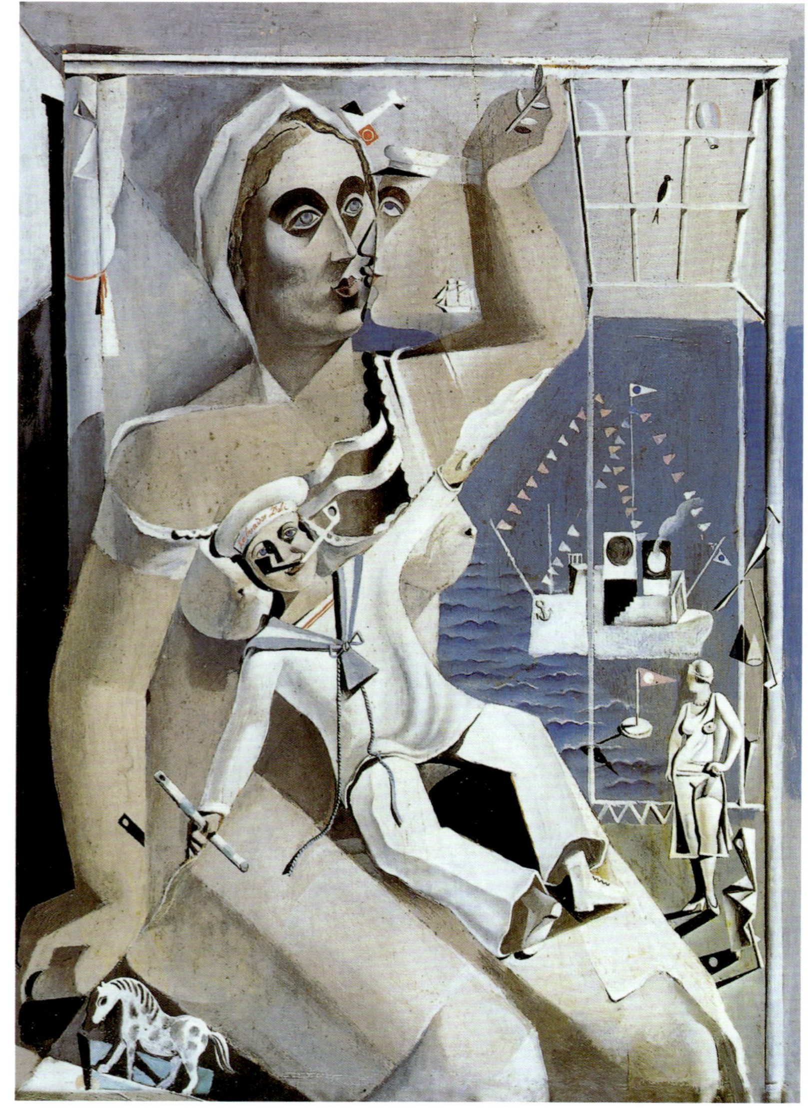

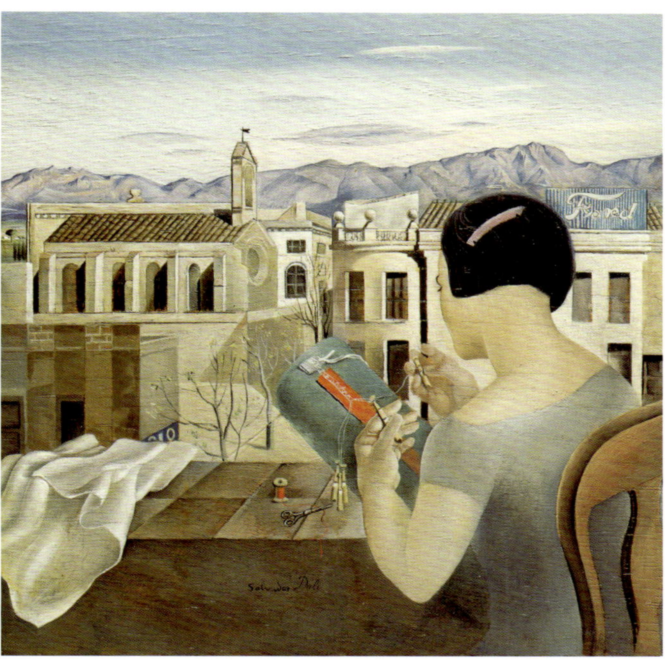

For Dalí, the prosthetic vision of film broadened
the understanding of the material world beyond
the limits of sensory, cognitive equipment.
The capacity of cinematographic equipment
to objectify is what makes it possible to capture
'the most humble and immediate facts, which
were impossible to imagine or to foresee before
cinema.'[11] In an article published as a continuation
and clarification of this one, Dalí stresses the
nature of this new poetry that emerges from the
prosthetic and dehumanised gaze of the camera:

The poetry of facts (the documentary)
The reference to the super-real cannot pass
unnoticed, since it introduces certain nuances to
Dalí's anti-artistic poetry and to his understanding
of film. Up until this time, the painter had been
mainly interested in the medium's photographic
qualities. Now, however, he identified a second
level of expression in its language: 'Film … offers
us a ready-made, constant, lavishly limited
language. This language is the first miracle; how
it is used, the second.'[13] By this, he was referring
to the montage and construction of film in
sequence. Having recognised the fragmentary
nature of filmic expression, Dalí abandoned the
stable forms of photographic immobility in his
painting in favour of applying his camera-like eye
to a disorderly muddle lacking connection but
which can be associated with the unconscious. In
Apparatus and Hand and *Honey Is Sweeter than Blood*
for example, the elements accumulate in space in
a manner reminiscent of the sharp, intermittent
and, at the same time, rhythmic and dynamic
expression of cinematographic montage.

In this process of radicalisation, Dalí also
distanced himself from the great names of film,
such as Chaplin, and replaced them with others
such as the unclassifiable Harry Langdon (fig.25):
'one of the purest flowers of the cinema and even
of our civilization.'[14] A middle-of-the-road
vaudeville actor whom Mack Sennett wanted to
launch as a new star of comic film, Langdon failed
to win a mass audience. His director, Frank
Capra, described him as someone endowed with
the 'intransigence of inanimate objects',[15] thus
underlining the mechanical nature of a character
driven by blind determination. In his aspiration
to comply with the rules of society, the childish,

17
Letter to Lorca dated 18/20 January
1927
Ink and collage on paper
21.1 x 16.5 cm
Fundación Federico García Lorca,
Madrid

Opposite:
18
Apparatus and Hand 1927
Oil on panel 62.2 x 47.6 cm
Salvador Dalí Museum,
St Petersburg, Florida

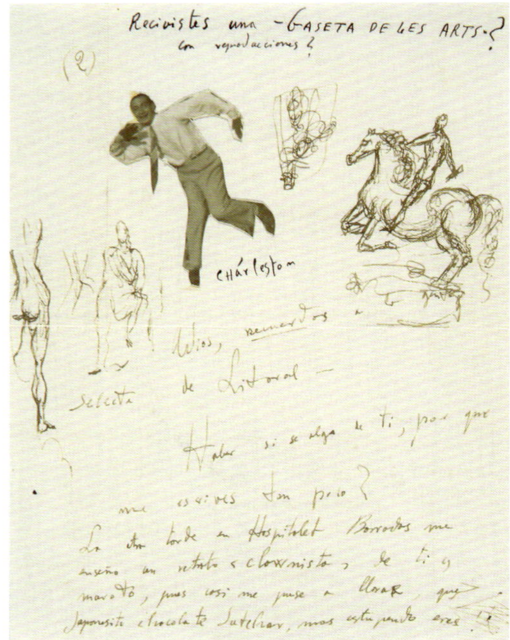

almost Beckettian Langdon ended up by becoming a diminutive but effective incarnation of social disorder. By championing this comic actor, admired by certain writers associated with Surrealism, Dalí moved a little nearer to André Breton's group.[16]

Breton himself had identified photography with automatic writing,[17] and Dalí was able to take advantage of this shared enthusiasm for objectivity to make the transition to Surrealist poetry with only a slight adjustment of his system of metaphor. In fact, Dalí's anti-art position coincided with Breton's intentions in its lack of aesthetic purpose and in its desire to record reality faithfully and objectively. Dalí also began to talk of the 'assassination of painting' (in the same way as Joan Miró), and to make paintings that were more object-like than objective, such as *Feminine Nude* 1928 (fig.20), in which a real piece of cork casts a painted shadow to represent a woman's torso. Towards the end of 1928 and throughout 1929, Dalí identified his new conception of reality with what he called 'facts'.

It is not necessary for me to insist how absolutely inadmissible appear to me today not only the poem, but any form of literary production that does not respond to the anti-artistic, faithful and objective documentation of the world of facts, from whose hidden meaning we constantly hope for and demand a revelation.[18]

This allusion to facts meant substituting a discursively constructed psychological reality for a world of phenomena, of superficial, external, secondary and often banal manifestations. These manifestations drew their strength from their randomness. Thus what makes a real fact different from a conventional literary fact was their enigmatic, absurd and unexplained nature. Buñuel (fig.14), who was greatly influenced by Dalí at the time, cited 'Adolphe Menjou's moustache' as an illustration of the 'facts' that make up 'authentic reality', while Dalí referred to the poetry of Benjamin Péret, which he saw 'as a document equally as real as a photo'.[19]

In championing facts, Dalí underlined his inclination towards documentary film at the expense of that of the imagination. 'My friends and I', he wrote in mid 1929, 'think highly of the sound film, especially in the documentaries.'[20] While they were working on *Un Chien andalou*, Dalí and Buñuel were convinced that the best way of making a film that obeyed the dictates of thought was by using the camera in the most impersonal way. Which is why, during the period that it took to make the film, Dalí spoke so often about documentaries as the equivalent of Surrealist texts. 'One violently anti-artistic tendency is defined in the exacerbated thrust towards the documentary', he wrote in a slightly earlier article, adding: 'We note the rigorous and powerful means that are today at the disposal of the documentary: the phonograph, photography, cinema, literature, the microscope,

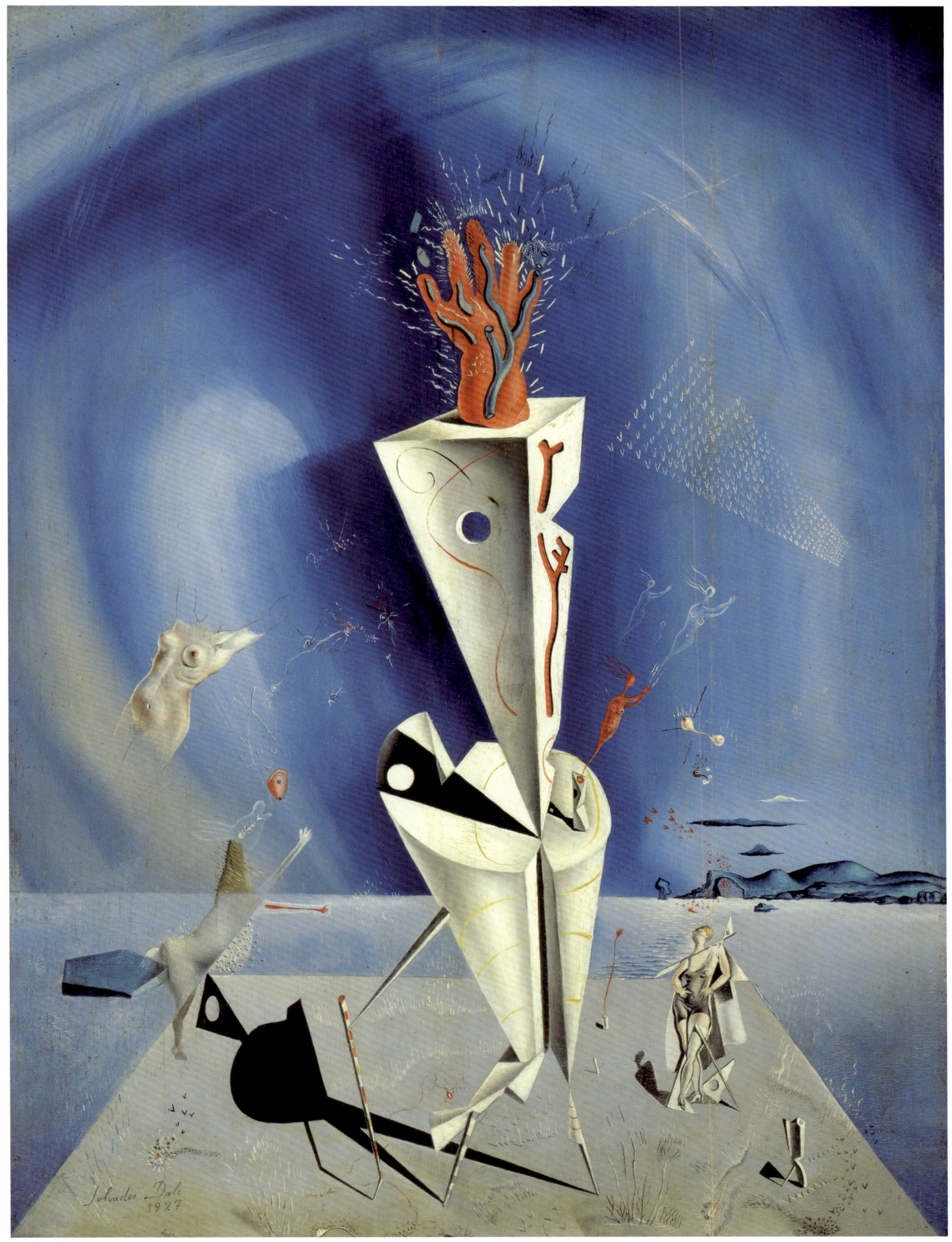

etc'.[21] Dalí did not see a conflict between objective documentary and Surrealist writing. On the contrary, he believed that they shared a common, essentially anti-artistic nature. In each creative process he suggested that

there is no intervention … on the part of the least aesthetic, emotive or sentimental purposes, these being the essential characteristics of the artistic phenomenon. The documentary notes in an anti-literary fashion things said to be in the objective world. In a parallel manner, the surrealist text transcribes, with the same rigour and in as much anti-literary sense as the documentary, the REAL and liberated functioning of thought, what actually goes through our mind, all this by means of psychic automatism and other passive states (inspiration).[22]

In this sense, *Un Chien andalou* can be seen as marking the point of arrival of the artist's thinking of that time. That the early part is a rerun in images of Dalí's anti-artistic theory is clear from the appearance, after the distressing slitting of the eye, of a reproduction of Vermeer's *The Lacemaker* (deliberately placed in the extreme foreground, which it shares with some sinister surgical instruments). Through it we are invited to explore the honest gaze, the chaste eye of which the Dutch painter was historically the representative and that, in these new historical circumstances, had been replaced by a medium with the technical capability of recording reality, that is to say, film. The slit eye stands as a metaphor for the replacement of man as

artistic subject by the camera; it is also a declaration of a new, technical, objective art, featuring formidable and rigorous prosthetic artefacts whose purpose is not reality itself but the inexplicable facts of that reality. As a result, the film, 'made apart from any aesthetic intention', presents a 'simple noting down, recording of facts',[23] in other words, an exploration of the real world without recourse to artistic or literary justifications.[24]

Surrealism in Hollywood

Budd Schulberg, in his Hollywood-set novel, *What Makes Sammy Run?* 1941, tries to explain the unexpected tears of an unfeeling character with a reference to Dalí: 'I wondered why I thought of surrealism when I saw him cry and then I remembered the Dalí exhibit of rain falling inside a taxicab. This was no less bizarre, no less grotesque.'[25] Presented as a critique of the film industry, Schulberg's novel aspired to reach a wide audience, and the future screenwriter drew his metaphors from a widely shared pool of cultural knowledge. By referring to the 'rainy taxi', he shifted Dalí and his images from the exclusive terrain of the modern art gallery to that of popular culture consumed by all.

In the middle of the 1930s, against the background of a Europe shaken by economic and social crises, Dalí described the cultural situation in terms of 'the cannibal frenzy of moral hunger' of masses ready to 'gnaw' at anything in order to

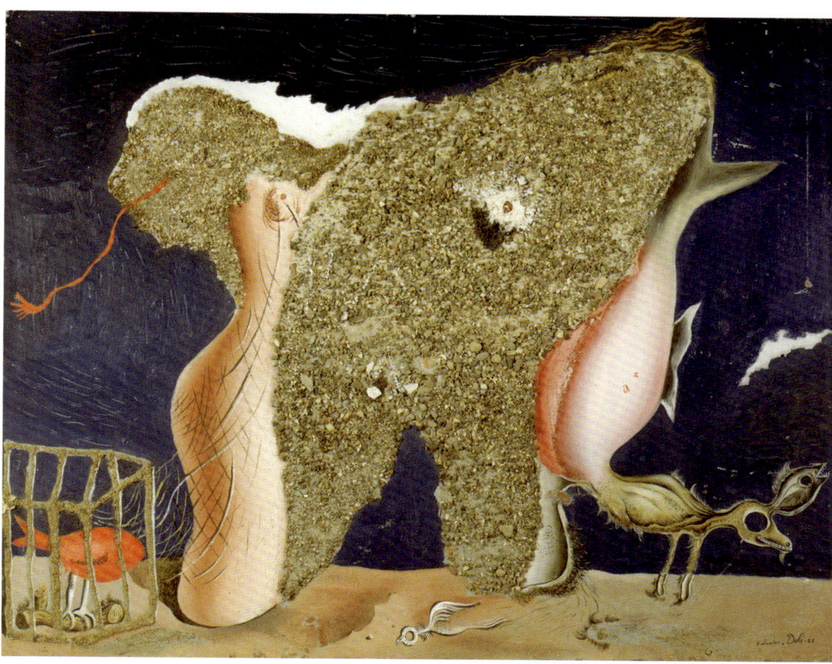

alleviate their appetite for totemic forms. The 'cultural banquet' offered only, 'the cold and insubstantial remains of art and literature' on the one hand and on the other, 'the red-hot analytical elucidations of the particular sciences'. The Surrealists – and Dalí himself – therefore found themselves faced with the challenge of a great 'nutritional responsibility' – that of satisfying the frenzied hunger before the starving masses should succumb to other less desirable foods.[26]

The metaphor of cannibalism would take on a new dimension in contact with American culture (with which Dalí had begun to familiarise himself during trips to New York from late 1934). The cinema, and Hollywood especially, would occupy an important role. The actress Mae West – considered scandalous because of her shameless sexual language – provided an early example of this appropriation. In 1934 Dalí reworked a photograph from a popular magazine and transformed her face into an apartment (fig.23). This picture continued the exploration of the paranoiac-critical method that Dalí began in 1929. The real disappeared to give way to a second image, which in turn gave rise to a third image, and so on. This negation of objectivism through a paranoid vision was in keeping with other transformations in Dalí's way of thinking towards the end of the 1920s.

Having been enthusiastic about the rationalism of Le Corbusier, Dalí moved on, under the influence of Surrealism, to defend completely opposing attitudes. The large wedge that he drove into the foundations of the modern edifice, effectively robbing it of its structure, was his tribute to the 'violently anachronistic' Modern Style or Art Nouveau architecture.[27] He discovered stimuli for his poetic imagination in the characteristic buildings of Barcelona. The ornamental nature of the work of Antoni Gaudí, Lluís Doménech i Montaner and Josep Puig i Cadafalch not only set their constructions apart from the principles of modern architecture but transformed them into receptacles for dreams and desires, introducing the realm of the unconscious with its associated phantoms, perversions and neuroses. By these means, which provided an opening to the expression of what has been repressed, a potent 'bad taste' emerged from the anti-modern, ornamental magma. Once he had discovered it in the Modern Style, Dalí did not hesitate to elevate it to an aesthetic level. And this has something in common with his gouache of Mae West. The carnal warmth of the actress's inviting, rounded curves are transformed into boarded flooring, the walls and the other rectilinear lines of the apartment, are designed to draw us back to the softness of her form as a place to inhabit – a space that finds in the actress's lips the point of convergence of all her comforting sensuality. In this way, a rigid, geometric architecture is contrasted with another that is tender and formless, an architecture of punishment with another of pleasure. Dalí explained this clearly in an article he wrote that year: 'I am very proud of having predicted in 1928, at the highest peak of

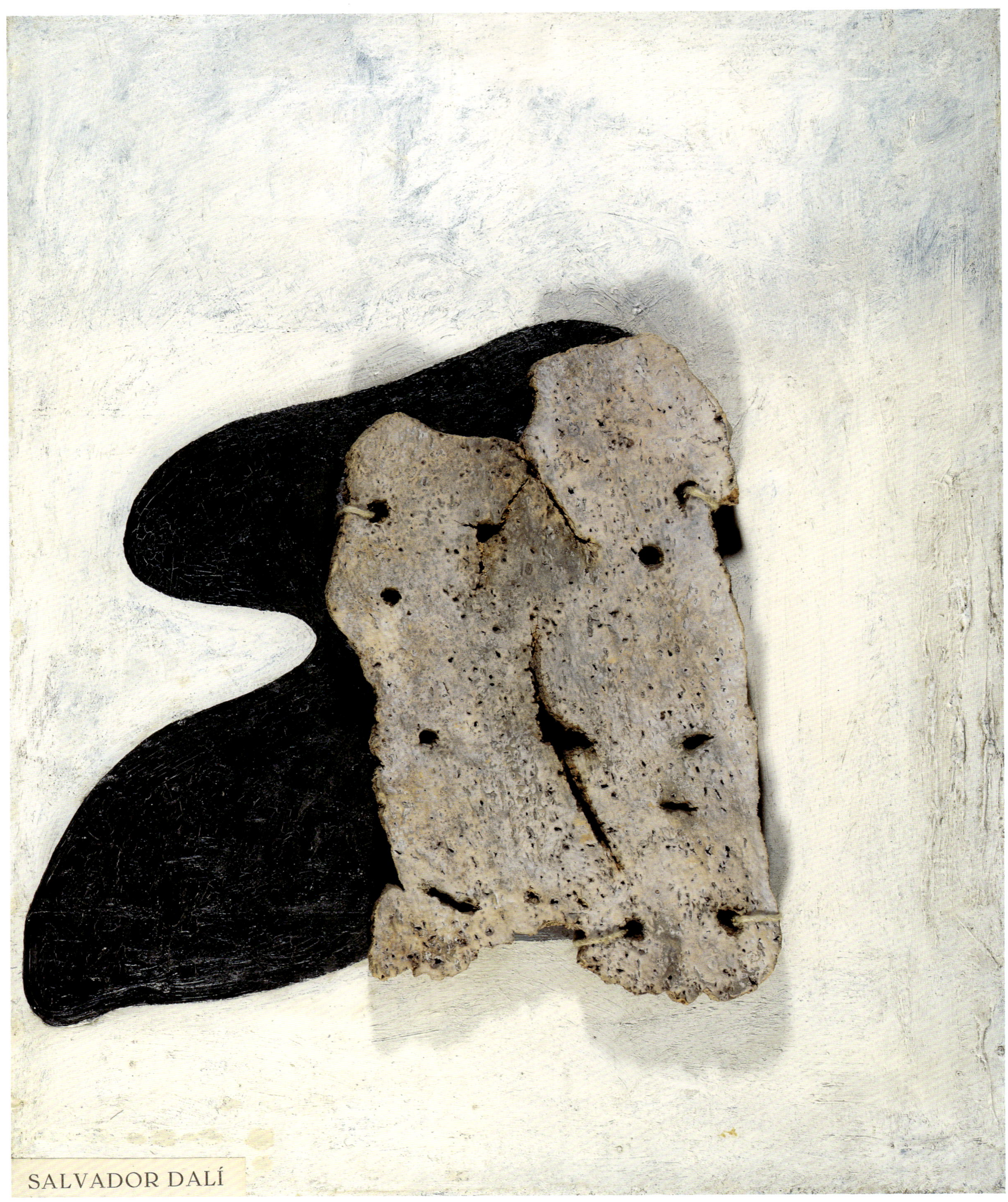

SALVADOR DALÍ

functional and practical anatomy, in the midst of the most scoffing skepticisms, the imminence of Mae West's rounded and salivary muscles, horribly slimy with biological ulterior motives.'[28] The apartment manufactured from the actress's face thus places Dalí firmly within an aesthetics in which dream, sensuality, the throbbing of life and the erotic occupy their own space. The cinema and Hollywood would also play an important role in this Surrealist aesthetic.

In January 1937, Dalí travelled to the west coast of America, and the time he spent in Los Angeles opened his eyes. 'I am just back from Hollywood', he wrote in June of that year, 'and there I have heard the word surrealism in every mouth.'[29] The dream-like nature of the films, the spectral world of mechanical fantasy, the lethargy of the unreal environments, all led him to think that

the cinema can only develop in the direction of the 'wireless imagination' and 'paralysing fantasy' – the very prey and food of the immense 'famine of illusion' of the public and the masses in general. Reduced to idiocy by the material progress of a mechanical civilization, the public and the masses demand urgently the illogical and tumultuous images of their own desires and their own dreams.[30]

Some months earlier, while he was still in Los Angeles, Dalí had sent a postcard to André Breton saying: 'I'm in Hollywood where I've made contact with the three American surrealists, Harpo

Marx, Disney and Cecil B. DeMille. I believe I've intoxicated them suitably and hope that the possibilities for surrealism here will become a reality.'[31]

The first of these three whom Dalí got to know was Harpo Marx. The painter had become aware of him when he saw the film *Animal Crackers* in 1932, which he recognised as the 'summit of the evolution of comic cinema'.[32] The Marx Brothers' film impressed many of the Surrealists (Breton described it as a 'midnight feast of sunshine').[33] Having sent Harpo a harp wrapped in cellophane and covered in small spoons a meeting took place in January 1937 which led to two projects: a portrait of Harpo, of which a couple of drawings survive (fig.83), and a screenplay written by Dalí himself and known as *The Surrealist Woman* or *Giraffes on Horseback Salad*.[34] Dalí admired the purity of Harpo's primitivism. 'Harpo Marx', he wrote, 'is the least modern of contemporary figures'.[35]

While the reference to Harpo Marx is unsurprising – even the very serious T.S. Eliot succumbed to the charms of those outrageous brothers[36] – the inclusion of Walt Disney as an 'American surrealist' is rather more unexpected. Despite feeding the childhood imaginations of many generations, the 'magician of Burbank', as he was known, did not and still does not enjoy a good press among the intellectual elite. The sentimentality of his plots, the idealised nature of his drawings, as well as his liking for merging high culture with popular culture in productions as surprising as *Fantasia* 1940 could all explain this response. There are at least two notable exceptions to this view: the Soviet filmmaker Sergei Eisenstein and Salvador Dalí himself. The creator of *The Battleship Potemkin*, who came to know Disney personally during his stay in Hollywood, wrote several pages on the work of the American filmmaker. 'Disney is an extraordinary filmmaker and an unsurpassed genius at creating audiovisual equivalence with music through the autonomous movement of line and the graphical interpretation of the interior process of the music (even more often with melody than rhythm!)', he wrote. He singled out the short film *Skeleton Dance* 1929 – based on the *Danse Macabre* by Saint-Saëns and the first of Disney's *Silly Symphonies* – as 'a masterpiece of musical movement-equivalence'.[37] Dalí, too, considered that the man who had popularised Mickey Mouse was an extraordinary creator and, like Eisenstein, ranked his *Silly Symphonies* above the rest of his work, describing these as a 'stunning and cataclysmic rainbow'.[38] As in the case of the Marx Brothers, this admiration would lead to a joint film project, *Destino*, although the final results would take longer to materialise.[39]

The poetry of bad taste
If it is surprising that Disney should be cited as one of the three 'American surrealists', this is nothing compared with the unexpected reference to DeMille. Considered to be the father of historical cinema, his movies have always been seen

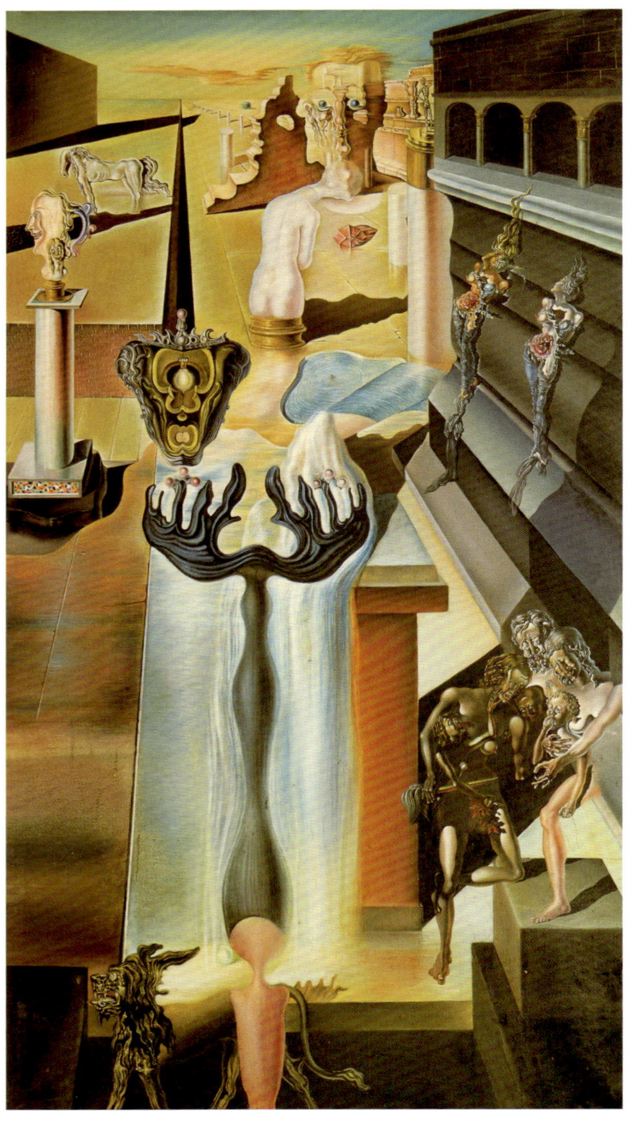

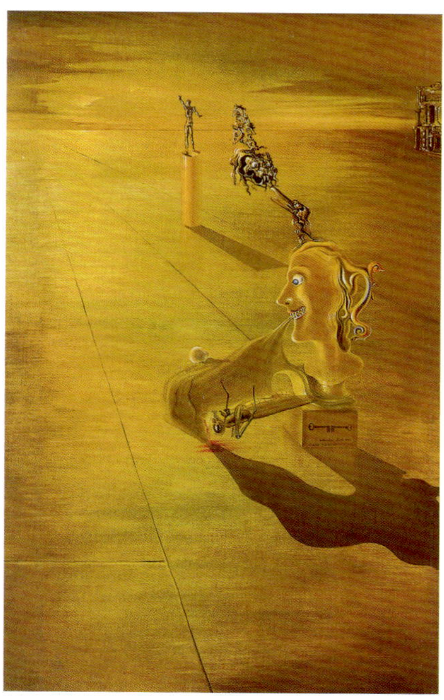

as a triumph of high-class papier mâché over expressive naturalism. After directing religious films such as *The Ten Commandments* 1923 and *The King of Kings* 1926 in the 1920s, during the first half of the 1930s he produced three movies – *The Sign of the Cross* 1932, *Cleopatra* 1934 and *The Crusades* 1935 – that established his reputation as a maker of period films. The ornamental excess and the choreographic representation of history, not to mention the pomposity of his characters, have, more than those of any other filmmaker, led his films to be labelled as kitsch.[40] But where some saw bad taste in massive measure, Dalí perceived a mysterious 'hallucinatory celluloid' from which sprang 'images of delirium, chance and authentic dreams' (as in the scene in *The Sign of the Cross* when Claudette Colbert immerses herself in a bath of asses' milk).[41] And, in his introductory notes to the Marx Brothers' film, he writes: 'The general idea of the script is to transfer to the contemporary period all the imaginative magnificence, splendour and epic character of Cecil B de Mille's films on antiquity.'[42] Dalí did not undertake any projects with DeMille, but it would be a mistake to interpret his admiration for the American director as purely anecdotal. While Dalí was able to find a counterpoint to the immutable and pragmatic logic of modern civilisation in the crazy irrationality of Harpo and the destructive childishness of Disney's drawings (those of the early period at least),[43] in the absurd gigantism of DeMille he appears to have discovered devices that were useful to him for other purposes – probably in relation to aesthetic confrontation. In his fight against good taste, Dalí no doubt saw the creator of *The Sign of the Cross* as an ally. His empty grandeur, his superfluous ornamentation, his recourse to the great subjects of sacred history, transformed the American director into an interesting survivor of past times. Dalí, who was keen to blaze a trail that would lead him far away from the rigidity of modern taste, found DeMille's visual world an inexhaustible source of ideas.

As Breton had already suggested in *Nadja*, one of the most significant sources of bad taste is 'anachronism', which allows us to view what was once in vogue as something that is now 'extravagant', 'unusual', 'impossible', and therefore once again as something 'living'.[44] Indeed the cinema championed by the Surrealists, and from the early 1930s by Dalí, is essentially anachronistic. To the serial films that were so popular around the time of the First World War but completely out of fashion by the end of the 1920s – such as *Les Vampires*, *Fantômas* and *Les Mystères de New York*[45] – Dalí added his own discoveries: the 'hysterical' Italian melodramas of 'Francesca Bertini, Gustavo Serena, Tullio Carminati and Pina Menicelli'.[46] These were films representing what he describes as the 'authentic golden age of cinema' in an essay in which, significantly, he relegates the once applauded 'dynamism, playfulness and standard of American cinematography' to the wretched condition of 'mythological sorrows'.[47]

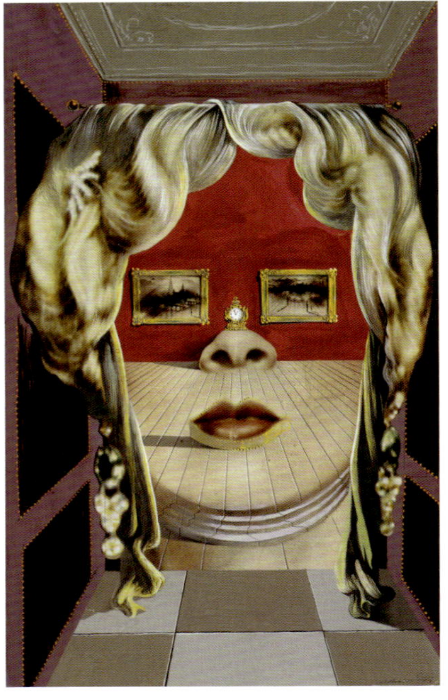

This 'anachronistic' attitude placed the Surrealists in general and Dalí in particular in an aesthetic and political position that was at odds with those around them. Aesthetically they were championing objects that were doubly obsolete – in belonging to popular culture and also in being outmoded – which distanced them from some of the immutable principles of the modern canon, such as originality and the necessary subjugation to the history of high culture as being the only acceptable tradition. Politically they were standing against the general flow of progress, striking out very specifically through their choice at the illusory nature of commodities which, as Marx (not Groucho but Karl) had explained, constituted one of the most powerful sources of social bedazzlement. By attacking the delusion of the consumer object, they were taking an ambitious stand against the snares of a phantasmagorical reality. The relationship with the outdated in any case formed part of the Surrealist poetics. It is in this context that Dalí considered writing, in the autumn of 1934, a film featuring the characters of Richard Wagner, Ludwig II of Bavaria and Sacher Masoch.[48] In fact, these characters would eventually appear in a ballet called *Bacchanal* that was premiered at the Metropolitan Opera House in New York on 9 November 1939.[49] Ludwig II has the most prominent role. As the programme notes put it:

The 'Tannhauser Bacchanale' is shown through the deliriously confused brain of Ludwig II of Bavaria who 'lived' all of Wagner's myths with such profound hyperaesthesia as to verge on madness. As the real protagonist of the ballet he identifies himself with those legendary heroes, and the plot represents the hallucinations and emotions he was a prey to.[50]

Against a backcloth painted with a large swan, a mountain cave (probably Tannhauser's), some clouds extending outwards like the tentacles of an octopus, the moribund frame of an old fishing boat and various piles of crates, a series of phantasmagorical figures wanders about the stage. These include a Venus, apparently nude, emerging from her shell, a timeless Lola Montez dressed as a skull, a volatile Sacher Masoch and his beaten wife, a group of satyrs from whose heads emerge vine stalks bearing grapes, a group of wild fauns crazily pursuing anything in a skirt, mermaids with codfish tails and crutches, umbrellas with skulls engaged in macabre dances, and so on. And in the midst of this unbridled fantasy was Ludwig II, the mad king of Bavaria, Wagner's patron, the architect of palaces that rivalled the splendour of Versailles, the devotee of extravagant luxury, the Romantic dreamer, the repressed homosexual, probably the most 'anachronistic' of the great European figures of modern times inasmuch as his plan for a 'decorative' monarchy coincided with the profound transformations taking place during the final third of the nineteenth century: industrialisation, the decline of absolute power, and social egalitarianism.

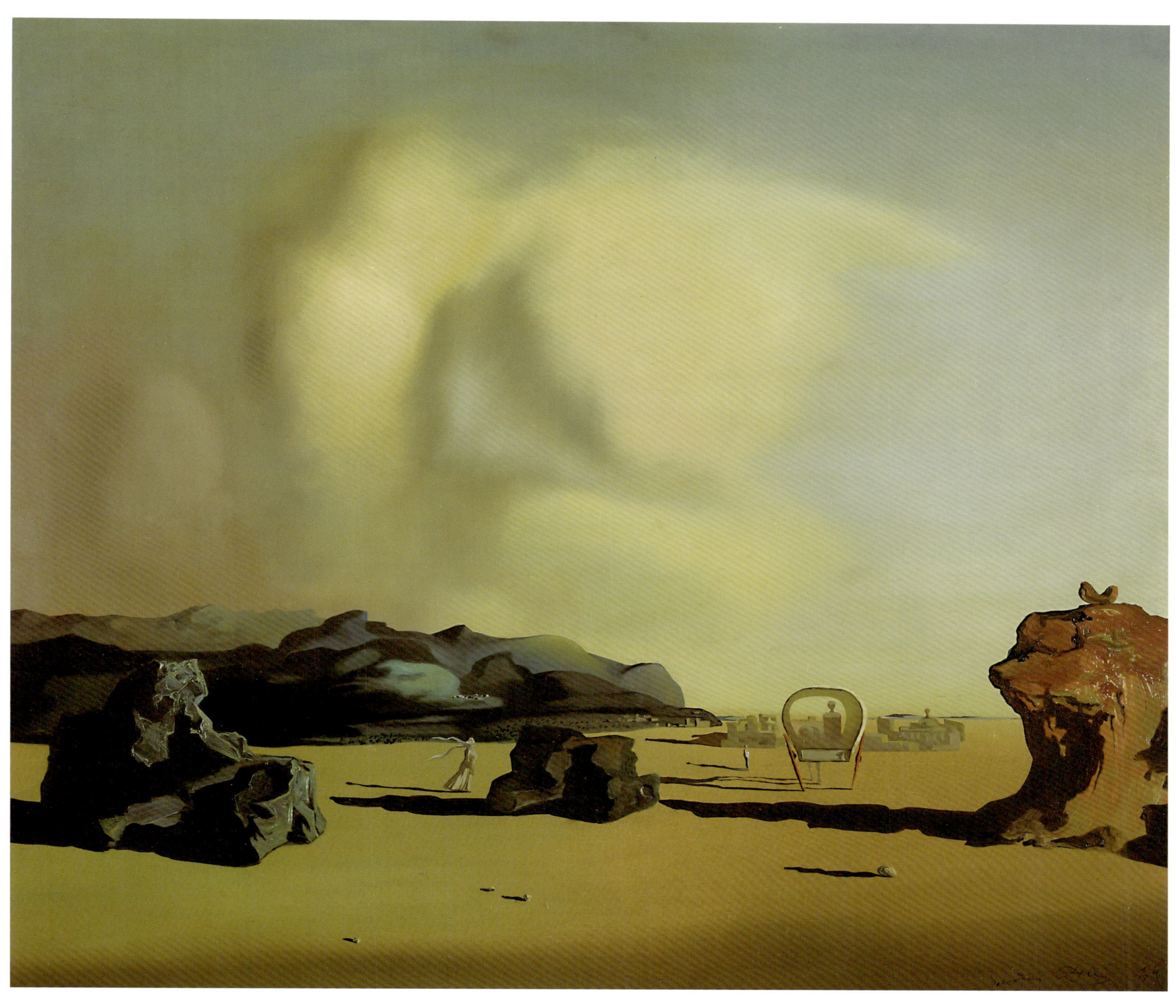

24
Moment of Transition 1934
Oil on canvas 54 x 65 cm
Collection Viktor and Marianne Langen

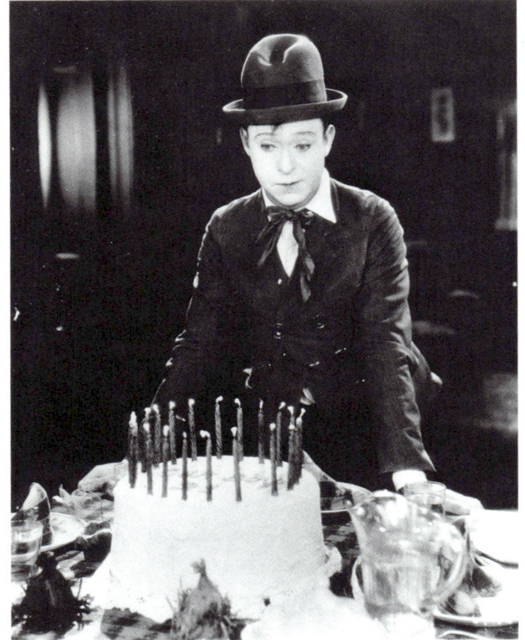

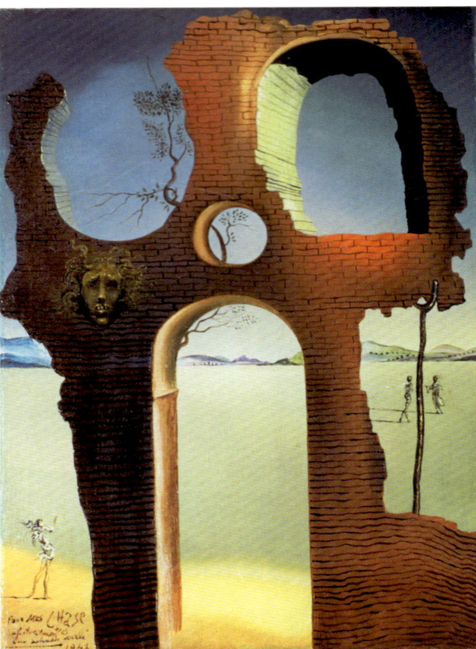

Popular taste soon transformed the figure of the monarch into an icon that was kitsch and perverse. Postcards, novels, plays and films elevated the pathetic figure to the ranks of a modern myth onto which the masses could project their fantasies. And Dalí, who saw this clearly, made use of the figure in his own particular battle. The mad king's world offered a bottomless arsenal of ridiculous ugliness, disproportionate artifice and syrupy sentiment with which, once again, he could assault established aesthetic rules. When discussing the ballet, a critic of the period wondered whether Dalí, 'by using the poor king in this way – who was already the victim of so many assaults on good taste – was not adding a new chapter to the long list of aberrations in which the monarch had already played a starring role'.[51]

Painting as ruin

Dalí was already entertaining these attitudes by the mid-1930s. Hollywood only served to feed him with the new devices that he had been seeking for some time: the replacement of the old anti-artistic poetics with a new type of negativity based on the struggle against modern beauty. He saw this as based on an 'aesthetics' that was 'intellectualist', 'immutable', 'never out of date', 'in a good state of health', 'abstract', 'well groomed', 'eternal' and provocative of 'elevated sentiments'.[52] Dalí contrasted this beauty with an art that was 'traumatic', 'extravagant' and 'blind', that made it 'possible to snatch raw and living lumps from that hard and extremely thick thing which is the sentimental fog from which are formed the very cheeks of memory'. One of the ways of achieving this was to use the anachronistic, which Dalí does not see as something antiquated and harmless to be kept in the junk room, but as a 'mark of the real bites of poetry' provoking a 'pain [that] must assuredly reach the finest and deepest roots of the human mind'.[53]

To this anachronistic aesthetics, liberator of the lowly and repressed, belongs a figure that occurs frequently in Dalí's painting of that period – that of the ruin. As the painter's interest in the outdated and outmoded grew in parallel with his cinematographic reorientation towards the extreme phenomena of Harpo, Disney and DeMille, he began producing a series of paintings in which the most important element appears to show the destructive power of the passage of time. From the Romantic skeleton in *The Horseman of Death* 1935 (private collection), with the lugubrious iconography of Böcklin in the background, via the direct representation of decaying architecture in *Ruin with Head of Medusa and Landscape* 1941 (fig.26), to the desolate frame of the abandoned boat (another type of skeleton) in *Shirley Temple, the Youngest, Most Sacred Monster of the Cinema in her Time* 1939 (fig.98), Dalí's painting is tinged with decay and pessimism. Even the radiant design objects that he had celebrated only years before now appear chipped, full of cracks, covered in weeds. We can see this in the half-broken telephone of *The Sublime Moment* 1938 (Museo Nacional, Centro de Arte Reina Sofía, Madrid) and in the enshrouded Cadillacs of *Clothed Automobiles* 1941 (Fundació Gala-Salvador Dalí, Figueres). Nor does film escape from this image of decay and death. Towards the end of 1944, Dalí painted seven large canvases with the generic title of *The Seven Lively Arts*, which featured drama, ballet, concert music and opera, as well as new forms of popular entertainment like boogie-woogie, radio and film. In the latter, Dalí painted a very large eye and ears (as an allegory of sound movies) resting on an unconnected body of dilapidated boxes and drawers: the decay eating into everything appears to have reached even the modern cameras that feed the fantasies of the masses. Coincidentally these works were accidentally destroyed, but Dalí retained this characteristic decay when he revisited the theme for *Rhapsodie moderne* 1957 (fig.96).

This cadaverous vision of reality – allegorical according to Walter Benjamin[54] – would eventually shape Dalí's painting, which, like DeMille's films, increasingly came to resemble an ornamental, historical vacuousness. This tendency is seen most clearly in the *grandes machines* that he began to produce from 1950 onwards. Such large-scale paintings as *The Discovery of America by Christopher Columbus* 1958–9 (Salvador Dalí Museum, St Petersburg, Florida) have less in common with the old history painting of which they are reminiscent than with the no less ancient technique of *pasticcio*, which is neither original nor a copy, but rather a strange invention that aspires to imitate the inimitable.[55] In the case of Dalí, the most interesting thing about his recourse to *pasticcio* is his use of a dead pictorial language (seventeenth-century painting) to reconstruct an equally dead form (the history genre) with the aim of endowing what was for Dalí a moribund modern art with a new mask (that could only be that of death). Definitively transformed into a flesh and blood, and hence a traumatic, anachronism in the early 1960s, the figure of Dalí grew before the eyes of a generation of artists who had just appeared on the scene. These young painters, not wishing to submit themselves to the dictates of the modernist canon, headed into unexplored territories, generally related to film and other forms of mass-media communication. This was true of Andy Warhol, among others, who, in his cult of superficiality and non-originality saw in Dalí a forerunner of the new taste that arose from the growing mass-consumerism. It is hardly surprising, then, that Warhol captured Dalí in two of his *Screen Tests* (fig.148). By showing him head down, he was no doubt acknowledging, not without ironic malice, Dalí's resistant attitude. Following pathways as original as they were strange, Dalí had succeeded in keeping alive the flame of creative possibility on the margins of the rules imposed by the rigid modern aestheticism, taking film, always, as his metaphor.

Translated by Alayne Pullen

Notes

1

This essay extends my earlier research published in *Dalí: Cultura de masas*, exh. cat., CaixaForum, Barcelona, Museo Nacional Centro de Arte Reina Sofía, Madrid, Salvador Dalí Museum, St Petersburg (Florida) and (as *It's All Dalí*), Museum Boijmans Van Beuningen, Rotterdam 2004–5, as well as *Salvador Dalí: la construccion de la imagen 1925–1930*, Madrid 1999 and trans. as *Salvador Dalí: The Construction of the Image, 1925–1930*, New Haven and London 2007.

2

The adjective 'superficial' was used by Krakauer in 'Kult der Zerstreuung', *Frankfurter Zeitung*, 4 March 1926, republished in Siegfried Krakauer, *The Mass Ornament*, Cambridge, Mass. 1995, pp.323–8. The term 'distracted' comes from Benjamin's 'Work of Art in the Age of Mechanical Reproduction' (1936), republished in Walter Benjamin, *Illuminations*, New York 1968 and London 1970, pp.219–53.

3

Dalí letter to Federico García Lorca, early June 1927, published in *Salvador Dalí escribe a Federico García Lorca, 1925–1936*, ed. R. Santos Torroella, Madrid 1978, p.59; and trans. in Christopher Maurer (ed.), *Sebastian's Arrows: Letter and Mementos of Salvador Dalí and Federico García Lorca*, Chicago 2004, p.73.

4

The article by Sebastià Gasch was published under the title 'Salvador Dalí' in *La Gaseta de les Arts* (Barcelona) 1 Nov. 1926. The letter from Dalí to Gasch was published by the critic in his book *L'expansió de l'art català al món*, Barcelona 1953, p.142.

5

Dalí, 'Sant Sebastià', *L'Amic de les Arts*, 31 July 1927, trans. as 'San Sebastian', in Haim Finkelstein (ed.), *The Collected Writings of Salvador Dalí*, Cambridge 1998, pp.22–3.

6

Dalí, 'Poesia de l'útil standarditzat', *L'Amic de les Arts*, 31 March 1928, trans. as 'Poetry of the Mass-Produced Utility', ibid., p.57.

7

Dalí, 'La fotografia, pura creació de l'esperit', *L'Amic de les arts*, 30 Sept. 1927, trans. as 'Photography: Pure Creation of the Spirit', ibid., p.46.

8

Dalí, 'Art català relacionat amb el més recent de la jove intel·ligència' (Catalan Art in Relation to the Latest from the Young Intelligentsia), *La Publicitat* (Barcelona), 17 Oct. 1928.

9

Dalí letter to Sebastià Gasch, 21 Nov. 1927, private collection.

10

Dalí, 'Film-arte, film anti-artístico', *La Gaceta Literaria*, 15 Dec. 1927; see full translation republished in this volume from Finkelstein 1998.

11

Ibid.

12

Dalí, 'Films antiartísticos. La gran duquesa y el camarero. El traje de etiqueta (por Adolf Manjou [sic])' (Anti-Artistic Films. The Great Duchess and the Waiter. Formal Wear (by Adolphe Menjou)), *La Gaceta Literaria*, 1 March 1928, p.188.

13

Ibid.

14

Dalí, 'Sempre, per damunt de la música, Harry Langdon', *L'Amic de les Arts*, 31 March 1929, p.3, trans. as 'Always, above Music, Harry Langdon', in Finkelstein 1998, p.70.

15

Frank Capra, *The Name above the Title*, New York 1971, p.83.

16

Robert Desnos wrote: 'There is false laughter, crying with laughter, the outburst of laughter, the concealed laugh, laughing in your face, the crazy laugh. But how can one describe the sorrowful laugh that appears on the lips of the astonishing actor Harry Langdon?' in 'Harry Langdon', *Le Soir*, 30 May 1928, republished in Robert Desnos, *Les Rayons et les ombres. Cinéma*, Paris 1992, p.127.

17

André Breton, 'Max Ernst' (1921), in *Oeuvres complètes*, vol.1, Paris 1988, p.245.

18

Dalí, 'L'alliberaments dels dits', *L'Amic de les arts*, 31 March 1929, trans. as 'The Liberation of the Fingers', in Finkelstein 1998, p.99.

19

Luis Buñuel letter to Pepín Bello, 17 Feb. 1929, published by Augustín Sánchez Vidal, *Dalí, Lorca, Buñuel. El enigma sin fin*, Barcelona 1988, pp.193–8, and letter from Dalí to Luis Montanyà, Jan. 1929, private collection.

20

Dalí, 'Documental – Paris – 1929 [VI]', *La Publicitat*, 28 June 1929, trans. as 'Documentary – Paris – 1929' in Finkelstein 1998, p.117.

21

Dalí, 'Revista de tendències antiartístiques', *L'Amic de les arts*, 31 March 1929, trans. as 'Review of Antiartistic Tendencies', ibid., pp.103, 104.

22

Dalí, 'Documental – París – 1929 [I]', *La Publicitat*, 26 April 1929, trans. ibid., pp.105–6.

23

Dalí, 'Un Chien andalou', *Mirador*, 24 Oct. 1929, tr., ibid., p.134.

24

For a more detailed study of Dalí's development during this period, see Fèlix Fanés, *Salvador Dalí: The Construction of the Image, 1925–1930*, New Haven and London 2007.

25

Budd Schulberg, *What Makes Sammy Run?*, New York 1941, p.268.

26

Dalí, *La conquête de l'irrationel*, Paris 1935, trans. as *Conquest of the Irrational*, New York 1935, p.9.

27
Dalí, 'De la beauté terrifiante et comestible de l'architecture modern style', *Minotaure* (Paris), nos.3–4, 1933, trans. as 'Concerning the Terrifying and Edible Beauty of Art Nouveau Architecture', in Finkelstein 1998, pp.193–200.

28
Dalí, 'Les Nouvelles Couleurs du sex-appeal spectral', *Minotaure*, 15 May 1934, trans. as 'The New Colors of Spectral Sex-Appeal, ibid. p.206.

29
Dalí, 'Surrealism in Hollywood', *Harper's Bazaar*, June 1937, republished in full in this volume.

30
Ibid.

31
Dalí postcard to André Breton, Feb.–March 1937, Bibliothèque Litèraire Jacques Doucet, Paris.

32
Dalí, 'Abrégé d'une histoire critique du cinéma', *Babaouo*, Paris 1932, trans. as 'Short Critical History of Cinema' in Finkelstein 1998 and republished in full in this volume. Five years later, he would refer to *Animal Crackers* as a 'biological, hysterical and cannibal frenzy' in 'Surrealism in Hollywood', also republished in this volume.

33
André Breton, 'It's a Bird', *Minotaure*, no.10, winter 1937.

34
See the essay 'Surrealism and Hollywood', 1937 by Michael R. Taylor in this volume.

35
See 'Surrealism in Hollywood' 1937, republished in this volume.

36
What Eliot really found fascinating was Groucho and his use of language; see David E. Chinitz, *T.S. Eliot and the Cultural Divide*, Chicago 2003, pp.188–9.

37
Eisenstein mixed criticisms with his praise. The most important of these referred to 'the complete stylistic breach between the impotent childishness of the pictorial simplification of the backgrounds and the surprising perfection of the movement and drawing of the moving characters in the foreground'. S.M. Eisenstein, *La Non-indifférente Nature* (1945–7) (Non-indifferent Nature), vol.2, Paris 1978, pp.342–3.

38
Dalí, 'Surrealism in Hollywood'.

39
See my essay on *Destino* in this volume.

40
Lotte H. Eisner, 'Il kitsch cinematografico' (Kitsch in the Cinema), in Gillo Dorfles, *Il Kitsch. Antologia del cattivo gusto*, Milan 1968, pp.210 et seq.

41
Dalí, 'Surrealism in Hollywood'.

42
Dalí, *Giraffes on Horseback Salad* 1937, manuscript, Musée National d'Art Moderne, Centre Pompidou, Paris.

43
We should remember that at the time Dalí visited Hollywood (early in 1937), Disney was known mainly for two series of short films: *Mickey Mouse* and *Silly Symphonies*. Other famous characters such as Donald Duck, Pluto and Goofy did not begin their careers until that year (Goofy in 1939). As for the full-length films, the first, *Snow White and the Seven Dwarfs*, also dates from 1937.

44
André Breton, *Nadja*, Paris 1928, in *Oeuvres complètes*, pp.676, 679.

45
As one of the characters in 'Trésor des Jésuites' comments, 'It is in *Les Mystères de New York* and *Les Vampires* that the great reality of this century should be sought.' See André Breton and Louis Aragon, 'Le Trésor des Jésuites', *Variétés* (Brussels), June 1929, pp.47–61. In *Fantômas* Robert Desnos saw 'for the first time, the presence of the marvellous' in twentieth-century culture, see 'Imagerie moderne', *Documents*, vol.1, no.7, Dec. 1929.

46
Dalí, 'Short Critical History of Cinema' in this volume.

47
Ibid.

48
'It is in fact a film project that brings me to New York. The characters are Wagner, Ludwig II of Bavaria and Sacher Masoch. It's a film that appears absolutely normal, extraordinarily sentimental, capable of making everyone cry. But that is only the appearance, the outer form. Without realising, the viewers will be intoxicated by this film whose poison will go on working on them as time goes by. It's a *time bomb*. I'm taking it on just in case: I don't know if I'll be able to do it.' J.C. [Just Cabot], 'Una estona amb Dalí', *Mirador*, 18 Oct. 1934, trans. in Fanés 2007, p.199. Dalí had mentioned Richard Wagner and Ludwig II of Bavaria publicly for the first time in 'Objets psycho-atmosphèriques-anamorphiques', *Le Surréalisme au service de la révolution*, no.5, 1933, pp.45–8.

49
See Robert S. Lubar, 'Surrealism on Stage', in *It's all Dalí*, Museum Boijmans van Beuningen, Rotterdam 2005, pp.359–62.

50
I have taken this information and reconstructed some of the moments of the production from press cuttings in the archives of the Fundació Gala-Salvador Dalí, Figueres.

51
E. Downes, 'Surrealist Ballet', *Boston Transcript*, 18 April 1940.

52
Dalí, 'Derniers modes d'excitation intellectuel pour l'été 1934', *Documents 34*, June 1934, Brussels, pp.34–5, trans. as 'The Latest Modes of Intellectual Stimulation for the Summer of 1934', in Finkelstein 1998, pp.253–5.

53
Ibid., pp.253–4.

54
Walter Benjamin, *Ursprung des deutschen Trauerspiels* 1928, trans. as *The Origin of German Tragic Drama*, trans. John Osborne, London 1977, p.183.

55
For *pasticcio* and its presence in contemporary art, see Ingeborg Hoestery, *Pastiche: Cultural Memory in Art, Film, Literature*, Bloomington and Indianapolis 2001.

In Darkened Rooms

Matthew Gale

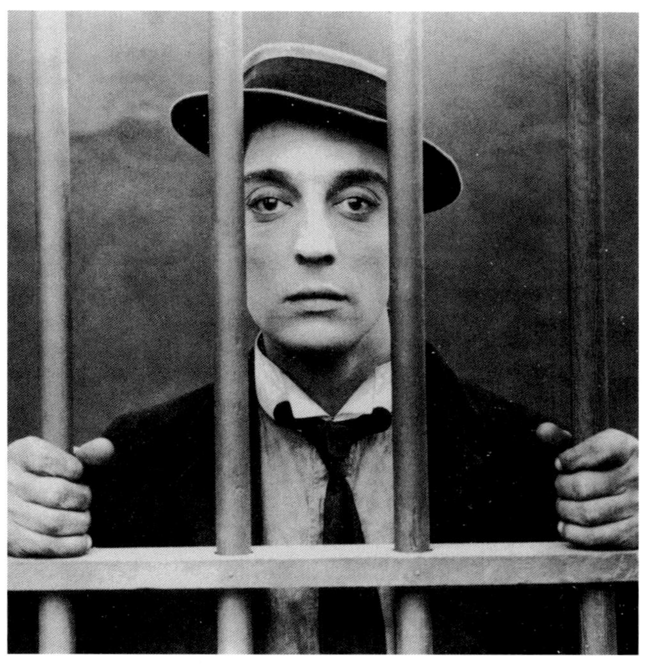

27
Buster Keaton in *The Goat*
1921
Ronald Grant Archive

Here is pure poetry

A man sits with his straw boater on his knees, his collar and tie tellingly askew. It is Buster Keaton. The still comes from *Seven Chances* 1925, in which the hero must marry before evening in order to secure an inheritance. Given Keaton's famed impassivity, he conveys his failure in this task entirely through his pose. Salvador Dalí included this image, and another of the actor in *The Navigator* 1924, in his collage *The Marriage of Buster Keaton* (fig.34a, b) of 1925.[1] In the following year, the painter expressed his admiration simply by declaring: 'Buster Keaton – here is Pure Poetry, Paul Valéry!'[2] Dalí's close associates Luis Buñuel and Federico García Lorca (the recipient of the collage) were also fans, and Keaton appears to have been a determining model for the central figure in *Un Chien andalou* in 1929.[3] As the evidence of the collage suggests, it was the subtle energy of Keaton's restraint that thrilled his contemporaries. The 'little man' of classic cinema narratives, he exemplified a daring inventiveness that struck a chord with the European avant-garde. Although more explicit in their challenge to authority and the comfortable assumptions of the viewer, Dalí and Buñuel adopted some of these strategies in both *Un Chien andalou* and *L'Age d'or*, not least in the struggle of the will and desire of the individual in the face of convention. The allegiance that they simultaneously proclaimed to Surrealism framed both films' receptions in the wider world and built an initially unlikely bridge between painting, Surrealism and cinema.

By the time of the public release of *Un Chien andalou* in late 1929, there was a wide awareness of Surrealism as a cultural force. Even if relatively few read André Breton's *Second manifeste du surréalisme* that appeared at that moment,[4] the movement was well known for interventions that regularly attracted press attention. Two years earlier, and reflecting their fascination with cinema, they had published 'Hands Off Love'. Primarily written by Louis Aragon, the manifesto defended Charlie Chaplin against his wife's claims of sexual deviancy in their divorce case.[5] One consequence of this defence appears to have been the group's sequence of discussions of sexual practice, the first of which took place on 27 January 1928.[6]

On 2 February 1928, within days of that meeting, the Surrealists attended the Cinéma des Ursulines for the premiere of *La Coquille et le clergyman* (The Seashell and the Clergyman). The film was directed by the leading filmmaker Germaine Dulac, with a script by Antonin Artaud. Despite his cooperation on the project, Artaud had become disenchanted by Dulac's end-product, which reflected her view of cinema as 'a visual symphony made of rhythmic images.'[7] Seeing his script as a revolutionary challenge to reality, he was especially angered by the qualification that she had added to the titles: 'from a dream by Antonin Artaud'.[8] The Surrealists, with whom Artaud had been active and was again passing through a brief period of reconciliation, attended the premiere to support Artaud by disrupting proceedings.

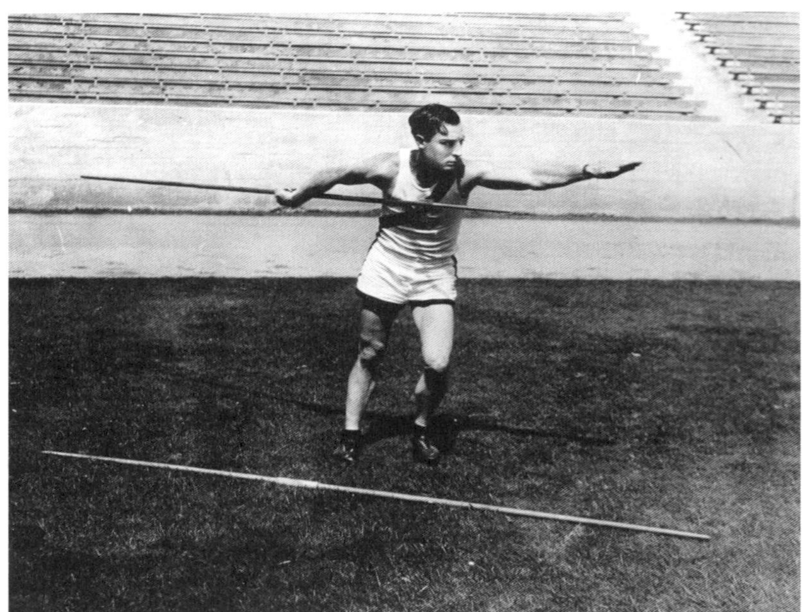

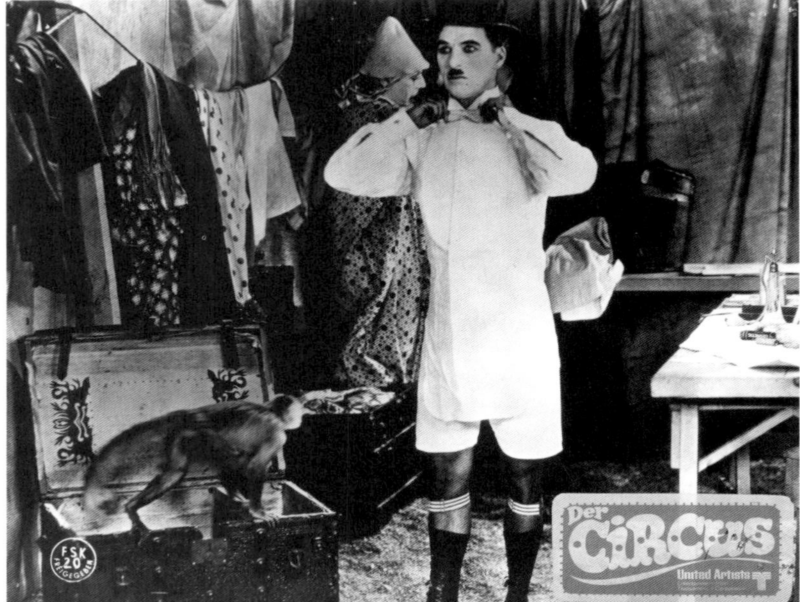

28
Buster Keaton in *College* 1927
Ronald Grant Archive

29
Charlie Caplin in *The Circus*
Ronald Grant Archive
1928

According to various accounts, Breton read aloud from the script throughout the screening and, after having insulted the director, the group was ejected, 'smashing the house mirrors as they went'.[9]

Beyond the extraordinary misogyny aimed at one of the few women directors working at this time, this disruption deserves consideration.[10] It is a measure of the unpredictability of such outbursts that Buñuel loaded his pockets with stones at the 1 October 1929 public premiere of *Un Chien andalou*, held at the same cinema: even though the film had been welcomed by the movement, he felt he needed to be forearmed against a similar Surrealist protest.[11] His precautions turned out to be unnecessary, but the action at *La Coquille et le clergyman* presaged the equally destructive intervention by the right-wing activists, the Ligue des Patriots, who protested against *L'Age d'or* in 1930 by slashing Surrealist canvases in the cinema foyer. While a distinction should be made between the Surrealists' protest on behalf of the author of *La Coquille et le clergyman* and the political machinations that resulted in the police ban of *L'Age d'or* (thus exposing an official sympathy with the action of the neo-Nazis), there seems relatively little to choose from between the Surrealists' mirror-smashing in 1928 and the Ligue's painting-slashing two years later.[12]

In addition to the tactics of disruption, the Surrealists' intervention over *La Coquille et le clergyman* hints at a chain of associated ideas about what film should be *in their view* and at that particular time. Breton's reading of Artaud's original scenario over the projected film signalled a hierarchy of values, whereby the original literary conception was more significant than the cinematic vision. Such an argument was rooted in a preference for the literary, and in the potential of automatism, the creative process that was liberated from conscious control and allowed, in Breton's words, the 'disinterested play of thought'.[13] The script represented a single poetic expression impoverished by the laboriously constructed film.

The unedited texts of automatic writing and the flowing line of automatic drawing had been the dominant means of liberation from convention through the early years of Surrealism. In an aside in his 1924 text 'Les Yeux enchantées' (The Enchanted Eyes), published in *La Révolution surréaliste*, Max Morise had proffered cinema as a solution to the difficulties presented in throwing-off conscious control in painting. Film offered the possibility for a constant flow of ideas: 'The cinema – a perfected cinema that would release us from technical formalities – could open the way towards a solution to this problem.'[14] Morise may have had in mind Man Ray's *Emak Bakia*, completed earlier that year, in which one fragmentary experience was supposedly captured by throwing the running camera over a flock of sheep; or he may have been thinking of the quite different nature of Keaton's physical comedy (as implied through a publicity still for *One Week* published in the preceding article).[15]

As such examples make clear, the Surrealists' regard for the primacy of unfettered imagination encountered difficult 'technical formalities' that critically undermined the project of automatism. However, as Dalí's key text of 1927, 'Film-arte, film-antiartistico', published in *La Gaseta Literaria*, demonstrated (though still from outside Surrealism), it was possible to address the problem that Morise had identified from a different perspective.[16] In favouring the 'anti-artistic' aspects of cinema – a practice of film-making beyond aesthetic pretension – he was able to set aside the very 'perfected cinema' that Morise had foreseen. He criticised the pretensions of genius and identified the 'anti-artistic film' as an alternative that reveals 'the entirely new poetic emotion of all the most humble and immediate facts, which were impossible to imagine or foresee before cinema'.[17] For Dalí, at this crucial moment, the potential of cinema lay in an anonymous creativity. It may be this challenge to the translation of narrative onto the screen that helped to encourage an upsurge in documentaries. The recording of the factual in films, such as would occur in Jean Vigo's Surrealist-inspired *A propos de Nice* 1930, enclosed potential for spontaneity through the unscripted reaction of those upon whom the camera's gaze was turned. Indeed, it was the documentary character, the 'anti-artistic' in Dalínian terms, of *Un Chien andalou* that allowed its extravagance to achieve naturalness.

The faithful translation of an authorial vision into film had already been achieved in Man Ray's inventive collaboration with Robert Desnos on *L'Etoile de mer* (Star Fish), made in 1928. According to the photographer's account at the time, he set out to complete a film based on one of Desnos's poems before the latter returned from a two-month trip. Stimulated by his long experience of cinema-going and his practice as a critic, Desnos had written 'a poem in the form of a scenario, full of very photogenic images'.[18] Significantly, however, Dalí and Buñuel had already come to the verge of condemning the poetic aspect of Man Ray's vision. Their comments suggest that they only held back in this condemnation out of respect for his pioneering role in film. In the same 1927 article, 'Film-arte, film-antiartistico', Dalí coupled Man Ray's *Emak Bakia* with Fernand Léger's *Ballet mécanique* (*Mechanical Ballet* 1923–4), but identified in them a 'fundamental misunderstanding', since 'the purest emotion still within the realm of vision (Man Ray's film is directed solely at the senses) does not have to be sought in the world of invented forms'.[19]

In published responses to questions posed by Dalí in March 1929, Buñuel expressed an admiration for what they termed 'the industrial anti-artistic film' of Hollywood. He was asked whether he felt that Man Ray had the 'wonderful intuition that the Americans have' or whether he showed an 'incomprehension of Surrealism, despite his adherence to the group?' To this very loaded question, Buñuel replied that Man Ray 'is full of *spirit*. Much closer to us and to Surrealism are Pollard, Menjou, Ben Turpin.'[20] This interview

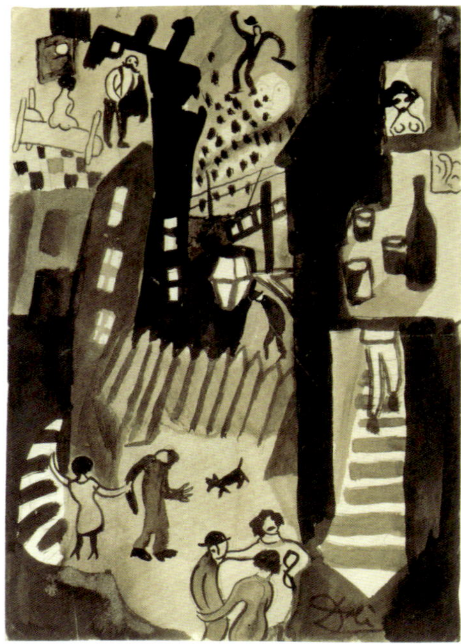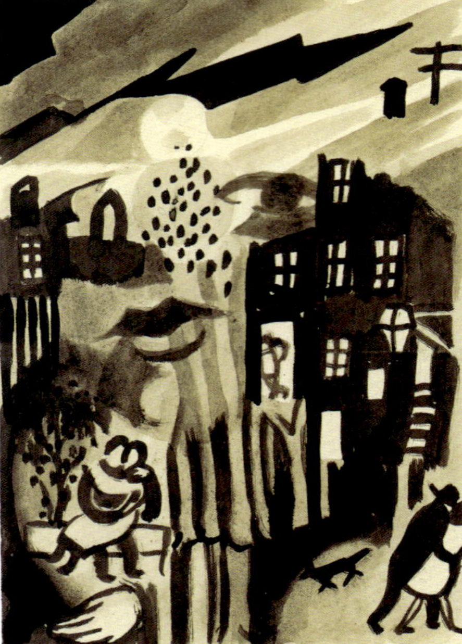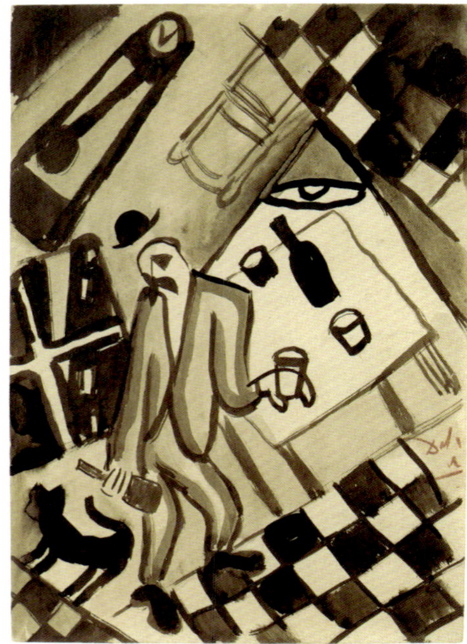

dates from the friends' closest collaboration, between the writing and shooting of *Un Chien andalou*, which began on 2 April 1929.[21] Buñuel had almost certainly seen *L'Etoile de mer*, which had been premiered nearly a year earlier (May 1928) and, in emphasising Man Ray's 'spirit', seems to refer to Desnos's contemporary discussion of the artist.[22] While the Spaniards were aware that their project was distinct, it is striking that they were confident of its alignment with Surrealism, even before any official contact with the group.

Their view of the objective possibilities of cinema fed into the formative thinking that underpinned *Un Chien andalou*. Although their sources were very heterogeneous, their difficulty with film 'directed solely at the senses' eliminated the formalism of much avant-garde cinema. It is, by contrast, the documentary elements, partly informed by the mechanistic aesthetic of the periodical *L'Esprit nouveau*, that appealed.[23] The innocent inventiveness derived from 'things themselves' was, from around 1927, a source of elaborate extrapolation within Dalí's associative imagination. First in his paintings and then in his film projects, ordinary 'things' were the trigger for images that were rooted in reality but pushed beyond it into an adjacent, highly charged, sphere.[24]

While this complex imagery was very personal to Dalí, its associative structure bears comparison with the techniques of the cinema. The visual power of the slapstick 'sight gag' necessarily drove the narrative of silent comedies, and aspects of their condensed overlaying of images appear to be echoed in his work. This may be seen in considering one memorable sequence from Keaton's *The Goat* 1921, in which the hero climbs onto an equestrian statue without knowing that it is only a clay model; the horse slowly gives way under his weight and buckles over the plinth. The softening of a realistic representation of nature anticipates Dalí's fascination with morbidity and decay. More specifically, Keaton's conceit directly evokes the soft forms of the painter's paranoiac-critical horse, lion, woman paintings of 1930, in which multiple realities are revealed.[25] Dalí's challenge was to achieve this multiplicity through the visual complexity of his static image, which, in film, Keaton secured through time (and timing).

The vitality of a Hispano

Dalí's generation was the first to grow up with the cinema and it was no longer the question of *whether* film was an art but rather the nature of that art and its aesthetics that was debated in the late 1920s. The cinema was regarded as a democratic art since it reached out to all walks of life. Already in 1923, René Clair (who would make his first film, *Paris qui dort*, later that year) had asserted that 'the screen masterpieces are almost always its greatest successes'.[26] In the appreciation of Hollywood's mass-produced movies, therefore, lay a residual egalitarianism that, despite its paradoxical nature, was founded in popularity.

30
Brothel 1922
Ink wash on paper 20.8 x 15 cm
Fundació Gala-Salvador Dalí, Figueres

31
Summer Night 1922
Ink wash on paper 20.8 x 15 cm
Fundació Gala-Salvador Dalí, Figueres

32
The Drunkard 1922
Ink wash on paper 20.8 x 15 cm
Fundació Gala-Salvador Dalí, Figueres

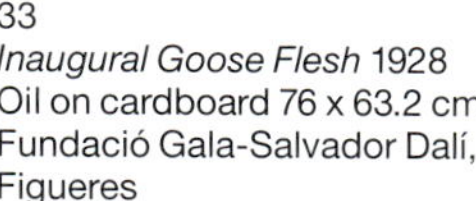

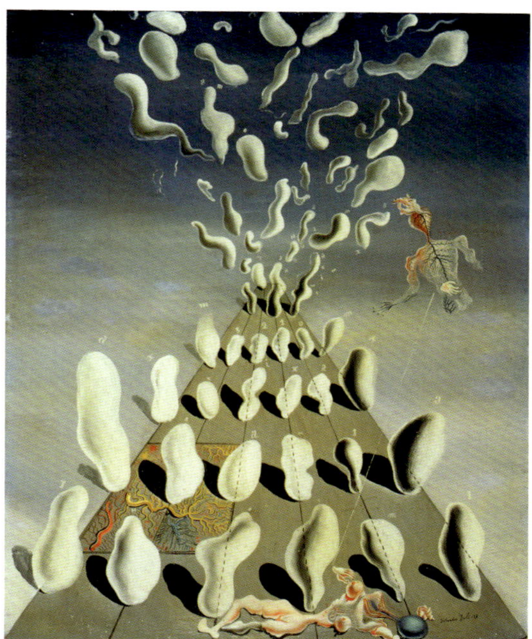

The broad aesthetic distinction in film remained that laid out by the pioneers of the turn-of-the-century: between a photographic art, founded on Louis Lumière's records of everyday events, and a theatrical art, as explored by Georges Méliès in his burlesque narratives. The cinema-goer of the late 1920s could experience all permutations in remarkable films that continue to have a resonance today. When the writers Ernesto Giménez Caballero and Ramón Gómez de la Serna established the Cineclub Español in Madrid in 1928,[27] its programme (as reported in *La Gaceta Literaria*) was broadly based. American films ranged from W.D. Griffiths's *Broken Blossoms* and Fred Niblo's *Mark of Zorro* (both 1919) to Robert Flaherty's documentary *Moana* 1926. Among the European films screened were Clair's *Entr'acte* 1924, Walter Ruttmann's *Berlin: Symphony of a City* 1927, Abel Gance's *La Roue* 1922 and Dulac's *La Coquille et le clergyman*.[28] They promised, too, full programmes of Chaplin's and Keaton's productions. Among those associated with the Cineclub was Buñuel, who returned to lecture at the Residencia de Estudiantes (where he, Lorca and Dalí first met as students),[29] and wrote reviews simultaneously for *La Gaceta Literaria* and for *Cahiers d'art* in Paris.

The reviews (by Buñuel and others) in these two periodicals are representative of the debate around the direction for film as an art during the period leading up to the making of *Un Chien andalou*. Necessarily, the opinions varied. The fabled expenditure on Niblo's three-hour Roman epic *Ben-Hur* 1925 yielded, according to one *Cahiers d'art* critic, only fifteen minutes of real cinema (seven and a half minutes on the galley battle and the same on the chariot race).[30] This observation reflected the tendency towards an appreciation of formalism, or at least those qualities that were unique to film, that characterised the journal more widely and circumscribed the way in which the cinematographic could be identified. In this vein, another critic in the same journal – although not overlooking the political message of Sergei Eisenstein's revolutionary film – welcomed *Battleship Potemkin* 1925 as the first film 'in which the harmonious image and rhythm are achieved with a fine amplitude'.[31] It was widely proclaimed as a masterpiece. Buñuel had already praised it as the most remarkable film he had seen, and later recalled its profound influence upon his work.[32] His enthusiasm for Eisenstein, as well as for Vsevolod Pudovkin and Dziga Vertov, acknowledged the fundamental ability to combine popularity with remarkable techniques and radical politics. Such popularity was, as Dalí pointed out in 1932, also felt among the 'most catholic and conservative' circles oblivious to the revolutionary message.[33]

Jacques-Bernard Brunius, who was a fellow-traveller of Surrealism, reviewed both Fritz Lang's *Metropolis* 1926 and Gance's *Napoléon* 1927 in *Cahiers d'art*. He admired Lang's complex vision of urban enslavement, although he observed that the 'remarkable' technical effects 'pass unseen, drowned-out by their abundance'.[34]

The Marriage of Buster Keaton 1925
Collage and ink on paper
each sheet 21.3 x 16.8 cm
Fundación Federico García Lorca,
Madrid

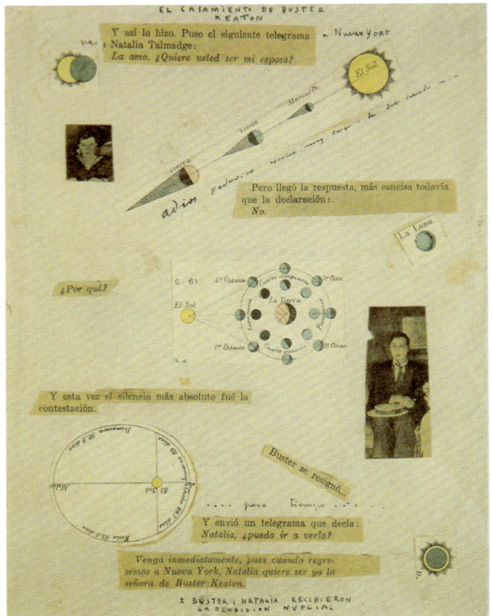
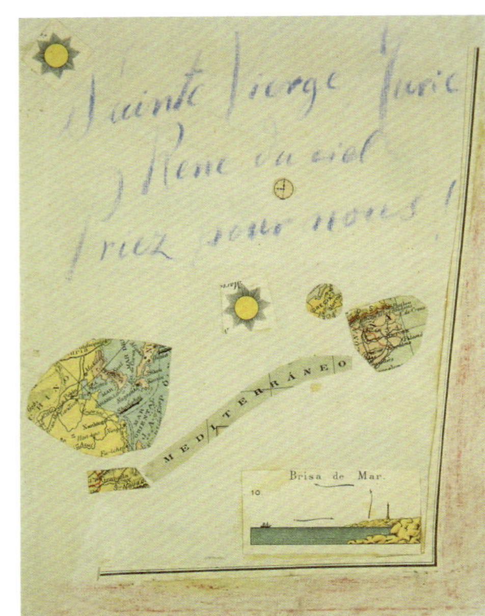

The sentimental ending lay in contrast to such mastery as well as the underlying story of labour and capital. Writing in *La Gaceta Literaria* towards the end of the year, Dalí echoed these views, comparing Lang's spectacle 'with all the theatricalism of the worst history painting'.[35]

Brunius reserved greater criticism, however, for Gance's *Napoléon*, which had arrived as the great French epic, complete with the unique device of tripartite screens that resulted in massive length and expenditure.[36] Its virtuosity appeared pointless. 'More powerful that *Metropolis*?', Brunius asked rhetorically: 'You would like to say less awful.'[37] He concluded: 'M. Abel Gance is a great director, a great musician, a great romantic, a divine practitioner. Anything you like, but he still has not completely understood cinema.' Such a criticism emphasised a desire for an interaction of parts characteristic of cinema (and implicitly exposing Gance's theatrical background), and was informed by Brunius's experience as a filmmaker himself (he would be an assistant director on *L'Age d'or*).[38] Buñuel was even more disdainful of *Napoléon* (although he had been urged by his mentor Jean Epstein to assist Gance and this review broke their relationship).[39] He called the film a failure, and added: 'in a way, it even represents the failure of the Latin spirit in the face of the modern form of expression that is the cinema'.[40] Piling on the pressure, he concluded that the audience should be warned on arrival: '"Sirs," we should tell them, "this is not cinema. This turns away from cinema. Go and

see *The Ingénue* instead, an American film about a young horsewoman in love, that ends with a discrete kiss. At least it is light, fresh, full of rhythmic images cut with a truly cinematic vision."'[41] Like Brunius, Buñuel looked in vain for the cinematic in Gance's work. The combination of heroic romanticism and mystical nationalism in *Napoléon*, reminiscent of the post-war moment, must already have appeared anachronistic. Neither was likely to be supported by those connected with international modernism or Surrealism. Brunius and Buñuel were connected to both. To his review of this epic, Brunius even added the postscript: 'When will people make small films?' *Un Chien andalou* was one answer.

As we have seen, Dalí also expressed an admiration (shared with Buñuel) for American film in 'Film-arte, Film-antiartistico' later in 1927. There he identified 'the entirely new poetic emotion' of the immediate.[42] In a subsequent article, simply entitled 'Films antiartísticos', he proposed that 'the cinema is the most unreal way to express reality'.[43] He enlarged upon this paradox, which implied his growing sympathy for Surrealism, by declaring: 'The force and poetry of cinema, like that of photography, is precisely this naturalness in the marvellous capturing within the naked screen of the strictest objectivity with its continuous and isolated manner of fantasy.' Dalí cited the films of the actor Adolphe Menjou in this relation to the ordinary, thus continuing the debate between serious cinema and popular entertainment. In most cases Dalí, Buñuel and their colleagues found

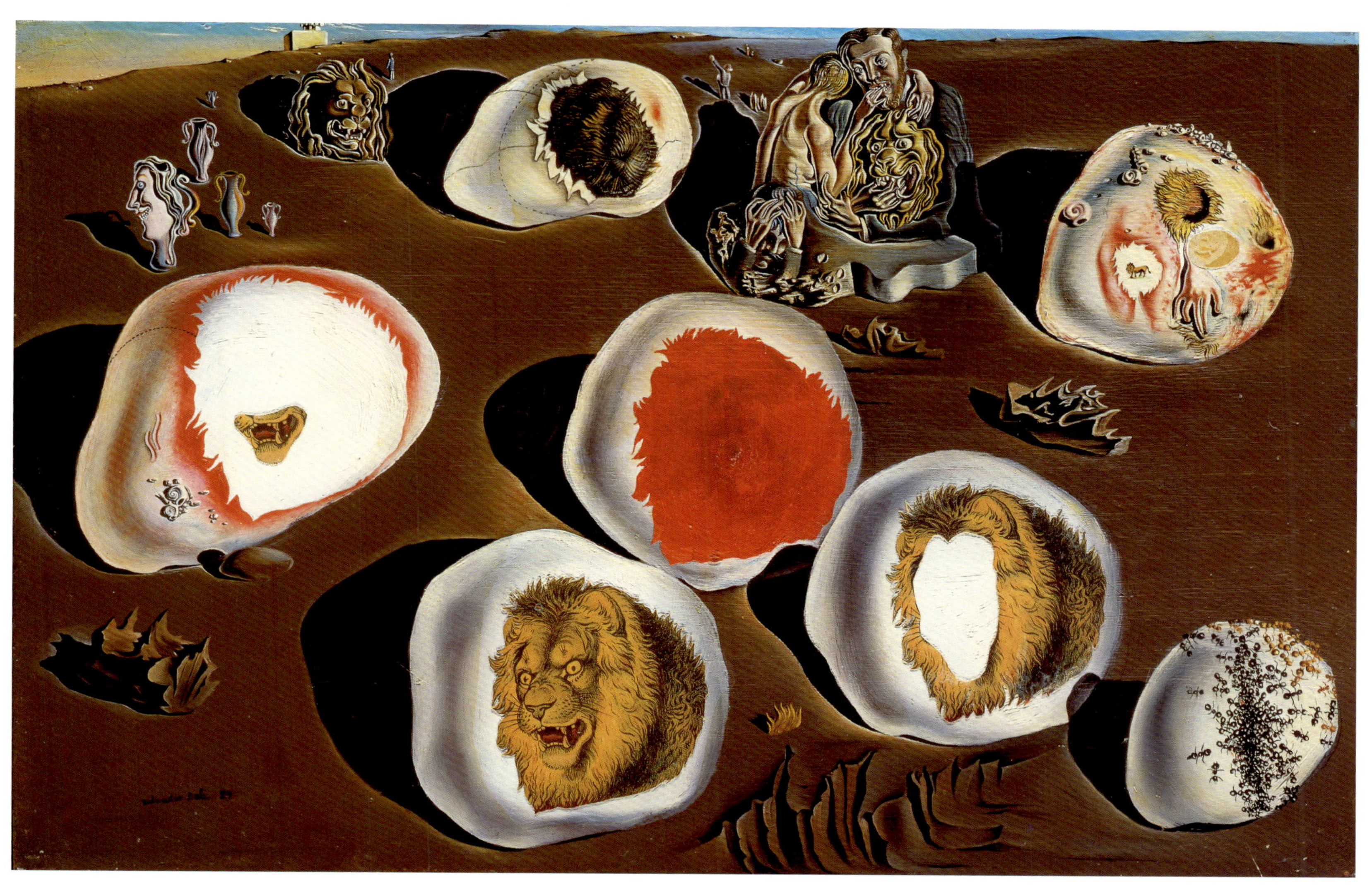

35
The Accommodations of Desire 1929
Oil and cut and pasted printed paper on
cardboard 22.2 x 34.9 cm
Metropolitan Museum of Art, New York.
The Jacques and Natasha Gelman
Collection, 1998

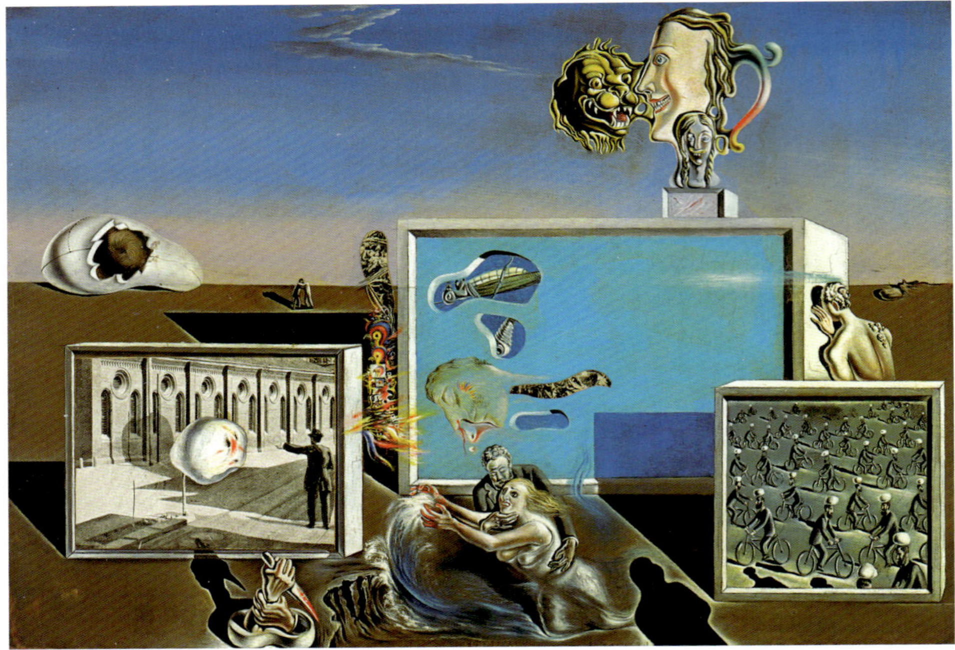

the 'high' art wanting in the face of the poetics of mass-production in Hollywood.[44] This was certainly the evident strength of Keaton and of Chaplin, whose works transcended classes and nations. Catching a reshowing of Keaton's *Sherlock Jr.* in 1927 (by which time it was already three years old), Brunius called for its return to the repertoire: 'It contains all cinema and its analysis, all humour, all poetry, all genius.'[45] Some months later, Buñuel wrote glowingly of *College* 1927, in which Keaton (playing a scholar trying to become a sportsman to impress a girl), performed a huge variety of physical stunts (fig.28). Behind the humour, Buñuel recognised a filmic technique comparable to the more demonstrative qualities of *Metropolis* and *Napoléon*. Though *College* is driven by romance, he also admired the disavowal of sentiment. 'The film was as beautiful as a bathroom', he declared in tones reminiscent of F.T. Marinetti's Futurist manifestoes 'with the vitality of a Hispano [car]', adding: 'Buster Keaton's expression is as modest as that of a bottle.'[46]

In his article, Buñuel pitted Keaton's 'anti-virtuosity' against Chaplin's sentimentality. For an earlier generation in Europe, Chaplin's films had been the apogee of American cinema, because, as Blaise Cendrars recalled,[47] they had been discovered by soldiers on leave from the trenches. The animated puppet of Chaplin with which Léger prefaced *Ballet mécanique*, harks back to that moment of solidarity between the avant-garde and popular culture.[48] A continuing admiration was demonstrated by the six-page supplement to *Cahiers*

d'art in early 1928 on the release of Chaplin's *The Circus* (fig.29).[49] This compendium extracted texts by Cendrars and a variety of others, ranging from the director Louis Delluc (author of a Chaplin biography) and the English writer John Middleton Murry to the Surrealist René Crevel. The popularity of such films seemed to point to an unconscious connection with the audience that was simply lacking in those who aspired to a grand style.

The comparison between Keaton and Chaplin was, by then, habitual. In the Catalan periodical *La Gaseta de les Arts*, Dalí's associate Sebastià Gasch used Keaton's *College* as a measure of Chaplin's *The Circus*, distinguishing between 'the plastic and the expressive' respectively.[50] While it was Keaton's impassivity that Dalí and Buñuel so admired – and Gasch cited the latter's comparison of the actor to a bottle – the result was deemed too 'dehumanised'. For Gasch: 'Chaplin's [expression], by contrast, is multiple, infinitesimal'.[51] However, as Chaplin expanded his movies of the later 1920s towards drama, so – for some – he appeared to succumb to the pretensions of high art. The question 'Chaplin or Buster Keaton?' posed by Dalí to Buñuel (in their interview of March 1929) is typical of the response that this shift elicited. So is Buñuel's answer: 'Chaplin no longer makes anyone but the intellectuals laugh.'[52] Perhaps Buñuel was targeting his former colleagues at *Cahiers d'art* as much as Gasch and others, or perhaps he had in mind the report that Chaplin wanted to make a 'Life of Christ' based on a script by Giovanni

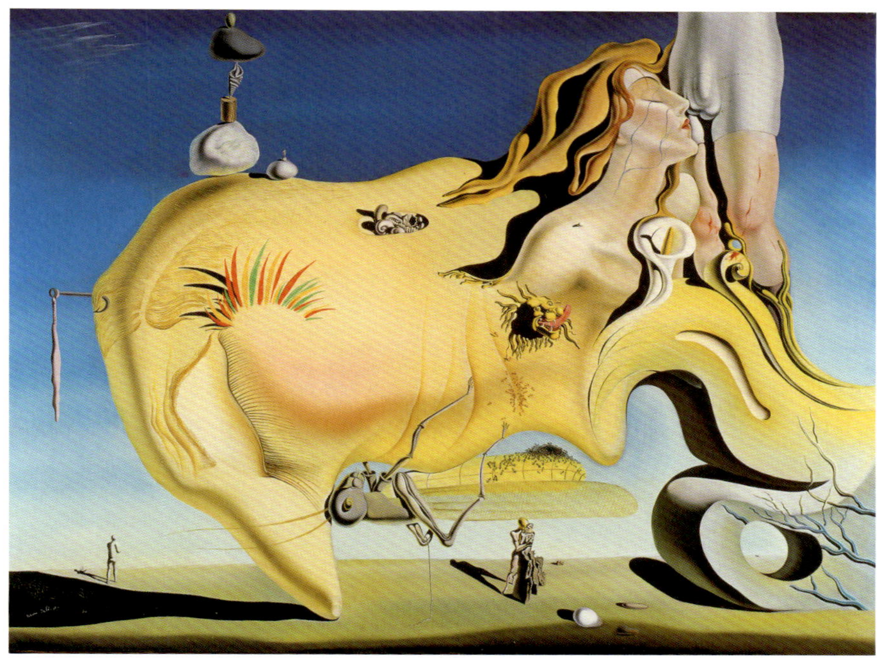

Papini.[53] Whatever the case, this dismissal came about after *The Circus* won an Oscar in 1928, an acceptance that came close to breaking the spell among European radicals. By 1932, Dalí would attack Chaplin's sentimental ending to *City Lights* as 'pseudo-transcendentalism'.[54]

The sense of a popular engagement through film remained powerful. It shaped publicly expressed tastes at a time of social unease across much of Europe. Through a shared entertainment, modernists fashioned a connection for themselves even if the people in the street were generally oblivious to such efforts. The political necessity of the Surrealists' engagement with the Communist party lay behind the immediate circumstances faced by Breton's group when Dalí and Buñuel joined them in 1929. Certainly this desire was fuelled by the potency of the films coming out of the USSR, which immediately became celebrated in the West. However, in contrast to the message of ideologically loaded group action in *Battleship Potemkin*, the Hollywood movies were politically anodyne, though democratic, in their portrayal of the individual struggling with authority (the ever-present policemen) and convention.

The appetite for stories of the battle with adversity extended beyond comedy to what are now more marginal figures such as Menjou and Tom Mix. The films of Mix, a circus-cum-western star, enjoyed considerable popularity. The writer Alberto Savinio identified the pretensions of French films as the cause behind audiences rushing to the cinemas 'promising either the froth of Tom Mix or the cut-price Ariosto-ism of Douglas Fairbanks'.[55] As early as 1927, Dalí evoked Menjou, Keaton and 'Tom Mix's white glove which touches black, pure like the latest amorous interlacements of the fish, crystals and stars of Marcoussis.'[56] Even as Dalí's references are abstruse, to measure Mix against the Cubist painter Marcoussis was to force contemporary worlds of 'low' and 'high' culture together provocatively. In so doing, he engaged in a wider current of cultural activity long underway within modernism, from the admiration of Guillaume Apollinaire for detective fiction to the strategy of the sensational and the new in popular magazines.

Because of the darkness

With only slight exaggeration, Buñuel wrote in February 1930 of the 'great crisis of cinema at present'. For an art still in the process of development, such a crisis seemed premature, but it hinged around the technical leap into sound. Buñuel's comments were addressed to the Vicomte de Noailles, his patron and backer on *L'Age d'or*, and his distinction between talking films, called *sonore-parlant* in French, and the more paradoxical *muet-sonore* (literally 'mute-sound') on which sound was added in post-production, represented both a financial and an ideological choice bound up with a struggle between rival sound systems from either side of the Atlantic.[57] In the event, de Noailles offered the extra funding,

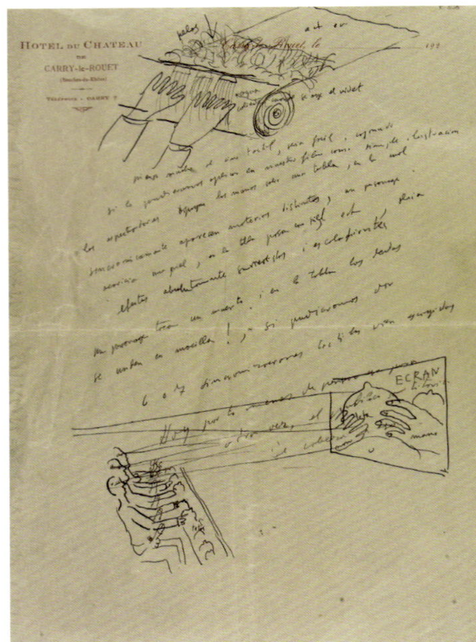

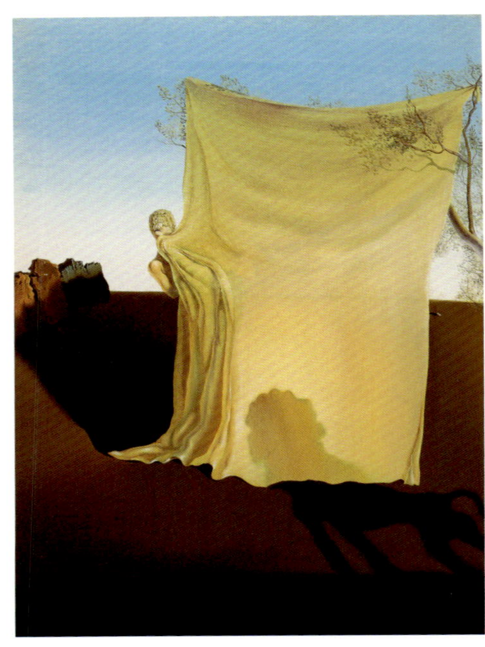

and *L'Age d'or* was made as one of the first sound movies in France. Others recognised in the 'crisis of cinema' a watershed. Asked in late 1929 if he would use sound, Man Ray demurred and commented of silent film: 'film-makers are far from having exhausted all of its possibilities … silent cinema is being abandoned just at the moment that it is becoming interesting to work with'.[58] Later still, his attitude hardened as he remarked: 'the cinema is primarily a banking operation these days'.[59] In so saying, Man Ray identified the financial shift from the project still within reach of the amateur or patron in the 1920s, to the studio productions of the 1930s, and from the quick turnaround of the early silents to the later multilingual versions of Hollywood movies.

Of course, the experience of silent cinema had not been silent. Musicians supplied an accompaniment, with all the potential inconsistencies from place to place. In 1925, the journalist Joseph Roth witnessed an audience revolt: 'They want a different tune. The pianist gets up, walks out, and the film continues without music.'[60] A member of the audience then physically retrieves the pianist and forces him to play the popular choice. In this context, Desnos commented that 'there is nothing more ominous … than a film projected in silence. Noise is necessary, yet every attempt at imitative orchestration has been pitiful.'[61] It was perhaps this localised performance that helped to induce a sense of continuity across the wide variety of

popular film. While Desnos could remark upon some cinemas as 'the meeting-place of the lowest company … [that] get the films they deserve', some of his other companions were more omnivorous in their tastes. In early 1929, the poet Paul Eluard wrote to his wife Gala of the 'mad eroticism' of a 'cinéma obscène' that he has just visited.[62] Beyond the challenge to convention that such illicit establishments provided, the unplanned discovery of film embedded within the city was a common theme. A year later, by which time Gala was living with Dalí, Eluard wrote melancholically: 'I go to the cinema alone all the time, because of the darkness.'[63]

In his 1928 novel *Nadja*, Breton laid out the potential to be found in the chance sampling of the continuous film programmes:

For this system which consists, before going into a movie theatre, of never looking to see what is playing – which, moreover, would scarcely do me any good, since I cannot remember the names of more than five or six actors – I obviously run the risk of missing more than others, though here I must confess my weakness for the most absolutely absurd French films. I understand, moreover, quite poorly, I follow too vaguely.[64]

Chance was a talismanic element within Surrealist circles in the 1920s, as indicated by the unattributed statement: 'Cinema is the bringing into play of chance'.[65] In *Nadja* Breton combined this with a distance, even a disinterest, that allowed him to

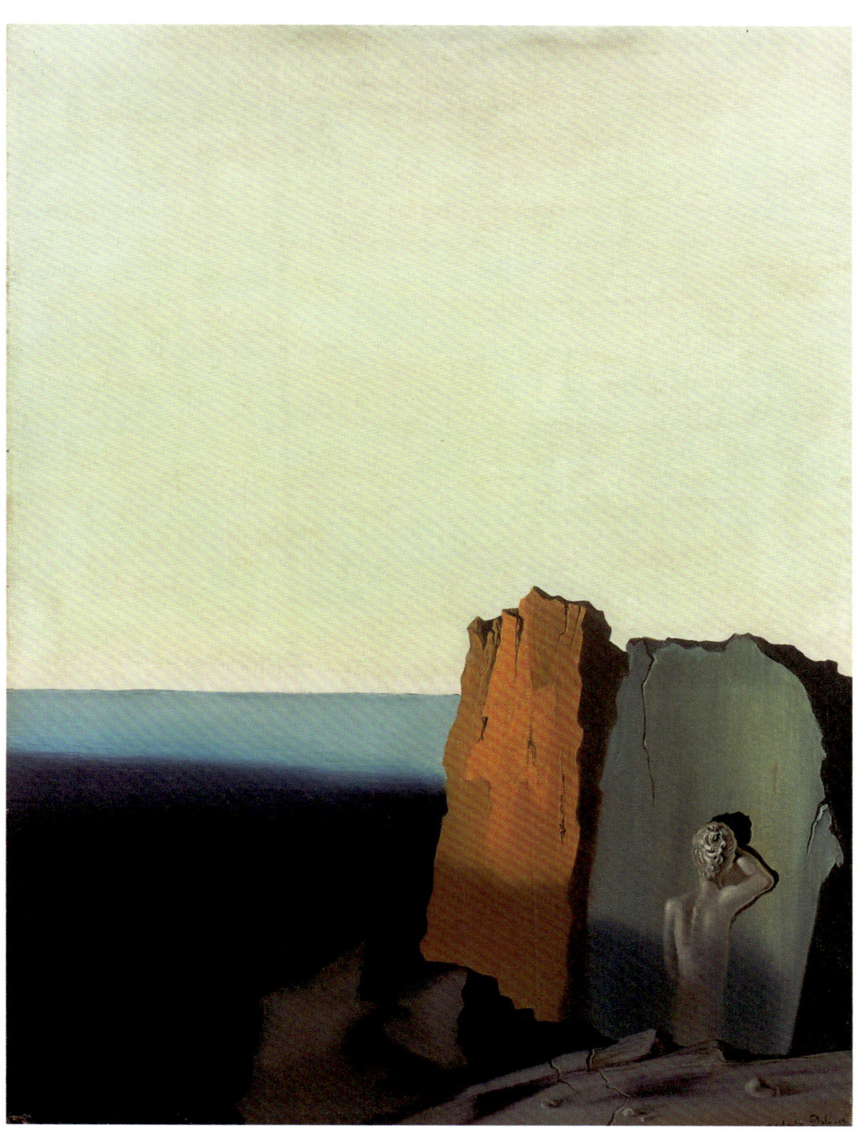

appreciate the disjunctive quality of the experience rather than the narrative thread of any individual production. Although covered by a suggestion that these were cheap pulp movies, it is notable that he disregarded the intentions and achievements of the filmmaker. Indeed, they seem to have been imagined as lacking the construction recognisable in more ambitious movies. Breton could make a virtue of understanding 'quite poorly' because he approached film as an immersive experience. As noted in relation to his criticism of Gance, Buñuel, by contrast, recognised that even the standard Hollywood movie was constructed cinematically.

For many, it was René Clair who presented the best prospects for a similarly cinematic sensibility in France. Buñuel had even concluded his review of *Napoléon* by citing him: 'If you want a French national cinema, encourage youth, those who perhaps through their age and their temperament are able to transfer our sensibility onto the screen: René Clair for instance.'[66] This was a vote of appreciation for a director of the same generation, who shared a similar humour and anti-authoritarianism cemented in his collaboration with Francis Picabia on *Entr'acte*. Above all, he infused his comedies with the pacing and techniques of Hollywood. This, however, did not save him from a mauling from the Surrealists in 1931 over *À nous la liberté* (For us, Freedom), his film about a prison break, which came only a year after the suppression of *L'Age d'or* by the police. They criticised Clair – in an article bitterly entitled

'A commercial film' – for making the authorities too humane.[67]

A different challenge to Surrealist aspirations lay in the first film of their favourite *bête noir*, Jean Cocteau. Long disparaged by them for his fashionable effeteness, he nevertheless managed to sustain a trajectory that remained disturbingly parallel to theirs, and this was made acute when he was commissioned by the Vicomte de Noailles to make a film at the same time as Buñuel's *L'Age d'or*.[68] In contrast to Artaud's experience with Dulac, Cocteau maintained control of *Le Sang d'un poète* (The Blood of a Poet, 1930), conceiving, casting and overseeing the shooting, on the basis of his theatrical experience. It shared some of its imagery with the collaborations of Dalí and Buñuel and with other Surrealist productions, but it was still the subject of the usual vilification.[69]

What distinguished *Le Sang d'un poète* from *L'Age d'or* was Cocteau's inherent tendency towards the baroque, encapsulated in one critic's over-generous appreciation: 'Symbolic cinema is born.'[70] Desnos identified Cocteau's 'exaggerated respect for art and mystique of expression' that placed him firmly within the role of self-consciously 'artistic' filmmaker.[71] For his part, Cocteau staked a claim for this pretension by asserting that his film 'is a realist documentary of unreal events'.[72] This was a commonly held understanding of the potential for fantasy in cinema, but it had, as we have noted, been specifically inverted by Dalí's recognition that 'the cinema is the most unreal way to express reality'.[73]

In this reversed word-play lies a fundamental divergence in outlook that marked the two projects supported by de Noailles: a documenting of theatricality as opposed to an unmasking of reality. *L'Age d'or* was released first, and Cocteau, who was among the guests at the premiere,[74] seemed to remark admiringly upon it despite this fundamental difference in approach: 'Scenes like those with the cow or the leader of the orchestra in Buñuel's *L'Age d'or* should be considered as a major event, the arrival of the tragic *gag*. I have no doubt that they will raise a bitter laugh … nothing can hold back the black stream of which they are the source.'[75]

The public will swoon
If films typically offered an escape from the everyday that the Surrealists admired, and which ordinary people sought out (especially as escapism in the 'dream factory' years of the 1930s depression), the assault that Dalí and Buñuel made on cinema was far from comforting. Both *Un Chien andalou* and *L'Age d'or* were, in their different ways, brittle with tension. Dalí had long foreseen a cinema that could provide this unsettling, sensual experience. In 1927, he had identified a 'cinema that is dumb, deaf, blind … since the best cinema is the kind that can be perceived with your eyes closed'.[76] In proposing this inner intensity, the painter touched upon both the power that he sought to harness for the screen and the weakness that he recognised in its

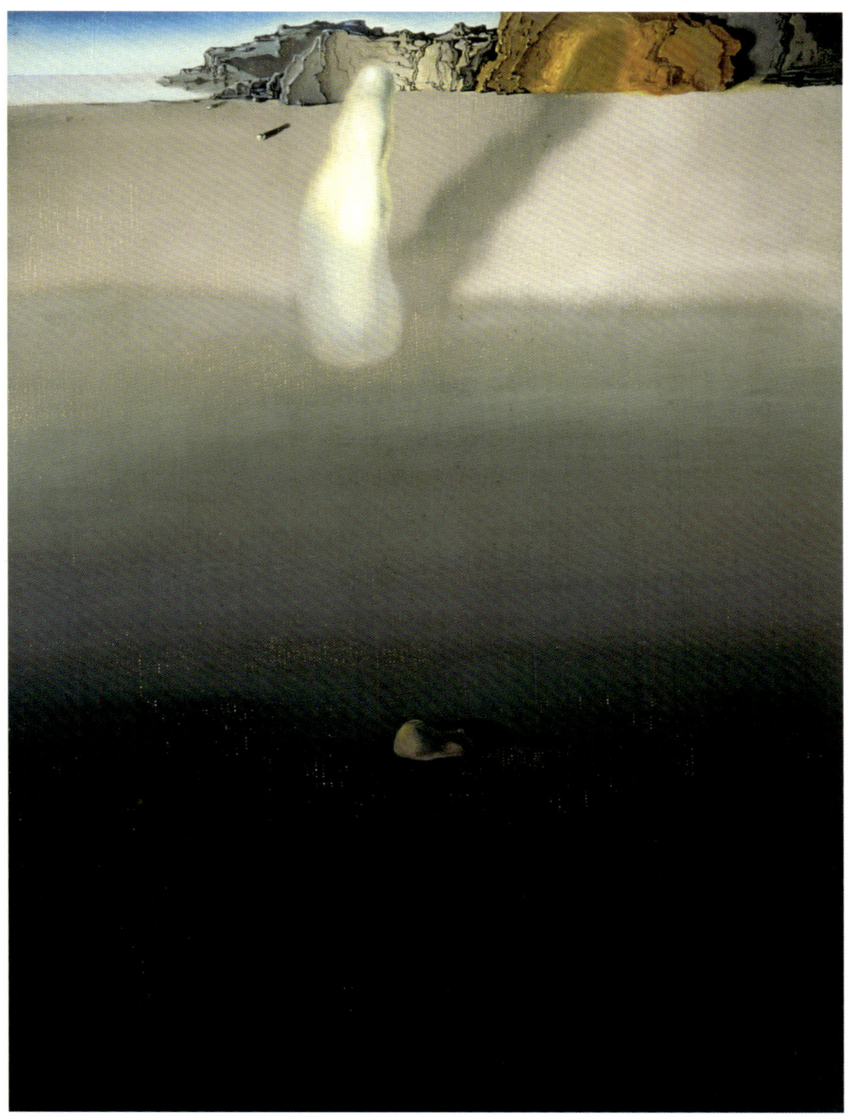

inability to match his own reveries. It may be for
this reason that he continued to paint, since his
extraordinary illusionism allowed the impossible
realities of his imaginings to be made public.[77]

    Early in 1930, and in direct opposition
to the 'senseless' cinema earlier imagined, Dalí
proposed 'tactile cinema' to Buñuel (fig.38).
Extending the sequences of rough fondling in
Un Chien andalou, the idea echoed Man Ray's
experiments with perfumed films four years
earlier.[78] The term recalled Marinetti's Futurist
manifesto *Il Tattilismo* 1921 and subsequent
'tactile poems' of which Dalí was probably aware.[79]
Even more than Marinetti, Dalí loaded his
proposal with a fervid tension:

*The spectators place their hands on a shelf over which
pass various materials simultaneously [with the film];
a character caresses skin: on the shelf skin passes. This
would have a totally surrealist effect and give one a
frisson. A character touches a dead body and fingers on
the shelf sink in, as into butter! This could be done with 6
or 7 well-chosen tactile synchronisations. It will have to be
considered for another time, [but] the public will swoon.*[80]

Dalí had been concerned with the fertility of
touch since the crisis in his painting in 1926–7. At
that moment, his concentration upon photography
and film as anaesthetic media ran parallel with the
exploration of texture in such works as the cork
Feminine Nude (fig.20) or the elements coated in
fine gravel. These were the direct ancestors of his

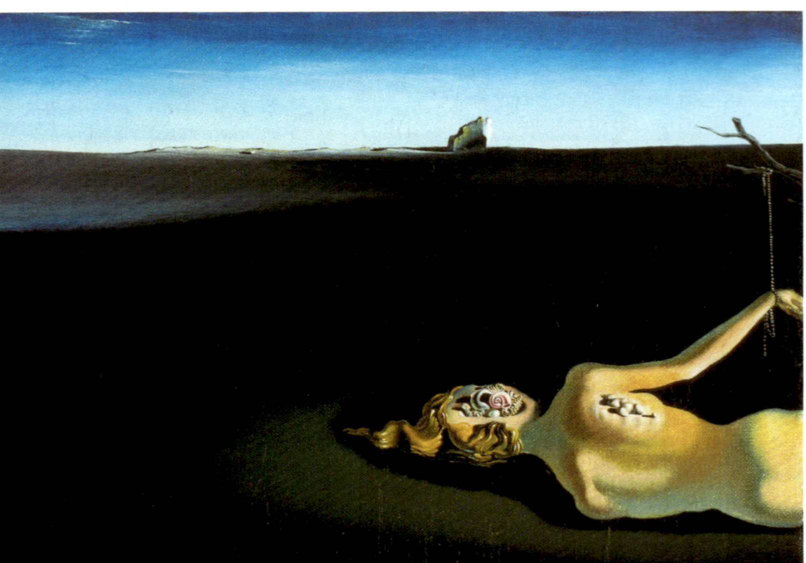

development of the Surrealist object launched in December 1931.[81] Here the soft watches were proposed as 'transubstantiated objects', but it is notable that the 'machine objects (experimental fantasies)', stimulated by the latent eroticism of Alberto Giacometti's sculptures, demanded a physical interaction already anticipated in the notion of the tactile cinema. Of course, tactility was, as Dalí acknowledged, technically impossible in 1930, when the control of sound was enough of a challenge. Nevertheless, Dalí's desire for a multi-sensual film embraced the potential for cinema as *Gesamtkunstwerk* or total artwork, an ideal previously of operatic proportions, but here given a physical presence that Wagner had not achieved.

Dalí could move with ease across media by ignoring boundaries between them. An idea sketched out in a marginal drawing might resurface in a scenario, on screen or on a canvas – or, in the case of the repeated image in his works of a stone/baguette balanced on the head, all three.[82] To see the seeds of imagery in his paintings emerge in the films is relatively unproblematic and this is hardly surprising given the different levels of opportunity to complete work in the two media. The throbbing hand in the painting *Apparatus and Hand* 1927 and isolated thumb in *The Wounded Bird* 1928 (figs.18, 50), therefore, seem to anticipate the inanimate hand in the box in *Un Chien andalou*. Both imply the confessional aspect made more explicit in the painting *The Great Masturbator* 1929 (fig.37). This transference continued for later

projects, such as the sofa bearing impressions of reclining figures that appear in the painting *Singularities* c.1935 (fig.89) and relate to *Giraffes on Horseback Salad*.[83] Images are tested and refined, adapted for the static or the temporal.

Although much less obvious, it is not surprising that the experience of film appears to have wrought a transformation in the way in which Dalí envisaged his painting. In other words, the experience of the cinematic helped to inform his pictorial vision. As a perceptive critic of cinema he was open to the unpretentiousness of standard Hollywood movies, and the opportunity to work with Buñuel appears to have heightened his awareness of what he could adopt for his own means. This cinematic element is perhaps most easily seen in the panoramas that emerge in Dalí's work in the late 1920s. Following the fragmented narrative space of his watercolours of Madrid nightlife (figs.13, 30–2), which are so reminiscent of the artificial structures of Robert Wiene's *The Cabinet of Dr Caligari* 1919, a new sense of space emerges even in the smallest of Dalí's paintings. Such paintings as *The First Days of Spring* 1929 (fig.7) show a familiarity with the work of René Magritte and Yves Tanguy, while their panoramic scope can be linked to the breadth of the big-screen image that embraces the spectator. From the plunging perspective of the centred railway tracks on which Keaton hurtles towards the viewer of *The Goat*, to the diminishing figure of Chaplin, abandoned, at the end of *The Circus*,

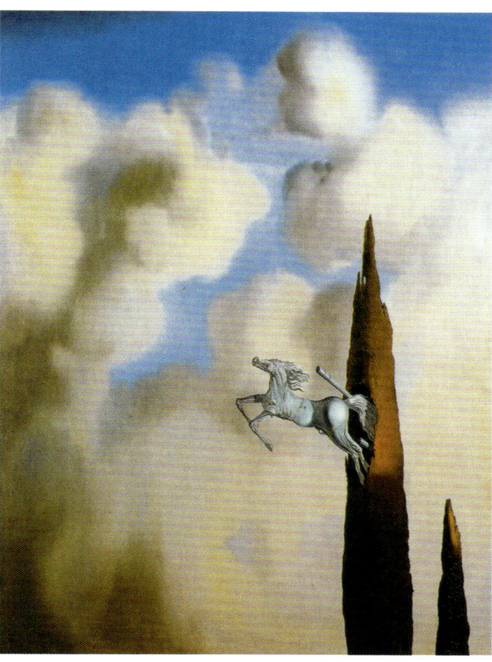

the spaciousness of the cinema screen was used to dramatic effect. By modifying the scale of his objects – often to a miniature size – and especially by raising and lowering the horizon, Dalí was able to manipulate his spaces in a way that echoes this practice but individualises it into a concentrated personal experience. The raised horizon of such works as *The Accommodations of Desire* (fig.35) has the effect of the filmic close-up that helps to drive narrative through a tightly focused world requiring concentration, delectation. By contrast, the lowered horizon afforded a vast sky in a way that, allied to his extraordinary pictorial ability to capture the sharp Mediterranean light of Port Lligat, transcends scale. More radically, in the later *Morning Ossification of the Cypress* 1934 (fig.43), no ground-plane is offered at all.

Especially from 1929 onwards, Dalí also made use of steeply angled pictorial spaces and threatening shadows. Again, there are artistic precedents for the steep spaces – most notably in the boarded platforms of de Chirico's 1914 paintings, which Dalí admired and to which he returned in his drawings for *Moontide* in 1941 (fig.100). Other works display a curious sense of layering, as if the ground-plane is a springboard to another, deeper, space beyond the elevated horizon. In *The Tower of Pleasure*, also known, appropriately, as *Vertigo* 1930 (private collection), a view is offered into this abyss from an unfeasibly high structure to the anthropomorphic landscape below. The image appears to insert a skyscraper

into the Catalan landscape, but also recalls the exaggerated camera angle of Harold Lloyd adventures, through which the danger is made ever-present in the mind and eye of the audience. Closely associated with this charged use of space is the use of the cast shadow. Again indebted to works by de Chirico, especially *The Enigma of a Day* 1914,[84] Dalí transformed the effect by having the shadow cast from the foreground, from the viewer's space. This is the classic suspense-filled device of the thriller and the murder mystery. It fuels anticipation. Dalí uses it in the figure's shadow in *Illumined Pleasures* 1929 (fig.36), and in a sequence of paintings associated with the theme of William Tell, the shadow of a lion is cast onto a cloth partially concealing the sexual activities of various figures: the shadow, the screen, the image revealed (fig.10).

The variety of these devices and the frequency with which Dalí used them indicates a crucial shift from his insistent differentiation between cinema and painting in 1927 to an accommodation of the cinematographic within his painting and within his activities at large. Thereafter, he moved seamlessly between media, exploring ideas in different ways and with different techniques as he saw appropriate. Between a cinema 'perceived with your eyes closed' and tactile cinema, he found a common denominator applicable to all his modes of practice.

Notes

The title of this text is indebted to André Breton's aside: 'The cinema? Three cheers for darkened rooms.' (*Manifeste du surréalisme*, Paris 1924, in *Manifestoes of Surrealism*, trans. Richard Seaver and Helen R. Lane, Ann Arbor 1969, 1972, p.46.) I should like to thank my family for their support, especially my father and my mother, without whom …

1
Only *Seven Chances* 1925 is identified by Ricard Mas Peinado in Dawn Ades, *Salvador Dalí: The Centenary Exhibition*, exh. cat., Palazzo Grassi, Venice, and Philadelphia Museum of Art 2004, p.78. *The Navigator*, in which Keaton and his fiancé are set adrift on a deserted liner, was made in 1924. Dalí sent Lorca the collage in February or March 1926, see Christopher Maurer (ed.), *Sebastian's Arrows: Letters and Mementos of Salvador Dalí and Federico García Lorca*, Chicago 2004, p.48. The texts all seem to come from a movie magazine, as they give a condensed version of the star's the real-life marriage, in 1922, to Natalie Talmadge (his co-star in *Our Hospitality* 1923).

2
Dalí, 'Sant Sebastià', *L'Amic de les Arts*, 31 July 1927, trans. in Haim Finkelstein (ed.), *The Collected Writings of Salvador Dalí*, Cambridge 1998, p.23. The text is dedicated to Lorca. Dalí's citation of Valéry may reflect a misapprehension upon which the poet himself reported in 1926: 'People always believe … that I have the same ideas as Mallarmé'; see Adrienne Monnier, 'The Voice of Paul Valéry', *Le Navire d'argent*, February 1926, trans. in Richard McDougall (ed.), *The Very Rich Hours of Adrienne Monnier*, New York 1976, p.209.

3
See the text on *Un Chien andalou* in this volume.

4
André Breton, *Manifeste du surréalisme*, Paris 1924, and *Second manifeste du surréalisme*, Paris 1929, in *Manifestoes of Surrealism*, trans. Richard Seaver and Helen R. Lane, Ann Arbor 1969, 1972.

5
'Hands Off Love', *La Révolution surréaliste*, no.9–10, 1 Oct. 1927, pp.1–6, originally published in English by Eugene Jolas (one of the co-signatories) in *Transition*, Sept.1927. While the manifesto made much of Mrs Chaplin's complaint about fellatio, its argument revolved around the rejection of the conventions of marriage in favour of the liberation of love.

6
See José Pierre (ed.), *Recherches sur la séxualité*, Paris 1990, trans. as *Investigating Sex: Surrealist Discussions 1928–1932*, trans. by Malcolm Imre, afterword by Dawn Ades, London 1992.

7
Germaine Dulac in *Les Cahiers du mois* 1925, cited by Ian Christie, 'French Avant-garde Films in the Twenties: From "Specificity" to Surrealism', in Phillip Drummond (ed.), *Film as Film: Formal Experiment in Film 1910–1975*, exh. cat., Hayward Gallery, London 1979, p.39.

8
See Sandy Flitterman-Lewis, 'The Image and the Spark: Dulac and Artaud Reviewed', in Rudolf E. Kuenzli (ed.), *Dada and Surrealist Film*, New York 1987, 2nd ed. Cambridge, Mass., and London 1996, pp.110–27; and Haim Finkelstein, 'Dalí and *Un Chien andalou*: The Nature of a Collaboration', ibid., p.130.

9
Mark Polizzotti, *Revolution of the Mind: The Life of André Breton*, London 1995 p.293 cites various accounts including Thomas Maeder, *Antonin Artaud*, Paris 1978, p.110, Denise Tual, *Le Temps dévoué*, Paris 1980, p.43, and Antonin Artaud, *Oeuvres complètes*, vol.3, Paris 1978, pp.326–7.

10
For Dulac see, among others, Ester Carla de Miro, 'Germaine who?', trans. Lucinda Hawkins in Drummond 1979, pp.127–8. Women remained absent from Surrealism at this moment, especially from the discussions on sex, as Ades notes (Pierre 1992, p.187).

11
Polizzotti 1978, p.333, citing Tual 1980, p.65, and Luis Buñuel, *My Last Breath*, London 1984, p.106 an abridged (though not identified as such, as noted by Hammond) version of *Mon Dernier soupir*, Paris 1982.

12
See my text on *L'Age d'or* in this volume.

13
Breton, *Manifeste du surréalisme*, 1924, in Seaver and Lane 1972, p.26.

14
Max Morise, 'Les Yeux enchantées', *La Révolution surréaliste*, no.1, 1 Dec. 1924, p.26, trans. in Marcel Jean (ed.), *The Autobiography of Surrealism*, New York 1980, p.194.

15
Morise cited Man Ray's rayographs (camera-less photographs), but Keaton's image accompanies Louis Aragon's 'L'Invention' four pages before (ibid. p.22).

16
Dalí, 'Film-arte, film-antiartistico', *La Gaceta Literaria*, no.24, 15 Dec. 1927, see full translation republished in this volume from Finkelstein 1998.

17
Ibid., for further discussion of Dalí's anti-art see Fèlix Fanés, 'Film as Metaphor' in this volume.

18
Man Ray, 'Un Film étonnant: L'Etoile de mer', *Vu*, no.46, 30 Jan. 1929, p.74, reproduced in Jean-Michel Bouhours and Patrick de Haas, *Man Ray: Directeur du mauvais movies*, exh. cat., Centre Georges Pompidou, Paris 1997, pp.79, 157–8; my trans.

19
Dalí, 'Film-arte, film-antiartistico', 1927. See translation in this volume.

20
Buñuel, interview, *L'Amic de les arts*, 31 March 1929, quoted in French in *Salvador Dalí: rétrospective 1920–1980*, exh. cat., Musée d'art national moderne, Centre Georges Pompidou, Paris 1979, p.66.

21
See Ian Gibson, *The Shameful Life of Salvador Dalí*, London 1997, p.202.

22
Desnos, 'The Work of Man Ray', *transition*, no.15, Spring 1929, pp.264–6; see also Dougald McMillan, *Transition 1927–38: The History of a Literary Era*, London 1975, p.86.

23
See Fanés, 'Film as Metaphor' in this volume.

24
See Dawn Ades, 'Why Film?' in this volume.

25
The implication that Keaton can escape his usual pursuers by melding with a work of art presents a sophisticated questioning of reality/realism worthy of Dalí.

26
René Clair, 'Exemples', *L'Intransigeant*, 13 Jan. 1923, cited in Christopher Green, *Léger and the Avant-Garde*, New Haven and London 1976, p.277.

27
Noted in C.B. Morris, *Surrealism and Spain, 1920–1936*, Cambridge 1972, p.17.

28
'Convocatoria a los cineastas: Cineclub español', *La Gaceta Literaria*, 1928, p.269.

29
In *My Last Breath* he recalls showing *Entr'acte*, the dream from Jean Renoir's *La Fille de l'eau* and Cavalcanti's *Rien que les heures*; Buñuel, 1984, p.103.

30
E.A. 'Ben-Hur', *Cahiers d'art: Feuilles volantes*, no.4–5, 1927, p.4.

31
S. Romoff, 'Cinématographe: Le Cuirassé Potemkine', *Cahiers d'art: Feuilles volantes*, no.1, 1927, p.4.

32
Buñuel reviewed it in *Cahiers d'art* 1926 (see Buñuel 1984, p.87).

33
Dalí, letter to Breton, March 1932, cited in Vicent Santamaria de Mingo, *El pensament de Salvador Dalí en el llindar dels anys trenta*, Barcelona 2004, p.71.

34
Bernard Brunius, 'Cinématographe: Metropolis ou "Plein la Vue"', *Cahiers d'art: Feuilles volantes*, no.2, 1927, pp.4–5; the author is also given as J. Bernard Brunius or Jacques-Bernard Brunius, he was also a contributor to *La Revue du cinéma* founded in 1928.

35
Dalí, 'Film-arte, film-antiartistico' 1927, see translation in this volume.

37
See Norman King, *Abel Gance*, London 1984, especially 'Gance and his Critics', pp.12–54; the film was shown at half-length on 7 April 1927, and complete (11,000 metres) on 9–12 May 1927. Reduced to a third, it went on general release in November, ibid. p.239.

37
Bernard Brunius, 'Notes sur Napoléon, vu par Abel Gance', *Cahiers d'art: Feuilles volantes*, no.3, 1927, pp.4–5.

38
Soon afterwards, Brunius made the documentary *Un Voyage aux cyclades* (announced in *Cahiers d'art*, no.1, 1932) with the ex-Surrealist Roger Vitrac and the photographer Eli Lothar – a collaborator on Buñuel's documentary *Las Hurdes: Tierra sin pan* 1933.

39
The break with Epstein, whom he assisted on *La Chute de la Maison Usher*, is cited in Joan M. Minguet Ballori, *Salvador Dalí, cine y surrealismo(s)*, Barcelona 2003, p.45.

40
Louis Bunuel [sic], 'Cinématographe: Napoléon, par Abel Gance', *Cahiers d'art: Feuilles volantes*, no.3, 1927, p.4.

41
Ibid. See also King 1984, p.49.

42
Dalí, 'Film-arte, film-antiartistico' 1927, see translation in this volume.

43
Dalí, 'Films antiartisticos: La Gran Duquesa y el camarero – El traje de etiqueta (por Adolf Manjou [sic]', *La Gaceta Literaria*, no.29, 1 March 1928, p.188.

44
Ibid.

45
Bernard Brunius, 'Sherlock Junior Détective', *Cahiers d'art: Feuilles volantes*, no.1, 1927, p.4. *Sherlock Jr.*, dated from 1924.

46
Louis Bunuel [sic], 'Sportif par amour', *Cahiers d'art: Feuilles volantes*, no.10, 1927, pp.4–5.

47
Blaise Cendrars, in 'A propos du "Cirque" de Charlot', *Cahiers d'art: Feuilles volantes*, no.1, 1928, p.39.

48
The Chaplin section survived from an 'unrealised film project'; see Carol E. Eliel, *L'Esprit Nouveau: Purism in Paris, 1918-1925*, exh. cat., Los Angeles County Museum of Art, 2001, p.44.

49
Cendrars 1928, pp.39-44.

50
Sebastià Gasch, 'El Circ', Gaseta de les Arts, vol.3, June 1928, pp.24-5; this text would be published in Spanish in *La Gaceta Literaria*, August 1928.

51
Ibid.

52
L'Amic de les arts, 31 March 1929, quoted in *Salvador Dalí*, exh. cat. 1979, p.66; my trans. This did not stop Buñuel, when he reached Hollywood, spending his Sundays with Chaplin; see Luis Buñuel, letter to Charles de Noailles, 2 Dec. 1930, Musée national d'art moderne, Paris, published in Jean-Michel Bouhours and Nathalie Schoeller, 'L'Age d'Or: Correspondance, Luis Buñuel – Charles de Noailles, Lettres et documents (1929–1976)', *Les Cahiers du Musée national d'art moderne*, hors-série, 1993, p.91.

53
'Noticiario', *La Gaceta Literaria*, 15 Dec. 1927, p.8; Papini was the former Futurist.

54
'Short Critical History Of Cinema' in Salvador Dalí, *Babaouo*, Paris 1932, see full translation from Finkelstein 1998 in this volume.

55
Savinio, 'Cinéma et théâtre', 5 December 1931, in *Souvenirs*, Milan 1976 and Paris 1986, p.154.

56
Dalí, 'Sant Sebastià', 1927, trans. in Finkelstein 1998, p.23.

57
Buñuel to Charles de Noailles, letter, 26 Feb. 1930, Musée national d'art moderne, Paris, published in Bouhours and Schoeller 1993, p.57.

58
Man Ray interview with André Gain, *Cinéa-Ciné pour tous*, no.144, 15 Nov. 1929, p.27, reprinted in Bouhours and de Haas 1997, p.169; my trans.

59
Man Ray, 'Answer to a Questionnaire', *Film Art*, vol.3, no.7, 1936, p.10.

60
'A Cinema in the Harbour', in *Frankfurter Zeitung*, 4 Nov. 1925, in Joseph Roth, *The White Cities: Reports from France 1925–39*, trans. and intro by Michael Hofman, London 2004, p.66.

61
Desnos, 'Picture Palaces', *Le Soir*, 28 May 1927, trans. in Paul Hammond (ed.), *The Shadow and its Shadow: Surrealist Writings on Cinema*, London 1978, p.46.

62
Eluard to Gala, [end April–beginning May 1929] in Paul Eluard, *Lettres à Gala, 1924–1948*, ed. Pierre Dreyfus, Paris 1984, letter 46, p.67.

63
Eluard to Gala, 27 [April 1930], ibid., letter 79, p.109.

64
Breton, *Nadja*, Paris 1928, trans. Richard Howard, New York 1960, p.37.

65
La Révolution surréaliste, no.3, 15 April 1925, p.7.

66
Bunuel [sic], 'Cinématographe: Napoléon', 1927, p.5.

67
René Crevel and Paul Eluard, 'Un film commercial', *Le Surréalisme au service de la revolution*, no.3/4, Dec. 1931, p.29.

68
It is unclear whether they were at the de Noailles' house at Hyères in the South of France at the same moment in January 1930. André Gide notes Cocteau's presence there on 3 January (*Journals 1889–1949*, trans. and ed. Justin O'Brien, Harmondsworth 1967, p.465); that day, de Noailles wrote to Buñuel about travel arrangements, but the latter does not appear to have set out for the south until 10 January (see Charles de Noailles letter to Luis Buñuel, 3 Jan. 1930, Musée national d'art moderne, Paris, in Bouhours and Schoeller1993, p.44, and 'Chronologie', ibid., p.177.

69
Man Ray, for instance, was said to have been furious on discovering that Lee Miller had undertaken a central role; see Antony Penrose, *The Lives of Lee Miller*, London 1985, p.35. Long afterwards, Dalí seems to have quoted Cocteau's film. The idea of reversing the film was used in *Le Sang d'un poète* to bring to life a statue played by Miller; Dalí and Hitchcock shot, though eventually rejected, a similar sequence of Ingrid Bergman for *Spellbound* in 1945.

70
Richard Pierre-Bodin, 'Le premier film de Jean Cocteau: La Vie d'un poète', *Figaro Film*, 9 Nov. 1930; my trans. This article predates the banning of *L'Age d'or* by a month (it fell in early December), a suppression that was enthusiastically supported by *Figaro* on 7 Dec. 1930, cited in Helena Lewis, *Dada Turns Red: The Politics of Surrealism*, New York 1988 and Edinburgh 1990, p.93.

71
Desnos, 'Avant-garde cinema', *Documents*, no.7, 1929, trans. in Hammond 1978, p.36.

72
Jean Cocteau, 'La Vie d'un poète', *Figaro Film*, 9 Nov. 1930.

73
Dalí, 'Films antiartisticos: La Gran Duquesa…', 1 March 1928, p.188.

74
The seating plan (Bouhours and Schoeller 1993, p.83), shows Cocteau on one side (row O) and Breton, Eluard, Maurice Heine and Tanguy seated, judiciously, on the other side of the cinema (row H). As Buñuel was absent in Zaragossa, the seat in his name must be for his wife Jeanne Rucar.

75
Cocteau, *Figaro Film*, 9 Nov. 1930; my trans.

76
'Film-arte, film-antiartístico', 1927, see translation in this volume.

77
For Dalí's continuation of painting see Dawn Ades, 'Why Film?' in this volume.

78
'Bonsoir Man Ray', extracted from *Entretiens avec Pierre Bourgeade*, Paris 1972, in Bouhours and de Haas 1997, p.175; my trans.

79
For a discussion of *Il Tattilismo*, 1921 and *I nuovi poeti futuristi* 1925, see Cinzia Sartini Blum, *The Other Modernism: F.T. Marinetti's Futurist Fiction of Power*, Berkeley and Los Angeles 1996, pp.133–7.

80
Dalí letter from Bouches-du-Rhône to Buñuel, undated (Jan.–Feb.? 1930), Filmoteca Española, published in French in Bouhours and Schoeller, 1993, p.54; my trans.

81
Dalí, 'Objets surrealistes', *Le Surréalisme au service de la revolution*, no.3, Dec. 1931, pp.16–17.

82
An early sighting is on the statue and passer-by in *L'Age d'Or*, but it recurs on *Retrospective Bust* (fig.97) and on the cyclist in the scenario for *Babaouo*.

83
See Michael R. Taylor's text in this volume.

84
At that time owned by Breton and the subject of the Surrealist enquiry 'Sur les possibilites irrationelles de pénétration et d'orientation dans un tableau Georgio [sic] de Chirico: L'Enigme d'une journee', *Le Surréalisme au service de la revolution*, no.6, 15 May 1933, pp.13–16.

DALÍ'S FILM PROJECTS

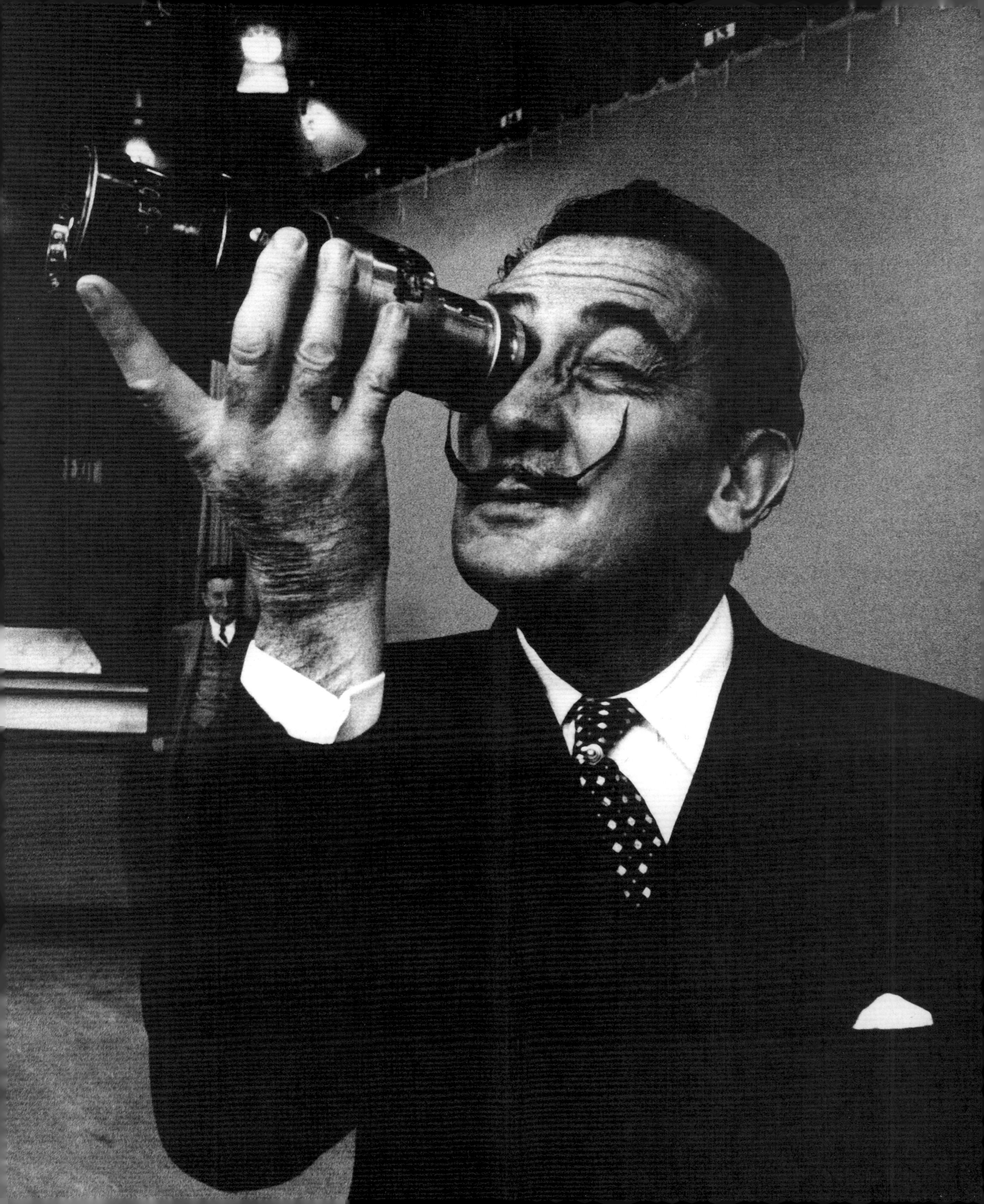

To Luis Buñuel, filmmaker

Careful! A lot of birds are coming forth!

The film bird, like that of photography, does not have to be hunted in far away places; it is everywhere, in any location, in the most unexpected site. The film bird, nevertheless, commands such subtle and perfect mimicry that it remains invisible in its flights through the naked objectivity. Because of this, discovering it is a matter of high poetic inspiration.[1]

There is no more spiritual a hunt than that of this bird, whose presence we are unable to perceive. No hunt is less gory or draws more blood; it is at the same time almost a game, with the bird imprisoned, shut within a *camera obscura* and liberated anew by the crystalline lens, free of anilines and having chloroformed wings.

If we care to listen, we would hear the black and white music of the different velocities of these birds as they come out from the electric milky way of the film projector. Then it would be sweet to notice how the most dizzying flights form a succession of quietudes, and the most inspired beating of the wings, a continuity of anesthetized calms; each new light, a new anesthesia.

The light of the cinema is at the same time wholly spiritual and wholly physical. Cinema captures unusual and mysterious beings and objects, more invisible and ethereal than spiritualist muslins. Each image of the cinema captures an undeniable spirituality.

In the cinema, a tree, a street, a game of rugby, are transubstantiated in a disturbing manner; a sweet yet restrained giddiness leads us to specific sensory transmutations. The tree, street, or the game of rugby may be sampled slowly like slush with a straw. The very vivid fluttering of the wind in *her* light dress might be collected, just like mercury, in a small aluminum box.

The cinema bird is a timbre, the cinema bird is yet the breeze emanating from a fan.

It takes more imagination to shoot at a tree full of invisible birds that at another one with birds that were arranged there beforehand disguised as Cubist birds; the film bird, for all that, is transparent and delicate, and it dies instantly whatever disguise it has on, under no matter what layer of paint.

The antiartistic filmmaker shoots at a brick wall and bags unexpected and authentic Cubist birds.

The artistic filmmaker shoots at false Cubist birds and captures a useless brick.

The antiartistic filmmaker ignores art; he shoots in a pure manner, obeying only the technical requirements of his apparatus and the childlike and joyful instinct of his sporting physiology.

The artistic filmmaker understands art almost always in a crude manner and obeys the

Art Film, Antiartistic Film [1927]
Salvador Dalí

sentimental arbitrariness of his genius.

The antiartistic filmmaker limits himself to emotions that are psychological, primary, constant, standardized, and thus aims at the suppression of anecdote. When monotony is reached, and when it is repeated, when you know what is going to happen, then you begin to feel the joy of unforeseen technical and expressive diversity. The antiartistic filmmaker arrives at constant action and signs.

The good guy's clean-shaven face; the very pointed and thin mustache of the bad guy; the chase and the gunshots aimed at the car, etc., etc.

Pipe, fruit bowl, guitar, bunch of grapes, small bottle of rum, sheet music, etc., etc.

It is known that the great Greek tragedians wrote skillfully, one following the other, on the very same subjects. Their audiences were not about to get excited by the sight of unexpected events; they sought their pleasure, their thrill, in the unexpected unfolding of events that were expected since they had already been familiar.

By a similar route, antiartistic cinema has created a wholly characteristic and very differentiated world of emotions and image types, that are appropriate, completely defined and clear for the conceptions that are shared by the thousands of people who comprise the great cinema audiences. Moreover, this whole creation is organic and homogeneous, the product of anonymous contributions and perfection attained by the route of standardization.

The mask of the bad guy, his gestures, his wardrobe, the hand knocking at the door, all become more and more refined in imparting dramatic and visual emotion; all this is getting to be more polished and better with each new film, perfection being approached by a process that is analogous to the increasingly disconcerting embellishment of airplanes.

Artistic cinema, on the other hand, has not managed to establish any universal type of emotion; quite the contrary, each new film tends toward the highest degree of rupture, to the most absolute dissociation, to the most uncontrolled inorganism.[2]

The artistic filmmaker, spoiled by the unassimilable absorption of literature and with a laughable urge for originality, tends toward the maximum complexity of psychological and expressive conflicts, embroiled with the greatest and most varied assortment of often uncinematic recourses; all this naturally leads directly to the anecdote with its semblance of transcendentalism,

which, deep inside, is perfectly innocent and puerile.

The anonymous antiartisic filmmaker films a white coffee shop, any kind of anodyne and simple room, a railroad signal box, a policeman's star, a kiss inside a taxi. Once the reel is projected, we know that a whole world of fairy tales of inexpressible poetry has been filmed.

Fritz Lang organizes a grand spectacle: architects, engineers, the crisscrossing of very powerful searchlights, grandiose Dantesque settings, so-called grandiose proportions, where multitudes, lights and machines, etc., etc., move about, with all the theatricalism of the worst history painting. It hardly matters to us whether one Moreno Carbonero paints the Middle Ages or a skyscraper. Cinema, in this manner, becomes an instrument which is expressive of the most gratuitous and vulgar anecdote; its pure, newborn throbbing is frightfully infected by all the germs of artistic putrefaction.

Be careful also with the innocent concept of grandiosity. Michelangelo with *The Last Judgment* is not greater than Vermeer of Delft with his *Lacemaker* in the Louvre, however small its dimensions are. Taking into account its plastic dimensions, Van der Meer's *Lacemaker*, alongside the Sistine Chapel, can be rated as having grandiose dimensions.

A lump of sugar on the screen can *become* larger than the interminable perspective of gigantic buildings.

For the artistic filmmaker, cinema, through its rich technical resources, can give us the concrete and exciting vision of the most grandiose and sublime spectacles that were until now the unique privilege of man's imagination. Thus, the film turns out to be pure illustration of what the artist of genius imagines.

The antiartistic film, on the other hand, remote from any concept of grandiose sublimity, rather than showing us the emotion exemplifying artistic delirium, reveals indeed the entirely new poetic emotion of all the most humble and immediate facts, which were impossible to imagine or foresee before cinema, and that are born of the spiritual miracle of the capture of the bird-film.

The artistic 'metteur en scène' is in need of innumerable and singular circumstances for his realizations; he needs, for example, to transfer himself a thousand years into the future and film

the cosmic emotion (always illustrative) of
the imposing rhythm of a monstrous mass
demonstration, parading between immense
armored buildings … but how far more moving
and exciting for us is the agile but slow rise of
absinthe through the sunny capillarity of a lump
of sugar found in our midst. And we won't feel any
less cosmic an emotion because of the simple and
humble physics of our drama; on the contrary, the
pulvarized nickel-plated trembling of the point of
the phonograph stylus made of saccharine mica
brings our pupils spiritually closer to the soft
pulsation, remote and weak, of the constellations.

Oh, Fritz Lang! who seeks the
spectacular in the most extreme and grandiose
settings while possessing a spectacle of unique
emotion that tickles the flesh. The fly sauntering
through the hair of your arm with the sleeve just
now rolled up, quick and calm on legs that are
sensorimetric instruments, is on the point of
flying off and describing over the limpid and
freezing morning sky a calligraphy that is more
lively and unsuspected than what your crude
imagination could ever form.

The best attempts at artistic film, a few
selected instances, to mention those of Man Ray and
of Fernand Léger, start off from an inexplicable,
fundamental misunderstanding; the purest
emotion still within the realm of vision (Man Ray's
film is directed solely at the senses) does not have to
be sought in the world of invented forms. The world
of cinema and that of painting are very different.
Precisely so, the possibilities of photography and
cinema are to be found in that unlimited fantasy
which is born of things in themselves.

Other film creations, which are more of less
artistic, exhibit the beginning of weariness,
tedium and sadness, characteristic of artistic fact;
only the antiartistic cinema, the comic cinema in
particular, produces films that are more and more
perfect, conveying the newest and the most
intense and diverting emotion.

Antiartistic cinema, extremely cheerful, bright,
sunny, a production of the greatest sensuality which
is asleep by dint of an abundance of injections of
the anti-opium that is the naked objectivity.

Cinema that is dumb, deaf, blind, I say, since the
best cinema is the kind that can be perceived with
your eyes closed.

First published as 'Film-arte, film-antiartístico', *La Gaceta Literaria* (Madrid), 15 December 1927, p.4. A note at the end specifies that it was 'Translated by the author from Catalan expressly for *La Gaceta Literaria*.' This translation is from *The Collected Writings of Salvador Dali*, edited and trans. Haim Finkelstein, Cambridge University Press 1998, pp.53–7.

Notes

1
[Translator's note:] Two illustrations of works by Dalí are integrated into the text, one, following the first two lines, is a drawing (or woodcut) of a head; the other, about five paragraphs before the ending, is a drawing or woodcut based on *Honey Is Sweeter than Blood* [see fig.2]. Both have the caption 'Cinematismo de Dalí', that is to say, visualization of his cinematic approach or style, although there is nothing specifically cinematic about either of them.

2
[Translator's note:] The word 'inorganismo' is Dalí's own coinage.

Contrary to common opinion, the cinema is infinitely poorer and more limited, with regard to the expression of the real functioning of thought, than writing, painting, sculpture, and architecture. There is hardly anything below it unless it is music, whose spiritual value, as is well known, is practically nil. The cinema is consubstantially bound, by its very nature, to the sensory, base, and anecdotal side of phenomena, to abstraction, to rhythmical impressions; in a word, to harmony. And harmony, a sublime product of abstraction, is, by definition, at the antipodes of the concrete, and, consequently, of poetry.

The rapid and continuous sequence of the images of cinema, the implicit neologism of which is in direct proportion to an especially generalizing visual culture, hinders any attempt at a reduction to the concrete and discounts more often than not (on account of the memory factor) the intentional, affective, and lyrical character of the concrete. The mechanism of memory, at which these images are directed in an exceptionally acute way, already tends by itself toward a disorganization of the concrete, toward idealization.

During wakefulness, the latent intention and the frenzy of the concrete almost always fall into amnesia, but they frequently crop up in dreams. The poetry of cinema requires more than any other a traumatic unbalancing toward the concrete irrationality in order to reach the true lyrical work.

The beginnings of the cinema having an experimental nature, up to and including Méliès,[1] constitute (by dint of the contemplative and questioning exhibition of things and phenomena as of the presence of an action set forth as a simulacrum) its metaphysical stage. Following the dull years during which the technique improved, the cinema, which has timidly approached a form of fleeting pseudo-naturalism, suddenly reaches its true golden age in the achievement of the first materialist films of the Italian school (prewar and the beginning of the war). I am referring here to the grandiose period of hysterical cinema with Francesca Bertini, Gustavo Serena, Tulio Carminati, Pina Menichelli etc.[2] … the cinema that is so marvellously, so justifiably, close to theatre, and that has not only the great merit of presenting us real and concrete documents of psychic disturbances of all kinds, of the true course of infant neuroses, of the fulfilment in life of the most impure aspirations and fantasies that prior to it were embodied in the admirable Art Nouveau architecture),[3] but also the merit of having achieved complete mastery of its basic technical means. From that moment on, the cinema will quickly go into decadence.

The actors actually lived these films in a continuous and shameless way that the boastful contemporary humour would no longer tolerate. It was then clever feminine exhibitionism in all its splendour. I remember these women with unsteady and convulsive walk, their hands of castaways of

Short Critical History of Cinema ¹⁹³²

Salvador Dalí

love groping along the walls, along the corridors, clinging to all the curtains, to all the shrubs; these women with a low neckline perpetually slipping off the most naked shoulders on screen, in an uninterrupted night of cypresses and marble banisters. In this turbulent and transitory period of eroticism, palm trees and magnolias were materially bitten, uprooted with the teeth by these women, whose fragile and pre-tubercular complexion did not exclude bodies daringly molded by precocious and fiery youthfulness.

In is in one of these films entitled *La Flamme*,[4] that Pina Menichelli could be seen quite naked in a dress made of feathers representing an owl, this for the sole purpose of justifying, with the coming of the twilight, a quite simplistic and pathetic symbolic comparison between the owl she embodied and a flame – the flame of love – that she had just ignited with her fatal hands before the ruined eyes, incommensurably circled with the dark rings of guaranteed onanism, of Gustavo Serena, who, from that moment on, did not make any movements other than the necessary, automatic and depressive ones enabling him to increasingly and jerkily descend into the water of the lake, until the usual expanding concentric circles subsided and the calm of the water was restored, following the suicide that constituted the moral of the film. These were automatic and depressive movements, solely comparable to those of William Tell in his old age, dazzled by the coppery light of the setting sun, William Tell, who is by now ready for death, his knees bloodied, his eyes swimming with tears, still walking, a pair of fried eggs (without the pan) carelessly placed on his shoulder.

Following the Italian cinema and the extraordinary *Mysteries of New York*,[5] the dynamism, the sports, and the so many other dreary mythologies brought to us by the budding American cinematographic standard, will keep on imponderably setting up continual osmoses with their own avant-garde artistic-literary applications, which will delight the Catholic and modern European intelligentsia. The cinema consciously chooses the absurd and stupid road to abstraction. It creates a boring language based on cumbersome visual rhetoric of an almost exclusively musical character, reaching its peak in the rhythmical use of close-ups, tracking shots, dissolves, double exposures, the hideous splitting of *découpage*, the allusive and sentimental spirituality of *montage* and the thousand other depravities that, running through the pathetic pre-sound films

throughout the world, and leading to a cinema that becomes more and more 'cinema' (films of the avant-garde, especially the Belgian ones), would have reached, but for the sudden intervention of sound film, the mark of genuine 'pure cinema' – in other words, of a more comfortable and complete shame, if this is possible, than that of pure painting – in the strict and precise sense of the word.

Sound film brings with it a marvelous impurity and considerable confusion which enable us to witness dialogues in one shot that are just a little bit longer than those in the silent cinema. It also brings us, before literature and art intervene (an imminent intervention and already discernible), the restoration of certain notions of the concrete that are capable, at least momentarily, of creating confusions and complications based on the persistence in memory of words over the images, to the grand detriment of the latter.

Throughout the history of cinema and, in particular, of contemporary cinema, a single tendency, the *concrete irrationality*, the delirious and pessimistic aspiration towards gratuitousness, continues in an upward surge, more and more sterilized, more and more conscious, in films incorrectly named film comedies, this for the sole and insufficient reason that they generally provoke laughter, albeit an infinitely distinctive laughter, and without this implying well-known tears that such laughter should hypothetically hide – an abominable and false invention of scribblers that is corroborated by pigs like Bergson who polish off all the *Ridi Pagliaccio*,[6] an inexhaustible and almost always substantial source of literature and art, that, in the cinema, becomes the subject par excellence, the unique, obligatory, solemn, all-mighty, majestic, imperial, necessary subject, one of consubstantial necessity, of apotheosized rigor, of mortal rigor.

The analysis of the history of the so-called film comedies tends to show precisely the progressive elimination of the *Ridi Pagliaccio*, which postulates, in a very latinized, colourfully messed-up manner all the supposedly transcendental germs of abstraction in the domain of life.

For us to confine ourselves to contemporary cinema, this psychological, artistic, literary, sentimental, humanitarian, musical, intellectual, spiritual, colonial, departmental and Portuguese filth, for us, I say, to confine ourselves to this complete filth of *Ridi Pagliaccio*, which is cultivated indistinctly and with the same fondness by the Sternbergs, Stroheims, Chaplins, Pabsts, etc.… etc.…, we must state that the irrationally inclined film comedies are the only ones to show the true path of poetry. Such are the unusual Mack Sennett films, all the minor film comedies with little-known actors who have no special talents, and also all those films indebted to the genius of a few, of Harry Langdon, for instance, or William Powell, who is as comic, or as little comic, as Langdon. Quite recently, it is *Animal Crackers* with the Marx Brothers, that is situated at the summit of the evolution of comic cinema.[7] All the desires of the latent systematic and concrete irrationality throughout film comedies reach their peak in this admirable film – desires that progressively cast off any justification, pretext, subjective humor, etc., these being mitigating circumstances that have prevented a realisation of these films' violent moral quality through which they become *films à these. Animal Crackers* achieves these kinds of solemn, persistent and exhausting, cold and diaphanous, predispositions and contagions so rarely reached, and this only after having gone past the all too psychological stage of humor, the stage of frivolous solutions, not to say entertaining schizophrenias; once the terrain of concessions to instantaneous mental hypotheses is crossed, attaining at last the true and palpable lyrical amazement, that, for myself, is effectively provoked by certain passages by Raymond Roussel.[8] It is equally possible for me to bring myself closer to this state of amazement by certain notions derived from love, which can appear to me in the form of a sudden and furious rain of six or seven average Anna Kareninas, dressed as Portuguese cups, the handles covered whether partially or not with curdled, nunlike-fucked-up milk.

The face of the one of the Marx Brothers having curled hair, this face which is that of persuasive and triumphant madness, as much at the ending of the film as at the very short moment when he endlessly plays the harp, pushes back – beyond the horizon of literary initiations into psychological pseudo-transcendentalism, the infinitely prosaic look of Charlie Chaplin at the ending of *City Lights*, a look of sweet go-getting that knows no equal other than the alleged look of revolting blind men or that of the smug and springlike, phenomenal and smelly, legless cripple.

In 1929, we, Buñuel and I, wrote the scenario of *Un Chien andalou*, and in 1930, the scenario of *L'Age d'or*. These are the two first surrealist films.

Apart from the films of Communist revolutionary propaganda, which are justified by their propaganda value, nothing merits consideration but that which might be expected of Surrealism and what might be awaited from a certain so-called comic cinema.

First published in French as 'Abrégé d'une histoire critique du cinéma', in *Babaouo: Scenario inédit précéde d'un Abrégé d'une histoire critique du cinéma et suivi de Guillaume Tell ballet portugais*, Editions des Cahiers Libres, Paris 1932, pp.11–21. This translation is from *The Collected Writings of Salvador Dalí*, edited and trans. Haim Finkelstein, Cambridge University Press 1998, pp.137–41.

Editor's Notes

1
Georges Méliès made film in the fantastic tradition of burlesque theatre before the First World War; his work underwent a revival in Paris in the late 1920s .

2
Francesca Bertini starred in the detective series *Nellie the Gigolette* begun in 1915 and *La Dame aux Camelias* 1916. For Pina Menichelli, see below.

3
'Modern Style' in the original, the term used in Spain to denote Art Nouveau.

4
Dalí used the French title in his original text, although Saurí identifies the original Italian film as *Il fuoco* [The Fire], and gives the following details: made 1915 by director Piero Fosco (pseudonym of Giovanni Pastrone) with Pina Menichelli and Febo Mari. (See Salvador Dalí, *Babaouo*, bilingual French and Spanish, trans. and annotated by Esteban Riambau Saurí, Barcelona 1978, p.147. Pastrone also collaborated with Gabrielle D'Annuzio on the historical epic Cabri in 1914 (released internationally in 1915)

5
[Dalí's footnote:] I make an exception here for ENTR'ACTE, because of the historical interest it presents. In spite of René Clair, the film in fact sums up some ideas of Marcel Duchamp, Man Ray, Francis Picabia; ideas that represent an isolated tendency that parallels the achievements of the American film comedies, but that, due to the poetical, negativist and nonconformist preoccupations of the authors of ENTR'ACTE, bear witness, on philosophical grounds, to a kind of agnosticism that is hardly conscious – that is, if we consider these authors' distrust of phenomena and of any attempt at a total reduction of them, as well as their distrust of the very particular notion of the elusive, and of any theoretical absence of knowledge beyond the ruinous aphrodisiac vertigos of the accidental.

6
This refers to Leoncavallo's opera *Pagliacci* (as notd by Saurí 1978 p.148) and, in particular, the exhortation to the clown to laugh despite the tragedy in the aria 'Vesti la giubba'. It is likely that Dalí had in mind Enrico Caruso's famous 1907 recording, which was characteristically melodramatic.

7
For the Marx Brothers see Michael R. Taylor's text in this volume.

8
For Dalí's admirations for Raymond Roussel, see Elliott H. King's text in this volume.

The chronology outlines the projects in which Dalí was involved, placing them in relation to films that he saw, read about or, more speculatively, had the opportunity of seeing. It draws on many sources, but the details about Figueres are reliant upon Josep M. Bernils i Mach, 'Els cinemes de Figueres' (*Annals de l'Insitut d'Estudis Empordaneos*, no.28, 1995) and research undertaken by colleagues at the Fundacío Gala-Salvador Dalí.
Matthew Gale

1904

<u>11 May</u>
Salvador Dalí born in Figueres.
<u>21 December</u>
Sala Edison, first cinema in Figueres, opens; screenings include Georges Méliès's *A Voyage to the Moon* 1902. The first travelling cinemas come to *Festes i Fires de la Santa Creu* (Fairs and Fiestas of the Holy Cross) in the following year.

1908

<u>January</u>
Birth of Ana Maria Dalí, the artist's sister. Dalí attends the infant school of Esteban Trayter Colomer, who owns a stereoscope with coloured slides which he recalls in *The Secret Life*. At some stage the Dalí family acquire a hand-cranked projector: the artist later recalled watching *The Fall of Port Arthur*, and *The Enamoured Student* as well as Charlie Chaplin and Max Linder films (*Unspeakable Confessions of Salvador Dalí*, London 1977, p.32).
<u>April</u>
Cinematógrafo Nuevo opens in Figueres showing, among others: *Adelante con la música* (On with the Music), hand-coloured; *Catástofe ferroviaria* (Rail Disaster); *El perro y sus sonrisas* (The Dog and its Smiles).
<u>June</u>
Open-air *Cine a l'aire lliure* established at Horta Gaiolà; films shown include: *El puñal árabe* (The Arab Dagger); *En China Shang Hai* (In Shang Hai, China); *Mariposas japoneses* (Japanese Butterflies).

1909

<u>Easter</u>
Sala del Jardí shows *The Life, Passion and Death of Our Lord Jesus*.
Sala Edison shows: *Una ráfaga de viento sobre la playa* (A Gust of Wind on the Beach); *Entre el deber y el dolor* (Between Duty and Temptation); *Entre los Tuareg* (Among the Tuareg); *Un mujer celosa* (A Jealous Woman).
<u>15 May</u>
Sala Edison shows *La venganza de la gitana* (The Gypsy's Revenge), hand-coloured.
Screenings begin at Teatre Municipal in Figueres (the future Teatro-Museu Salvador Dalí).

1910

Dalí studies at Colegio Hispano-Francés de la Inmaculada Concepción in Figueres.
Pablo Picasso summers in Cadaqués.

1913

Festes i Fires de la Santa Creu showing of Enrico Guazzoni's Roman epic *Quo Vadis?* 1913.

1914

<u>August</u>
Outbreak of First World War. Neutral Barcelona becomes a haven for Parisian avant-garde.
In his 'Short Critical History of Cinema' 1932, Dalí recalled the wartime melodramas produced by the 'hysterical' Italian cinema and *The Mysteries of New York* 1914.

1916

Dalí studies at the Instituto and Escuela Municipal de Dibujo, in Figueres.

1919

Dalí shows paintings in Societat de Concerts, in Teatro Municipal, Figueres.
In Paris, Charlie Chaplin's *Shoulder Arms* and Cecil B. DeMille's *The Cheat* are voted the best films on general release.

1921

<u>6 February</u>
Death of Felipa, Dalí's mother.

1922

<u>January</u>
Dalí exhibits at Associació Catalana d'Estudiants, Galerie Dalmau, Barcelona.
In Berlin, Robert Wiene's *The Cabinet of Dr Caligari* is released.
<u>October</u>
Dalí enrols at Real Academia de Bellas Artes in Madrid; at Residencia de Estudiantes meets Luis Buñuel, Federico García Lorca, and Pepín Bello.
<u>17 November</u>
André Breton delivers lecture to accompany Francis Picabia's exhibition at Galerie Dalmau, Barcelona.
<u>22 December</u>
Dalí's father marries Felipa's sister, Catalina, in Barcelona.
In USA, Buster Keaton completes *Our Hospitality* and Harry Langdon makes *Picking Peaches*.

A Cinematic Chronology of Dalí
1904–1940

1924

21 May–11 June
Dalí imprisoned in Figueres and Gerona for political activism; on return home, he later claimed, he ate and 'immediately after I went to the movies'. (*The Secret Life*)
September
Dalí returns to the Academia in Madrid, from which he was temporarily expelled in October 1923.
November
Breton's *Manifeste du surréalisme* published in Paris.
December
Coliseum, Barcelona, shows W.D. Griffith's *Ten Commandments* 'which all of Barcelona has seen' (*Gaseta de les Arts*, 15 Dec. 1924).
In USA, Erich von Stroheim's *Greed* is released; Buster Keaton completes *Sherlock Jr.* and *The Navigator* (directed by Donald Crisp).

1925

Easter
Federico Garcia Lorca visits Dalí in Cadaqués.
18 April
Louis Aragon lectures at Residencia de Estudiantes in Madrid.
28 May
Ten works by Dalí shown in *Primera Exposición de la Sociedad de Artistas Ibéricos* in Madrid.
14–27 November
Dalí's first solo exhibition at Galerie Dalmau, Barcelona.
In USA, Chaplin's *The Gold Rush* and Frank Niblo's *Ben-Hur* are released.

1926

11–28 April
Dalí visits Paris and Brussels with sister and stepmother, sees Buñuel and meets Picasso.
In Figueres, the Teatro Municipal installs large projectors and shows *La Cruzada de la Humanidad* (The Crusade of Humanity), *La Fiera del Mar* (The Festival of the Sea), and Fritz Lang's *Die Nibelungen* 1924.
14–20 June
In Madrid, refusing to be examined at the Academia, Dalí is definitively expelled.
October – December
For a second solo show (31 Dec. – 14 Jan. 1927) at Dalmau, Dalí spends a month in Barcelona.
In Paris, Luis Buñuel is assistant director on Jean Epstein's *Mauprat*.
November
In New York, death of Rudolph Valentino, a role model for Dalí.

1927

February
Dalí's military service in Figueres.
July
Dalí declares his enthusiam for *Fox Movietone*, Tom Mix, Adolphe Menjou and Buster Keaton in 'Sant Sebastià' (*L'Amic de les Arts*).
September
Surrealist tract *Hands off Love* published.
October
Dalí shows *Apparatus and Hand* (fig.18) in Barcelona.
Casino Menestral, Figueres shows Hollywood films: (on 9 October) the comedy *Peligros de un conquistador* (*Tin Hats* 1926, dir. Edward Sedgwick) with Claire Windsor and Conrad Nagel, and the melodrama *El soldado desconocido* (*The Unknown Soldier* 1926, dir. Renaud Hoffman) with Margarita de la Motte and Henry B Walthall; (on 23 October) Blanche Sweet in *La secretaria particular* (*Diplomacy* 1926, dir. Marshall Neilan); (on 29 October) *Choque afortunado* (The Unfortunate Shock), and Johnny Hines in *Blancos y rojos* (White and Red); and (on 30 October) Buster Keaton's *La casa encantada* (*The Haunted House* 1921).

December
Dalí's 'Film-arte, film-antiartístico' published.
In Paris, Jean Epstein's *La Glace à trois faces* and Man Ray's *Emak Bakia* shown at Studio des Ursulines. Other films shown during 1927 include: Eisenstein's *Battleship Potemkin*; Buster Keaton's *Sherlock Jr.* 1924 and *College*; Abel Gance's *Napoléon*; Frank Niblo's *Ben-Hur* 1925; Lupu Pick in *Le Dernier Fiacre de Berlin*; Alberto Cavalcanti's *En rade.*
In Berlin, Walter Ruttman completes *Berlin – Symphony of a City* and Fritz Lang releases *Metropolis.*
In Los Angeles, Harry Langdon stars in *Long Pants.*

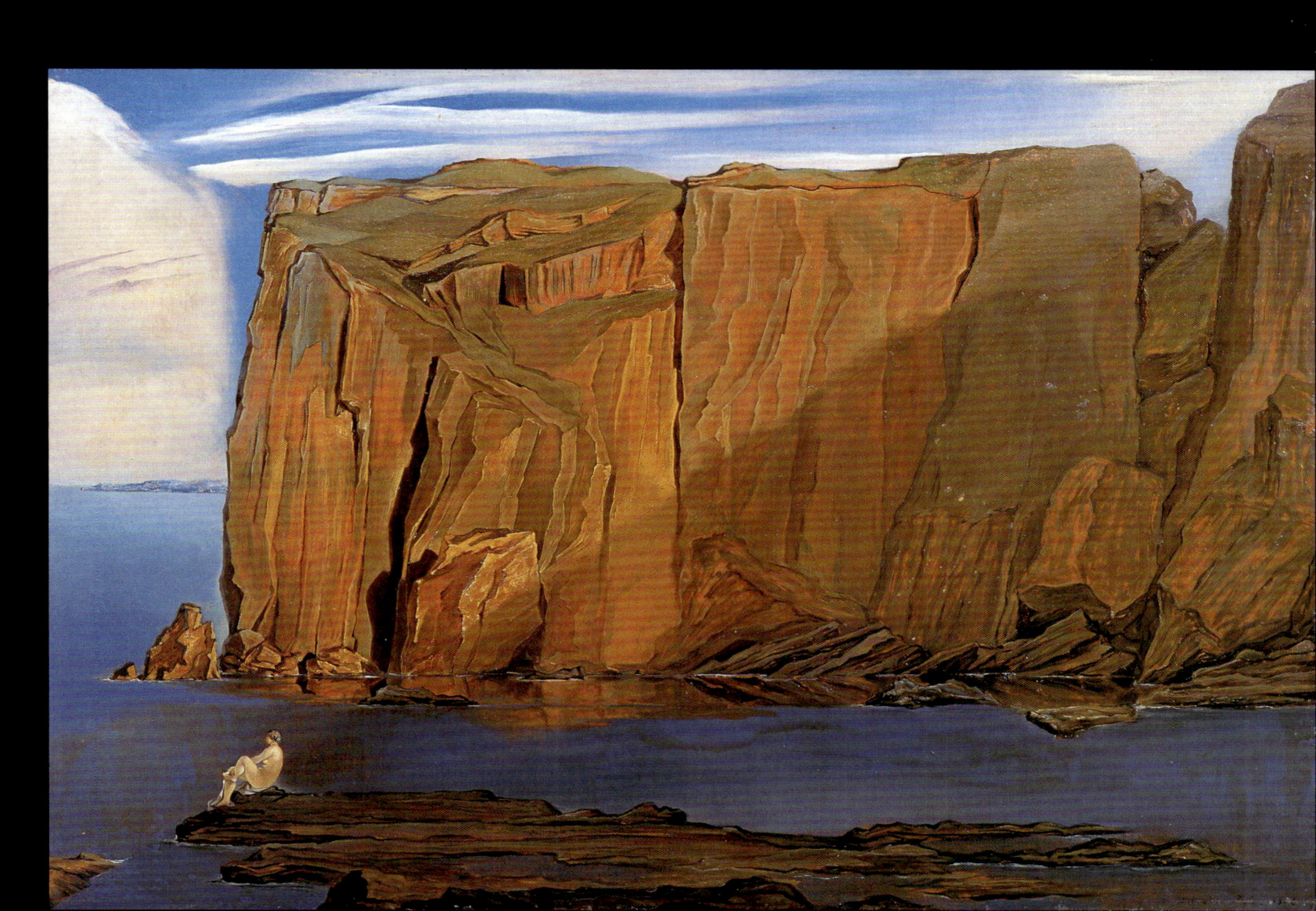

44
Penya segats 1926
Oil on panel 27 x 41 cm
Private collection

1928

2 February
Surrealists disrupt premiere of
Dulac's *La Coquille et le clergyman*
(The Seashell and the Clergyman),
shown with Murnau's *Nosferatu the
Vampire* at Cinéma des Ursulines,
Paris. *Cahiers d'Art* publishes a six-
page supplement on Chaplin's *The
Circus*; the film goes on to win one
of the first Academy Awards.
March
Dalí, Lluis Montanyà and Sebastià
Gasch publish *Manifest Groc*.
May
Breton publishes *Nadja* with
photographs by Man Ray; it is
much admired by Dalí.
June
Chaplin's *Circus* and Keaton's *College*
shown in Barcelona and reviewed by
Gasch (*Gaseta de les Arts*, June 1928).
Teatro Municipal in Figueres shows
first locally made film: *Figueras
industrial y artistica*, by Josep Pagès.
December
Cineclub Español established in
Madrid, at first evening Ramón
Gómez de la Serna presents Man
Ray's *L'Etoile de mer*, Stroheim's *Greed*
and Alan Crossland's *Jazz Singer*.
Films shown in Paris include: Jean
Epstein's *La Chutte de la Maison Usher*
(on which Buñuel worked). Pierre
Prévert, Marcel Duhamel, Man Ray
and Jacques-André Boiffard work on
Souvenirs de Paris (also called *Paris-
Express*); Gaston Modot directed
La Torture par l'espérance.
In Los Angeles, Walt Disney
makes first Mickey Mouse
cartoon *Crazy Plane*.

1929

January
Buñuel and Dalí write *Un Chien
andalou* in Figueres.
February
Dalí publishes 'La dada fotografica'
in *La Gaseta de les Arts*.
April – June
Dalí in Paris for the shooting of *Un
Chien andalou*. Joan Miró introduces
him to Surrealists. He sees W.S. Van
Dyke and Robert Flaherty's *White
Shadows of the South Seas*, one of the
earliest sound films. He leaves before
6 June premiere of *Un Chien andalou*
(shown alongside Man Ray's *Les
Mystères du Château de Des*) at the
Studio des Ursulines.
3–7 September
Congrès du cinema indépendant at La
Sarraz, Switzerland; *L'Etoile de mer*,
Un Chien andalou and Joris Ivens's
Le Pont and *Pluie* shown. Paul and
Gala Eluard and other Surrealists
visit Dalí in Cadaqués.
1 October – 23 December
Un Chien andalou shown at Studio 28,
Paris with Frank Borzage's *The River* (as
La Femme au corbeau), Jean Painlevé's
Oursin, Donald Crisp's *The Cop*.
24 October
Un Chien andalou shown in Barcelona
to great acclaim.
November
Dalí in Paris preparing his exhibition
at Galerie Goemans (20 Nov.–5 Dec.)
and for which Breton writes the
catalogue preface; however, Dalí
leaves before opening.

December
Breton announces expulsions in
Second Manifeste du surréalisme
published in *La Révolution surréaliste*
(15 Dec.), where Dalí and Buñuel
publish the scenario of *Un Chien
andalou*. Georges Bataille, one of
Breton's targets, publishes 'Le Jeu
lugubre' in *Documents*, no.7. Dalí
returns to Paris at the end of
December after argument with his
father; works with Buñuel on the script
for *L'Age d'or*.
Movies released that year in Paris
include *Passion of Joan of Arc* with Ivan
Mosjoukine, and Yerofeiev's *Le Coeur
de L'Asie*. Jacques-Bernard Brunius
assists Henri Chomette on *Le Requin*
and Claude Heymann assists Jean
Renoir on *Deux Balles au Coeur*; both
assistants would work on *L'Age d'or*.
Movies released elsewhere include:
(in the USA) Tom Mix in *Son of the
Golden West*; Douglas Fairbanks Jr. in
The Jazz Age; Greta Garbo in *A Woman
of Affairs*, *Wild Orchids* and *The Single
Standard*; the Marx Brothers in the
'musical farce-comedy' *Coconuts*; (in
UK) Alfred Hitchcock's *Blackmail*;
and Anna May Wong in *Piccadilly*.

March
L'Age d'or shown at New York
Film Society.
Buñuel makes *Tierra sin pan*
(*Land Without Bread* 1933). Domingo
Pruna directs first Catalan sound film
El Café de la Marina.
December
Dalí publishes 'De la beauté
terrifiante et comestible de
l'architecture modern style'
in *Minotaure*, no.3–4.

30 January
Dalí and Gala marry in civil
ceremony in Paris.
5 February
Breton places Dalí on trial among his
Surrealist colleagues in Paris for
'Hitlerianism', though he is
'acquitted'. An attempted Fascist
coup the following day brings street
protests (10 Feb.)
4–6 October
General strike and declaration of a
Catalonian republic in Barcelona.
Dalí speaks of a film project about
Ludwig II of Bavaria.
24 October – 10 November
Dalí's first solo show in London
(Zwemmer Gallery).
14 November
Dalí and Gala, accompanied by
Caresse Crosby, arrive in New York for
his exhibition at Julien Levy Gallery.
16 December
Dalí begins publishing illustrated
texts in *American Weekly* which
stimulate his scenario *Les Mystères
surréalistes de New York*, and continue
after his return to Europe
(18 January 1935).

3 March
Dalí reconciled with his father.
June
Suicide of René Crevel. Dalí
publishes *The Conquest of the Irrational*.
August
Breton, Eluard and Man Ray film
project 'Essai de simulation du délire
cinématographique'.
The Marx Brothers' *A Night at the
Opera* is released in the US.

Jean Renoir *Une Partie de compagne*
released in France.
11 June – 4 July
International Exhibition of Surrealism in
London. Dalí's diving-suited lecture
(1 July), was to have covered Harpo
Marx, whom he met that summer.
Dalí has a solo exhibition at Alex
Reid and Lefevre.
7 December
Dalí arrives in New York for the
Museum of Modern Art's exhibition
Fantastic Art, Dada, Surrealism (9 Nov. –
17 Jan.). He disrupts a screening of
Joseph Cornell's *Rose Hobart* as it is
close to his ideas.

January
Dalí visits Harpo Marx in Hollywood
on the set of *A Day at the Races*.
Writes the scenario called *Giraffes on
Horseback Salad* or *La Femme surréaliste*.
February
Breton publishes *L'Amour fou*.
March
In Austria, Dalí paints and writes
The Metamorphosis of Narcissus (fig.95).
June
Dalí publishes 'Surrealism
in Hollywood'
July
Solo show at Renou & Colle, Paris,
includes images relating to the
Marx brothers project.
In the USA Walt Disney releases
Snow White and the Seven Dwarfs
September
In Italy with Edward James.
October
Dalí introduces Roberto Matta to
Breton.

January
Dalí creates *Rainy Taxi* for *Exposition
internationale du surréalisme* in Paris.
September
Painting at Coco Chanel's villa
in South of France.

February
In Paris, Breton breaks with Dalí.
Dalí goes to New York for solo
exhibition, makes (and breaks) Bonwit
Teller store window, and designs
Dream of Venus pavilion for New York
World Fair. US film releases include:
Little Princess with Shirley Temple,
Wuthering Heights with Merle Oberon
and Laurence Olivier, *Each Dawn I Die*
with James Cagney, *The Wizard of Oz*
with Judy Garland, the Marx Brothers'
At the Circus and Garbo in *Ninotchka*.
1 September
German invasion of Poland
precipitates Second World War.
Dalí and Gala move to Arcachon
in South of France.

May
German invasion of France; Paris
occupied on 14 June. Dalí and Gala
flee through Spain to Lisbon.
16 August
Dalí and Gala arrive in New York.

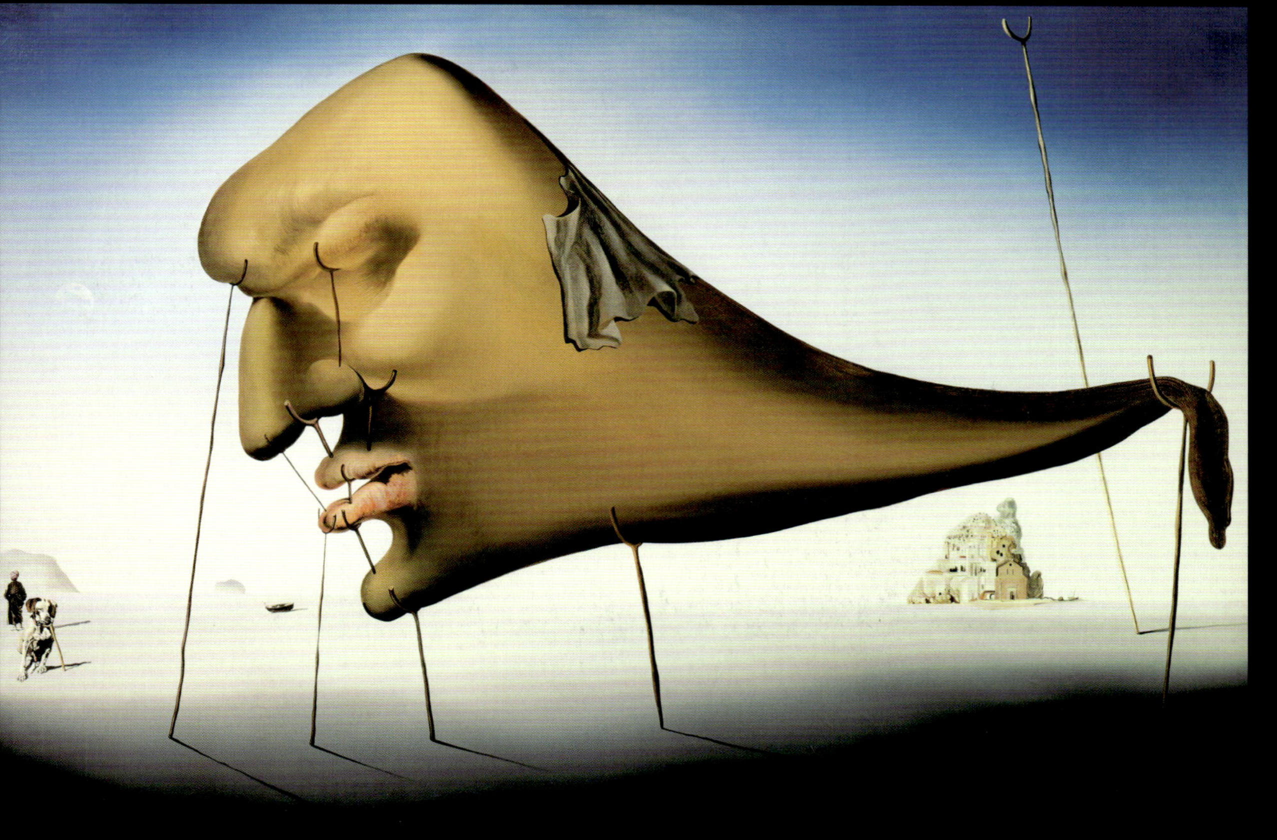

45
Sleep 1937
Oil on canvas 51 x 78 cm
Private collection

Un Chien andalou 1929

Matthew Gale

In July 1929, at the invitation of the poet and patron Victoria Ocampo, the Romanian writer Benjamin Fondane delivered his 'Presentation of Pure Films' to an audience in Buenos Aires. The film programme included the collaboration between Salvador Dalí and Luis Buñuel *Un Chien andalou,* fresh from its 6 June premiere in Paris (where it had been shown with Man Ray's *Les Mystères du château de dés* and a Harold Lloyd and Bébé Daniels film).[1] In Argentina, it was shown with *Entr'Acte* by René Clair and Francis Picabia, Germaine Dulae's *La Coquille et le clergyman* and Man Ray's *L'Etoile de mer.*[2] Having published the unrealisable *Trois scenarios ciné-poèmes* in the previous year, with a photograph by Man Ray,

Fondane was well qualified to discuss the current state of European avant-garde film.[3] Even his title assured this, by doubly alluding to the purity of abstract film (represented in the selection by Man Ray) and to debates around the nature of the specifically cinematographic (as opposed to the theatrical). The inclusion of *Un Chien andalou* is significant in relation to these alternative meanings, although, as their writings indicate, Dalí and Buñuel would only have accepted the purely cinematographic as a definition for their work.[4] Like many of his contemporaries, Fondane understood silent film as an egalitarian, poetic language of movement that was on the point of extinction through the introduction of sound.[5]

Discussing the film programme within this wider scope of avant-garde provocation, he declared: 'To the attentive eye, the modern spirit, including Dada and Surrealism, is characterised … as an *agent provocateur*, obliging European civilisation to produce, at an accelerated rate, the acts of suicide necessary to make way finally for something else.'[6] Fondane's 'attentive eye' seems to acknowledge the opening of *Un Chien andalou*.

If any single sequence can stand for a film, it is this introductory act. On a balcony on a moonlit night, a heavy-lidded man (Buñuel) calmly uses a razor to bisect the eye of a young woman. The impact of this action remains with every renewed viewing, the initial shock living on in visceral horror, never entirely defused by the warning of the cloud passing across the moon, nor even by knowledge of the (quite evident) substitution of a cow's eye (fig.48a, b). Freud, as Dalí (already an avid Freudian in the early 1920s) must have known, identified an assault on the eye as a primary childhood fear. Seen through his theory of Oedipal desire, the act in *Un Chien andalou* was overlaid with transgressive sexual tension, and it is a short step to castration anxieties.[7] Georges Bataille, the writer and editor of the para-Surrealist periodical *Documents*, added a further gloss when he identified a conjunction of horror and seduction: 'In this respect, the eye could be related to the cutting edge, whose appearance provokes both bitter and contradictory reactions;

this is what the makers of *Un Chien andalou* must have hideously and obscurely experienced when … they determined the bloody loves of these two beings.'[8] Hinting at the obsessive eroticism exposed in *The Story of the Eye*, which he had published pseudonymously the year before, Bataille imagined the eye both as the source of seduction – 'the dazzling eye of a young and charming woman' – and as a cannibalistic sacrifice.[9]

It remains uncertain whether either Dalí or Buñuel had consciously made these associations (even if it is possible that they had read Bataille's clandestine novel). They certainly had meant *Un Chien andalou* to require an adjustment from its audience that was revolutionary in ambition. Beyond a desire to shock through restrained violence (perhaps, grimly, inspired by films of pioneering eye surgery),[10] they offered the lacerated eye as a comment on, and denial of, the visual and the rational. In this context, it alerted the audience to the very nature of the film, perhaps even staking a claim to a greater radicalism than that made by André Breton in relation to painting: 'the eye exists in a savage state'.[11] More startling than Man Ray's imposition of an eye in the camera lens at the beginning of his film *Emak Bakia*, the introduction to *Un Chien andalou* acknowledged film as parallel to, rather than a record of, reality. The 'pure film' of Dalí and Buñuel was, therefore, a provocative alternative to the rational, from which the viewer, transfixed in the cinema, had little escape. Bataille

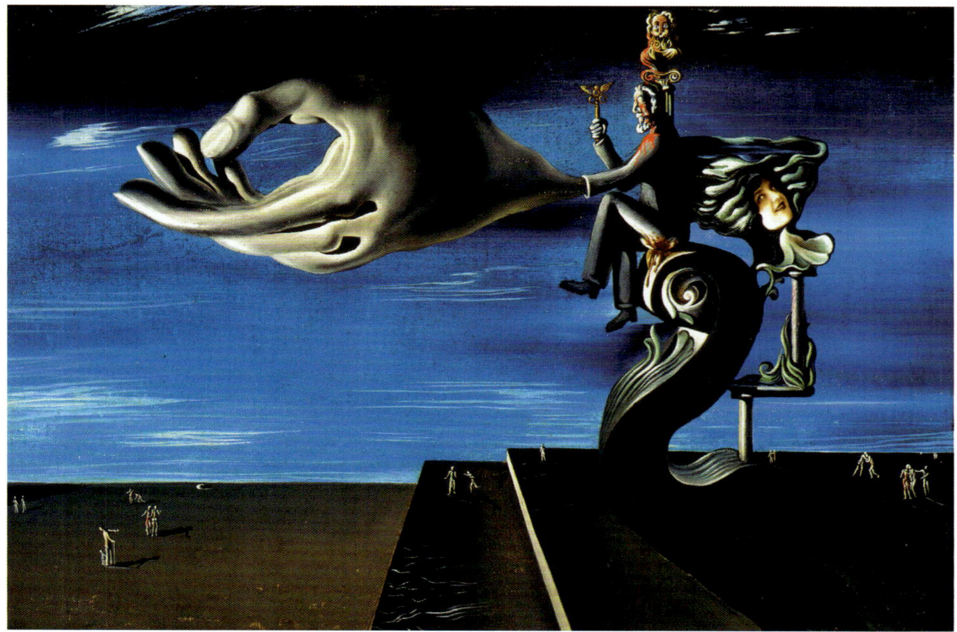

46
La Main (Les Remords de conscience) 1930
Oil and collage on canvas
41.3 x 66 cm
Salvador Dalí Museum,
St Petersburg, Florida

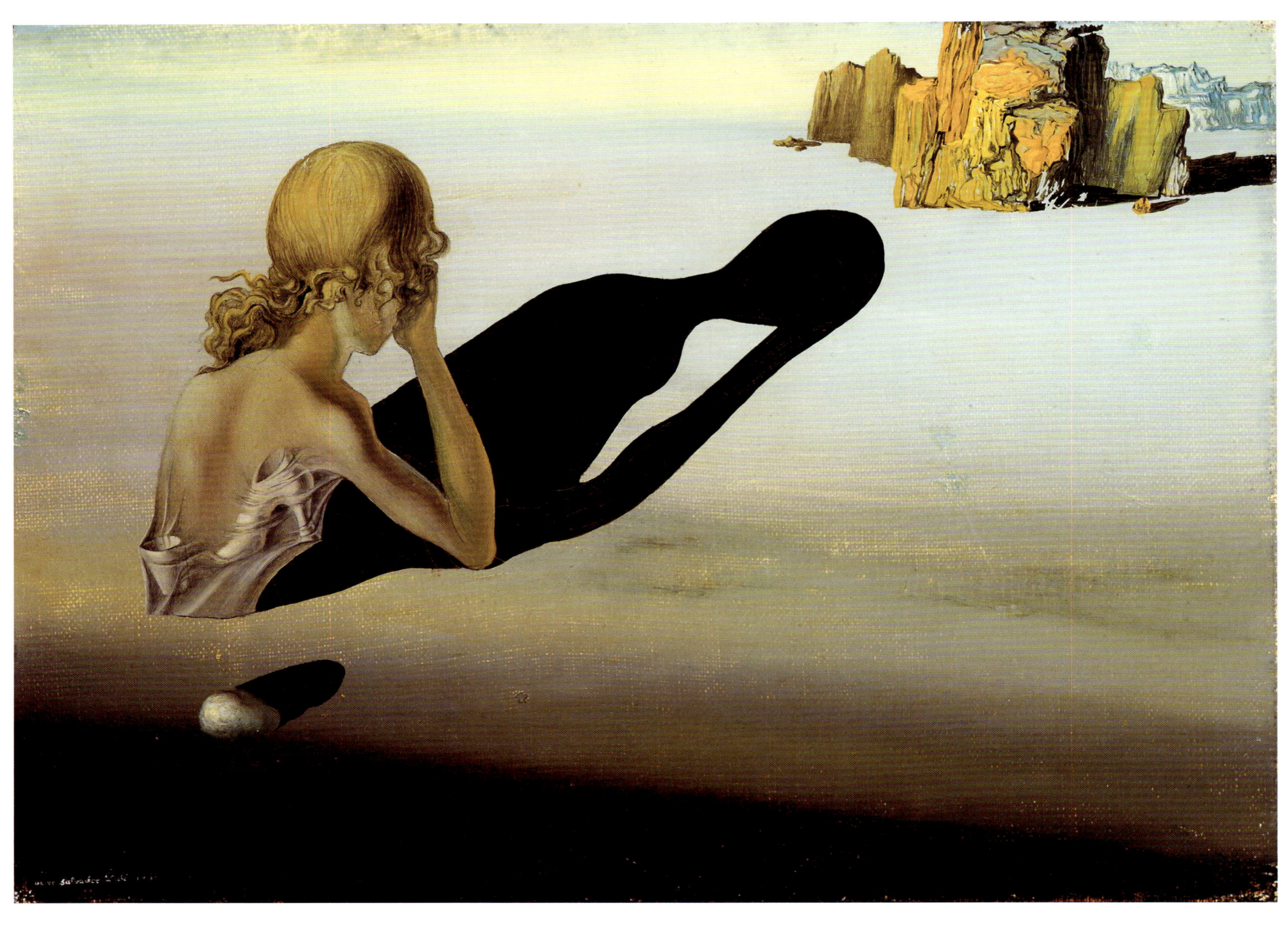

47
Remorse or *Sphinx Embedded
in Sand* 1931
Oil on canvas 19.1 x 26.7 cm
Kresge Art Museum, Michigan
State University, East Lansing.
Gift of John F. Wolfram

wrote of the spectators 'caught by the throat',[12] while the film director Jean Vigo acknowledged that this opening 'assures us that, in this film, we will have to look with – if I may put it this way – more than an everyday eye'.[13]

Although the origins of the project have been recounted a number of times, they remain somewhat obscure. Buñuel persuaded his mother to finance his first film following his apprenticeship to Jean Epstein (for whom he worked as an assistant director on *La Chutte de la Maison Usher* 1928).[14] It is unclear whether he actively sought Dalí's collaboration even though they had both been publishing on the potential of film as seen from their different perspectives. 'Buñuel', the painter later recalled, 'one day outlined to me an idea he had for a motion picture that he wanted to make'.[15] This initial idea, to be called *Caprichios*, was to use the device of editing a newspaper to link unrelated stories by Ramón Gómez de la Serna, and it may have been stimulated by the latter's presentation at the first evening of the Cineclub Español in December 1928.[16] Dalí – perhaps wary of the echoes of Madrid Ultraism rather than any anticipation of Parisian developments – declared this too tame. He immediately wrote a brief outline of his own, which encouraged Buñuel to travel to Figueres in January 1929.[17] They entered a collaboration of unusual creativity. At the end of the month, Buñuel told a local journalist: 'No other collaboration could come together more intimately; in this way, by amending or suggesting ideas or concepts to one another, it was exactly like self-criticism.'[18]

The resulting film, by then provisionally entitled *Vaya marista* (Go Marist), would be made on the basis of the ideas brought together in Figueres and Cadaqués.[19] Dalí anticipated the project's significance, writing to Sebastià Gasch: 'I am collaborating with Buñuel on a film that will be, I am convinced, the most important attempt in European film.'[20] Just as Buñuel's earlier project had relied upon Gómez de la Serna, so it may be assumed that their fervid imaginations were fed by other sources, amongst which may have been Antonin Artaud's published script for *La Coquille et le clergyman*, arguably the most 'Surreal' film up to that moment.[21] That they set out to challenge its shortcomings and restrictions appears to be confirmed by Buñuel's claim (in the same interview) that they hoped 'to make visible certain subconscious states which we believe can only be expressed by the cinema'.[22] Lying behind the accounts of the free collaboration between Dalí and Buñuel, may have been a more concerted strategy that may give credence to the – very *un*Surreal – idea that 'they worked hard and methodically'.[23] One possibility is that the pair constructed scenes through Freudian word-plays in order to attain this programmatic result.[24] Whatever the case, in this process another working title *Dangereux de se pencher en dedans* (It Is Dangerous to Lean Inside) was abandoned for the more mysterious *Un Chien andalou* (which their Andalusian friend the poet and playwright Federico García Lorca took as a personal affront).[25]

Not unexpectedly, accounts of the individual input into the scenario differ and attempts have been made to disentangle and to attribute particular ideas or sequences to one or the other.[26] These include the laceration of the eye, which does not appear in the original scenario, though is generally attributed to Dalí,

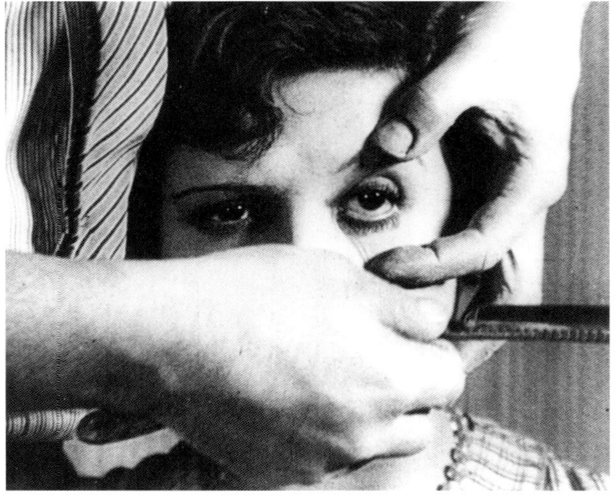

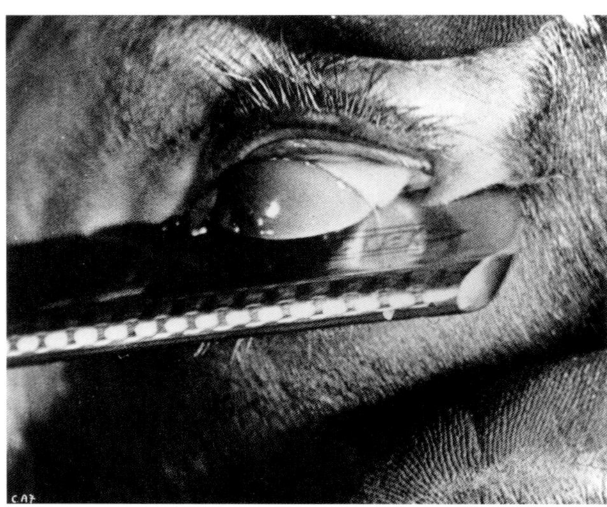

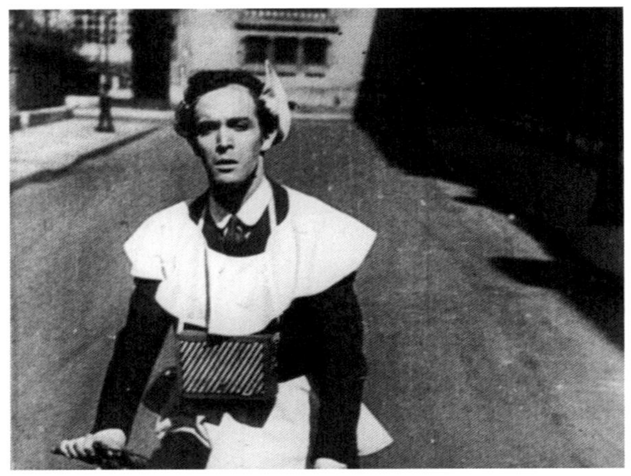

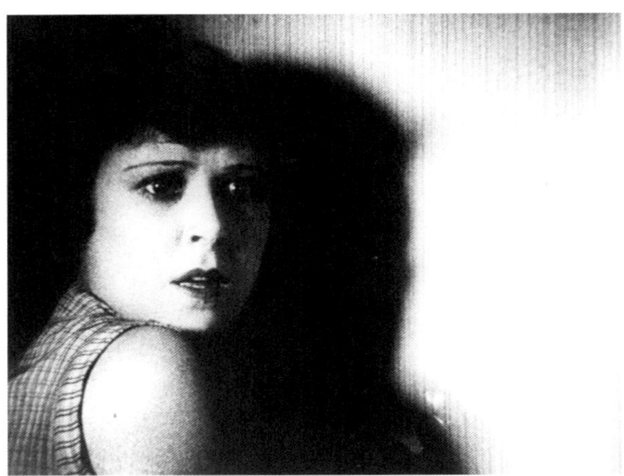

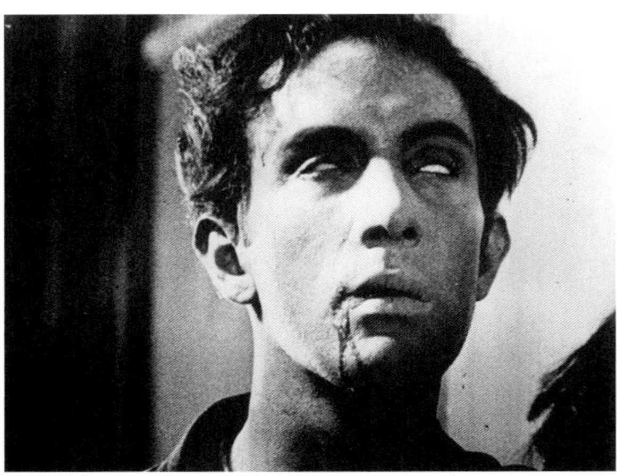

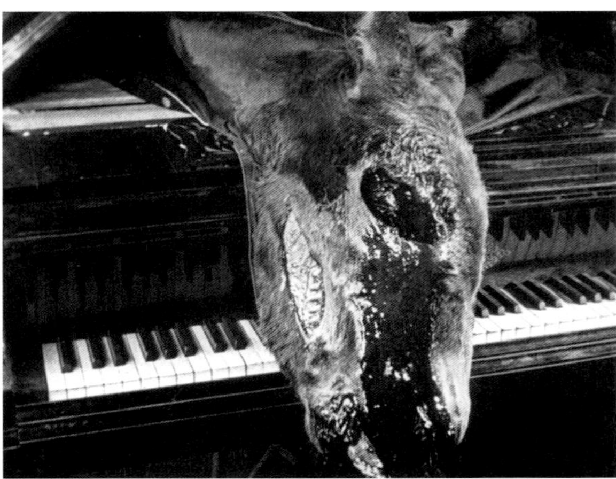

who anticipated it somewhat in the idea of a 'wide open eye with a hair across it' in his prose piece 'Nadal a Bruselles' (Christmas in Brussels, 1927).[27] The strongest evidence for this lies in Buñuel's contemporary attribution of the sequence to Dalí, as reported by Bataille.[28] It is in the nature of the collaboration that neither held exclusive claim to it, at the time at least, but that ideas arose from a broader seedbed. This included not only their own texts but those of their intellectual circle in Madrid; the writings of José Moreno Villa and of Rafael Alberti carried related imagery.[29] They were blended, perhaps, with Parisian precedents such as Max Ernst's collage illustration for *Répétitions* 1921, with an eye on a thread, and the examples of Man Ray's *Emak Bakia* and Bataille's *The Story of the Eye*.[30]

The appearance of other specific images, both in Dalí's paintings and in *Un Chien andalou*, show how the complex exchange of ideas reached back much further than the writing session in Catalonia. The inspiration may run in various directions and from various sources. A key example is found in the rotting donkeys in the film, famously laid out (along with priests, corks and other items) on the grand pianos that the protagonist drags across the room (figs.49d, 53a). At the time, Dalí wrote of his fascination on encountering a fly-strewn corpse of a donkey on the Ampurdan plain, and the motif is found and developed in a range of paintings of 1926–9.[31] The enucleated eye-sockets of the beasts feature in *Honey Is Sweeter than Blood* (fig.2), where they are shown with a disconcerting precision. Dalí would recall making the dripping heads of the donkeys used on the film set even more unctuous (before acting as one of the priests, fig.53a).[32] However, he was also aware that he shared this fixation with a number of his former companions at the Residencia de Estudiantes in Madrid, including Buñuel, Lorca and Pepín Bello (who, at one stage, laid claim to an unacknowledged contribution to *Un Chien andalou*).[33] This related to a shared and privileged language of rebellion and disparagement of which 'putrefaction' was the key term. Initially used as a term of abuse, its associations were fashioned by Dalí into an obsession with softness and morbidity. Thus an individual idiom derived from a shared language, and the painter elaborated upon this imagery in his work in the 1930s.

Perhaps, as a number of scholars have concluded, attempts to establish the lineages of ideas for parts of *Un Chien andalou* are rarely fruitful because of the particular factors that characterised the collaboration: the shared friendship since the Residencia, the intense writing experience, and the fact that each would draw upon the film's imagery in their subsequent work. Disentanglement appears to be born primarily of retrospective revisionism in the wake of the bitterness over the removal of Dalí's name from their collaborations.[34] Instead, Haim Finkelstein's broad assessment remains convincing: that the collaborators shared 'parodistic' and 'psychological concerns', but that Buñuel was 'largely responsible for the overall narrative framework and … cinematic character', while Dalí 'contributed to the figural activity … as well as to some of its narrative procedures'.[35] The balance between flashes of brilliance from the painter and filmic structure from the director rings true insofar as any such separation is possible.

After their moment of chemistry, each of the collaborators reverted to his established role. Buñuel was eager to return to Paris to test what he had learned with Epstein and to run his own project. He booked the crew, the studio time and the cast. He chose an experienced leading man, Pierre Batcheff, and an attractive, though less experienced, leading woman, Simone Mareuil (fig.49a, b). The shot-by-shot shooting script was also his and would serve as the text that he and Dalí published in *La Révolution surréaliste* in late 1929 as part of their absorption into Surrealism.[36]

For Dalí, it seems that the throwback to the halcyon spirit of his student life with Buñuel helped to refine and codify the imagery that would make a sudden upsurge in his paintings of the second part of 1929 and establish his characteristic style: illusionistic, mysteriously allusive, sexually charged, and disturbing. Among the works that he made over the next twelve months were *The Lugubrious Game, The Accommodations of Desire*, and *The Illumined Pleasures* (figs.8, 35, 36). These (and other) works show Dalí adapting imagery revisited in and developed for *Un Chien andalou*. The infestation of ants that crawl from the man's hand in the film (where he is both mesmerised and horrified) features recurrently in writings (notably the contemporary 'Núm.1 bis 6')[37] and in paintings beginning with *Accommodations of Desire*, where they congregate on one stone-like object. Like the film's fade between a sea urchin and a hairy armpit, their configuration in the painting is allusive of pubic hair though not entirely explicit. The other passage in the film involving

underarm hair – in which the man's mouth is haired-over and the woman checks her armpit – also carries some of this perverse and disturbing sexual tension.

A different echo may be found in a figure in *The Illuminated Pleasures*, whose head rests against one of the fictive box constructions. The pose suggests the individual viewer (or, perhaps, voyeur) of an early cinematic device such as a zoetrope or a praxinoscope, which demanded a concentration and isolation symmetrical to that of a cameraman. Dalí was familiar with such devices: he adorned his object *Retrospective Bust of a Woman* 1933 (fig.97) with an animated strip (derived from Léger's animation of Chaplin at the beginning of *Ballet mécanique*) and a praxinoscope remains in his studio at Port Lligat. This would support the sense of the illusionistic boxes in the painting as encapsulating condensed narratives. At the same time, the man's pose in *The Illumined Pleasures* relates to the punished or shamed figures that appear in other paintings, including *The Lugubrious Game*. A reference to Adam in Masaccio's *Expulsion from the Garden of Eden* may be intended, as sexual awareness brings remorse. In Dalí's work, the concealed face is often associated with a reciprocal sexual exposure. This was not – could not be – achieved in the film, though the cyclist punished for wearing the effeminate cape and apron assumes a comparable position when sent to stand in the corner. When he turns to shoot his oppressor, who falls against the girl in the park (fig.53b), the Oedipal nature of this act of aggression is emphasised by the revelation that the shot man is identical in appearance. The painter was just beginning to explore the Oedipal myth of William Tell and this murder appears to be part of that pursuit.

In *Un Chien andalou*, this complex of sexual tensions is captured, in all its ambiguity, by Pierre Batcheff's performance, alternately predatory and pathetic. He demonstrated a mercurial shift between these characteristics, not least in his lustful pursuit of the girl in her room (fig.49c). Batcheff had come to prominence through roles in Abel Gance's *Napoléon* 1927 and in Clair's comedy *Les Deux Timides* 1928, of which one critic observed that he 'even sports Charlot's [Chaplin's] moustache and "quotes" certain of his gestures'.[38] In line with Dalí and Buñuel's preferences, his performance in *Un Chien andalou* seems to draw upon this adaptability by taking Buster Keaton, rather than Chaplin, as the model.

50
The Wounded Bird 1928
Oil and sand on cardboard 55 x 65.5 cm
Tel Aviv Museum of Art,
The Mizne-Blumental Collection

51
Luis Buñuel and Salvador Dalí
Still from *Un Chien andalou* 1929
Courtesy of Contemporary Films

52
Ants 1929
Gouache, ink and collage
11.5 x 16.4 cm
H. Amigorena Collection, Paris

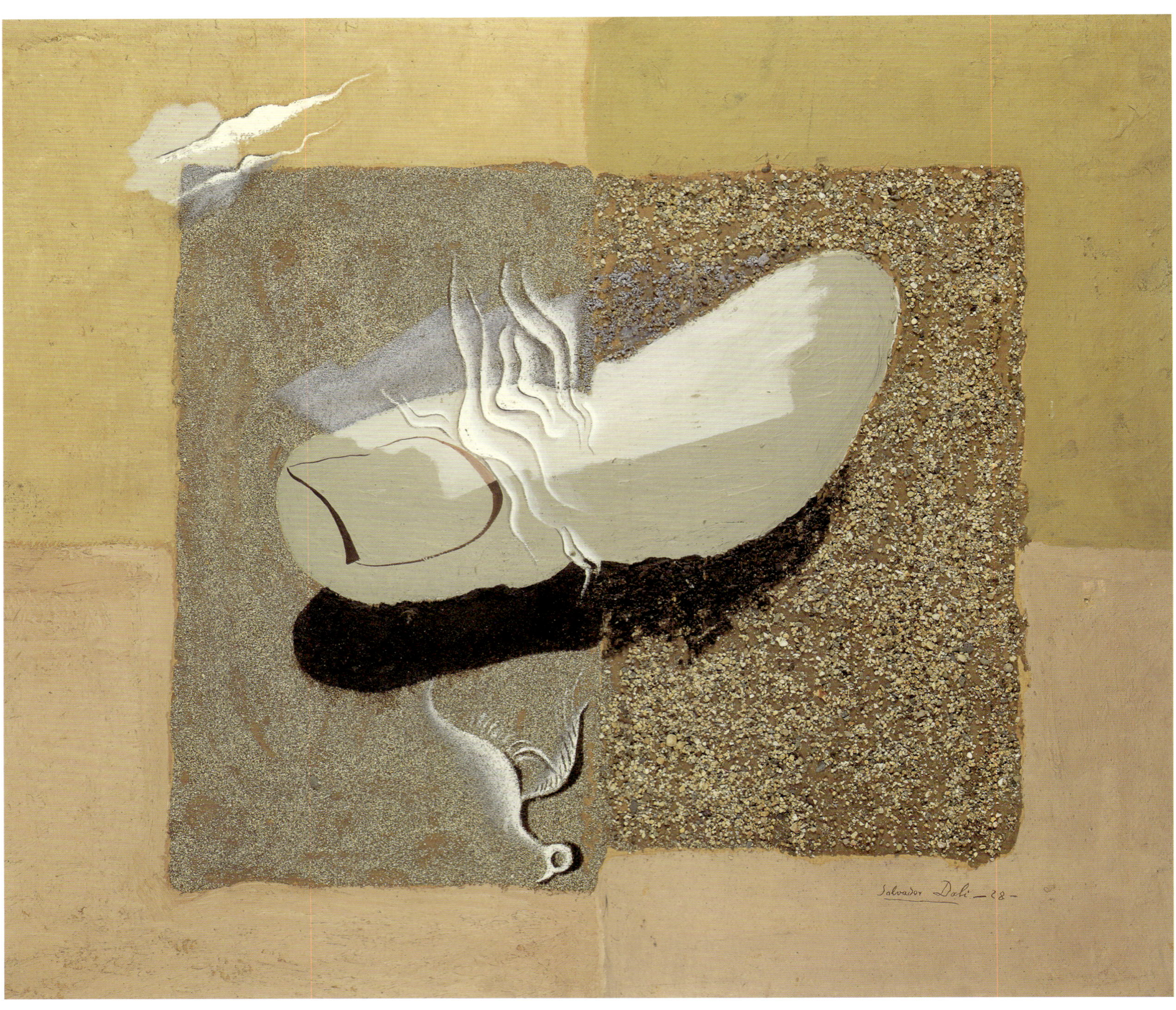

Though not unadulterated, there are aspects of homage in the graphic white face that highlights his heavily made-up eyes and mouth, and his Keatonesque gauntness (fig.27). Particular gestures also evoke the comedian. One example of such quotation comes towards the end of the shooting script: 'He suddenly clasps his hand to his mouth as though his teeth were falling out. The young woman looks at him disdainfully. When the man takes his hand away, we see his mouth has disappeared.'[39] Batcheff's peculiar high-elbowed gesture of revelation here evokes Keaton's disbelieving wiping of his eyes, part of a vaudevillian repertoire that he used in *The Electric House* 1922, *Sherlock Jr.* 1924 and elsewhere. In this, and other instances, such as the connection between the piano-dragging and Keaton's single-handed installation of a grand piano using pulleys in *One Week*,[40] Batcheff conveys, through evocation, the admiration shared with Dalí and Buñuel. This is very deliberate and was surely understood by the contemporary audience and, as others have remarked, was seen as part of a wider response to Hollywood conventions recognised at the time.[41]

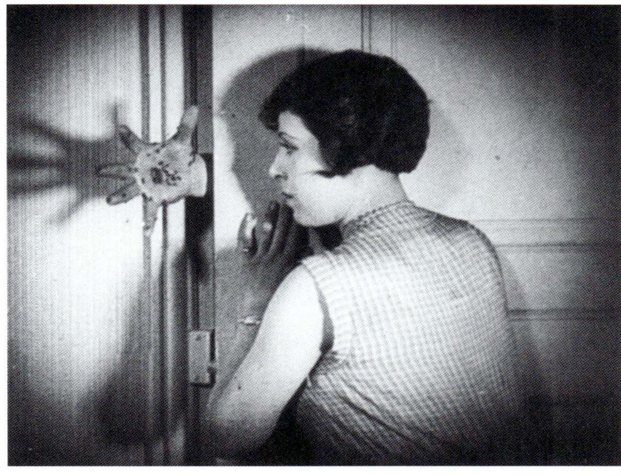

This is not to suggest that *Un Chien andalou* was anything other than deliberately disturbing. Fondane suggested that it acted like 'a magnificent crime'.[42] What the film shared with Hollywood comedies was an episodic structure. However, the inter-titles deliberately subverted the narrative by disruptive chronological vaults, such as 'Once upon a time', 'Twelve years earlier', or 'In springtime', a phrase that simultaneously evokes the advertisements for the Parisian department store Printemps.[43] Buñuel's colleague Jacques-Bernard Brunius, who reviewed the film for *Cahiers d'art* in mid-1929, recognised that until *Un Chien andalou*, 'it had not been understood that a film can be neither romantic nor anecdotal'.[44] By this, he implied its quality as a totally cinematic experience. It is part of its fascination that the episodic nature of *Un Chien andalou* makes it mysterious and perplexing. As well as being a function of Buñuel's extraordinarily fast cutting ('every three seconds' according to Hammond),[45] which heightens the sense of density in such a short film, the deliberate undermining of a sequential logic opens the film to multiple memories or reconstructions for the audience. In this sense, although distinguished by its slippery nature, it parallels a dream narrative, a form of text much in evidence in the early numbers of *La Révolution surréaliste*.

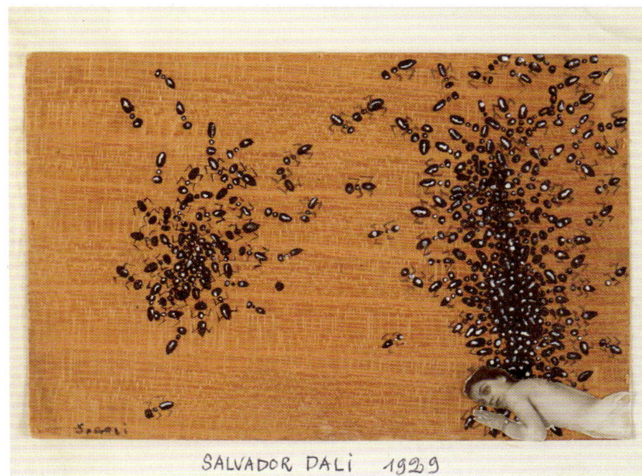

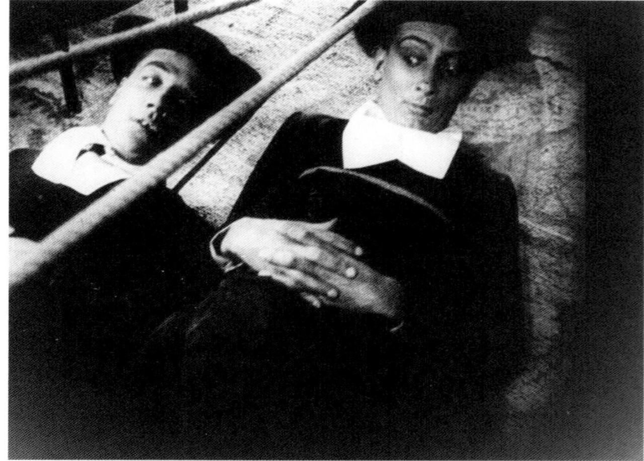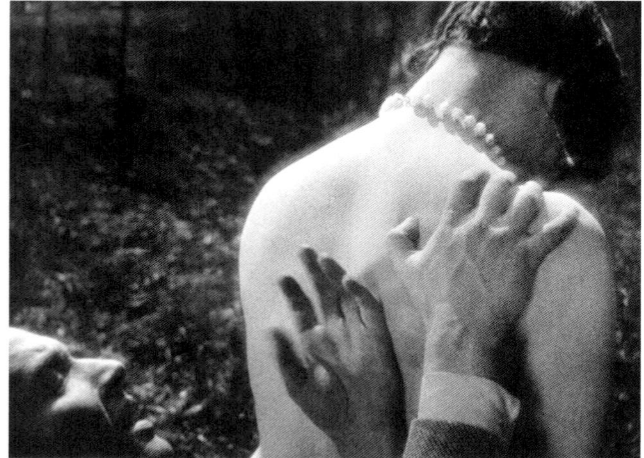

Although polymorphous, *Un Chien andalou* has an underlying concern with obsessive love – that would be re-visited in *L'Age d'or* – played out between the cyclist (fig.49a), soon stripped of his unexpected garments, and the girl (fig.49b), robust equally in her desires and strategies of self-defence. She is, by turns, concerned at the cyclist's collapse, and fascinated by the dangerous isolation of the girl in the street who mistily cradles the boxed hand and is oblivious to the traffic that eventually knocks her down. The man, already in the room, is aroused to greater aggression by this sight and instigates a series of assaults and claustrophobic chases through the room. That these are circular, and potentially perpetual, is indicated by the woman's escape through the door (in which she, famously, traps his ant-ridden hand (fig.51) only to turn round into the same room. That the passions unleashed are circumscribed by convention is confirmed by the obvious, though parodic, symbolism of the piano-dragging scene, in which religion and moral decay are literally embodied by priests and donkeys (fig.49d).

Behind the lust and (mock) symbolism lies a dark melancholia that critics of the day tended to reduce to the fact that the collaborators were Spanish. The profound flavour of mortality closes the film abruptly, when the girl's idyllic walk on the beach with her new man concludes with a shot ('In springtime') of them embedded up to their chests in sand, rotting. Their putrescence and abandonment echo the partially buried figures in many of Dalí's contemporary paintings (e.g. *Remorse* 1931, fig.47) and play to a bitter humour that has been identified with an undertow of masculine crisis: 'the film appears … fissured by references to the romantic stereotype of the lover which is constantly undermined by the frankly comic'.[46] It may be argued that it is just such an assault on the authority of stereotypes that Dalí and Buñuel admired in Hollywood films and sought to sharpen in their own.

Due to Buñuel's efficient planning, shooting of *Un Chien andalou* began on 2 April 1929 and it was privately premiered a little over two months later on 6 June at the Studio des Ursulines.[47] Arriving just after shooting started, Dalí made his first extended stay in Paris (he had visited briefly in 1927) in order to be on hand at the Billancourt studios and on location, which included the trip to Le Havre to shoot the closing scenes on the beach. The first weeks of his stay were taken up by the film and by intense sessions of modification shared with Buñuel and Batcheff.[48] Some sense of the painter's experience is captured in his series of articles 'Documental – Paris 1929' that he sent back for *La Publicitat* in Barcelona, which included his visit to the first talkie shown in Europe, *White Shadows of the South Seas* by W.S. Van Dyke and Robert Flaherty.[49] Infiltrating the Surrealist milieu, Dalí frequently visited Joan Miró, who had encouraged his Parisian ambitions, and became friendly with Robert Desnos. Dalí left Paris before the 6 June screening but, in securing the film in the same programme as Man Ray's *Les Mystères du château de dés*, Buñuel ensured their long-anticipated entry into Surrealism. Through Man Ray and Aragon (who vetted the film for the group), the door opened to the inner core of the movement and to Breton, who is reputed to have commented: 'C'est un film surréaliste!'[50]

The two collaborators seemed both thrilled and disgusted – perhaps to different degrees – by the success of *Un Chien andalou* once it reached a wider audience in October.[51] Dalí soon protested that the film's success was born

of a snobbish acceptance of anything avant-garde.
'This public', he declared in an article published
late that month, 'has understood nothing of the
moral basis of the film, which is aimed directly
against it, with a total violence and cruelty'.[52]
Introducing the shooting script in *La Révolution
surréaliste* in December, Buñuel took up this
theme, believing that the film's popularity implied
a misunderstanding of the fact that it was 'a
desperate, passionate call to crime'.[53] Interestingly
even this echoed the promotion of the film; the
poster for the Studio 28 screening stated, in the
form of an anonymous quotation: 'This film is a call
to murder.'[54] That both collaborators sought to
repel popular acceptance with violence is indicative
of the extreme misapprehension that they believed
had occurred. Even as they benefited from the
notoriety that *Un Chien andalou* brought, giving
them an instant *entrée* into Parisian intellectual and
social circles, their objection fuelled the ferocity
that they poured into their next project, *L'Age d'or*.
They played a delicate game between commitment
and hypocrisy as they capitalised upon the benefits
– chiefly in the form of entry into the circle of the
Vicomte de Noailles – while protesting the
radicalism of their values.

Un Chien andalou
Cast in order of appearance

Man (smoker)	Luis Buñuel
Woman	Simone Mareuil
Man (cyclist)	Pierre Batcheff
Youth in street	Fano Messan
Seminarists	Salvador Dalí, Jaime Miravitlles, Marval
Man (on beach)	Robert Hommet
Script	Salvador Dalí and Luis Buñuel
Photography	Albert Duverger
Set designer	Pierre Schildknecht
Editor, Director	Luis Buñuel

Black and white, silent (soundtrack *Les Grands Films Classiques* 1960),
24 min., 432 metres.*
Shot at Billancourt studios, Epinay, Paris and on location Le Havre
First shown: Film Studio des Ursulines, Paris, 6 June 1929, and Studio 28,
Paris, 1 October – 23 December 1929
Original negative, Cinemathèque Française, gift of Buñuel 1946

* These details, from Yasha David (ed.), *¡Buñuel! La Mirada del siglo*, exh. cat.,
Museo Nacional Centro de Arte Reina Sofía, Madrid and Museo de Palacio de
Bellas Artes de México 1996, p.340, reflect the restored version, which runs at
16 frames per second.

Notes

1
Ian Gibson, *The Shameful Life of Salvador Dalí*, London 1997, p.210.

2
For the two programmes see Patrick de Haas, 'Chronologie', in Jean-Michel Bouhours and Patrick de Haas, *Man Ray: Directeur du mauvais movies*, exh. cat., Centre Georges Pompidou, Paris 1997, pp.187–8.

3
See Benjamin Fondane, *Ecrits pour la cinema: le muet et le parlant*, ed. Michel Carssou, Paris 1984, and Leonard Schwartz, 'Benjamin Fondane & the Genesis of the Cine-Poem', *Frank: International Journal of Contemporary Writing & Art*, no.5, Spring 1986, pp.24–6.

4
See the texts cited in 'In Darkened Rooms' in this volume.

5
Eric Freedman, 'The Sounds of Silence: Benjamin Fondane and the Cinema', *Screen: Surrealism and Cinema Issue*, vol.39, no.2, Summer 1998, p.165.

6
'Présentation de films purs', 1929, in Fondane 1984, p.64, cited in Peter Christensen, 'Benjamin Fondane's "Scenarii intournables"', in Rudolf E. Kuenzli (ed.), *Dada and Surrealist Film*, New York 1987, 2nd ed., Cambridge and London 1996, p.73 (whose translation is slightly modified here).

7
Sigmund Freud, *The Uncanny* 1919, cited in Jean Clair, 'Alberto Giacometti: *La Pointe à l'oeil*', *Cahiers du Musée national d'art moderne*, no.11, 1983, p.71. See also Gibson 1997, p.195, *The Collected Writings of Salvador Dalí*, ed. Haim Finkelstein, Cambridge 1998, p.121, and Linda Williams, *Figures of Desire: A Theory and Analysis of Surrealist Film*, Urbana 1981, and Phil Powrie, 'Masculinity in the Shadow of the Slashed Eye: Surrealist Film Criticism at the Crossroads', *Screen: Surrealism and Cinema Issue*, 1998, pp.156–7.

8
'L'Oeil', *Documents*, no.3, June 1929, as 'Eye' in Georges Bataille, *Visions of Excess: Selected Writings, 1927–1939*, trans. and ed. Allan Stoekl, Minnesota and Manchester 1985, p.17. See, among others, Yve-Alain Bois, 'Abattoir', in Yve-Alain Bois and Rosalind E. Kraus, *Formless: A User's Guide*, New York 1997, p.43, and William Jeffett, 'Salvador Dalí', in Dawn Ades and Simon Baker (eds.), *Undercover Surrealism: Georges Bataille and DOCUMENTS*, exh. cat., Hayward Gallery, South Bank Centre, London 2006, p.101.

9
'Eye', ibid.; see also Lord Auch [Georges Bataille], *Histoire de l'oeil*, Paris 1928, as *The Story of the Eye*, trans. Joachim Neugroschel, Harmondsworth 1982.

10
Joan M. Minguet Batllori, *Salvador Dalí, cine y surrealismo(s)*, Barcelona 2003, pp.92–4, speculates on the link to the filmed operations of the Barcelona ophthalmologist Ignacio Barraquer made in 1917.

11
Breton, 'Le Surréalisme et la peinture', *La Révolution surréaliste*, no.4, 15 July 1925, p.26.

12
'Eye', ibid., p.19, n.1.

13
Jean Vigo, *Vers un cinema social*, Paris 1930, extracted in *Salvador Dalí: rétrospective 1920–1980*, exh. cat., Musée d'art national moderne, Centre Georges Pompidou, Paris 1979, p.99; my trans.

14
See Gibson 1997, pp.191–2.

15
Dalí, *The Secret Life of Salvador Dalí*, trans. Haakon M. Chevalier, New York 1942 and London 1948, p.205.

16
The programme at the Cineclub Español in Madrid, including Erich von Stroheim's *Greed* and Man Ray's *L'Etoile de mer*, Bouhours and de Haas 1997, p.187.

17
The Secret Life of Salvador Dalí 1942, 1948, p.206.

18
Buñuel interviewed in Puig Pujades, 'Un film a Figueres. Una idea de Salvador Dalí i Luis Buñuel', *La Nau*, 28 Jan. 1929, cited in Minguet Batllori 2003, p.67; also cited, slightly differently, in Gibson p.193. The memoirs of each maintain this sense of harmony, as do those of Dalí's sister Ana Maria Dalí, *Salvador Dalí visto par su hermana*, Barcelona 1949.

19
'¡Vaya Marista!', typescript, Fonds Buñuel, Filmoteca Española, Madrid, published in Alfonso Puyal, '"¡Vaya Marista!": La version literaria de *Un perro andaluz*', *Cuadernos de la Academia*, no.5, May 1999, pp.237–55; see also Agustín Sánchez Vidal, 'Notas', in Salvador Dalí, *Obra Completa, vol.III: Poesía, Prosa, Teatro y Cine*, ed. Agustín Sánchez Vidal, Barcelona 2004, p.1271.

20
Dalí letter to Gasch, undated [Jan. 1929], Archivo Gasch, cited in Minguet Batllori 2003, pp.71–2.

21
See Haim Finkelstein, 'Dalí and *Un Chien andalou*: The Nature of a Collaboration', in Kuenzli 1987, pp.130, 132.

22
Buñuel to Pujades, 28 Jan. 1929, trans. in Gibson 1997, p.193.

23
Stuart Liebman, '*Un Chien andalou: The Talking Cure*', in Kuenzli 1987, pp.143–4.

24
Ibid. Liebman assumed that they wrote in French, but the surviving typescript is mainly in Spanish; see 'Desglose de *Un perro andaluz* escrito por Luis Buñuel en colaboración con Salvador Dalí', typescript with annotations, Cinémathèque Française, published in David 1996, pp.201–12.

25
Ibid.; see also *Obra Completa, vol.III*, 2004, p.1272. For the humour in the film see Finkelstein 1987, pp.133–5; the allusion to the Andalusian Lorca is explored by Gibson 1997, pp.195–6. For the early titles see 'Introducción' in *Obra Completa, vol.III*, 2004, pp.111–12.

26
For differing assessments see Finkelstein 1987, and Minguet Batllori 2003, pp.69–78.

27
'Nadal a Bruselles', *L'Amic de les Arts*, 30 Nov. 1927, trans. in Finkelstein 1987, p.25; noted in Dawn Ades, *Dalí*, London 1982, p.51.

28
Bataille, Dec. 1929, discussed by Minguet Batllori 2003, pp.85–90.

29
Minguet Batllori 2003, pp.85–6.

30
A number of these sources and parallels are discussed in Clair 1983, pp.67–80, others are illustrated in David 1996, pp.59–95.

31
Salvador Dalí, 'L'allibements dels dits', *L'Amic de les Arts*, no.31, 31 March 1929, p.6, cited in Agustín Sánchez Vidal, 'De *L'Age d'or* à *La Ruée vers l'or*', in Jean-Michel Bouhours and Nathalie Schoeller, '*L'Age d'or*. Correspondance, Luis Buñuel – Charles de Noailles, Lettres et documents (1929–1976)', *Les Cahiers du Musée national d'art moderne*, hors-série, 1993, p.13.

32
The Secret Life of Salvador Dalí 1942, 1948, p.213.

33
'L'allibements dels dits', 1929; for Bello's claim see Minguet Batllori 2003, p.79.

34
See Agustín Sánchez Vidal, *Buñuel, Lorca, Dalí: el enigma sin fin*, Barcelona 1988, pp.248–50; Bouhours and Schoeller 1993, pp.162–4, and Minguet Batllori 2003, pp.71–6. See also my text on *L'Age d'or* in this volume.

35
Finkelstein 1987, p.139.

36
Luis Buñuel and Salvador Dalí, 'Un Chien andalou', *La Révolution surréaliste*, no.12, 15 Dec. 1929, pp.34–7.

37
'Núm.1 bis 6', *L'Amic de les Arts*, no.4, 31 March 1929, pp.5, 12, 13, trans. in Finkelstein 1998, p.127.

38
André Levinson, 'René Clair, Les Deux Timides', *L'Art vivant*, 1 Jan. 1929, p.37; Powrie 1998, p.162 notes that Batcheff modelling on Chaplin is picked up in Richard Abel, *French Cinema: The First Wave, 1915–1929*, Princeton 1984, p.231.

39
Luis Buñuel and Salvador Dalí, 'Un Chien andalou', *La Révolution surréaliste* 1929, in *Classic Film Scripts: 'L'Age d'or' and 'Un Chien andalou', films by Luis Buñuel*, trans. Marianne Alexandre, London 1968, p.89.

40
Noted by Phillip Drummond, 'Textual Space in *Un Chien andalou*', *Screen*, vol.18, no.3, 1977, p.79.

41
See Michael Richardson, *Surrealism and Cinema*, Oxford and New York 2006, p.28.

42
'Présentation de films purs', 1929, cited in Freedman 1998, p.167.

43
Observation of Annette Michelson made to Stuart Liebman (in Kuenzli 1987, p.154, n.1) cited by Jean-Michel Bouhours, 'Ambushed Advertising', in Fèlix Fanés, *It's All Dalí*, exh. cat., Museum Boijmans Van Beuningen, Rotterdam 2004, p.393. It is a sign of refinement that this was originally given as 'avec le printemps' in the shooting script published in *La Révolution surréaliste*, no.12, 15 Dec. 1929, p.37.

44
Bernard Brunius, 'Un Chien andalou: Film par Louis Buñuel', *Cahiers d'art*, no.5, 1929, pp.230–1.

45
Paul Hammond, *L'Age d'Or*, London 1997, p.40. This depends on the film speed. *Un Chien andalou* has habitually been shown at 24 frames per second, making it 17 minutes long, but the 2003 version restored by Ferrán Alberich for the Filmoteca Española sets it at 16 frames per second, more usual in silent films, which extends it to 24 minutes. Minguet Batllori 2003, p.121 n.50, notes that at the slower speed the film's technical shortcomings are more apparent.

46
Powrie 1998, p.162. There is an evident connection to the iconography of the *Angelus* of Millet that fascinated Dalí, see, for instance, Sánchez Vidal 1993, p.17.

47
See Gibson 1997, p.202.

48
According to the latter's wife Denise Tual, cited by Gibson, ibid.

49
Ibid., p.204; for the articles see also Dawn Ades's 'Why Film?' in this volume.

50
According to James Bigwood, 'Cinquante ans de cinéma dalinien', in *Salvador Dalí: rétrospective 1920–1980*, p.345.

51
It was in an alternating programme at Studio 28, 1 Oct. – 23 Dec. 1929.

52
Dalí, '*Un Chien andalou*', *Mirador*, 29 Oct. 1929, cited in Emmanuel Guigon, *Luis Buñuel y el surrealismo*, exh. cat., Museo de Teruel 2000, p.12.

53
Buñuel in *La Révolution surréaliste*, no.12, 15 Dec. 1929, p.54.

54
Repr. Guigon 2000, p.9.

L'Age d'or ¹⁹³⁰

Matthew Gale

L'Age d'or is a bitter masterpiece, combining –
sometimes with evident tension – the most
aggressive critical instincts of Salvador Dalí and Luis
Buñuel. 'My general idea in writing the scenario
of *L'Age d'or* with Luis Buñuel', Dalí claimed in the
film's programme, 'was to present the pure straight
line of the conduct of one who pursued love in spite
of the ignoble humanitarian and patriotic ideals
and other miserable mechanisms of reality.'[1] The
nature of this pursuit can be summarised by the
efforts to which the protagonist goes in order to kick
a dog, an action that drew objections from the actor
playing the part, Gaston Modot, and, subsequently,
from the audience. On an immediate level, the
kicked dog may stand for the fashionable success of

Un Chien andalou, as well as providing the animal
missing from that film. On a grander level, the dog
is kicked by a man literally in the grips of official
restraint (he is being manhandled by detectives),
for whom this assault confirms his determination to
act independently, just as, within the limitations of
the cinema in 1930, Dalí and Buñuel laid down their
most extreme challenge through this film. What is
poignant about the protagonist's act, however, is
its impotence. It is symbolic defiance, petty anger
passed down the chain of power to one even more
powerless than himself.

There is no doubt that this film was
intended to be read politically. The ceremony of
the 'Foundation of Rome', which occurs near the

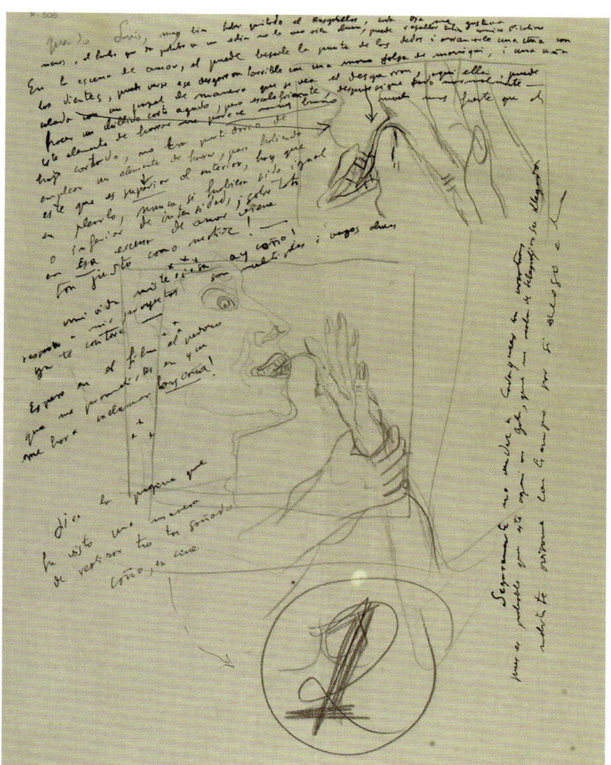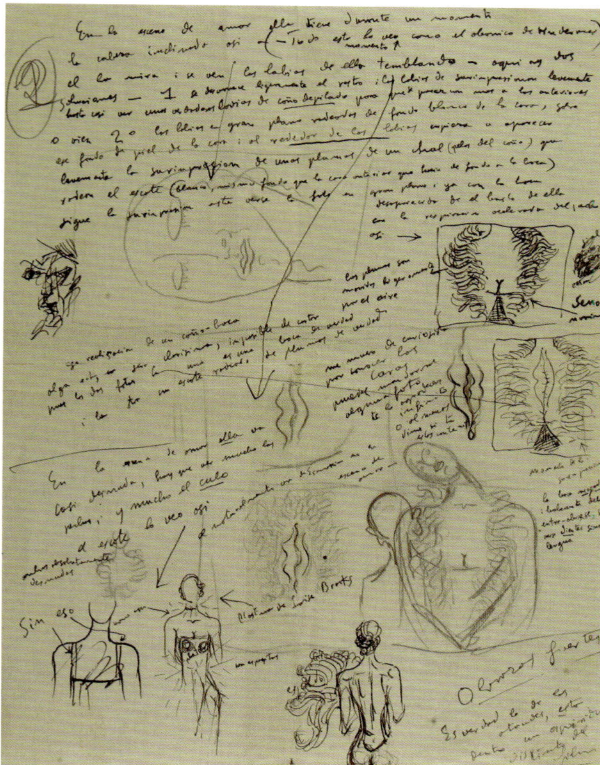

54 a,b
Letter from Salvador Dalí to Luis Buñuel detailing ideas for *L'Age d'or* 1930
Ink on paper 26.5 x 21 cm
Filmoteca Española, Madrid. Fondo Buñuel

beginning, is a parody of Italian Fascism. Its pretensions are lampooned in the procession of Mallorcans, the bishops seated amongst the bandit-infested rocks of Cap de Creus, and the subsequent glimpse of the bishops as mitred skeletons (fig.56).[2] Even the mismatched official couple was recognised at the time as a send-up of the King and Queen of Italy (eliciting a protest from the Italian Embassy).[3] The broader context for this conjunction of religion and politics would appear to be the reconciliation between the Vatican and the Kingdom of Italy recently fashioned by Benito Mussolini in the Lateran Pacts of February 1929.[4] A French audience would have recognised this as a warning about the rising conservatism on their doorstep that allowed the police chief Jean Chiappe to hold 4,000 militants in order to prevent them from partici-pating in the May Day parades that year.[5] Through such explicitness, *L'Age d'or* was immediately controversial. Both Dalí and Buñuel had yearned for a *succès de scandale* over *Un Chien andalou*; now they left no room for misunderstanding. All establishment values were under attack: from the ironic title (evoking, it has been argued, Don Quixote's misguided idealism),[6] and the prologue of the rat killed by scorpions, to the epilogue in which the Marquis de Sade's predilections are played out by a Christ-like figure.[7]

The conception of the film came at an especially complex time in the lives of both collaborators, although their fundamentally different circumstances converged as both committed to Surrealism. The last quarter of 1929 was a personal watershed for Dalí, a moment at which the still partially repressed imagery of his work was liberated into total exposure. The personal catalyst has often been seen to be Gala, who arrived in his life in September among those who made the famous Surrealist visit to Cadaqués. She was a married mother, sexually liberated and a foreigner. All attributes generated extreme distrust in the painter's father and Dalí stoked this disapproval with the Picabian canvas inscribed 'Sometimes I spit with pleasure on the portrait of my mother' (fig.55). He was disinherited.[8] That he did not recant is evidence of the new security that he had found in his relationship and in Surrealism. This remained the case even when he was under the severe pressure of being banned from Cadaqués by the Guardía Civil, an action reflecting his father's influence and which was echoed in the arrest of the protagonist in *L'Age d'or*.[9]

As well as Gala's arrival, Cadaqués was filled that late summer with Surrealists for Dalí to impress: Paul Eluard, the dealer Camille Goemans and his wife, René and Georgette Magritte, and

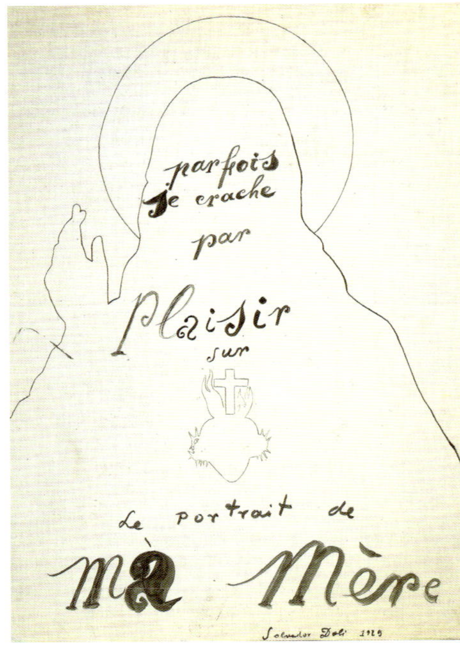

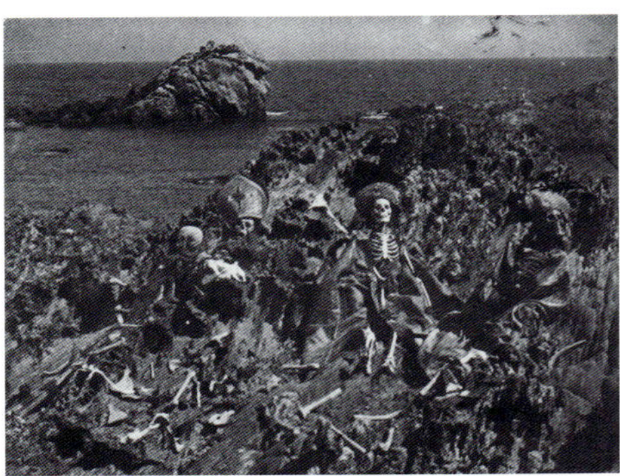

Buñuel. With only one misjudgement – a momentary contact with Georges Bataille's rival group around the periodical *Documents* – Dalí immediately engaged with the movement.[10] His official acceptance was signalled in *La Révolution surréaliste*, which carried the script of *Un Chien andalou*, as well as illustrations of his paintings *The Accommodations of Desire* and *The Illumined Pleasures* (figs.35, 36), completed for his debut exhibition at the Galerie Goemans in November.[11] In the accompanying catalogue, André Breton barely hesitated in calling Dalí a genius,[12] and conjured up the powerful effect of his visual manipulations:

We are literally snatched up, and the fact is just as grave in the face of this lion's head, large as anger, or of this mask with a handle to it … both of which seem to want to go on turning round indefinitely, without any change of expression, not only within these pictures but also within us – yes, in a kind of interior showcase – and which go on reverberating, to our terror, in the air, as though the latter suddenly revealed itself as a mere play of mirrors.[13]

Such images evoke certain paintings and, through the description of movement within the 'interior showcase', aspects of the filmic, though without specifying either.

For Buñuel, also committed to his companion Jeanne Rucar, this was an important moment. He arrived within Surrealism just as Louis Aragon, one of the key founding figures, shifted towards Stalinism and the radicalisation of the movement's political engagement. Although this second film as director would allow Buñuel to pursue possibilities in Hollywood in 1930–1, he followed Aragon's path towards Stalinism in 1932; this was evident in his documentary *Tierra sin pan* (*Land without Bread*, 1933), which highlighted the engrained poverty of the region of Las Hurdes.[14] *L'Age d'or*, therefore, acted as a channel for Buñuel's emerging social protest as well as his professional ambition.

In late November 1929, the Vicomte de Noailles, who had been deeply impressed by *Un Chien andalou*, promised to fund the new project, and in the weeks before Christmas, Buñuel joined Dalí in Cadaqués.[15] The new scenario was to be an extension of *Un Chien andalou* and was initially named *La Bête andalou* (The Andalusian Beast) and then *Abajo la constitucion!* (Down with the Constitution!).[16] However, the creative intensity shared in Figueres nine months earlier had evaporated, and virtually no progress was made. Buñuel then embarked upon the scenario alone, though several scholars have shown how Dalí's letters to his friend were filled with ideas that were broadly incorporated.[17] It is likely that an element of financial responsibility in terms of the film's budget combined with the inspiration that shaped Buñuel's writing. This was evident in his correspondence with Charles and Marie-Laure de Noailles during the winter and early part of 1930, and his visit to their house at Hyères – the modernist building immortalised in Man Ray's *Les Mystères du château de dés* – where he discussed and developed the scenario with his backers.[18] That Dalí's contribution remained confined to correspondence made it no less effective. However, the later arguments between the two stemmed from this discrepancy in their relative contributions.[19] Buñuel clearly did the detailed work, but Dalí felt that he was an equal partner since his ideas had been absorbed in the scenario. History has tended to move towards supporting the latter position, though it remains clear that the film could not have been shaped without Buñuel.

It is through these letters to the de Noailles that so much is known of the conception of *L'Age d'or*. Buñuel notified Charles de Noailles regularly about the progress of the project and its mounting costs as it became more ambitious. As with *Un Chien andalou*, he secured an experienced leading man, Gaston Modot, and a pretty newcomer as the woman, Lya Lys.[20] He made a bid to keep up with the latest technology of sound film and called-in two experienced assistant directors, Jacques-Bernard Brunius and Claude Heymann.[21] De Noailles had little hesitation in backing this expansive approach.[22] At the same time, ideas poured in from Dalí as he pushed the images previously tested for *Un Chien andalou* to the limits of propriety. In one notable letter (fig.54a, b), he detailed how he could 'solve' the problem of Buñuel's desire to show a woman's sex on screen. The fade between a mouth seen on its side and a woman's cleavage surrounded by a feather shawl would, according to the painter, allow a momentary superimposition that would be simultaneously recognisable and impossible to censor.[23] Since Buñuel was aware that the French authorities had banned Eisenstein's *The General Line* 1929, he must have repressed this desire. Nevertheless, the exchange makes clear how Dalí continued to visualise the film and to offer new ideas.

In his witty analysis of *L'Age d'or*, Paul Hammond has established a convincing parallel between the film's structure and the segmented body of the scorpion identified in the opening sequence ('five prismatic articulations' and 'a sixth vesicular joint, the poison sack').[24] The need for a distinct structure may have been driven by the accumulation of elements, which resulted in a step up in length and ambition from *Un Chien andalou*, although it echoes that film in using a prologue and epilogue. The scorpion sequence of the prologue is a readymade scientific film, in which the creature's killing of a rat anticipates the emphasis on the bodily and the violent that is played out over the course of the film.[25] The found inter-titles are in the spirit of the popular entomologist Jean-Henri Fabre. This material replaced a sequence about scorpions that was to have been shot at Cadaqués, where Buñuel took the cast and crew in April 1930 to film the other opening scenes: the arrival of the Mallorcans, the Foundation of Rome, the bandits and the bishops.[26] Dalí was absent, having been banned from the town by his father. Buñuel acted as intermediary between the two, and his diplomatic efforts extended to taking time (and film stock) to shoot a five-minute domestic short of the painter's father and step-mother, now known as *Menjamt garotes* (Eating Sea Urchins).[27] The eating of sea urchins seems deliberately ritualistic in the circumstances.

Like the prologue, the conclusion of *L'Age d'or*, very obviously shot in the studio back in Paris, is detached from but reflective upon the main narrative. The famous and controversial scene of the Duc de Blangis, who is clearly identifiable as Christ (as Dalí noted in the film's programme),[28] emerging with companions from an orgy in the Château de Selligny is only made more sacrilegious by the Duc's return to the orgy with a youth and the accompanying screams and implication of a scalping before he re-emerges clean-shaven. Both the Fabrean prologue and the epilogue provide the film with a philosophical underpinning founded in humanity's animal passions.[29] This reinforced the 'Freudo-Marxist' instincts of sex and death identified by the collaborators' new Surrealist colleagues in the supporting programme notes.[30]

Between these scenes of violence is a narrative of unconsummated desire and lust, an *amour fou* of the sort chronicled by Breton in *Nadja* 1928. The film's narrative was described by the Surrealists in 1931 as 'dominating … the constructions of the spirit and the logic of the flesh'.[31] Slippages in time are indicated by the inter-titles, just as in *Un Chien andalou*, but the underlying story of unsatisfied desires is more structured. Ecstatic cries first announce the couple as they embrace in the mud on a beach and interrupt the ceremony of the Foundation of Rome. They are forcibly separated and the man is arrested. The rest of the film charts their struggle to be reunited. The varied interruptions they face stand for a catalogue of conventional taboos. Beginning with this near-climactic public embrace, the action moves through increasingly private spaces: the streets, the woman's house, her garden, and, eventually, her bedroom. Rather than facilitating intimacy, however, these are the sites for a sequence of thwarted encounters. Even when the lovers eventually find themselves alone in the garden, this key scene is what Dalí called 'an unaccomplished love scene'.[32] The greatest intimacy is achieved through the sexually loaded sequence in which the woman sucks a statue's toe (fig.57b), and she and the man suck each other's fingers. His caressing hand is briefly, and deliberately lacking continuity,

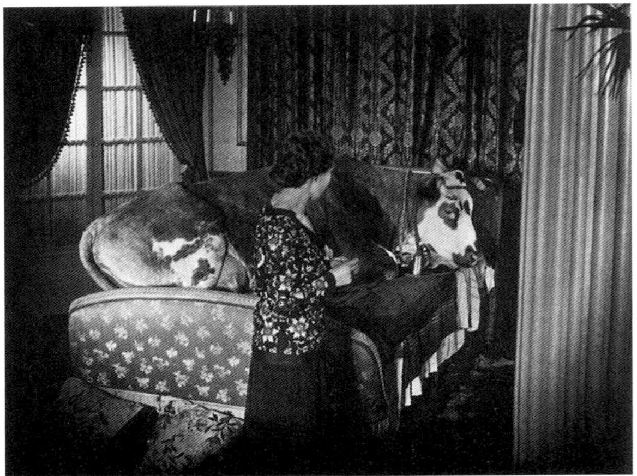

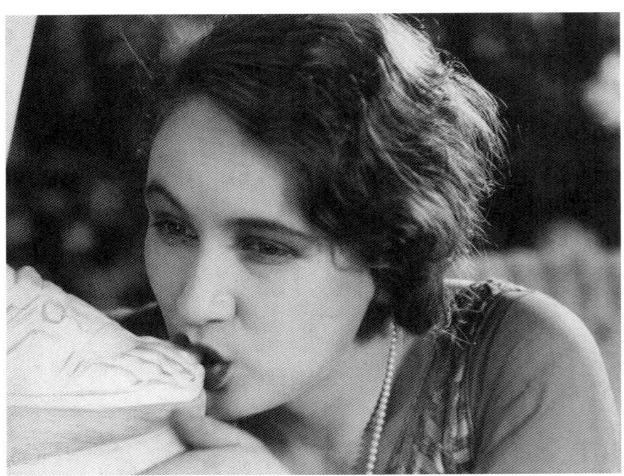

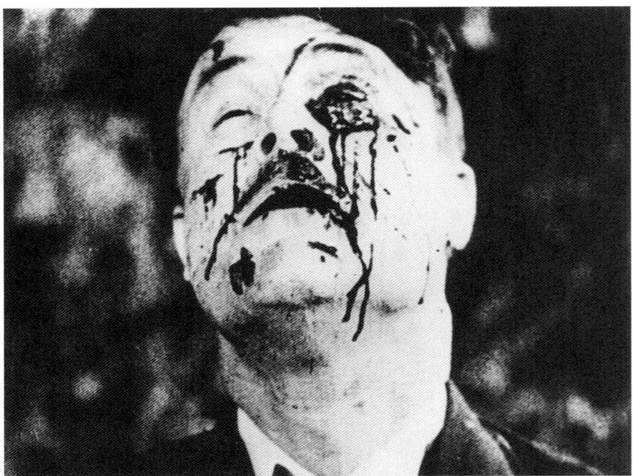

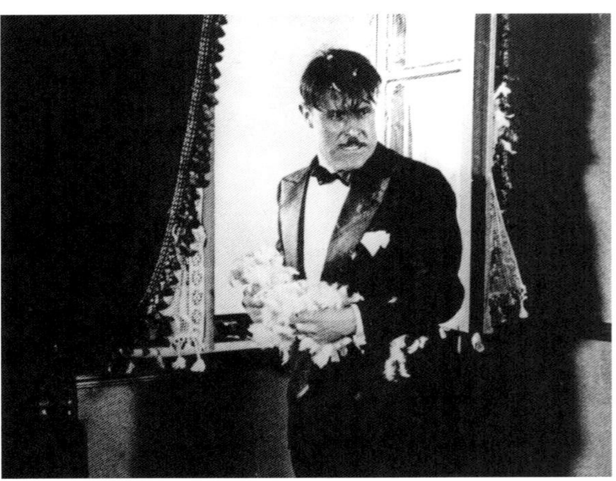

shown as fingerless. While evoking a violent finger-biting scene in Erich von Stroheim's *Greed*,[33] this sequence is a condensed version of Dalí's more savagely ecstatic suggestion that one of the lovers should bite off the fingernails of the other (fig.54a).[34] Something of this is felt when the man suddenly appears blood-splattered and accompanied by the impassioned voice-over '*mon amour, mon amour*' (actually spoken by Paul Eluard), which heightens the perverse relation between violence and romance (fig.57c). Characteristically, this is rapidly inverted to become a moment of abandonment, as the woman goes off with a conductor and the man wrecks her room.

The air of melodrama that might have dominated the narrative of *L'Age d'or*, and is emphasised by the romantic music of Wagner's *Tristan and Isolde*,[35] is undercut by the use of non-sequitor and the generally dead-pan style of acting. The latter reflects the collaborators' admiration for Hollywood silent comedy,[36] while the factual is played on, and subverted, through the documentary elements (there are also newsreels of a riot and a flight over Rome). The effect is to lend veracity to the narrative, and this is further reinforced by a much steadier pacing than was found in the frantic inter-cutting of *Un Chien andalou*. Although these technical distinctions may be attributed to Buñuel, they bear interesting parallels with Dalí's painting. Just as the juxtaposition of images in the earlier film had close connections with the accumulations of 'little things' in Dalí's contemporary canvases,[37] so the more controlled structure of *L'Age d'or* echoed his subsequent compositions of 1930–1, in which the impact is vested in a tense narrative concentration (fig.58). Of course, the additional layer of sound in the second film allows for complexity on another plane, experienced most effectively in the drums of Calanda (Buñuel's home) that mark the Sadean ending.

The obstacle to the lovers' *amour fou* is, of course, convention in all its forms: church and state, law and order, tradition and family. Dalí and Buñuel assault all these values in *L'Age d'or* with brutal efficiency and purpose. The gamekeeper's shooting of his mischievous son for knocking away his cigarette is shockingly casual; it is also embedded in the painter's concurrent concerns with the Oedipal interpretation of the William Tell myth (figs.10, 39). The film's attack is at its most focused in the woman's bedroom. The cow that she finds on her bed is both disturbing and hilarious (fig.57a). On being deserted, the man's enraged destruction of the room (again impotent, in the throwing of feathers, fig.57d) indicates a darker violence only retrieved by the absurdity of the items thrown from her window. Like the scene of dragging the piano in *Un Chien andalou* these items – feathers, a plough and a bishop – catalogue the burdens of convention (class comfort, landed wealth and religion). Together with the burning giraffe (an animal much used by both collaborators),[38] they reappear in Dalí's paintings, where the plough, for instance, is a key element in his complex deconstruction of the iconography of Millet's *Angelus*.

L'Age d'or is almost as famous for being banned after six days of public viewing as it is for its impact. Indeed, one is often measured by the other, since many knew it only as a legend. The film was completed in May, and the de Noailles were satisfied by the result when they saw it in screenings at their private cinema at Place des Etats-Unis in early July 1930.[39] Though the dichotomy between its message and the opulence of the patrons' home caught the Surrealists' attention at a special preview, the film's virulence generated extreme enthusiasm.[40] Many years later, Breton asked rhetorically: 'What does this film respect, if not, as always, love in its most carnal aspects, freedom pushed to the point of delirium, and, in the context of a morality without obligation or penalty, a worship for the pathos that might enter into certain of life's moments?'[41] In July 1930, Buñuel was confident and explicit, telling a Spanish journalist that he wanted 'a moral scandal, that will consist in revolutionising the bad habits of a society in open conflict with nature'.[42] The carnal was set to be revolutionary.

The engagement of *L'Age d'or* with the political concerns of Surrealism at that moment, seen especially in the group tract produced for the programme, has even led to the suggestion that Buñuel consulted Breton and others in writing the scenario.[43] Whatever the case, the film was an instrument in the negotiation with the Communist Party, as well as becoming a victim of the conflict with the right in all its forms. The programme notes framed the film's political radicalism within the rising sense of crisis in the wider world. Not the least of the brazen claims was Dalí's identification of the Duc de Blangis with Christ, which would cause uproar.[44] This lay in direct contradiction to the stealth with which the film impresario and owner of Studio 28, Jean Mauclaire, had secured the original censor's licence. Having committed to the expense of installing the appropriate sound system, he had provided a résumé of the film for the censors that glossed over its contentious aspects and passed others off as humour.[45]

The Surrealists turned out for the private premiere at the Cinema du Panthéon on the morning of 22 October 1930, and the seating plan shows a fashionable array alongside a wide range of artistic guests including Picasso, Georges Braque, Gertrude Stein and Constantin Brancusi.[46] Just as Dalí had returned to Figueres before the premiere of *Un Chien andalou*, so Buñuel was absent in Spain, preparing to leave for New York on 28 October; however, he reported the cool reception that the film received from the de Noailles' friends.[47] With Buñuel in Hollywood, Dalí became the spokesman when the public screenings began exactly a month later, on 28 November at Studio 28, and rumblings of discontent erupted into assault on 3 December. Looking back twelve days later, Dalí told Giménez Caballero: 'the scandal seemed inevitable to us. For six days all the Surrealists and a large number of sympathisers went to all the presentations of the film.'[48] Their presence was to no avail. Dalí's account of the evening to Charles de Noailles (safely returned to Hyéres),[49] closely matches the report issued soon afterwards by the Surrealists. The trigger for the protest by the neo-Nazi Ligue Anti-Juive and Ligue des Patriotes was the juxtaposition of a lady's foot and an ostensory.[50] This had probably been identified as a convenient signal. Ink was thrown at the screen and smoke-bombs forced people from the auditorium, the Surrealist paintings exhibited in the foyer were slashed and the telephone lines cut. It was a classic example of neo-Fascist intimidation. The audience returned to the screening, however, and defiantly watched to the end, which was greeted, according to Dalí, 'with warm applause from the public who unanimously signed a protest against the aggression'.[51] Although there were arrests of the Ligue protesters, a campaign was stoked up by the right-wing press for the withdrawal of the film's certificate. There followed a week of official investigations and requests to resubmit to the censorship board and cut certain scenes before, on 10 December, *Le Figaro* carried the news that the film would be banned.[52] Its certificate was withdrawn two days later, when Chiappe ordered the seizure of all copies at Studio 28 and at the director's home. Although the Surrealists' pamphlet *L'Affaire de L'Age d'or* was a powerful

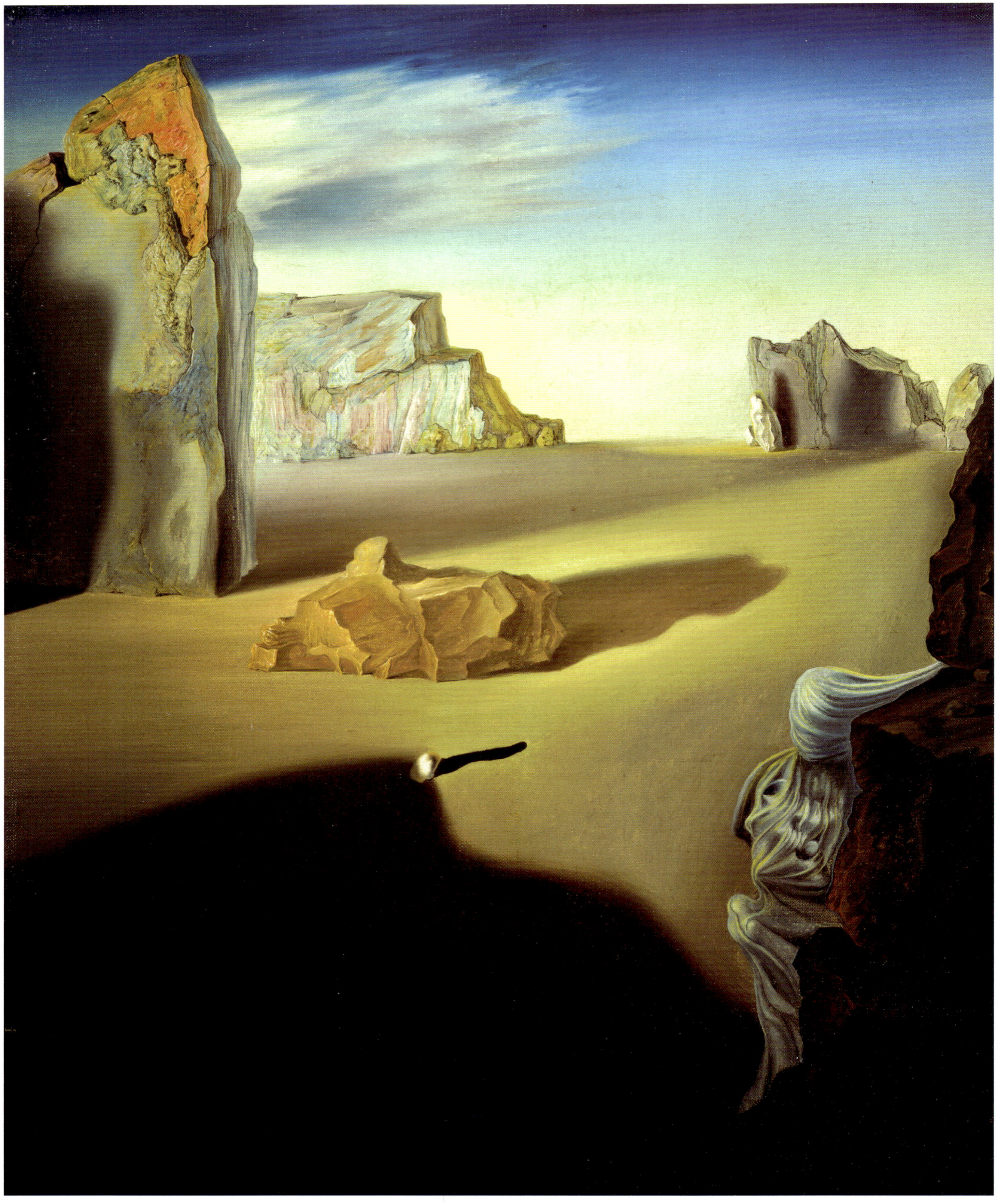

rhetorical counter-blast to these events, it had no effect on their course, and the film became a victim of intolerance.

Somewhat uncharacteristically, Buñuel tried to find ways of getting round the censors by removing offensive passages and later by re-editing it under the new title (taken from Marx): *Dans les eaux glacées du calcul égoïste* (In the Frozen Waters of Egotistical Calculation). Breton recalled it as a forlorn attempt.[53] After the disintegration of his friendship with Buñuel, Dalí also dismissed it in a footnote: 'when Buñuel abandoned Surrealism, he expurgated *L'Age d'or* of its frenzied passages and made a number of other alterations without asking me my opinion. This altered version I have never seen.'[54]

It is sometimes said that *L'Age d'or* was not seen again in France for fifty years, and the scandal was certainly so widely reported that cinemas abroad feared similar interventions. However, neither the French police confiscation of copies nor the official ban was as thorough as legend suggests. A limited number of clandestine screenings occurred in film clubs. Nancy Cunard, who was at the 22 October 1930 showing, organised a screening in Wardour Street in London on 2 January 1931, for which Aragon is said to have smuggled a copy across the Channel.[55] By March 1933, *L'Age d'or* had also crossed the Atlantic to be shown at the New York Film Society.[56] Under similar circumstances, screenings even occurred in France in 1931–2 and in Spain (where Buñuel himself presented it in late 1931).[57] Although Breton failed in his attempt to show it in Tenerife at the time of the Surrealist exhibition in 1935, his hosts at *La Gaceta de Arte* eventually succeeded the following year.[58] Of course, such private distribution did lead to confusion, and David Gascoyne, writing in 1935, could even conclude (mistakenly) that its radicalism made it 'impossible to imagine what would happen were this film to be shown in England, even to a Film Society audience.'[59]

For those who had been able to see it in the violent days of its first screening, *L'Age d'or* took on a mythic status as a film of critical importance in its attack on society and its oppression of the individual. In the later 1930s and marked by intervening events (including the outbreak of the Spanish Civil War and the election of the Popular Front government in France), Henry Miller saw the film as Buñuel's creation, lamenting the director's current obscurity while declaring his suspicions regarding Dalí's successes. Despite these prejudices, he sought to identify the film's power. 'I want to repeat', Miller wrote, '*L'Age d'or* is the only film I know of which reveals the possibilities of the cinema! It makes its appeal neither to the intellect nor to the heart: it strikes at the solar plexus. It is like kicking a mad dog in the guts. And though it was a valiant kick in the guts and well aimed, it was not enough!'[60]

L'Age d'or
Cast in order of appearance

Bandits	Max Ernst, Pierre Prévert, Francisco Cossio, Pedro Flores, Joaquín Roca, Juan Esplandiu, Jean Aurenche, Jaime Miravitlles
Governor	Josep Llorens Artigas
Governor's wife	Mme Hugo
Man	Gaston Modot
Woman	Lya Lys
Policemen	B. Aliange, Gilbert
Marquis of X	Bonaventura Ibáñez
Marquisse of X	Germaine Noizet
Maid	Caridad de Laberdesque
Guests	Marie-Berthe Aurenche-Ernst, Roland Penrose, Domingo Pruna, Simone Cottance-Brunius, Joan Castanyer, Joaquín Peinado, Raymond de Sarka, Jacques-Bernard Brunius, Joan Castanyer, Jacques Prévert
Gamekeeper	Manuel Angeles Ortiz
Bishop	Marval
Conductor	A. Duchange
Duc de Blangis	Lionel Salem
Script	Salvador Dalí and Luis Buñuel
Photography	Albert Duverger
Set designer	Pierre Schildknecht and Serge Pimenoff [1]
Sound	Peter Paul Brauer
Production Manager	Marval
Production Assistant	Jeanne Rucar
Assistant directors	Jacques-Bernard Brunius, Claude Heymann
Editor, Director	Luis Buñuel
Producers	Vicomte and Vicomtesse de Noailles

Black and white, sound, 63 min, 1715 metres
Shot at Studios de Billancourt (silent sequences, 3–26 March 1930), Studios de la Tobis, Epinay-sur-Seine (sound sequences, 31 March – 1 April), and on location Cap de Creus, Catalonia (5–9 April), Montmorency and Paris, 16eme (19–24 May).
Additional footage from *Le Scorpion languedocien* (André Bayard or J. Javault / Éclair, 1912), *The White Sister* (Henry King / Metro Pictures, 1923) and newsreel form Actualités Pathé and Eclair-Journal *

* Details modified from Yasha David (ed.), *¡Buñuel! La Mirada del siglo*, exh. cat., Museo Nacional Centro de Arte Reina Sofía, Madrid, and Museo de Palacio de Bellas Artes de México 1996, pp.341–2, Paul Hammond, *L'Age d'or*, London 1997 and Robert Short, *Un Chien andalou / L'Age d'or*, DVD booklet, London 2003.

Notes

1

Dalí, 'Le scénario', *L'Age d'or* (programme), Nov. 1930, reprinted in *Salvador Dalí: Rétrospective 1920–1980*, exh. cat., Musée d'art national moderne, Centre Georges Pompidou, Paris 1979, p.100.

2

For the significance of the Mallorcans, see Agustín Sánchez Vidal, 'De *L'Age d'or* à *La Ruée vers l'or*', in Jean-Michel Bouhours and Nathalie Schoeller, '*L'Age d'or*. Correspondance, Luis Buñuel – Charles de Noailles, Lettres et documents (1929–1976)', *Les Cahiers du Musée national d'art moderne*, hors-série, 1993, pp.13–15. In this connection, Paul Hammond (1997, p.18), notes the 1926 pact between Primo de Rivera and Mussolini, which allowed for an Italian base on Mallorca.

3

Paul Hammond, 'Lost and Found: Buñuel, *L'Age d'or* and Surrealism', in Peter William Evans and Isabel Santaolalla, *Luis Buñuel: New Readings*, London 2004, p.17.

4

For the Lateran Pacts, see Adrian Lyttleton, *The Seizure of Power: Fascism in Italy 1919–1929*, London 1973, 1989, pp.416–21; see also Paul Hammond *L'Age d'or* 1997, p.25.

5

This context is emphasised by Hammond (2004, p.17).

6

Sánchez Vidal 1993, p.19.

7

Although Maurice Heine, the Sade expert, found one that was overlooked and asked why the film held back from attacking other religions cited by Sade, in 'Lettre ouverte à Luis Buñuel', *Le Surréalisme au service de la revolution*, no.3, Dec. 1931, pp.12–13.

8

For accounts of this complex and charged situation see *Salvador Dalí : An Illusrated Life*, London 2007, pp.61–71, as well as Ian Gibson, *The Shameful Life of Salvador Dalí*, London 1997, pp.218–24.

9

See Salvador Dalí Cusí (the painter's father), letter to Buñuel, March 1930, trans. in *Salvador Dalí : An Illustrated Life*, London 2007, pp.66–71.

10

Georges Bataille, 'Le Jeu lugubre', *Documents*, no.7, Dec. 1929, pp.297–302, trans. and ed. Allan Stoekl as 'The Lugubrious Game' in Georges Bataille, *Visions of Excess: Selected Writings, 1927–1939*, Minnesota and Manchester 1985, pp.24–30. See also William Jeffett, 'Salvador Dalí', in Dawn Ades and Simon Baker (eds.), *Undercover Surrealism: Georges Bataille and DOCUMENTS*, exh. cat., Hayward Gallery, South Bank Centre, London 2006, p.101.

11

La Révolution surréaliste, no.12, 15 Dec. 1929 reproduced *The Accommodations of Desire* (pp.19, 20) and *The Illuminated Pleasures* (pp.29, 64), and carried the script for *Un Chien andalou* (pp.34–7).

12

André Breton, 'Salvador Dalí', Nov. 1929, trans. David Gascoyne in Franklin Rosemont (ed.), *André Breton: What is Surrealism? Selected Writings*, New York 1978, p.44; Breton describes Dalí as 'a man who hesitates (and whose future will show that he did not hesitate) between talent and genius'.

13

Ibid., p.45.

14

For *Tierra sin pan* see Mercè Ibarz, 'A Serious Experiment: *Land Without Bread*, 1933', in Evans and Santaolalla 2004, pp.27–42, as well as Jordana Mendelson, *Documenting Spain: Artists, Exhibition Culture and the Modern Nation, 1929–1939*, Pennsylvania 2005. The 'Aragon Affair', which culminated in his defection to the Communist Party, has been retold many times; a fundamental account remains Maurice Nadeau, *The History of Surrealism*, Paris 1964, trans. Richard Howard, Harmondsworth 1973, pp.169–99.

15

All the letters between Charles de Noailles and Buñuel are held in the Musée national d'art moderne, Paris, and published in Bouhours and Schoeller 1993. The funding was confirmed in de Noailles to Buñuel, 19 Nov. 1929, ibid., p.35; the newspaper *Sol Ixent*, 15 Dec. 1929 (ibid., p.40) reported that Buñuel was in Cadaqués.

16

Sánchez Vidal 1993, p.21.

17

Among others see Sánchez Vidal 1993, Hammond 1997, Jean-Michel Bouhours, 'Nunca más la edad de oro', in Emmanuel Guigon (ed.), *Luis Buñuel y el surrealismo*, exh. cat., Museo de Teruel 2000, Joan M. Minguet Batllori, *Salvador Dalí, cine y surrealismo(s)*, Barcelona 2003, and Hammond 2004.

18

Buñuel to Charles de Noailles, receipt, 16 Jan. 1930, in Bouhours and Schoeller 1993, p.44 was written in Hyères.

19

The collapse of the friendship was linked to disputes over the authorship of the two films, but lay in a fundamental divergence of ideology as Buñuel moved towards Communism and Dalí kindled an interest in Hitler and, later, Franco. In 1933, Dalí complained bitterly to Buñuel that he had just seen *Un Chien andalou* in Paris but found that his name had been removed from the credits (Dalí to Buñuel, two undated letters, Filmoteca Española, Madrid, in Bouhours and Schoeller 1993, pp.162–3). The bitterness festered and may be traced through the lowest point of their relationship when Dalí, at the height of his fame in America in 1939, refused to help Buñuel when he was in dire financial straits (Gibson 1997, pp.392–5; see also Javier Herrera Navarro, 'The Decisive Moments of Buñuel's Time in the United States: 1938–40. An Analysis of Previously Unpublished Letters', in Evans and Santaolalla 2004, pp.49–50). At the end of their lives the project for *Little Demon* suggests that reconciliation was not impossible (see Elliott H. King's text in this volume).

20

Buñuel to de Noailles, 8 Feb. 1930, ibid., p.47, reported on Modot. For their previous histories, see Nancy Berthier, 'Fantasmas de carne y hueso: Actores de *L'Age d'or*', in Guigon 2000, pp.39–48.

21

Buñuel to de Noailles, 8 Feb. 1930, Bouhours and Schoeller 1993, pp.47–8, reported the financial ambition, and Brunius's engagement; Brunius had been a fellow critic on *Cahiers d'art* with Buñuel, see 'In Darkened Rooms' in this volume.

22

De Noailles to Buñuel, 11 Feb. 1930, Bouhours and Schoeller 1993, p.49.

23

Dalí to Buñuel, undated letter, Filmoteca Española, Madrid, ibid., p.53, repr. p.52.

24

Hammond 1997, p.9; he also quotes Heymann on the fact that the structure follows that of bourgeois films, ibid., p.40.

25

The footage is from *Le Scorpion languedocien* by André Bayard or J. Javault, for Éclair, 1912; ibid., p.8. Its acquisition is mentioned in Buñuel to de Noailles, 21 April 1930, Bouhours and Schoeller 1993, p.67.

26

Buñuel to de Noailles, 2 April 1930, Bouhours and Schoeller 1993, p.66, is from Cadaqués.

27
For *Menjamt garotes* (Eating Sea Urchins), see Fèlix Fanés, 'Antes de Las Hurdes', in Guigon 2000, pp.188–213.

28
Dalí, in *Salvador Dalí* exh. cat.1979, p.100.

29
Sánchez Vidal 1993, pp.17–18, and Hammond 1997, pp.11–12.

30
Hammond 2004, p.16.

31
'Manifesto on *L'Age d'or*', 1931, trans. in Rosemont 1978, p.327.

32
Dalí, in *Salvador Dalí* exh. cat., 1979, p.100.

33
As noted by Fèlix Fanés, 'Más allá de la pintura', *La Pintura y sus sombras: Cuatro estudios sobre Salvador Dalí*, Museo de Teruel 2004, p.62. In 1937, *Greed* was called 'the apotheosis of the ugly, the sordid, in human beings', in Herman G. Weinberg, 'Erich von Stroheim', *Film Art*, no.10, vol.4, Spring 1937, pp.8–15.

34
Dalí to Buñuel, undated letter, Filmoteca Española, Madrid, ibid., p.50, repr. p.51.

35
Columbia records issued a twenty-disc recording of *Tristan and Isolde* in 1929, according to Florent Fels, 'Phonographe', *L'Art Vivant*, 1 April 1929, p.296; Mendelssohn, Beethoven and Debussy were also used; see Bouhours and Schoeller 1993, pp.28–9.

36
See my text 'In Darkened Rooms' in this volume.

37
See Dawn Ades, 'Why Film?' in this volume.

38
See text by Michael R. Taylor in this volume.

39
Buñuel to de Noailles, 24 May 1930, Bouhours and Schoeller 1993, p.70, announces its completion. A preview on 30 June faltered on technical grounds (Buñuel to de Noailles, 30 June 1930, ibid., p.73), and Buñuel left for Spain on 1 July. The de Noailles's private screenings ran 1–7 July 1930, as noted in Javier Herrera Navarro, 'La recepción de *Un Chien andalou* y *L'Age d'or* en España', in Guigon 2000, p.117.

40
Georges Sadoul, 'Souvenirs d'un témoin', *Etudes cinématographiques*, nos.38–9, 1965, extracted in Gianni Rondolino, *L'occhio tagliato: Documenti del cinema dadaista e surrealista*, Turin 1972, p.110.

41
André Breton interview with André Parinaud [1951], in *Entretiens*, Paris 1952 and 1969, trans. Mark Polizzotti, in André Breton, *Conversations: The Autobiography of Surrealism*, New York 1993, p.121.

42
Buñuel, interview with Andrés Ruiz Castillo, *Heraldo de Aragon*, 20 July 1930, quoted in Sanchéz Vidal 1993, p.19.

43
Hammond 2004, pp.15–16.

44
Dalí, in *Salvador Dalí* exh. cat. 1979, p.100 and abridged (though presented as the scenario) in Dalí, *The Secret Life*, New York 1942, and London 1948, p.411, where no mention is made of the Duc de Blangis and Christ. Bouhours and Schoeller 1993, p.86, indicate that this text post-dates the screening of the film.

45
Mauclaire's text is included in Buñuel to de Noailles, 29 Sept. 1930, Bouhours and Schoeller 1993, pp.80–1.

46
Ibid., p.83.

47
Buñuel, *My Last Breath*, London 1984, p.118.

48
Ernesto Giménez Caballero, 'El escándalo de *L'Age d'or* en Paris: Palabras con Salvador Dalí', *La Gaceta Literaria*, 15 Dec. 1930, p.3, press cutting from Archivio Buñuel, Filmoteca Española, repr. in Guigon 2000, p.23.

49
Dalí to de Noailles, undated (4 Dec. 1930), Bouhours and Schoeller 1993, pp.92–3, partly trans. in Gibson 1997, pp.270–1.

50
'Exposé des faits', in *L'Affaire de 'L'Age d'or'*, 1930, reprinted in *Salvador Dalí* exh. cat. 1979, p.115.

51
Dalí to de Noailles, undated (4 Dec. 1930), Bouhours and Schoeller 1993, p.93. The petition is published in ibid. p.103.

52
Ibid., pp.94–103.

53
This is noted in André Breton, *L'Amour fou*, Paris 1937, p.114, trans. Mary Ann Caws as *Mad Love*, Lincoln (Nebraska) and London 1987, p.78. See also Hammond 1997, pp.67–8.

54
Dalí, *The Secret Life*, 1942, 1948, p.284 n.1.

55
Anne Chisholm, *Nancy Cunard*, Harmondsworth 1981, pp.218–19; the preparations were detailed in Juan Vicéns letters to de Noailles, 30 Dec. 1930 and 7 Jan. 1931, Bouhours and Schoeller 1993, pp.109, 110. The precise date derives from the invitation card, ibid., p.118. This undermines the premise of Michel Remy, '*L'Age d'or* y Gran Bretaña: Historia de una ausencia', Guigon 2000, pp.120–9.

56
Fernando Gabriel Martin, 'El conocimiento de Buñuel en la cultura anglosajona de los años treinta y cuarenta', in Guigon (ed.) 2000, pp.154–5. Buñuel's correspondence with de Noailles (17 Sept. 1931) shows that Victoria Ocampo requested it for Buenos Aires; Bouhours and Schoeller 1993, p.147.

57
Emmanuel Guigon (Guigon 2000, p.21) publishes a poster for a showing on 15 Feb. 1932 at Ciné Art; Navarro (ibid., pp.118–19) lists screenings in Madrid (23 Nov. 1931) and Barcelona (Dec. 1931). Buñuel to de Noailles, 5 Dec. 1931, Bouhours and Schoeller 1993, p.149, reports on the Madrid showing.

58
Breton 1937, p.114; Martin, in Guigon 2000, p.160, notes the showing in May 1936 in Tenerife, which was reviewed in *La Gaceta de Arte*.

59
David Gascoyne, *A Short Survey of Surrealism*, London 1935, p.96.

60
Henry Miller, 'The Golden Age', in *The Cosmological Eye*, New York 1939 and London 1945, p.61.

La Chèvre sanitaire 1930–1

Agustín Sánchez Vidal

'La Chèvre sanitaire' (The Hygienic Goat) is a title shared by two pieces of writing by Salvador Dalí: a short essay that forms part of his first book *La Femme visible* (The Visible Woman), and a rough draft of a film script written at around the same time, but which remained unpublished until 2004.[1] In *La Femme visible*, 'La Chèvre sanitaire' is placed between another theoretical essay, 'L'Ane pourri' (The Rotten Ass), and the poem 'Le Grand Masturbateur' (The Great Masturbator), which in turn is followed by a piece of prose writing entitled 'L'Amour' (Love).[2] This provides us with an initial context: the second half of 1930, when Dalí began living with Gala and broke his ties with his family, moved to Paris and adopted

French as his habitual language. As he recounts in the tenth chapter of *The Secret Life of Salvador Dalí*, it was Gala who 'gathered together the mass of disorganised and unintelligible scribbling that I had made throughout the whole summer in Cadaqués, and brought to them a "syntactical form" that was more or less communicable'.[3] In these notes, he sketched out the 'paranoiac-critical method' and its various consequences. While he abominated representations of putrefaction in 'L'Ane pourri', in 'La Chèvre sanitaire' he contrasted this with an exaltation of the gratuitous, and his exhortation to overcome the onanistic solipsism of 'Le Grand Masturbateur' led to the celebration of 'L'Amour'.[4]

The essay 'La Chèvre sanitaire' is certainly not one of Dalí's best, but it is of particular interest in assessing the importance he gave to the arbitrariness of subjective mechanisms in allowing the paranoiac method to operate free from external distortions: 'The gratuitous would constitute something like a geometric point perfectly sheltered from any contamination and from all psycho-sensory influence; it is, in other words, isolated from any carnal or affective intercourse, and it lies outside psychology.'[5] He proposed that, for want of a better name, this point should be called 'the hygienic goat', because 'I have not found any conscious or unconscious relationship between this name and that which it serves to designate. I do this in the hope that in such a fashion true relationships will be established in this case in a natural (apologies!) manner.'[6] This leads him to one of his most radical ideas: 'Everything leads us to believe that reality, in the very near future, will be considered solely as a simple state of depression and inactivity of thought, and, consequently, as a series of moments of absence during wakefulness.'[7]

Film seemed to Dalí an ideal medium for accessing this new vision, going beyond the fragmented and static knowledge of various snapshots, since: 'Natural history, when going through a special state of intuition, might be considered a film of enormous dimensions'.[8] Always assuming, of course, that we have already rejected 'the thousand and one kinds of filthiness that the avant-garde film has obscenely inflicted on us'.[9] Thus, in the theoretical essay 'La Chèvre sanitaire' we see expressed the reasoning that would lead Dalí to translate his beliefs into film. And as the essay, written in Port Lligat, is dated 13 August 1930, it is possible to surmise that the screenplay of the same name might have been written during the second half of that year or early in 1931.

The first thing to note about the film script is that it is merely a rough draft, heavily influenced by other productions of the time, the most obvious and inescapable being *L'Age d'or*, the film shot by Buñuel in the spring of 1930, to which Dalí contributed numerous ideas and which caused such a scandal that it was banned on 10 December of that year. Throughout *La Chèvre sanitaire* there are repeated allusions to *L'Age d'or*, with certain passages containing recognisable quotations from the film or else ideas that Dalí had sent to Buñuel for inclusion in it. Some were taken up, others were discarded and reclaimed by Dalí in his later film projects. One example is the self-propelled coffin, one of the 'gags' that Dalí sent to Buñuel for *L'Age d'or*.[10] The idea was not used by Buñuel at that time,

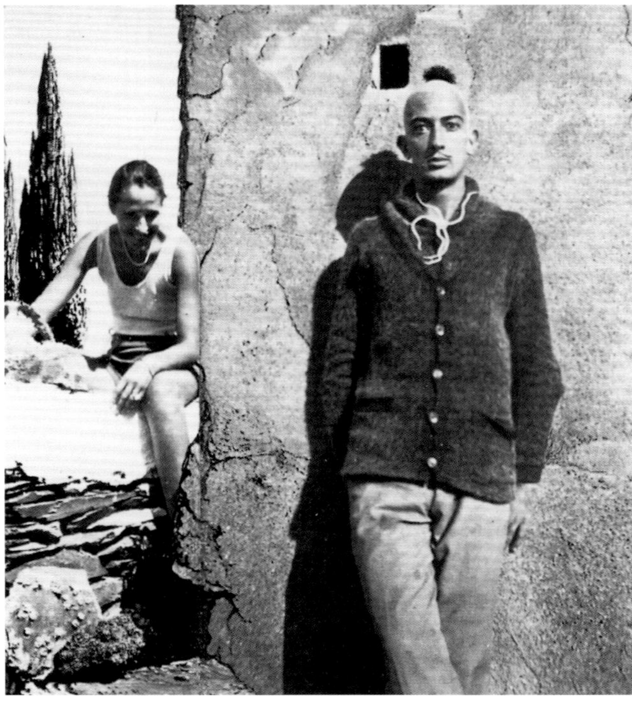

59
Frontispiece for *L'Amour et La memoire* 1931
Photomontage
Fundacío Gala-Salvador Dalí,
Figueres

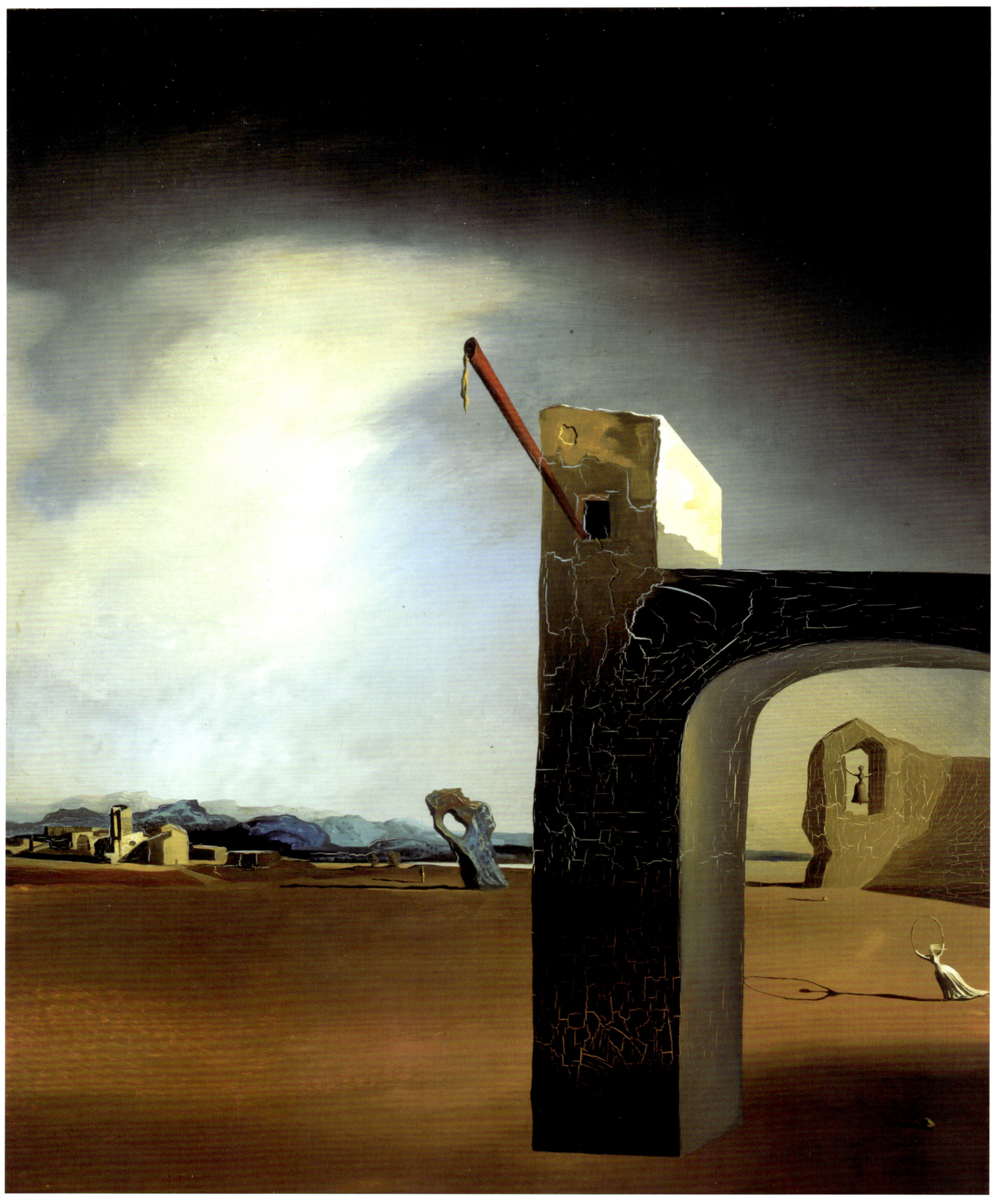

but he did pick it up later in his Surrealist text *La Agradable Consigna de Santa Huesca* 1933 (The Pleasant Instruction of Santa Huesca), and in his film *Simon of the Desert* 1965.[11] Dalí reclaimed it in his film script *Babaouo*, published in Paris in 1932, which he longed to film, perhaps even with Buñuel himself as director.[12]

All these endeavours form part of Dalí's many tireless efforts to disseminate Surrealism and to remove it from the ghetto of the avant-garde, something he would only gradually achieve within the mass culture of the United States. With this in mind, he seized every opportunity to develop the potential of the paranoiac-critical method. And it is in this method that the deepest connection can be found between two projects as disparate and distant as *La Chèvre sanitaire* and *La Carretilla de carne* (The Wheelbarrow of Flesh) 1948–52.[13] Both screenplays demonstrate that this method, explored in his painting, could also be applied to film, producing a corresponding array of double images by means of double plots, double subjects and other ways of subjecting reality to scrutiny and suspicion. At the same time, with his growing number of film projects in the early 1930s, Dalí was also seeking to establish his own presence in the field of cinema, alongside Buñuel, who had eclipsed his contributions to the conception and writing of *Un Chien andalou* and *L'Age d'or*.

Dalí wrote the draft of the screenplay *La Chèvre sanitaire* in French, sketching it out in ink and pencil in an exercise book with notes and drawings that are not always related to the script. It begins with twenty-six sections, which often display clear links with the essay of the same name: 'The spirit of the film must be focused on the principles of *La Chèvre sanitaire* and, consequently, must be directed towards the idea of the gratuitous'.[14] Accordingly, he envisages 'fixing and setting the most unstable passages',[15] taking as his model the convulsive geology of the Cap de Creus, already seen in *L'Age d'or* and in paintings of 1929 such as *The Great Masturbator* (fig.37) and *Imperial Monument to the Child-Woman* (Centro de Arte Reina Sofía, Madrid). Through this 'mineralisation', he sought to give concrete, tectonic and architectonic form to paranoid delirium in a way that was similar to what Antoni Gaudí had achieved in Modern Style (or Art Nouveau) buildings such as La Pedrera in Barcelona (fig.61). Dalí had already referred to this idea back in 1928, when he wrote: 'What we could hardly dream of breaking is smashed

with the most absolute lesson in mutilation, and that which is the softest becomes hardened as an ore.'[16]

To illustrate this, in *La Chèvre sanitaire*, sculptors were to be shown in their studios observing what was happening in front of them and capturing these changes in their modelling. This was an idea close to Dalí's heart, always seeking, as he did, to give solid form to the mutable and perishable:

I wanted to flood the Place de l'Opéra in Paris with plaster so that I could then take casts of the people there drinking coffee, with their scarves, their wraps, their buttons, all the little details … dogs taking a piss, cyclists falling off their bikes, the tram, the cars … everything! To take a monstrously monumental cast and then transfer it to Carrara marble, because … I want ephemeral and entirely unusual ideas to be made eternal, like the pyramids of Egypt. This would be something sublime, a marble snapshot of a day like any other in the Place de l'Opéra in Paris.[17]

Another striking image in *La Chèvre sanitaire* is that of a character playing a harmonium with his feet in the sea who looks like André Breton but wears his hair in a woman's bun and 'when he stands up you can see a dark stain in the seat of his white trousers'.[18] This recalls the excrement-spattered underpants of *The Lugubrious Game* 1929 (fig.8), a painting by Dalí that the Surrealists found problematic.[19] It was also a malicious reference to his father, who suffered a violent attack of diarrhoea, fouling his trousers after stuffing himself with fruit in Figueres market.[20] This image seems to suggest that Dalí has here transferred to Breton the paternal image, which he also assigned to some of his patrons.

Other ideas appear aimed at blowing sky high the system of synchronism, continuity and correspondence used in the standardised language of silent film and in the newly emergent sound film and which had already been sabotaged in *Un Chien andalou* and *L'Age d'or*. In *La Chèvre sanitaire*, a grandiloquent sound is undermined by some anodyne images; the door of a house situated in a town leads on to the rugged, mineral landscape of Cap de Creus; or an implausible number of objects, animals and people come pouring out of a tiny room, anticipating the cabin scene in the Marx Brothers' film *A Night at the Opera* 1935.[21]

In terms of plot, *La Chèvre sanitaire* aims to develop three themes of fatal love in three acts: 'a) forbidden love (brother and sister); b)

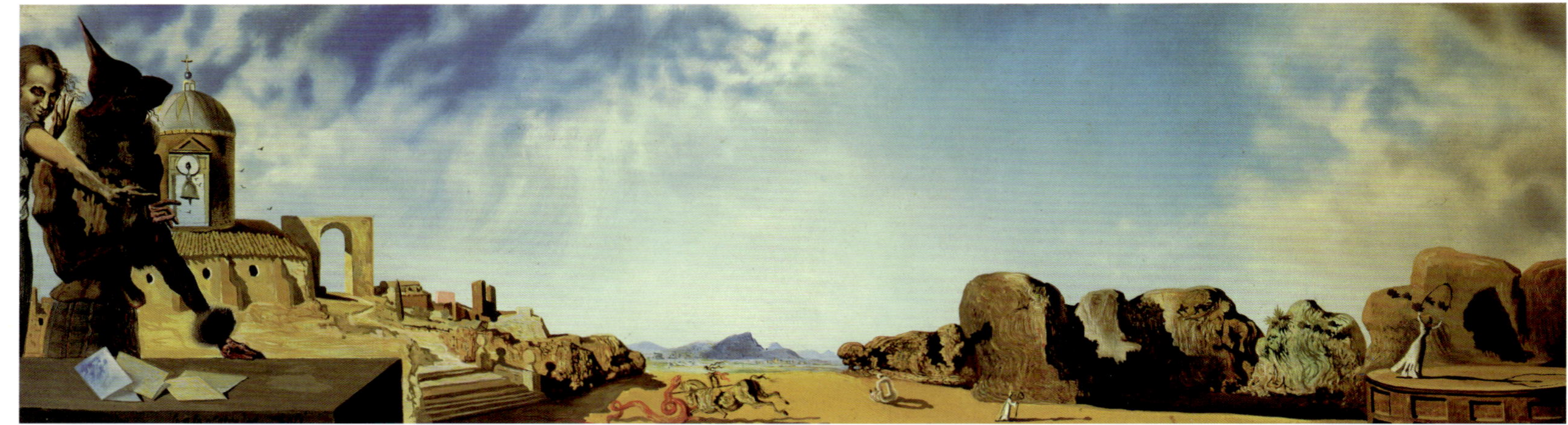

reciprocal love (Romeo and Juliet); c) love for love's sake (Don Juan)'.[22] Within this framework, special importance is given to the incestuous butterfly scene in an evocative echo of Dalí's troubled family relationships, already captured in the 1929 drawing entitled *The Butterfly Hunt* (private collection, Paris) which is a sketch for part of his unfinished canvas *The Invisible Man* of 1930 (fig.21) .[23] This painting was the artist's first attempt to produce the double images that his paranoiac-critical method would so tangibly project. In a similar way, in *La Chèvre sanitaire* Dalí was seeking to construct a plot 'composed of three absolutely different subjects' at the same time and constructed like *The Invisible Man*.[24] This triple variation on the same theme is developed through three stages – infancy, the couple and the family – that allow us to glimpse to what extent Dalí's expulsion from the family home and his partnership with Gala brought him a fresh sensibility and perception.

The emotional dislocation it provoked was translated into his painting and his poetry in the form of double or triple images that headed off into all kinds of narcissistic metamorphoses and interchanges between the various visual forms. These found expression in the dialectic of two of his titles of the period, the painting *The Invisible Man* and the poem 'The Visible Woman'. Later, in his narrative writing, this disparity would be expressed through the emergence of masks and hidden faces. In film, it involved a broad and dynamic range of mechanisms of change, riddled with dissonance. Initially this was achieved through the distortion of musical rhythm and of the conventional logic of montage. After the introduction of sound, it found expression in a contradiction between the image and the soundtrack, achieved in *L'Age d'or* and proposed in *Babaouo*. These were disarticulations of a kind that were also strongly anticipated in *La Chèvre sanitaire*, thanks to Dalí's open-minded exaltation of gratuitous acts.

Translated by Alayne Pullen

61
Anthropomorphic Echo 1938
Oil on panel 14.3 x 51.7 cm
Salvador Dalí Museum,
St Petersburg, Florida

Notes

1
The original manuscript, in French, is held in the Fundació Gala-Salvador Dalí, Figueres; a full publication appears (in Spanish translation) as 'La Cabra sanitaria', in Salvador Dalí, *Obra Completa, vol.III: Poesía, Prosa, Teatro y Cine*, intro. and notes by Agustín Sánchez Vidal, Barcelona 2004, pp.1085–98. I am grateful to Montse Aguer, Director of the Centre d'Estudis Dalinians de Figueres for enabling me to consult the originals.

2
On 15 Dec. 1930, Dalí stated in *La Gaceta Literaria*, that this book 'will comprise three theoretical articles and a long poem that will be entitled *El gran masturbador*'.

3
Salvador Dalí, *The Secret Life of Salvador Dalí*, New York 1942 and London 1948, p.250.

4
The essay 'La Chèvre sanitaire' has not attracted much critical attention, although it was picked up by Louis Pauwels in *Les Passions selon Dalí*, Paris 1968. See *Obra completa, vol.II: Textos autobiográficos 2*, ed. with notes by Montse Aguer, Barcelona 2004, pp.257–65; and trans. as 'The Sanitary Goat' in Haim Finkelstein (ed.), *The Collected Writings of Salvador Dalí*, Cambridge 1998, pp.226–31.

5
Ibid. pp.228–9.

6
Ibid., p.229.

7
Ibid., p.230.

8
Ibid.

9
Ibid., pp.227–8.

10
Dalí letter Buñuel, first published in Agustín Sánchez Vidal, *Buñuel, Lorca, Dalí: El enigma sin fin*, Barcelona 1988, p.237.

11
Ibid, p.257.

12
See Buñuel letter to Charles de Noailles, 18 Aug. 1932, in Jean-Michel Bouhours and Nathalie Schoeller, 'L'Age d'or: Correspondance, Luis Buñuel – Charles de Noailles, Lettres et documents (1929–1976)', *Les Cahiers du Musée national d'art moderne*, hors-série, 1993, p.158. For *Babaouo* see William Jeffett's essay in this volume; the scenario was made into a film in 2000, directed by Manuel Cussó-Ferreras.

13
For *La Carretilla de carne* see my text in this volume.

14
Obra Completa, vol.III, 2004, p.1085.

15
Ibid.

16
Dalí, 'Realidad y sobrerrealidad', *La Gaceta Literaria*, 15 Oct. 1928, trans. as 'Reality and Surreality', in Finkelstein 1998, p.97.

17
Wolf Vostell, *El fin de Parzifal, Museo Vostell*, Malpartida de Cáceres 1989, p.19.

18
Obra Completa, vol.III, 2004, pp.1088–9.

19
The Secret Life of Salvador Dalí, p.231.

20
Ian Gibson, *The Shameful Life of Salvador Dalí*, London 1997, p.46.

21
Obra Completa, vol.III, 2004, p.1092.

22
Ibid., p.1093.

23
See also Dawn Ades, 'Why Film?' in this volume.

24
Obra Completa, vol.III, 2004, pp.1089–90.

Cinq Minutes à propos du surréalisme *1931–3*

Dawn Ades

In the early 1930s Dalí planned two documentary films of very different kinds: *Cinq Minutes à propos du surréalisme* (Five Minutes about Surrealism) and *Contre la famille* (Against the Family).[1] They were conceived when Dalí's prestige within the Surrealist movement was at its height: fizzing with propositions, he was producing an astonishing variety of works and ideas that, as André Breton acknowledged in *Qu'est que le surréalisme?*, brought new life to the movement.[2] *Cinq Minutes à propos du surréalisme* is a promotional film to explain the movement as a whole, and relies on the participation of Breton himself, who was to appear, speaking, at the end of the film. Surrealism was already an avidly discussed phenomenon throughout Europe, but at the same time was in danger of acceptance at a superficial level which Breton had explicitly warned against in his *Second Surrealist Manifesto* 1929.[3] Controlling the reception and understanding of the movement became a priority, and Dalí's scenario forms part of a broad campaign to clarify its intentions and serious ambitions.

 Cinq Minutes … is described as 'A documentary film by Salvador Dalí with the effective collaboration of the surrealist group.' The typescript, in impeccable French, is untitled and undated.[4] It was almost certainly not typed by Dalí himself, who had a free and inventive attitude towards spelling. The title *Cinq minutes à propos du*

SURREALISME is derived from an introductory text that would have preceded the film proper on the screen. The scenario is incomplete. A letter signed by Dalí to an unknown recipient (and that serves as an introduction) explains that this 'very rapid schema' is only a rough and general sketch of basic ideas, and lacks the 'gags' of the moving drawings and important Surrealist documents that would be crucial to the definitive version. From its tone, this letter seems to have been addressed not to Breton or the Surrealist group, but to a potential funder or producer of the film. In addition to the ten numbered pages of the scenario there is a floating page about 'surrealist composition', including part of Breton's poem from the first *Surrealist Manifesto* constructed from fragments of newspaper, for which Dalí had evidently not yet found a place, and three photographs: a page of six studies for Dalí's *Invisible Sleeping Woman, Horse, Lion* (figs.62, 63), a black and white reproduction of *The Persistence of Memory* 1931 (fig.74) and an original photographic print of Man Ray's *Indestructible Object* 1923.[5]

The typescript, with pen and ink drawings by Dalí, is divided into three columns: 'Words', 'Images', 'Sounds' (fig.64a, b). Dalí therefore conceived it as a 'talking film', but at the same time separated words from sounds, the latter constituting a separate strand, which would create 'an ambiance of "surrealist disorientation"'. The 'Sounds' start with music: not the Wagner and tangos of *Un Chien andalou*, but Havana rumbas and blues, followed by alarm clocks, the wind, the noise and whistles of the Metro, laughter, and the shrieks of a chicken whose throat is cut. These sounds will reappear in later scenarios, as in *Babaouo*, where Dalí draws them into his paranoiac effects, with heavy breathing resolving into the sound of the sea.[6] The 'Images' column includes both written descriptions and drawings, the latter sometimes spilling over into 'Sounds' or expanding to occupy a full page. The visual effects were heterogeneous and included moving graphics as well as filmed events and still photographs. The 'movements' of the graphics were important for Dalí, who must have conceived them as animated cartoons, and they were to be based on two different graphic images: the tree and a human silhouette, as he explains in the introductory letter.

The talking script starts in orthodox Surrealist fashion with Freud and the concept of conscious and subconscious thought. A portrait of Freud was to have headed the 'Images' column, followed by a frame divided horizontally into

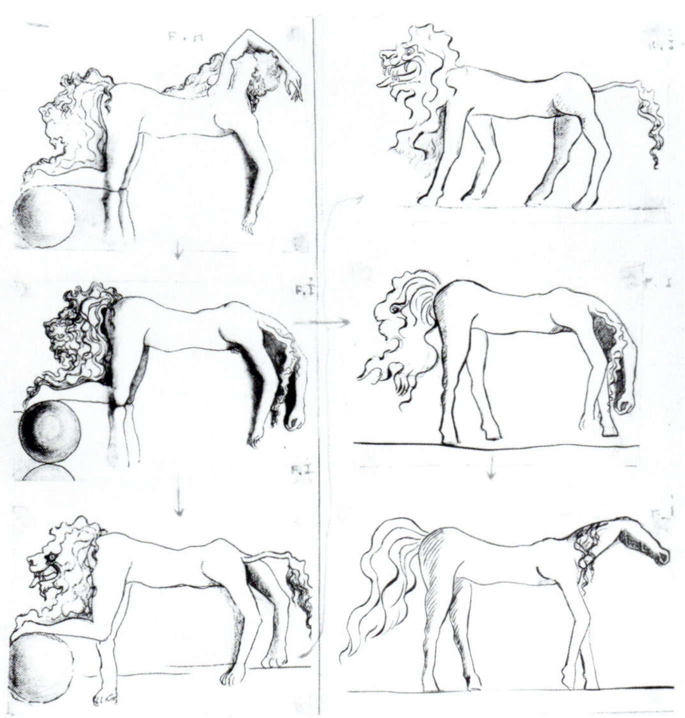

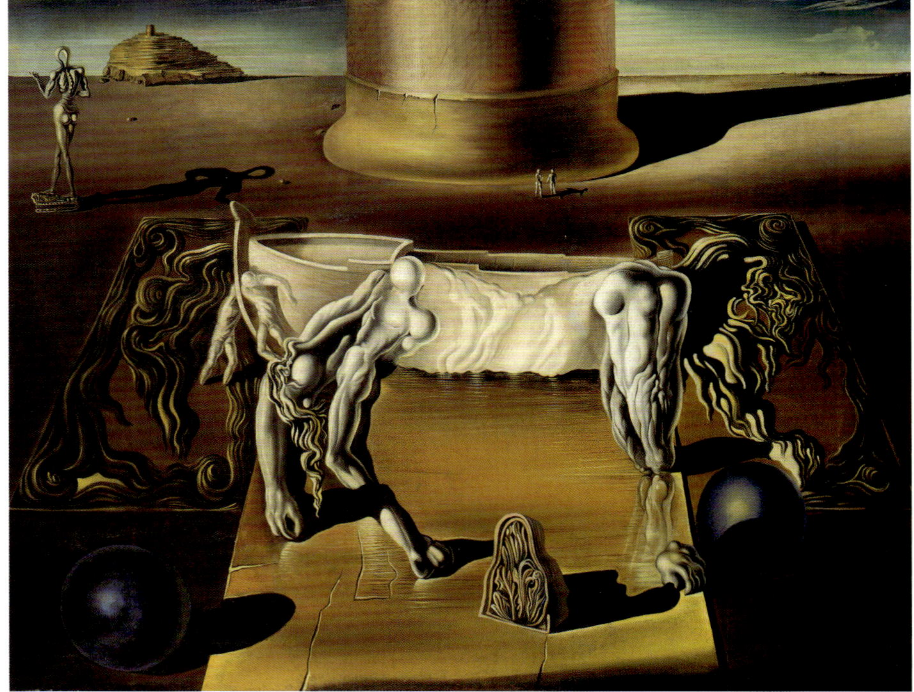

<table>
<tr><th>PAROLES</th><th>IMAGES</th><th>SONS</th></tr>
</table>

PAROLES

Le savant autrichien Sigmund Freud a découvert que chez l'homme, en plus de sa pensée <u>consciente</u> qui est celle qu'on connait, il existe une autre pensée aussi réelle que celle-ci, mais que nous ne connaissons pas, appelée pensée <u>subconsciente</u>.

* *

Le conscient et le subconscient seraient deux choses aussi différentes et antagonistes que le froid et le chaud, que le blanc et le noir.

* *

L'esprit humain pourrait être comparé à un arbre dont les racines se formeraient dans les ténèbres du subconscient et nourriraient les branches, le feuillage et les fruits qui émergeraient à la lumière de la conscience.

* *

IMAGES

Portrait de Sigmund Freud

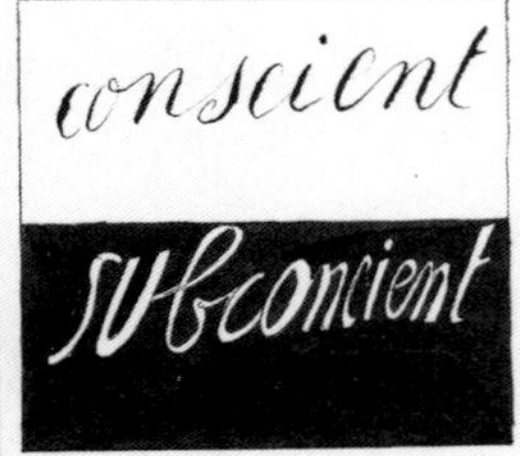

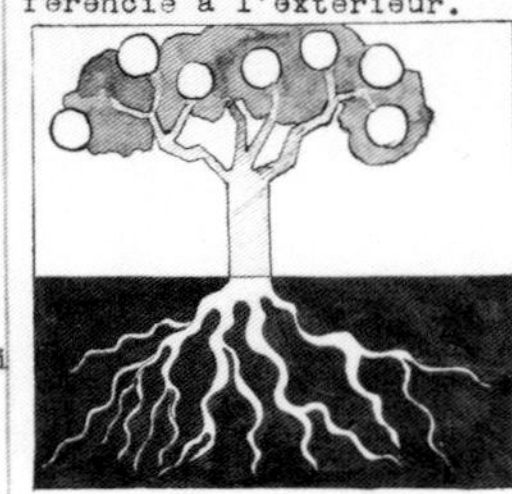

On voit, par des mouvements du graphique, l'arbre se former à partir de ses racines. Le dessin est très différencié à l'extérieur.

SONS

l'exploration du sub- conscient est entreprise par l'activité collective de "l'expérimentation sur- réaliste". Elle illumine le monde symbolique des rê- ves.

Le sommeil occupe la moitié de la vie de l'hom- me. Le rêve se continue encore, même en dehors du sommeil, à travers la vie éveillée, par les rêveries, fantaisies, délires, désirs irrationnels. On rêve sans interruption. Les images de rêve fourmillent dans la vie humaine mais l'homme ferme devant elles les yeux de sa conscience. Son sens pratique et rationnel refoule tout ce qui est langage symbolique du subconscient. Le rêve est le langage du subconscient. Les images et les récits de rêves sont scrupuleusement transcrits par les surréalistes. Ils ne sont qu'une vengeance contre la réalité pratique,

Une moitié de ce qui était entièrement noir devient blanc et réapparait alors le dessin de l'arbre du début. Dans une forme apparaissent ces mots: expérimentation surréaliste. Cette forme, (à déterminer) par un mouvement qui "exca- ve" la partie noire du sub- conscient illumine soudaine- ment une forme déterminée où s'inscrit le mot "rêve". Ce mot avance et occupe tout l'écran.

On passe à une silhouette humaine dont une moitié est remplie de formes mouvantes correspondant aux rêves et aux centres desquelles se trouvent des images concrè- tes les plus hétéroclites et irrationnelles. Ces for- mes envahissent irrégulière- ment l'autre moitié de l'hom- me qui est divisée en casiers rectangulaires portant des inscriptions correspondant aux diverses activités de la vie quotidienne: rendez-vous d'affaires, être aimable a- vec madame X., surveiller l'heure du dernier autobus, avoir le temps de se raser, être un honnête homme, aller être au bureau de poste, té- léphoner à la banque, etc... Quelques-unes de ces images de rêves correspondant aux tableaux ou dessins surréa- listes de rêves, s'approche- ront en prenant toute la grandeur de l'écran. Entre ces images se trouvent des phrases de rêves, qui elles aussi en- vahiront tout l'écran. Une d'entre elles sera un ins- tantané du "Chien Andalou" lequel s'animera pendant un instant suffisant à faire voir la scène du meurtre.

64 a, b
Cinq minutes à propos du surréalisme c.1931–3
Two pages from the film scenario
Scottish National Gallery of Modern Art, Edinburgh. Bequeathed by Gabrielle Keiller 1995

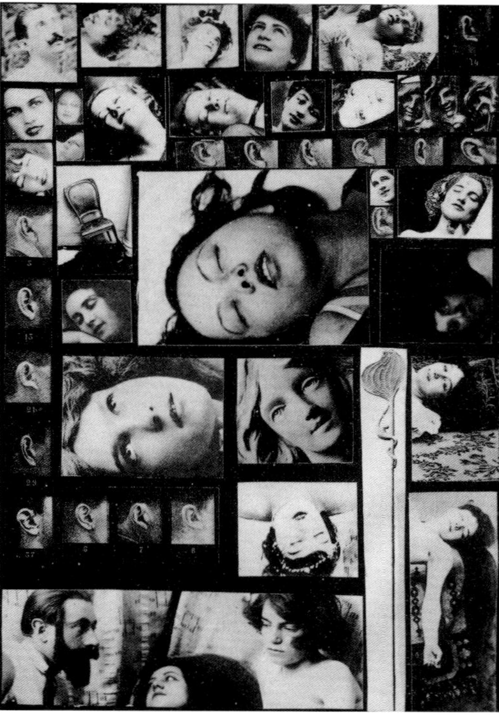

black and white sections inscribed with the words 'conscious' and 'subconscious', then the image of a tree (fig.64a). 'The human mind could be compared to a tree whose roots form in the darkness of the subconscious and nourish the branches, foliage and fruits which emerge into the light of the conscious.' No less than three versions of a tree are illustrated: the first, quite stiff and stylised, arises, 'with graphic movements', from its roots. In the next version 'convulsive undulations' in the roots, corresponding to Freud's 'pleasure principle', are matched by the contrary tendency, the 'reality principle', in the branches. Wiggly arrows underground, following the movement of the roots, are countered by sharply angled arrows in the branches above. The spoken script accompanying these images follows Breton's argument in the first *Surrealist Manifesto* 1924, in distinguishing between the 'new scientific method of "psychoanalysis"', and artistic and poetic experiments inspired by Freud's ideas: the domain of 'the group called "SURREALIST"'. Breton had emphasised that the latter had just as much right to explore the unknown region of the 'subconscious' as the scientists, and that their research would run parallel to psychoanalysis. Following a scene with Surrealists grouped round a table piled with bizarre objects appears the third tree, shown in a full-page drawing with various headings: 'reality principle' and 'pleasure

principle' at the top and bottom, and in the roots underground: 'paranoiac images', 'collages', 'dreams', 'automatic writing', with 'surrealist experiment' in two boxes at the level of the interface between upper and lower zones. In 1933, writing in the Surrealist-oriented periodical *Minotaure*, Maurice Heine used a similar image of a tree to demonstrate the psycho-biological classification of sexual perversions.[7]

The 'descent' into the 'prohibited, deep, obscure and unknown' regions of the human mind are then visualised with a sudden switch to a modern metaphor: the Surrealists descend 'the metro steps of pre-sleep', entering the underground train while opening their umbrellas, accompanied by 'living automata' and a half-nude woman. Then total blackness, the sound of a high wind, followed by the noise and whistle of the metro. The text here echoes the language of Dalí's 1930 book, *La Femme visible*, with for example the striking phrase, to describe the underground voyage into the subconscious, as 'the land of treasures'.[8]

Dreams, 'the language of the sub-conscious', are illustrated with a silhouette of the human body divided into light and dark sections and numerous compartments containing signs and symbols (fig.64b). The 'Images' text describes the clash between the rational world and the desires hidden in dreams in detail, listing dream images, interspersed with 'phrases from dreams', which 'fill the whole screen' and a snatch from the murder scene of *Un Chien andalou*. The emphasis on the contrast between daily life and unconscious desires presages the later scenario *La Femme surréaliste* or *Giraffes on Horseback Salad*, whose plot turns on the incompatibility between regular daily life and the free world of the Surrealists.[9]

Surrealist activity is then demonstrated with the collective game 'Cadavre exquis' (which Dalí played with the group in the early 1930s, when he uniquely used to sign his contribution to the otherwise anonymous collective drawings), collage, and the Surrealist object. The latter is described in terms close to those used by Dalí in his 1931 text 'Objets surréalists', which similarly announces the idea of 'objects of symbolic function', visibly demonstrated in the scenario: 'a hand enters the field of vision to set [the surrealist objects] in motion.'[10] Dalí finally explains his own paranoiac images, which arise from a 'delirium of interpretation': 'an odalisque can be at the same time a horse and a lion.' Using the potential for mobile graphics in film, he describes the woman arriving, reclining lazily, then becoming first a horse, whose tail twitches, then reverting to the image of the odalisque, before becoming a lion. The six stages of the drawing are illustrated on a separate sheet (fig.62), while the 'Images' column returns to the idea of roots emerging from darkness, culminating in 'blackness troubled by distant explosions, luminous, cloudy signs, vague forms which disappear immediately', a visual formlessness to correspond with the continuing mystery of the unknown subconscious. The film ends with the appearance of Breton himself speaking about the effect of Surrealism's irrational and poetic activity on the world of the future – a rather wild and incoherent speech that seems more Dalí than Breton.

The film is 'constantly tugged away from its orthodox explanation of surrealism by Dalí's innate unorthodoxy'.[11] His desire completely to over-ride 'reality' is exacerbated by the violence of the language. Dream images are 'a vengeance against practical, logical and rational activity': 'WATCH OUT for the poisonous and FATAL images of SURREALISM.'

Notes

1

Cinq minutes à propos du SURRÉALISME, original in French, formerly in the collections of Georges Hugnet and then Gabrielle Keiller, who bequeathed it to the Scottish National Gallery of Modern Art, Edinburgh 1996. Published, with an introduction by Dawn Ades, in *Studio International*, vol.195, no.993–4, 1982, and, with Spanish translation, in Salvador Dalí, *Obra Completa, vol.III: Poesía, Prosa, Teatro y Cine*, intro. and notes by Agustín Sánchez Vidal, Barcelona 2004, pp.1050–76. For *Contre la famille*, see my text in this volume.

2

Breton, *Qu'est que le surréalisme?* Brussels 1934, trans. in André Breton, *What is Surrealism? Selected Writings*, ed. Franklin Rosemont, New York 1978, p.136.

3

Breton, *Second Manifeste du surréalisme*, Paris 1929, in *Manifestoes of Surrealism*, trans. Richard Seaver and Helen R. Lane, Ann Arbor 1969, 1972, pp.177–8.

4

My argument in 1982 for dating it between 1930 and 1933 rested on the presence of *Invisible Sleeping Woman, Horse, Lion* of 1930 and Dalí's use of the term 'paranoiac' rather than 'paranoiac-critical' which he preferred after 1933. Agustín Sánchez Vidal (2004, pp.1273–4) agrees with Ian Gibson (*The Shameful Life of Salvador Dalí*, London 1997, p.243) and Paul Hammond (personal communication) that the absence of any mention of *L'Age d'or* implies a date not later than 1930. However, references within the script to the Surrealist object in terms very close to Dalí's 1931 text ('Objets surréalistes', *Le Surréalisme au service de la revolution*, no.3, Dec. 1931, pp.16–17) make it unlikely that it was earlier than this, and the photograph of *The Persistence of Memory* (although not included in the first publication of the script in *Studio International*), confirms 1931 as the earliest possible date. Elizabeth Cowling, in *Surrealism and After: The Gabrielle Keiller Collection* (Edinburgh 1997, p.158) suggests that it might even be a few years later, noting Breton's 'determined efforts to open Surrealism up to a significantly larger audience' around 1933–4, and his abortive attempt to organise a series of public lectures on Surrealism in 1935.

5

The photographs of *The Persistence of Memory* and *The Indestructible Object* were not included in the scenario published in *Studio International* in 1982. At what date they were bound in with the scenario is unclear, but they could plausibly have been among the 'important surrealist documents' that Dalí planned to include.

6

For *Babaou* see William Jeffett's text in this volume.

7

Maurice Heine, 'Note sur un Classement Psycho-Biologique des Paresthésies sexuelles', *Minotaure*, no.3, 1933, p.36.

8

Dalí, *La Femme visible*, Paris 1930.

9

For which see Michael R. Taylor's 'Giraffes on Horseback Salad' in this volume.

10

Dalí, 'Objets surréalistes', *Le Surréalisme au service de la revolution*, no.3, Dec. 1931, p.16.

11

Ades 1982, p.62.

Contre la famille 1932

Dawn Ades

Contre la famille (Against the Family), is a short sketch for a documentary film intended to expose the family as a historical construct and breeding ground for neuroses and psychological conflict. The preoccupations are recognisably Dalí's own, although inflected by Surrealism's larger political concerns.

The scenario can be dated to 1932. Dalí was at the time in regular correspondence with his friend the Catalan poet and journalist J.V. Foix, keeping him up to date with Surrealist activities, especially his own, and eager for their dissemination in Catalonia. On 25 February Foix published a note in his regular column 'Meridians' in the prestigious cultural section of *La Publicitat,* under the heading *Surrealist Activism.* There he announced a new publication by Dalí: '*Vive le surréalisme!* (surrealist novel) with Gala, Dulita, André Breton, Marlene Dietrich, René Crevel, Buster Keaton, Kaergiki, surrealist objects etc. Just now he tells me he is writing a "scenario" against the family.'[1]

Contre la famille confirms not only Dalí's obsessional interest in the conflict between father and son, exemplified in the William Tell paintings from 1930 (fig.10), but his desire to analyse the psychological damage inflicted on the individual by the family in the light of its historical and socio-political history. It is a remarkable attempt to unite a psychoanalytical approach with a Marxist analysis of a dominant social institution.

66
Portrait of my Father 1925
Oil on canvas 104.5 x 104.5 cm
Museu Nacional d'Art de
Catalunya, Barcelona

The short scenario could, however, just as well have been a plan for a treatise, since it almost entirely lacks any visualisation of actual scenes, and mainly consists of headings and brief notes outlining the key subjects.[2] Dalí's chief reference-points are Freud and Engels, but primarily the former. The scenario treats the idea of family in terms of an individual passing through the stages of sexual development. It is in two sections: a summary of the main points (as well as a 'bibliography' of the film), which are then more fully developed under the heading 'The Film'.

The introduction begins: 'Intrauterine dreams. Freud … The birth trauma of Otto Rank. Beginning of the pre-natal sexual life. Theory of the polymorphous perverse …' Later, in *The Secret Life*, Dalí was to devote a chapter to 'Intra-uterine memories' in which he claims that his personal memories of the womb 'corroborate on every point' Dr Rank's 'sensational book', which 'identifies the said intra-uterine period with paradise, and birth – the traumatism of birth – with the myth, so decisive in human life, of the "Lost Paradise".'[3] Rank's *Das Trauma des Geburt* (*The Trauma of Birth*) was published in 1924 and translated into French in 1928. The 'polymorphous perverse' is a reference to the idea, developed by Freud in *Three Essays on the Theory of Sexuality* (1905), that 'a disposition to perversions is an original and universal disposition of the human sexual instinct' and that the potential

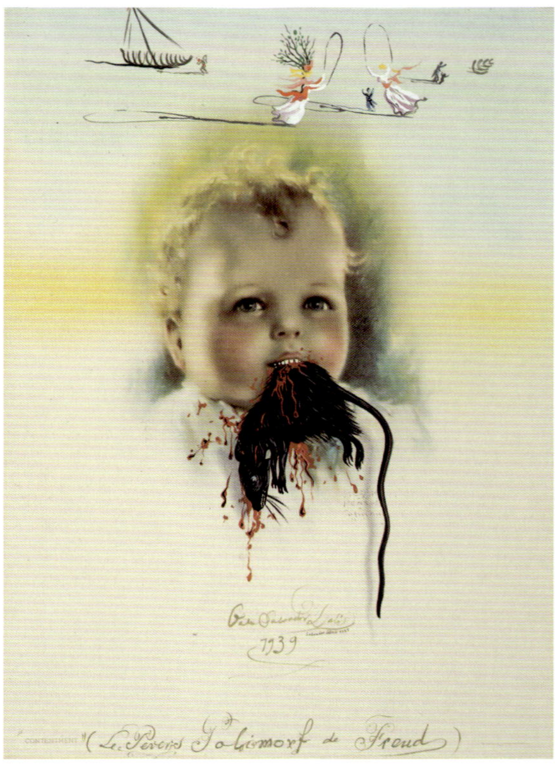

67
*Freud's Perverse Polymorph
(Bulgarian Child Eating a Rat)* 1939
Mixed media on paper
48.7 x 36.3 cm
Fundació Gala-Salvador Dalí,
Figueres

Opposite:
68
The Average Bureaucrat 1930
Oil on canvas 81 x 64.8 cm
Salvador Dalí Museum,
St Petersburg, Florida

for sexual excesses is innate in children.[4] Dalí later made a curious 'assisted readymade' entitled *Freud's Perverse Polymorph* 1939, depicting a child eating a rat (fig.67). The prologue to the scenario continues 'Infancy, formation of the Oedipus complex, castration – Freud … Intervention of the social and economic factors, Engels' history of the family.' After mentioning 'Eumenides – Oedipus at Colonnus', it ends 'Legal prostitution of matrimony.'

Dalí starts the second section, 'The Film', with two 'scenes' but then swiftly reverts to notes. The first 'scene' is obscure but contains a telling slippage from 'husband' to 'father': 'Scene of the neurosis which explodes at the moment of the cure of the husband whom they have been treating – passage – the father deals with tomorrow, the son starts a speech about the next day.' This odd temporality is somewhat clarified further on when Dalí elides historical and evolutionary progress: 'The simple fact of his later birth situates the son on a level historically more developed in the future. Fathers, in Marx's words, should be educated by their children.' The second scene introduces an image recurrent in Dalí's paintings and drawings of the period: 'Prologue-scene of the butterfly hunt.'[5] This is not elaborated but is immediately succeeded by a reiteration of the stages of the individual's development, from intra-uterine life, the birth trauma (Rank), infancy and the 'formation of complexes – the Oedipal complex, castration complex, knowledge of death and birth of the aversion feeling'.

In a relatively discursive passage, Dalí accounts for one of the recurrent themes in *Contre la famille*: the inhibition of desire and of the faculty of the imagination. Here he makes reference to Freud's idea of repression: 'Reality principle against the pleasure principle, theory of repression – all vital human aspirations are repressed by the social conventions incarnated by the family.' Dalí plans to treat familial relationships via Freudian case studies: 'All the situations develop on the basis of registered and analysed clinical cases.' Among these, he mentions son and mother ('Oedipus complex which prevents love'), brother and sister, and again the 'Eumenides'. These are the Furies, 'avengers of crime, especially crime against the ties of kinship',[6] who figure most famously in the Greek story of Orestes, who murdered his mother Clytemnestra. The 'Electra complex' was proposed by Jung as the female equivalent to the Oedipus complex, Electra being Orestes's sister who assisted

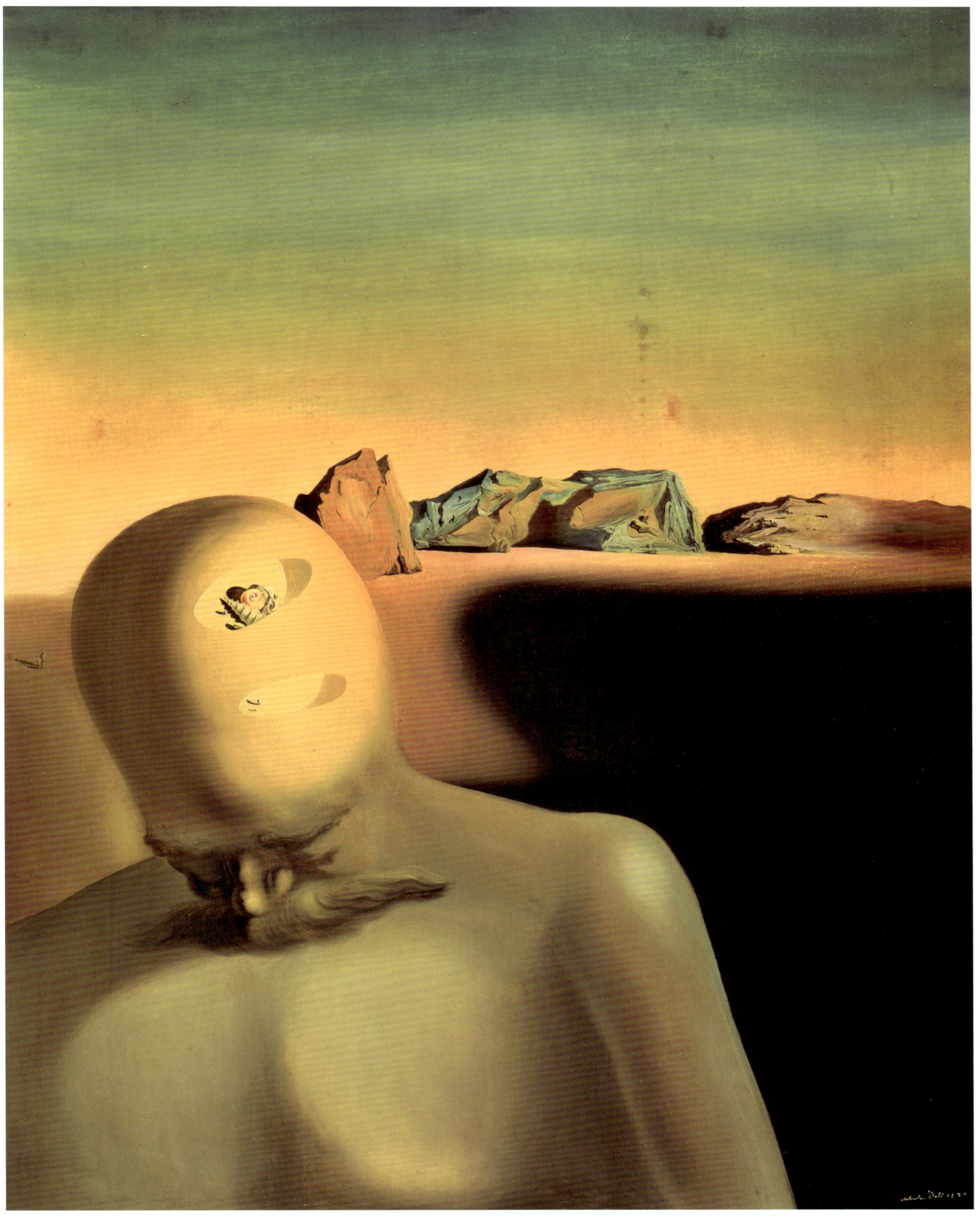

in the killing of the mother. But it is not this basic inversion of father/son to mother/daughter that Dalí invokes, but rather the more general notion of the child rebelling against the parent (potentially son against mother) and suffering for it. Dalí began, very shortly after this unresolved scenario, to explore his obsession with Millet's *Angelus*, the simple devotional painting of a couple pausing to pray at the sound of the Angelus bell (fig.132). His paranoiac-critical analysis of this obsession, which involves the slippage of the man in the couple from husband to son, concluded that it represented (for him) the maternal equivalent of the terrible paternal myth of the father devouring his own son. Since Dalí is always the protagonist, this is thus the mother annihilating the son.[7]

Although Dalí ignores the issue of class in the history of marriage as Engels analysed it in *The Origin of the Family: Private Property and the State* 1884, his note 'Prostitution of marriage … Evolution from maternal to paternal relationship' draws on Engels, who wrote that the 'marriage of convenience turns often into the crassest prostitution'.[8] Dalí also seems to reflect Engels's acceptance of the argument of the German social anthropologist Johann Jakob Bachofen that women had once held power under a maternal rather than paternal order:

We have seen how right Bachofen was in regarding the advance from group marriage to individual marriage as primarily due to the women. Only the step from pairing marriage to monogamy can be put down to the credit of the men, and historically the essence of this was to make the position of women worse and the infidelities of men easier.[9]

Freud's harnessing of Greek myth to his identification of enduring human instincts and complexes had provided a model for Dalí's attempt to tell the history of the family through the individual, in which he relies on theories of ontogenesis and phylogenesis. In the final passages of the film, this guide is lacking. Dalí evidently intended to represent the psychological, social and sexual implications of the 'myths' of Christianity and of Communism. In doing so, the 'problem of woman' presents itself to him in a different light. Rather than taking familial relationships (mother, sister, wife etc.) he introduces female types. Christianity itself is relatively straightforward: 'Paternal authority. Repression of pleasure, Christian idea of the nobility of suffering', but Dalí moves immediately from this to the contrasting ideas of the *camarada*

(female friend) and the 'exotic woman' – 'cases which could present themselves – Realisation of desires' and then to Communism.

Communism has 'conquered love and with it, the full liberty of the imagination'. Presumably he means that love has been released from its sordid links to property and money and perhaps this was intended to propitiate the PCF (Parti communiste français) which had recently been outraged by Dalí's erotic text 'Rêverie'.[10] The scenario ends with two ideas: the son as agent of change and the condition of 'woman' in the modern era. The 'son' will 'reproduce the conflict provoking the crisis of transition, the eruption of utopian ideas heralded by the concept of total liberty of the imagination, imagination which is directly proportional to the humanity and spirituality of love'. However, Dalí's attitude to the utopia of Communism is ambivalent and he ends with notes on the unresolved condition of woman: 'Social deviation, condition of the woman as object to be made use of, opposed to the communist idea of the companion, in which erotic relations are discarded.' Neither, it would appear, is satisfactory to him.

Dalí's animus against paternal authority and its incarnation in the family was doubtless inspired by his recent experience with his own family: in 1930, his father (figs.66, 69) disowned him and threw him out of the family home, leaving Dalí and Gala homeless and penniless. *Contre la famille* provides an interesting theoretical basis for paintings such as *The Birth of Liquid Desires* (Peggy Guggenheim Collection, Venice) or *William Tell* (Centre Pompidou, Paris), but, despite his practice in scenario writing at this moment (notably for *Babaouo*), it is hard to imagine *Contre la famille* evolving into a complete film.

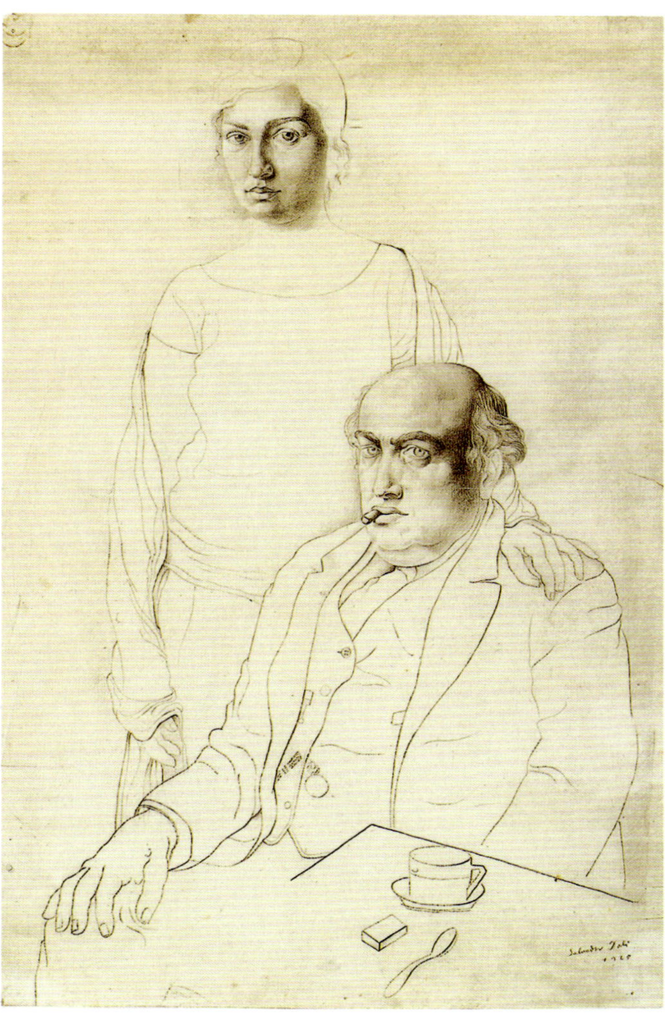

69
Don Salvador and Ana María Dalí
*(Portrait of the Artist's Father and
Sister)* 1925
Pencil on paper 50 x 33 cm
Juan Abelló Collection, Madrid

Notes

1
Rafael Santos Torroella, *Salvador Dalí:
Corresponsal de J.V. Foix 1932–1936*,
Barcelona 1986, p.84. Unaware of the
existence of this scenario, Santos
Toroella made the reasonable
suggestion that the reference was to
Dalí's William Tell theme, especially
the 'Guillame Tell: ballet portugais',
which concludes the *Babaouo*
scenario (for which, see William
Jeffett's text in this volume).
However, what Dalí had evidently
communicated to Foix was the plan
for a film 'against the family'.

2
The original manuscript, in French,
is held in the Fundació Gala-Salvador
Dalí, Figueres; a full publication
appears (in Spanish translation) as
'Contra la familia', in Salvador Dalí,
*Obra Completa, vol.III: Poesía, Prosa,
Teatro y Cine*, ed. Agustín Sánchez
Vidal, Barcelona 2004, pp.1079–82.

3
Salvador Dalí, *The Secret Life of
Salvador Dalí*, New York 1942
and London 1948, p.26.

4
Sigmund Freud, 'Three Essays on the
Theory of Sexuality', *On Sexuality*,
The Pelican Freud Library vol.7,
Harmondsworth 1977, p.155.

5
For a detailed discussion of this
theme in relation to *La Chèvre
sanitaire* see my essay 'Why Film?'
in this volume.

6
Paul Harvey, *The Oxford Companion
to Classical Literature*, Oxford 1951.

7
Le Mythe tragique de l'Angélus de Millet
was written c.1933 but not published
until 1963, as *Le Mythe tragique de
l'Angélus de Millet: Interpretation
'paranoïaque-critique'*, Paris 1963;
trans. as *The Tragic Myth of Millet's
Angelus*, St Petersburg (Flo.) 1986.

8
Frederick Engels, *The Origin of the
Family: Private Property and the State*,
London 1972, p.134. Dalí remained
quite indifferent to Engels's extensive
discussion of non-Western – specifically
Iroquois – notions of kinship.

9
Ibid., p.144.

10
'Rêverie', *Le Surréalisme au service de la
revolution*, no.4, Dec. 1931.
Dalí's text was regarded by the PCF
as pornographic and Breton was
criticised for publishing it. Relations
between Surrealism and the
Communist Party deteriorated during
the early 1930s, the former insisting
on retaining their independence and
the latter on the need to subsume
personal/artistic practices to the
interests of the Party.

Babaouo 1932

William Jeffett

When Dalí wrote the scenario *Babaouo* in 1932,[1] he had already realised, in collaboration with Luis Buñuel, the Surrealist films *Un Chien andalou* 1929 and *L'Age d'or* 1930. The screenplay for *Un Chien andalou* that they published in the final number of *La Révolution surréaliste* (December 1929) was written as if it described the finished production, and it took advantage of cinema terminology indicating location, framing and the sequence of shots and plans.[2] This confirms that, in conceiving *Babaouo*, Dalí was already practiced in visualising film narrative in terms of a series of images. This experience also followed the pattern of such surrealist poetic prose as André Breton's *Nadja* published in 1928, and Tristan Tzara's *L'Homme approximatif* 1931 which was published alongside the screenplay for *Un Chien andalou*.[3]

Babaouo tells a story with a start and finish, of a conventional sort commensurate with classical categories stretching back to Aristotle's *Poetics*. Its sequences, however, are punctuated with gratuitous and irrational events that do not advance the narrative, but serve as temporal delays and enigmatic intrusions into the unfolding of the otherwise coherent, linear structure. The underlying story is straightforward. In a hotel, Babaouo (whose name evokes a folk simplicity)[4] receives a message from his lover Mathilde Ibañez summoning him to the Château de Portugal where she needs his help.[5] He takes the

Metro (encountering a number of eccentric actions along the way) and then a taxi. Along the road, the taxi driver stops to climb a tree, placing Indian feathers on his head and shouting. Babaouo, having continued his journey alone, arrives at the château to find the beautiful Mathilde beside a shrouded white object, 'infinitely larger than a corpse' and 'too horrible' to expose. They undress, but as Mathilde's mother appears (together with a group of friends) they throw the white packet on top of her. They then escape by car, passing patrols of communist soldiers and hearing machine gun fire in the forest. When Mathilde grabs Babaouo (in a scene reminiscent of Breton's *Nadja*), he crashes the car, leaving her dead and himself blind. In the epilogue, Babaouo slowly recovers in a seaside village where he paints as a therapy, but eventually, as we shall see, he dies, in a manner foretold earlier in the film.

The film scholar Christian Metz has viewed such delays, or what he calls 'suspenses', as essential to the erotic economy of cinema:

The cinema's directly erotic subject … voluntarily plays on the limits of the frame and on the progressive unveilings, necessarily incomplete, that the camera allows when it moves … The framing and its displacements (which determine the placement) are by themselves 'suspenses' … The mode by which the cinema, with its strolling frames, finds the means of unveiling space has something to do with a sort of permanent undressing, of a generalised strip-tease[6]

Dalí's emphasis on syntactic narrative structure (diachronic), while injecting irrational semantic structural elements (synchronic), was typical of Surrealist devices in other poetry and poetic prose writing. This is found most notably in Tzara's Surrealist poetry made between 1929 and the mid-

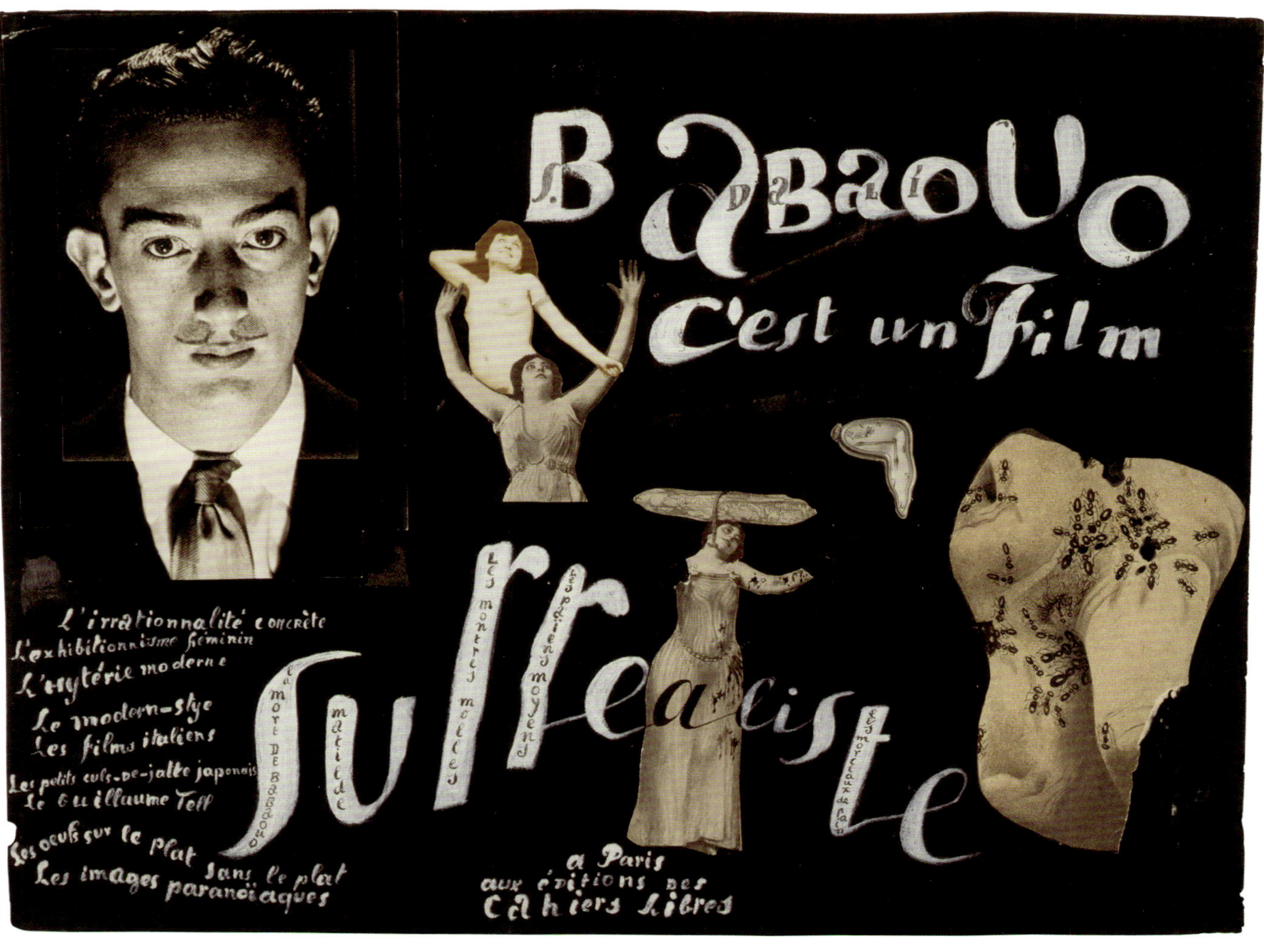

70
Design for a poster for
Babaouo, C'est un film surrealiste 1932
Mixed media on cardboard
27 x 37.1 cm
Fundació Gala-Salvador Dalí, Figueres

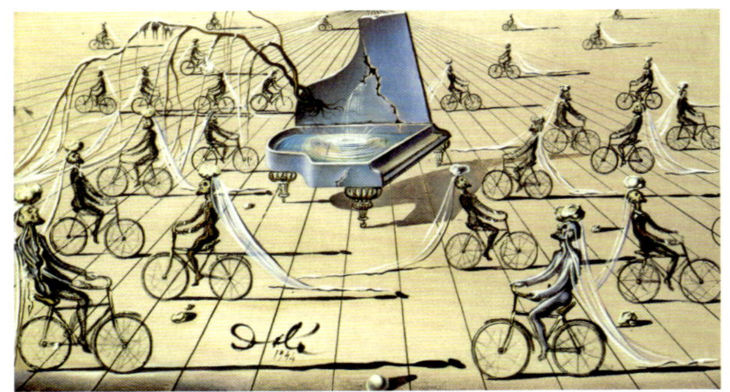

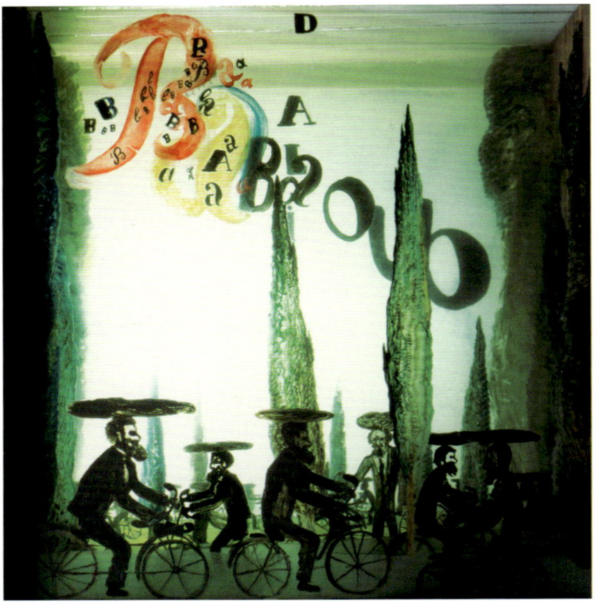

71
Sentimental Colloquy 1948
Oil on canvas 26 x 47 cm
Salvador Dalí Museum,
St Petersburg, Florida

72
Babaouo 1932
Wood and painted glass
25.8 x 26.4 x 30.5 cm
Fundació Gala-Salvador Dalí,
Figueres

1930s, with an early example being the poem
L'Homme approximatif 1931. The fragment of
this text that appeared in the final number
of *La Révolution surréaliste* was seen alongside a
reproduction of Dalí's *The Accommodations of Desire*
1929 (fig.35), while the screenplay for *Un Chien
andalou* was illustrated with *The Illumined
Pleasures* 1929 (fig.36). In both paintings filmic
narrative is suggested through doubled images
and through vignettes which occupy discrete areas
of the canvas. In *The Illumined Pleasures* one of
these vignettes, which are separated by what appear
to be picture frames, includes the images of cyclists
riding with stones on their heads, which also
appear as an early scene in *Babaouo*, where they are
blindfolded (fig.71).[7] This image is later repeated
in the scenario's coda, 'Guillaume Tell, Ballet
Portugais (extrait du film précédent)' (William
Tell: Portuguese Ballet (extract of the preceding
film)), where loafs of bread replace the stones.[8]
A sequence of a gentleman with a loaf of bread
balanced on his head had already occurred in *L'Age
d'or*, where he is seen walking in the country beside
a statue which also has a loaf on its head. No
explanation is offered for this recurrent device.

In Tzara's poetry, the phrases similarly
draw the reader inexorably from line to line,
like the unfolding of sequences of filmed images.
For example, he writes:

The return of Tzara to Surrealism in 1929–30 is
of interest for our understanding of the young
Dalí and specifically to the painter's approach to
writing. Their connection culminated in Dalí's
design of the frontispiece etching for Tzara's
Grains et Issues 1935. This work, written in a poetic-
philosophical prose, is of enormous importance
to Surrealist writing of the 1930s and is notable for
both its semantic derangement and its syntactic
coherence, qualities we find equally in Dalí's
approach to cinema. It is not without interest
that its first chapter, 'rêve expérimental', was
published in *Le Surréalisme au service de la Révolution*
where Dalí's paintings *Meditation on a Harp* 1933–4
(fig.133) and *Gala and the Angelus of Millet Preceding
the Imminent Arrival of the Conical Anamorphoses*

1933 (fig.132) were also reproduced. Tzara even appropriated, as a narrative device, the early moment from *L'Age d'or* where the couple wrestle in the mud citing the specific number of the scene and the address of Studio 28.

A young man, horribly deformed down the whole left side of his body … holds the young girl's hands in his for a long time. The evident sense of politeness is transformed into such a delirious joy that it cannot be hidden from the people around them. Now standing back to back, with their legs slightly out, they prop each other up. This will last for at least an hour, while the gaping crowd encircle, pass and disperse, but none will doubt to what sort of communion of experimental emotions the two lovers will thus be devoted, the more so that they will separate without, perhaps ever, having the chance to meet again.[10]

Apart from this literal reference to *L'Age d'or*, Tzara's derangement of semantics paralleled Dalí's own use of conventional pictorial devices in painting and his own approach to writing as an extended chain of images. For example, Tzara writes:

Sleep will turn empty and dry, for the dreams will no longer come to crush the stones of existence with their Archimedean screw, the desires being heaped up during the time of waking …
      Time will no longer be imprisoned in the system of all too-well-known hammers, alas! To our period that forms an alliance with the excremental odour of the idea of death and of regret. Time liberated from the bony embrace of religion being effaced from the circle of human representations, the metros will be at the disposition of the laboratory of suffering and cruelty.[11]

Tzara's narrative on balance remains poetic, its syntactic structure providing an architecture for poetic images, while Dalí leans towards an unfolding chain of events and sequences of images, despite their irrationality.

However, Dalí's *Babaouo* is written neither as poetry nor as pure screenplay. Rather, it is narrative prose into which have been injected periodic references to location, framing and plans. As with *Un Chien andalou*, most typically Dalí prefers a simplified cinematic language which includes three set-ups: *gros plan* (close up), *plan Américain* (three-quarter length) and *suivi en tram* (tracking shot). The montage cutting between different shots allowed Dalí both to use narrative and to disrupt it. Gratuitous and often violent events take place within this broad scheme which expand the temporal flow, such as the killing of the chickens in the background of one scene set in the hotel at the beginning. Other examples include the famous cyclists with stones on their heads, dancers on the stairs of the metro, and an orchestra performing on the metro platform. This passage is exemplary:

Babaou now … arrives at a large square full of bicycle-riders criss-crossing it slowly. They are blindfolded and they bear a large stone on the head … Babaouo crosses the square passing cautiously between the cyclists. He goes down a Métro entrance, not refraining from greeting with a familiar wave of the hand a middle-aged woman wearing a shirt, who makes a great deal of noise while sawing wood at the entrance. The camera follows Babaouo in a tracking shot as he walks for a very long time down the stairs. At times, a couple of tango dancers cross a landing in one exalted skid. Babaouo arrives at a platform on which are waiting a great many passengers, mingled with a huge orchestra that is installed there and is getting ready to play the overture to 'Tannhauser'.[12]

Such expansions (or suspensions) may be likened to the idea of condensation in the dream work as described by Sigmund Freud.[13] They are certainly meant to provide a comic backdrop for the unfolding of the narrative architecture, though clearly it is comic also in the sense of the black humour that Dalí had explored previously in his collaborations with Buñuel.

Stock images in Dalí's paintings also make an appearance, such as the soft watches and fried eggs on a plate without the plate. Painted versions of the soft watch (*The Persistence of Memory* 1931 (fig.74) and *Anthropomorphic Bread – Catalan Bread* 1932 (Salvador Dalí Museum, St Petersburg, Florida), preceded its appearance in *Babaouo*, while in the case of *Fried Eggs on a Plate without the Plate* 1932 (private collection), the painting was executed the same year as the text, suggesting an osmosis between word and image in terms of artistic production. In this way, textual strategies converged with pictorial ones.

In the poster that Dalí designed for the film (fig.70) these images are clearly indicated through texts to signify, if not the force of the unconscious, the presence of Surrealism somehow deployed as Dalí's signature. It is significant that *Babaouo*, unlike *Un Chien andalou* and *L'Age d'or* is subtitled: 'c'est un film surréaliste'; although this cry 'it's a surrealist film' is said to have been Breton's reaction to *Un Chien andalou*. Another textual reference to William Tell appears in the poster and refers to a nexus of painted images which first appeared in 1930 (see fig.10). The collage-image of ants appears earlier, both in *Un Chien andalou* (fig.51) and swarming on the pocket watch in *The Persistence of Memory*. Consequently, a painted pictorial space achieved around 1929–30 informed Dalí's construction of cinematic narrative, here the disjointed images providing a bizarre effect of delay, while the filmic sequence in turn was introduced back into painting and its pictorial structure. Despite the static nature of painting, narrative was evoked in the simultaneous presentation of scenes or the doubling of images, suggesting a collapsing of linear filmic time into a dream space, or dream landscape, informed by memory (fig.75).

Moreover, there is a circular structure to the narrative which approximates the stasis of painting and in which a sequence of events predicts the future. This includes the final sequence and death of the protagonist *Babaouo*. This sense of the structure folding in on itself recalls the prose writing of Jorge Luis Borges and may be linked the Ultraist literary context of Madrid in the mid-1920s, in which Dalí first matured.[14] His Madrid drawings of dark, sceno-graphic night life (figs.13, 30–2) evoke the derangement of endless drunken excursions through the Spanish capital's bars and night clubs and are a pictorial precedent for the mature use of similar narrative devices in the 1930s.

Babaouo concludes with an 'Epilogue' and is followed by a coda called 'Guillaume Tell, Ballet Portugais (extrait du film précédent)', where Dalí shifts from a filmic to a theatrical language. Here the origin of comic cinema in vaudeville is foregrounded. Again devices which appear in the paintings, such as the image of a giant spoon, reappear as a stage curtain. This sense of the origin of an anti-artistic cinema in popular theatrical forms is complemented by specific references to popular songs: the sardana *Per tu Ploro*, the rhumba *Le Vendeur de cacahuètes* and the tango *Renacimiento*.

A striking feature of *Babaouo* is the atmosphere of impending violence and the generalised sense of the setting. Though published in June 1932, it carries the qualification: 'The action takes place in 1934 in any European country during the Civil War'.[15] The choice of date was prophetic, for even as early 1932 there was a sense of crisis in both Spain and France with the arrival of the economic recession and growing unease of the European political situation.

The formation of the Second Republic (14 April 1931) in Spain was born of political crisis, the collapse of the Dictatorship of Primo de Rivera and exile of King Alfonso XIII, compounded by the world-wide economic crisis. A generalised climate of fear at the rise of a new mass culture which threatened established canons of intellectual and aesthetic value is seen in Ortega y Gasset's *España*

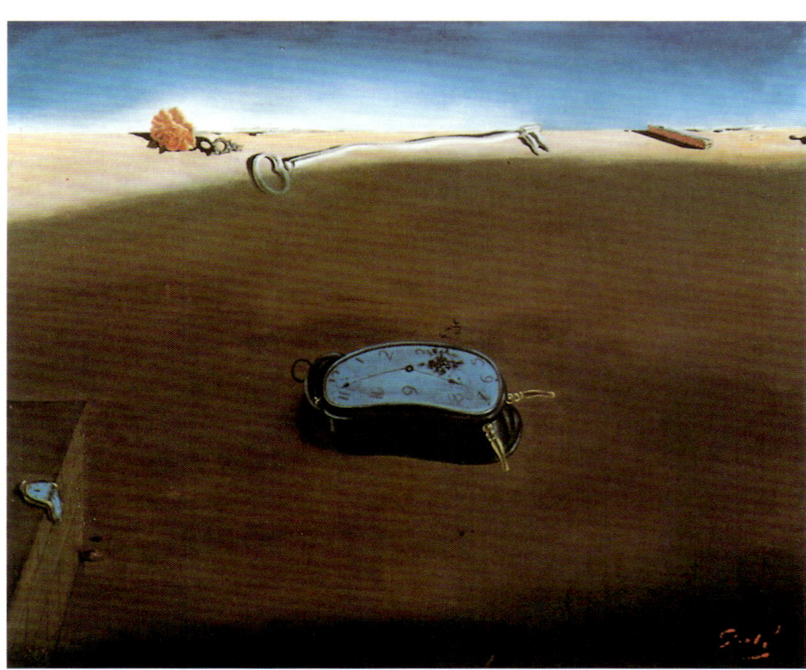

73
Soft Watches 1933
Oil on canvas 81 x 100 cm
Private collection

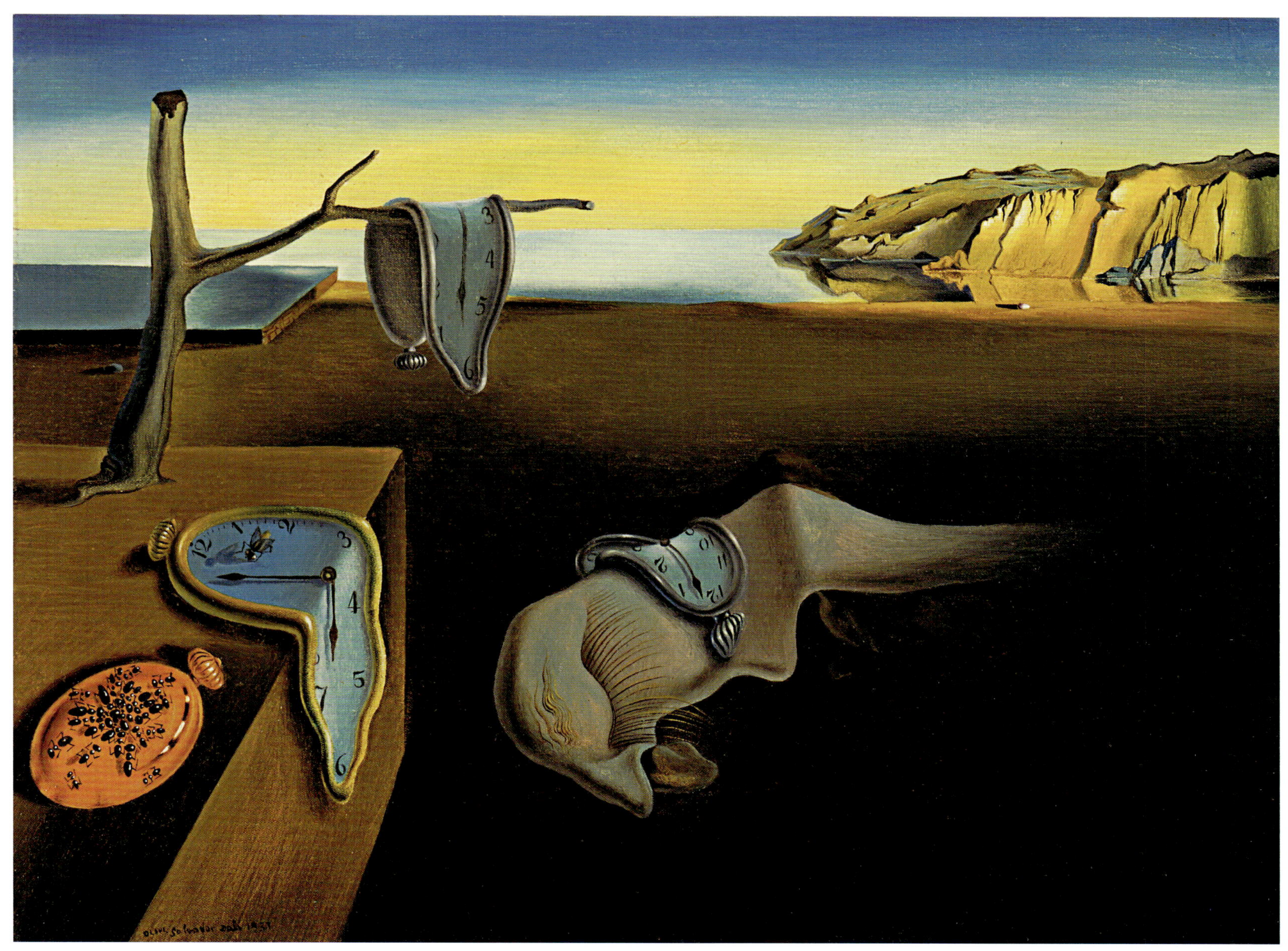

invertebrada 1921 and *La Rebelión de las masas* 1930, both written well in advance of the turmoil of the failed revolution of October 1934. For Ortega, even a decade earlier, Spain was soft and impotent, 'in the midst of an extreme case of historical invertebration'.[16] More worrying is his assessment of the 'violence and illegitimacy' of Fascism.[17] He observed: 'a realist would discover, under the affirmative mask that fascism wears, its predominantly negative character. Its apparent force consists actually in the weakness of others.'[18] In this context, it is interesting to consider the importance of soft images in Dalí's painting. Clearly, it was precisely mass culture which Dalí was prepared to embrace in *Babaouo*. By 1930, things were no better and Ortega wrote that 'the whole world - nations and individuals - is demoralised'.[19] His explanation is based on the conservative idea that the masses, or bourgeois culture, no longer know their place. Ortega again addresses the growing presence of Fascism and Communism. He identifies both as mass movements and is particularly concerned with the replacement of the rule of law by aggression. He argues that the thoughtless masses feel they know what is best and are prepared to impose it through direct action.[20] Ortega's judgement on Spain and Spaniards is harsh and pessimistic: 'it is impossible to change into healthy normality what is of its essence unhealthy and abnormal.'[21]

In France, too, the economic crisis began to bite and consequently introduced a period of instability. Dalí even was the target of social and political violence when, in December 1930, Studio 28 where *L'Age d'or* was showing was attacked by proto-fascist thugs, and the artworks on display in the foyer were either damaged or destroyed. In 1931, Germany suspended reparation payments to France. Prime Minister André Tardieu's unsuccessful calls for constitutional reform lead to elections in 1932, which brought a left-wing coalition government to power with the Radical majority and a Socialist minority. Meanwhile, the surprise assassination by a crazed white Russian of President Paul Doumer in May provoked a second election, with Albert Lebrun becoming President and the Radical Édouard Herriot becoming Prime Minister. Shortly following the elections, the Lausanne Conference considered the question of German reparations, an issue which would plague the rest of the year. In November 1932, Herriot signed a non-aggression pact with the Soviet Union, at the same time cutting military spending because of the economic crisis. Timing was bad given the rising influence of the Nazi Party in Germany. By December, Herriot was out of power over the issue of paying allied war debts to the US.

The atmosphere of crisis in France can be seen in the political or economic publications of the period 1929–32. It is explicit in the translation of Marxist Carl Steuerman's *La Crise mondial* 1932 or Raymond Patenôtre's *La crise et le drame monétaire* 1932.[22] From a firmly right-wing perspective, Robert Aron and Arnaud Dandieu's *Décadence de la nation française* 1931 suggested the despair of political instability, and Thierry Maulnier's *La Crise est dans l'homme* 1932 adopted a more profoundly pessimistic position.[23] In academic philosophy, Jean Wahl's *La Malheur de la conscience dans la conscience de Hegel* 1929, proposed that the self was in a continual state of self division, striving for an impossible unity, but suspended in a state of negativity.[24] This state of perpetual negativity was characterised by suffering and was tragic, as the implied unity of the dialectic was never resolved in absolute consciousness. In abstraction Wahl saw a 'dismemberment of life', and his study was devoted to Hegel's concept of the 'unhappy consciousness'. Finally, the publication of Céline's first novel *Voyage au bout de la nuit* 1932[25] offered the most relentless vision of mankind's despair and set the tone for the years to come. Georges Bataille's response was jubilant: 'the magnitude of *Voyage au bout de la nuit* consists in this, that it makes no appeal to the demented emotion of pity that Christian servility has linked to the consciousness of misery.'[26] Other reactions were more measured, 'There is nothing in the world but baseness, rottenness, and the march towards death, with some impoverished amusements: popular festivals, brothels, onanism. Céline, in this novel of despair, sees no escape other than death.'[27]

Dalí's pessimism was one which sought actively to exacerbate the crisis with the idea of enthusiastically promoting a catastrophe. The self was divided and doubled; the concept of reality was bankrupt and discredited. Paranoiac thought superseded reality. At the end of the 'Epilogue' of *Babaovo*, appropriately our hero is summarily exterminated: 'He then arrives alongside an automobile stopped beside the road. From the interior of this automobile, a machine gun shoots at him. *Babaouo* falls dead.'[28] A footnote reiterates the subtitle of the scenario: 'It's a surrealist film'.[29]

The prefatory 'Short Critical History of Cinema' may be understood, when taken together with 'Guillaume Tell, Ballet Portugais (extrait du film précédent)', as a conceptual frame for *Babaouo*. It situates the scenario between the comic traditions of popular vaudeville theatre and slapstick films. In this sense 'Abrégé d'une histoire …' is not so much a historical study as a theoretical explanation of Surrealist film of which *Babaouo* is an example.[30] According to Dalí, cinema by its very nature was abstract and rhythmic, and this went against the grain of Surrealism's tendency towards the concrete and the poetic. Therefore, for Dalí, 'The poetry of cinema requires more than any other a violent and traumatic unbalancing toward the concrete irrationality in order to reach the true lyrical fact'.[31] It was talking film, with all of its 'marvellous impurity',[32] that kept the medium from falling into the error of pure cinema, by recovering 'certain notions of the concrete that are capable … of creating confusions and complications based on the persistence in memory of words over images, to the grand detriment of the latter.'[33]

Furthermore, he declares: 'a single tendency, the concrete irrationality, the delirious and pessimistic aspiration toward gratuitousness, continues in an upward surge.'[34] As we have seen, gratuitousness was an essential feature of the narrative structure of *Babaouo*.

This quality, for Dalí, was achieved most clearly in comic cinema through the vehicle of laughter and best exemplified in films such as the Marx Brothers' *Animal Crackers* 1930. This takes cinema to the lyrical equivalents of Raymond Roussel. Dalí concludes by seeing the future of cinema in Surrealist films (consisting entirely of his and Buñuel's work) and comic cinema. Indeed, taking 'A Short Critical History of Cinema' as a conceptual guide, one can only surmise that *Babaouo*, despite the death of the protagonist, is both a Surrealist film and a hilarious comedy.

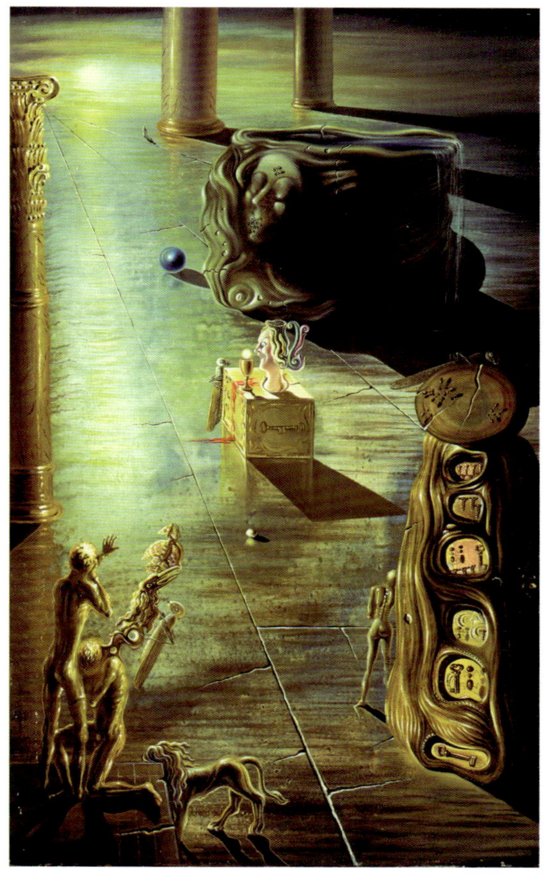

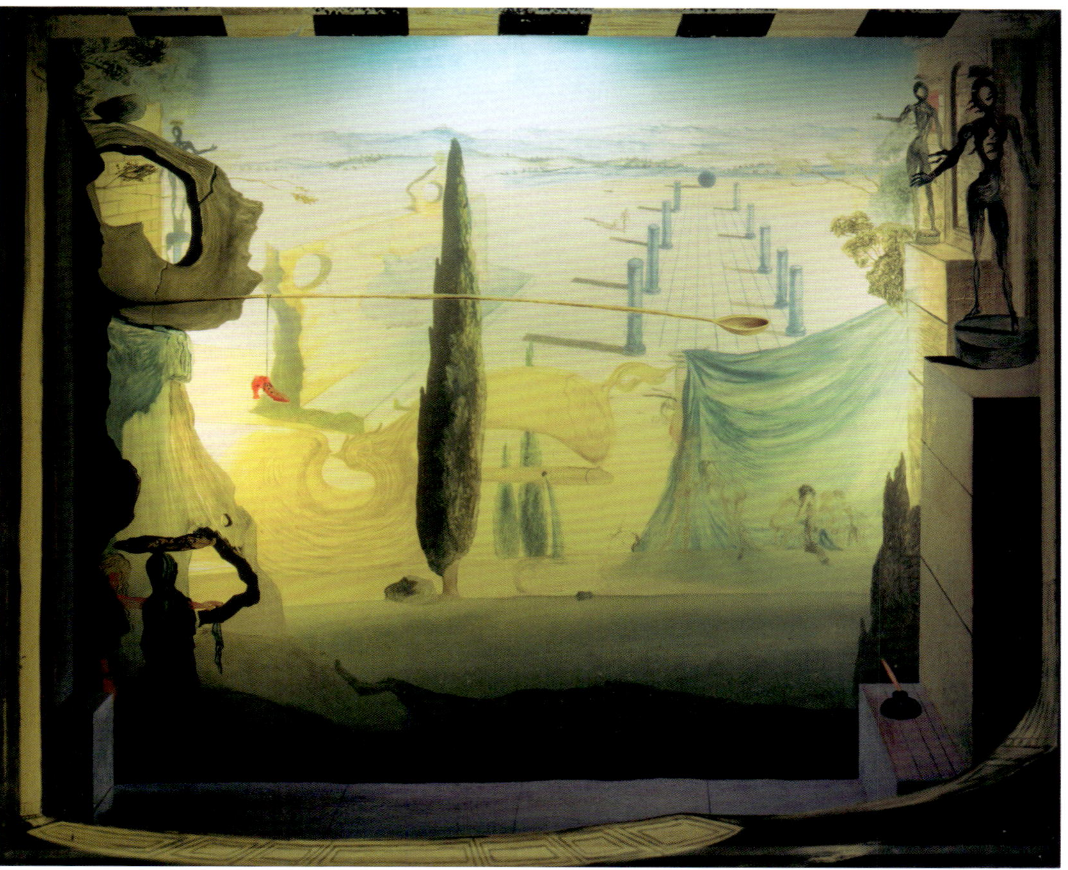

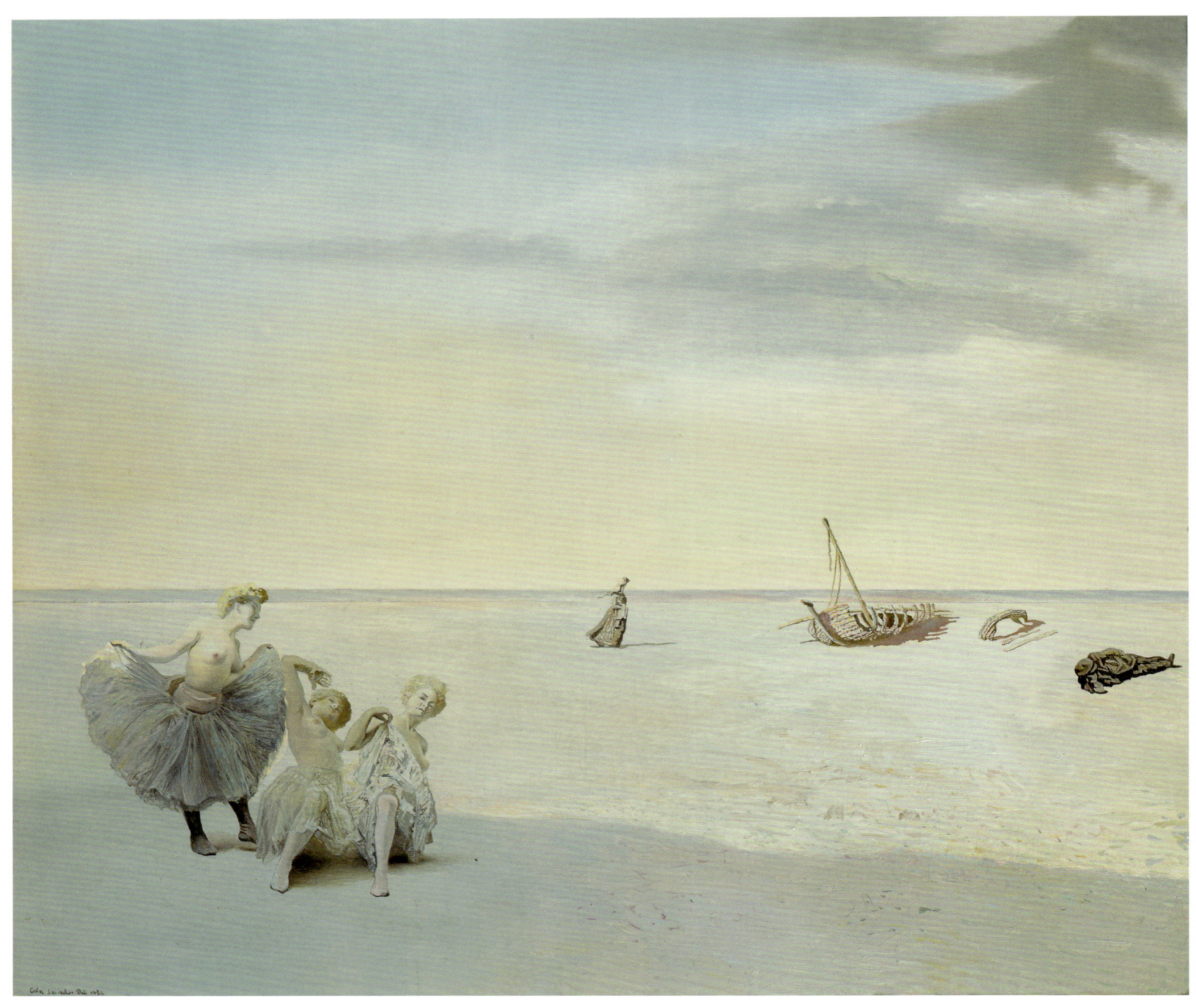

77
Forgotten Horizon 1936
Oil on wood 22.2 x 26.7 cm
Tate. Bequeathed by the Hon.
Mrs A.E. Pleydell-Bouverie
through the Friends of the
Tate Gallery 1968

1
Salvador Dalí, *Babaouo, Scenario inédit, précédé d'un abrégé d'un histoire critique du cinéma, et suivi de Guillaume Tell ballet portugais*, Paris 1932, bilingual French and Spanish ed., ed. Esteban Riambau Saurí, Barcelona 1978 .

2
Luis Buñuel and Salvador Dalí, 'Un Chien andalou', *La Révolution surréaliste*, no.12, 15 Dec. 1929, pp.34–7.

3
Tzara, 'L'Homme approximatif', Breton had published extracts from Nadja in *La Révolution surréaliste*, no.11, 15 March 1928, pp.9–11. ibid., pp.18–20.

4
Augustín Sánchez Vidal, *Salvador Dalí, Obra completa, III: Poesía, prosa, teatro y cine*, Barcelona 2004, p.1275.

5
According to Ian Gibson (*The Shameful Life of Salvador Dalí*, p.301) Matilde Ibáñez was the name of a girl Dalí knew in Barcelona; oddly the actor who played the father in *L'Age d'or* was also called Ibañez.

6
Christian Metz, *Le Signifiant imagincire: psychanalyse et cinéma*, Paris 1977, p.105; my trans.

7
Babaouo 1932, p.29.

8
Ibid., p. 56.

9
Tristan Tzara, 'L'Homme approximatif (fragment)', *La Révolution surréaliste*, no.12, 15 Dec. 1929, p.19, trans. in Tristan Tzara, *Approximate Man and Other Writings*, trans. Mary Ann Caws, Detroit 1973, p.128.

10
Tristan Tzara, 'Grains et issues: Rêve expérimental', *Le Surréalisme au service de la Révolution*, no.6, 15 May 1933, p.54; my trans.

11
Ibid., p.52.

12
Babaouo, trans. extracted in Haim Finkelstein (ed.), *The Collected Writings of Salvador Dalí*, Cambridge 1998, p.143.

13
Sigmund Freud, *The Interpretation of Dreams* 1900.

14
Juan Manuel Bonet, *El Ultraísmo y las artes plasticas*, Valencia 1996.

15
Babaouo, trans. extracted in Finkelstein 1998, p.141, though translated there as 'a civil war'.

16
José Ortega y Gasset, *España invertebrada*, Madrid 1921, trans. as *Invertebrate Spain*, New York 1937, p.63.

17
Ibid., p.195.

18
Ibid., p.199.

19
José Ortega y Gasset, *La Rebelión de las masas*, Madrid 1930, trans. as *The Revolt of the Masses*, London 1961, p.104.

20
Ibid., p 97.

21
Ibid., p. 107.

22
Carl Steuermann, *La Crise mondial, ou vers capitalisme d'État*, Paris 1932; Raymond Patenôtre, *La Crise et le drame monétaire*, Paris 1932.

23
Robert Aron and Arnaud Dandieu, *Décadence de la nation française*, Paris 1931; Thierry Maulnier, *La Crise est dans l'homme*, Paris 1932 and 1935.

24
Jean Wahl, *Le Malheur de la conscience dans la philosophie de Hegel*, Paris 1929. See also Bruce Baugh, *French Hegel: From Surrealism to Postmodernism*, New York 2003, pp.2–6, 19–24, esp. p.22.

25
Louis-Ferdinand Céline, *Voyage au bout de la nuit*, Paris 1932.

26
Georges Bataille, from *La Critique Social*, no.7, Jan. 1933, in *Oeuvres complètes*, Paris 1979, vol.2, p.53; my trans.

27
Anonymous, 'Sur *Voyage au bout de la nuit*', *L'Humanité*, 9 Dec. 1932; my trans.

28
Babaouo 1932, p.49; my trans.

29
Ibid.

30
'Abrégé d'une histoire critique du cinema', see full translation as 'A Short Critical History of Cinema', republished in this volume from Finkelstein 1998.

31
Ibid.

32
Ibid.

33
Ibid.

34
Ibid.

Les Mystères surréalistes de New York 1935

Matthew Gale

'New York is a totally Böcklinian city', Dalí reported to the poet J.V. Foix on 17 November 1934, 'full of monumental tombs, cypresses, dogs and fossilized humidities.'[1] He had been in the city three days, and this response tempered his initial excitement on arrival. An honourable mention at the Carnegie Prize and the acquisition, a year earlier, of *The Persistence of Memory* 1931 (fig.74) by the Museum of Modern Art ensured that he was already a celebrity there.[2] However, Dalí's reference to Arnold Böcklin evokes his famous painting *The Isle of the Dead* of 1880 and appears to be an indication of the sense of anxiety that he carried with him from Catalonia.[3] A shift to the right in the central

government had precipitated a general strike called on 4 October and the declaration of a Catalan Republic two days later, which brought a swift military response. With strikers and soldiers on the streets, Dalí abandoned his plan to give a lecture in Barcelona on 5 October and rushed to France with his paintings, which were destined for a show at the Julien Levy Gallery, New York, in November.[4]

Violence underpinned this experience and, almost certainly, Dalí's expectations of the United States. Although he and Gala travelled with their American patron Caresse Crosby, it is likely that Dalí anticipated New York primarily through its varied portrayal in the cinema.[5] This connection may be suggested by the fact that just before leaving Europe he had professed to have a film in mind (it would feature more Germanic references: Wagner, Sacher-Masoch and Ludwig II of Bavaria), and that, on arrival, he also mentioned a film plan to Foix; it did not come to (immediate) fruition.[6] In films, the depiction of the social extremes of New York ranged from the down-at-heel street-life of Chaplin's *The Immigrant* 1917 to the luxury of Keaton's stockbrokers in *The Saphead* 1920. This disparity was more evident after the Wall Street Crash of 1929 and the onset of the Depression. At the same time, the vogue for jazz had raised European awareness of the Harlem Renaissance, which reached Paris through Josephine Baker, the Blackbirds and films like *The King of Jazz* 1930 (which included George Gershwin's *Rhapsody in Blue*). Nancy Cunard, who had arranged for *L'Age d'or* to be seen in London, had just issued her vocal condemnation of racial discrimination, *Negro Anthology* 1934.[7] Dalí certainly anticipated that New York would be exciting, shaped by the criminal underworld portrayed in *The Mysteries of New York* movie series of 1914, starring Pearl White, that he had enjoyed as a boy and, perhaps, the more recent anti-heroes of such gangster movies as *Little Caesar* 1930 and *Scarface* 1932.[8]

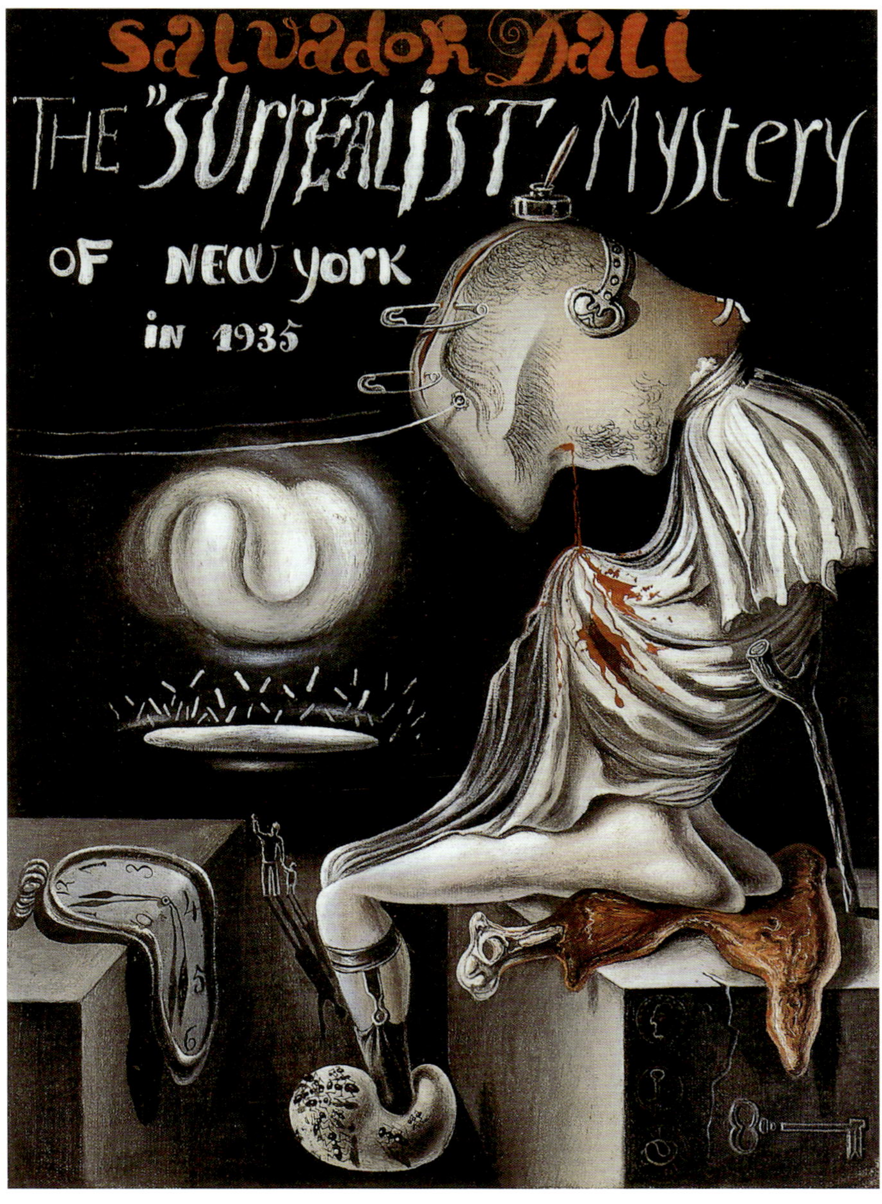

78
The Surrealist Mystery of New York 1935
Oil on canvas 40 x 30 cm
Private collection

Famously preparing for his first encounter with the American press on 14 November 1934 by getting the ship's cook to bake him a two-and-a-half-metre long baguette, Dalí fulfilled all expectations of Surrealistic eccentricity. His paintings, some of which he unwrapped for the awaiting journalists, proved a popular and critical success when the exhibition at the Julien Levy Gallery opened a week later.[9] Levy also published Dalí's anticipatory text *New York Salutes Me*, which affirmed his self-appointed role as the embodiment of Surrealism. From the point of view of the movement's internal politics, this was a particularly risky position, since on 5 February 1934, André Breton had called Dalí to account for the ambiguous treatment of Lenin in his recent paintings (e.g. fig.81) and, worse, for 'counter-revolutionary acts tending towards the glorification of Hitlerian Fascism'.[10] While the painter was exonerated from these charges, his relationship with the movement remained precarious. In establishing himself as Surrealist ambassador in America, however, he stood a chance of recuperation.

Certainly, Dalí's importance was widely accepted in New York, and the paintings in his show were admired as 'startling symbols of psychopathic phenomena'.[11] During his stay, Dalí gave lectures at the Casa de las Españas, and (through interpreters) at the Museum of Modern Art and the Wadsworth Atheneum in Hartford, Connecticut, where *Un Chien andalou* was shown. The whole visit was rounded off, on the eve of his departure on 19 January 1935, by a fashionable *Bal onirique* (Oneiric Ball) organised by Crosby and Joella Levy where New York went Dalinian.[12]

The ability to maintain a balance between the elite society to which he was drawn and his fascination for popular culture is seen in Dalí's engagement on the series of illustrated articles for the magazine *The American Weekly* and their close association with his film scenario *Les Mystères surréalistes de New York*. The evidently sensationalist publishing arrangement began on 16 December 1934 (a week after the show at Levy's closed), with the article 'Written by a Madman, Illustrated by a Super-Realist'. It was followed by six installments running into the following summer, well after Dalí's return to Europe.[13] As published in fragmentary form in the magazine, the illustrations appear to be a rather casual stroll through the artist's repertoire of familiar motifs, with a liberal distribution of

79
Study for the Scenario for 'Les Mystères surréalistes de New York' 1935
Pencil, charcoal and Indian ink on paper 55 x 41 cm
Fundació Suñol, Barcelona

Right:
80
Gangsterism and Goofy Visions of New York 1935
Graphite pencil and ink on paper 54.6 x 40 cm
Courtesy of Menil Collection, Houston

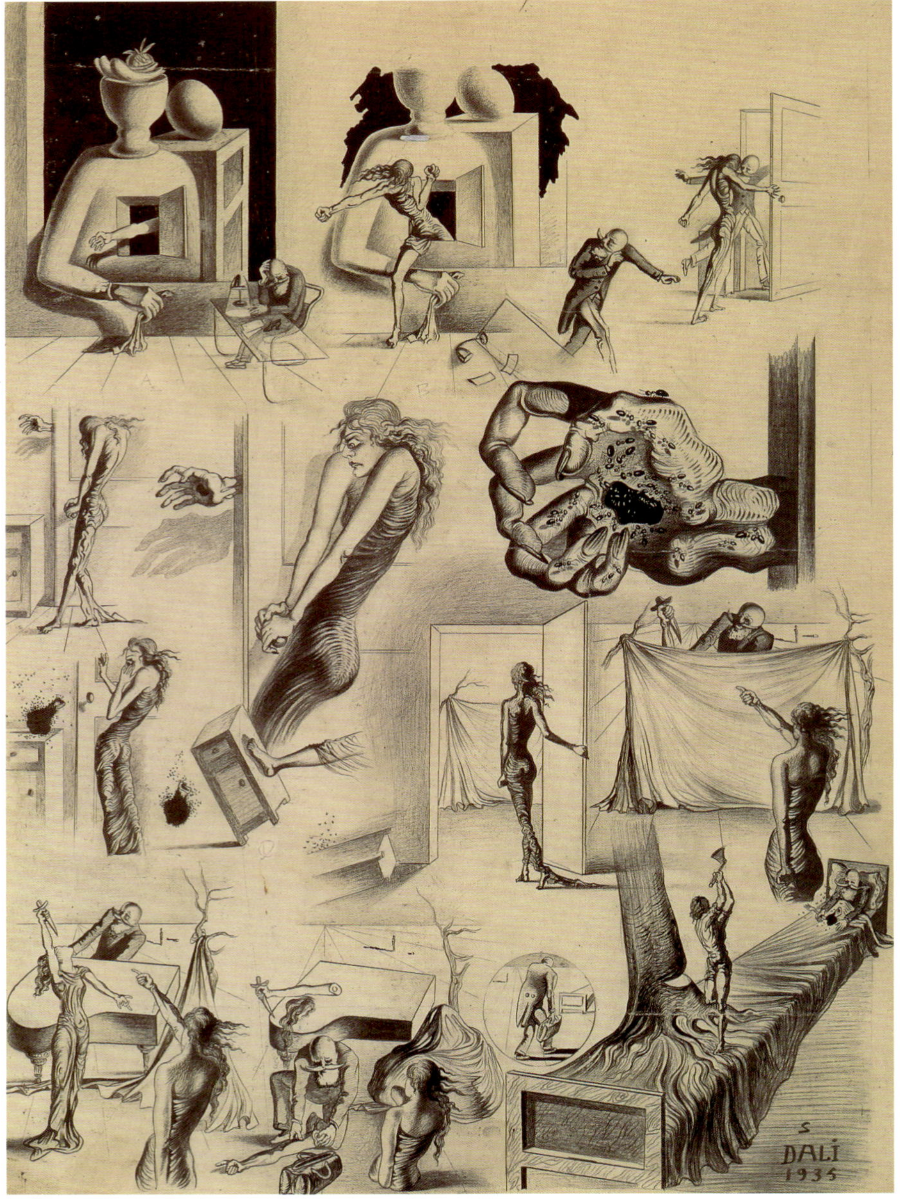

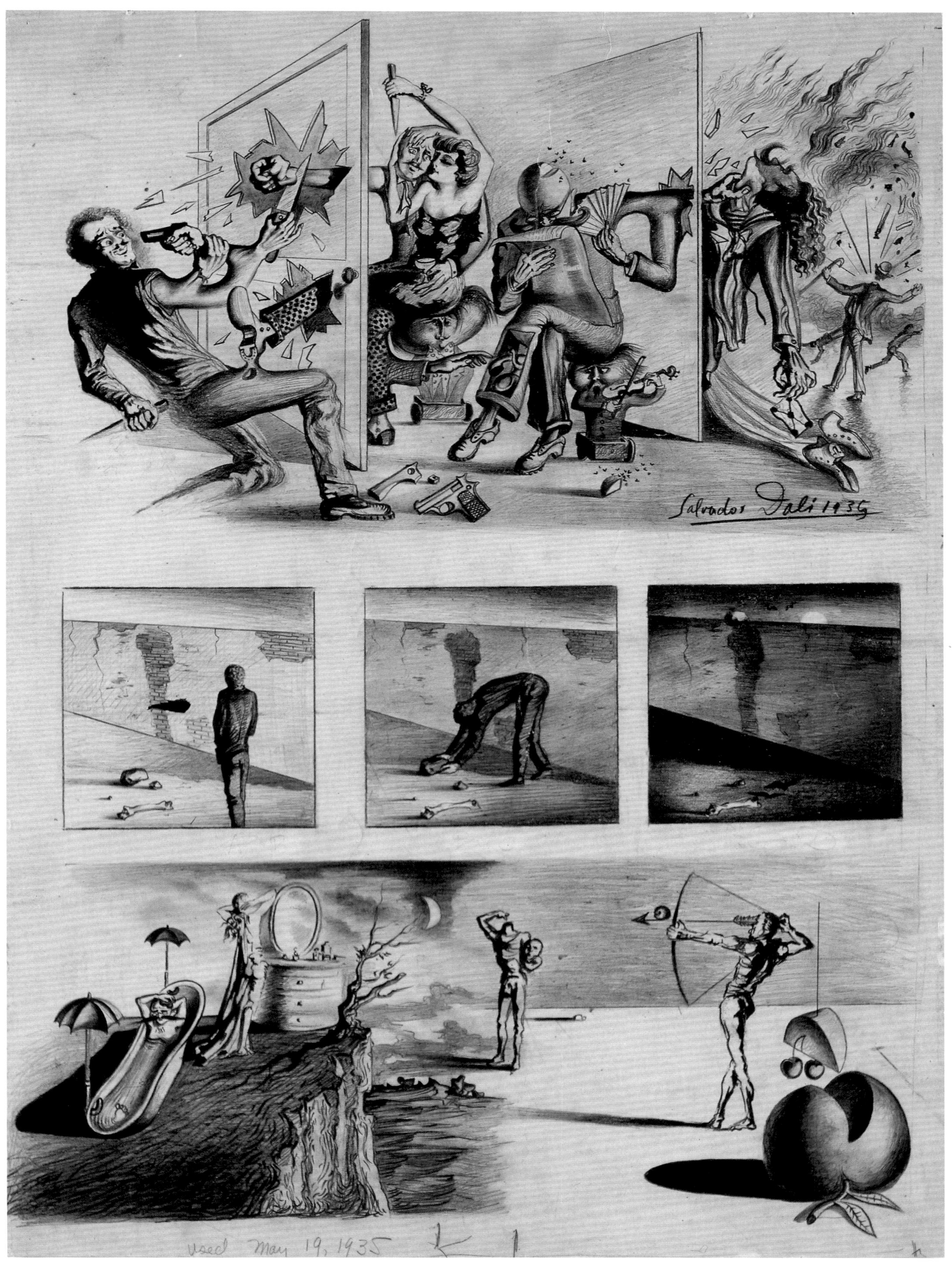

Salvador Dali 1935
used May 19, 1935

pianos, anamorphic skulls, soft watches and early incarnations of his lobster telephones (fig.82). Even as there was an overt commercial motivation in the report 'New York as seen by the Super-Realist' (24 February 1935), it is reminiscent of the series of 'Documentaries' that he wrote for *La Publicitat* on his first extended visit to Paris six years earlier.[14] Both played on the mode of the subjective reportage of an outsider.

A painting and a number of drawings with sequential images survive for the closely associated scenario of *Les Mystères surréalistes de New York*, written in French.[15] Despite the shared imagery there is no indication that was anything other than a speculative exercise. The painting, which is often described as being in preparation for a poster, bears the English inscription 'THE "SURREALIST["] MYSTERY OF NEW YORK IN 1935' (fig.78). Like the finished drawings, it combines familiar motifs – a figure with a gartered leg and a safety-pinned sleeper's head, beside a soft watch – though set against a striking dark ground that suggests a nocturnal setting for the narrative. Dalí adopted the violence, sexuality and criminality of popular gangster movies for his project, although – like so many of his scenarios – it remains fragmentary in nature. Scenes located across the city, and similarly packed with Dalínian objects, act as a preliminary section to the surviving scenario; these include Fifth Avenue, Radio City and the Museum of Natural History, but begin in Harlem, possibly as a deliberate evocation of Federico García Lorca's *Poeta en Nueva York* 1930.[16] Brief numbered and titled scenes then follow, including 'The Adorers of the New Fear', 'The Aging of New York' (in which a Surrealist monument to the end of prohibition is erected), and 'The Cannibalism of American Films', in which a 'severed arm pursues its cannibalistic desires'.[17] It is among these sections that the silent *Les Mystères de New York* series, originally made in 1914, is first cited and transmuted into a Surrealisation of the city.

Beyond these fragmentary passages, the fullest part of the scenario bears the heading '"Film script" of the prologue of the "Surrealist mysteries of New York"'. It too employs the violence of contemporary movies evoked in Dalí's drawing *Gangsterism and Goofy Visions of New York* (fig.80). The narrative is even more closely followed in *Study for the Scenario for 'Les Mystères surréalistes de New York'* (fig.79), which

illustrates the action in the office of the 'head of a secret organisation set up to sow Surrealist mystery in New York':

Outside his window, an anthropomorphic skyscraper is used for breeding hysterical mediums. One of these mediums escapes from the cataleptic glacier and enters the head's room and rushes towards him threateningly. He prudently flees, but in her fury, the medium shuts the door, ripping off his hand.
The medium is terrified to discover the horrible hole at the centre of the hand through which thousands of ants begin to emerge.
The hand writhes in agony and now becomes a horrible ball crawling with ants and a swarm of bees that have also come out of the hole.[18]

The re-use and melodramatisation of the scene from *Un Chien andalou*, which Dalí had just shown in America, parallels the self-quotation in the drawings, but there are also elements that are new to his repertoire. The anthropomorphic skyscraper, which also appears in the related *Study*, seems to be a response to New York, as is its horizontal mutation into the bed 'as long as a skyscraper' to which the medium of the story repairs to eat the rogue hand. This structure, like the mysterious woman, would reappear in Dalí's proposal for the Marx brothers, which brought his enthusiasm for America to a new pitch.[19]

The 'Explanation' that concludes the scenario again alludes to the Pearl White series and claims that: 'These scenes materialise the subconscious necrophilia that animates secret clubs and that translates into the truculent success of New York.'[20] All of this suggests that, just as Dalí identified the cannibalism of American films, so he conceived *Les Mystères surréalistes de New York* as a symmetrically self-referential exercise.

In the months following his return to Paris, Dalí attempted to reassert the paranoiac-critical method at the heart of Surrealism through *The Conquest of the Irrational*, a text in which the edible analogy already present in the scenario is elaborated. 'Salvador Dalí's famous soft watches', he wrote in the imperious third person, 'are nothing else than the tender, extravagant and solitary paranoiac-critical camembert of time and space.'[21] It was, perhaps, the conjunction of Dalínian and Einsteinian worlds that led Breton to quote this passage in his *Anthologie de l'humour noir* 1939, as something

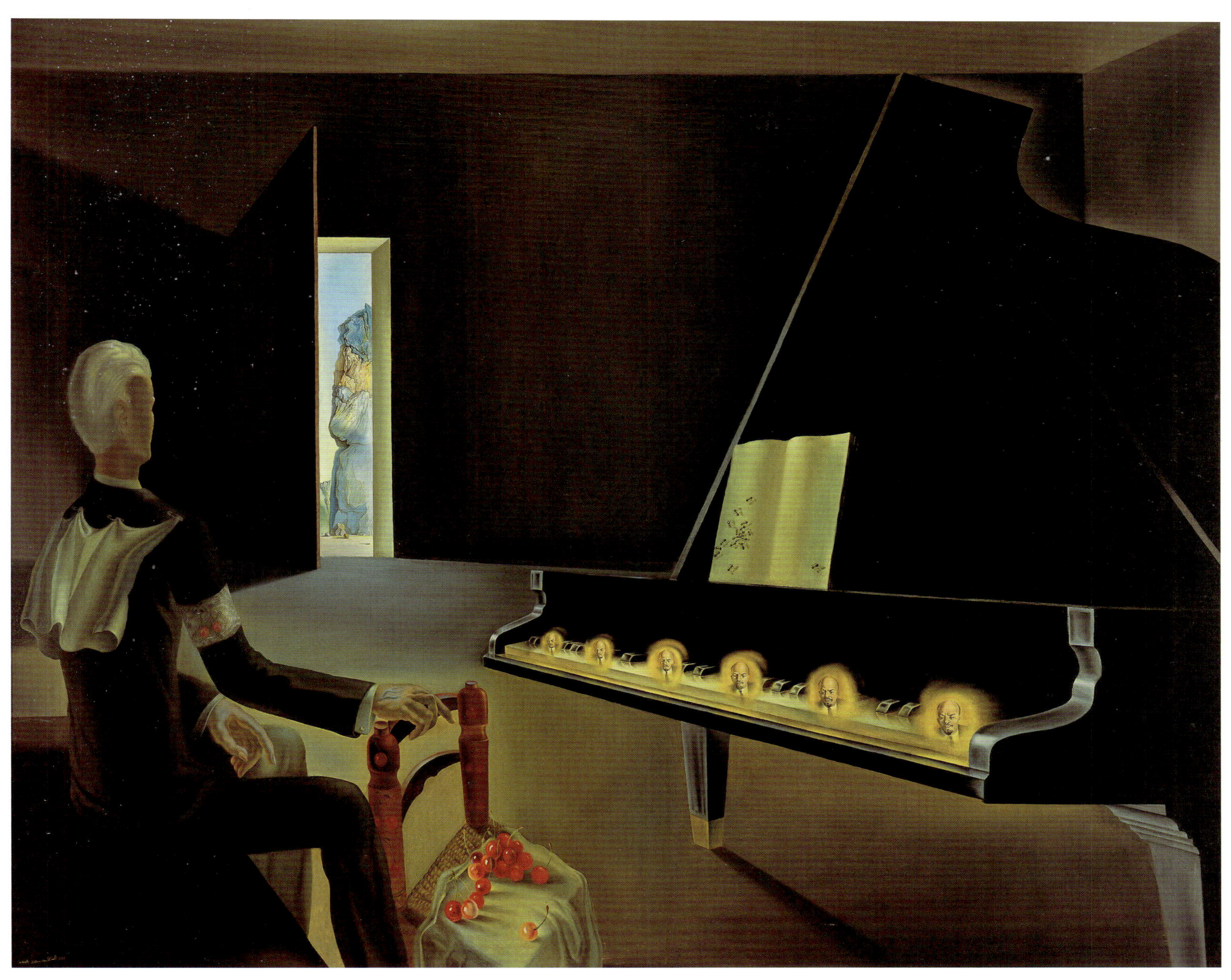

81
*Partial Hallucination. Six Apparitions
of Lenin on a Grand Piano* 1931
Oil on canvas 114 x 146 cm
Centre Pompidou, Paris.
Musée national d'art moderne /
Centre de création industrielle

of a farewell to the painter's commitment to the movement just as he was definitively expelled.[22]

For his part, Dalí's appetite for New York and America had been whetted by his visit, and he would return in 1936, and thereafter with increasing frequency. The clearest passages of *Les Mystères surréalistes de New York* barely mask, however, a sense of anxiety and violence that reflects back on the artist's precarious position within Surrealism, the urban tension of the city and the premonitions of civil war at home.

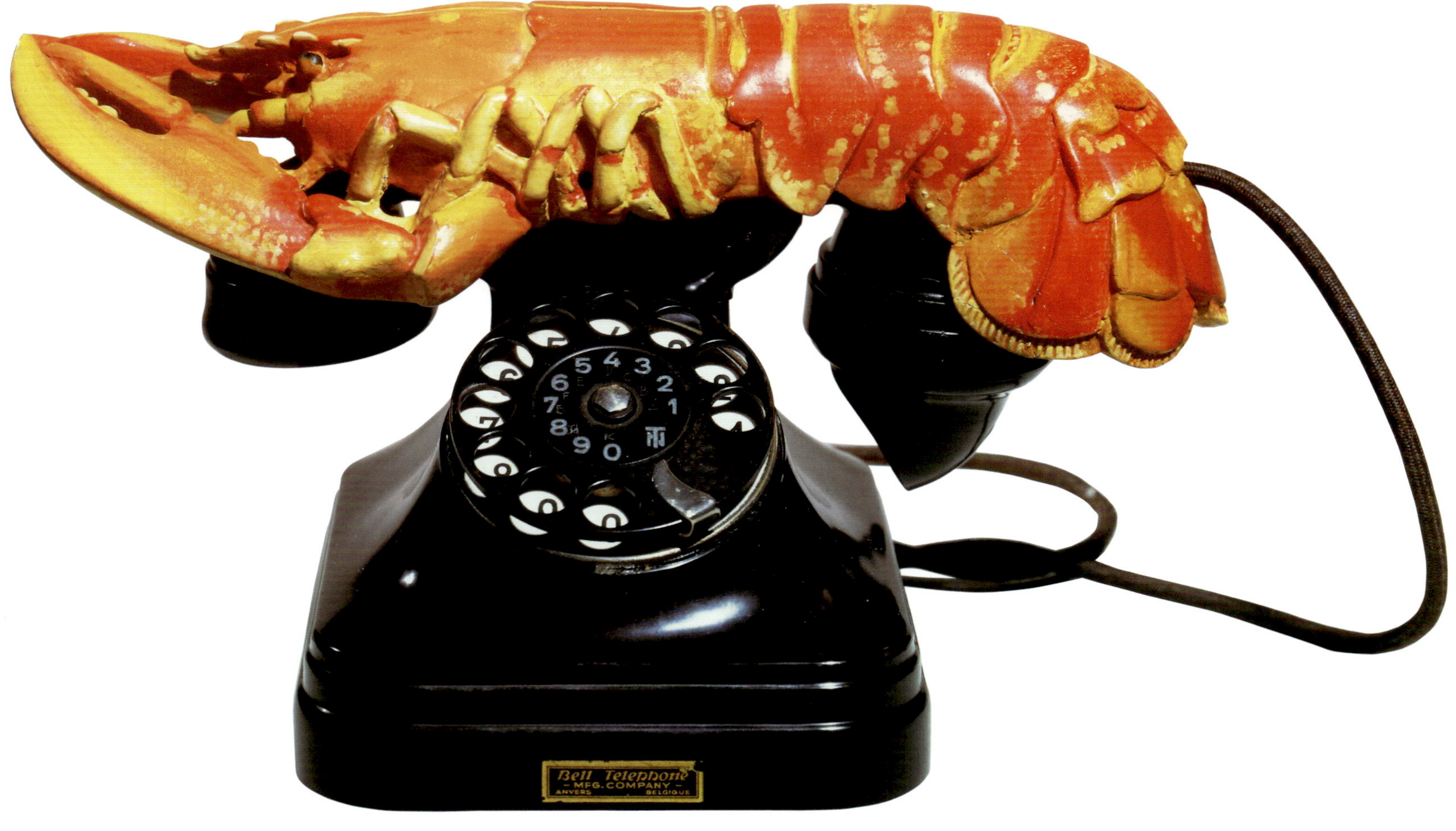

82
Lobster Telephone 1936
Plastic, painted plaster and mixed media
17.8 x 33 x 17.8 cm
Tate. Purchased 1981

Notes

1
Salvador Dalí, card to J.V. Foix, New York, 17–18 Nov. 1934, published in Rafael Santos Torroella, *Salvador Dalí corresponsal de J.V. Foix 1932–1936*, Barcelona 1986, p.137, trans. in Ian Gibson, *The Shameful Life of Salvador Dalí*, London 1997, p.338.

2
For a detailed study of Dalí's early fortunes in America see Eric M. Zafran, '"I am not a madman": Salvador Dalí in Hartford', in Dawn Ades (ed.), *Dalí's Optical Illusions*, exh. cat., Wadsworth Atheneum Museum of Art, Hartford (Conn.), Hirshhorn Museum and Sculpture Garden, Washington D.C. and Scottish National Gallery of Modern Art, Edinburgh 2000, pp.38–61.

3
In an adjacent note he asks Foix for news of events there; Santos Torroella 1986, p.137. Dalí conflated Böcklin, Millet's *Angelus* and skyscrapers in the illustration *New York?* 1938 made for *The Secret Life of Salvador Dalí*, trans. Haakon M. Chevalier, New York 1942 and London 1948, p.331. The original drawing is now in the Gala-Salvador Dalí Foundation; see *La Vida Secreta de Salvador Dalí*, exh. cat., Fundació Gala-Salvador Dalí, Figueres 2004, no.100.

4
Gibson 1997, pp.330–2. This and a later hurried departure are confused in *The Secret Life*, pp.320–4, 354–7. The original text of the lecture in Catalan is held in the Gala-Salvador Dalí Foundation, it has been translated as 'The Surrealist and Phenomenal Mystery of the Bedside Table' in Fèlix Fanés, *Salvador Dalí: the Construction of the Image, 1925–1930*, New Haven and London 2007, Appendix 6, pp.198–200.

5
Crosby may have acquainted Dalí with the writing of her husband Harry (who committed suicide in New York on 11 Dec. 1929), who wrote about New York and published in *transition* (e.g. 'Sleeping Together', republished in Noel Riley Fitch (ed.), *in transition: A Paris Anthology*, London 1990, p.241).

6
Just Cabot, 'Abans d'anar a Nova York: Una estona amb Dalí', *Mirador*, 18 Oct. 1934, republished in Santos Torroella 1986, pp.212–13 and trans. in Fanés 2007, p.199; Dalí mentions a film project in the 17–18 Nov. letter to Foix, ibid., p.137. For the extension of this idea as the ballet *Bacchanal* see Fèlix Fanés, 'Film as Metaphor' in this volume.

7
For Cunard's *Negro Anthology* see Petrine Archer-Straw, *Negrophilia: Avant-garde Paris and Black Culture in the 1920s*, London 2000, pp.159–70. See also my text 'L'Age d'or' in this volume.

8
The Mysteries of New York and related *Exploits of Elaine* are discussed by Fèlix Fanés, *It's All Dalí*, exh. cat., Museum Boijmans Van Beuningen, Rotterdam 2004, p.119, and Agustín Sánchez Vidal in Salvador Dalí, *Obra Completa, vol.III: Poesía, Prosa, Teatro y Cine*, ed. Agustín Sánchez Vidal, Barcelona 2004, pp.1282. For the 1930s gangster movies see Michael R. Taylor, 'Gangsterism and Goofy Visions of New York, 1935' in Dawn Ades (ed.), *Salvador Dalí: The Centenary Exhibition*, exh. cat., Palazzo Grassi, Venice and Philadelphia Museum of Art (London) 2004, pp.240–2, citing David E. Ruth, *Inventing the Public Enemy: The Gangster in American Culture, 1918–1934*, Chicago 1996.

9
On 21 Nov.; see *Secret Life*, pp.329–30; see also Gibson 1997, pp. 336–9.

10
See Karin von Maur, 'Breton et Dalí, à la lumière d'une correspondance inédit', in Agnés Angliviel de la Beaumelle and Isabel Monod-Fontaine, *André Breton: La Beauté convulsive*, Musée national d'art moderne, Centre Georges Pompidou, Paris 1991, pp.196–202.

11
Anon, 'Dalí to Lecture at Avery Tuesday', *Hartford Times*, 14 Dec. 1934, quoted by Zafran 2000, p. 47.

12
Ibid., pp.47–8, and *Secret Life*, pp.337–8.

13
See Taylor 2004, p.242, n.1. Three issues (24 Feb., 12 March and 31 March 1935) are reproduced in Fèlix Fanés, *Dalí: cultura de masas*, exh. cat., CaixaForum, Barcelona, Museo Nacional Centro de Arte Reina Sofía, Madrid, and Salvador Dalí Museum, St Petersburg (Flo.) 2004, p.199.

14
For the relation to 'Documental – Paris – 1929', see Sánchez Vidal 'Introduccion', in Dalí, *Obra Completa, vol.III*, p.128.

15
The original manuscript, in French, is held in the Fundació Gala-Salvador Dalí, Figueres; a full publication appears (in Spanish translation) as 'Los Misterios Surrealistas de Nueva York', in Dalí, *Obra Completa, vol.III*, pp.1157–66.

16
Ibid.; see also Sánchez Vidal's accompanying assessment, ibid., pp.127–9, and Federico García Lorca, 'El Rey de Harlem', *Poeta en Nueva York* 1930, trans. in J.L. Gili (ed.), *Lorca: Selected Poems*, Harmondsworth 1960, pp.69–75.

17
Dalí, *Obra Completa, vol.III*, pp.1161–2.

18
Ibid., p.1165, trans. Fèlix Fanés, *It's All Dalí*, exh. cat., Museum Boijmans Van Beuningen, Rotterdam 2004, p.132.

19
See Michael R. Taylor, 'Giraffes on Horseback Salad', in this volume.

20
Dalí, *Obra Completa, vol.III*, pp.1166.

21
Dalí, *La Conquête de l'irrationnel*, 1935, republished as *The Conquest of the Irrational* in *The Secret Life*, p.423.

22
Breton, *Anthologie de l'humour noir*, Paris 1939, 3rd ed., Paris 1966, p.379. Dali extrapolated on his current interest in Einstein's findings (as a modification of Cartesian and Euclidian space) in his abandoned lecture of Oct. 1934, in Fanes 2007, p.199.

Giraffes on Horseback Salad 1937

Michael R. Taylor

In his 1932 essay 'A Short Critical History of Cinema', Salvador Dalí placed the Marx Brothers' movie *Animal Crackers* 1930 'at the summit of the evolution of comic cinema' (fig.85).[1] The artist went on to describe the deep kinship he felt with the 'concrete irrationality' of Groucho, Harpo, Chico, and Zeppo, whose humorous antics and anarchic behaviour he likened to his own Surrealist art practice.[2]

In the same year, Dalí's admiration for the Marx Brothers' movies was shared by two former Surrealists, Antonin Artaud and Philippe Soupault. Artaud celebrated the liberating quality of films such as *Animal Crackers* and *Monkey Business* 1931, which he viewed as authentic additions to the anti-rational poetics of Surrealism in their complete 'destruction of all reality in the mind'.[3] In a January 1932 review, which Dalí probably read, Artaud argued that their comedy functioned on two levels. The first involved their 'poetic and revolutionary' jokes, stunts and pirouettes that were intoxicating but also dangerous, in that this slapstick humour 'always leads toward a kind of seething anarchy, a total breakdown of reality by poetry'.[4] In addition, Artaud claimed that these cinematic hymns to revolt were accompanied by an underlying sense of 'something disquieting and tragic, a fatality (neither fortunate nor unfortunate, but difficult to express), which would hover over it like the cast

83
Harpo Marx 1937
Pencil and ink on card 45.5 x 35.6 cm
Philadelphia Museum of Art

84
Dalí drawing Harpo Marx 1937
Fundació Gala-Salvador Dalí, Figueres

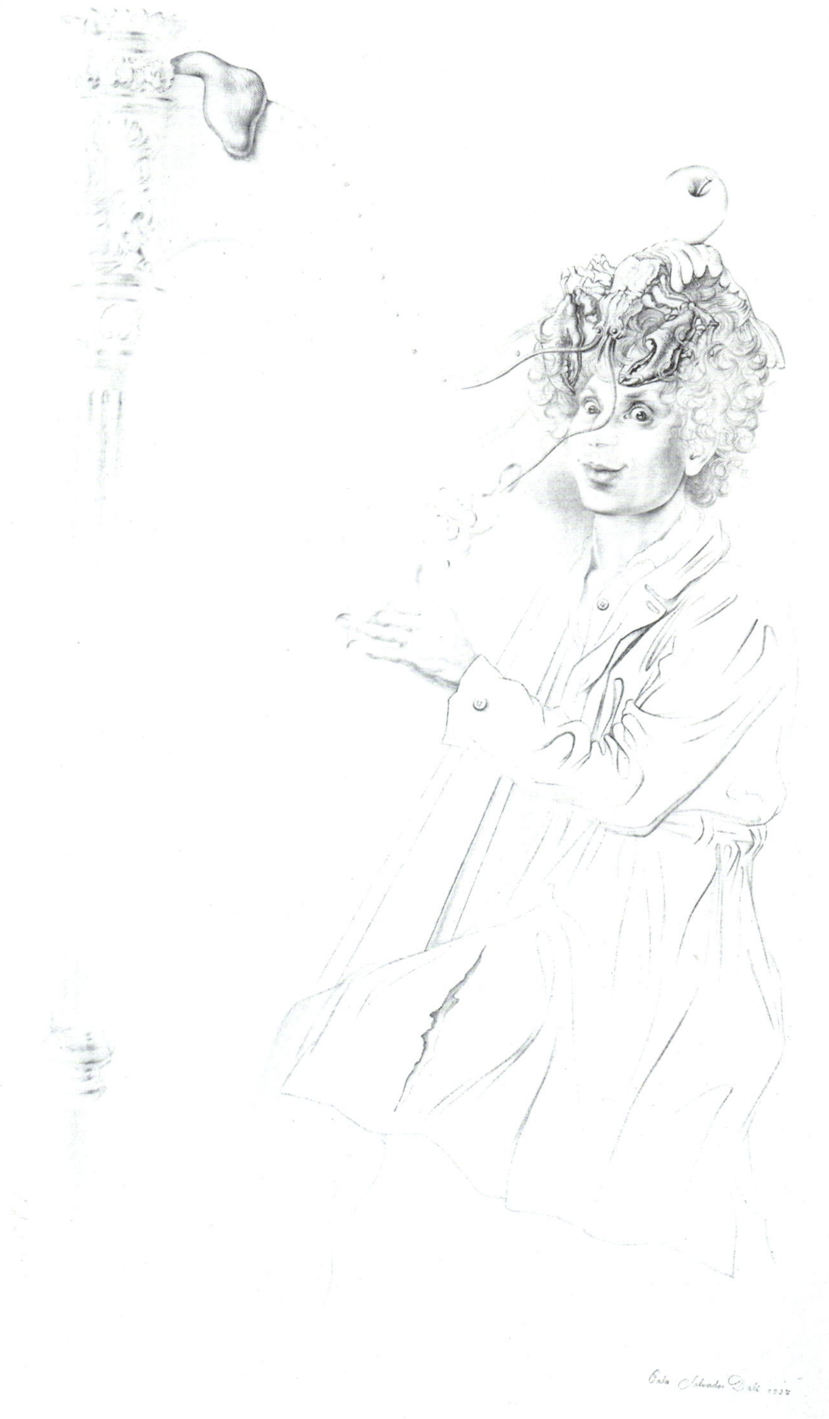

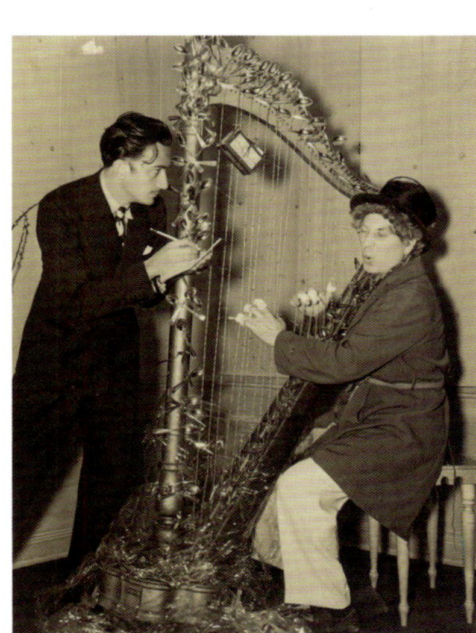

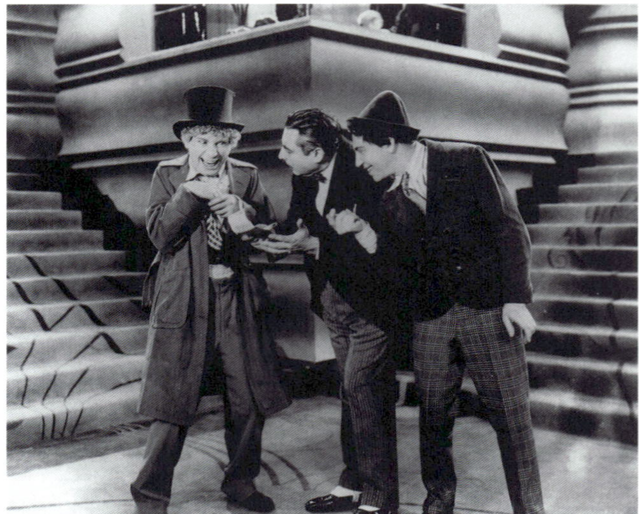
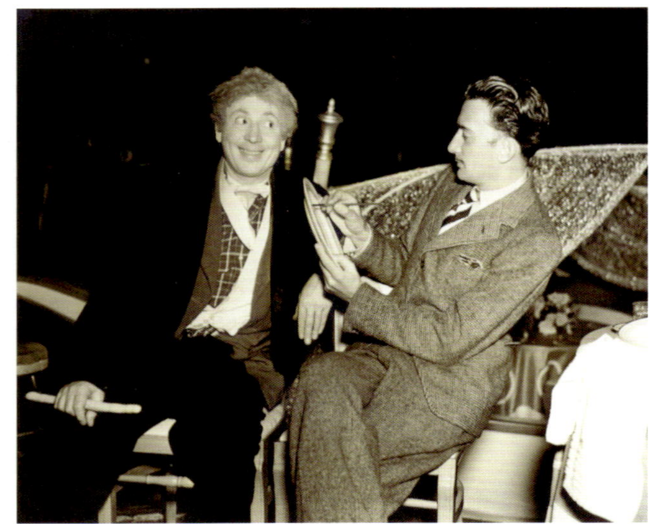

of a dreadful illness upon an exquisitely beautiful profile.'[5] Soupault similarly praised the satiric comedy of *Horse Feathers* in a review of October 1932. There he claimed that the film 'lifts us out of reality by exaggerating our peculiarities and aggravating our habits. The real quality of the Marx Brothers and of their extravagant, excessive comedy remains human. They are exactly like ordinary people and act just as we should act if social regulations did not prevent us from behaving in that way.'[6]

    Like Soupault and Artaud, Dalí believed that the Marx Brothers' actions symbolised an absolute freedom from society's conventions. This notion was carried to its extreme in the figure of Harpo, who was singled out for special praise in Dalí's essay: 'The one with the curly hair, whose face is that of persuasive and triumphant madness, as much at the end of the film as during the too short moment when he interminably plays the harp.'[7] Harpo's sight gags and pantomime actions, a hangover from Vaudeville and silent films, may have been easier for European audiences to follow, as the rapid-fire repartee of Groucho and Chico would have been blunted in translated subtitles. This may be why Dalí admired Harpo's split-second timing and unconventional sense of humour over that of the other Marx Brothers.

    Harpo's appearance and hyperactive persona perfectly matched Dalí's carefully cultivated self-image as the living embodiment of Surrealism, which may owe a significant debt to the American and his vaudeville props. The mute performer delighted audiences by producing a steaming hot cup of coffee from his trouser pocket or a candle lit at both ends from inside his trench coat. Indeed, the irrational quality of the Marx Brothers' humour was favourably compared to Surrealist filmmaking and painting by the American film critic Joseph Alsop Jr., in a 1935 review. He believed that *A Night at the Opera* surpassed *Un Chien andalou* in expressing the workings of dreams and the unconscious, especially in the delirium of the movie's closing chaos.[8] Alsop's association of this 'strange lunatic humor' with the Surrealist movement was shared by Groucho Marx, who explained in 1946 that the Marx Brothers' antics aimed at 'the overthrow of sanity, to give the brain a chance to develop'.[9]

    When Harpo Marx visited Europe in the summer of 1936 Dalí sought him out at a party in Paris. This meeting was by all accounts a great success, and the artist decided to cement their friendship with a handmade Christmas present. He designed an elaborate harp with barbed-wire strings and teaspoons and forks for tuning knobs, all covered with Saran Wrap cellophane.[10] Harpo was so delighted with this instrument that he responded with a photograph of himself with bandaged fingers, thus pretending that he had unwittingly plucked the barbed-wire strings. This was followed by a telegram on 31 December 1936, in which Harpo informed Dalí that he was a great admirer of *The Persistence of Memory* (fig.74) and that, if ever the artist visited California, he would be 'happy to be smeared by you'.[11]

    Dalí did not wait long to take Harpo up on his invitation, arriving in Hollywood in January 1937, where he announced to newspaper reporters that he intended to make a portrait of the sweet-natured comedian. As one art critic speculated: 'it is not stated whether Dalí will endeavour to balance two broiled chops on the silent redhead's shoulders or to merely infest his countenance with ants, but one thing is certain, the stunt will be worth many columns of publicity for both artist and subject.'[12] Their meeting took place in the garden of Harpo's Los Angeles home and confirmed Dalí's impression that the comedian was the most surrealistic character in Hollywood: 'He was naked, crowned with roses, and in the centre of a veritable forest of harps (he was surrounded by at least five hundred harps). He was caressing, like a new Leda, a dazzling white swan, and feeding it a statue of the Venus of Milo made of cheese, which he grated against the strings of the nearest harp.'[13] Although Dalí no doubt exaggerated the event, it is clear that Harpo enjoyed playing the buffoon around the artist and raised his manic energy to new levels of hysterical frenzy.[14]

Dalí completed two exquisite portrait drawings of Harpo in February 1937, along with a, now-lost, painting of the performer posed in the manner of Frans Hals's *The Laughing Cavalier*.[15] The surviving portraits were made from quick sketches in pencil and ink, carried out at Harpo's home and during the making of *A Day at the Races*. Photographs taken for the *Los Angeles Examiner* document these sessions, showing Dalí sketching a beaming Harpo as he plucks his harp, or recreating the earlier photograph in which the grimacing performer strums the barbed-wire strings of this instrument of torture (fig.84).[16] In the drawing completed for the June 1937 issue of *Harper's Bazaar* (fig.83), Harpo is shown with a beatific smile and wide, unblinking eyes, as he plays the harp with his long, graceful fingers.[17] Dalí painstakingly observed every fold of the comedian's trench coat, while his curly locks were lovingly delineated with the detailed illusionism that the artist had perfected. This conventional image of the celluloid clown was then embellished with the familiar Dalinian props, such as the piece of tongue-like meat draped over the top of the harp, which may relate to the comedian's onscreen muteness, or the lobster and apple that rest on Harpo's head, which refer to the artist's earlier interest in the themes of edible beauty, cannibalism, and the legend of William Tell. The second portrait drawing was reproduced in *Time* magazine in December 1938, where it bore the following description: 'In the centre foreground sits Harpo staring, sadly strumming on his harp.

His hair is golden fuzz, interwoven with fuchsia flowers and gay green leaves. He is not surprised by the company of three attentive giraffes – their backs on fire. In the distance are eight more giraffes, also burning, trying to get away from their own heat by running.'[18] The image of a giraffe on fire made its first appearance in the darkly ominous *The Burning Giraffe* of 1936–7 (Kunstmuseum Basel), and the slightly later *Inventions of the Monsters* (The Art Institute of Chicago), where it expressed his genuine fears that an impending global conflict would bring about the destruction of European civilisation.[19] However, when a journalist asked Dalí in 1939 about their presence in his portrait of the American comedian, he answered: 'Slapstick humour. How could that better be expressed than by these giraffes with their burning necks.'[20]

Dalí professed himself thunderstruck by the beauty of Harpo Marx during these sittings: Groucho would later joke that Dalí 'was in love with my brother – in a nice way'.[21] As neither spoke the other's language, Gala conversed in German with the comedian and then translated their conversations into French for her husband, and vice versa. Thus a close friendship grew and, with Gala as translator, the pair began working on ideas for a scenario for a Surrealist film starring the Marx Brothers, and possibly the artist himself. Dalí believed that it would rival and even surpass the 'biological, hysterical and cannibalistic frenzy of *Animal Crackers*.'[22]

Although their collaborative movie never reached production, the imagery and ideas that the artist explored with Harpo survive in two manuscripts, both written in Dalí's distinctive handwriting and featuring his inimitable drawings in the margins. The most substantial manuscript remains unpublished but has acquired the English title *Giraffes on Horseback Salad*. It consists of eighty-one handwritten pages, and is preserved in the Bibliothèque Kandinsky in Paris (fig.87a–c). The striking title would seem to look back to the Marx Brothers' 1932 movie *Horse Feathers*, as well as Harpo's recent role as a jockey in *A Day at the Races*, while also referencing Dalí's ongoing obsession with burning giraffes. Indeed, the scripts feature exploding giraffes, and even a memorable scene involving a stampede of burning giraffes wearing gas masks; one page is headed: 'The giraffe on horseback.'[23] Dalí began various revisions of the manuscript as a 'sketch for a scenario' or 'Scenario de Salvador Dalí – Marx brothers – musique de

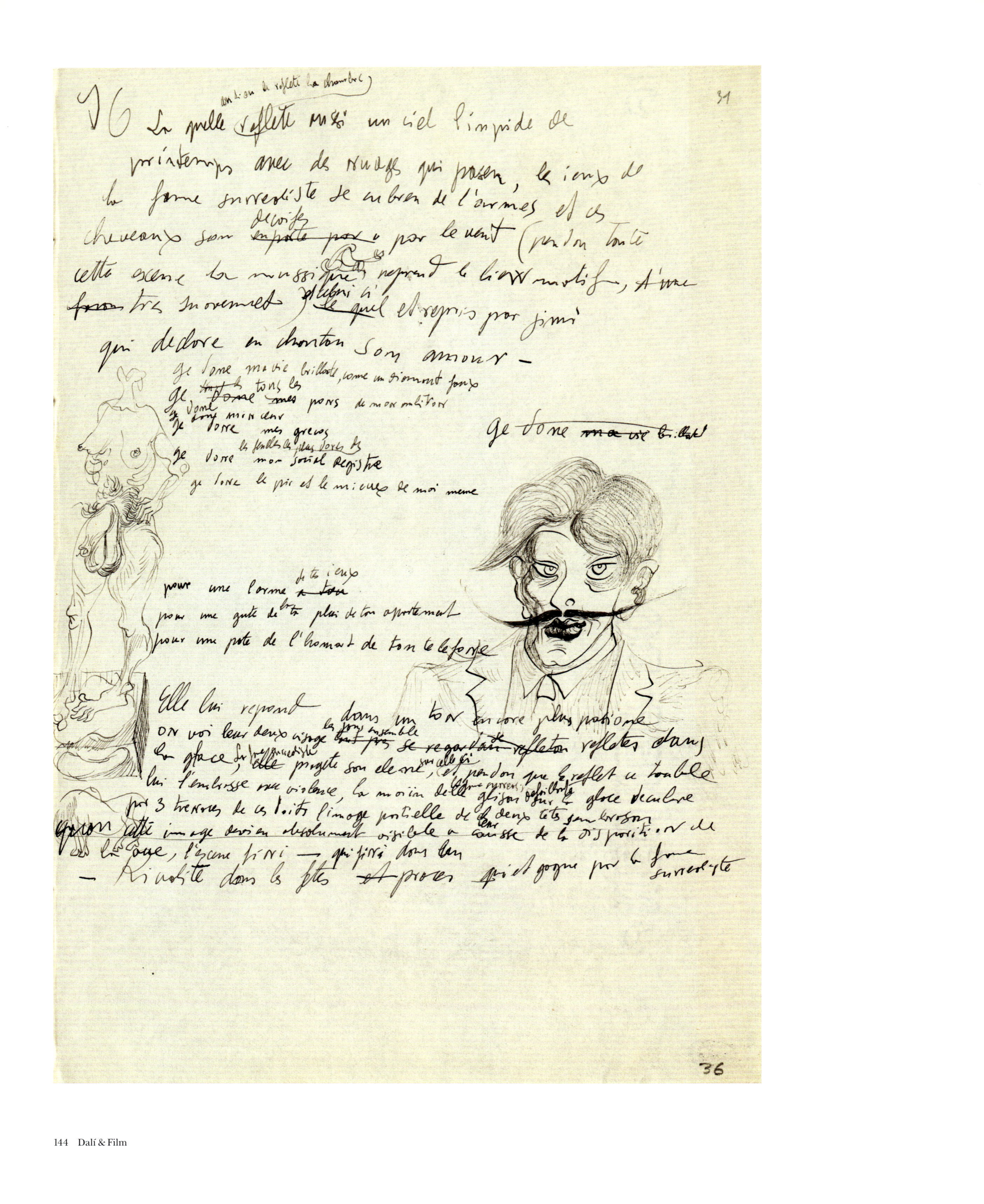

Cole Porter'.[24] To compound this mystery, a slightly shorter manuscript survives in the Fundació Gala-Salvador Dalí in Figueres, and it is entitled *La Femme surréaliste* (*The Surrealist Woman*). This sixty-five page manuscript was recently translated into Spanish.[25] Several prose fragments from the Figueres manuscript have also appeared in English, although a full translation of both manuscripts is badly needed.[26]

Both manuscripts were handwritten in French by the artist, with a few pages of English translation in another hand, as in the section headed 'Sketch for a Scenario' in the Paris text. Thankfully, large sections of the Paris and Figueres manuscripts are written on hotel stationery, thus allowing us to date accurately the development of the artist's ideas for the film. For example, the Château Frontenac stationery provides us with evidence that the artist began the film script before his meeting with Harpo in Los Angeles, since Dalí and Gala stayed at this Canadian Pacific Hotel in Quebec for a week at the end of December 1936, to escape from what the artist, in a letter to André Breton, termed 'the uninterrupted agitation of New York'.[27] Elsewhere, the letterhead of the Garden of Allah Hotel and Villas on Sunset Boulevard in Hollywood, California, informs us where the couple stayed during their extended visit to Los Angeles, after arriving in January 1937. Other hotel stationery, such as the Arizona Inn in Tucson and the Wrangler's Roost in Phoenix, Arizona (whose slogan was 'Out where the worst begins'), indicates the route taken by the couple in the spring of 1937 back to their final destination of the St Moritz on the Park Hotel in New York.

The impromptu drawings that accompany the text in the Paris and Figueres manuscripts reveal Dalí's mounting excitement in writing the film's scenario. It is imbued with an atmosphere comparable to those of the most dazzlingly decadent periods of history; the artist even envisioned a historical preface on Caligula to set the stage for the movie. Scattered throughout the texts are thumbnail sketches of androgynous nudes with large breasts and overripe vaginas and penises, as well as a deranged and haggard self-portrait (fig.87a). Clearly the debauched nature of the movie script was taking its toll on his imagination, as well as his libido, since the self-portrait is accompanied by a carefully rendered drawing of a standing nude, complete with pert female breasts and male genitalia of gargantuan proportions.

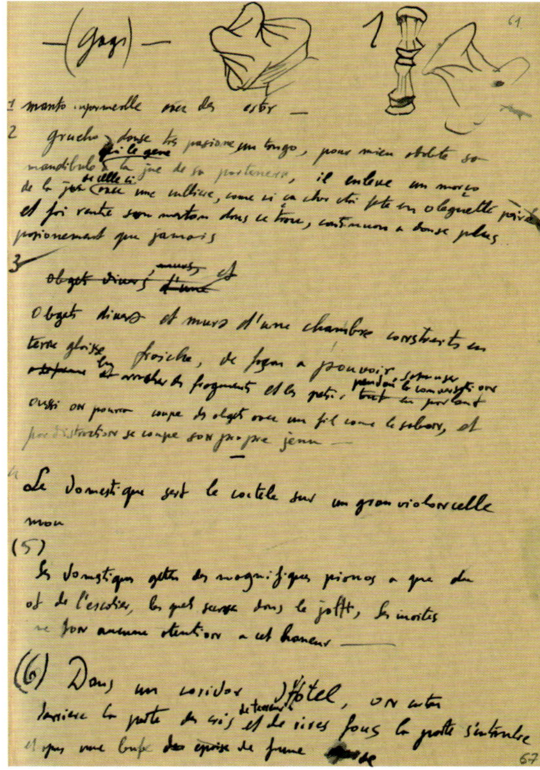

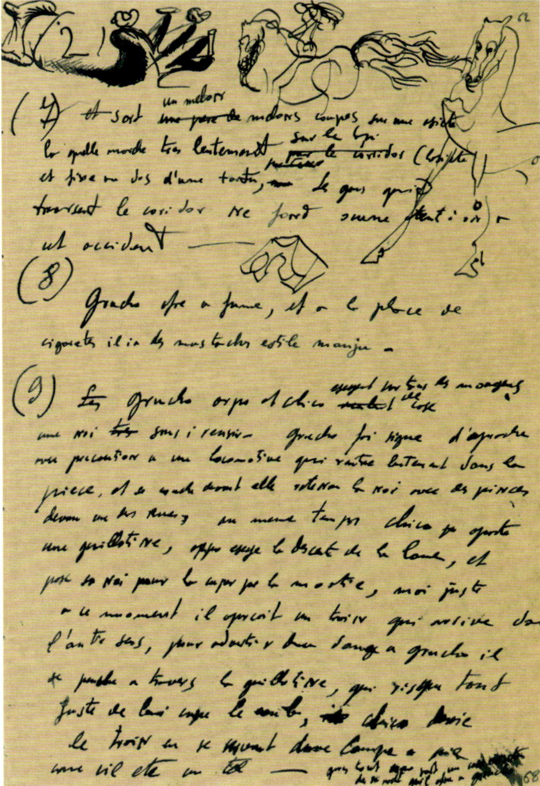

A cursory glance at the ideas in the illustrated manuscripts is sufficient to refute Ian Gibson's dismissal of the scenario as 'banal beyond belief'.[28] They reveal the artist's sophisticated understanding of the history of cinema, as well as his subversive aim to introduce his delusional fears and erotic fantasies to mainstream Hollywood audiences through the vehicle of a Marx Brothers' movie. The basic plot concerns a character called Jimmy, a thinly veiled self-portrait of the artist as a young Spanish aristocrat and businessman, who is forced to live in exile in the United States as a result of the catastrophic civil war then ravaging his homeland. Bored by his stuck-up, unimaginative fiancée Linda, who represents 'the world of convention', Jimmy falls in love with the mysterious and immensely wealthy Surrealist Woman, who personifies the 'world of fantasy, dreams and the imagination'.[29] Her friends are the Marx Brothers, Harpo (or 'Arpo' as Dalí repeatedly refers to him in the text and related drawings), Groucho, and occasionally Chico (whom he calls 'Beppo,' perhaps because he always spoke with an Italian accent in the movies), who are the film's real protagonists.[30]

Bewitched by the Surrealist Woman, Jimmy follows this spectral figure to her cabaret. It has red satin walls, sofas shaped like lips, and mirrors with holes out of which girls' arms snake out to entangle Groucho and Harpo, who deliriously writhe under their caresses. The decadent atmosphere of the cabaret is conveyed in Dalí's *Singularities* c.1935 (fig.89), that depicts the faceless Surrealist Woman presiding over her crimson domain, replete with Surrealist furnishings (fig.88) and an entrance made of long strands of white hair with a zipper down the middle. The love triangle between Jimmy, Linda, and the Surrealist Woman forms the basis of the scenario, which can be seen as a struggle between convention and the imagination that Dalí envisioned would be presented with 'all the imaginative pomp, splendour and epic character of historical films as typified by Cecil B. de Mille'.[31]

The scenario often draws upon Dalí's by-now-familiar wellspring of psychosexual themes and obsessions. These include his signature soft watches, lobster telephones, and troupes of cyclists with smooth stones or loaves of bread balanced on their heads. These cyclists first appeared in his 1929 painting *Illumined Pleasures* (fig.36) and later featured prominently in the script for *Babaouo* of 1932.[32] While the early pages of the 1937 manuscript are strongly indebted to

Babaouo, the later film-script also contains several instances in which Dalí's delirious ideas anticipate his subsequent works, such as the snail-infested *Rainy Taxi* that was placed at the entrance of the 1938 *Exposition Internationale du Surréalisme* at the Galerie Beaux-Arts in Paris:

Groucho comes out and sits at his desk. He takes out a magnifying glass and a palmist's book and scrutinizes each hand, one by one. In one of the hands he finds something which interests him but which he cannot see properly because of the light, so he tries to bring the lamp on his desk but this is a fixture. Impatiently, he pulls at [a girl's] arm but naturally cannot pull it far, so that in exasperation, he takes up a large pair of scissors from the table as if to cut off the hand. At this moment, Chico comes into the room, clothed in a rain-soaked mackintosh and calls to him, 'Come and see the latest accessory on my car.' Groucho lets go of the arm and the scissors. They go down to the street where Harpo is waiting in front of the car. Chico says to them, 'I have just installed indoor rain.'[33]

Other scenes include an interlude in which Harpo plays his harp ecstatically, like a modern Nero, while Chico accompanies him on the piano, dressed in a deep-sea diving suit. This looks back to Dalí's own near-death experience while giving a lecture in a similar diving outfit during the *International Surrealist Exhibition* at the New Burlington Galleries in London in 1936.[34] This sequence, for which Dalí made an exquisite sketch, takes place on a viewing platform shaped like the prow of an enormous gondola overlooking a sea of crisscrossing cyclists who are competing to see who can ride the slowest with a rock balanced on their head (fig.90). Also discernible on the deck of the judges' tower is the reclining figure of Groucho, lazily smoking a cigarette, while nearby Jimmy and the Surrealist Woman, lying side by side, watch the spectacle of the competition below, which takes place in front of the dramatic backdrop of a fierce brush fire.[35]

The manuscripts for *Giraffes on Horseback Salad* almost exclusively gave the spotlight to Harpo, who, in one scene is dressed as Nero, restrained by chains and put on trial for 'using money for mad and immoral ends.'[36] The artist's decision to give top billing to Harpo reversed the traditional hierarchy of the Marx Brothers' movies, which gave centre stage to Groucho. On rare occasions, Dalí reverted to the traditional format of the Marx Brothers' films. In one sequence Groucho invites the owners of a

88
*Study for 'Singularities'.
Surrealist Furniture* c.1934–5
Pencil on paper 25.3 x 37.3 cm
Fundació Gala-Salvador Dalí,
Figueres

89
Singularities c.1935
Oil and collage on board
40.5 x 50 cm
Fundació Gala-Salvador Dalí,
Figueres

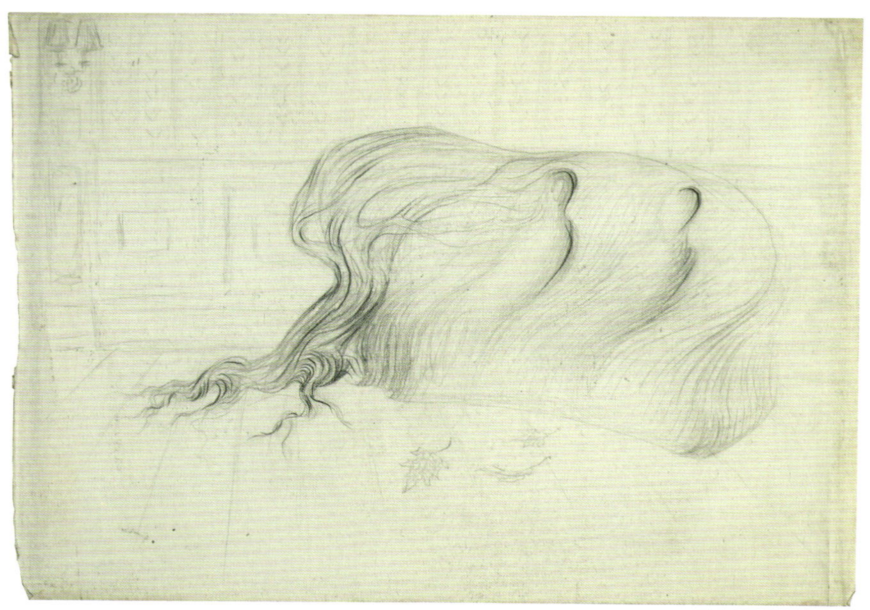

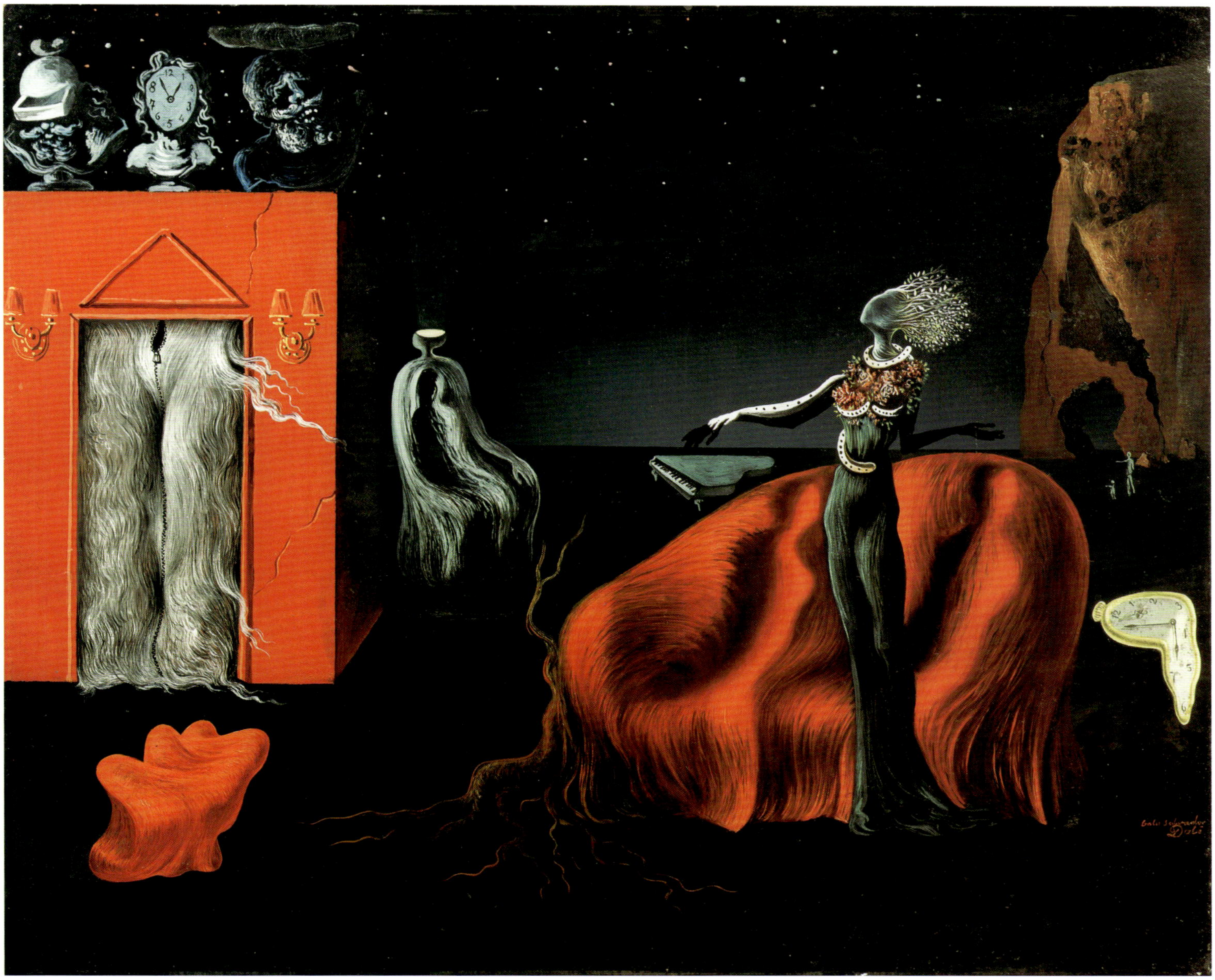

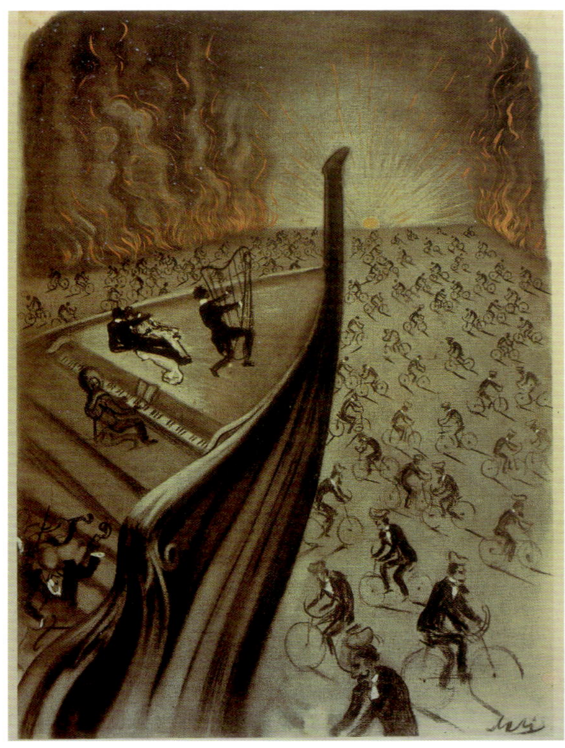

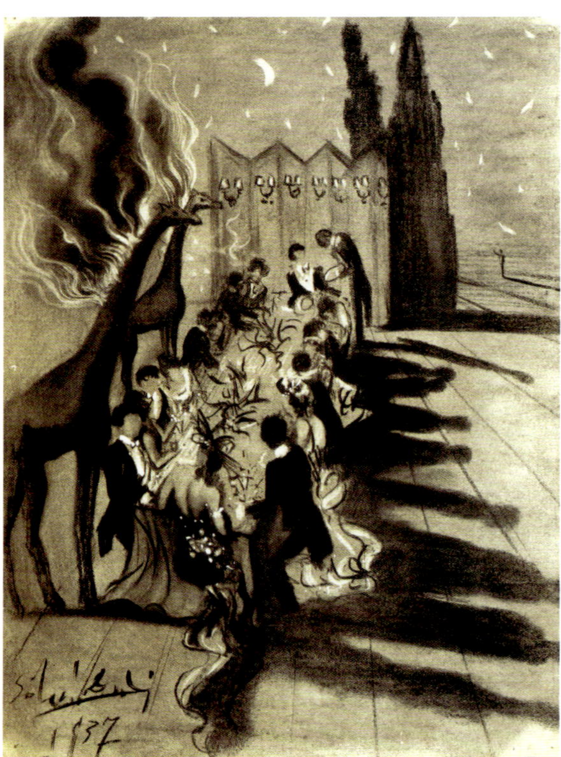

sumptuous villa on a picnic, during which he brings a gun and begins taking pot shots at the old man's house. After the first shot, he hands a large pair of field glasses to the panic-stricken fellow so that he can more easily watch the destruction, at which point his wife faints.

These scenes reveal that Dalí had fully grasped the underlying anarchy of the Marx Brothers' comedy, which exhibits a primordial potential for disrupting the ordering systems of conventional bourgeois society. He imagines Groucho giving:

a series of orders, each more absurd and incomprehensible than the other, to his three brothers who answer the telephone, and rush from one end of the town to the other carrying out his orders. For instance, Groucho tells Harpo: 'Bring me the eighteen smallest dwarfs in the city.' Harpo, armed with a large butterfly net, goes out, finds the dwarfs in a circus and on the street and catches them. These he piles into a car, and takes to the best hairdresser where their hair and whiskers are arranged in the most fantastic way possible, and beauty masks are applied.[37]

The Figueres manuscript provides invaluable insights into Dalí's ideas for the Surrealist Woman. The character was derived from the mysterious, flower-headed woman that he depicted in works such as *Necrophiliac Springtime* 1936 (private collection), and who took human form on 11 July 1936 when Sheila Legge walked through Trafalgar Square with her face completely covered with roses. Legge's performance as the *Surrealist Phantom*, which was clearly orchestrated by Dalí as a spectacular addition to the Surrealist exhibition in London, anticipates the faceless, extravagantly dressed Surrealist Woman whose identity was to be carefully concealed in *Giraffes on Horseback Salad*. The artist's stage directions call for the Surrealist Woman to be 'photographed from behind or in circumstances where the face is hidden, in order to increase the enigmatic atmosphere of her personality.'[38]

Together with these manuscripts, Dalí also produced more than a dozen drawings in a variety of media in the spring of 1937 (figs.92, 93). These images give us some idea of what the film's scenery and decor would have looked like, including a couch shaped like a pair of lips and an armchair overgrown by blooming flowers. Other drawings allow us to visualise some of the more bizarre sequences in *Giraffes on Horseback Salad*, such as *Dinner in the Desert Lighted by Giraffes on Fire* (fig.91), or *Surrealist Dinner on a Bed*, which depicts an elaborate banquet that takes place on a sixty-foot long bed, in which the dwarfs, caught by Harpo, hold lighted candelabra and change their positions every few minutes like living statues.[39]

Perhaps the most memorable drawing of all, *Groucho Marx as the Shiva of Big Business* (private collection, sketched in fig.93), depicts the comedian as the Hindu deity Shiva, calmly answering multiple telephones with his six arms. This suggests that the artist may have remembered a short entry on Shiva and his wife Kali by Georges Bataille in the critical dictionary of *Documents* in 1930. Bataille described Kali, the goddess of terror, destruction and night: 'She is represented adorned with a necklace of severed human heads, her belt consists of a fringe of human forearms. She dances on the corpse of her husband Shiva and her tongue, from which the blood of the giant she has just decapitated drips, hangs completely out of her mouth.'[40] This evocative account was accompanied by an image of Kali, triumphantly sticking out her tongue, and holding in her four hands a severed human head, a platter of dripped blood, and a scimitar. Dalí may have had this

image in mind when he portrayed Groucho as a rapacious, multi-limbed businessman, no doubt forgetting that the illustration accompanying Bataille's essay portrayed Kali rather than Shiva.[41]

Encouraged by Harpo's initial interest in the project, Dalí continued to work on the screenplay when he returned to Europe in March 1937. In an enthusiastic letter to Harpo, written at the Arlberg-Wintersporthotel in Zürs, Dalí confidently predicted that the film's 'sensational scenario made expressly for your genius, with extraordinary decorations and a very lyrical music, like Cole Porter's, would be something hallucinatory which in addition to amusing us could make a successful revolution in the cinema.'[42] Sadly, like so many of Dalí's film projects, *Giraffes on Horseback Salad* was never realised. Groucho claimed that he put the kibosh on it. 'Salvador Dalí wrote a surrealist movie for us', he later recalled. 'He approached me one day at the studio … "Groucho," he went on, "have I got a script for you." No, he didn't – it wouldn't play'.[43] When the artist himself was asked why the project never came to fruition, 'Dalí grew furious and began beating pigeons with his cane. "No one would *dare* to do

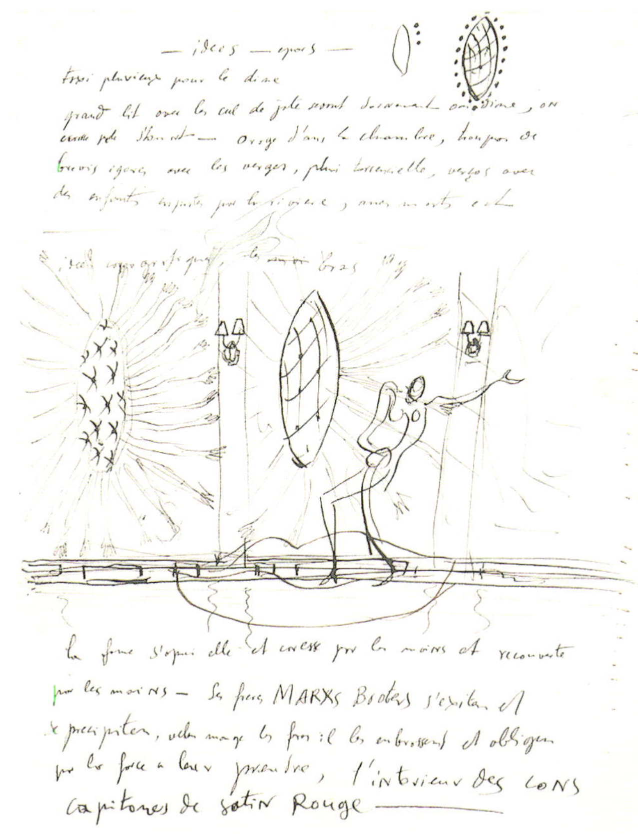

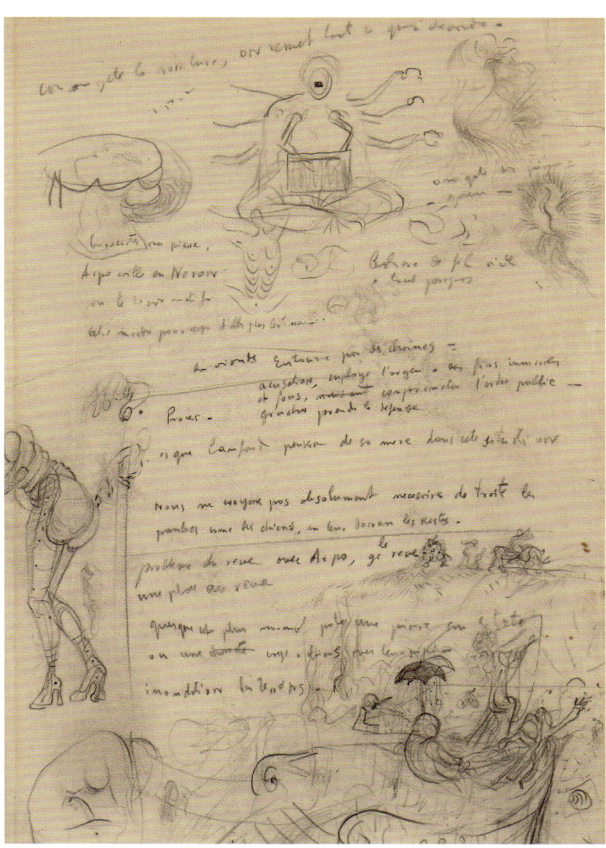

Dalí's script!" he expostulated, exasperated …
When asked if there wasn't someone who could
find affection for the script, his countenance
softened. "Harpo liked it," he said.'[44]

Never one to bear a grudge, Dalí continued
to praise the films of the Marx Brothers, especially
his beloved Harpo, whom he described in 1944 as
the funniest man in Hollywood.[45] It is clear from *The
Secret Life of Salvador Dalí* that he had not entirely
given up hope of producing *Giraffes on Horseback
Salad*. Its explosive potential can be gauged by the
following passage that can also, in retrospect, be
read as a mournful elegy to the project:

*And on Fifth Avenue Harpo Marx has just lighted the
fuse that projects from the behinds of a flock of expensive
giraffes stuffed with dynamite. They run in all directions,
sowing panic and obliging everyone to seek refuge pell-mell
within the shops. All the fire-alarms of the city have just
been turned on, but it is already too late. Boom! Boom!
Boom! Boom! I salute you, explosive giraffes of New York,
and all you fore-runners of the irrational – Mack Sennett,
Harry Langdon, and you too, unforgettable Buster
Keaton, tragic and delirious like my rotten and mystic
donkeys, desert roses of Spain![46]*

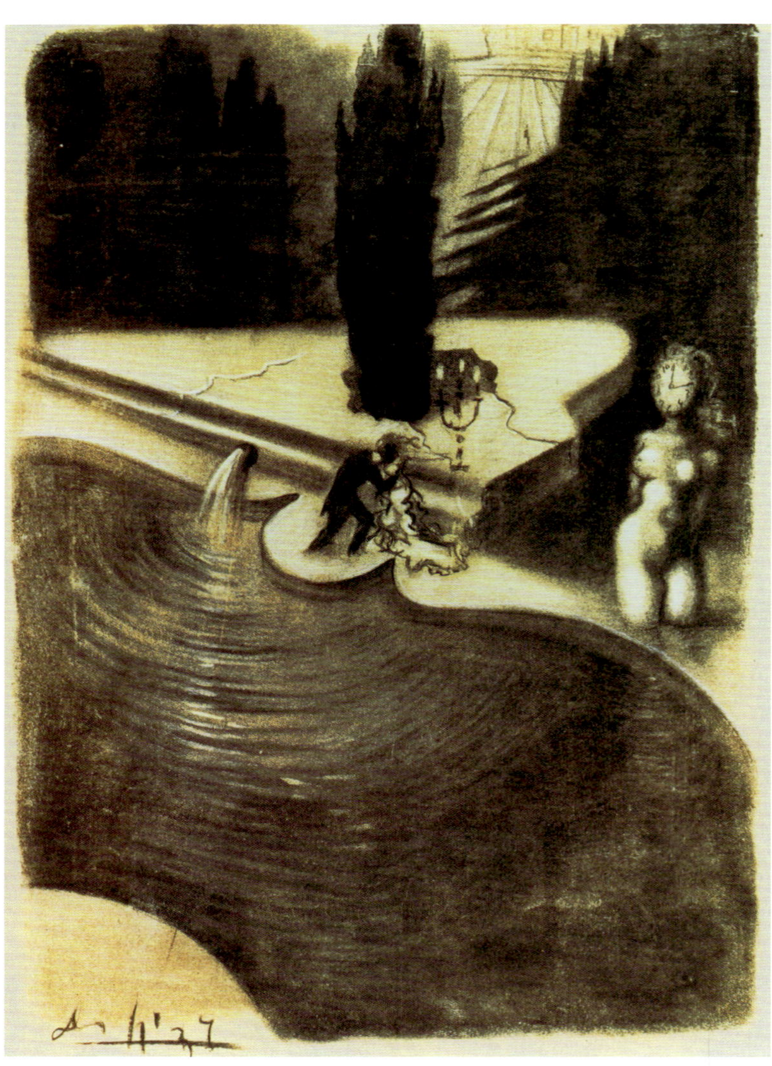

94
The Surrealist Piano 1937
Charcoal, watercolour and
pastel on paper 60 x 43 cm
Mugrabi Collection

95
Metamorphosis of Narcissus
1937
Oil on canvas 51.1 x 78.1 cm
Tate. Purchased 1979

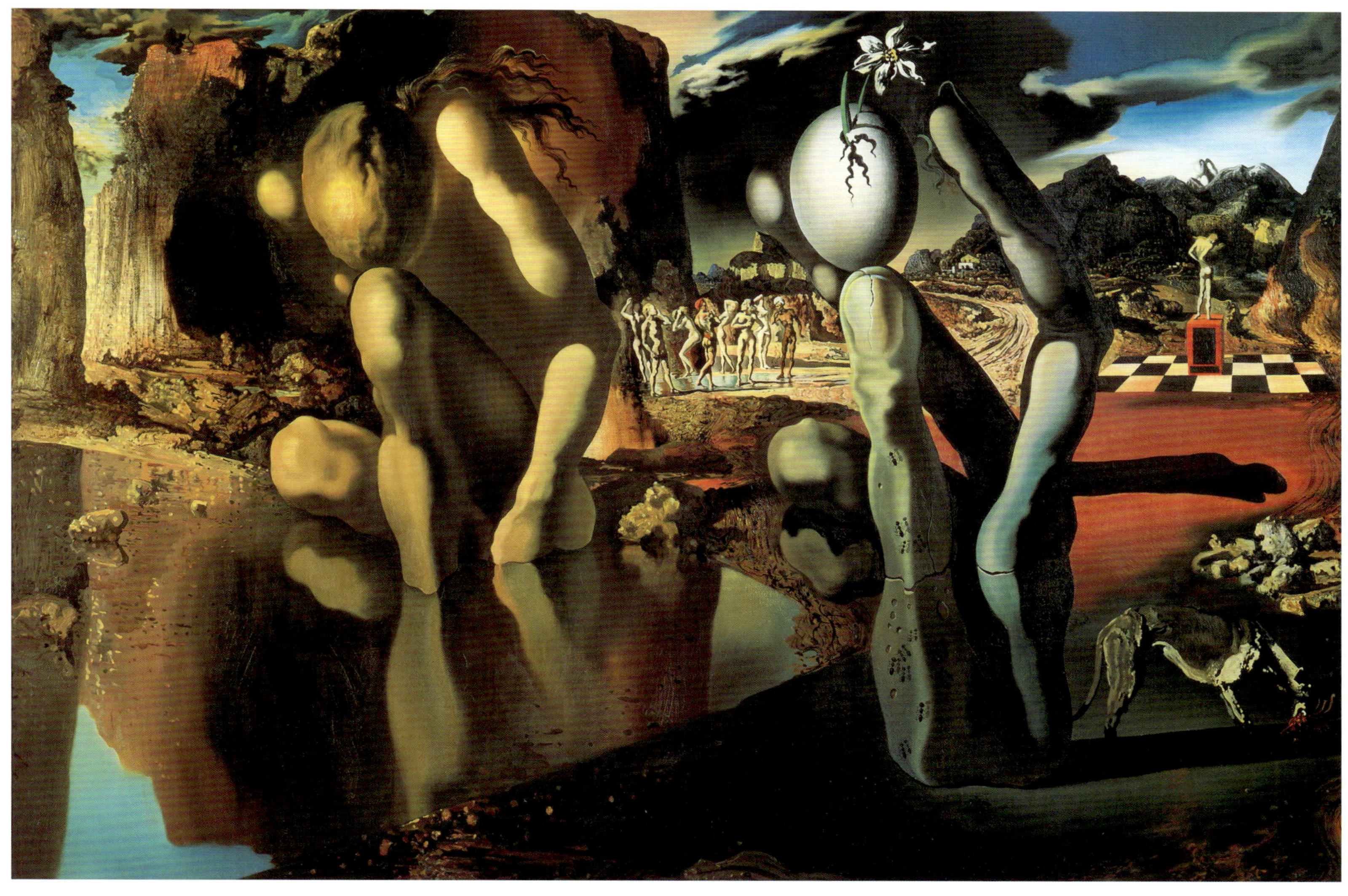

Notes

1
Salvador Dalí, 'Abrégé d'une histoire critique du cinema', in *Babaouo: Scenario inédit précédé d'un Abrégé d'une histoire critique du cinema et suivi de Guillaume Tell ballet portugais*, Paris 1932, pp.11–21: see full translation republished in this volume from Haim Finkelstein (ed.), *The Collected Writings of Salvador Dalí*, Cambridge 1998.

2
Ibid. For more on Dalí's humour and interest in comic cinema, especially in relation to the Marx Brothers, see Peter Tush, 'Salvador Dalí & Harpo Marx: Surrealist Shenanigans & Freudian Follies', in Hank Hine, William Jeffett, and Kelly Reynolds (eds.), *Persistence and Memory: New Critical Perspectives on Dalí at the Centennial*, St Petersburg (Florida) and Milan 2004, pp.37–44.

3
Antonin Artaud, 'Les Frères Marx au Cinéma du Panthéon', *Nouvelle Revue française*, 1 Jan. 1932, pp.156–8, reprinted in Susan Sontag (ed.), *Antonin Artaud: Selected Writings*, trans. Helen Weaver, New York 1976, p.240.

4
Ibid., p.241. Translation slightly modified by the author.

5
Ibid., p.240. Translation slightly modified by the author.

6
Philippe Soupault, 'Horse Feathers', *L'Europe nouvelle*, 8 Oct. 1932, reprinted in Joe Adamson, *Groucho, Harpo, Chico, and Sometimes Zeppo: A History of the Marx Brothers and a Satire on the Rest of the World*, New York 1973, p.160.

7
Dalí, 'A Short Critical History of Cinema' republished in this volume.

8
Joseph Alsop Jr., 'Surrealism Beaten at its Own Game', *New York Herald Tribune*, 15 Dec. 1935, p.17.

9
Hedda Hopper, 'Interview with Groucho Marx', *Los Angeles Times*, 31 March 1946, reprinted in Adamson 1973, p.160.

10
Marie Seton, 'S. Dali + 3 Marxes =', *Theatre Arts Monthly*, vol.23, Oct. 1939, p.734.

11
Harpo Marx, Radiogram Cable to Salvador Dalí, 31 Dec. 1936, reprinted in Robert Descharnes, *Salvador Dalí: The Work, The Man*, trans. Eleanor R. Morse, New York 1984, p.158.

12
Anonymous, 'Dali Goes Hollywood', *Art Digest*, 1 March 1937, p.17.

13
Dalí, 'Surrealism in Hollywood', trans. George Davis, *Harper's Bazaar*, June 1937, republished in this volume.

14
Although often dismissed as pure fantasy, Wes D. Gehring has argued that Dalí's admittedly exaggerated account should not be dismissed out of hand, since Harpo 'was known for sometimes playing his harp in the nude, with guests occasionally being introduced into the most revealing of first impressions,' see Wes D. Gehring, *The Marx Brothers: A Bio-Bibliography*, New York 1987, p.173.

15
Fleur Cowles, in her biography of Dalí, refers to this third portrait of Harpo Marx as being painted in the style of Frans Hals's *The Laughing Cavalier* 1624, with lace ruff, satin shirt, huge hat and two coal-black dots for eyes. Sadly this painting has long since disappeared, and one wonders if this was not also a surrogate self-portrait, given that Hals's famous portrait features a goatee and handlebar moustache not unlike the antennae-like forms of the artist's own trademark moustache, see Fleur Cowles, *The Case of Salvador Dalí*, London 1959, p.249.

16
Anonymous, 'S-u-r-r-e-a-l-i-s-m or One Way to Make Merry', *Los Angeles Examiner*, 17 Feb. 1937, reprinted in Descharnes 1984, p.158.

17
The caption accompanying the drawing reads: 'Portrait of Harpo Marx, drawn in Hollywood for Harper's Bazaar by Salvador Dalí', see Dalí, 'Surrealism in Hollywood', *Harper's Bazaar*, June 1937, p.68.

18
Anonymous, 'Dali's Harpo', *Time*, 12 Dec. 1938, p.50.

19
When the Art Institute of Chicago acquired *Inventions of the Monsters* in 1943, Dalí sent a telegram congratulating the museum and commenting on the work's genesis and symbolism: 'Am pleased and honored by your acquisition. According to Nostradamus the apparition of monsters presages the outbreak of war. This canvas was painted in the Semmering mountains near Vienna a few months before the Anschluss [the annexation of Austria by Nazi Germany in March 1938] and has a prophetic character. Horse women equals maternal river monsters. Flaming giraffe equals cosmic masculine apocalyptic monster. Cat angel equals divine heterosexual monster. Hourglass equals metaphysical monster. Gala and Dalí equal sentimental monster. The little blue dog alone is not a true monster. Sincerely, Salvador Dalí'; see Anonymous, 'Dali's Heterosexual Monster Invades Chicago', *Art Digest*, 15 Oct. 1943, p.13.

20
S.J. Woolf, 'Dali's Doodles Come to Town', *New York Times Magazine*, 12 March 1939, p.16.

21
Stefan Kanfer, *Groucho: The Life and Times of Julius Henry Marx*, New York 2000, p.227.

22
Dalí, 'Surrealism in Hollywood', republished in this volume.

23
'Giraffes on Horseback Salad', ms., Bibliothèque Kandinsky, Centre Georges Pompidou, Paris [p.65].

24
Ibid. [pp.12, 39].

25
Salvador Dalí, 'La Mujer Surrealista', in Salvador Dalí, *Obra Completa, vol.III: Poesía, Prosa, Teatro y Cine*, ed. Agustín Sánchez Vidal, trans. Ferran Esteve, Barcelona 2004, pp.1169–88. In addition to the manuscripts, a typescript entitled 'Dossier d'un projet de film avec les frères Marx' is held at the Salvador Dalí Museum, St Petersburg, Florida.

26
Short passages from the Figueres manuscript have appeared in English translations in the following books and articles: 'The Surrealist Woman' in Descharnes 1984, p.158; Anonymous, 'A (Very Strange) Day at the Races,' *Harper's Magazine*, vol.292, no.1752, May 1996, pp.32–3; Fèlix Fanés, 'The Marx Brothers', in *Dalí: Mass Culture*, trans. Sue Brownbridge, Barcelona 2004, p.95; and Simon Louvish, *Monkey Business: The Lives and Legends of The Marx Brothers: Groucho, Chico, Harpo, Zeppo with added Gummo*, London 1999, pp.241–2.

27
Ian Gibson, *The Shameful Life of Salvador Dalí*, London 1997, p.369. That Dalí had begun work on the manuscript before his meeting with Harpo is confirmed by a cryptic reference in the radiogram that the comedian sent him on 31 Dec. 1936. Harpo's cable informed the artist that he had 'received wire from Jo Forrestal saying you interested in me as victim', which probably relates to an early draft of Dalí's film scenario in which Harpo, playing the role of the deposed Emperor Nero, is arrested and put in prison for compromising public morals. Harpo's radiogram announced that he was 'thrilled with idea'; see Harpo Marx, Radiogram Cable to Dalí, 13 Dec. 1936, reprinted in Descharnes 1984, p.158.

28
Gibson 1997, p.371.

29
Fanés 2004, p.95.

30
As Simon Louvish has pointed out, Chico Marx was often erroneously referred to as Beppo in Europe, where an 'Italian' clown was expected to have an Italian name, see Louvish 1999, p.241.

31
'Giraffes on Horseback Salad'.

32
See William Jeffett's essay in this volume.

33
'Giraffes on Horseback Salad', [p.65].

34
Salvador Dalí, *The Secret Life of Salvador Dalí*, trans. by Haakon M. Chevalier, New York 1942 and London 1948, p.345.

35
Anonymous, 'A (Very Strange) Day at the Races,' *Harper's Magazine*, vol.292, no.1752, May 1996, p.33.

36
James Bigwood, 'Salvador Dalí, Reluctant Filmmaker,' *American Film*, vol.5, no.2, Nov. 1979, p.63.

37
Louvish 1999, p.241.

38
Salvador Dalí, 'The Surrealist Woman' in Descharnes 1984, p.158.

39
Anonymous, 'A (Very Strange) Day at the Races' 1996, p.32.

40
Georges Bataille, 'Kali,' *Documents*, vol.2, no.6, 1930, n.p., reprinted in Alastair Brotchie (ed.), *Encyclopaedia Acephalica*, trans. Iain White, London 1995, p.55.

41
This argument is strengthened by the fact that Bataille ends his entry on Kali with a reference to Dalí's 1929 painting *The Lugubrious Game*, ibid.

42
Meredith Etherington-Smith, *Dalí*, London 1992, p.262. Dalí sent a draft of this letter to Edward James, requesting that he translate it into English. It is not known if the letter, which is now preserved at the Edward James Foundation, West Dean, was ever sent to Harpo.

43
Groucho Marx, *The Groucho Phile: An Illustrated Life*, New York 1976, p.147.

44
Adamson 1973, p.161.

45
Earl Wilson, 'It Happened Last Night: Dalí Confides in Me: He's Not Mad – Just Crazy', *New York Post*, 20 Nov. 1944, p.32.

46
The Secret Life of Salvador Dalí, 1942, 1948, p.332.

Nothing seems to me more suited to be devoured by the surrealist fire than those mysterious strips of 'hallucinatory celluloid' turned out so unconsciously in Hollywood, and in which we have already seen appear, stupefied, so many images of authentic delirium, chance and dream.

Indeed, one always more or less believes to have 'dreamed' it when one recalls Claudette Colbert bathing in a pool filled with asses' milk at the beginning of de Mille's 'Sign of the Cross',[1] one believes to have 'dreamed' it when one recalls all the biological, hysterical and cannibalistic frenzy of 'Animal Crackers' which created a new, perfectly original and fascinating form of Marxism in the history of cinema,[2] one always believes to have 'dreamed' those dazzling 'cataclysmic rainbows' which are the Silly Symphonies of Disney,[3] one always believes to have 'dreamed' that phantom, real an unreal among them all, the most evanescent and the most sensual, the most 'camellia' and the one most drenched with silvery *arrière-pensées*, the mythological and surrealistic phantom Garbo.[4]

I am just back from Hollywood,[5] and there I have heard the word surrealism in every mouth. They have even officially announced surrealistic passages in forthcoming films. This only goes to prove that Hollywood has suddenly discovered all that it has always dimly desired in the subconscious.

Because the cinema can only develop in the direction of 'wireless imagination' and 'paralysing fantasy' – the very prey and food of the immense 'famine of illusion' of the public and the masses in general.[6] Reduced to idiocy by the material progress of a mechanical civilization, the public and the masses demand urgently the illogical and tumultuous images of their own desires and their own dreams. It is for this reason that today these crowds press hungrily around surrealism's rescue table, digging their nails into the living flesh of morsels of dream which they offer them that we may 'save our fantasy' and proclaim the 'rights of man's madness'. Thus do we try to keep them from sinking forever in that thick leaden sea which is the everyday vulgarity and stupidity of the so-called 'realist' world.

It is possible that in Hollywood we shall see imitations of surrealism before true surrealism, but true surrealists already exist in Hollywood. Naturally the most fascinating and surrealistic character in Hollywood in Harpo Marx.

I met Harpo for the first time in his garden. He was naked, crowned with roses, and in the center of a veritable forest of harps (he was surrounded by at least five hundred harps). He was caressing, like a new Leda, a dazzling white swan, and feeding it a statue of the Venus de Milo made of cheese, which he grated against the strings of the nearest harp. An almost springlike breeze drew a curious murmur from the harp forest. In Harpo's pupils glows the same spectral light to be observed in Picasso's.

Surrealism in Hollywood [1937]
Salvador Dalí

Harpo adores eating avocadoes, which are served to him with a sauce that is absolutely of the same color as his red wig (the films of the Marxes lose much by not being in color). He adores 'soft' watches.[7] He adores those tiny and appealing furry 'trombones' that fly like cockchafers above flowers. He adores his beautiful wife. He adores flowers. He adores the vague forms of humidity stains on the walls of houses not yet finished. And he adores the landscapes of Watteau, to which he corresponds chronologically and poetically.

Because Harpo is the least modern of contemporary figures, he brings with him always that relaxed light, the duet of all those imponderable moths of the past; and this to such a point that he succeeds miraculously in transforming any place where he may be into an astounding atmosphere of legend. Harpo makes an appearance, marvelously out of his element, in the most modern gleaming apartments, nickel tubing everywhere, carrying hitched behind him all the straw, the erotic hay, all that odor composed of lambs, butterflies and heliotrope which constitutes the secret of the troubling perfume of Watteau and his century. Harpo arrives, and there clings to his hallucinatory curly wig all the snuff, the songs of the nightingale and the swallows' droppings of the shadowed parks of the Embarkment for Cythera – that painting astounding among all others because it is painted like a true opera,[8] with music from all the invisible harps of light and from the plain chant of the landscape, all the culminating in the deep chest tones that the sinking sun exhales over the disarranged tresses of the great trees; and these in their turn are lived in by a thousand passages of Harpo, which serve as a nest for the languorous, strident, passionate duets of the thousand couples of blackbirds, canaries, lambs and minute steaks (because for Harpo there exists no essential difference between a butterfly and a minute steak, anything which bleeds with truly poetic truculence is his prey – Harpo devours all with the aid of that corrosive saliva *par excellence* that is 'imaginative phosphorescence'). Because one must say for once and all: 'HARPO IS A SPECTER'.

If Harpo is a specter, Garbo, his antagonist, is a phantom.[9] A phantom is a body that seems unreal, and yet can be lighted like any ordinary physical body. A specter does not absorb light, nor does it reflect light; it shines, it is phosphorescent. There is as much difference between a specter and a phantom as there is between a yellow chicken that has just broken through its shell and a greasy boiled potato that has just been lifted from the *marmite*. The sun is a specter *par excellence* as the name of its specter would indicate, the moon is the phantom among the heavenly bodies because it does nothing but let itself be lighted, it sends forth the image of its own reflection, its own phantom.

And that is why, as Harpo may be considered the sun of Hollywood, Garbo may be considered it moon, whence springs the lunar light of Garbo, that reflection that orientates itself from afar (from childhood?), that reflection which fades, is troubled, grows dim, at the approach of intimacy, of lips, of sentimental tempests, with the same fragile, imponderable and subtle sensibility of an authentic reflection in a mirror upon which one breathes. The faintest emotions, the least drop of melancholy cloud the bright celestial body of Garbo with the same purplish fog that invades a glass of transparent water when one pours into it a single drop of anisette.

If one were to turn out the light, Harpo, the specter, would continue to shine, one could in the blackest night continue to read a newspaper by the phosphorescent glow of his wig alone. But Garbo would be extinguished with the light, like a gardenia with the coming dusk; she is *mate*, silvery, and dressed in the cosmic mourning of all the nights of the moon and love.

One of the rarest things in the world is to find specters among women: generally they are moons phantoms. Gala, my wife, is a great exception to every rule, because I find myself married to an authentic rainbow. The mixture of suns and moons can lead to terrible consequences from every point of view. I invite my readers to try to distinguish between the specters and phantoms among their friends and the Hollywood stars.

SPECTRAL AND SURREALIST ANALYSIS
OF THE HOLLYWOOD HEAVENS

SPECTERS
Cecil de Mille is surrealist in his sadism and fantasy.[10]
Harpo Marx is surrealist in everything.
Adolphe Menjou's moustache is surrealist.
Clark Gable is not surrealist.
Et cetera.

PHANTOMS
Gary Cooper is surrealist in that film of dream
and delirium 'Peter Ibbetson', also with his tuba
in 'Mr Deeds'.[11]
Garbo's ecstasy is surrealist.
William Powell is surrealist in the ruins of his regard.
Robert Taylor is not surrealist.
Groucho Marx is surrealist in his cynicism
and his Marxism.
Et cetera.

Salvador Dalí, 'Surrealism in Hollywood', *Harper's Bazaar*, vol.71, no.6, June 1937, pp.68, 132, trans. George Davis. The original manuscript, in the Fundació Gala-Salvador Dalí, Figueres, is in French but dedicated to the British collector and patron Peter Watson.

Editor's Notes

1
Alongside Colbert, Charles Laughton played Nero in Cecil B. DeMille's *Sign of the Cross* 1932.

2
For the Marx Brothers' (hence Dalí's punning 'Marxism') *Animal Crackers* 1930, which includes the art expert Abby the Fishmonmger, see Michael R. Taylor's text in this volume.

3
For Walt Disney's early *Silly Symphonies* see Fèlix Fanés' 'Destino' in this volume.

4
Dalí may have Garbo's *Queen Christina* 1933 in mind.

5
Dalí went to Hollywood in February 1937, visiting the Marx Brothers on the set of *A Day at the Races*. He passed through New York to Europe in March; he was already in the Tyrol by 27 March (when he wrote to Breton). See *Salvador Dalí: Obra completa; vol.III: Album*, Barcelona 2004, pp.118, 120. This article appeared in June, which also saw the publication of *Métamorphose de Narcisse*.

6
'Wireless imagination' is a term that Dalí borrows from Marinetti.

7
For this see Michael R. Taylor's text in this volume.

8
Watteau's *Embarkation for Cythera* 1717, in the Louvre.

9
Dalí distinguished between spectres and phantoms in the titles of his paintings. The subject of his diving-suit lecture in London on 1 July 1936 was to have been 'Authentic Paranoiac Phantoms'; see *The Secret Life of Salvador Dalí*, trans. Haakon M. Chevalier, New York 1942, London 1948, p.345.

10
The rhythm of this list echoes one in Breton's *First Manifesto of Surrealism*.

11
Dalí and the Surrealists adopted Henry Hathaway's *Peter Ibbetson* 1935 as a Surrealist film as early as Jacques-Bernard Brunius's article, 'Dans l'ombre où les regards se nouent', *Minotaure*, no.11, Spring 1938, pp.38–42; Frank Capra's *Mr Deeds goes to Town* 1936 was a screwball comedy.

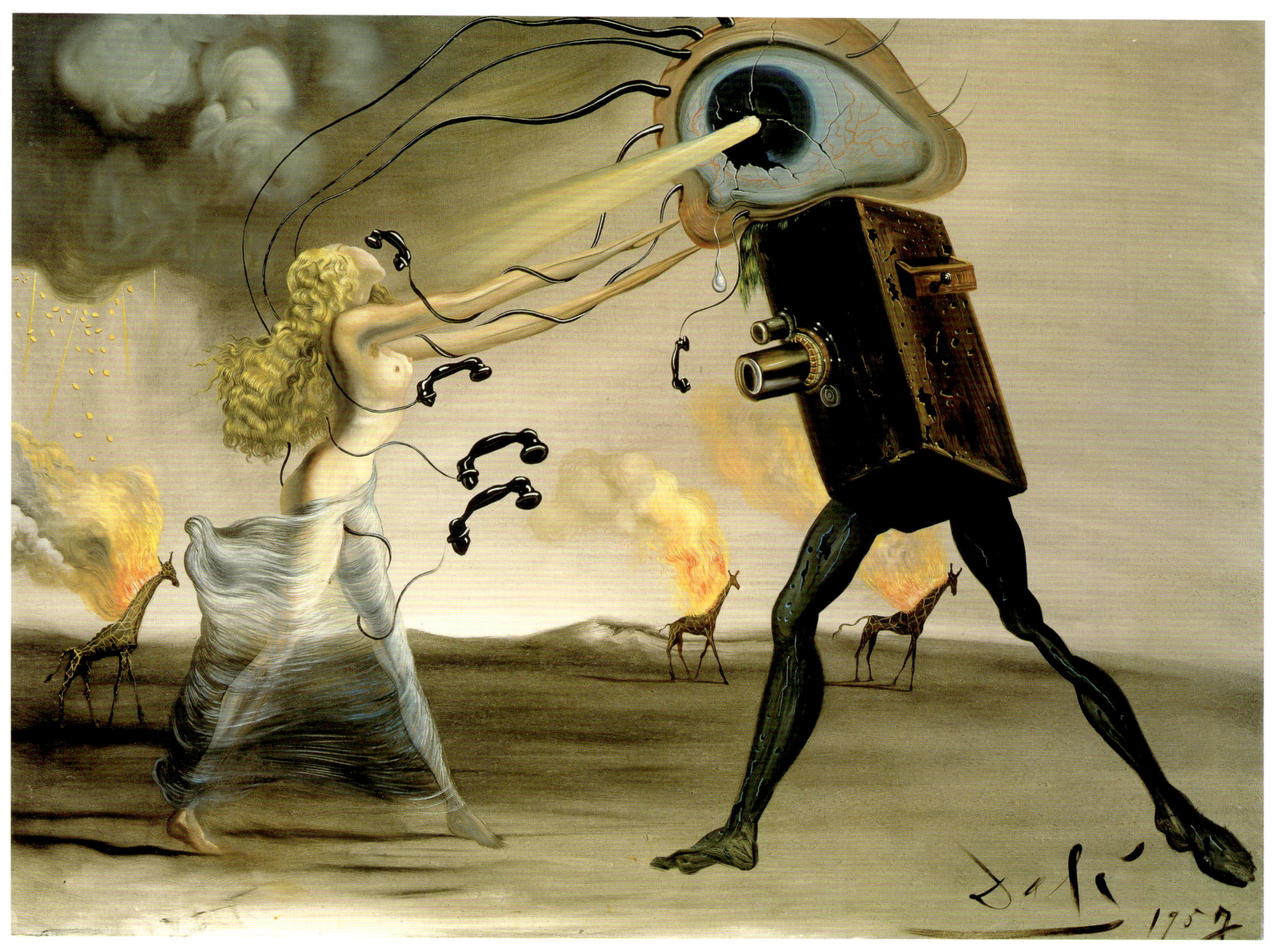

96
Rhapsodie Moderne
(Les Sept Arts) 1957
Oil on canvas 84 x 114 cm
From the collection of
Jake Shafran, London

I discovered a week ago that, with everything in my life, films included, I am about twelve years behind. For instance, for eleven years now I have been meaning to make a film that would be wholly, utterly, 100 per cent hyper-Dalinian. According to my reckoning, it is therefore probable that this film will finally be shot next year.

I am exactly the opposite of the hero of La Fontaine's fable of *The Shepherd and the Wolf*. For As in my life, and even during my adolescence, I have achieved so many sensational things, and it now happens that whatever I announce – as, for example, my liturgical bullfight, where courageous priests will have to dance in front of a bull that will be borne to heaven by a helicopter after the fight – everybody, except me, believes in the project which however – and this is the most surprising part – will end up, as sure as fate, by becoming a reality.

At the age of twenty-seven, for my arrival in Paris, I made two films in collaboration with Luis Buñuel which will remain historic: *Le chien andalou*[1] and *L'age d'or*. Since that date, Buñuel has worked alone and directed other films, thereby rendering me the inestimable service of revealing to the public who it was who was responsible for the genius and who for the elementary aspects of *Le chien andalou* and *L'age d'or*.

If I create my film, I want to be sure that it will be, from beginning to end, a succession of wonders, because there is no point in bothering to see shows that are not sensational. The more numerous my public, the greater the fortune my film will bring its author, who has so justly been baptised 'Avida Dollars'. But for a film to seem marvellous to its audience, the first indispensable requisite is that the audience can believe in the marvels that are revealed to them. One must therefore abandon, first of all, today's repulsive cinematographic rhythm, that conventional and boring rhetoric of camera movements. How can one believe, even for a second, in even the most banal melodrama when the camera follows the murderer everywhere, travelling even into the washroom where he goes to wash the blood off his hands? That is why Salvador Dalí, before he so much as begins his film, will take care to immobilise his camera, to nail it to the floor like Christ on the cross. Too bad if the action moves out of the visual field! The public will wait - distressed, exasperated, breathing heavily, stamping their feet, in ecstasy or, better still, bored to death – for the action to come back into the visual field. Unless some very beautiful and completely unrelated images distract the audience by parading before the immobile, bound, hyperstatic eye of the Dalinian camera, which will then finally be restored to its true purpose of being slave to my prodigious imagination.

My next film will be exactly the opposite of an experimental *avant-garde* film, and especially of what is nowadays called 'creative', which means nothing but a servile subordination to all the commonplaces of our wretched modern art. I shall

My Cinematographic Secrets [1954]

Salvador Dalí

tell the true story of a paranoid woman in love with a wheelbarrow which successively takes on all the attributes of the beloved whose dead body has served as a means to transport. In the end, the wheelbarrow is reincarnated and becomes flesh. That is why my film will be called *The Flesh Wheelbarrow*.[1] Sophisticated or ordinary, all the audience will be forced to participate in my fetishist delirium, because it is something that is strictly true and that will be told in a way no documentary could have managed. In spite of its categorical realism, my work will contain some really extraordinary scenes, and I cannot resist communicating some of them to my readers in advance, for the sole purpose of making their mouths water. They will see five white swans explode one after the other in a series of minutely slow images that develop according to the most rigorous archangelic eurhythmics. The swans will be stuffed with real pomegranates that have been filled in advance with explosives, so that it will be possible to observe with all due precision, the explosion of the birds' entrails and the fan-shaped burst of pomegranate seeds which will hit the cloud of feathers as one might imagine the corpuscles of light bump into each other,[2] so that, in my experiment, the seeds will have the same realism as in the paintings of Mantegna, and the feathers the flowing vagueness which made the painter Eugène Carrière famous.

In my film there will also be a scene representing the Trevi Fountain in Rome. The windows of the houses round the square will open, and six rhinoceroses will fall into the water one after the other. After each rhinoceros falls, a black umbrella will rise, open, from the bottom of the fountain.

In another scene, the Place de la Concorde will be shown at daybreak, slowly being traversed in all directions by two thousand priests on bicycles carrying placards with the very vague but still recognisable effigy of Malenkov.[3] And then, at the right moment, I shall show one hundred Spanish gypsies killing and cutting up an elephant in a Madrid street. They will leave only its fleshless skeleton, in this way transposing an African scene that I once read about in a book. At the point that the pachyderm ribs become visible, two of the gypsies who, in spite of their savage frenzy, do not for a moment stop singing flamenco, will penetrate the carcass to appropriate the best giblets, the heart, the kidneys, etc. They will begin fighting over them with knives, while those who stayed outside will continue cutting the elephant into pieces,

occasionally wounding the fighters inside, who with a horrible, piercing joy stuff the animal's interior, now transformed into a great bloody cage.

Nor should I forget a singing scene in which Nietzsche, Freud, Ludwig II of Bavaria and Karl Marx will sing their doctrines with incomparable virtuosity, answering each other antiphonally, to some music by Bizet. This scene will unfold on the banks of Lake Vilabertran, in the middle of which, shivering with cold, the water up to her waist, a very old woman, dressed as a torero, will be balancing an *omelette aux fines herbes* on her shaven head. Each time the omelette slides off and falls into the water, a Portuguese will replace it for here with a fresh one.

Towards the end of the film, we shall see the globe of a candelabra that alternatively swells and shrinks, then is covered with ornaments, then fades, burns bright again, turns liquid, hardens anew, etc. I have been thinking for almost a year about this summary of the entire political history of materialist humanity, symbolised by the morphological transformations of a marsh-mallow, simple and recognisable in the outline of the candelabra's globe. That long and very precise study lasts exactly one minute in my film and corresponds to the vision of a man overwhelmed by the sun, closing his eyes and painfully pressing them against the palms of his hands.

All this I alone can achieve – being, of course, inimitable – because I am the unique being, with Gala, who possesses the secret which enables me to create my film without ever having to cut or to use montage. That secret alone will bring endless queues to the doors of cinemas where my work will be shown. Because, contrary to the expectations of the naive, *The Flesh Wheelbarrow* will not only be the work of a genius, but it will also be the most commercial film of our age, since there is one quality that always rivets everybody's attention – the prodigious!

First published in French as 'Mes Secrets cinématographiques', *La Parisienne; Revue Littéraire Mensuelle*, Feb. 1954. pp.165–8; this translation appears as 'June' [1953] in Salvador Dalí, *Diary of a Genius*, foreword and notes by Michel Deon, trans. Richard Howard, Hutchinson Press, London 1966, pp.91–4.

Editor's Notes

1
The film project is *La Carretilla de Carne*: see Agustín Sánchez Vidal's text in this volume.

2
Rather than 'imagine', the original French gives 'one can dream – or, better, day-dream'.

3
The original French gives 'George Malenkov'.

The chronology outlines the later projects in which Dalí was involved, placing them in relation to films that he saw, read about or, more speculatively, had the opportunity of seeing. After returning to Port Lligat in 1948, Dalí established a seasonal pattern of migration from late 1949. He spent spring and summer at Port Lligat and autumn and winter between New York and Paris. The films noted below include those Dalí was known to have admired, and he may have seen them in any of these countries.
Elliott H. King

A Cinematic Chronology of Dalí

1941–1989

1949

23 November
At an audience with Pope Pius XII in Rome, Dalí has his painting, *The Madonna of Port Lligat* 1949 (The Patrick and Beatrice Haggerty Museum of Art, Marquette University, Milwaukee), blessed.

1950

Dalí begins the unrealised film script, *Le Sang Catalan*.
16 June
US release of *Father of the Bride*, directed by Vincente Minnelli and starring Spencer Tracy and Elizabeth Taylor, with a dream sequence inspired by Dalí.
25 June
Outbreak of Korean War.
21 September
Dalí's father, Salvador Dalí i Cusí, dies.

1951

15 April
In Paris, Dalí announces his turn to 'nuclear mysticism' in his *Manifeste mystique* (*Mystical Manifesto*).
28 July
Walt Disney's *Alice in Wonderland* released in the USA (France, 21 December; Spain, 17 April 1954).
19 September
A Streetcar Named Desire, directed by Elia Kazan, released in the USA (France, 16 January 1952).

1953

16 January
French release of *Manon des sources*, directed by Marcel Pagnol, whom Dalí admired.
25 February
French release of *Les Vacances de Monsieur Hurlot* (*Mr Hulot's Holiday*), directed by Jacques Tati (US, 16 June 1954). Amanda Lear recalls Dalí enjoying the film very much.

1954

February
Dalí's publishes 'Mes sécrets cinematographiques' in *La Parisienne*.
11 May
Dalí turns fifty.
October
With Philippe Halsman, publishes *Dalí's Mustache*.
20 November
Dalí paints a copy of Jan Vermeer's *Lacemaker* at the Louvre in Paris (fig.142). Robert Descharnes's film of the event initiates eight years of production on the unfinished *L'Histoire prodigieuse de la Dentellière et du rhinocéros*.

1955

Dalí paints *Portrait of Laurence Olivier in the Role of Richard III* (fig.140) to promote the film *Richard III*, directed by Alexander Korda.
30 April
Dalí stages a spectacle at Vincennes Zoo in Paris in which he progresses on *Paranoiac-Critical Study of Vermeer's 'Lacemaker'* (fig.142) from within the rhinoceros pen.
17 December
Dalí delivers a lecture at the Sorbonne, 'Aspects phénoménologiques de la métode paranoïaque-critique', analysing connections between sunflowers, cauliflowers, rhinoceros horns and *The Lacemaker*.

1956

23 October – 10 November
Hungarian Revolution.
November
Suez Crisis erupts.

1957

16 October
French release of *Le Notti di Cabiria*, directed by Federico Fellini, produced by Dino De Laurentiis (USA, 28 October; Spain, April 1958).

1958

9 May
Hitchcock's *Vertigo* released in the USA (France, 12 December).
1 August
Cinemages (New York) publishes an excerpt from *Babaouo* 1932.

1959

29 March
US release of *Some Like It Hot*, directed and produced by Billy Wilder and starring Marilyn Monroe (France, 9 September).
3 June
Les Quatre Cents Coups, directed by François Truffaut, released (USA, 16 November; Spain, 29 August 1960).
6 August
Hitchcock's *North by Northwest* is released in the USA (France, 21 October).
15 December
Official opening of the *Exposition international du surréalisme (EROS)* exhibition at the Galerie Daniel Cordier in Paris.

1960

16 March
French release of *À bout de souffle*, directed by Jean-Luc Godard (USA, February 1961).
April
Dalí films *Chaos and Creation* with Philippe Halsman at Videotape Productions, New York. The film is presented at the Fifth International Annual Conference on Visual Communications, at the Waldorf in New York.
11 May
French release of Federico Fellini's *La Dolce Vita* 1960.
28 November
Surrealists' Intrusion in the Enchanters' Domain opens at the D'Arcy Galleries, New York. Other Surrealists express their disapproval of Dalí's participation in the exhibition.

1961

March
Walt Disney visits Cadaqués to discuss projects including an animated film of Dante's *Inferno* and of Cervantes's *Don Quixote*.
May
Buñuel's *Viridiana*, made on his return to Spain, premieres at the Cannes Film Festival. It is released in France on 28 August, (USA, March 1962; Spain, May 1977).

1962

7 March
French release of *Les sept péchés capitaux* 1962, directed by Philippe de Broca, Claude Chabrol, Jacques Demy, Sylvain Dhomme, Max Douy, Jean-Luc Godard, Eugène Ionesco, Edouard Molinaro and Roger Vadim.
18 October
Francis Crick, James Watson and Maurice Wilkins win the Nobel Prize for their work on the structure of DNA.
24 October
US release of *The Manchurian Candidate*, directed by John Frankenheimer.
16 December
US release of *Lawrence of Arabia*, directed by David Lean and produced by Sam Spiegel. (France, 15 March 1963; Spain, 1 October 1963).
16 December
Buñuel's *El Ángel exterminador* is released in Spain (France, 1 May 1963; USA, 21 August 1967). Dalí recommends the film to Mia Farrow.

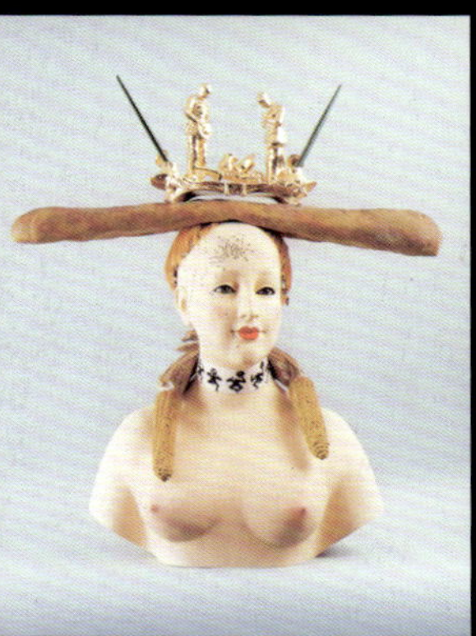

97
Retrospective Bust of a Woman
1933
Porcelain display bust with ears of corn, strip of cardboard used as a necklace, gilded sponge, and couple from Millet's *Angelus* with wheelbarrow and two calamai with quills 54 x 45 x 35 cm
Private collection. Courtesy Galerie Natalie Seroussi

May
Fellini's *8 1/2* is shown at the Cannes
Film Festival (released U.S.A. 25 June).
25 October
In Paris. Dalí publishes *Le Mythe
tragique de l'Angélus de Millet*, originally
written in the 1930s. He adds in the
opening: 'For anyone who would dare
to make the most ambitious of films.
this book contains the most
revolutionary of "secret" scenarios'.

1964

29 January
Stanley's Kubrick's *Dr Strangelove*
is released in USA (France as
Docteur Folamour, 10 April; Spain
as *¿Teléfono rojo?, volamos hacia Moscú*.
10 January 1966).
May
Dalí publishes *Journal d'un génie* in
Paris. He turns sixty.
8 September
Major Dalí retrospective opens at the
Tokyo Price Hotel. Japan.

In New York. Andy Warhol films
his two Dalí *Screen Tests*.
February
Twentieth Century Fox employs Dalí
to promote *Fantastic Voyage*, starring
Raquel Welch. The delivery of one
of his paintings is filmed as *Dalí's
Fantastic Dream*.
5 May
Jean-Luc Godard's *Alphaville* is
released in France (U.S.A. 25 October)
and Dalí reveals that it comes highly
recommended by Marcel Duchamp
(Alain Bosquet. *Entretiens avec Salvador
Dalí*, Paris 1966).
18 November
An important Dalí retrospective
opens at the Gallery of Modern Art.
New York.

22 March
Jean-Luc Godard's *Masculin féminin* is
released in France (U.S.A. September).
November
Jean Christophe Averty's *Autoportrait
Mou de Salvador Dalí* is produced by
Seven Arts Television in the USA:
Orson Welles narrates the English
version. Seven Arts also makes the
hour-long *The World of Salvador Dalí*.

1967

24 May
Belle de jour, directed by Buñuel
and starring Catherine Deneuve.
is released in France (Spain.
December; U.S.A.10 April 1968).
6–30 December
Dalí participates in *Homage to Marilyn
Monroe*. Sidney Janis Gallery. New York.

6 April
US premiere of Stanley Kubrick's
2001: A Space Odyssey is released in the
USA (released in France. 27
September).
June
Dalí designs the cover of *TV Guide*.
which includes the article. 'Salvador
Dalí's View of Television'.
4 September
Pier Paolo Pasolini's *Teorema* premieres
at the Venice Film Fesitval (France.
January 1969: U.S.A. April 1969).

1969

Dalí buys Puból Castle. which
he decorates and presents as
a gift to Gala. Dalí frequently visits
filming in Cadaqués of Jules Verne's
The Light at the Edge of the World (1971)
with Kirk Douglas. Samantha Eggar
and Yul Brynner.
15 March
French premiere of Buñuel's *La Voie
lactée* (U.S.A. January 1970).

Brynner photographs Dalí
painting *Roger Freeing Angelica*
1970–4 (Fundació Gala-Salvador
Dalí. Figueres).
11 March
Fellini's *Satyricon* 1969 released in
the U.S.A. Donyale Luna. who had
appeared in *Autoportrait mou de
Salvador Dalí* is among the film's actors.
29 March
Buñuel's *Tristiana* is released in Spain
(France. 29 April: U.S.A. September).
Lear recalls Dalí admiring Catherine
Deneuve's performance.
1 April
In Paris. Dalí announces the creation
of the Teatre-Museu Dalí in Figueres.
21 November
Dalí's visit to his major retrospective
at the Museum Boijmans Van
Beuningen in Rotterdam is filmed.
December
Peau d'âne. directed by Jacques Demy
is released in France. Dalí is said to
have told Catherine Deneuve (with
reference to its title. *Donkey Skin* or
Ass's Skin): 'My dear. you are truly the
most beautiful ass I've ever seen'.

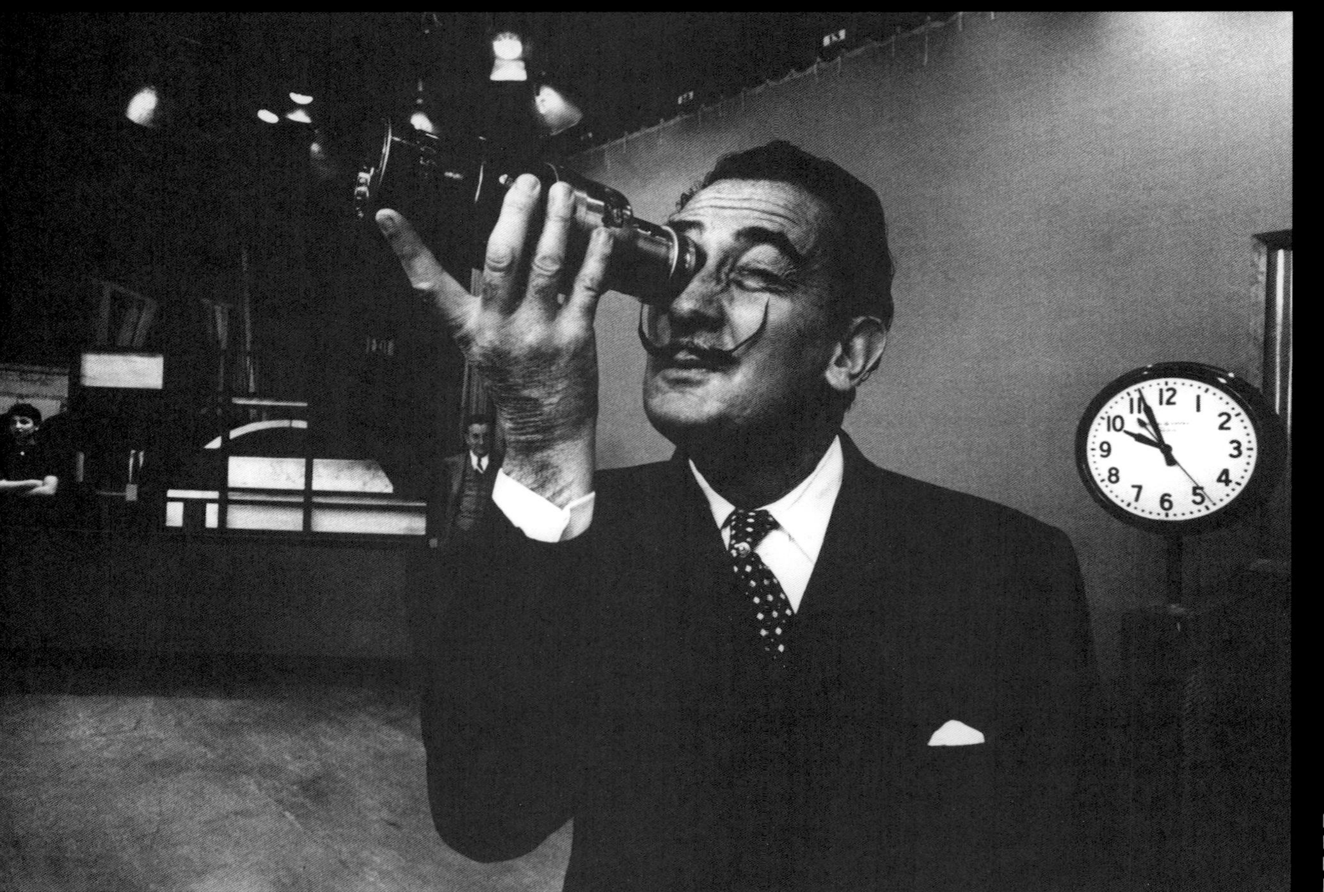

Dalí on the set of the CBS
Morning Show. photographed
by Philippe Halsman 1956
Halsman Archive / Magnum Photos

1971

7 March
Inauguration of Eleanor and
A. Reynolds Morse collection
at the Salvador Dalí Museum
in Cleveland, Ohio.
19 December
A Clockwork Orange, directed by
Stanley Kubrick, premieres in the
USA (France, April 1972; Spain,
16 June 1975). Dalí later uses the
soundtrack, based on Beethoven's
Ninth Symphony, as the score for
*Impressions de la Haute Mongolie –
Hommage à Raymond Roussel* (1975).

1972

Dalí is asked to design a Tarot deck
for the James Bond film, *Live and
Let Die* 1973.
April–May
Dalí's 'first world exhibition of
holograms' is held at the Knoedler
Galleries, New York.
15 September
Buñuel's *Le Charme discret de la
bourgeoisie* is released in France
(USA, 22 October).
December
The artist expresses disapproval in the
press after the presentation of the 1966
film, *Autoportrait mou de Salvador Dalí*.
11 December
US release of Jacques Tati's *Traffic*,
a film Lear recalls Dalí enjoying.

1973

Dalí's conversations with André
Parinaud published as *Comment
on devient Dalí* (Paris).
8 April
Death of Picasso.
24 May
Bruce Gowers directs *Hello Dalí*,
featuring Russell Harty, for London
Weekend Television, broadcast on
UK television on 8 November. In
1975, the Salvador Dalí Museum and
the Teatre-Museu Dalí jointly publish
Dalí's comments about the film.
December
Jacques Tati visits Dalí in Paris.

1974

Dalí is approached by Alejandro
Jodorowsky to play Emperor Shaddam
IV in his film based on Frank
Herbert's science-fiction novel, *Dune*.
Dalí is also asked by director Pier
Paolo Pasolini to make a poster for
Salò o le 120 giornate di Sodoma 1976.
January
In New York Dalí enlists director
José Montes Baquer to direct
*Impressions de la Haute Mongolie –
Hommage à Raymond Roussel* 1975.
August
Dalí organises a Happening
in Granollers that serves as the
closing sequence for *Impressions
de la Haute Mongolie.*
28 September
Opening of the Teatre-Museu
Dalí, Figueres.

1975

January
*Impressions de la Haute Mongolie –
Hommage à Raymond Roussel* is
presented at the Avoriaz International
Fantasy Film Festival in France.
27 September
Dalí's public endorsement of General
Franco's execution of five alleged
terrorists leads Jodorowsky to
withdraw his invitation for the artist
to appear in *Dune*.

1978

Dalí films *1001 Visions de Salvador Dalí*
for French television, directed
by Alain Ferrari.
He publishes a deluxe edition
of *Babaouo* in Barcelona.

1979

9 May
Dalí is inducted into the Académie
des Beaux-Arts de l'Institut de France
in Paris.
18 December
Dalí's retrospective at the Centre
Georges Pompidou, Paris; it travels to
the Tate Gallery in London in 1980.

1982

7 March
Inauguration of the Salvador Dalí
Museum in St Petersburg, Florida.
10 June
Death of Gala.

1983

January
Luis Revenga films a few minutes of
'The Little Demon' to send to Buñuel.
29 July
Death of Buñuel.

1989

23 January
Dalí dies at the Torre Galatea, Figueres.

Moontide 1941

Ilene Susan Fort

It was inevitable that Salvador Dalí and Hollywood should meet. By the 1940s, he was the most celebrated Surrealist, and Los Angeles was the world's most popular entertainment capital, where the border between reality and fantasy merged. But even alliances that at first appear so natural can encounter problems: such is the story of Dalí in Hollywood.[1]

Carey McWilliams, the most astute commentator on Southern California, explained in 1946 that 'Hollywood is neither a town, nor a city … Despite its nebulous geographical status, however, Hollywood does exist as a community, but a community that must be defined in industrial rather than geographical terms.'[2] He goes on to discuss it as a physical place, a commercial industry, and a creative sphere. It is these multiple geographies that constitute Dalí's Hollywood. The studios rapidly outgrew the place and, by the 1930s, Hollywood was a somewhat ragged neighbourhood of transients, opportunists and tourists. Unlike the American Surrealist Man Ray, who lived there during the 1940s, Dalí was merely a sporadic visitor. When he was in California, he would stay in other neighbourhoods of Los Angeles or Beverly Hills, or even further afield in the desert community of Palm Springs or at Pebble Beach on the Monterey coast (some 350 miles to the north), communities that were popular with the upper echelon of the motion-picture industry who sought privacy. When he was in Los Angeles, it was primarily for business appointments with motion-picture executives and directors, and for social events that were an essential part of the movie business. Dalí thrived on such get-togethers, his natural theatrical instinct and need to be centre stage prompting him to take full advantage of opportunities for self-promotion.

Dalí's direct experience of Hollywood was with the industry and its creative spirit. The commercial film community existed largely separately from other Angelinos, who tended to be conservative and traditional in attitude and life style. However, the industry also remained apart from most painters, sculptors and art teachers who lived and exhibited throughout the region. Some worked for the studios full-time or on special projects, but most did not, and this was especially true of the more progressive artists. Yet, the avant-garde and the industry did at times influence each other, despite their psychological distance. Hollywood attracted other European artists besides Dalí, among them Eugène Berman and Ruth Bernhard, and it was the home of the foremost American patrons of the European avant-garde, Walter and Louise Arensberg.[3] Also based there were the founders of Post-Surrealism,

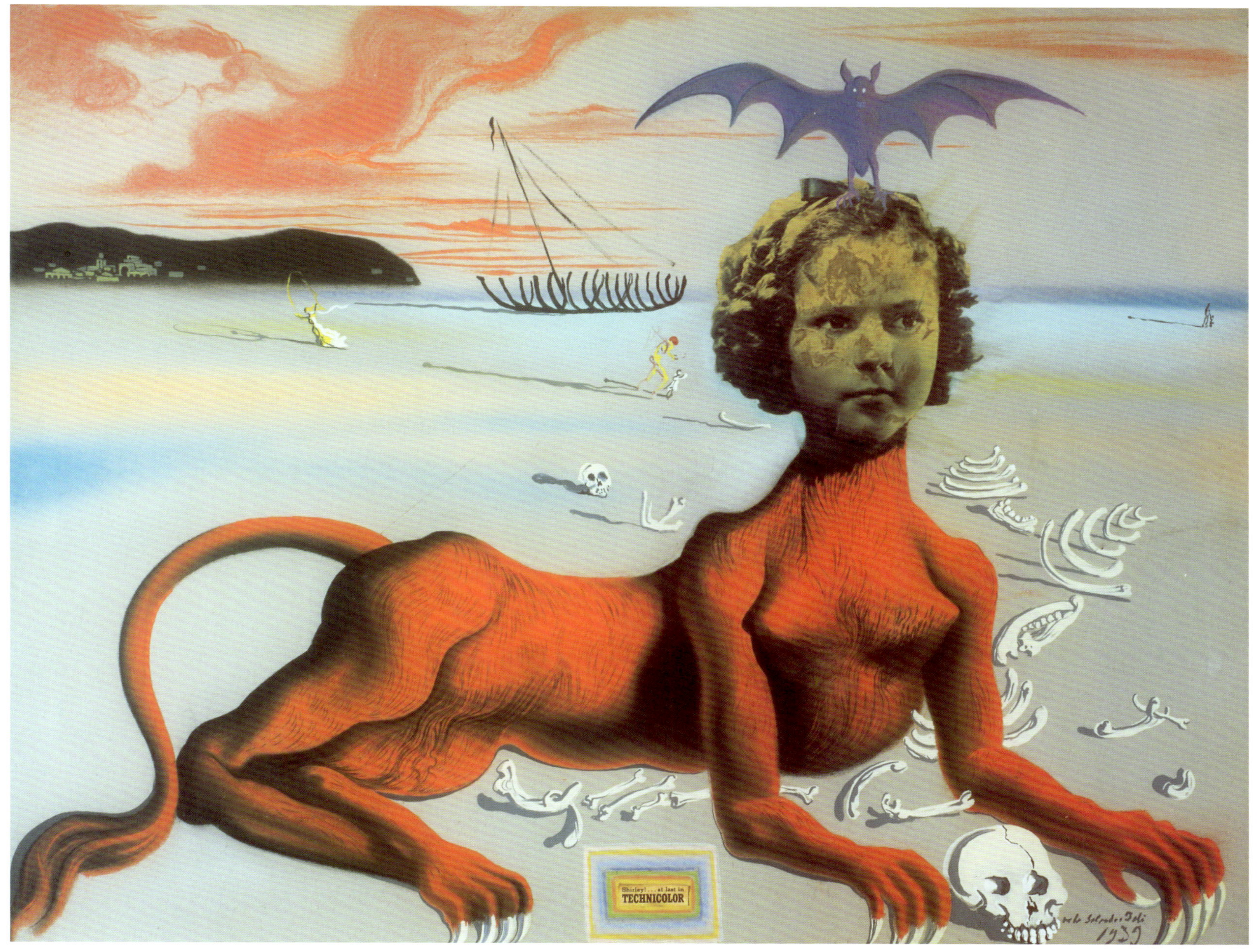

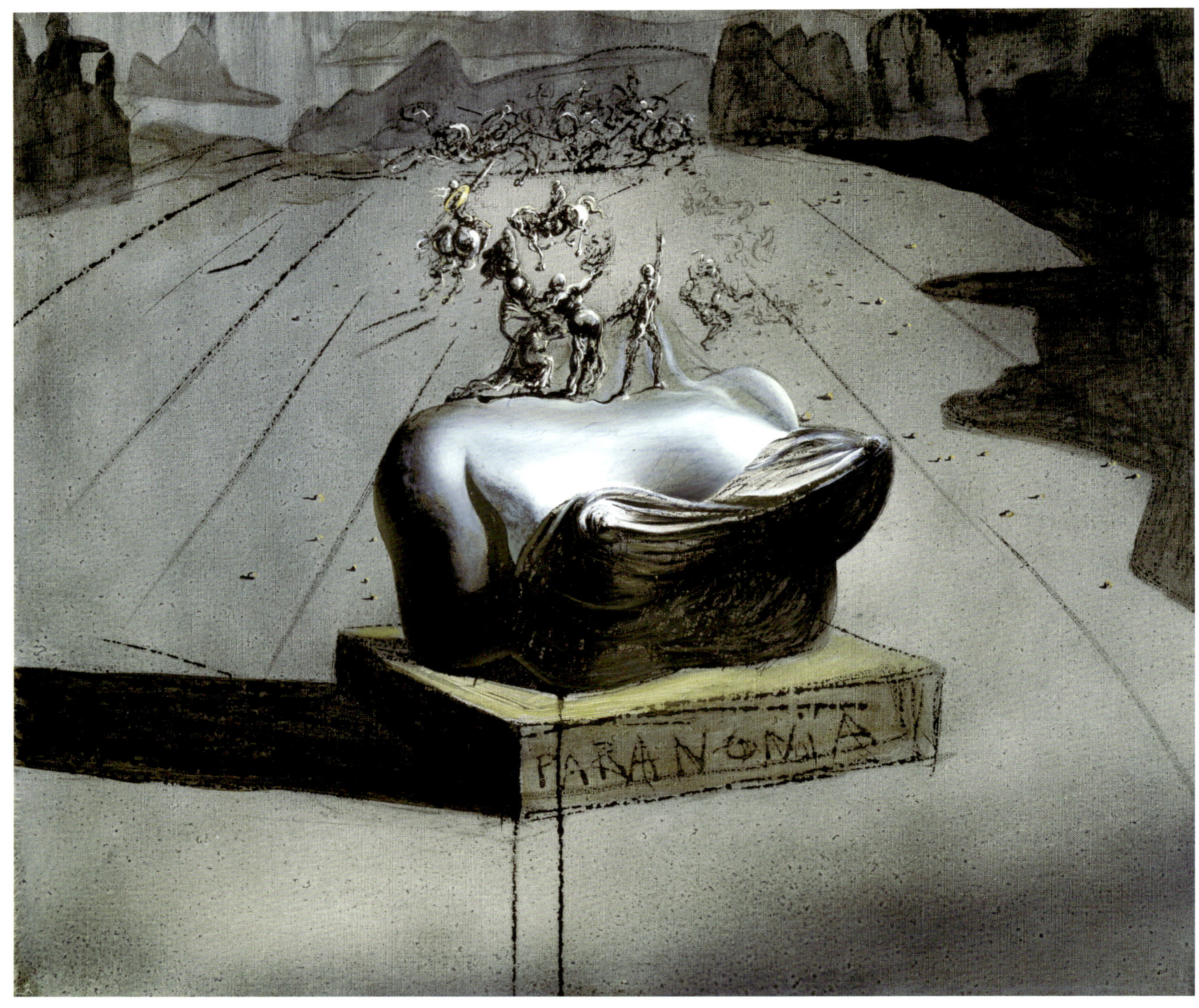

99
Paranonia c.1935
Oil on canvas 38 x 46 cm
Salvador Dalí Museum,
St Petersburg, Florida

Lorser Feitelson and Helen Lundeberg, the only American followers of the European movement to have issued a manifesto.[4] Through the activities of Oskar Fischinger, Curtis Harrington, and John and James Whitney, the region was simultaneously becoming one of the country's most active centres of experimental film.[5]

Numerous early writers noted that Hollywood was a state of mind, an idea that eventually led it to become known as 'the dream machine'. Dalí attributed this aspect to Surrealism:

I am just back from Hollywood, and there I heard the word surrealism in every mouth. They have even officially announced surrealistic passages in forthcoming films. This only goes to prove that Hollywood has suddenly discovered all that it has always dimly desired in its subconscious.[6]

Many of the European Surrealists loved American cinema. A decade earlier, in 1927, both Dalí and Luis Buñuel wrote articles about films in which they explained their enthusiasm. Buñuel praised the 'School of Buster Keaton' as full of 'vitality, photogeny' and with 'no culture', and Dalí extolled it as 'anti-artistic'.[7] Indeed, Hollywood movies satisfied their demands for a medium without a tradition, one that was truly modern and authentic.

Dalí first crossed the Atlantic in 1934 to attend the opening of his solo exhibition at the Julian Levy Gallery in New York. Although Dalí needed no encouragement, Levy was instrumental in publicising him. During the 1930s, the dealer almost single-handedly introduced the movement to the United States with his series of group and solo exhibitions and his 1936 publication *Surrealism*.[8] Levy shared the Surrealists' passion for cinema. As the first president of the Film Society of New York, he was instrumental in screening Dalí's early joint ventures with Buñuel, *Un Chien andalou* and *L'Age d'or* in 1932[9] (they would be shown at Charlie Chaplin's home in California the following year). In his book *Surrealism*, Levy devoted an entire section to cinema, presenting translated scenarios of Dalí's early films as well as the following explanation:

The surrealist attempts to explore the realm of the subconscious, to examine it not with the eye of the scientist … but with the eye of the poet and artist, without the recourse to the logic of everyday reality. It can readily be seen that the cinema offers the perfect medium for such a purpose. Thoughts and dreams almost universally operate as a sequence of moving images … not to mention the tricks so accessible to the camera such as

superimposed concepts or the double exposure, flash-backs of memory, and tentative forecasts into the future … Buñuel and Dalí are the first to attempt using the film as a medium for metaphor and ideology.[10]

By the time of Dalí's 1937 visit to Hollywood to meet the Marx Brothers, he was already a household name – as famous as the comic actors whom he so admired.[11] His reputation had been accomplished by several means: exhibitions at the Levy Gallery leading to a well-publicised acquisition by the Museum of Modern Art, an appearance on the cover of the popular American weekly magazine *Time*, and theatrical antics that made headline news.

In 1941, Levy could no longer deny the lure of Hollywood and so, accompanied by Dalí, he travelled west for a season. He rented the Los Angeles gallery space of Dalzell Hatfield, where, in early autumn, he presented his Dalí show that had recently been on view in New York and Chicago. Levy wrote to James Soby, curator at the Museum of Modern Art: 'Hollywood is exciting and the Gallery is alive and selling.'[12] On 2 September, shortly before the show, Dalí hosted a masquerade fundraiser party in Pebble Beach. It was attended by many of the Hollywood elite, among them Bob Hope, Bing Crosby and Ginger Rogers, and it may have been there that Dalí first discussed the project for a nightmare sequence for the film *Moontide*. By 15 September, Twentieth Century Fox had issued a written agreement with the artist, through Hatfield as his agent, establishing the details of his services and payment of $5,000.[13] Significantly, the agreement allowed the artist to retain all the sketches and paintings that he made for the project.

It appears that Dalí developed his ideas over the next two months. Before attending the opening of his first retrospective (a joint exhibition with Joan Miró) at the Museum of Modern Art in New York on 18 November, he had secured a postponement of the original filming schedule specifically so that he could return to Hollywood to present his ideas to the studio in person. According to the *Hollywood Reporter*: 'Salvador Dalí, he of the pixilated paint brush, arrives Thursday [20 November], from New York to discuss with Twentieth Century a nightmare montage he will do for "*Moon tide*".'[14] He brought with him what was probably the final one of three versions of the dream scenario, typed-up for the studio executives as a four-page presentation in

English.[15] On 21 November, three days before filming began, Dalí reported to the studio; they had thought it, 'advantageous if he can spend a day or two before commencement of the photography, with our director and producer, arranging the details of the Nightmare Sequence'.[16]

Moontide, produced and distributed by Twentieth Century Fox, starred the French actor Jean Gabin (in his first English-speaking role and first American film) and Ida Lupino. It was a drama based on the 1940 novel *Moon Tide* by Willard Robertson. The story concerned Bobo, an alcoholic dockworker with a violent temper, who rescues and falls in love with a down-and-out young woman. The movie was to be directed by Fritz Lang, whose films Dalí knew, but had criticised. A sober tale of good and evil on the fringes of society, the story was perfect for Lang, who had received critical acclaim in the 1920s for dark films about human loneliness. Refusing to work for the Nazis, Lang had left Germany in 1933 and within a year had settled in Hollywood under contract to David Selznick at MGM. The Austrian was one of many celebrity directors, artists and writers to flee Nazi Europe for the safety of California and employment in the American film industry. By the early 1940s, the émigrés – among them René Clair, who had crossed the Atlantic Ocean in 1940 on the same passenger ship as Dalí and Man Ray – constituted a significant group in Hollywood.

Lang continued to infuse his American films with the same bleak worldview that dominated his German cinema, focusing on the themes of revenge, hatred and the inequities of life.[17] As a creator of nightmares, Dalí was one of Lang's few peers. From the very start, the Surrealists had been conscious of the analogical role played by film language: it could simulate a dream. If only part of a film was to be Surrealistic, it was inevitable that it should be a dream sequence, since fascination with the unconscious dominated Surrealist ideology. Buñuel admitted, 'I love dreams, even when they're nightmares … My *amour fou* is the single most important thing I shared with the surrealists. [And] *Un Chien andalou* was born of the encounter between my dreams and Dalí's.'[18] Dalí concurred, and related the idea to the Hollywood experience: 'Nothing seems to be more suited to be devoured by the surrealist fire than those mysterious strips of "hallucinatory celluloid" turned out so unconsciously in Hollywood, and in which we have already seen appear, stupefied, so many images of authentic delirium, chance and dream.'[19]

Around the time of *Moontide*, both commercial and avant-garde filmmakers in Los Angeles were utilising the device of the dream. *The Wizard of Oz* 1939 presented almost the entire story as a dream (in colour compared to the black-and-white prologue), while the independent *Meshes of the Afternoon* 1943 by Maya Deren and Czech filmmaker Alexander Hammid mystified the viewer by merging dream with reality. Their approaches, however, differed. Commercial directors usually recounted a dream as a logical

100
Sewing Machine and Umbrellas. Drawing for the film *Moontide* c.1941
Ink on canvas 20.3 x 25.8
Fundació Gala-Salvador Dalí, Figueres

101
Window Display with Umbrella and Sewing Machine. Drawing for the film *Moontide* c.1941
Pencil on Indian paper
8.8 x 12.8 cm
Fundació Gala-Salvador Dalí, Figueres

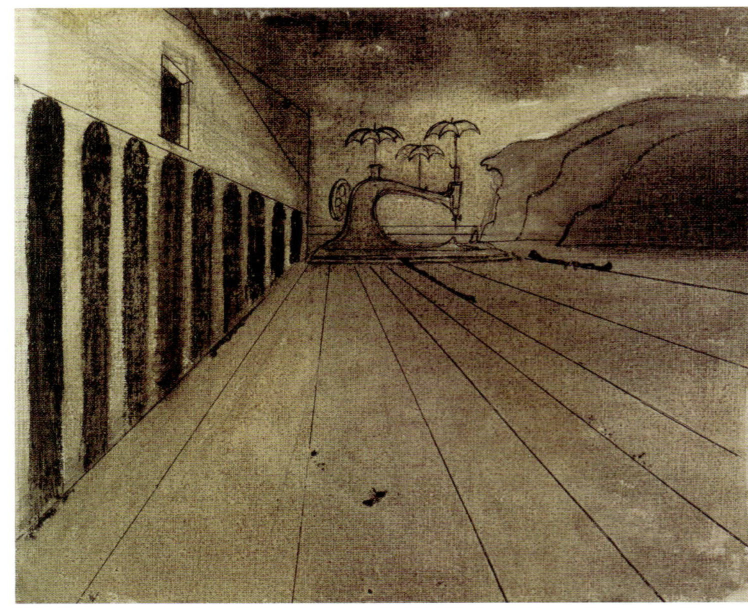

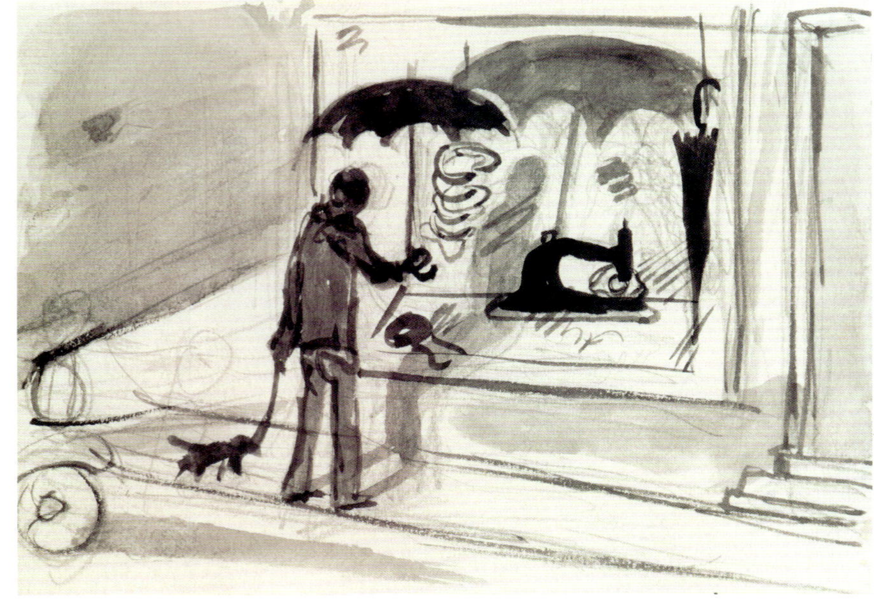

segment of an orderly narrative, in contrast to the experimental filmmakers. The latter tended to present their plots out of sequence or with repetitions. As Buñuel declared in a lecture delivered in San Francisco in 1947, irrationality was a 'result of a CONSCIOUS psychic automatism', and profited from 'a mechanism analogous to dreams'.[20] The influence of Sigmund Freud's psychoanalytic interpretation of dreams and the Surrealist pictorialisation of them reached its pinnacle in commercial Hollywood films only two years after *Moontide*, when Hans Richter wrote, produced and directed *Dreams that Money Can Buy* 1944–6, a story about a psychiatrist who sees his patients' dreams and desires as images on their retinas (Richter, Man Ray, Max Ernst and others contributed the dream imagery).[21]

The hallucination of Bobo's mind distorted by alcohol and guilt in *Moontide* was a perfect theme for Dalí. In paintings such as *The Persistence of Memory* 1931 (fig.74), he had begun to depict such disturbing psychoses through a meticulously rendered realism combined with a macabre mood and misshapen forms. Dalí had read Freud's writings avidly in the 1920s and found his ideas about human neuroses a rich font for his own imagery.[22] As he explained in his scenario presented to Twentieth Century Fox, he conceived Bobo's nightmare 'in terms of scientific symbols – Freudian, Surrealist, and Dalínian'.[23]

Dalí planned to have the dockworker walk through a bordello-like restaurant, a bedroom and finally a large public square, experiencing a variety of emotions from confusion to disgust, fury and horror. An enormous sewing machine in which the spirit of a murdered sailor resided was to be the central motif. Throughout the nightmare, Bobo would experience the transformation of ordinary people and objects into fantastic creatures, including sirens. Dalí took full advantage of the filmic devises of fade-ins and -outs and abrupt changes for these metamorphoses. Just as the machine's needle was about to pierce the eye of one of the sirens, the eye would dissolve into the rising sun and Bobo would awake. 'All the images and symbols employed are intended to convey the unbroken sensation of leaden expression weighing' upon Bobo, Dalí wrote. Typical of the artist was his recycling of imagery that he and other Surrealists had used in books, paintings and films. The needle and eye refer to *Un Chien andalou*, a flying giraffe to *L'Age d'or*, and the seductive floating women to Dalí's 1939 New York World's

Fair installation, the *Pavilion of Venus*. The sewing machine combined with umbrellas echoes the famous juxtaposition expressed by the Comte de Lautréamont: 'as beautiful as the chance encounter of a sewing machine and an umbrella on an operating table'.

Dalí created five drawings and three paintings for *Moontide*.[24] Two drawings seem to relate to the central motif of the dream. In one, a man with an umbrella and a dog (also in the nightmare) are on a street, looking at a sewing machine in a storefront window (fig.101). The reflection of the umbrella over the sewing machine is also related to Dalí's unusual placement of huge umbrellas on the top of the monumental machine in the second drawing, which depicts a public square with a de Chirico-like colonnade (fig.100). Two other preparatory drawings are of a single human skull. In one, the skull has vacant eye sockets and sits incongruously on a round table beside which are two wire Victorian chairs, the structure and eyes coalescing as two seated figures (fig.102a). The other shows a skull whose open mouth is filled with smaller screaming skulls (fig.102b). Although the double-image of the skull with chairs may refer to the bar where Bobo began his drunken brawl, a skull was not part of Dalí's proposed scenario.

Dalí's visibility had led the motion picture industry to hire him, but ultimately it may have deemed his art too scary for the general public. John Russell Taylor has suggested: 'It often seemed as though [foreign] intellectuals in Hollywood were not so much bought as bought off.'[25] Hollywood motion pictures were profit-making first and foremost, controlled by high-level businessmen, who were often not concerned with the opinions of their writers, musicians and painters, distanced from the executives by their lowly position in the highly stratified studio hierarchy. The studio chief had final authority over every aspect of the film. The idea that an artist could write, design, film and produce a movie – as Buñuel and Dalí had done in the 1920s – was completely antithetical to the Hollywood mentality. It was for this reason that Man Ray refused to work for the studios.[26] As *Moontide* showed, Dalí was more willing to be part of the system. He was prepared to work under contract on a small part of a film. Although Twentieth Century Fox allowed him to keep his artworks, his contract ensured that the studio retained sole and exclusive rights to and ownership of his ideas, and

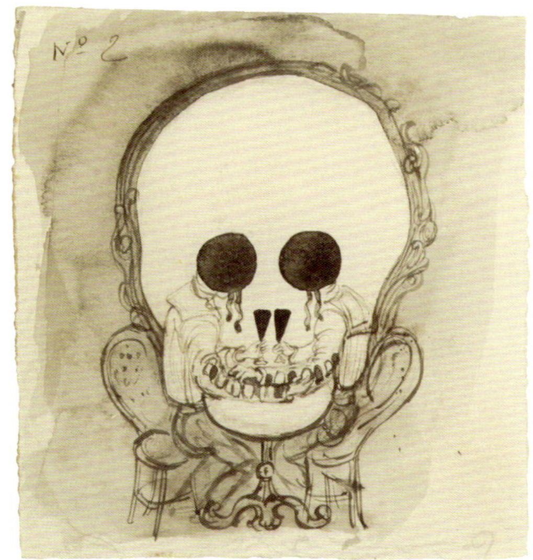

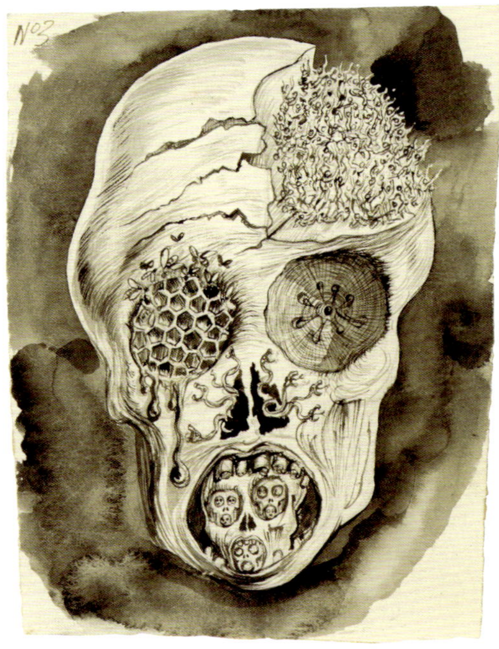

102a
Cafe Scene. Drawing for the film
Moontide 1941
Pencil, wash and Indian ink on paper
13.6 x 12.6 cm
Fundació Gala-Salvador Dalí, Figueres

102b
Face of War. Drawing for the film
Moontide 1941
Pencil, wash and Indian ink on paper
17.5 x 13.2 cm
Fundació Gala-Salvador Dalí, Figueres

could 'add to, subtract from, arrange, revise, adapt, rearrange, make variations of said property, [and] change the sequence.'[27]

The disparity between the attitudes of the avant-garde Dalí and the capitalist film business might have seemed enough to doom the association, but it was another circumstance that killed off his contribution to *Moontide*: the timing. *Moontide* started production on Monday 24 November 1941. Thirteen days later, on the morning of 7 December, Japan attacked Pearl Harbor, sweeping the United States into the Second World War. The country, both populace and government, was galvanised into a single focus – victory – and the film industry became an essential factor in this momentum.

Entry into the war had an immediate impact on the nature of the film business. The American public had long considered an afternoon at the local movie theatre a necessary luxury, even when family finances drastically shrunk during the preceding depression years. In 1938, motion pictures ranked fourteenth among American industries by volume of business and eleventh in total assets, and in Los Angeles, it was the region's leading industry from 1920 until the war.[28] Just a cursory glance at one of the industry's newspapers, *The Hollywood Reporter*, demonstrates the repercussions of Pearl Harbor: the 9 December issue was devoted to the war's effect on Hollywood, and a major front-page article insisted that the making of motion pictures was 'just as important as the production of ammunition, planes, or boats.' Using the traditional American mandate, the church, the article went on:

We heard a priest, speaking to his pulpit here last Sunday: 'The influence of motion pictures is the greatest of all influences on the public's mind and in the daily conduct of that public's life … Your task is … to keep the American chin up – to keep our people entertained. And keep them laughing.'[29]

For days afterwards, articles were devoted to describing the different activities and changes that the studios had already implemented for the war effort, including the making of more patriotic and comic films.

Lang directed a series of powerful anti-Nazi films for Hollywood, such as *Man Hunt* 1941. They shared the grim perspective of the world that he had intended to underscore in *Moontide*. However, the dockworker's tale lacked any of the redeeming qualities of his pro-Ally films. Since he insisted on retaining the novel's original bleak ending, Lang was quickly removed from the film, the studio citing 'a disagreement over treatment of the story'.[30] Neither *Moontide* nor the dream sequence was entirely scrapped. Instead, the new director, Archie Mayo, softened their intensity and transformed the ending into a typical American fable: the dockworker and his girlfriend marry. Significantly, the art directors Richard Day and James Basevi presented Bobo's delirium as far less frightening or perverse than envisaged in Dalí's proposal.

The final filmed hallucination was more a montage of clips of Bobo's activities during the pandemonium of his drunken stupor, all presented in a manner echoing the dockworker's confusion over what had happened. It contained only one oblique reference to sex, compared to Dalí's typical pervasive usage. In a 1931 painting, *The Dream* (The Cleveland Museum of Art, Ohio), Dalí replaced the mouth of a woman with an ant-infested, pubis-like expanse of flesh, thereby alluding to repression and anxiety. He intended similar sirens with swirling hair to allure Bobo and the viewer into the dream space. Since Bobo's hallucination occurs immediately after he has an altercation in a bar over a floozy, the sexual innuendoes suggested by Dalí would have been blatant and completely antithetical to the wholesome character promoted by the Hollywood industry. Dalí's proposed seductresses were replaced by a single female, who magically loses her head, thereby becoming nothing but a dress, which in the story symbolised sexuality. Ironically, the disappearance of her head was the only Surreal element in the filmed version of the so-called nightmare.

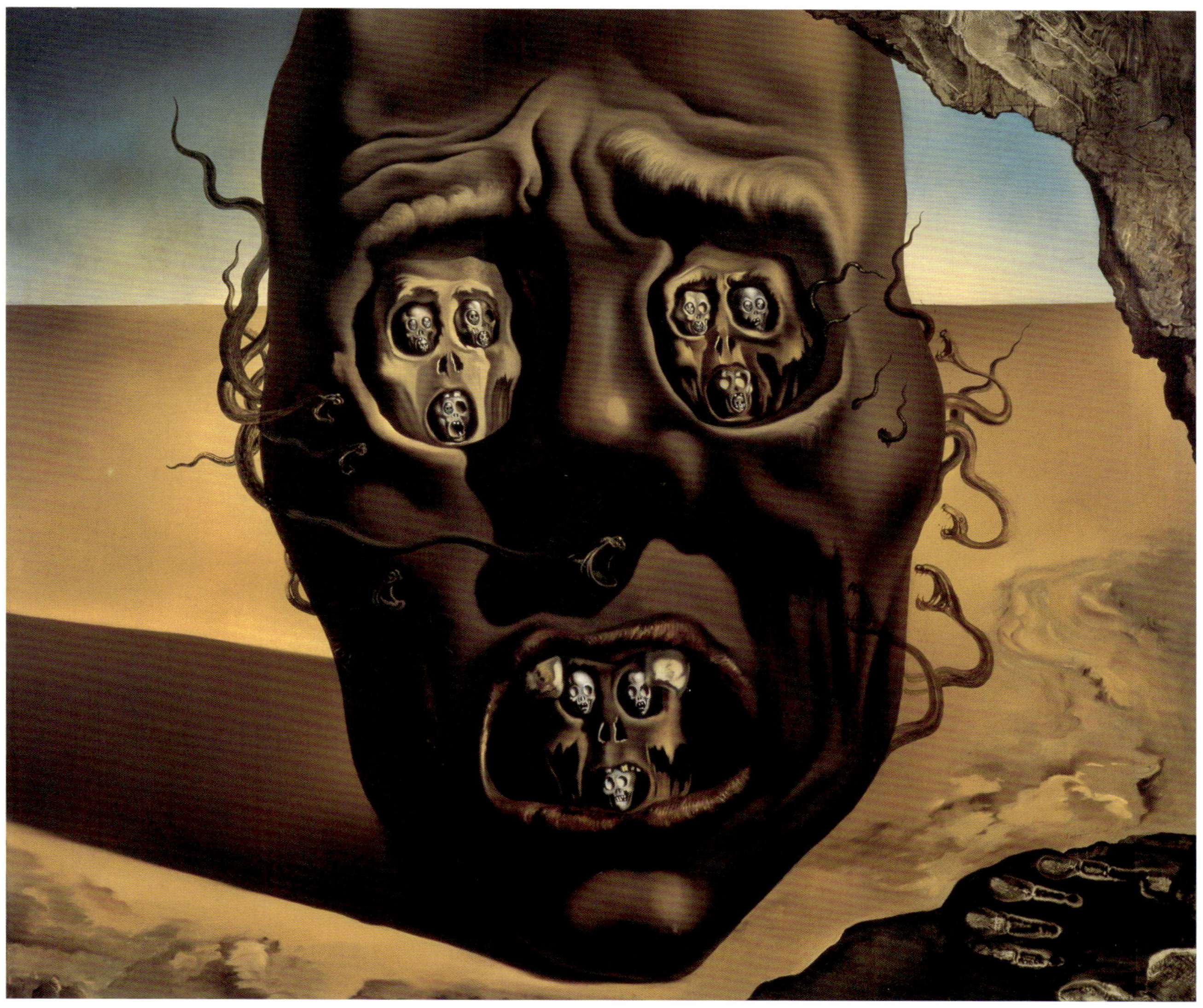

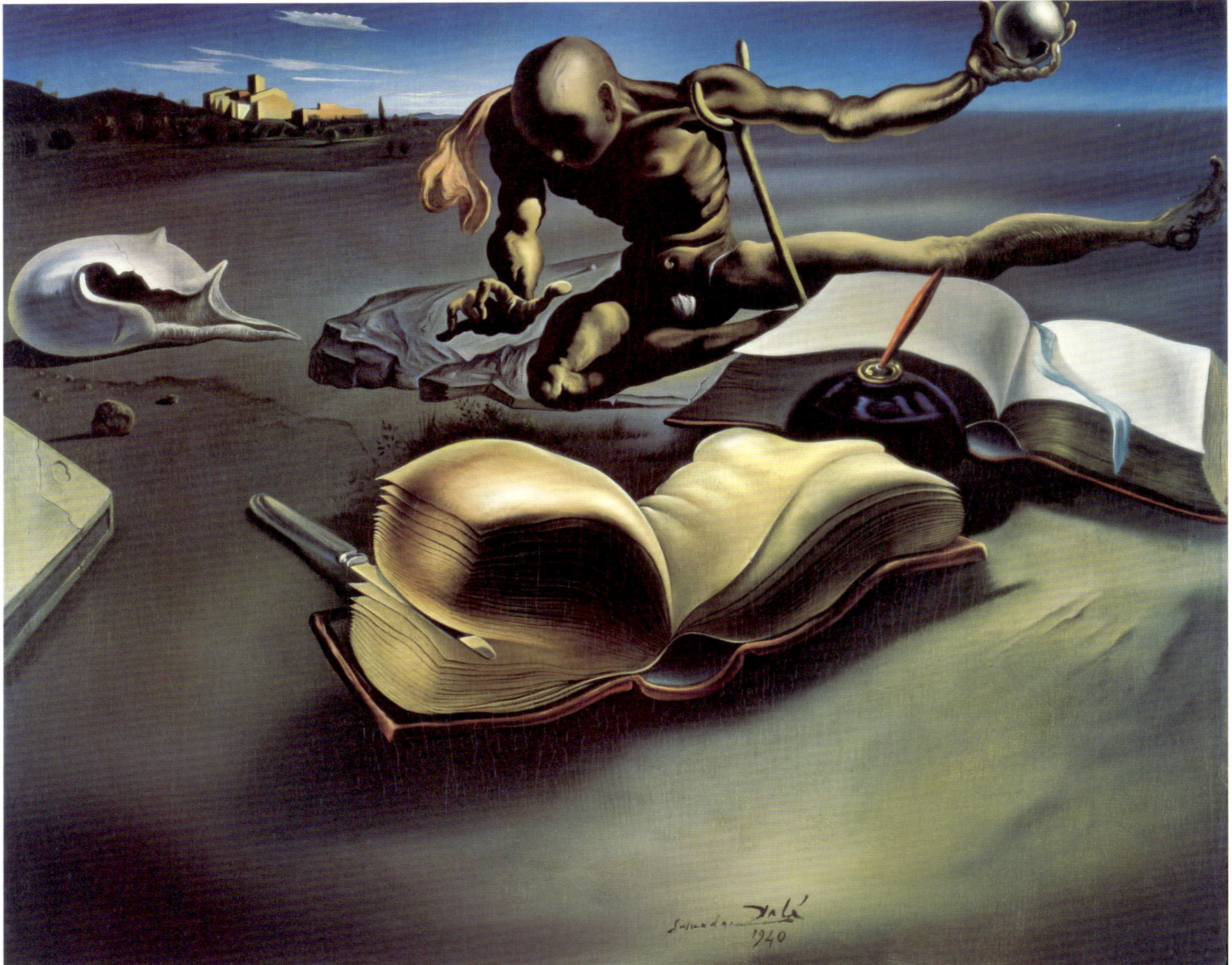

Twentieth Century Fox's decision not to use Dalí's ideas was more than a matter of art or social mores. During the month of December 1941, just after he had presented his scenario and sketches to the studio, Dalí's Fascist leanings came under attack in the American art press when American Social Surrealist Walter Quirt issued the leaflet *Wake Over Surrealism: With Due Respect to the Corpse*.[31] Although Dalí had signed various Surrealist manifestoes against colonialism and war in the 1930s, and painted several canvases related to the European political situation as late as 1940, when he began *Face of War*, a powerful indictment of war whose iconography he later may have considered using for *Moontide* (fig.103), his political affiliations were repeatedly questioned.[32] The 1941 debate would not have encouraged the Hollywood film industry to continue its association with him. Dalí's notoriety, as well as his admiration of popular culture and his willingness to subsume himself in a commercial group venture, was not enough, therefore, to guarantee success in Hollywood.

Notes

1
Dalí's experiences in Hollywood have been mentioned in recent publications on the artist and Surrealism, such as Fèlix Fanés, *Dalí: Mass Culture*, exh. cat., Fundació 'la Caixa', Barcelona 2004, pp.83–5, and Lewis Kachur, *Displaying the Marvelous: Marcel Duchamp, Salvador Dalí, and Surrealist Exhibition Installations*, Cambridge, Mass. 2001, pp.161–3. Brief discussions have also appeared in Susan Ehrlich (ed.), *Pacific Dreams: Currents of Surrealism and Fantasy in California Art, 1934–1957*, exh. cat., Los Angeles 1995; and Robert S. Lubar, 'Salvador Dalí in America: The Rise and Fall of an Arch-Surrealist', in Isabelle Dervaux et al., *Surrealism USA*, exh. cat., National Academy Museum, New York 2005, pp.20–9. The latter presents a largely negative opinion of Dalí's American experiences, especially his film work, declaring that the artist had 'sold out' with his commercialism.
I should like to acknowledge the help of Jenny Romero of the Academy of Motion Picture Arts and Sciences in my research for this publication.

2
Carey McWilliams, *Southern California: An Island on the Land*, New York 1946, and reprinted Salt Lake City 1973, p.330.

3
The Arensbergs were the first major American collectors of Dada and Surrealist art (they also bought Cubist and Pre-Columbian art). Their collection is now in the Philadelphia Museum of Art. See *The Louise and Walter Arensberg Collection*, Philadelphia 1954.

4
Feitelson was one of the leaders of modernism in Los Angeles from the late 1920s through the 1950s, first encouraging Surrealism then Hard-edge abstraction. See *Lorser Feitelson and Helen Lundeberg: A Retrospective Exhibition*, exh. cat., San Francisco Museum of Modern Art 1980.

5
Fischinger was one of the few who bridged the gap between the commercial and independent film worlds. He emigrated from Germany on receiving a studio contract with Paramount. For years he was best known for his contribution to Walt Disney's *Fantasia*. See William Moritz, *Optical Poetry: The Life and Work of Oskar Fischinger*, Eastleigh 2004, for a complete discussion of his films and paintings.

6
Salvador Dalí, 'Surrealism in Hollywood', trans. George Davis, *Harper's Bazaar*, June 1937, p.68 and republished in this volume.

7
Luis Buñuel, 'Buster Keaton's "College"', *Cahiers d'art*, no.10 (1927), trans. David Robinson, in Paul Hammond (ed.), *The Shadow and its Shadow: Surrealist Writings on Cinema*, London 1978, p.35; and Salvador Dalí, 'Film-arte, film-antiartistico', *Gaceta Literaria*, 15 Dec. 1927, no.24, 15 Dec. 1927, see translation by Haim Finkelstein, republished in this volume from Haim Finkelstein (ed.), *The Collected Writings of Salvador Dalí*, Cambridge 1998.

8
Julien Levy, *Surrealism*, New York 1936 and 1968.

9
Ingrid Schaffner, 'Alchemy of the Gallery', in *Julien Levy: Portrait of an Art Gallery*, Cambridge, Mass. 1998, pp.21, 36–7.

10
Levy 1968, p.65.

11
See Michael R. Taylor's essay in this volume.

12
Julien Levy to James Soby, 27 Oct. 1941, in Box 3, folder 16, no.910128, James Thrall Soby Papers, Special Collections, The Getty Research Institute, Los Angeles.

13
The details of the negotiations about Dalí's services and scheduling are recorded in contracts, letters and interoffice memos in the Twentieth Century Fox Archives. See Dalí file, Legal Department Records, Twentieth Century Fox Collection, Box FXLR 1264, Collection 95, on deposit University of California Los Angeles Art Special Collections. I should like to thank Lauren Buisson of the Arts Library Special Collections and David F. Miller of Twentieth Century Fox for their help.

14
Hollywood Reporter, 18 Nov. 1941, p.7.

15
Salvador Dalí, 'Jean Gabin's Nightmare for *Moontide*, for Twentieth-Century Fox Film Corporation, Beverly Hills, Hollywood', 4 November [1941], typescript, in English, Ms. 53, in Archives, Centro de Estudios Dalíanos, Fundació Gala-Salvador Dalí, Figueres. All versions, MSS 53–6, are in the Foundation archives; they are in both French and English. All future discussion in this essay of Dalí's dream sequence is based on this manuscript version.

16
George Wasson [Studio Counsel], typed letter to Dalzell Hatfield, 29 Oct. 1941, Legal Department Records, Twentieth Century Fox Collection, on deposit UCLA Special Art Collections.

17
Peter Bogdanovich, *Fritz Lang in America*, London 1967, pp.6–10.

18
Luis Buñuel, *Mon dernier soupir*, Paris 1982; trans. Abigail Israel as *My Last Breath*, London 1984, and *My Last Sigh*, New York 1984, p.92. Buñuel devotes an entire chapter of his autobiography to 'Dreams and Reveries'.

19
'Surrealism in Hollywood', republished in this volume.

20
Luis Buñuel, 'Notes on the Making of UN CHIEN ANDALOU', trans. Grace L. McCann Morley, in Frank Stauffacher (ed.), *Art in Cinema: A Symposium on the Avantgarde Film*, San Francisco 1947, p.29. Capitalisation is in original. Morley was director of the San Francisco Museum of Art, the sponsor of the film symposium.

21
'Program Note: Dreams that Money Can Buy', in Frank Stauffacher (ed.), *Art in Cinema: A Symposium on the Avantgarde Film*, pp.89–90.

22
David Lomas, 'Encyclopedia: Sigmund Freud', in Dawn Ades (ed.), *Dalí: The Centenary*, exh. cat., Palazzo Grassi, Venice and Philadelphia Museum of Art 2004, p.435.

23
Salvador Dalí, 'Jean Gabin's Nightmare …', p.1.

24
Memos from Dalzell Hatfield to Jason S. Joy, 3 Dec. 1941, typed, *Moontide* file, Legal Department Records, Collection 95, Twentieth Century Fox Collection, Box FXLR 325, on deposit UCLA Art Special Collections.

25
John Russell Taylor, *Strangers in Paradise: The Hollywood Emigres, 1933–1950*, New York 1983, pp.115–16.

26
Man Ray stated in a 1943 talk, 'the movies will become a great art one day', when film production 'will really be in the hands of one mastermind'. Quoted in Dickran Tashjian, 'Man Ray in Hollywood, 1940–1951', *Man Ray: Paris, LA*, Los Angeles 1996, p.83.

27
Items 4 and 10 of 15 Sept. 1941 agreement, Dalí file, Box FXLR 1264, Legal Department Records, Collection 95, Twentieth Century Fox Collection, on deposit UCLA Art Special Collections.

28
McWilliams 1973, pp.339, 341.

29
'War's Effect on Hollywood: Get out of the Dumps! Hollywood! Jump Out of It!', *Hollywood Reporter*, 9 Dec. 1941, pp.1, 5.

30
'Mayo Takes Lang's Meg on *Moontide*', *Hollywood Reporter*, 9 Dec. 1941, p.1.

31
Quirt first attacked Dalí in 1937 when they both participated in the symposium 'Surrealism and Its Political Significance' at the Museum of Modern Art in New York. The 1941 debate in the editorial column of *Art Digest* also involved the American Social Surrealist O. Louis Guglielmi. *Wake Over Surrealism: With Due Respect to the Corpse* was published by the Pinacotheca Gallery, New York. For a discussion of the controversy, see Ilene Susan Fort, 'American Social Surrealism', *Archives of American Art Journal*, vol.22, no.3, 1982, pp.17, 20, and notes 66–8.

32
Helena Lewis, *The Politics of Surrealism*, New York 1988, pp.92–5, 151–2.

Spellbound 1944

Sara Cochran

On 17 August 1944, Salvador Dalí signed a contract with Vanguard Films in Los Angeles to make designs for the film *Spellbound* – then called *The House of Dr Edwards*. The document stipulated that, for $4,000, Dalí would 'create, draw and paint all sketches and/or designs required in connection with the so-called "Dream Sequence" in the picture *The House of Dr Edwards* (four (4) paintings).'[1] The proposition was straightforward, but the fate of this sequence before the film's release in 1945 was not.

The film's director Alfred Hitchcock and its producer David O. Selznick were contemplating hiring Dalí by the time the script was finalised on 7 July 1944.[2] A year later, the artist reported: 'My movie agent and excellent friend, Fefe (Felix Ferry), ordered a nightmare from me by telephone. It was for the film *Spellbound*.'[3] Despite Dalí's levity, the negotiations were complicated. The studio appeared more interested in his notoriety than in his artistic contribution. On 6 July, Selznick explained in a memo: 'If we make a deal for the celebrated artist we have in mind … we should not let this leak out in publicity as I think we can get some sensational breaks on it.'[4] Almost two weeks later, he 'confidentially' named 'Dalí the famous painter' but was clearly worried about costs: 'The price we would have to pay would be considerably in excess of what it would be worth to us strictly for production purposes … We would make the deal with Dalí only if there is an important publicity value to be obtained.'[5] These concerns lessened when the studio assessed the commercial value of Dalí's name to be about $50,000 and that it would assure free coverage in national magazines, which had developed something of an obsession with him. It was noted, for instance, that Dalí had appeared in *Life* magazine six times over the previous twelve months.[6]

The Dalí name was indeed a bankable asset. The mid-August announcement of his hiring garnered an article in *Life* and four in the local press over the course of less than a month, and it is interesting that their readers were clearly familiar with Dalí's personality and work. The *Motion Picture Herald* joked about limp watches, and the *Hollywood Citizen News* made reference to ants.[7] The article in the *Los Angeles Times* highlighted the painter's jarring mixture of French and English, his love of strange juxtapositions and his droopy mustachios.[8] Adding to the coverage, Dalí stage-managed a minor controversy by stating that women inherently lacked artistic abilities.[9]

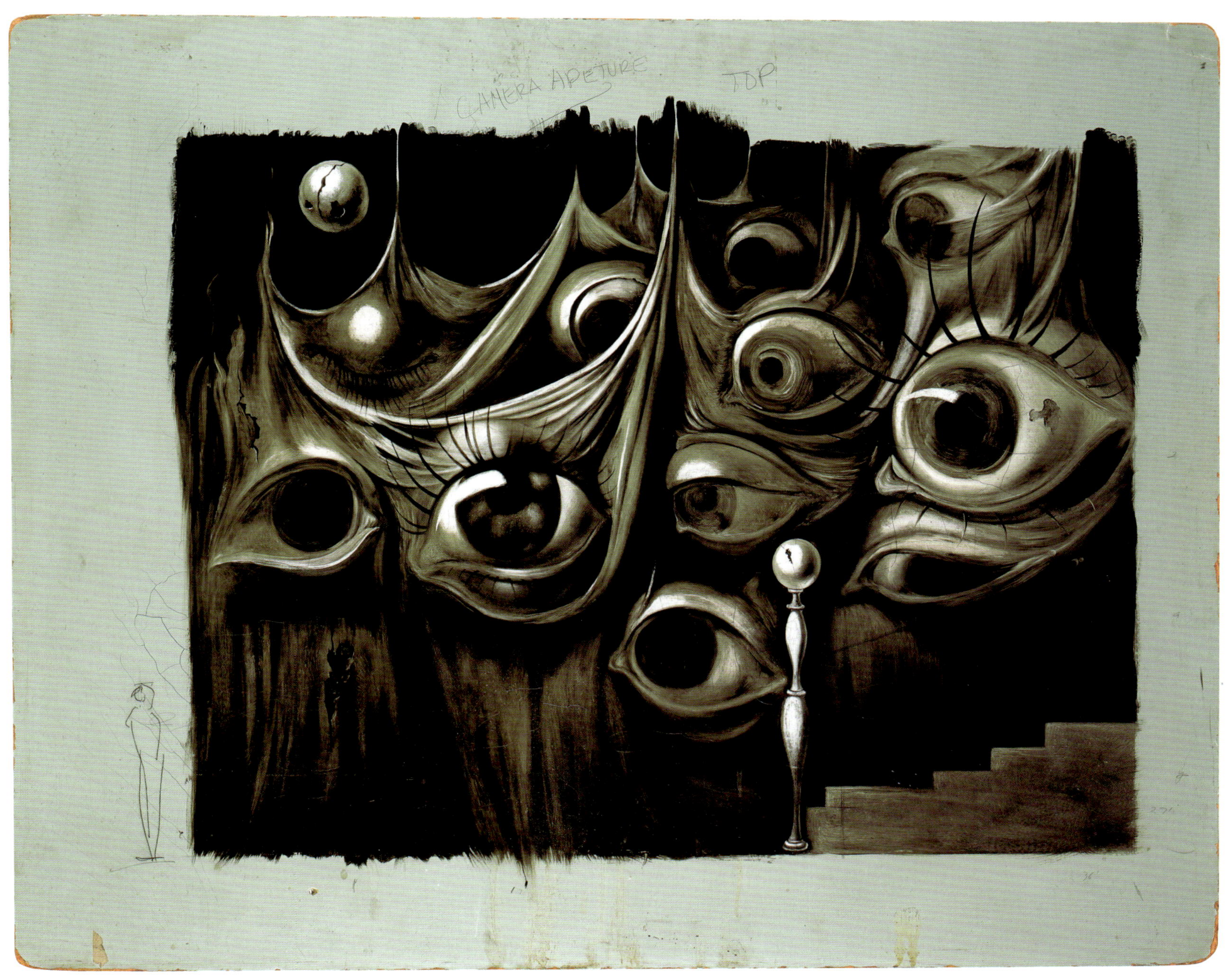

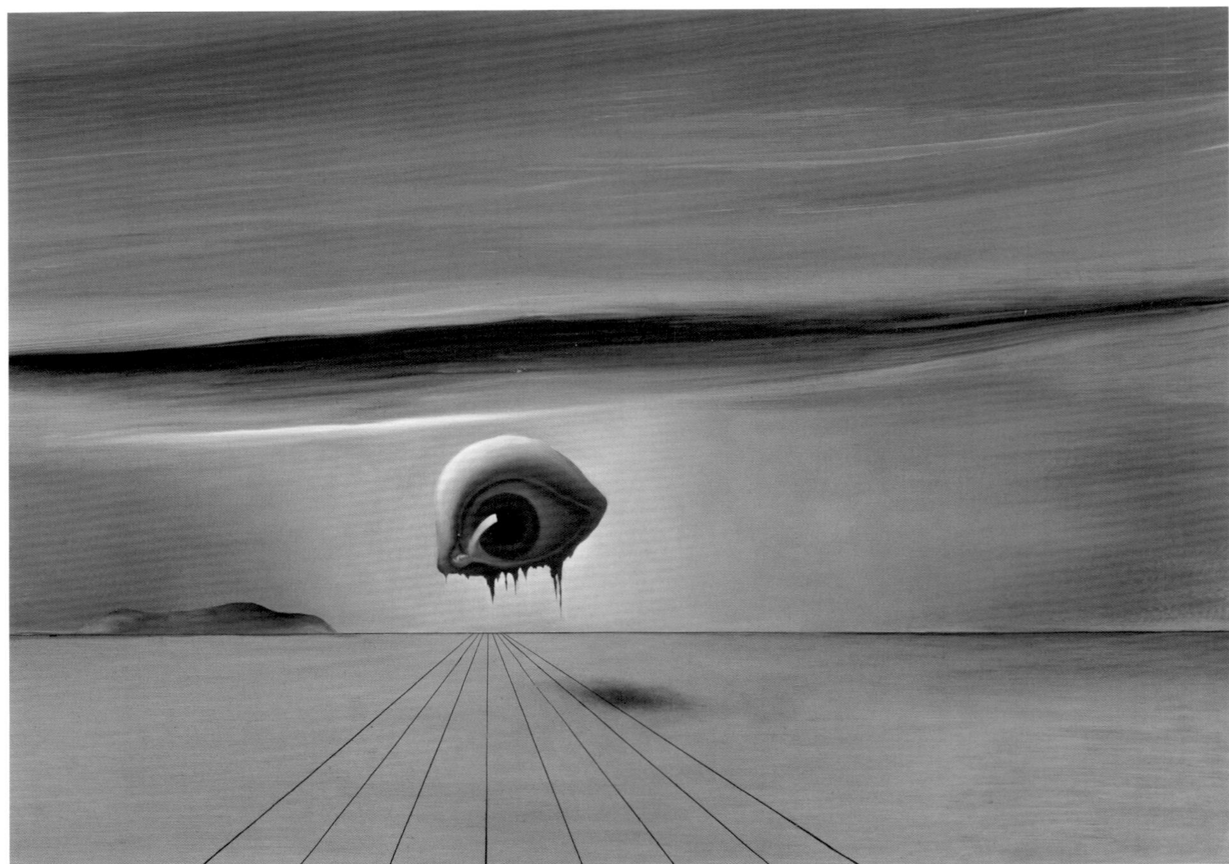

106
Study for the dream sequence in
Spellbound 1944
Oil on panel 58.7 x 84 cm
Private collection

Opposite:
107
Dalí supervising the making of the
drop curtain for *Spellbound*
Harry Ransom Humanities
Research Center, University of
Texas at Austin

Despite these publicity successes, Selznick bridled at the stipulation that Dalí was to retain ownership of all his sketches and paintings:

I think the Dalí deal is absurd, that we have been jockeyed into a silly position and that this is probably the first time in History that an artist has been paid more than top price for his work in order for him to keep his work … none of Dalí's work, or very, very little of it, will remain in the finished picture and it is my fear that he will only lead us astray and into a lot of expense over and above what he gets for film that will wind up on the cutting room floor.[10]

This was Dalí's *modus operandi.* As Felix Ferry explained to Selznick, the artist always kept his theatre or ballet works because even sketches had such great commercial value.[11] More importantly, although Selznick probably did not know it, Dalí's 1941 contract with Twentieth Century Fox for the nightmare sequence in *Moontide* had granted him full ownership of all that he produced.[12] Ultimately, Vanguard Films and Dalí would compromise: they agreed to divide the works equally, with the studio making the first choice.[13]

Spellbound is premised on the idea that a repressed experience can directly trigger a neurosis.

Although its approach now appears dated, it was then considered an ambitious exploration of Freudian analysis and was nominated for the 'Best Picture' Academy Award. Selznick had undergone psychoanalysis himself, and he hired a therapist, Dr May E. Romm, as a technical advisor. The film's 'scientific' character was actively promoted. On-set publicity shots of the director and stars – including Dalí – were sent to the press with the explanation that a dream sequence 'analysed according to Sigmund Freud's *Interpretation of Dreams*' contained all the clues to the film's mysteries.[14] In addition, a solemn announcement opened the film: 'Our story deals with psychoanalysis, the method by which modern science treats the emotional problems of the sane.'

The story begins in a psychiatric asylum, where the brilliant Dr Constance Peterson (Ingrid Bergman) works with the retiring director Dr Murchison (Leo G. Carroll). However, upon the arrival of the new director, Dr Edwards (Gregory Peck), it is apparent that all is not well: he becomes catatonic whenever he happens to see parallel lines on a white background. Although she quickly realises that he is an imposter, Peterson falls in love with this lost man and helps him to discover that

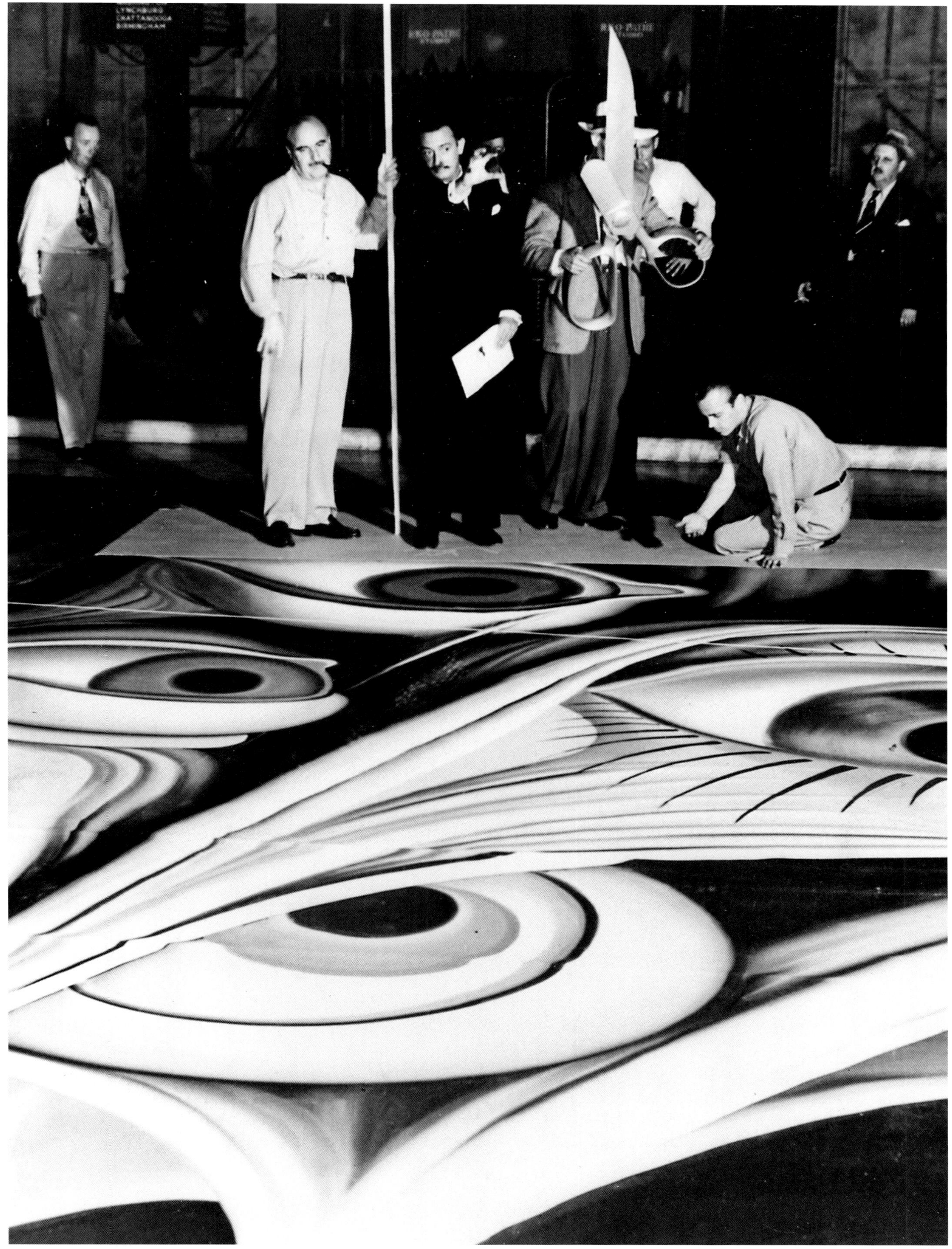

he is John Ballentine, an amnesic and the possible murderer of the missing Dr Edwards. The couple seek refuge with Peterson's former professor, Dr Alex Brulov (Michael Chekhov), and use the elements of Ballentine's dream to unravel the mysterious death of Dr Edwards, unlock the trauma of Ballentine's childhood, cure his neurosis and clear his name by proving the guilt of Dr Murchison.

Almost twenty years later, Hitchcock told François Truffaut that it was 'just another manhunt story wrapped up in pseudo-psychoanalysis'. Since Hitchcock was instrumental in shaping the project, this account was perhaps disingenuous. He had owned the rights to the novel, which he sold to the studio,[15] and wrote to the author of the first script, Angus McPhail, to explain the changes they were making in the second version.[16] *Spellbound* was also Hitchcock's first exploration of the psychotic or neurotic repercussions of a psychological shock, a subject that later inspired *Vertigo* 1960, *Psycho* 1960 and *Marnie* 1964. Finally, it was Hitchcock who wanted to work with Dalí (fig.150). In a later television interview, he explained:

I requested Dalí. Selznick, the producer, had the impression that I wanted Dalí for the publicity value. That wasn't it at all. What I was after was … the vividness of dreams … [A]ll Dalí's work is very solid and very sharp, with very long perspectives and black shadows. Actually I wanted the dream sequence[s] to be shot on the back lot, not in the studio at all. I wanted them shot in the bright sunshine. So the cameraman would be forced to do what we call stop it out and get a very hard image. This was again the avoidance of the cliché. All dreams in the movies are blurred. It isn't true. Dalí was the best man for me to do the dreams because that is what dreams should be.[17]

In contrast to the standard, vaporous dreams, then, Hitchcock wanted a heightened contrast that would give his sequence a sharper focus than the rest of the film – almost ironic ultra-realism.[18] The film's budget curtailed these aspirations. Selznick preferred to use only miniatures and painted backdrops,[19] and hoped that this effect could be achieved on a sound stage. However, art director James Basevi advised him that instead of being luminous, the effect would be merely photographic.[20]

Discussions between Dalí and Hitchcock began in early August 1944, more than two weeks before the artist signed his contract.[21] The two men got on well, and Dalí recalled: 'Hitchcock is one

of the rare personages I have met lately who has some mystery.'[22] As described in the final script, Ballentine's dream was set in four very different locations: 1) a gambling house in which Ballentine plays cards with the bearded man (a cipher for Dr Edwards) and meets the angry, faceless proprietor (a stand-in for Dr Murchison), who accuses the bearded man of cheating with blank cards; 2) a high, sloping roof, off which the bearded man falls as the faceless proprietor appears from behind the chimney holding a small wheel; 3) a ballroom in which Ballentine dances with Peterson and kisses her before she turns into a statue; 4) a huge slope down which Ballentine tries to escape from the beating wings of a flying statue.[23] Drawing on his discussions with Hitchcock, Dalí completed four grey-tone paintings and one in colour. He made two designs featuring eyes for the gambling house scene: the first, with many eyes (fig.105), is cut in half to reveal the second colour image of a single eye, set within a receding perspective (fig.106). He also made a strange landscape with a high rooftop and chimney (fig.116); a barren landscape for a new scene set in a 'weird and desolate place' that, initially, included a desk at which Peterson was seated (fig.109); and an image of two abutting pyramids, down which Ballentine escaped and which are overshadowed by an enormous pair of pliers (figs.108, 110). Each of these paintings served as a backdrop for the different scenes. There was no backdrop for the ballroom scene. It was to be filmed on a set, and the scene in a 'weird and desolate place' was added as a transition to Ballentine's flight down the slope.

In the finished film, the dream sequence was reduced to three scenes: the gambling house, the roof top, and the slope. The ballroom and the bridging element were cut. The gambling scene most closely follows the original dream sequence in the script, with one element immediately standing out: a pair of oversized scissors cutting through an eye painted on to the curtain. Any viewer with a passing knowledge of cinema or of Surrealism would have recognised the reference to the shocking scene of the razor slicing through a woman's eye in Dalí's previous collaboration with Buñuel, *Un Chien andalou*. This allusion is further emphasised by the fact that before the dream sequence, Ballentine, in a trance, walks out of a white bathroom holding a razor in his hand, evoking Buñuel on the moonlit balcony in the earlier film. However, the cutting of the eye on the curtain was described in the script and actually pre-

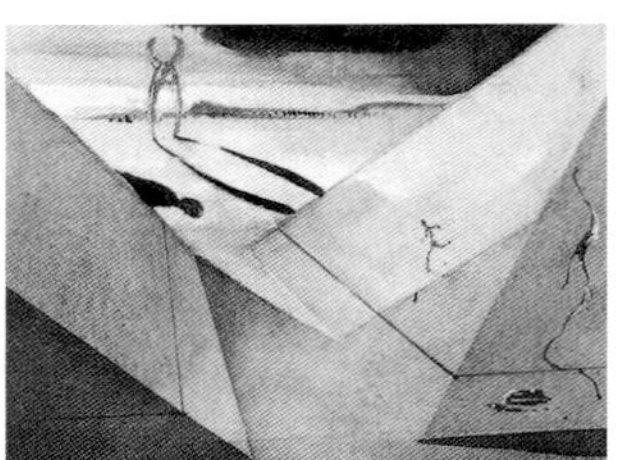

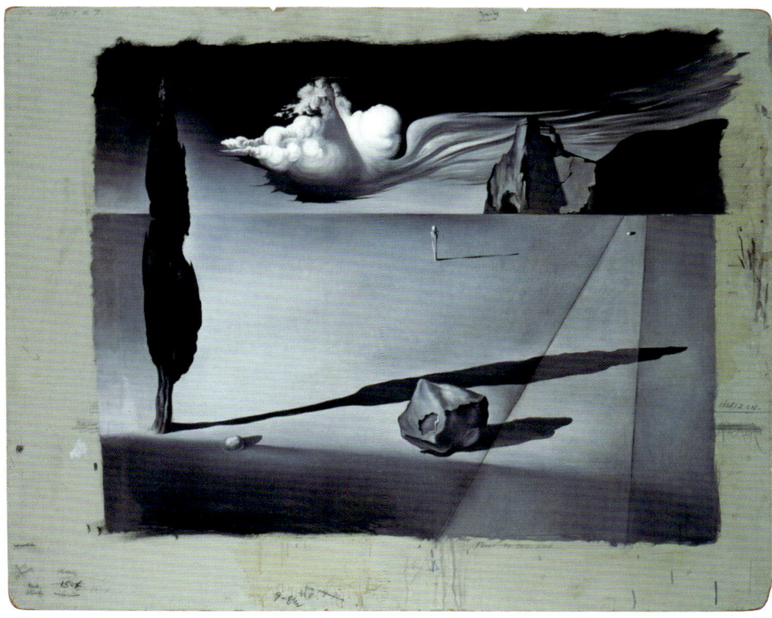

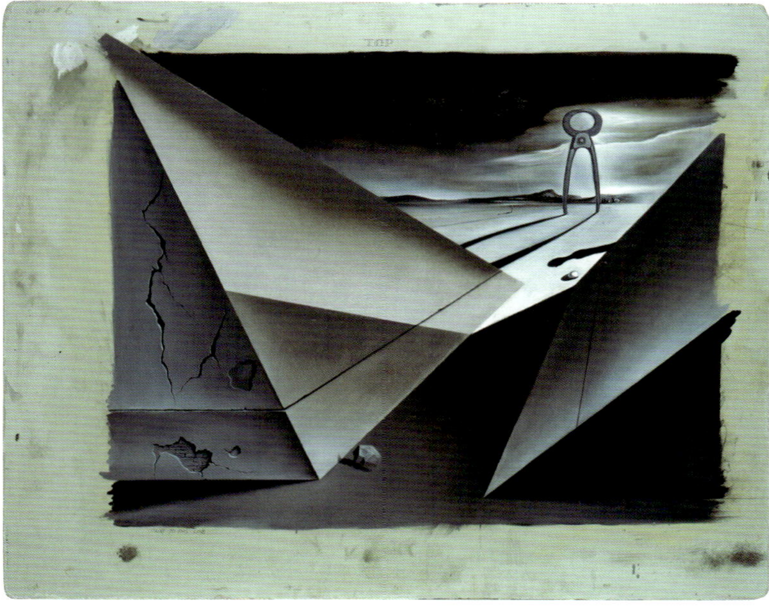

dated Dalí's involvement. This is a testament to the widespread influence of *Un Chien andalou*, seen, for example, in the 1937 short film *Even – As You and I* by Roger Barlow, Harry Hay and LeRoy Robbins.[24]

Dalí's major contribution was to create the scene's disquieting atmosphere. He painted the two backdrops with eyes, and was photographed tracing the scissors' path through the curtain that had been professionally reproduced by the local billboard painters Grosh Scenic Studio (fig.107). His revealing costume (a ripped Dior negligée) for the so-called 'kissing bug' (Rhonda Fleming), who ran around kissing the men in the gambling house, fell foul of the censors.[25] Dalí also designed the tables and chairs with plaster legs shaped to look like woman's legs in stockings and high heels that paid homage to Kurt Seligmann's 1938 *Ultra-Furniture*. Other Surrealist references include a balustrade for the stairway that resembles the 'bilboquet' in Magritte's early paintings, like *Annunciation* 1928, and metronomes with eyes that cite Man Ray's 1932 *Object to be Destroyed*. Even the masked proprietor recalls the faceless men and women who inhabit Man Ray's 1929 film *Les Mystères du château du dé*. However, it is hard to know if Dalí included these elements as a homage or parody of the originals.

In the other two scenes, Dalí's creative influence resided principally in his paintings. These were used as backdrops for the actors, who were filmed against blue screens. However, there is one interesting detail in the scene in which the bearded man falls from the high roof: the script called for the angry proprietor to emerge from behind the chimney carrying a small wheel – a emblem for the revolver with which Dr Murchison kills the real Dr Edwards. The wheel is round in the drawings for the re-shooting of the scene made after Dalí left, but in the final film it is distorted into an uneven oval shape that resembles the melting watches in *The Persistence of Memory* 1931 (fig.74). Again, it appears that this allusion did not come from Dalí, suggesting that Hollywood was entirely familiar with his imagery.

The painter had hoped to make more of a mark on *Spellbound*. He had proposed sticking the image of an eye on the backs of cockroaches running across the bearded man's blank cards. He also hoped to include some of his trademark ants in the scene where Bergman turned into a statue (figs.113, 114), but, as the *Hollywood Citizen News* reported: 'It'll be a plain statute without ants: Dalí wanted 'em. Miss Bergman proved non-cooperative.'[26]

111
Dalí on the set of *Spellbound*
1944
Harry Ransom Humanities
Research Center, University
of Texas at Austin

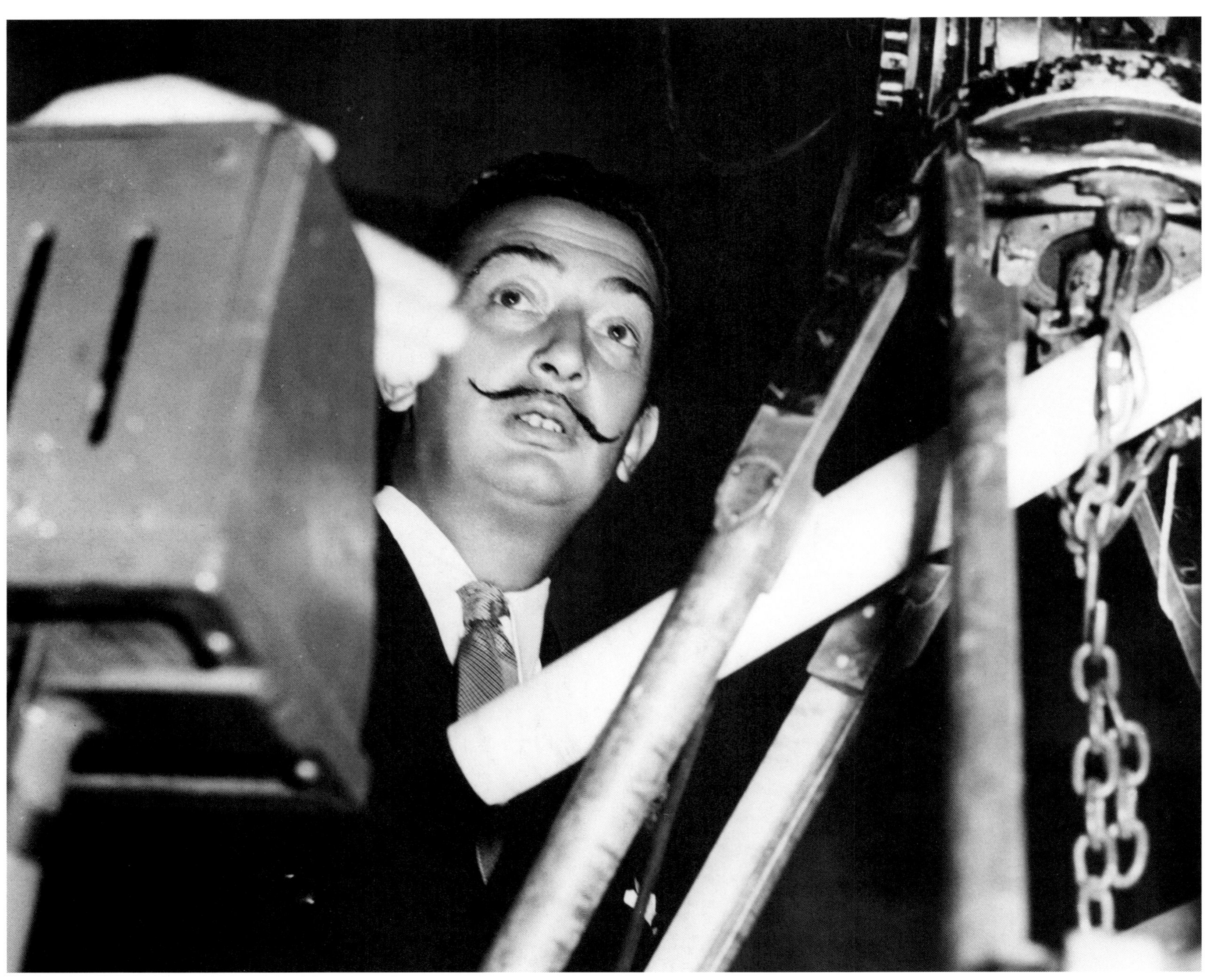

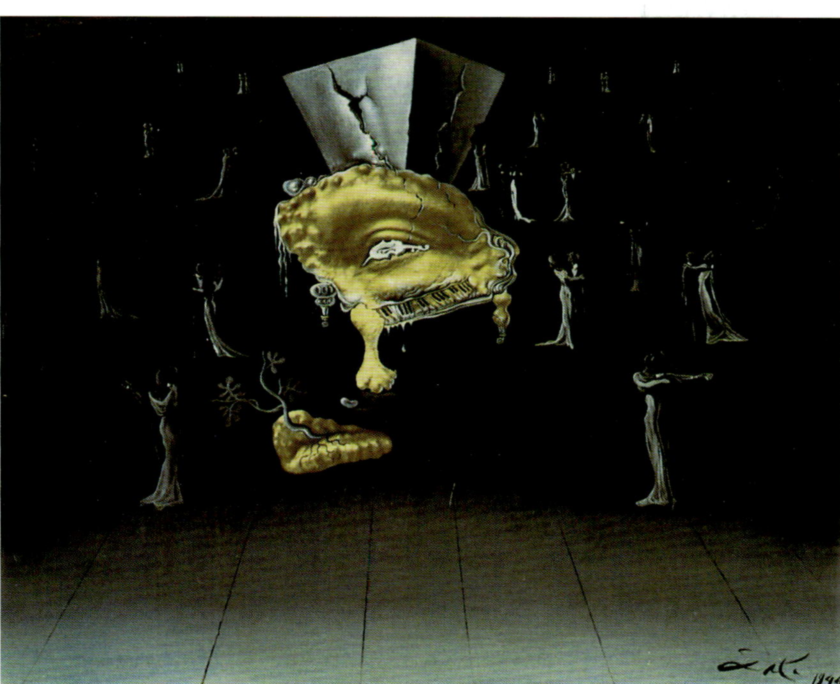

Had it survived, Dalí's great contribution to the film would have been the ballroom scene (fig.112). Though exaggerating the time-span, Bergman recalled:

It was a wonderful, twenty-minute sequence that really belonged in a museum. The idea for a major part of it was that I would become, in Gregory Peck's mind, a statue. To do this, we shot the film in the reverse way in which it would appear on the screen … I was dressed in a draped, Grecian gown, with a crown on my head and an arrow through my neck.[27]

The statue was made by the studio, and existing photographs document a room full of dancers under a suspended orchestra and the breaking of the plaster cast with Bergman behind. Writing in *Dalí News* a year later, the artist explained:

In order to create this impression [of oppressiveness and unease], I will have to hang fifteen of the heaviest and most lavish pianos possible from the ceiling of the ballroom, swinging very low over the heads of dancers. These would be in exalted dance poses, but they would not move at all, they would only be diminishing silhouettes in very accelerated perspective, losing themselves in infinite darkness.[28]

Selznick, who was worried about costs, decided to make miniature pianos and suspend them from the ceiling. To correct the consequent problems of perspective, the studio employed forty dwarfs to dance in the scene. Dalí was devastated:

The [miniature] pianos didn't at all give the impression of real pianos suspended from ropes ready to crack and casting sinister shadows on the ground … and the dwarfs, one saw, simply, that they were dwarfs. Neither Hitchcock nor I liked the result and we decided to eliminate this scene. In truth the imagination of Hollywood experts will be the one thing that will ever have surpassed me.[29]

On 8 September 1944 it was determined that if a close up of Gregory Peck was added to the footage already shot for the dream sequence, the filmed images would match the length of the narration of the dream itself and the scene would be complete.[30] Four days later, Hitchcock stated his satisfaction with all Dalí's work and, after a little over a month at the studio, he was paid his fee in full.[31] He and Gala left for Pebble Beach before travelling east to New York. Filming ended soon afterwards, and Hitchcock also left Los Angeles for New York. This left Selznick to edit the film. However, as he reviewed the footage, certain problems became evident, especially with the dream sequence. By 25 October Selznick was forced to admit:

It's not Dalí's fault, for his work is much finer and much better for the purpose than I ever thought it would be.

It is the photography, set-ups, lighting, etc., all of which is completely lacking in imagination and all of which is about what you would expect from [the production company] Monogram.[32]

At this point, Selznick enlisted the legendary art director William Cameron Menzies (with whom he had worked on *Gone with the Wind*) to reorganise the dream sequence, match the footage they could use and reshoot scenes as necessary.

By December, Menzies had mapped out a new version of the dream sequence, and his plans were sent to Hitchcock and Dalí, who were both staying at the St Regis Hotel in New York. Through Ferry, the artist expressed a desire to be further involved:

[Dalí] is anxious to see [the plans] as he would like to submit any suggestions in case he thought that would improve them. Some more drawing could be submitted for which there would be no extra charge. I want you to realize how anxious he is that his first American picture should be perfection. He is so anxious that the entire work have the usual Dalí quality.[33]

Selznick expressed interest in this surprising offer from 'Avida Dollars' (André Breton's nickname for the avaricious painter), but the studio did not want to expend any more time or money, keen to release the film on its given date. By February 1945, Selznick was resigned to finishing the film and expressed no surprise when Menzies declined a credit for his work.[34] The film was released with only Basevi (who had also worked as the art director for *Moontide*) named as art director, and the dream sequence described as 'based upon the designs by Salvador Dalí'.[35]

Despite all of its travails, *Spellbound* was favourably received in the press. However, not everyone was so kind. In Paris, the former Dadaist Georges Ribemont-Dessaignes wrote in 1946: 'For sometime now Dalí appears to have downgraded the Surrealist doctrine to the level of fashion; he is now employed in Hollywood, but all he is doing is holding an everything-must-go Surrealist rummage sale.'[36] Interested in images and their influence, however, Dalí recognised cinema as a potent (and potentially very lucrative) conduit to the masses. In criticising Dalí's work on *Spellbound*, Ribemont-Dessaignes forgot the Surrealists' interest in cinema as a free-form experience, entered at any time and left as soon as they were bored.[37] This fragmented approach mirrors Dalí's vision of the dream sequence as a series

113
Scene deleted from *Spellbound* 1944
Harry Ransom Humanities Research Center, Univeristy of Texas at Austin

114
Ingrid Bergman in costume for the deleted dream sequence for *Spellbound* 1944
Harry Ransom Humanities Research Center, University of Texas at Austin

115
Dream Caused by the Flight of a Bee around a Pomegranate, a Second before Awakening 1944
Oil on panel 51 x 41 cm
Museo Thyssen-Bornemisza, Madrid

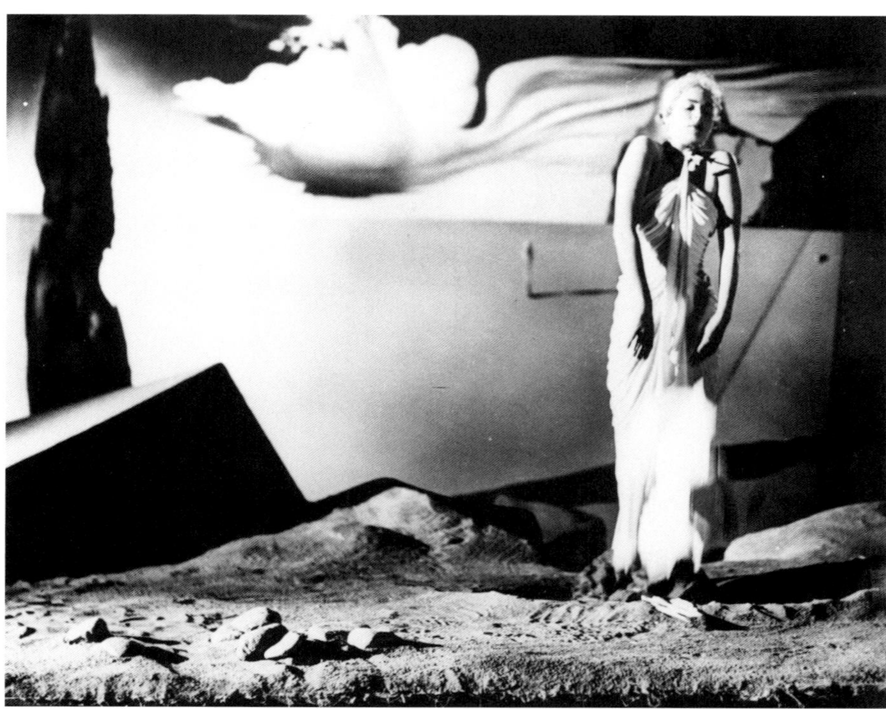

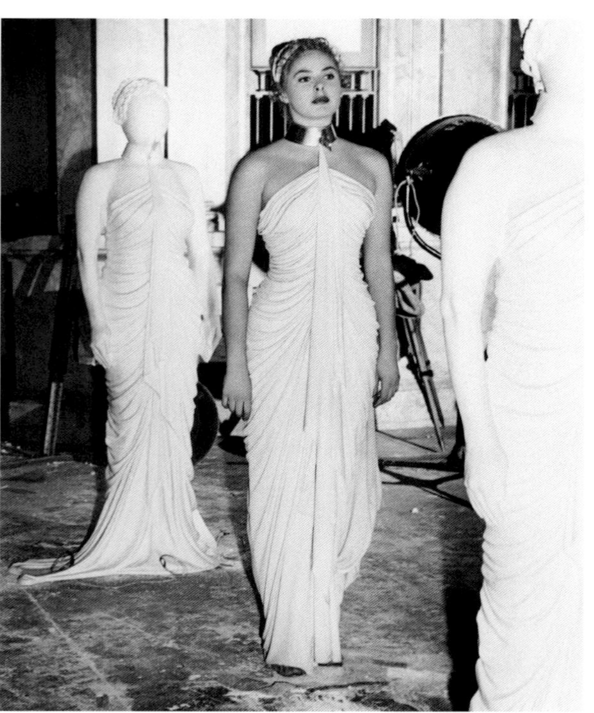

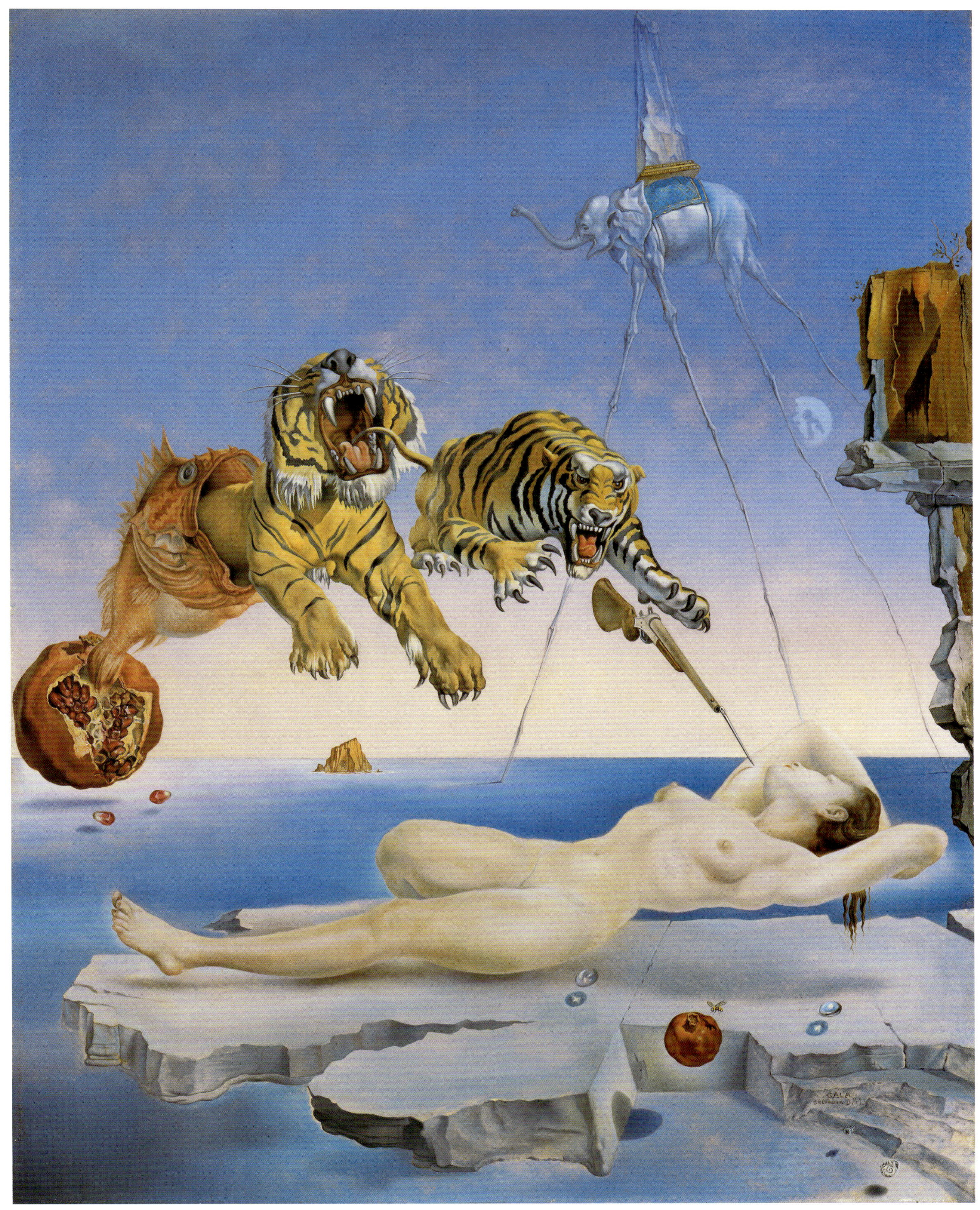

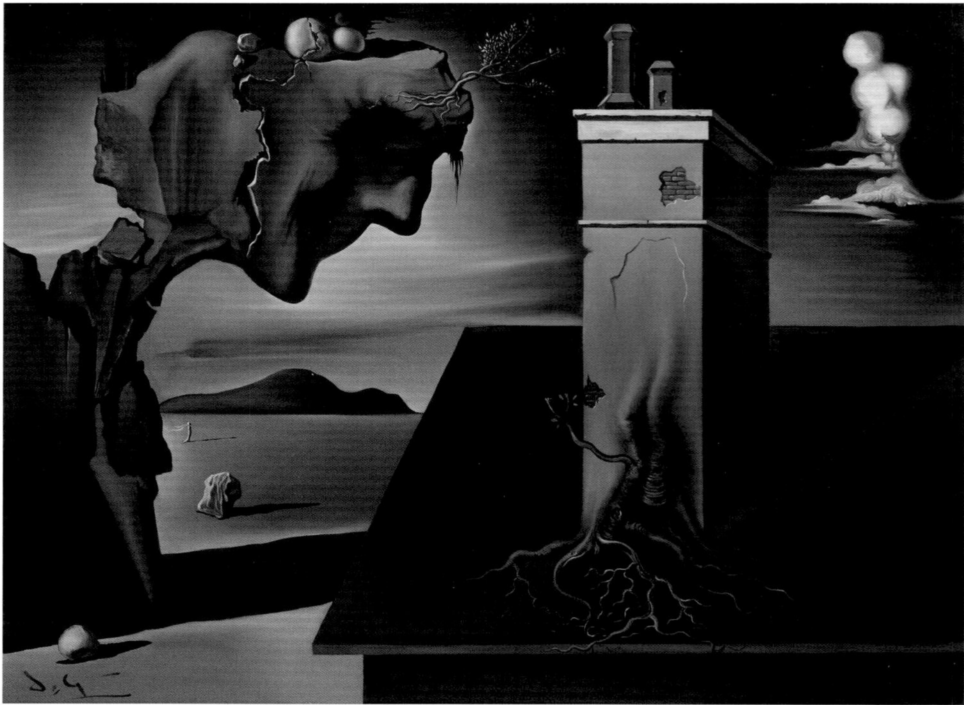

116
Spellbound
Oil on panel 73 x 92 cm
Private collection

of spectacular images that marked a pause in the film, allowing confusion and the irrational to dominate, if only for a brief moment.

However, Dalí's dalliance with celluloid dreams was a golden cage. In 1950, his name surfaced again in Hollywood in connection with the MGM domestic comedy, Vincente Minnelli's *Father of the Bride*. The film contains one moment of fantasy. The night before the wedding, the father (Spencer Tracy) of the bride (Elizabeth Taylor) dreams that a cluster of disembodied eyes watches him as he walks down the aisle. The floor turns soft and drags him down, ripping his clothes, pulling off his trousers and rendering him an abject, crawling mess who makes his daughter scream in horror and shame. In its humour and pathos, this scene recalls the moment in *Un Chien andalou* in which the protagonist struggles across an apartment, pulling an assemblage of objects including two bound priests and two grand pianos topped with dead donkeys. However, Dalí was not directly involved in *Father of the Bride*. Rather, it seems that Hollywood had assimilated his aesthetic and imagery, which MGM felt no shame in reproducing without involving the artist.

The Hollywood studios certainly appreciated the unpredictability and sense of danger associated with Dalí's name. Regardless of Hitchcock's ideas, Selznick had ultimately hired Dalí for *Spellbound* because of his shock – and therefore commercial – value. Assessing this, one early memo joked about the striking contrast between the libidinous artist and the decorous Bergman:

I am not certain that Dalí's Phallic frescoes would be a nice juxtaposition with our Christmas tree, Miss Bergman. We would, of course, get kicks against the pricks from the Holy Men, who are undoubtedly convinced by now that Dalí is a very unsavoury character.[38]

But the studio also feared Dalí's volatile qualities. The publicity photographs of Dalí for *Spellbound* vacillated between portraying the painter as mad genius and as obsessive craftsman. In the end, he must have been frustrated by his involvement. Perhaps the handsome pay cheque made up for it, but if Hollywood had a place for his creativity, it was a marginal one: the space of fantasy and nightmares.[39] In this way, Dalí's irrationality was kept firmly in check by a dream factory aware that its business relied on a delicate balance between reality and fantasy.

Notes

1
File: Spellbound, Salvador Dalí – Contracts and Correspondence, Selz 864.15. David O. Selznick Archive, Harry Ransom Center, The University of Texas at Austin, hereafter cited as Selznick Archive. I should like to thank Steve Wilson of the Harry Ransom Center for his help.

2
After the success of their first collaboration, *Rebecca* 1940, it was Selznick who had brought Hitchcock to Hollywood and put him under contact with the studio.

3
Dalí's shameless self-promotional publication *Dalí News*, 20 Nov. 1945, p.2.

4
Memo from Selznick to King (cc. Hitchcock and Daniel O'Shea) dated 6 July 1944 (dictated 5 July 1944) File: Spellbound Sequences, Selz 230.14, Selznick Archive.

5
Memo from Selznick to King (cc. O'Shea) dated 18 July 1944 (dictated 17 July 1944). File: Spellbound Sequences, Selznick 230.14, Selznick Archive.

6
Memo from Cameron Shipp (Public Relations) to Daniel O'Shea dated 19 Aug. 1944 in response to Selznick's request for an opinion about the commercial value of Dalí. File: Spellbound Production, Selz 611.14, Selznick Archive.

7
Unsigned notice in the column 'Art Director', *Motion Picture Herald*, 19 Aug. 1944, p.144 and Frederick C. Othman 'About Dreams: Especially in Technicolor', *Hollywood Citizen News*, 28 Aug. 1944.

8
Philip K. Scheuer, 'Dalí Now Dreams for Movie', *Los Angeles Times*, 10 Sept. 1944.

9
'Novelist Flays Dalí's Charge', *Hollywood Citizen News*, 6 Sept. 1944.

10
Memo from Selznick to Daniel O'Shea, dated 4 Aug. 1944. File: Spellbound Production, Selznick 611.14, Selznick Archive.

11
Letter Ferry to Selznick, dated 2 Aug. 1944. File: Spellbound Sequence, Selznick 230.14, Selznick Archive. Herbert Cerwin, who worked with Dalí at the Del Monte Hotel in Pebble Beach on the organisation of Dalí's 1941 party 'Surrealism Night in an Enchanted Forest', held Gala responsible for Dalí's greedy control of his work: 'When we were sitting at the dinner table and Dalí was talking, he occasionally would draw a sketch to illustrate a point he was making; Gala would always destroy these drawings or drop them in her purse.' Herbert Cerwin, *In Search of Something: The Memoirs of a Public Relation Man*, Los Angeles 1966, p.159.

12
Twentieth Century Fox interoffice memo from George Wasson to Jason S. Jay, dated 15 Sept. 1941. Box: FXLR 1264, Salvador Dalí File – 4725, Twentieth Century Fox Archive, Special Collections, University of California, Los Angeles. I should like to thank Lauren Buisson of the Arts Library Special Collections for her help.

13
Letter of agreement from Vanguard to Salvador Dalí, c/o Hayward-Deverich Agency, 9200 Wilshire Blvd, Beverly Hills. File: Spellbound Production, Selz 611.14.

14
File: Selznick 4582.44/ SHEX 275.

15
Contract between Hitchcock and Vanguard Films for a nominal $1, dated 17 July 1944. Alfred Hitchcock Collection, Folder 651 – Spellbound (misc.), Special Collections, Academy of Motion Picture Arts and Sciences. I should like to acknowledge the help of Jenny Romero of the Academy.

16
Undated draft of a telegram from Hitchcock to Angus McPhail in London. Alfred Hitchcock Collection, Folder 651. Academy of Motion Picture Arts and Sciences, Special Collections.

17
Film Profiles: Alfred Hitchcock, undated interview by Philip Jenkinson for BBC TV, cited in Nathalie Bondol-Poupard, 'Such Stuff as Dreams Are Made On: Hitchcock and Dalí, Surrealism and Oneiricism', in Guy Cogeval and Dominique Paint (eds.), *Hitchcock and Art: Fatal Coincidences*, exh. cat., Montreal Museum of Fine Arts 2000, p.156.

18
He may have wanted an affect like that achieved in the films of avant-garde cinematographer and choreographer Maya Deren, such as in her 1943 *Meshes of the Afternoon*.

19
He had stated this in a memo as early as 7 July 1944. File: Spellbound Sequence, Selz 230.14, Selznick Archive.

20
Selznick memo to Basevi, 21 Nov. 1941; Basevi to Selznick Eight days later. File: Spellbound Sequence, Selz 230.14, Selznick Archive.

21
Letter from Ferry to Selznick, dated 2 Aug. 1944. File: Spellbound Sequences, Selz 230.14, Selznick Archive.

22
Dalí News, 20 Nov. 1945, p.2.

23
The script was originally dated 29 June 1944, but it was finalised on 7 July. File: Selznick 511.5, Selznick Archive. A first version of the script (File: Selznick 510.14, Selznick Archive) had been submitted a few months earlier on 3 April 1944. These first and second versions differ greatly. The first version describes Ballentine fighting in a Japanese play before the sets fall down. Then, a dog howls and a woman comes on stage. He is frightened and tries to flee, but the woman says he will never get away because they have recorded everything.

24
Directed by and starring Roger Barlow (later known as a cinematographer in Hollywood in the 1960s), Harry Hay (better known as a major gay rights advocate in the United States after the Second World War) and LeRoy Robbins (a well known sound designer in Hollywood the 1960s and 1970s), this 12 minute, silent comedy was not publicly released until its inclusion the 2005 Kino Video double DVD set, *Avant Garde: Experimental Cinema of the 1920s & 1930s*.

25
In his illustrated essay *A Nightmare Ordered by Telephone* that is included on the 2002 Criterion DVD of *Spellbound*, James Bigwood stated that the censors asked for Fleming's midriff, left thigh and breasts to be further covered.

26
Othman 1944.

27
Donald Spoto, *The Art of Alfred Hitchcock: Fifty Years of his Motion Pictures*, New York 1976, p.158

28
Dalí News, 20 Nov. 1945.

29
Ibid.

30
Memo from Johnson to Kern. File: Spellbound Sequences, Selz 230.14, Selznick Archive.

31
Memo from Johnson to the studio's financial department, requesting Dalí's payment. File: Spellbound Production, Selz 611.14, Selznick Archive.

32
Memo from Selznick to O'Shea. File: Spellbound Sequences, Selz 230.14, Selznick Archive.

33
Letter from Ferry to Selznick dated 19 Dec. 1944. Spellbound Sequence, Selz 230.14, Selznick Archive.

34
Memo from Selznick to Dann dated 14 Feb. 1945. Spellbound SHEX 2001-210, Selznick 4265.8, Selznick Archive.

35
For *Moontide* see Ilene Susan Fort's essay in this volume.

36
Translated and cited in Bondol-Poupard 2000, p.166.

37
See Matthew Gale's essay 'In Darkened Rooms' in this volume.

38
Memo from Cameron Shipp to Daniel O'Shea dated 19 Aug. 1944. Spellbound Production, Selznick 611.14. Selznick Archive.

39
In the 2006 book *Exquisite Corpse: Surrealism and the Black Dahlia Murder*, Mark Nelson and Sarah Hudson Bayliss argue that this space could not contain him. They make a compelling visual argument that the inherent violence and eroticism of Dalí and Surrealism influenced the bizarre and gruesome murder of the young starlet Elizabeth Short in Los Angeles in 1947. The authors speculate that the crime was a deconstructed version of one of the Surrealist's favourite games: the exquisite corpse.

117
Study for the Walt Disney
film *Destino* 1946
Pencil on tracing paper 39.4 x 35.5 cm
Fundació Gala-Salvador Dalí,
Figueres

118
Study for the Walt Disney
film *Destino* 1946
Pencil and ink on paper 35 x 42.3 cm
Fundació Gala-Salvador Dalí,
Figueres

Opposite:
119
*Portrait of Pablo Picasso in the
Twenty-first Century* 1947
Oil on canvas 65.5 x 56 cm
Fundació Gala-Salvador Dalí,
Figueres

Destino ¹⁹⁴⁶

Fèlix Fanés

It is likely that Dalí came into contact with Walt Disney during the filming of *Spellbound* in 1944, even though he had shown an interest in the filmmaker since 1937, describing him then as a 'Surrealist'.[1] What perhaps attracted the painter to Disney was the less 'mimetic', less 'narrative', nature of his films. The fact that animated drawings do not reproduce 'real' movement has always set them apart in the world of cinema. The advent of sound cinema had played an important part in Disney's success. The real impact of Mickey Mouse came with the film *Steamboat Willie* 1928, the third in the series but the first with sound, and the triumphal path of the *Silly Symphonies* began with *The Skeleton Dance* 1929, based on the *Danse macabre* by Saint-Saëns. With *Snow White and the Seven Dwarfs* 1937, he raised the humble cartoon from a brief accompaniment to the feature film to its central role in cinema programming. Disney's films were also removed from the narrative realism of Hollywood by their narrative heterodoxy, their plots being determined by the rhythm of the music.

Whether or not this was what attracted Dalí to Disney's work, what is certain is that towards the end of 1945, the great animation studio invited him to work on a six-minute 'episode' (eight minutes according to some sources) that would combine real images with animated drawings. It was to be based on a song by the Mexican songwriter Armando Domínguez entitled 'Destino' (adapted

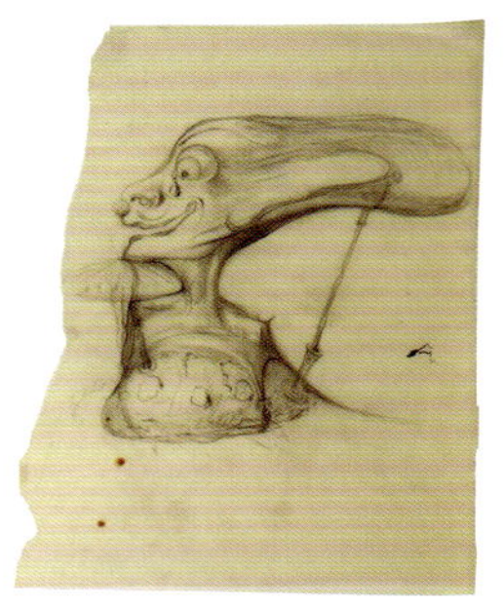

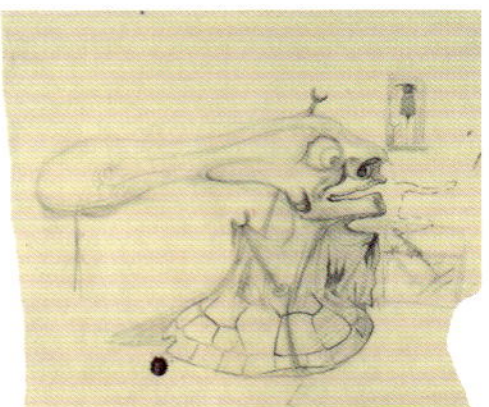

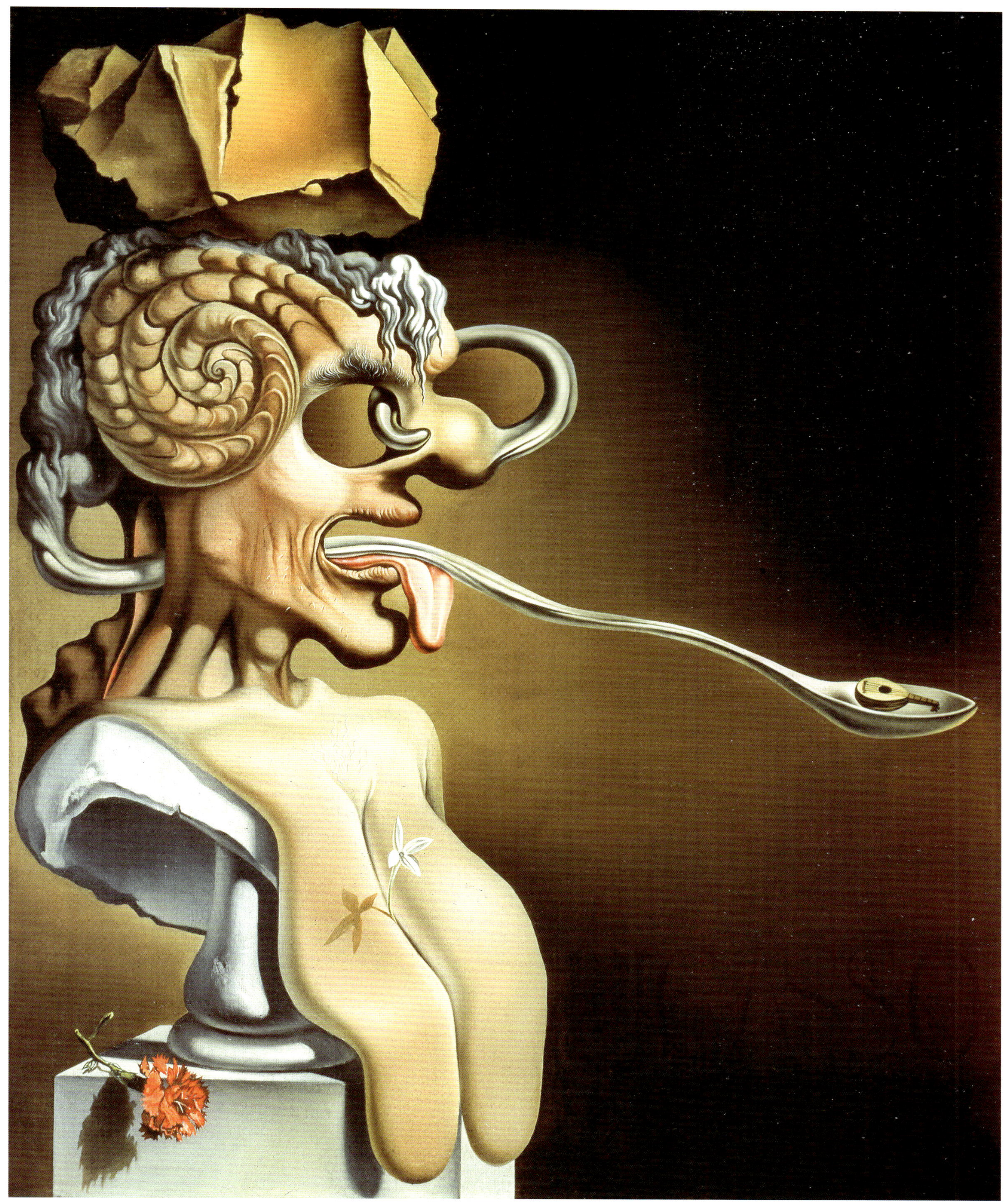

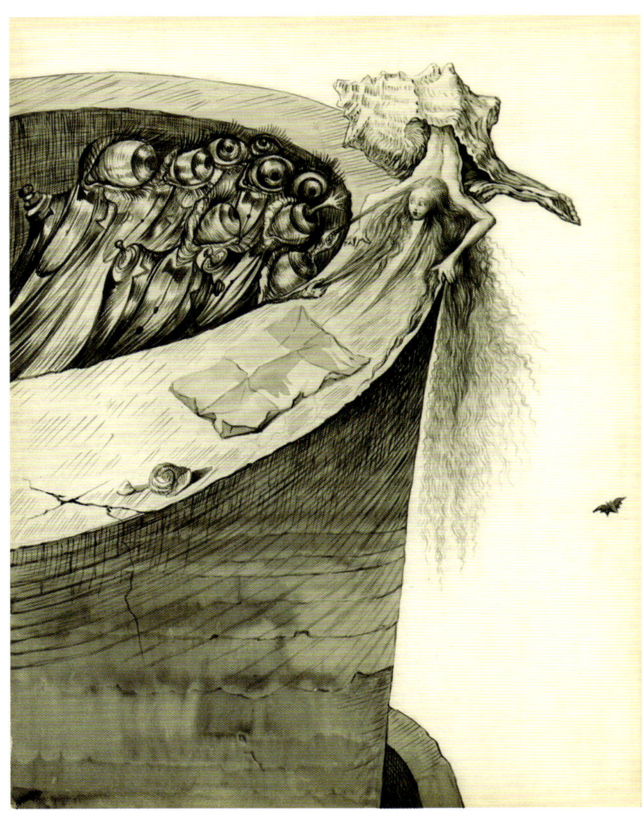

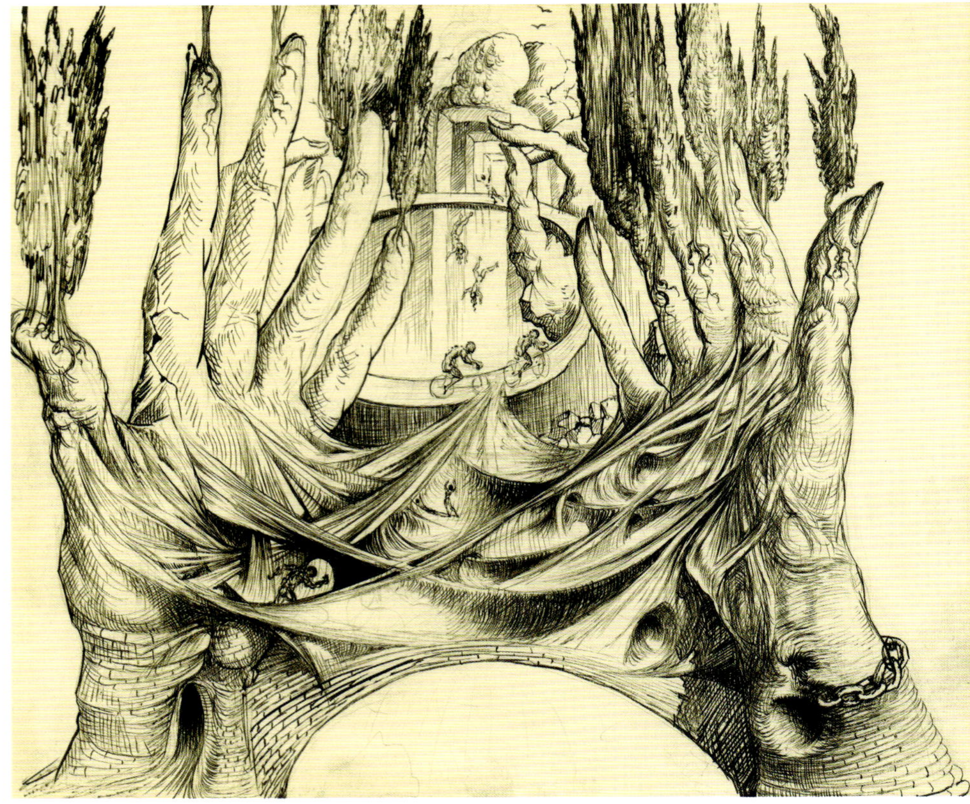

into English for Disney by Ray Gilbert as 'My Destiny in Love').[2] This episode was intended to form part of a composite feature film (known at the time as a 'package film'). Dalí signed a contract with Disney Studios on 14 January 1946. We know from a letter written a fortnight later by Gala to the curator James Thrall Soby, that Dalí soon began going to the studio. 'For ten days now', Gala reported, 'Dalí has been working with Disney'. She added optimistically: 'For the first time he seems to enjoy the greatest freedom to express his ideas. The film will no doubt be a success in this sense.'[3] Up until the middle of April 1946, Dalí went to work in the animation building on Dopey Avenue in Burbank, just like any other studio employee. Various photographs show him with his work tools in the studio offices (fig.149). Others show him with his closest colleagues in front of walls covered in the storyboard drawings. Although, according to the press of the time, Dalí's contract was for eight weeks, his work extended over a much longer period and he returned to the studios to complete a second period of work between July and August 1946.

Knowledge of the work that Dalí executed at the Disney Studios is variable. Alongside some definite information, some is conjectural based on imprecise documents, and some aspects we know nothing about at all. It is certain that Dalí produced the principal images for the film in the form of refined Indian ink drawings, elegant, polished watercolours, or even as medium-size oil paintings. This followed the pattern of those he made during his collaboration with Hitchcock.[4] As well as these carefully executed works, Dalí also produced a large number of images on lined studio paper as a visual guide to the unfolding action of the film. For this, he counted on the collaboration of John Hench.[5] Bob Cormack, another company employee, also worked on developing the continuity. It can therefore be said that Dalí was responsible to a large extent for the visual aspect of the film.

There never appears to have been a conventional script and the origin of the plot remains unclear. In the Disney Studios archives, however, there are five or six typed treatments of the script (depending on whether or not one counts repeats), one of them signed J.H. (John Hench). From these documents, it is possible to deduce that they were drawn up on the basis of conversations with Dalí. The writing style is not the artist's, but the content appears to have much in common with his extraordinary imagination. According to these documents, the film was to

120
Study for the Walt Disney film *Destino* 1946
Pen, ink and watercolour on paper 36.9 x 30.4 cm
Walt Disney Feature Animation and the Animation Research Library, Burbank, California

121
Study for the Walt Disney film *Destino* 1946
Pen and ink on paper 23.6 x 28.8 cm
Walt Disney Feature Animation and the Animation Research Library, Burbank, California

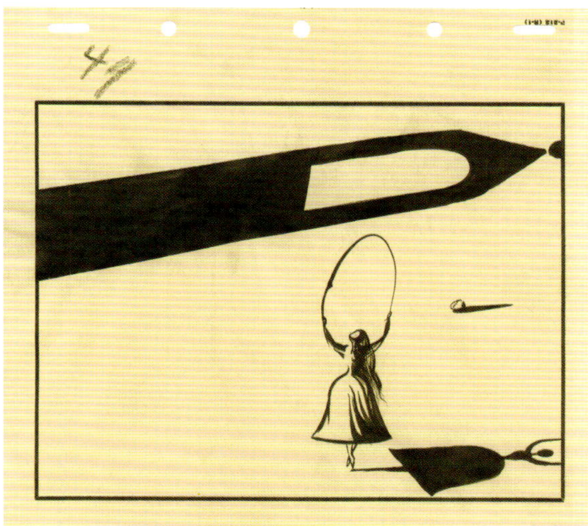

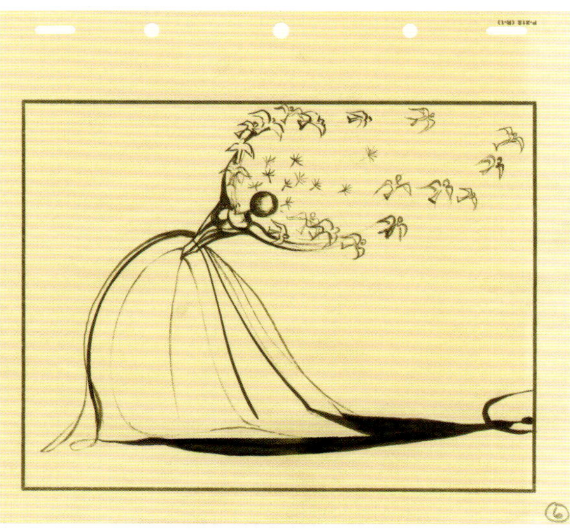

have a live-action prologue and epilogue. Dalí was
to appear in both sections to explain some of the
characteristic symbols of his work. The didactic
tone of these parts was confirmed by Dalí in an
interview in April 1946, in which he stated that
the film 'is an effort intended to initiate the public
into surrealism, better than painting or the
written word'.[6] The backdrop against which he was
to have filmed the prologue was a semi-circular
wall containing five niches, the central one of
which contained a fountain in the form of a swan.
The other niches would contain a huge and
slightly distorted drooping match; a chimera; a
strange being with drawers; and a sculpture of a
hand with ants that comes to life. The fountain
was a symbol of invisible destiny. As Dalí explained
at the end of the prologue, the theme of the film
was 'the search for true love, to find one's destiny'.

The story was composed of a series of
metamorphoses. The first part of the film – 'The
problem' – begins with a fountain representing
Chronos, the god of time (fig.124). On a triangular
base, a human figure leans against a clock placed
above a head of Medusa from which water is
spurting. Both the pyramidal base and the figure
appear in a state of ruin, as was common in Dalí's
images of the period. In a first transformation, the
fountain disappears into the pyramid. This in turn
becomes a road along which a young girl advances.
As her body moves forwards, it leaves behind a
series of after images (similar to the effect used by
Jules-Etienne Marey in his chronophotography)
until it fades from sight. From the figure of the girl
emerge the outlines of a man and a woman. The
skin of the man's face melts away, in a similar way
to certain paintings by Magritte, revealing within it
a series of objects such as crutches. We realise that
it is a mannequin, a symbol of false love. This is
the beginning of a number of symbolic events
experienced by the girl that are revealed to be
transitory seductions rather than her true destiny.
As she advances along the road, which becomes
an internal spiral staircase leading to the top of
the tower of Babel, the girl comes across a figure
holding a champagne glass (a symbol for partying
and frivolity). She then encounters a group of large
eyes that follow her around (symbolising curiosity,
attention, gossip) (fig.120). Finally she encounters
a woman with a head of roses that disintegrate into
a shower of petals (the spectre of motherhood).
Along the way, she also comes across a bride, whose
head is a baby in a crib; this figure glides forward
like a snail behind a small rainbow visible in light

Below:
123
Nude Torso on Building on Checkerboard. Study
for the Walt Disney film *Destino* 1946
Oil and collage on Masonite 45.5 x 60.3 cm
Walt Disney Feature Animation and the
Animation Research Library, Burbank, California

Right:
124
Study for the Walt Disney film *Destino* 1946
Watercolour on paper 29.7 x 37 cm
Walt Disney Feature Animation and the
Animation Research Library, Burbank, California

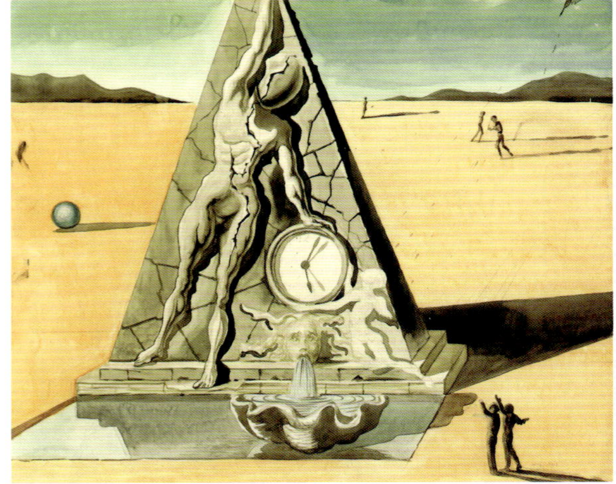

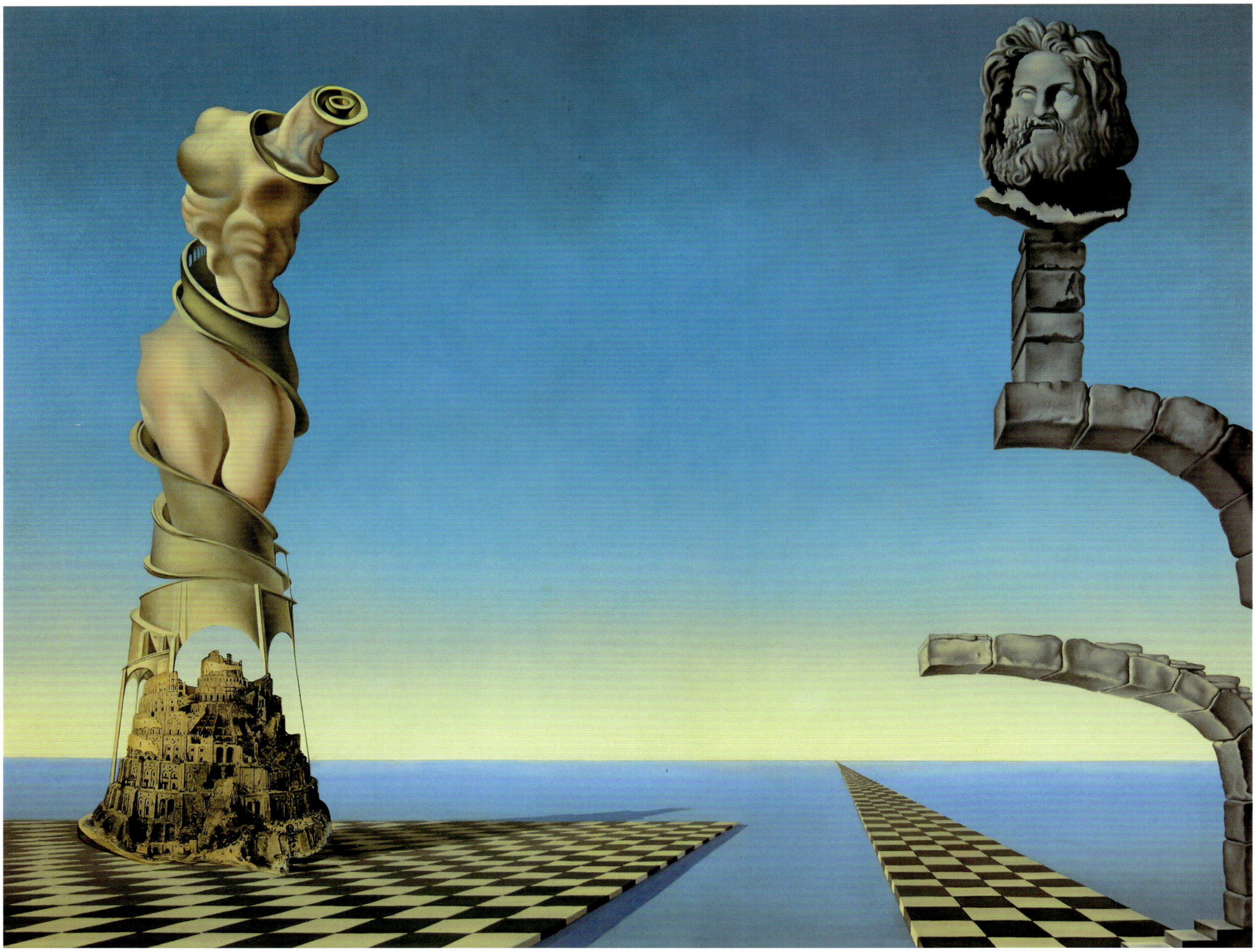

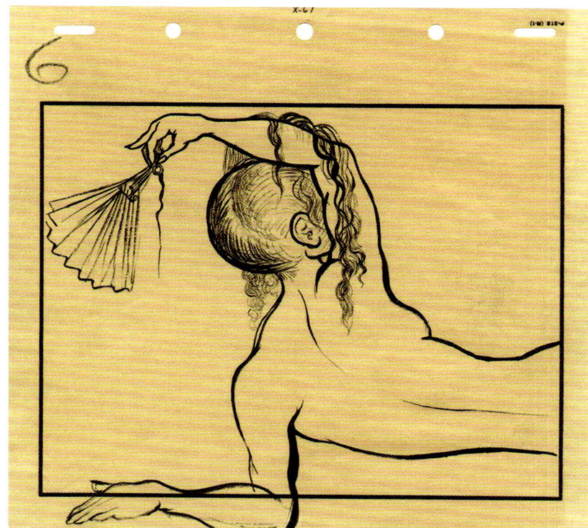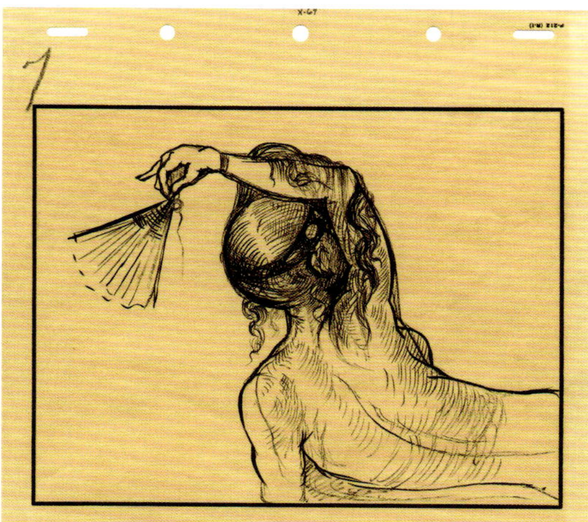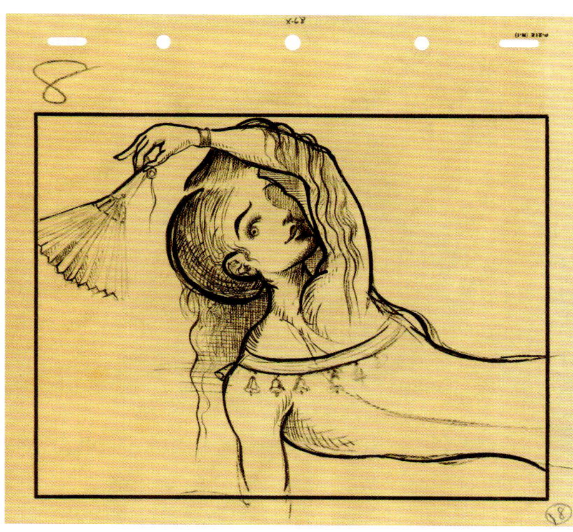

rain (fig.126) until, pursued by the eyes and stripped half naked by the rose thorns on the woman's head, she takes refuge inside a shell. At the very end of the road, driven forwards by this set of false appearances, she finally falls from the top of the Tower of Babel. Using various means, including a collection of fantastical telephones with spindly spider's legs, she reaches a wide, open plain, where the fountain of Chronos stands, along with a bell tower. In the background is a vast Surrealist arrangement of hands linked by the lines in their palms, combine to create a maze that leads to the temple of love (fig.121).

In the second part of the film ('Working out of the problem: search') the girl, fascinated by the silhouette of the bell hanging from the arch (fig.122), lies down in its shadow and takes on its shape, her head becoming a dandelion clock. Meanwhile, Chronos has begun to break away from the fountain, freeing himself from time (represented by the soft clocks stuck to his body like leeches, which, when pulled off, leave holes through which the background landscape can be seen). Brightly coloured humming birds emerge from the girl's head (fig.122a), bringing the statue of Chronos to life. As one of the treatments puts it: 'Time is withdrawn, he sees his own destiny and himself in his hand.' Once transformed into a living person, he takes on the appearance of a baseball player. He stares at his hand, which, in the foreground, can be seen covered in ants. The palm of his hand is transformed into the maze we saw earlier, and the ants metamorphose into cyclists, who race pointlessly around. Various rocks spin like a whirlwind, coming together to form

the face of Destiny (Jupiter) which, as a double image, also contains the girl as a ballerina (fig.129).

In the third part ('Solution or climax' – the part to which Dalí contributed least), Chronos dances a *pas de deux* with the girl, whose head has been transformed into a baseball. Suddenly, the transparent figure of a baseball catcher interferes with the couple's dance. The male dancer hits a ball at this menacing spectre, who then disappears. His body casts a shadow that is transformed into a door through which the ballerina – also created from the figure of the young man – passes, thus becoming the focal point of his thought or psyche. As one of the documents states: 'Desire is completely oriented.' Two white gazelles appear as the avalanche of love leads to the crystallisation of the human notion of happiness, which then shatters to reveal love as a cosmic phenomenon. The new space created – a form of celestial architecture representing the temple of love – appears to be inspired by Piranesi's mazes and intricate *Carceri*. The temple, which contains aspects of all civilisations (telephones in particular) becomes an island in a sea of passion. One heart is imprisoned within another (the female heart being a firmament for the male heart). At the centre of the heart, a dandelion blooms and within this microcosm extends the original plain with the fountain and the tower (symbolising man and woman, fig.123) and again, penetrating the fountain, the dandelion reveals the bell – the silhouette of the dancer planted in the heart. Finally, in the live-action epilogue, Dalí presents two young people in a room, a boy and a girl, whom we deduce are the film's protagonists.

125 a, b, c
Storyboard drawings for the Walt Disney film *Destino* 1946
Pen and ink on paper 20.3 x 22.8 cm
Walt Disney Feature Animation and the Animation Research Library, Burbank, California

According to some sources, only fifteen
to eighteen seconds of the film were actually made.
Curiously, these images are not found in the
storyboard nor in the various treatments. The
images are of two tortoises with enormous human
heads, which, as they come together, create a space
between them that is the outline of the body of the
dancer, the female protagonist (see figs.117, 118).
Were these perhaps executed during Dalí's second
period at the Disney Studios? We do not know. What
we do know for certain is that after this proof had
been made, a decision was taken to halt the film.
Whether or not this was because Dalí's aesthetics did
not comply with the company's standards (there
were nudes, monsters and a high level of symbolic
abstraction) is also unknown. Disney had just
produced two 'package films': *The Three Caballeros*
1945 and *Make Mine Music* 1946. Perhaps one or
both of these failed to produce the desired results.
It could also be that the formula was considered
overworked and exhausted. Whatever the case, the
Destino project was shelved and it was not until many
years later (in 2003), that with John Hecht, Dalí's
main collaborator, acting as consultant,the Disney
company finally completed it.[7]

Destino dates from a period when Dalí's
activities as a writer, scenographer, clothes
designer, creator of advertising campaigns,
collaborator on cinematographic sequences,
etc, had relegated his work as a painter to second
place. As was often the case, the film contains
many of the iconographic motifs that he had used
in his earlier works and which brought a certain
thematic coherence to all his work, regardless of
the medium used. Thus we find melting clocks,
girl-bells, ants, cyclists with loaves of bread on
their heads, crutches, shells, telephones and so
on. Even baseball cannot be considered a new
theme, since Dalí had used it in the oil painting
Melancholy, Atomic Uranic Idyll 1945 (fig.130),
and his 1947 *Portrait of Pablo Picasso in the
Twenty-first Century* (fig.119) extended the use
of metamorposed heads. The important role
played by double images in some of the many
transformations that occur in the film suggest that
he took advantage of the opportunity of working
with animation to introduce a temporal element
that up till that time he had only been able to
develop spatially (in his paintings). This may well
have been one of the challenges, perhaps the most
significant one, that attracted him to take part in
the project.

Dalí and Disney remained in contact

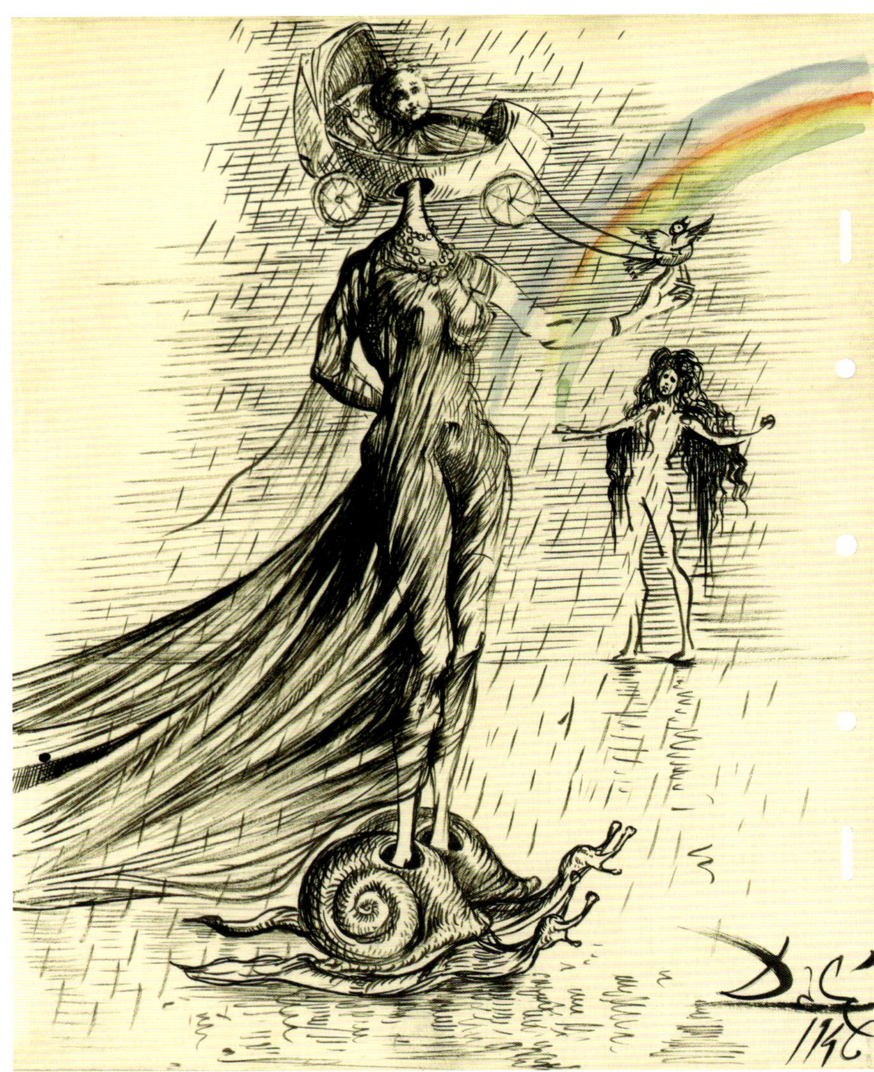

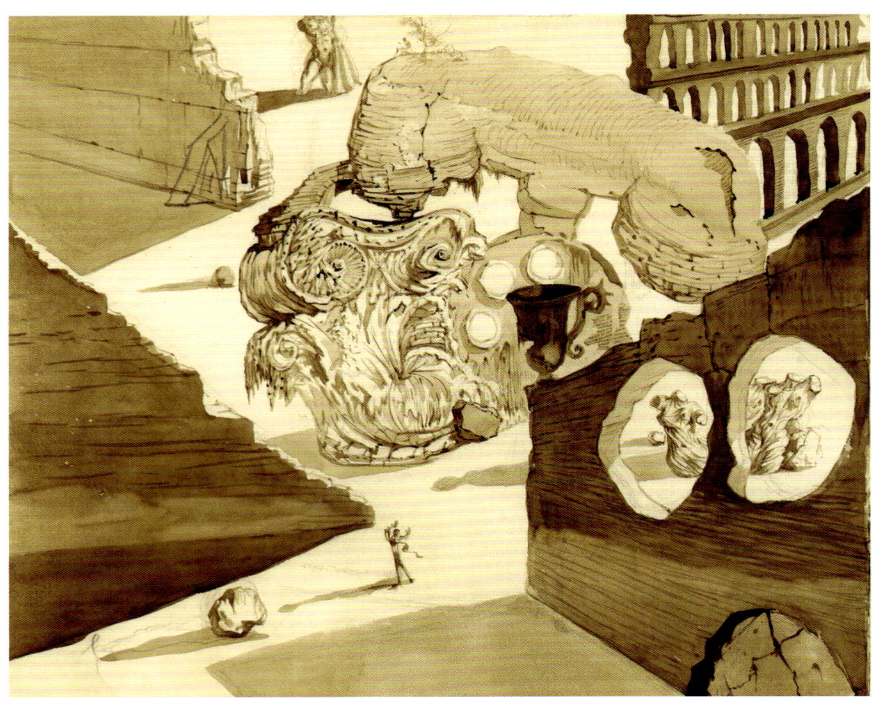

Left:
126
Study for the Walt Disney
film *Destino* 1946
Pen, ink and watercolour
on paper 30.6 x 25.5 cm
Walt Disney Feature Animation and
the Animation Research Library,
Burbank, California

127
Study for the Walt Disney
film *Destino* 1946
Watercolour on paper
29.2 x 37.3 cm
Walt Disney Feature Animation and
the Animation Research Library,
Burbank, California

Right:
128
Study for the Walt Disney film
Destino 1946
Mixed media on Masonite
50.5 x 63.5 cm
Fundació Gala-Salvador Dalí,
Figueres

129
Large Head of Greek God.
Study for the Walt Disney
film *Destino* 1946
Oil on Masonite 63.5 x 50.5 cm
Walt Disney Feature Animation and
the Animation Research Library,
Burbank, California

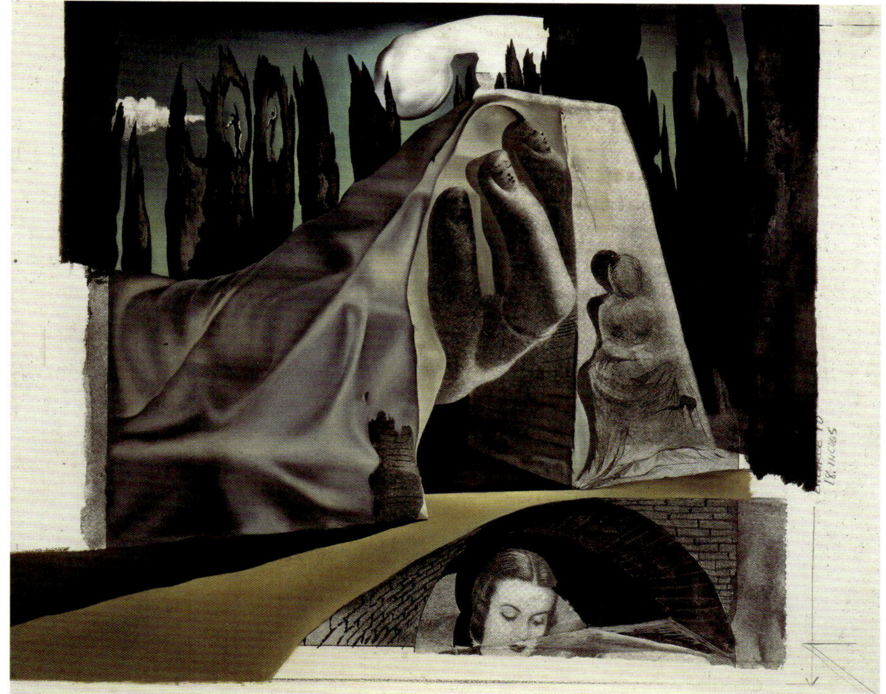

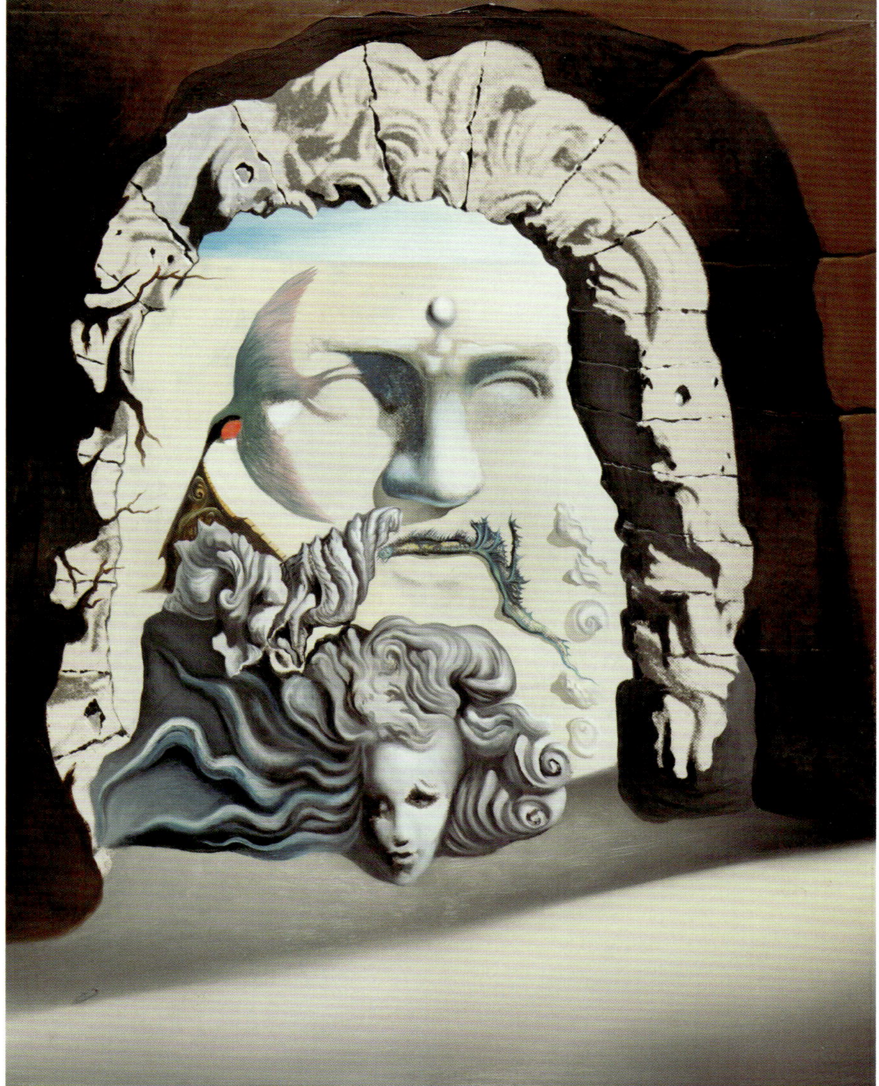

despite the abandonment of this project. A decade
later, in October 1957, Disney and his wife visited
Port Lligat.[8] They discussed the possibility of a
collaboration on a film based on *Don Quichote*,
reflecting the painter's current project for a suite
of lithographs. The idea was never pursued.

Translated by Alayne Pullen

130
Melancholy, Atomic Uranic Idyll 1945
Oil on canvas 66.5 x 86.5 cm
Museo Nacional Centro de Arte
Reina Sofía, Madrid

Opposite:
131
*Open Field with Ball in Centre and
Mountains in Rear*. Study for the
Walt Disney film *Destino* 1946
Oil on Masonite 50.5 x 63.5 cm
Walt Disney Feature Animation and
the Animation Research Library,
Burbank, California

Notes

1
Dalí, 'Surrealism in Hollywood', *Harper's Bazaar*, June 1937, republished in full in this volume; see also my essay 'Film as Metaphor' in this volume.

2
This and other information in this article is courtesy of material kept in The Animation Research Library of Walt Disney Feature Animation, Burbank, California. I should like to thank its director, Lela Smith and its chief archivist, Tim Campbell, for the assistance and friendship I was shown during my visit to this institution.

3
Gala Dalí letter to James Thrall Soby, 29 Jan. 1946, James Thrall Soby Papers, The Museum of Modern Art Archives, New York.

4
See Sara Cochran's text in this volume.

5
In the Disney archives there are two reconstructions of the film's storyboard produced years later by John Hench. These allow us to identify which images were drawn by which artist and help to determine the project's visual continuity and storyline. See also L. Shannon, 'When Disney Met Dali', *Modern Maturity*, Dec. 1978 – Jan. 1979.

6
With A. Frankenstein, *Arts*, 12 April 1946, quoted in *Salvador Dalí. 400 Obres. 1914–1983*, Barcelona 1983, vol.2, p.124.

7
Destino 2003, directed by Dominique Monferey, produced by Baker Bloodworth and art directed by Thierry Fournier.

8
Salvador Dalí: An Illustrated Life, London 2007, p.235.

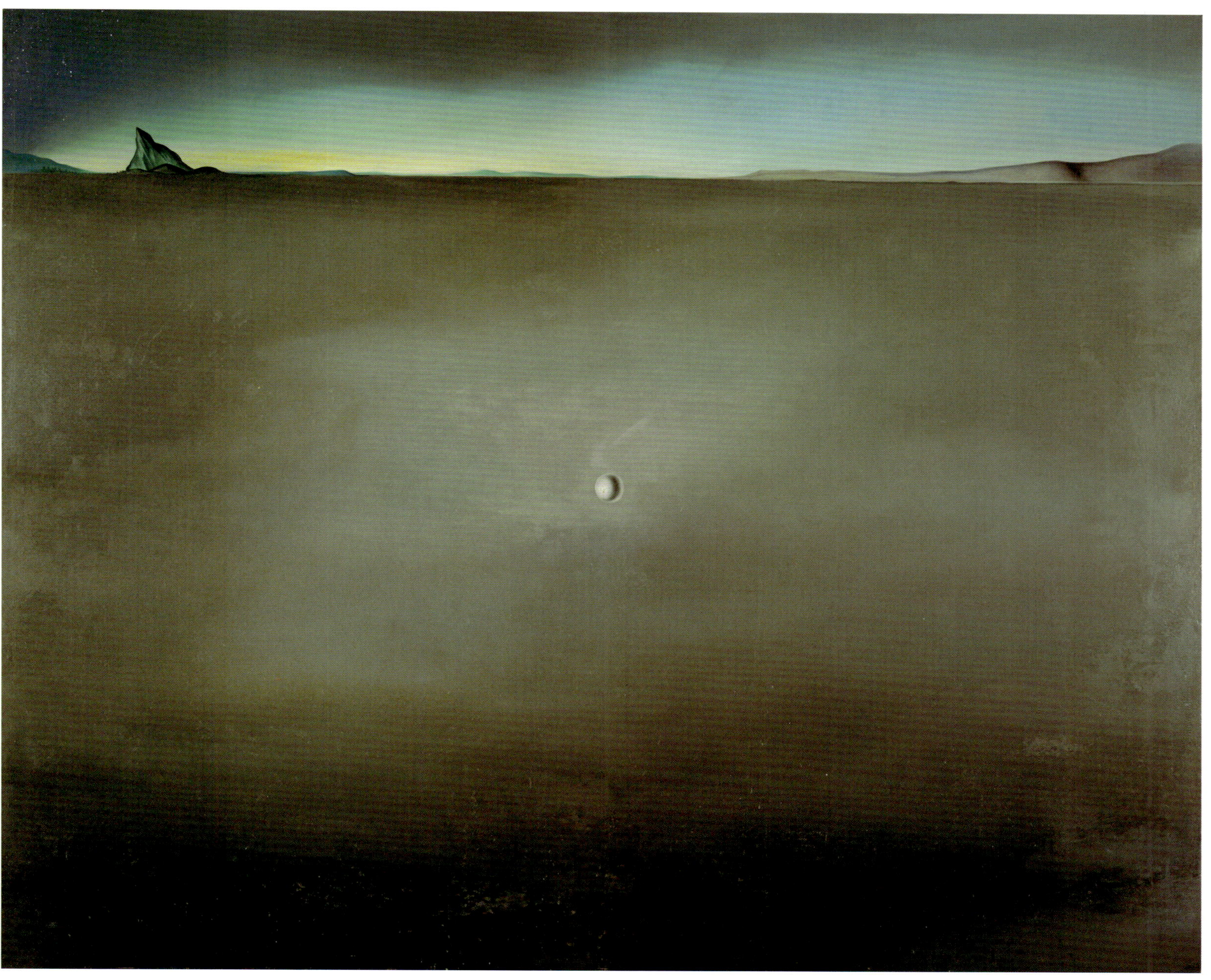

La Carretilla de carne 1948–52

Agustín Sánchez Vidal

La Carretilla de carne (The Wheelbarrow of Flesh) is one of Dalí's most substantial film projects, which he developed from 1948 to 1952 and which apparently came close to being filmed. It shares an important underlying connection with the much earlier and sketchier *La Chèvre sanitaire* (The Hygienic Goat): Dalí's attempt to transfer to the screen his paranoiac-critical method and his use of the multiple image. The approaches, however, are very different. *La Chèvre sanitaire* falls firmly within the phase of what may be called 'analytical Surrealism' that seeks to sever the threads of continuity and the logical and syntactical connections of film through a disarticulation equivalent to automatic writing or collage.[1]

La Carretilla de carne, on the other hand, can be ascribed to a 'synthetic realism', where the irrational ingredients form part of a narrative that is more naturalistic or even melodramatic.

The development of *La Carretilla de carne* may be traced through the successive versions that Dalí produced. The first, which is kept in the archives of the Fundacío Gala-Salvador Dalí, Figueres, consists of four pages typed in English with the title *The Wheelbarrow of Flesh: First Paranoiac Film by Salvador Dalí* and dated 1948. This was a significant date, since it was the year in which Dalí returned to Spain and set up home in Port Lligat. There is also a manuscript written in French, *La Brouette de chair: Premier film paranoïaque*, in Dalí's own handwriting, and partly on paper from Del Monte Lodge, where he stayed in Pebble Beach, California. In both, the subtitle underlines the use of the paranoiac-critical method. A third version, also handwritten by Dalí and kept with his papers, is twenty pages long; it is written in Spanish though full of Catalan spellings and has the title *La Carretilla de carne*; this too is on Del Monte Lodge paper and that of the St Regis Hotel, New York.[2] Another document, a synopsis entitled *El Alma* (The Soul), belongs to the archives of the filmmaker Luis Marquina.[3] Dalí spoke publicly about this project in 1953 and 1954, but without differentiating between the successive stages of its elaboration:

'I shall tell the true story of a paranoid woman in love with a wheelbarrow, to which she ascribes all the attributes of the person she loved and whose body it had served to carry.'[4]

The origins of the piece date back to the 1930s and to Dalí's own particular reading of Jean François Millet's painting *The Angelus*, which depicts a couple praying in a field, with a wheelbarrow in the background. The artist's manuscript on the subject was lost in 1941 and only recovered in 1962. On its publication the following year, Dalí clearly expressed the nature of the screenplay: 'I had gathered an entire collection of oppressive information on *rural eroticism* that was to conclude with my film of that time, *La Brouette de chair*.'[5]

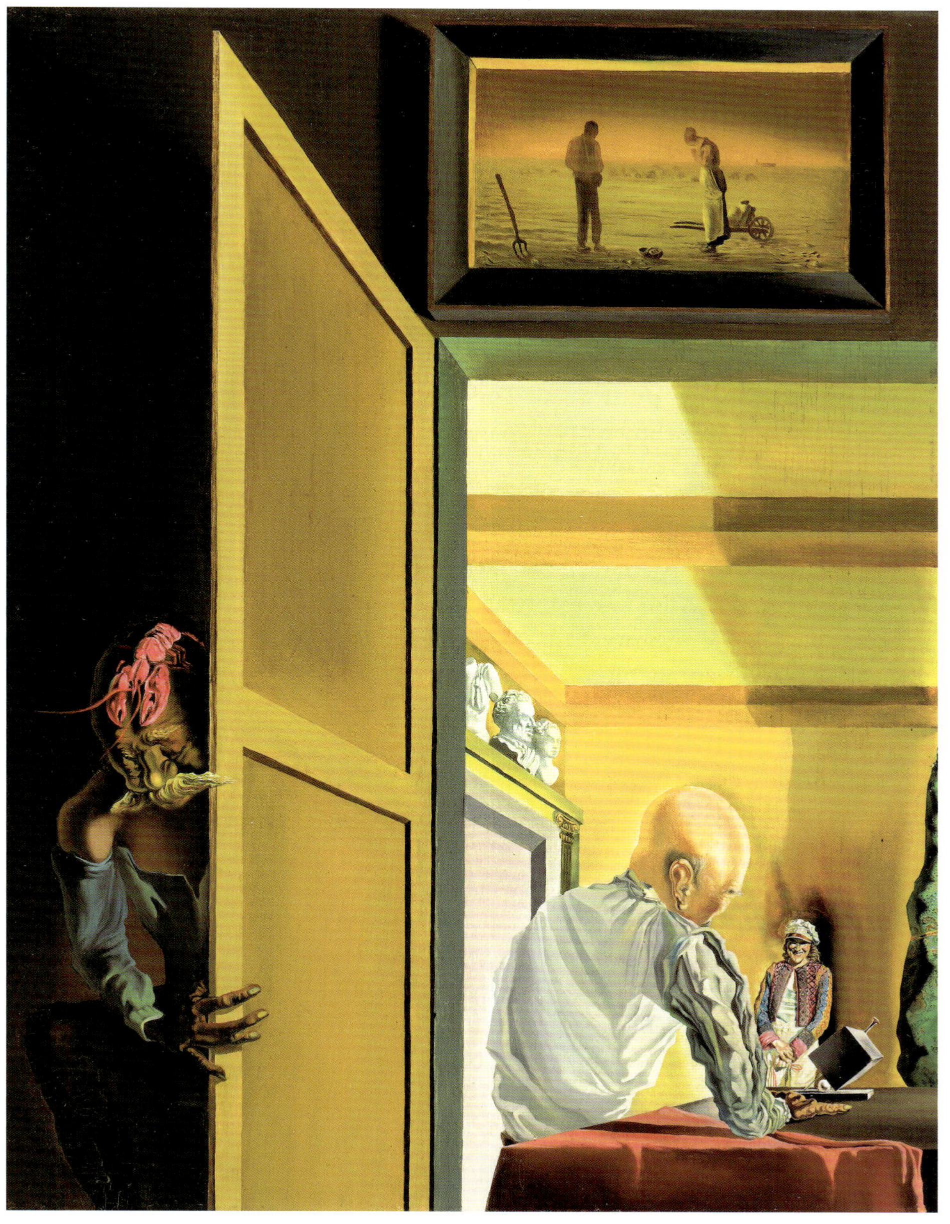

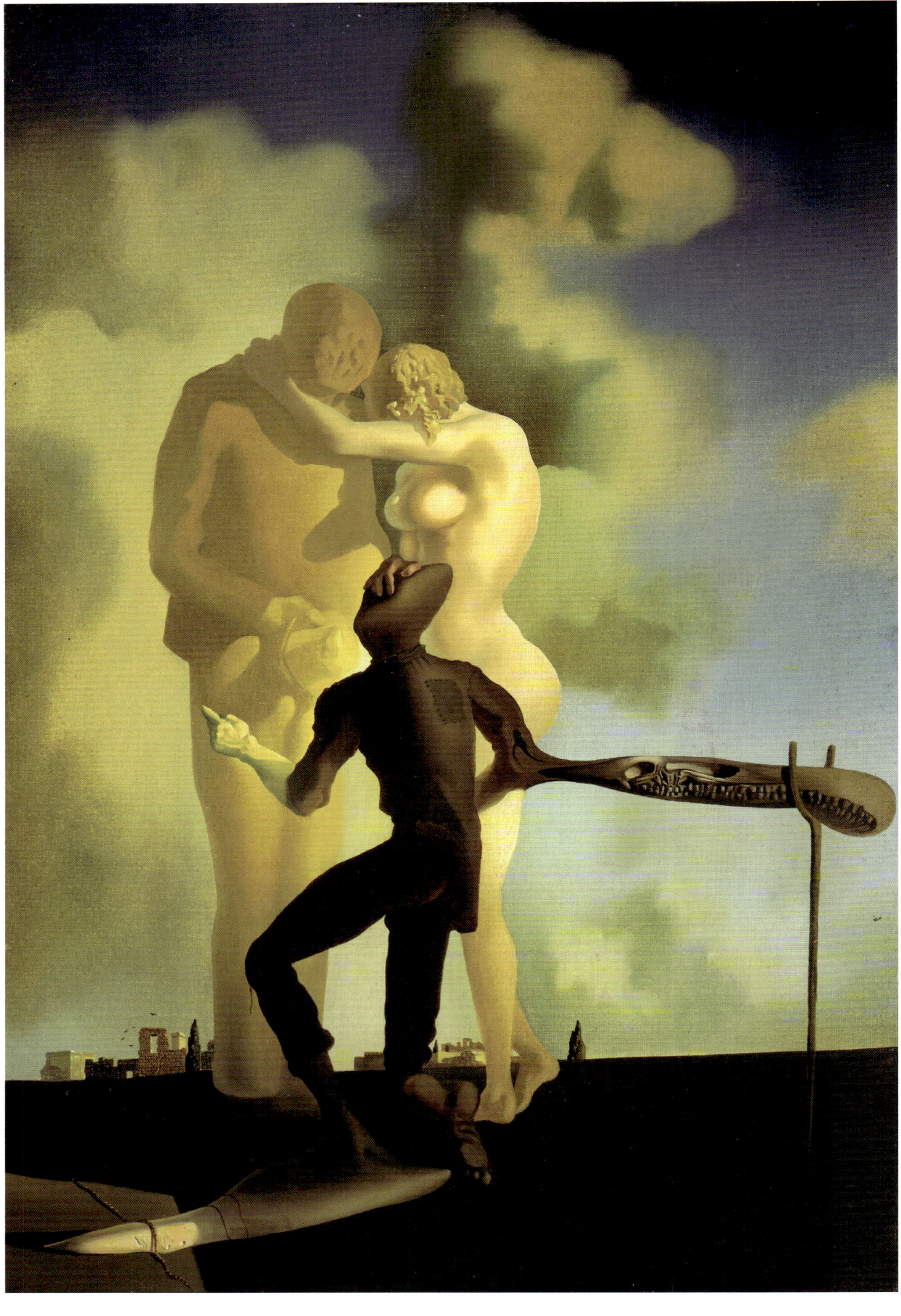

For the Spanish edition, Dalí added this revealing note describing it as: 'The most disturbing *secret* screenplay for he who is tackling the most ambitious film.'[6]

The time to which he refers must have been around 1948, when the script was still known as *Historia de una carretilla*. The following year, there were plans to film it on the Costa Brava with Paulette Goddard and Burgess Meredith in the principal roles, working with the Belgian cameraman André Cauvin. The English typescript, marked 'Famous Affairs Corporation', referred to above must have belonged to this phase. Later, the lead actress was changed to Anna Magnani and the project became Dalí's 'first neomystical film', following in the vein of the *Manifeste mystique* (Mystic Manifesto) that he issued in April 1951.[7] According to an interview he gave in August that year, the plan was to film it the following summer between Port Lligat and Palamós. He stated that Magnani was very enthusiastic about the film, which he conceived as 'based on exteriors, very cheap, mystical, like all my films, a film that will cause a great sensation. It will be my cinematic manifesto.'[8] A short while later, the project seems to have undergone a new metamorphosis, ending up with the title *El Alma*. Dalí was to be the scriptwriter, director and producer, and Joan Milá the cameraman. This is the version to which Dalí must have been referring in November 1951 at a press conference held at the Museo de Arte Contemporáneo in Madrid, when he talked about his film on St Teresa, starring Greta Garbo and with music by Jacinto Guerrero.[9]

The initial approach, seen in the English version, *The Wheelbarrow of Flesh*, appears to pick up on a central idea from his film project *La Chèvre sanitaire*, that is to say, to create a film that means several things at the same time, the cinematic equivalent of the multiple image. By then, Dalí was well aware how difficult this would be to achieve with a full plot line and he therefore decided to focus on a single fetishistic object, the wheelbarrow, which would be constantly reinterpreted by the protagonist in her paranoid delirium. It was made clear that the wheelbarrow is: 1) a dining table; 2) a marriage bed; 3) a coffin; 4) a cupboard; 5) a crib; 6) a nesting place for birds; 7) a bed for cats; 8) a wheelbarrow of flesh; 9) an altar for prayer; 10) a cross.[10]

The handwritten Spanish version entitled *La Carretilla de carne* must be slightly later and presents some important new ideas. A cripple was added – a limbless man introduced as the father of Magnani.[11] Since the film was going to be filmed in Franco's Spain, the theological aspects of the screenplay of this 'first neomystical film' were overseen by a priest. The tone here was more racially Iberian, with unmistakeable Mediterranean touches and something of the 'southern' register of films such as Jean Renoir's *Toni* or the Provençal atmosphere of films by Marcel Pagnol. Here, the central character becomes involved with a group of gypsies, who take her with them on their travels across the peninsula in what Dalí describes as an 'epic crossing through the geological and archaeo-logical sublimity of Spain'. This may be seen as a touristic and folkloric display to encourage official subsidies, but also a kind of pilgrimage or *via crucis* that parallels the article 'To Spain guided by Dalí' that the artist published in *Vogue* magazine in May 1950.[12] Other changes were structural. Unlike in the 1948 version, which was recounted via an extended flashback, here the narrative is linear. It begins in the institution in which the protagonist's father has been hospitalised and where he is moved around in a wheelbarrow. The girl, who is mute, takes care of her father, treating the wheelbarrow as if it were the crib of a newborn child. She rejects the advances of the men who desire her, remaining attentive to her filial duties. That is, until the father dies of typhus and the nuns at the home try to burn his clothes along with the wheelbarrow. The daughter objects and, pulling a cross from his pauper's grave, she attacks the nuns with it. She then goes to live with the gypsies, where she continues to unleash the passions of the men who come into contact with her, in particular the Andalusian gypsy Pacigán, who, when he sees the girl paying more attention to a road worker than she does to him, kills the unfortunate man.

It is then that the girl's peregrinations across Spain begin, ending with her settling in Cadaqués. There, she discovers a sack of hardened cement that reminds her of the limbless body of her father and she begins dressing it in scraps of clothing. But a time comes when she has piled so many useless bits and pieces into the wheelbarrow that it starts to fall apart. Once the vehicle has been stripped of its trimmings, she has to reinforce it with pieces of iron that take the shape of a cross and become a religious symbol that will be revealed to her as the reason for her *via crucis*. Dalí used this journey and symbolism to express his abhorrence of materialism, contrasting it with mysticism. The priest defending the protagonist resembles Freud, to underline the fact 'that even the most day-to-day Catholicism understands inherently more about the human spirit than the most elaborate psychoanalysis'.[13] And when the woman destroys the wheelbarrow with a mallet, as if dismantling her phantoms, she reveals the support in the form of a cross, which, as Dalí explained, is simply 'consciousness of her religious faith'.[14] She drags the cross all the way to the cemetery and returns it to the pauper's grave from which she seized it at the start of the film.

When seen in the context of his other projects, *La Carretilla de carne* appears to be the ultimate expression of Dalí's persistent obsession with Millet's *Angelus* (fig.132), expanded here to include that 'rural eroticism' that he was surprised to discover in paintings such as *The Hireling Shepherd* by the Pre-Raphaelite William Holman Hunt. That painting, which depicts a shepherd showing a country girl a Death's Head Moth, had already served as inspiration for the Death's Head Moth sequence in *Un Chien andalou* and Dalí's article on 'Le Surréalisme spectral de l'eternel féminin préraphaéliste' (The Spectral Surrealism of the Pre-Raphaelite Eternal Feminine). In that text, he alludes to the 'grandiose and *cannibal* Milletesque' aspect of Hunt's work, with the 'lustful summer heat of the quartered and bloody wheelbarrow of flesh'.[15] This may possibly be the source of the later version, *El Alma*, the title being a reference to the celebrated metaphor used by the Spanish mystic St Teresa, who compared the human soul to a larva that would be transformed into a butterfly. Here however, the moth that represents death in Hunt's work is transformed into a symbol of religious significance, an authentic Baroque *vanitas*.

As for the wheelbarrow, in addition to the one that appears in Millet's *Angelus*, there is another that had mythical significance for the Surrealists – that of the postman Ferdinand Cheval (1879–1912). For thirty-three years, Cheval laboured constantly – under the edifying motto 'God, Homeland, Work' – building with his own hands his Palace Idéal (Ideal Palace), a fantasy structure reminiscent of Modern style (Art Nouveau) architecture and in which he honoured his 'much-loved wheelbarrow', by putting it on display in its own niche. In 1933, both Dalí and André Breton wrote articles in the magazine *Minotaure* on the subject of modernist architecture. Breton concludes his with a photograph of

Cheval's Palais Idéal and these words on St Teresa: 'The very fact that she should see her wooden cross become transformed into a crucifix of precious stones, and that she should simultaneously take this vision to be *imaginative* and *sensory*, makes Teresa of Ávila acceptable to lead this procession composed of mediums and poets. Unfortunately she is still nothing more than a saint'.[16] Dalí set about rectifying this shortcoming in his novel *Hidden Faces* 1944, by providing the mystic and writer with the remaining attributes needed through Solange de Cléda, the central character. In the prologue he introduces her as 'a profane, St Teresa, Epicurus and Plato burning in a single eternal flame of female mysticism'.[17]

In *Le Mythe tragique de l'Angélus de Millet*, Dalí included a postcard celebrating the Cheval's Palais Idéal, thus underlining 'the manifest and extremely marked fetishistic fixation the postman Cheval had for his wheelbarrow'. Having spoken of the 'rural eroticism' of *La Carretilla de carne*, he added: 'My intention is to demonstrate how peasants exhausted by their work eroticise their instruments of labour and that the wheelbarrow in particular is specifically the prototype object of this symbolic function.'[18] As a final link, in 1956 – when the *La Carretilla de carne* project was still dragging on – Dalí constructed a Surrealist object, which he named *La Carretilla*, as totemic as that of Cheval himself. A wheelbarrow-monument was already present in the earliest (slightly eccentric) English version of the film scenario: 'In an unihabited landscape in the middle of rocks so accidented that walking is practically impossible, one discovers placed as an idol a large decrepit wheelbarrow. To explain the unwanted presence of this wheelbarrow in such surroudings the film will relate its story.'[19]

Translated by Alayne Pullen

134
The Spectre of Sex Appeal 1934
Oil on panel 18 x 14 mm
Fundació Gala-Salvador Dalí,
Figueres

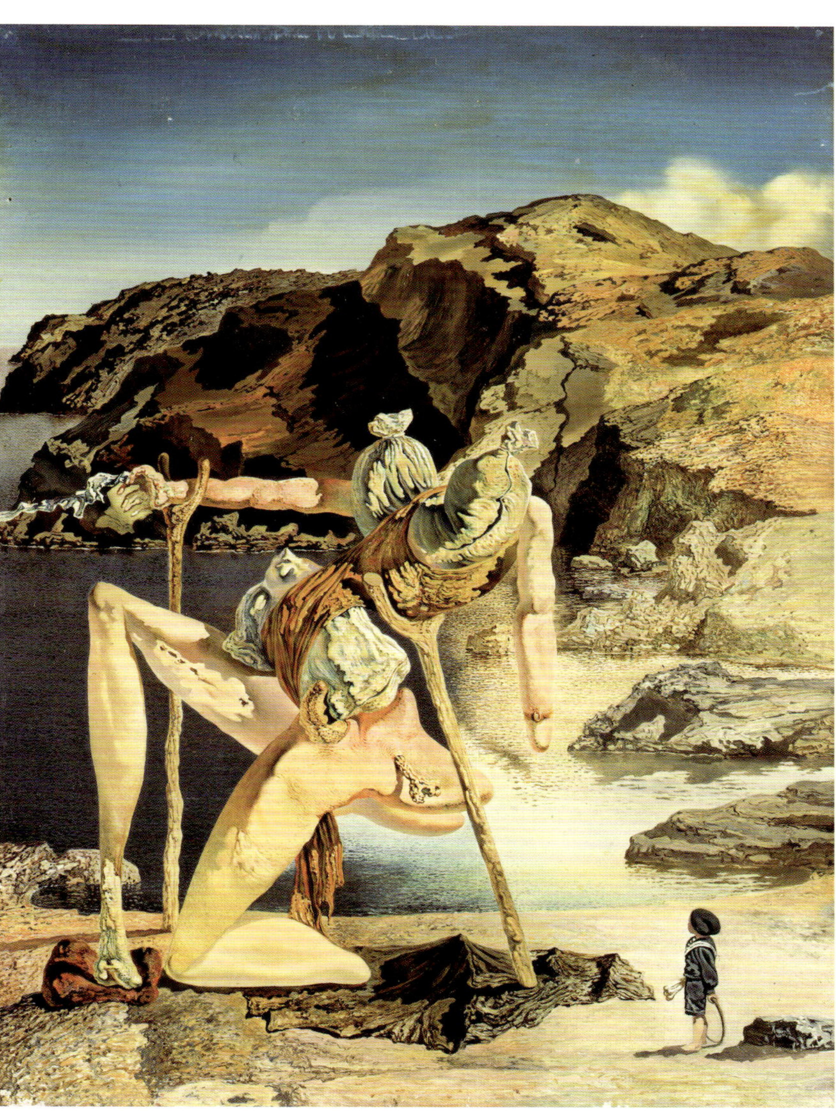

Notes

1
See my text on *La Chèvre sanitaire* in this volume.

2
The original manuscripts are held in the Fundació Gala-Salvador Dalí, Figueres; they are published (in Spanish translation) as 'La Carretilla de Carne', in Salvador Dalí, *Obra Completa ,vol.III: Poesía, Prosa, Teatro y Cine*, ed. Agustín Sánchez Vidal, Barcelona 2004, pp.1203–18, see also p.141–9.

3
Published in *Contracampo*, no.33, Summer–Autumn 1983, p.31. Luis Marquina Pichot was an old family friend and son of the dramatist and poet Eduardo Marquina who, in 1922, had provided a recommendation for Dalí to support his application to the Residencia de Estudiantes. In 1935 Luis worked with Buñuel in his production company Filmófono directing *Don Quintín el amargao* (Don Quintín, the Embittered).

4
Dalí, 'Mes secrets cinématographiques', *La Parisienne*, no.14, Feb. 1954, pp.165–8 and republished in this volume from *Diary of a Genius*, London 1966. This comment dates from June 1953 and he refers to the project again on 9 May 1956 (ibid. p.139).

5
Le Mythe tragique de l'Angélus de Millet: Interpretation 'paranoïaque-critique', Paris 1963; trans. as *The Tragic Myth of Millet's Angelus*, St Petersburg (Flo.) 1986.

6
El mito trágico del 'Ángelus' de Mille, Barcelona 1978.

7
Manifeste mystique, Paris 1951, and as *Manifiesto místico*, Port Lligat 1951.

8
See *Obra Completa ,vol.III* 2004, p.143.

9
'Picasso y Yo', 11 Nov. 1951, published in *Mundo Hispanico*, no.46, 1952, pp.37–42.

10
Obra Completa ,vol.III 2004, p.1205.

11
See 'Teresa y el hombre-tronco' (Teresa and the limbless man), in *Obra Completa, vol.III* 2004, pp.353–66.

12
'To Spain Guided by Dalí', *Vogue*, 15 May 1950, pp.54–7.

13
Obra Completa ,vol.III 2004, p.1217.

14
Ibid.

15
Dalí, 'Le Surréalisme spectral de l'éternel féminin préraphaélite' (The Spectral Surrealism of the Pre-Raphaelite Eternal Feminine), *Minotaure*, no.8, 15 June 1936, pp.46–9.

16
Dalí, 'De la beauté terrifiant et comestible, de l'architecture modern 'Style' (On the Terrifying and Edible Beauty of Modern Style Architecture), and André Breton, 'Le Message automatique', (The Automatic Message), *Minotaure*, no.3–4, 1933.

17
Hidden Faces, trans. Haakon Chevalier, New York and London 1947 and 1973, p.xii.

18
Le Mythe tragique de l'Angélus de Millet.

19
'The Wheelbarrow of Flesh', manuscript, Fundació Gala-Salvador Dalí, Figueres.

Le Sang catalan c.1950

Montse Aguer and Matthew Gale

In the summer of 1948, the Italian film director Luchino Visconti released *La terra trema* (The Earth Trembles), one of the key films of post-war Italian neo-realism. With amateur actors speaking an anachronistic dialect, the film emphasised locality and the interconnection between nature, subsistence and social structures. In so doing, it framed a drama of class struggle that had particular relevance in the political debates of Cold War Europe. That July also marked the return of Dalí and Gala from their exile of eight years in America (1940–8). It is very likely that Dalí saw Visconti's film, since by the end of 1948 he had visited Italy and agreed to make the set designs for the director's production of *As You*

Like It.[1] The painter travelled to Rome again for the premiere of the play on 26 November 1949.[2]

An undated typescript scenario for a folkloric documentary, Dalí's *Le Sang catalan* (Catalan Blood) seems to fall after these events and shares certain concerns with *La terra trema*: a sense of rootedness, historical locality and group identity. Moreover, the early images proposed in the script, of people gathering – with peasants walking and fishermen arriving by sea – evoke the communal imagery of Visconti's Sicilian tale. Significantly, on arrival in Spain, Dalí had renounced 'Freudian psychology' for an interest in 'the geography of the places where myths return to life'.[3] Like Visconti, the painter

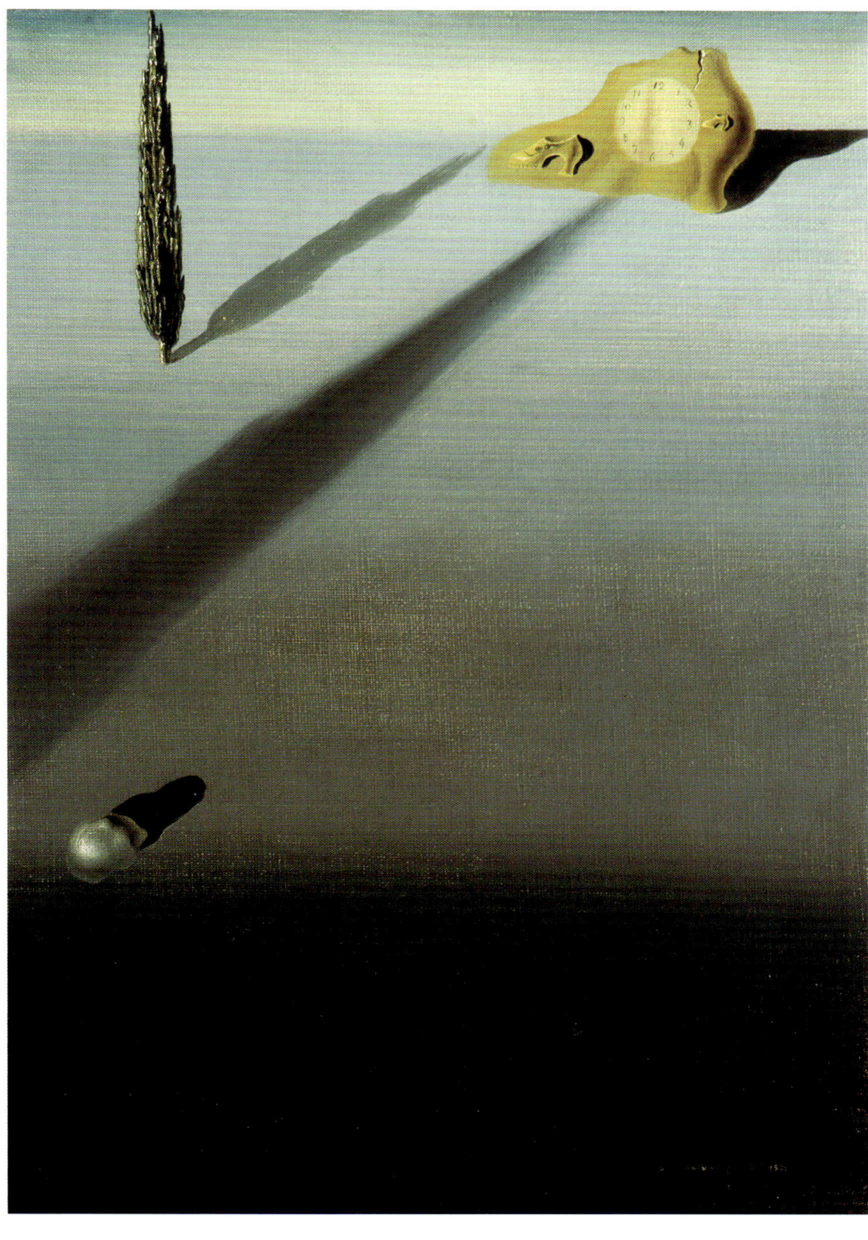

135
The Sense of Speed 1934
Oil on canvas 33 x 24 cm
Fundació Gala-Salvador Dalí,
Figueres

suggested that the region under scrutiny was overlooked. Dalí's claim for the neglect of Catalonia was made in the introductory speech that he scripted for himself in the scenario: 'Let us enter into the living reality of a country that is, above all, forgotten, above all phenomenal, above all original, violent and philosophical.'[4] In this connection, it is notable that Dalí had specifically contrasted his previous project *La Carretilla de carne* (The Wheelbarrow of Flesh) to current Italian film. 'I want to make a profoundly Spanish cinema', he declared in July 1949, 'that responds on a different plane to what Rosselini has done for Italian cinema … Everything [in *La Carretilla de carne*] takes place in Catalonia, on the Costa Brava and at Cap de Creus'.[5] This was also the context for *Le Sang catalan*.

Of course, Dalí's proposal was not circumscribed by the same political concerns that motivated either Visconti's explicit reference to the radicalism of the peasant occupation of land, or Buñuel's study of class and regional struggle in *Tierra sin pan* (Land Without Bread) 1933. Instead, the painter's return to Spain was part of his post-war revaluation of classicism, Catholicism and conservatism. After eight years in the United States, he was able to balance this with a fascination for the new, but his increasingly antagonistic relationship with modern art became more discordant as the 1950s wore on. Dalí's lecture, 'Picasso and I' at the Maria Guerrerro theatre in Madrid on 11 November 1951 set the tone, by comparing the 'geniuses' of the title as the 'two most antagonistic artists of modern painting'. There he also made his most recent concerns explicit: 'As my name Salvador indicates, I come to save modern painting from idleness and chaos; I want to integrate the experience of Cubism and Luca Paccioli's *Divina proporzione* and to sublimate atheist Surrealism, the last refuge of dialectical materialism, in the great Spanish tradition of mystical and realistic painting.' Lurching into politics, he characterised Franco in a uniquely Dalínian manner: 'In these days of grave crises and spiritual decadence, each great figure is an eccentric force who does exactly the opposite of his nearest predecessors. From this point of view, General Franco is one of the first to act in this way. To me, this seems highly "original".'[6] This opportunistic and oddly ambivalent lecture succeeded simultaneously in achieving acceptance at home and provoking disbelief abroad.

If Dalí's return to Spain provides the general context for *Le Sang catalan*, it is difficult to be more precise about its date.[7] The early 1950s was a period in which a number of film projects were set in train, notably *La Carretilla de carne* and the endlessly elaborated *L'Aventure prodigieuse …*[8] Like the former, in which a girl travels the country with a gypsy group (oddly reminiscent of that in Bizet's *Carmen*), *Le Sang catalan* had a folklorist, documentary and mythic aspect.[9] Dalí's opening speech in the film, which was set in the crypt of Antoni Gaudí's church of La Sagrada Familia in Barcelona, was to be witnessed by Christopher Columbus and Narcís Monturiol (the Catalan inventor of the submarine).[10] 'The life of this people', Dalí proclaimed by way of explanation of his title, 'has evolved under the biological sign of blood, is marked by authentic blood'.[11] This referred to the medieval origin of the Catalan coat-of-arms, formed by four fingers dipped in the blood of Catalonia's founding leader Wilfredo el Velloso, and dragged across a golden shield. In the ensuing narrative, the birth of the nation in suffering is closely related to the physical ruggedness of Dalí's favourite site: the fall of the Pyrenees into the Mediterranean at Cap de Creus, and the extrapolation of this ruggedness in the robust architecture of Gaudí. Other signs of nationhood are found in the music and dance of Catalonia that Dalí specifically mentions as bearers of historical continuity – the *sardana* and the national song 'Els segadors' – and in traditions such as the *Ball se bastons* dances, the human towers of the Xiquets de Valls or the traditional *caramelles* songs. For Dalí, this inheritance was found in the people who recur obsessively in his work, such as Gaudí, and the writer-philosophers Ramon Llull and Francesc Pujols. It was also located in the mythical places of his iconography: Gaudí's La Sagrada Familia and La Pedrera, the Barcelona of the Ramblas and the Paseo de Gracia, or the mountain and monastery of Montserrat, the key symbols of Catalan nationalism. Most fundamentally it was found in the nostalgia for the land, its locality and its timelessness.[12]

These were, of course, the very signs of nationhood that Franco had sought to repress within a centralised Spain resistant to the centrifugal forces of nationalism. However much the folkloric elements in *Le Sang catalan* could have been compared with the travelogue article for *Vogue* (May 1950), 'To Spain: Guided by Dalí',[13] the very premise of a film based in the recognition of Catalan identity was to some degree radical and subversive. The painter makes that explicit: 'Any efforts of a totalitarian regime are radically opposed to the profound and substantially ultra-individualist condition and origin of the Catalan spirit, and this same spirit is racked with convulsion.'[14] In this sense, no matter how conservative his outlook, Dalí remained able to undertake an individual subversion.

In *Le Sang catalan*, a monument is set up to the idea of nationhood. Such ceremonies occur in other texts, including *Les Mystères surréalistes de New York*, where there was a monument to the end of Prohibition. In *L'Age d'or*, to which the new project appears to have made particular reference, there was a ceremony for the Founding of Rome, and that earlier address seems to be reflected in Dalí's speech in Gaudí's crypt. One other aspect of this project that recalls his own films is the recourse to temporal circularity, most notably favoured in *Un Chien andalou*: *Le Sang catalan* concludes, in a rather musical way, by repeating the first paragraphs of the opening speech.

The images that Dalí conjured up in his writing explicitly return to some of his earlier film projects. The omnipresence of 'the desolate and savage landscape of the Cap de Creus, peopled by mysterious ruins', stands out in this respect. The bristling rocks, alongside disembowelled pianos and rotting donkeys or luxurious crystal spiders, form part of an iconography that is reinforced by the sound of the sea and the wind, often mixed with Catalan and Wagnerian music. Furthermore, the scenario is wrapped up in 'an atmosphere of "virtual" legend' that would be contrasted to a 'brutal realism', with people depicted crudely in order to attain a documentary sensibility that penetrates – as the final text echoes – 'the living reality of a country that is, above all, forgotten, above all … violent'.[15]

Notes

1

In an interview with *El correo catalan* on 5 Dec. 1948, Dalí explained that he had been to Italy to study the architecture of Palladio and that, while he was in Rome, Visconti had asked him to make the designs for *As You Like It*.

2

Ian Gibson, *The Shameful Life of Salvador Dalí*, London 1997, pp.452–3; this was also the moment of Dalí's audience with the Pope, to which he took *The Madonna of Port Lligat* (first version) 1949 (The Patrick and Beatrice Heggerty Museum of Art, Marquette University, Milwaukee).

3

In Juan Felipe Vila San Juan, 'Salvador Dalí, el gran pintor surrealista, ha regresado a España', *La Vanguardia*, 1 Aug. 1948; Dalí stated: 'I want to return to painting my mythology with concrete sites seen in a new way, in tune with new physics; I am no longer interested in Freudian psychology but rather in the geography of the places where myths return to life.'

4

The original manuscript, in French, is held in the Fundació Gala-Salvador Dalí, Figueres; a full publication appears (in Spanish translation) as 'La Sangre Catalana', in Salvador Dalí, *Obra Completa, vol.III: Poesía, Prosa, Teatro y Cine*, ed. Agustín Sánchez Vidal, Barcelona 2004, pp.1221–31.

5

Dalí, interview in *Solidaridad nacional*, 19 July 1949.

6

Dalí, 'Picasso and I', lecture at the María Guerrero theatre, Madrid 11 Nov. 1951.

7

Sánchez Vidal 2004, has proposed the mid-1950s; p.149.

8

See the texts by Agustín Sánchez Vidal ('La Carretilla de carne') and Elliott H. King in this volume.

9

In 'To Spain: Guided by Dalí', *Vogue*, May 1950, the artist spoke of an 'impressionist immersion'; it is possible to speak of a 'folkloric immersion' in the case of *Le Sang catalan*.

10

Dalí discussed the submariner in an interview in *Journal de Genève*, 7 July 1953: 'Did you know that it [the submarine] was also invented by a Spaniard? By Monturiol, who was born, like me, in Figueres, and who continues to play a great part in my thinking. So this is also a case of exalting a Spanish genius and for me the submarine has always represented the descent into the depths of the subconscious.'

11

Sánchez Vidal 2004, p.1221.

12

Dalí told the magazine *Destino* (1 April 1950): 'I need to be at Port Lligat, to see the sailors, the colour of the olives and the bread, feel the peace, the landscape, with its devotion and inner piety. I need the sense of the local at Port Lligat, just as Raphael needed Urbino, in order to reach the universal through the particular.'

13

Sánchez Vidal 2004, p.149.

14

Ibid., p.1226.

15

Ibid., p.1231.

Chaos and Creation [1960]

Helen Sainsbury

If the physicists are producing anti-matter, let it be allowed to the painters, already specialists in angels, to paint it.[1]

In April 1960, the Waldorf Hotel, New York, was the setting for the 5th Annual Convention on Visual Communications.[2] Although unable to attend on the day, Salvador Dalí found a way to accept the organisers' invitation to appear. Always ready to embrace new technology, he enlisted the services of Videotape Productions Inc. in New York and, with the collaboration of photographer Philippe Halsman, together they made a recording for presentation at the convention. The resulting film offers intriguing insights into Dalí's position in relation to modernism, a subject that had preoccupied him from the 1920s.

Documentary in style, the film takes the form of a lecture and performance that result in the creation of an artwork. Halsman, taking the role of commentator, translator and, to some extent, straight man to Dalí's chaotic and mercurial presence, opens by asking 'Do you paint?' After knocking over two easels with his cane, Dalí replies that he does not need to because the work on a third easel has already been 'finished' by Mondrian. He goes on to create a painting using two female models, a pigsty (a bespoke wooden structure divided up into compartments so that the view from above replicates the composition of the Mondrian, fig.137), an assortment of liquids, one 'slightly debauched motorcycle', four pigs and seven mealworms, who, rather touchingly, are credited in the opening sequence along with the models and production team. The finished painting is, according to Dalí, 'perhaps not one of the best abstract paintings but one of the most angelical'. He is then seen on the telephone, talking to the Director of the Guggenheim Museum, James Johnson Sweeney, offering the painting as something that would interest his museum. In the closing scenes, splashes of paint on the canvas, which bear some resemblance to musical notes, are interpreted on the piano by Leonardo Balada.

The film is littered with tongue-in-cheek references to art and artists both admired and criticised by Dalí. On the one hand, the jokes may be read as homages to works that he held in esteem. For example, the mealworms are superimposed over the writhing human beings depicted in Hieronymous Bosch's *The Garden of Earthly Delights* c.1505, a work much admired by Dalí, who refers to Bosch as the grandfather of Surrealism. The tone may be irreverent, but in this instance it is far from critical. Meanwhile, the white dress of one model is pulled off, caught in the turning wheel of the motorcycle, a humorous reference to Marcel Duchamp's *The Bride Stripped*

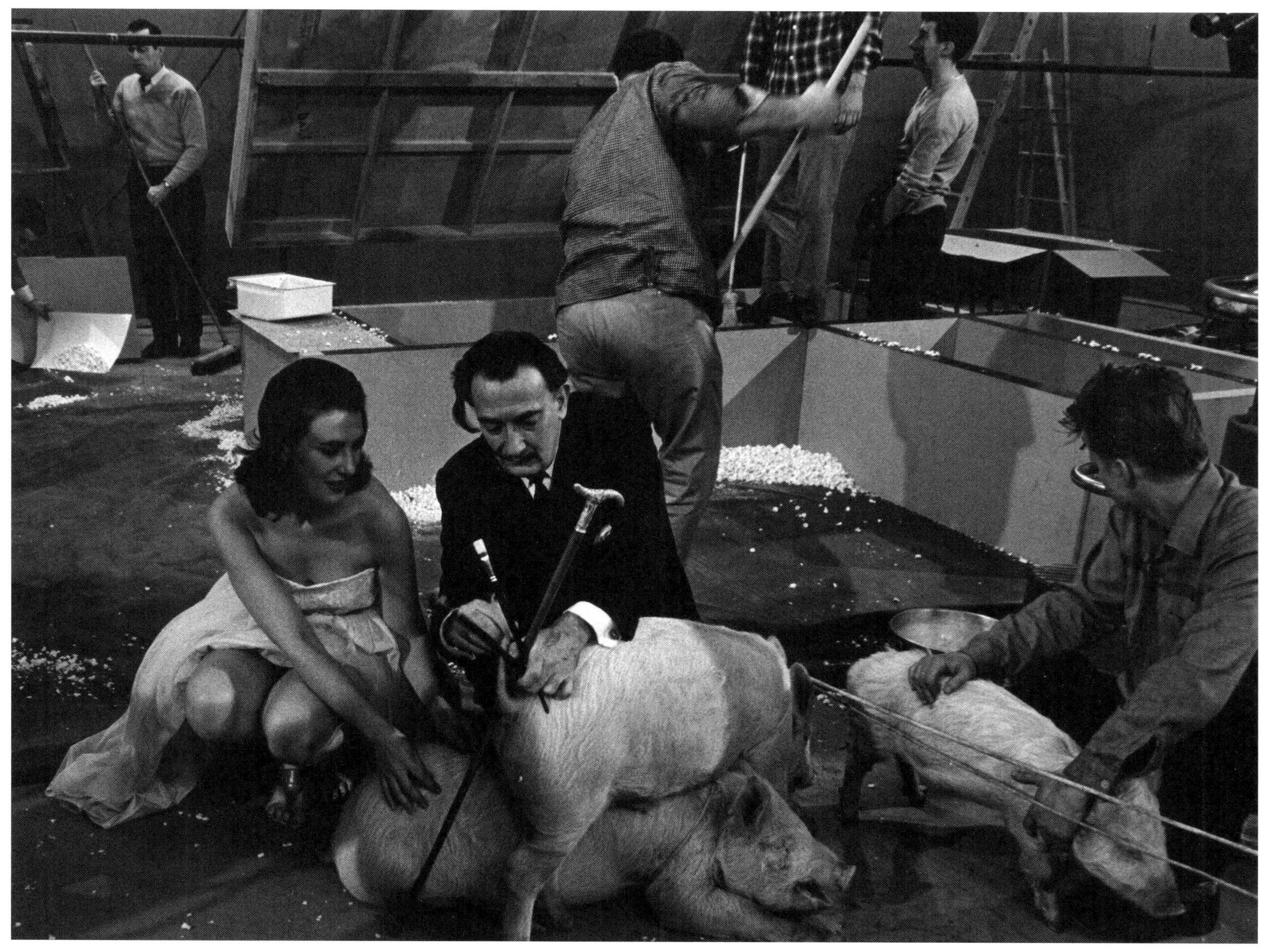

Bare by her Bachelors Even of 1915–23. Dalí and Duchamp had been friends since their participation in the Surrealist movement in the 1930s, and they saw each other frequently from 1958 onwards, since both artists would typically spend much of the winter in New York, their summers in Cadaqués, with visits to Paris en route between the two.[3] However, Duchamp's implied presence in *Chaos and Creation* cannot be due to friendship alone. As Dawn Ades has pointed out, although his readymades were currently being held up as instrumental in the development of Conceptual art, Dalí had recently reassessed Duchamp's brief but significant contribution to the history of painting. In the 1959 text 'The King and Queen Traversed by Swift Nudes', which takes its title from a Duchamp canvas, Dalí traced the lineage from Duchamp's early paintings of forms in motion or disintegration to his own 'post-atomic' period paintings.[4] Above all, Dalí saw Duchamp as grappling with the modern theories of physics that so fascinated him.

Piet Mondrian, on the other hand, was often on the receiving end of harsh criticism from Dalí. The very premise of *Chaos and Creation* – that of allowing order to emerge from chaos – gave Dalí an opportunity to attack what he saw as the cold rationality of modernism, and of Mondrian in particular. It also allowed him to align his own work with that of a younger generation of artists whom he admired, especially Willem de Kooning, whose intensely gestural paintings of women made in the 1950s seemed to Dalí to contain the same energy and fragmentation that he sought in his own paintings of the human figure around that time.[5] In *Chaos and Creation*, the painting that he created with this unorthodox assembly of materials and tools mimicked the acceptance of chance and gesture in Abstract Expressionism, which, as Dalí noted, had its roots in Surrealist practice (fig.138).

In the 1947 volume, *50 Secrets of Magic Craftsmanship*, Dalí had included a comparative table of values after 'Dalínian Analysis'.[6] Eleven artists were given marks out of twenty for nine different categories: craftsmanship, inspiration, colour, design, genius, composition, originality, mystery and authenticity. Vermeer scored the highest, dropping just one point for originality. Picasso occupied the middle ranks, whilst Mondrian attained a miserable five out of 180. *Dalí on Modern Art: The Cuckolds of Antiquated Modern Art*, published ten years later, contained a scathing attack on the practitioners and champions of modernism, asking 'what is more cuckolded, more betrayed, more afflicted with cracks than this modern art with its mania for the sterilised cleanliness of functional forms and aseptic surfaces?'[7] Again, Mondrian comes under particular scrutiny. The same work that was reproduced for the 1960 film, *Composition (B) in Blue, Yellow and White* 1936 (Kunstmuseum Basel) is here illustrated alongside Vermeer's *The Music Lesson*. Dalí confesses:

I find in Mondrian's order the chambermaid's cleanliness of Vermeer and even his retinian instantaneity of blues and yellows. I nevertheless hasten to say that Vermeer is almost everything and Mondrian almost nothing!

Completely idiotic critics have for several years used the name of Piet Mondrian as though he represented the summum of all spiritual activity.

Matter is discontinuous and any valid venture in modern painting can and must proceed only from a single idea, as concrete as it is significant: the discontinuity of matter.

Dalí's watches are soft because they are the masochistic product of the discontinuity of matter. Mathieu's signs are the royal decrees of the discontinuity of matter.[8]

In *Chaos and Creation*, Dalí amuses himself by making play with the two names. Piet [Mondrian] becomes Niet, Russian for no, whilst Dalí is equated with Da, or Yes, thereby affirming that he stands for everything and Mondrian for nothing.

The symbolic meaning of the images in *Chaos and Creation* has been explored by Fèlix Fanés.[9] The motorbike mimics the means of production of the mechanical age, the young women are clearly associated with the origins of life, whilst the pigs may be seen as representative of Dalí himself. It should be noted that the motifs of pigs, motorbikes and Mondrian also appear in parallel projects, such as the February 1960 issue of *Art News*, in which Dalí offered an alternative review of a new exhibition of Cartier-Bresson photographs. These, he asserts, are 'so "hyperestheticized" with moralities that it becomes morally necessary to extract at least four of them'.[10] A vibrant Cartier-Bresson photograph of Seville from 1933, a year in which the city suffered anarchist uprisings in the build-up to the Spanish Civil War, is reproduced directly above a photograph of a pig farm in Holland of 1956. The former image depicts

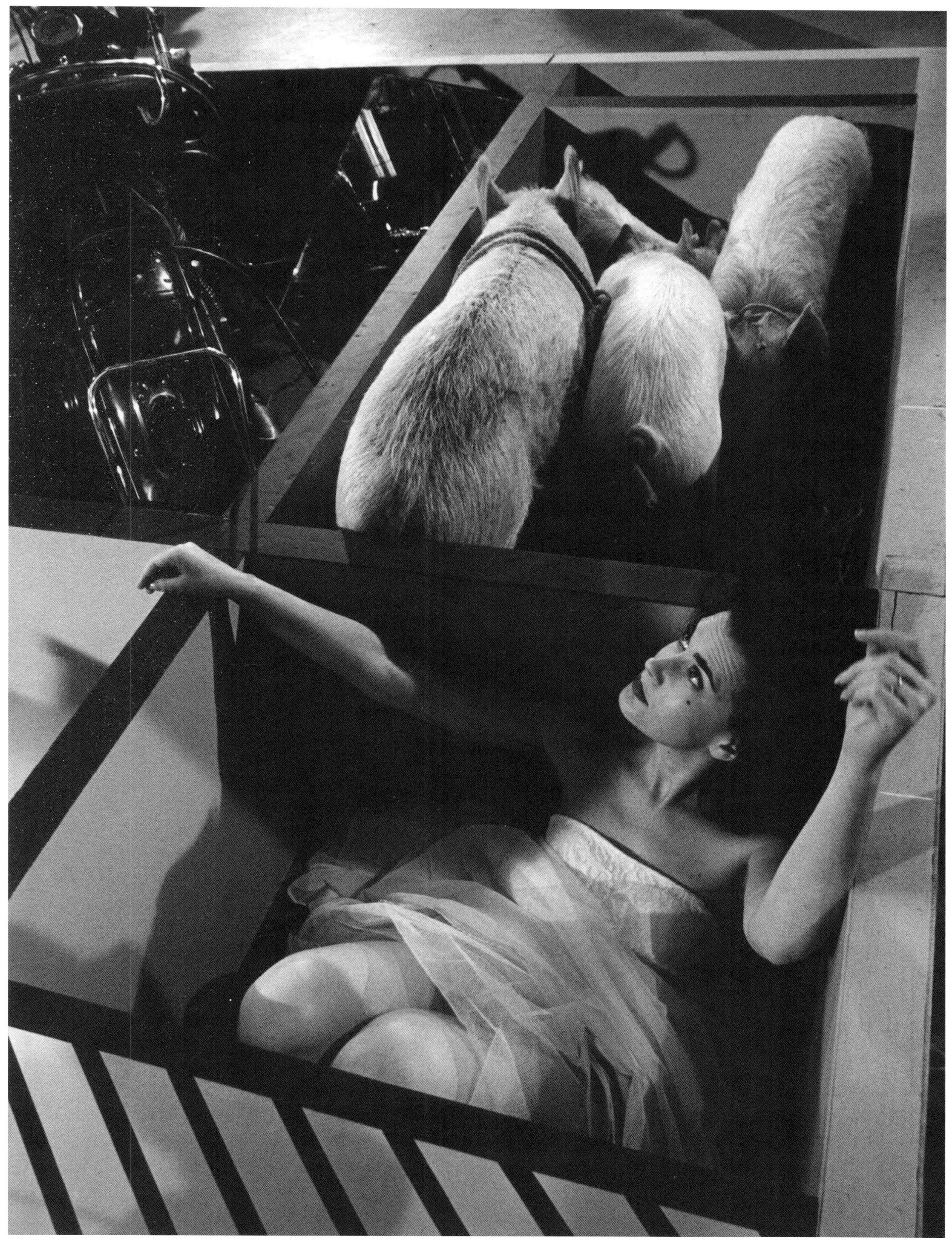

children playing in a ruined street, yet despite the apparent poverty and hardship of their situation, the exuberance of the youngsters is undeniably life-affirming. By contrast, the Dutch scene is one of calm and order, the pigs lined up in geometric pens. Even the landscape, which consists of parallel dykes and a straight line of trees, seems to have been subjected to order. Dalí, in the accompanying text, makes no secret of his desire to contaminate this world of order with something more visceral:

Holland: clarity, cleanliness, parallelism. The Holland of hogs, like a Mondrian or a Vermeer. In the famous opera I am writing at the moment, I want one hundred (100) hogs to be killed simultaneously against a background of 558 motorcyclists, the engines running. Now that I have seen Cartier-Bresson, I want the hogs to be prepared for slaughter in rigorously parallel lines, like a wonderful Mondrian – wonderful because pinked (the rose of pigs); each of the black lines will become tender, bleeding, deafening with sonorous volume.[11]

Dalí, a natural performance artist long before the term existed, would certainly have been tracking the significant changes taking place in art during the late 1950s. John Cage's performance evenings at Black Mountain College, the 'Happenings' prevalent on the New York scene, the activities of the Gutaï group in Japan and, not least, Dalí's close companion Georges Mathieu's public painting performances would, no doubt, have come under his radar. Indeed, in 1959 he described Mathieu, admiringly, as among the 'courageous group [who] rushed at top speed toward absolute nothingness'.[12] However, the spring of 1960 was notable for a number of significant events that took place over the few weeks preceding the April conference for which *Chaos and Creation* was made.

According to notes in the Philippe Halsman Archive, Dalí's videotape was recorded on 4 March 1960.[13] Just five days later, on 9 March, Yves Klein invited an audience to the Galerie Internationale d'Art Contemporain in Paris to witness a performance in which nude models painted themselves blue, then were instructed by the artist to press their bodies against canvases on the walls and floor of the gallery, creating imprints of their torsos and thighs.[14] For Klein, these were the areas of the body in which the creative energy of the universe could be found, and this was the first public performance of these works, which he called 'anthropometries'. Although they are very far from the chaotic creation of Dalí, it seems that both artists were grappling with the nature of the universe as well as celebrating the role of the body, especially through its imprint, as opposed to the intellect. Here too, music played a part in the performance. Klein's *Monotone Symphony* consisted of just one sound, drawn out for twenty minutes, followed by a similar period of silence. His performance concluded with a discussion in which Mathieu participated. Given that Dalí refused to cross the Atlantic by air, and was in New York on 4 March, it seems virtually impossible that he could have attended Klein's performance five days later, but it is conceivable that he would have heard about the forthcoming event from Mathieu.

Meanwhile, on the other side of the Atlantic, Swiss artist Jean Tinguely was preparing for another extraordinary event, which would take place in the gardens of the Museum of Modern Art, New York, on 17 March.[15] Much as Dalí railed against the dryness of Mondrian's lines, Tinguely reacted against the utopian grandeur of the architecture surrounding the garden. *Homage to New York* might be seen as a reversal of the process employed in *Chaos and Creation*. Tinguely constructed a complex machine from found materials, which, in the performance itself, proceeded to self-destruct. Although prevented from reaching its ultimate purpose by the intervention of an over-zealous fire-fighter, the remains nevertheless ended up in the bin.

Dalí's innate talent for showmanship ensured that his arrival in New York never passed unnoticed. Whenever he visited the United States, he endeavoured to find new ways of attracting publicity. On one occasion he disembarked from the liner with a 12-metre long baguette over his shoulder. In December 1959, his entrance had a more futuristic feel. Dressed in a gold leather boiler suit, Dalí negotiated the gangplank in his newly invented mode of transport, the 'ovocipede', a transparent bubble with a seat inside it that could be propelled by the user like a hamster wheel.[16] This vehicle, which was modelled on a detail from *The Garden of Earthly Delights*, was to reappear in *Chaos and Creation* as an unconventional bathtub for one of the models.

Despite the notoriety this generated with the general public, Dalí's aesthetic position was very much on the outside of the New York art scene at this time. He wrote extensively on what he saw as the shortcomings of modern art, and particularly of abstract art, which occupied such a hallowed position in the United States under the influence of distinguished wartime emigrés like Mondrian and Josef Albers. Hans Namuth's film of Jackson Pollock making one of his paintings had helped to raise the status of painting as an act in itself rather than a means to represent the world. However, for Dalí there was something of the cold calculation of Mondrian in the controlled way that Pollock executed his paintings. Moreover, Mondrian had clearly acknowledged his admiration for Pollock by advising a sceptical Peggy Guggenheim to support the artist.[17] Dalí saw the Solomon R. Guggenheim Museum (until 1952 called the Museum of Non-Objective Art) as the repository of this type of work. As recently as 1957 James Johnson Sweeney, who was director from 1952 to 1960, had organised a monographic exhibition on Mondrian.[18] He, therefore, appeared to champion all that Dalí despised in art.

Both Sweeney and Dalí had been invited to contribute to the symposium that accompanied the Museum of Modern Art's 1958 Antoni Gaudí exhibition.[19] Dalí contributed a series of taped proclamations in which he took the opportunity to berate the New York critics, whom he felt trivialised Gaudí's contribution whilst lamenting the lack of due consideration afforded to those 'heroic and neglected abstract painters such as

Klein, Mathieu, Tobey, Serpent [sic: Serpan] and others'. Although Sweeney comes in for some gentle mockery in the film, he went some way to redeem himself in Dalí's eyes when he published his 1960 monograph on Gaudí.

Chaos and Creation was one of several fruitful collaborations with Philippe Halsman, a friend of Dalí since the 1940s. Halsman's imagination and technical brilliance resulted in some memorable images, many developed in collaboration with the artist, such as the *Dalí Atomicus* portraits of 1940 and *Dalí's Mustache* 1956, an innovative book in the form of an interview.[20] The light-hearted tone of the book is echoed in *Chaos and Creation*, in which it becomes clear that the two friends enjoyed a shared sense of humour.

Balada, who provided the musical element of the film, had first met Dalí whilst studying music at Julliard College in 1957–8, through common friends who had also been exiled by the Spanish Civil War. He recalls that much of the performance was improvised and that Dalí had assembled the cast and props with no fixed idea of what their role might be.[21] Dalí presided over the proceedings, but the performers were able to contribute ideas as the action progressed. Unfortunately, the surviving copy of the film does not appear to be complete. It cuts out abruptly just as Balada begins to play the piano, but he remembers that there was further footage, which it seems may have been edited out or lost.

It is not known what exactly led Dalí to use videotape to make the recording, but the surviving copy, found at Dalí's house in Port Lligat, had been transferred to 16mm film.[22] It would have been necessary to project the film at the conference and it may be that the technology was not available at that time for projecting the film straight from videotape. However, as Fanés has pointed out, Dalí's use of videotape precedes that of Nam June Paik, generally credited with being the first video artist, whose earliest video work was exhibited in 1965.[23] It remains open to conjecture whether Dalí's choice of video was merely one of convenience or a conscious decision to move into a new medium.

Dalí may have been poking fun at the art world, but nevertheless, *Chaos and Creation* brings together a number of serious subjects that preoccupied him throughout his career. The first formal shot is of Dalí inviting the cameraman to focus on his eye, perhaps a reference to the slicing of the eye at the beginning of *Un Chien andalou*.

His broader interest in popular film and television is also hinted at through the use of popcorn and custard pies amongst the props. Here, as in his paintings, Dalí also plays with double images, by superimposing his own mouth onto an image of the eye of a classical sculpture, found in a magazine. The implication, interpreted by Halsman, is that 'Dalí's mouth has become his eye and through his mouth he will explain.'

Despite revisiting a number of earlier obsessions, *Chaos and Creation* nevertheless encapsulates Dalí's thinking in the late 1950s and early 1960s. As he had recently declared in his *Anti-Matter Manifesto*, Freud (and the subconscious) no longer served as the primary source for his imagery.[24] The artist's voracious appetite for new learning had led him to study the theories of contemporary physicists, and Werner Karl Heisenberg's *Uncertainty Principle*, in particular, had captured his imagination and may even have stimulated the film's title.[25] A world that, according to Heisenberg, was in such a state of perpetual motion that it was impossible to measure the location of anything at any point in time, offered infinite creative possibilities.

Notes

1
Salvador Dalí, *Anti-Matter Manifesto*, originally published in *Salvador Dalí*, exh. cat, Carstairs Gallery, New York 1958. See also Haim Finkelstein (ed.), *The Collected Writings of Salvador Dalí*, Cambridge 1998, pp.366–7.

2
Fèlix Fanés, *Dalí. Cultura de Masas*, exh. cat., CaixaForum, Barcelona 2004, p.117.

3
Anne d'Harnoncourt and Kynaston McShine (eds.), *Marcel Duchamp*, exh. cat., The Museum of Modern Art, New York 1973, pp.27–8.

4
Dawn Ades, 'Dalí and Duchamp', in Hank Hine, William Jeffett and Kelly Reynolds (eds.), *Persistence and Memory; New Critical Perspectives on Dalí at the Centennial*, St Petersburg (Flo) and Milan 2004, p.12. For 'The King and Queen Traversed by Swift Nudes', *Art News*, April 1959, see Finkelstein 1998, pp.366–9.

5
Jordi Falgàs, 'The "Chafarrinadas" of Modern Abstract Art: Dalí and Abstract Expressionism', in Hine, Jeffett and Reynolds 2004, p.35. In 1959 Dalí cited de Kooning along with Kline, Tàpies, Millarès and Mathieu ('The King and Queen Traversed by Swift Nudes', in Finkelstein 1998, pp.368.

6
Salvador Dalí, 50 *Secrets of Magic Craftsmanship*, New York 1947, 1992, trans. Haakon M. Chevalier, p.28.

7
Salvador Dalí, *Dalí on Modern Art: The Cuckolds of Modern Art*, New York 1957, trans. Haakon M. Chevalier, pp. 51–7.

8
Ibid., pp.59–61.

9
Fèlix Fanés, *Chaos and Creation: un film inédito de Salvador Dalí* in *Actas del V Congreso de la A.E.H.C.*, La Coruña, C.G.A.I., 1995, pp.19–25, also republished online at Biblioteca Virtual Miguel de Cervantes, 2002.

10
Salvador Dalí, 'Cartier-Bresson: Moralities', *Art News*, vol.58, no.10, Feb. 1960, pp.38–9.

11
Ibid. The right half of the photograph had been reproduced in André Breton's *L'Amour fou*, Paris 1937, 1983, p.169.

12
'The King and Queen Traversed by Swift Nudes', in Finkelstein 1998, pp.368.

13
I am grateful to Oliver Halsman Rosenberg for this information.

14
Sidra Stich, 'Anthropometry Painting', in *Yves Klein*, exh. cat., Museum Ludwig, Cologne 1995, pp.171–91.

15
Pontus Hulten and Jean Tinguely, *A Magic Stronger than Death*, New York 1987, p.68.

16
Montse Aguer, 'Chronology' in Dawn Ades (ed.), *Dalí*, exh. cat., Palazzo Grassi, Venice 2004, pp.522–4.

17
Ellen G. Landau, *Jackson Pollock*, New York 1989, p.105.

18
Mondrian: The Early Years, Solomon R. Guggenheim Museum, New York, Dec. 1957 – Jan. 1958 and San Francisco Museum of Art, Feb. 1958.

19
Aguer 2004, pp.521–2.

20
Salvador Dalí and Philippe Halsman, *Dalí's Mustache*, New York 1954.

21
Telephone conversation between the author and Leonardo Balada, 29 Jan. 2007.

22
Fanés 1995.

23
Fanés 2004, p.117.

24
Dalí, *Anti-Matter Manifesto*, see Finkelstein 1998, pp.366–7.

25
Ibid.

Crazy Movies that Disappear

Elliott H. King

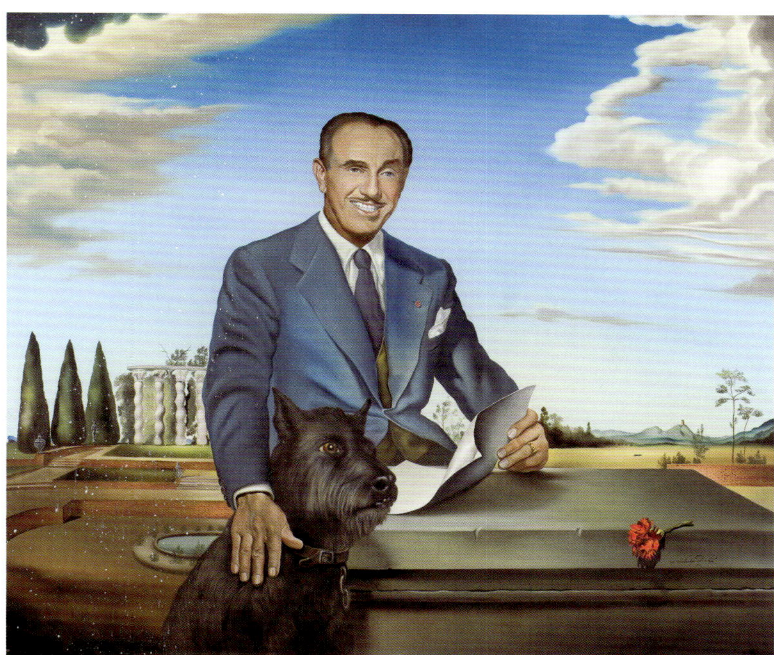

Gerard Malanga: I saw the film you were in where you put a piano in a tree. It was shown at the Caresse Crosby memorial at Gotham Book Mart.

Dalí: Bravo! Bravo! Bravo! Many crazy scenes are now lost. We had three living turtles and the turtles moved inside the piano with cats. And the tails of the cats were attached so when you made a certain sound the cats me-e-eeowed, and suffered very much. And after, we killed every cat with guns. After, we caught a swan and killed it. One beautiful white swan and put one bomb inside and the swan explodes in a thousand pieces … intestines in slow motion … going everywhere, and the feathers! The most beautiful explosion of the swan.

Malanga: And this is on film?

Dalí: Movies disappear and you can never recollect them … And now you have discovered one.

Malanga: The swan explosion sounds very romantic …

Dalí: Absolutely divine …[1]

Although some have questioned whether Dalí's grotesque vision of an exploding swan was ever truly put to film or if he was merely being provocative,[2] this 1975 interview with the artist Gerard Malanga, Warhol's former assistant, is a reminder that the Catalan artist's cinematic experiments went well beyond those that have entered popular consciousness or even for which we have acknowledged scenarios. The post-war era included some of the most prolific decades of Dalí's career, and while his *Portrait of Laurence Olivier in the Role of Richard III* 1955 has become emblematic of his amicable relationship with the film industry (fig.140), a number of his projects never made it past conception or simply failed to leave any lasting mark. These include: his proposal to Jack Warner to make a documentary about his book *50 Secrets of Magic Craftsmanship*[3]; his pitch to Federico Fellini to make a cinematic adaptation of *The Secret Life of Salvador Dalí*; the *Seven Wonders of the World* series that was commissioned for a movie launch in 1954 but never used;[4] the Pop art poster for *Fantastic Voyage* 1966 starring Stephen Boyd and Raquel Welch that he made but was unused; the tarot deck he designed – or asked his muse Amanda Lear to design for him – for *Live and Let Die* 1973, which was cut from the picture when a price could not be negotiated with Bond producer Albert R. 'Cubby' Broccoli;[5] and the poster for Pier Paolo Pasolini's controversial film *Salò, or the 120 Days of Sodom* 1975 that was ordered but apparently never completed.[6] He is also said to have worked on a stereoscopic television channel with the American company Video Head, and he apparently made a brief video in 1972 for which he used Marilyn Monroe's head and superimposed the facial features of American actress Denise Sandell, telling her that he planned to film the Paris *Vogue* cover he had designed in December 1971 using Philippe Halsman's collage photograph, *Mao Marilyn*.[7] For many of these projects no relics have surfaced, but as Dalí told Malanga, most of his 'crazy' experiments disappeared.

Happily, Dalí scholarship is far from stagnant. As the present exhibition testifies, it is very likely that long-forgotten anecdotes, clips and scenarios will continue to surface as more people turn their attentions towards Dalí's efforts with cinema and, more specifically, his work beyond the orthodoxy of Surrealism. This distinction is especially important for his work with film. Although the title 'Surrealist' was more or less bestowed (and revoked) at the discretion of André Breton, the aesthetic rupture between Dalí's Surrealist and, for lack of a better term, 'ex-Surrealist' painting (i.e. executed after his formal dismissal from the movement in 1939) was largely delineated by the artist himself. He directly opposed his new 'classical' work to his 1930s production, which he belittled in his 1941 essay, 'The Last Scandal of Salvador Dalí', as merely 'experimental'.[8] Over the next forty years, he would declare that his work was no longer Surrealist, yet he abandoned neither the paranoiac-critical method nor his identification of himself as the only legitimate Surrealist. While his 1941 partition may provide a convenient means of classifying a certain turn in his painting – thinly veiled Freudian symbols give way to geometrically organised, mythological and, later, religious subjects – closer examination reveals many unacknowledged continuities. Perusing the catalogue for his 1941 exhibition at New York's Julien Levy Gallery, one sees that *Old Age, Adolescence, Infancy (The Three Ages)* and *Slave Market (with Apparition of the Invisible Bust of Voltaire)* (both 1940, now in the Salvador Dalí Museum, St Petersburg, Florida) flaunt the double-imagery

he had employed earlier with *The Endless Enigma* 1938 (Museo Nacional Centro de Arte Reina Sofía, Madrid). And the handful of works that could be argued as classically influenced are not markedly different from earlier pieces in their union of meticulous technique and oneiric space.[9] His previous exhibition at the Julien Levy Gallery in 1939 had even included the painting *Saint Jerome*, suggesting that by this early date he had already adopted the Catholic subjects that would typify his work in forthcoming decades. In fact, the 1941 'classical' exhibition was largely denigrated in the press because they could not distinguish Dalí's classicism from his 'Surrealism'.

If the case can be made for some pictorial continuity, the evidence is all the more persuasive with regard to his film scripts, due largely to his habit of recuperating details from past projects, most of which had gone unrealised. His statement that *La Carretilla de carne* would capture 2,000 priests on bicycles traversing the Place de la Concorde recalled his designs for the ballet *Colloque sentimental* (Sentimental Symposium, 1944; fig.71),[10] drawn from the cyclists that had figured in his screenplay *Babaouo* (which themselves originated in his 1929 painting *Illumined Pleasures*; fig.36). The aforementioned exploding swan was also first put forward for *La Carretilla de carne* ('five white swans explode one after the other in a series of minutely slow images that develop according to the most rigorous archangelic eurhythmics'), and recalls the exploding giraffes cited in *The Secret Life*

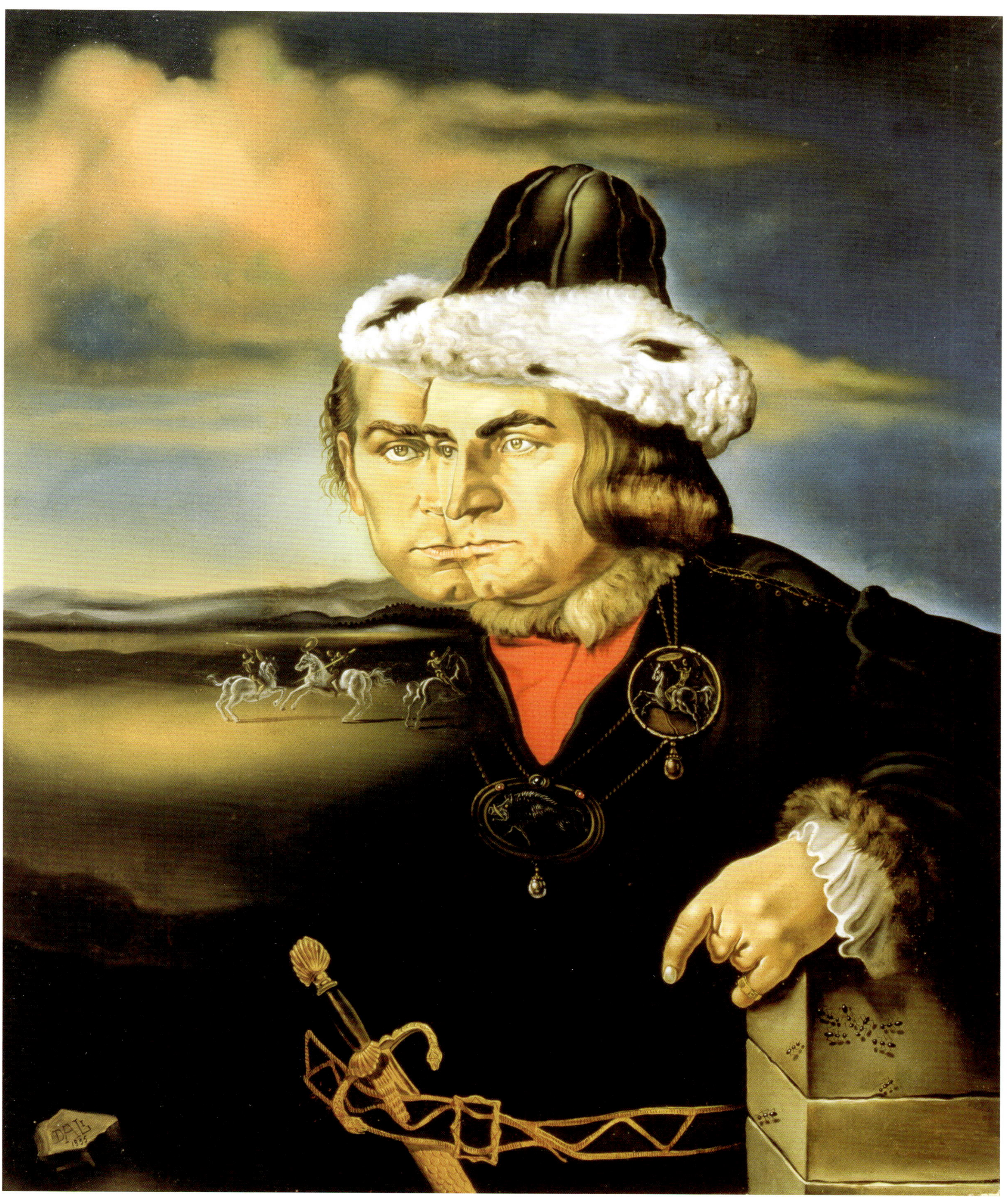

of Salvador Dalí in reference to *Giraffes on Horseback Salad*.[11] An image of an elongated bed was introduced in his illustrated frontispiece for his book *La Femme visible,* and went on to figure in his scripts *Babaouo, Les Mystères surréalistes de New York* and *Giraffes on Horseback Salad,* and his designs for the 1939 *Dream of Venus* pavilion. Pianos are another recurring subject, from *Un Chien andalou* through to numerous pictorial references from 1931 onwards.[12] While it remains open whether such repetition should be judged an asset or detrimental to Dalí's cinematic activity, these continuities confirm that the partitions that have been constructed between his early, Surrealist and long-censured 'late' work have been inappropriately and unnecessarily exaggerated.

One of the great examples of Dalí's recuperation and reinvention of previous material – and one of the few cases when his filmic vision actually made it to the shooting stage – is the unfinished motion picture, *L'Histoire prodigieuse de la dentellière et du rhinocéros* (Prodigious History of *The Lacemaker* and the Rhinoceros, 1954–62), one of the most widely misunderstood projects of the artist's post-war oeuvre. Filming on this rarely seen movie began in November 1954 hard on the heels of *La Carretilla de carne,* when Dalí returned to Paris from New York determined to make a copy of Jan Vermeer's famous painting in the Musée du Louvre, *The Lacemaker* 1669–70.[13] This was the first of many continuities; the artist had been attracted to Vermeer's depiction of a Dutch girl weaving

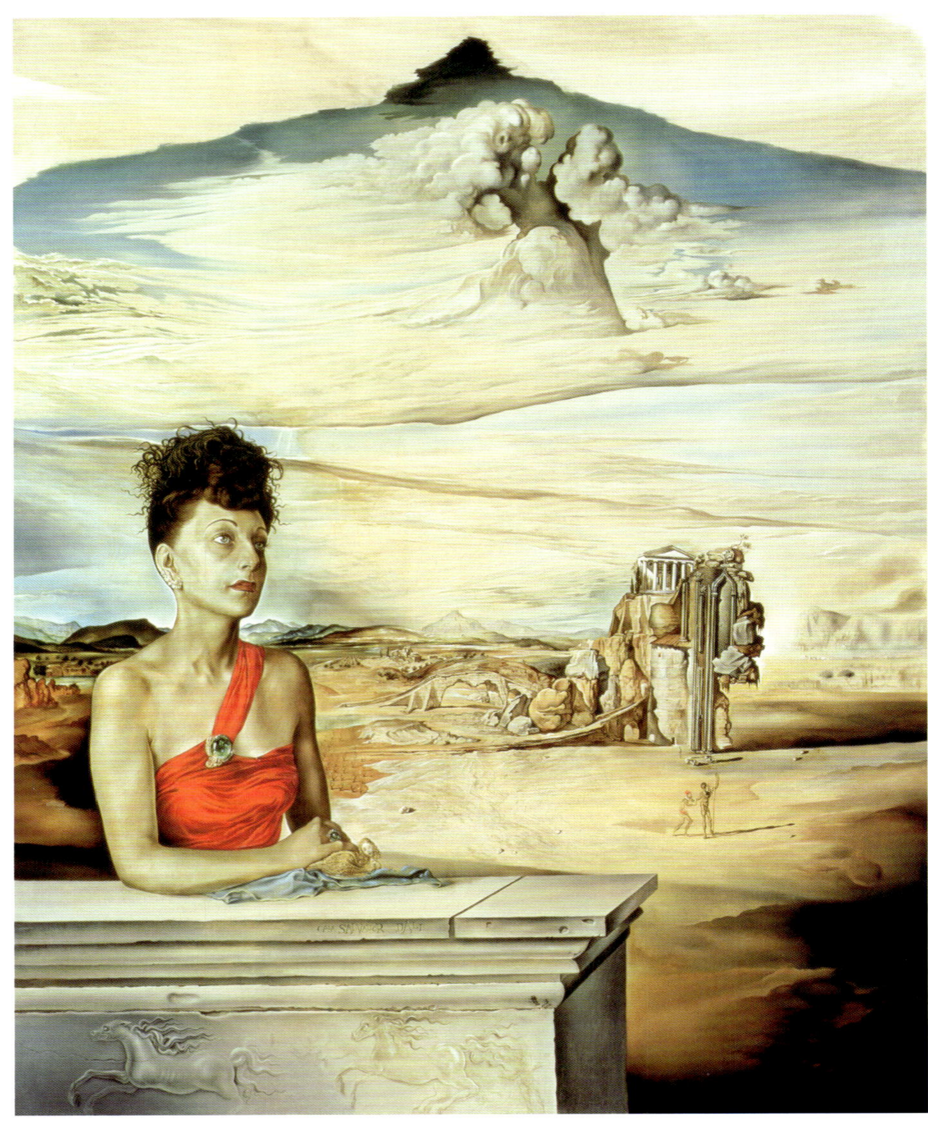

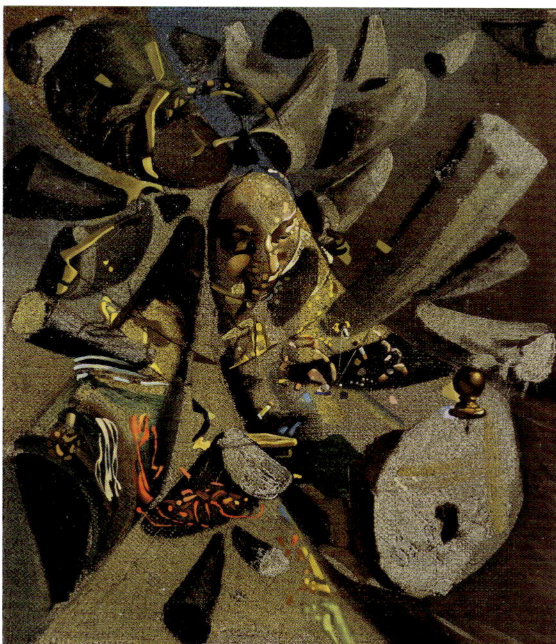

142
*Paranoiac-Critical Study of
Vermeer's 'Lacemaker'* 1954–5
Oil on canvas on panel
27.1 x 22.1 cm
The Solomon R. Guggenheim
Museum, New York. Anonymous Gift

multi-coloured threads for at least twenty-five years – one recalls its cameo in *Un Chien andalou*. He later reported having been fascinated by the image since the age of nine, when, he said in 1955, he was overcome by a 'lyrical ecstasy' provoked by pressing his elbow into some dried bread crumbs on the dining-room table while looking at a reproduction of *The Lacemaker* that hung on the wall of his father's office. He then 'began to become absolutely obsessed in a truly delirious way by the painting *The Lacemaker* … and the rhinoceros horn'.[14] Through his contact with the Louvre's conservator, Magdeleine Hours, Dalí organised a one-hour session to copy *The Lacemaker* and asked the French photographer Robert Descharnes, whom he had met in 1950 through the Tachist painter Georges Mathieu, to make a film. Descharnes recalls the day:

Wednesday, November 20[15] *at eleven in the morning, Dalí was welcomed in the Louvre's Grand Galerie by Monsieur Florisonne, the curator of the museum's department of paintings. He led him to a large room in the La Trémoille pavilion, which was generally reserved for laboratory work, where they had set up two easels and a chair. On one easel was an empty white canvas and on the other, Vermeer's Lacemaker. Dalí promised to copy it in one hour … Dalí then started to methodically copy the painting surrounded by Professor [Pierre] Roumeguère, Magdeleine Hours, who created the first great laboratory in the Louvre, the painter Georges Mathieu, Nicolas Tikomirkoff and myself – I was filming this scene because*

Dalí insisted that we follow his work step-by-step. Ultimately, he painted several copies of The Lacemaker, which were actually exercises in rhinoceros horns, because these copies had nothing more really to do with The Lacemaker. She represented the three rhinoceros horns or 'three converging rhinocessalesque bread crumbs'.[16]

Following Dalí's instructions, every stage of his visit to the Louvre was filmed, from his sober entrance through the Museum's ornamented galleries to his meticulous analysis of *The Lacemaker*, during which he pointed out to the conservator a renegade hair on the work's surface. Descharnes shot many close-ups of the painter's face, reminiscent of Paul Haesaert's *Visite à Picasso* 1950 – the film in which the artist whom Dalí often regarded as his arch-rival in Spanish genius painted on a vertical pane of glass to allow the camera to record his expressions.[17] After an hour of work, however, Dalí had not copied *The Lacemaker* at all. He had instead painted four converging rhinoceros horns.[18] Purporting to be mystified by this himself,[19] he then suggested to Descharnes that they collaborate on an extended film that would explore the psychic relationship between the rhinoceros horn and *The Lacemaker* in all its facets. The next few months would find Dalí adding to his developing *Paranoiac-Critical Study of Vermeer's 'Lacemaker'*. In April 1955 he arrived at Vincennes Zoo in Paris, where, enclosed within a rocky alcove barely separated from the zoo's rhinoceros François, he painted the second stage of the work – recorded in

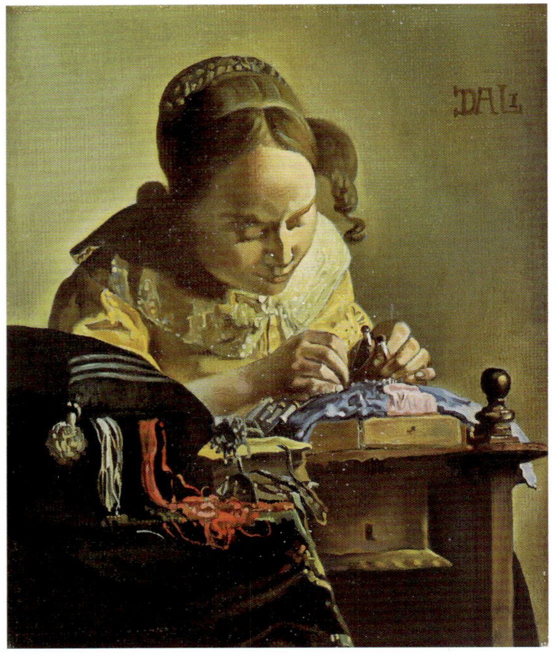

143
The Lacemaker
(after Vermeer) 1955
Oil on canvas 23.5 x 19.7 cm
The Metropolitan Museum
of Art, New York.
The Robert Lehman
Collection, 1975

one of the film's most familiar scenes. Dalí ultimately painted three versions of *The Lacemaker: The Paranoiac-Critical Study* (fig.142), the detailed study now in the Metropolitan Museum of Art (fig.143) and an unfinished version that he retained (fig.145). During the rigorous study that ensued at Port Lligat, it seems that Dalí discovered that rhinoceros horns, like sunflowers and cauliflowers, are constructed according to logarithmic spirals – forms frequently found in nature, where the distance between a spiral's turnings increases by a defined mathematical ratio, *Phi* (Φ). It is likely that he had already anticipated this, given his longstanding interest in morphology, and his near decade of correspondence with the Romanian mathematician Matila Ghyka, whose writings explored the inherent harmony and proportion present in nature and art by analysing the mathematical construction of certain growth patterns, including those of rhinoceros horns.[20] Armed as he was with this understanding of natural geometry and believing *The Lacemaker* to be 'formed' of rhinoceros horns, it was then a relatively simple leap for Dalí to 'see' *The Lacemaker* within the spirals of sunflowers and cauliflowers (fig.144).

Largely because the film is unfinished very few have seen the footage in its entirety, and the notion that the exploration of logarithmic spirals constitutes the core of the *L'Histoire prodigieuse* … has hitherto gone unchallenged. Descharnes compounds this view in his 1962 monograph *Dalí de Gala*, where he offers a formulaic chain for the film's movement: 'Nebulous = *Lacemaker* = rhinoceros horn = corpuscular and logarithmic granulations of the cauliflower = granulation of the sea urchin, this shiver of creation, etc.'[21] Watching *L'Histoire prodigieuse* … today, it is clear that things are not so straightforward. Dalí's passion for logarithmic forms, one finds, is only the springboard for a confounding ecstasy that introduces into the film a myriad of non sequitor sequences: Dalí struggling to paint within the strong winds of the Catalan *tramuntana* (an *homage* to a turn-of-the-century Figueres shoemaker who was reportedly driven mad by the winds and died trying to 'conduct' them on the city's Rambla); chairs pursuing Dalí and Gala across the Empordá plain; and Dalí – sporting a polyhydric hat inspired by Johannes Kepler – ferociously whipping nine canvases with a riding crop.[22] In another baffling sequence, Dalí, wearing a Catalan *barretina* cap, paints an abstract rendition of *The Lacemaker* whilst Emilio Puignau, his builder and then Mayor of Cadaqués, observes from a nearby shrub in the role of Hitler, sipping tea and offering the painter loaves of bread.[23]

It is difficult to imagine how Dalí could have intended such scenes to function in a coherent film, particularly with logarithmic forms as its subject. In many ways, it might be said that he was simply too excited by the prospects of cinema, and without a strong directorial presence like that which had been offered by Buñuel, he could not restrain himself from overlabouring his scripts with material. One sees this in both *La Carretilla de carne* and *L'Histoire prodigieuse*…[24] But according to Descharnes, the inchoate assemblage of scenes that now comprises *L'Histoire prodigieuse*… is not a shortcoming but a product of the film's nature; narrative cohesion was decidedly not the paramount criterion for shooting, at least after about 1956, when filming moved from Paris to Cadaqués. The film authentically began as a documentary of Dalí's work on the painting that would become *Paranoiac-Critical Study of Vermeer's Lacemaker* – creating an amalgam of art and performance that leads one to wonder how much it might be indebted to Hans Namuth's films and photographs of Jackson Pollock, and especially to *La Bataille de bouvines*, a film that Descharnes had made on 25 April 1954 of Georges Mathieu painting at the Salon de Mai. But priorities shifted as shooting continued, and the confines of a conventional movie were abandoned in favour of a virtual – and visual – forum for the artist's cinematic experiments. Dalí did whatever he liked, and Descharnes dutifully followed to see where the artist's imagination would turn next. This indulgence – as well as Descharnes' willingness to finance the film almost entirely on his own – encouraged Dalí to pursue inspirations that might never have been filmed otherwise; ultimately, this may be the most important and enduring aspect of the film. 'I was not thinking of filming for the cinema or for television', Descharnes explains. 'The goal was only to express his ideas. It was continually putting elements in a sack. For him, it was a space – just as if he decided to do a little text. But it continued, like a journal.'[25]

In this cinematic 'space', Dalí was free to refashion his previous ideas. Certain scenes in *L'Histoire prodigieuse*… bear a striking resemblance to *Un Chien andalou*, for example. Indeed, in the ultimate act of auto-pilfering, in 1959 Dalí went so far as to have his archivist Albert Field request permission from Buñuel for scenes from *Un Chien andalou* to be recycled for his ongoing film with Descharnes,[26] a connection that should perhaps be unsurprising given that both films were heavily influenced by the 'anti-art' attitude that Dalí had formed in the late 1920s.[27] One episode in particular, in which a needle presses against the eye of actress Martine Roussel, is inextricably linked not only to *Un Chien andalou*'s famous attack against the *oculus sinister*, but also to the unrealised scenario for *Moontide* that was to include a sewing-machine needle plunging into an actress' eye, and to his dream sequence for *Spellbound*, when a man cuts through the eyeball curtains with a pair of enormous scissors.[28] Other scenes invoke the Surrealist classic through transparent dissolves and visual puns. Directly quoting *Un Chien andalou*, a spiny sea urchin becomes a hairy armpit, and an erect nipple is submerged in milk to emerge as a sea urchin's crusty shell decorated with jasmine.

Some of Dalí's ideas for *L'Histoire prodigieuse*… were successfully employed elsewhere. His suggestion for an episode exploring micro-

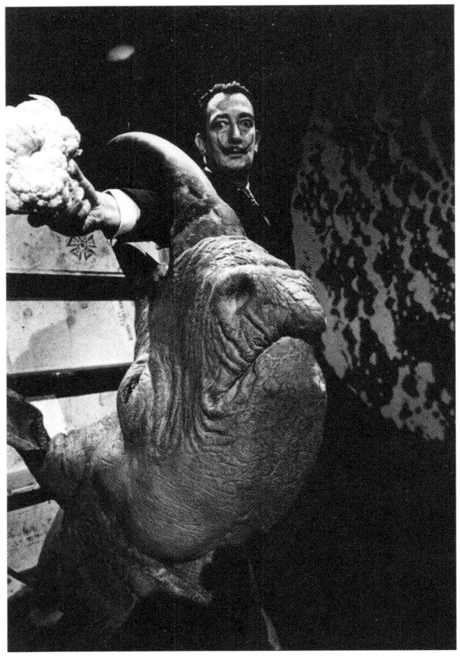

scopic scratches on the copper band of a ballpoint pen in which he 'saw' the Battle of Thermopylae provided sufficient fodder for *Impressions de la Haute Mongolie – Hommage à Raymond Roussel* 1975. This film also recuperated a sequence that Dalí designed in 1958, in which his bucolic painting *Moonlit Landscape with Accompaniment* 1958 (private collection) rotates ninety-degrees to reveal Hitler's nose and moustache.

The shooting of *L'Histoire prodigieuse…* continued sporadically for eight years, and by 1962, Dalí's attentions had moved away from finishing the film (if it could indeed truly be finished) towards the potential offered by television. The logic of that shift had already been evident in 1956, when Dalí appeared on CBS's morning show directing an elaborate sequence that included the head of a rhinoceros, twelve cauliflowers, a film clip of an atomic explosion, a reproduction of *The Lacemaker* and a photograph of a rhinoceros horn – in short, all the elements that were meant for *L'Histoire prodigieuse…* minus the nonplussing additions.[28] He was given atypical freedom with the programme, but there was only a limited time in which to film and he was surely somewhat constrained by the capabilities of the television studio. As a result, however, the CBS appearance succinctly encapsulated his associations between rhinoceros horns, sunflowers, cauliflowers and *The Lacemaker* in a way that ever eluded *L'Histoire prodigieuse…* (figs.144, 147).

Television offered freedom but also welcome limitations, and it is perhaps for this reason that of all Dalí's ideas to make it to film, none after *Father of the Bride* 1950 was actually for the cinema. *L'Histoire prodigieuse…* was less a cinematic project than a sketchpad, and *Chaos and Creation* 1960 was a video – perhaps the first artist's video.[30] By far his most elaborate ventures – *L'Autoportrait mou de Salvador Dalí* (1967, with Jean-Christophe Averty), *Impressions de la Haute Mongolie* (with José Montes Baquer) and *1001 visions de Salvador Dalí* (1978, with Alain Ferrari) – were made for television and in close collaboration with a professional director. According to Descharnes, who also worked with Dalí on *L'Autoportrait mou de Salvador Dalí* and *Les 1001 visions de Dalí*, the artist did not regard television any differently from cinema: 'For Dalí, a camera was a camera. The important thing was the film *when he intervened*.'[31]

In 1974, television would give Dalí the opportunity to explore one of his longstanding cinematic interests, the close-up. When director José Montes Baquer arrived at the St Regis Hotel to discuss with the artist a documentary he was shooting for Westdeutsche Rundfunk about audiovisual art in the United States, Dalí took the opportunity to show him a ballpoint pen on which he had been regularly urinating. Amanda Lear remembers that he had about twenty of these pens, which he kept in a drawer 'where he gloated over them'.[32] 'In this clean and aseptic country, I have been observing how the urinals in the luxury restrooms of this hotel have acquired an

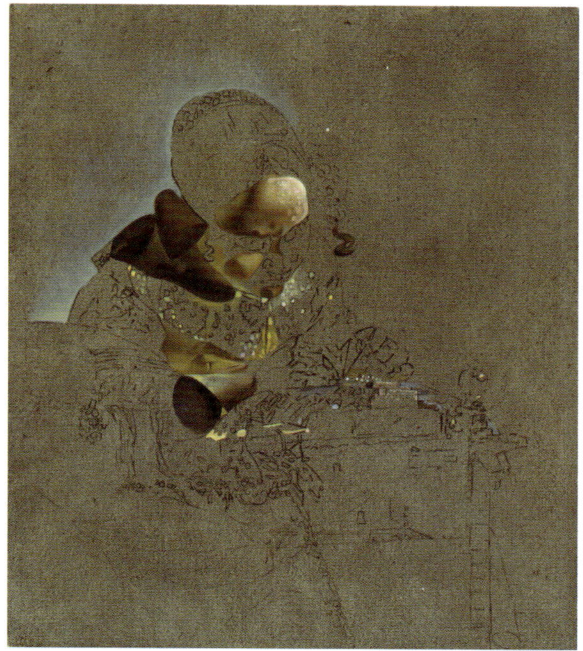

astounding range of rust colours through the interaction of the uric acid on the precious metals', Dalí told the director:

For this reason, I have been regularly urinating on the brass band of this pen over the past weeks to obtain the magnificent structures that you will find with your cameras and lenses. By simply looking at the band with my own eyes, I can see Dalí on the moon, or Dalí sipping coffee on the Champs Elysées. Take then this magical object, work with it, and when you have an interesting result, come see me. If the result is good, we will make a film together.[33]

The German team was invigorated by Dalí's challenge and spent one week filming all the Lilliputian forms that had developed on the pen's three-centimetre brass band. They presented their condensed, thirty-minute video to Dalí, who found it 'infinitely better' than anything he had expected.

The film, *Impressions de la Haute Mongolie – Hommage à Raymond Roussel*, vacillates between images of the newly inaugurated Teatre-Museu Dalí in Figueres and a fable that Dalí spontaneously invented upon seeing Montes Baquer's footage about an expedition to western upper-Mongolia in search of giant hallucinogenic mushrooms many times more powerful than LSD. In Dalí's tale, these soft, white mushrooms – which take six years to grow up to eighteen metres high – had once been administered by a princess to her subjects in the midst of a famine; the whole region had thence become 'cretinised', so that her subjects were no

longer able to distinguish reality from their visions. It is only at the end of the film that one discovers that all the strange scenes are actually extrapolated from the microscopic stains and scratches on the pen. The movie concludes with an outdoor 'happening': enthusiastic townspeople spray paint at an enormous canvas through high-pressure fire hoses while others brandish placards adulating the film's extraordinary *boligrafo*.

It is possible that *Impressions de la Haute Mongolie* was influenced by Pier Pasolini's *Teorema* 1968, a film in which one of the characters, inspired by Francis Bacon to become an artist, urinates on a canvas, and reportedly one of the few modern films that Dalí enjoyed.[34] However, given Descharnes's testimony that the artist had first sowed the seed of this idea in *L'Histoire prodigieuse …*, it would seem that it pre-dated Pasolini's film by several years. It is noteworthy, however, that when Andy Warhol described the 'oxidation paintings' that he began making in December 1977 by hiring friends to urinate on canvases primed with copper-based paint, Dalí criticised them as 'old-fashioned' and compared them to *Teorema*.[35] This is curious, since Warhol's method was essentially identical, though Dalí, of course, took the additional step of analysing the stains to construct a narrative. Warhol's paintings have been critically linked to the drip paintings of Pollock and even to Duchamp's *Fountain* 1917, but given the temporal proximity of Dalí's experiments, the frequent meetings between the two artists in New York and the presence of

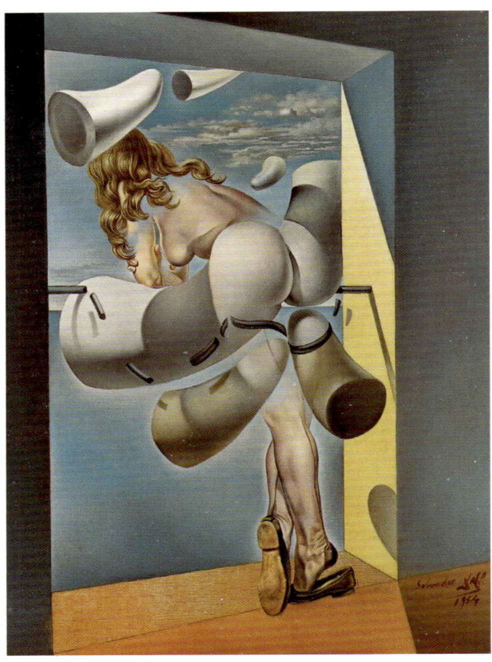

certain figures who oscillated between the Surrealist's 'court' at the St Regis and Warhol's Factory, it is reasonable to hypothesise that in fact Dalí may have been the most direct inspiration for Warhol's series.

The most direct influence on Dalí, meanwhile, was the eccentric French poet, novelist and playwright Raymond Roussel (1877–1933). Dalí insisted that *Impressions de la Haute Mongolie – Hommage à Raymond Roussel* should be so titled in order 'to better understand the work'.[36] Largely unpopular during his lifetime, though much admired in the 1930s by Michel Leiris, Duchamp and many of the Surrealists, Roussel is best known for his virtually impenetrable writing style, exemplified by *Impressions d'Afrique* 1910, *Locus Solus* 1914[37] and *Nouvelles Impressions d'Afrique* 1932. This last was a 1,274-line poem composed of four enormous cantos, each of which consists of only one, drawn-out sentence that is complicated by extremely lengthy footnotes and parenthetical associations that can run up to five levels deep. Despite (or, perhaps, owing to) its difficulty, Dalí was extremely enthusiastic about *Nouvelles Impressions d'Afrique* and, having sent Roussel a copy of his screenplay *Babaouo* in 1932,[38] published a review of the book in *Le Surréalisme au service de la revolution* in 1933, championing it as 'the dream journey of the new paranoiac phenomena':

Roussel's analogies are the product of the most direct, unmediated associations, quite anecdotal and random.

They allow us to witness the darkest and deepest conflicts anyone has ever lived through. Indeed we must look on the sequence of 'compound elements' as relations, since they unfold in a coherent, consecutive way, and remorselessly present a number of very clear, obsessive invariables; for example, fried eggs, multiple allusions to the smell of urine after the ingestion of asparagus, etc. The irrational nature of Roussel's book is established beyond doubt by its universe of relationships between elements.[39]

Thus in 1933, Dalí already recognised the parallel between his burgeoning paranoiac process of uncovering hidden relationships and the irrational associations that Roussel forged in his writing. This can also be inferred from Dalí's quotation of Roussel's title in his 1938 painting, *Impressions of Africa* – a work that premiered in the artist's 1939 exhibition at the Julien Levy Gallery, possibly under the title *Melancholic Eccentricity*.[40] Among Dalí's most memorable self-portraits, this impressive oil, executed in Italy, boasts some of the artist's most intricate double-images, suggesting a relationship between Roussel's 'irrational' sequences and the 'concrete irrationality' that Dalí was striving to capture in his work.

Dalí was also moved by other passages in Roussel's writing, notably the writer's description of the euphoria he experienced upon finishing *La Doublure* 1897:

What I was writing was wreathed by light, I closed the curtains for I was afraid that the slightest chink might

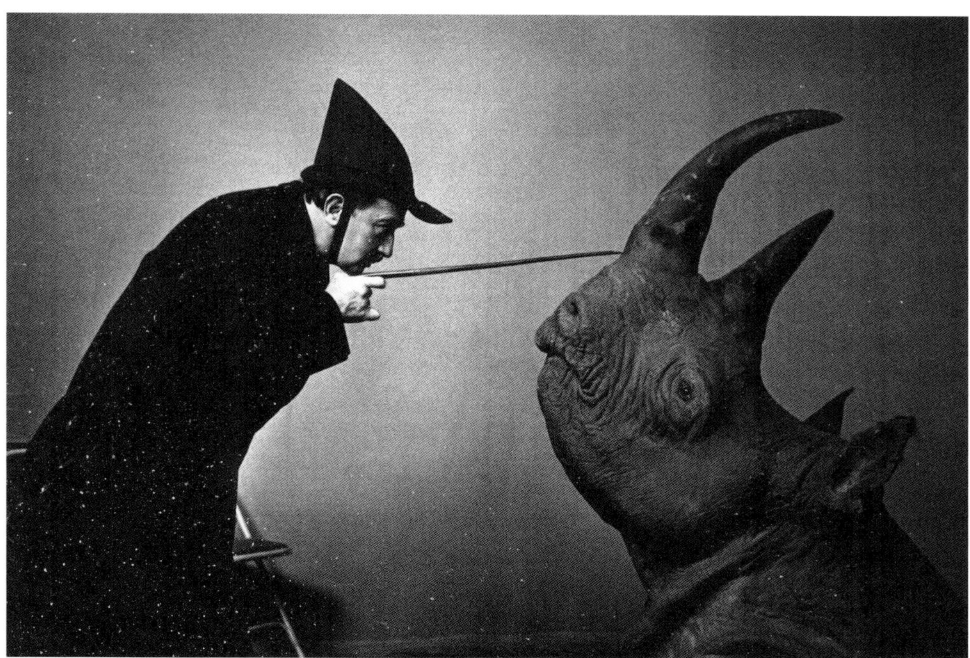

*let escape the luminous rays which emanated from my
pen, I wanted to pull back the screen suddenly and
flood the world with light. If I had left these sheets
of paper lying about, shafts of light would have been
created and would have travelled as far as China,
and the demented crowd would have burst into
the house.*

Roussel's description of the 'luminous rays' that
emanated from his pen was quoted in several
essays, including Pierre Janet's 'The Psychological
Characteristics of Ecstasy' 1926 (which Dalí
would have known given his interest in 'the
phenomenon of ecstasy'),[41] and André Breton's
essay published in 1937.[42] It seems likely that it
influenced *Impressions de la Haute Mongolie*, in
which a pen indeed transports the viewer 'as far
as China'.

Also pertinent to *Impressions de la Haute
Mongolie* is Roussel's description of his travels in
Comment j'ai écrit certains de mes livres 1933:

*in 1920–21, I travelled the world by way of India,
Australia, New Zealand, the Pacific archipelagi, China,
Japan and America … I already knew the principal
countries of Europe, Egypt and all of North Africa, and
later I visited Constantinople, Asia Minor and Persia.
Now, from all these voyages I never took a single thing for
my books. It seemed to me that the circumstance deserves
mention, since it proves so well how imagination counts
for everything in my work.*[43]

Referring to this passage, Breton reinforced this
claim, citing Michel Leiris' account that when
Roussel visited Beijing, he 'shut himself away after
the most cursory visit of the city'.[44] *Impressions de la
Haute Mongolie* also invokes a geographic location
that Dalí never saw – filming took place in New
York, Paris and Spain, but not in Mongolia
(though Dalí allegedly toyed with the idea
of travelling to Beijing).[45] But the film is not
completely isolated from reality. Dalí's position is
clarified by his earlier cinematic exploration of the
division between imagination and reality in *Giraffes
on Horseback Salad*, which opposed a 'Surrealist
Woman' to the unimaginative character, Linda.[46]
'The entire film takes place amidst the struggle
between these two women', Dalí wrote in 1937,
'who personify the world of convention and the
world of imagination. Their struggle culminates in
a process in which it becomes impossible to judge
which of the two worlds is more absurd than the
other.'[47] Dalí's agenda was arguably more militant
than Roussel's: where Roussel took refuge in
the chimerical, Dalí actively strove to 'discredit
reality'.[48] *Impressions de la Haute Mongolie*, like
Giraffes on Horseback Salad, conflates reality with
fantasy to the point where it is difficult to tell where
one ends and the other begins.

Ian Monk, who tackled the challenge
of translating *Nouvelles Impressions d'Afrique* into
English, writes, 'Perhaps one of the points of
the structure of *New Impressions* is to show how a
truly imaginative writer can use a fleeting

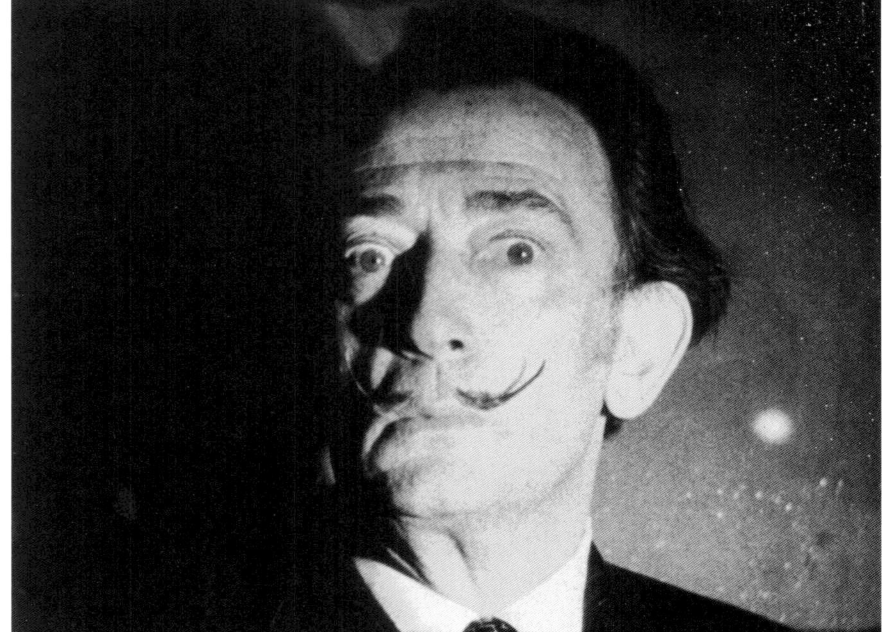

(and intrinsically not very interesting) experience to take his readers anywhere he wants and then take them back again'.[49] *Impressions de la Haute Mongolie* strives for something similar in forming all its fantasy voyages from something commercially produced that one sees without giving it a second thought (a pen).

Although Monk singles out Roussel for exploring 'the rich potentiality of this technique', one must not forget the work of another author whom Dalí revered, Marcel Proust, who launched into *Remembrance of Things Past* with something as seemingly trivial as a madeleine dipped in tea. The combined influence of Proust and Roussel on *Impressions de la Haute Mongolie* should not be underestimated. Attesting to the relationship that Dalí saw between these two writers is a group portrait, staged at his swimming pool in Port Lligat for the 1971 Christmas issue of Paris *Vogue*, in which members of his colourful entourage hoist three large photographs of Proust, Roussel and Chairman Mao Zedong.[50] Dalí noted that Proust's image of a mummy wrapped in gold in *In the Shadow of Young Girls in Flower*, was written despite the fact that Proust had probably never seen a mummy himself (prompting Dalí to conclude that Proust most likely gained his inspiration from a box of sardines).[51] This ability to envision something without having experienced it first-hand recurs in the *Vogue* issue in Dalí's adaptation of Albrecht Dürer's 1515 woodcut of a rhinoceros – possibly art history's most famous depiction of the animal and an image that Dürer is known to have made based on written descriptions without ever having seen a rhinoceros himself. Dalí was clearly taken aback by this, and may have likened it to Henri Zo's original fifty-nine illustrations for *Nouvelles Impressions d'Afrique*. As is well known, Zo was approached to illustrate Roussel's text through a detective agency, and he executed the drawings without knowing the author's identity or having the opportunity even to read the story. 'The choice of illustrations confirms once again the genius of Raymond Roussel', Dalí wrote in 1933.

After 1975, Dalí would continue to make programmes for French television, though none was as groundbreaking as *Impressions de la Haute Mongolie*. His final attempt at cinema would come in 1982, when he sought to rekindle a partnership with Buñuel with the ultimately unrealised short, *The Little Demon*. He sent the director a telegram:

Dear Buñuel, Every ten years I send you a letter with which you disagree, but I do not give up. Last night I had an idea for a film which we could make in ten days, not about the philosophical demon but about our beloved little devil. If you fancy it, come and see me at the Púbol Castle. I embrace you, Dalí.[52]

A second telegram quickly followed, giving Buñuel directions to the Castle, which suggests that Dalí was optimistic that his invitation would be accepted. Despite what Dalí says in his telegram, in forty years Buñuel had not once responded, vexed that Dalí had refused to give him a loan in 1939 when he was at his most desperate.[53] Perhaps it was because both were approaching the end of their lives, but Buñuel responded this time, though not in the affirmative: 'I received your two cables', he wrote. 'Great idea for a film *Little Demon*, but I withdrew from the cinema five years ago and never go out now. A pity. Embraces.'[54]

Dalí was touched by Buñuel's reply and in January 1983 invited the Spanish director Luis Revenga to come to Púbol to film a sample of *The Little Demon* that he planned to send to Buñuel to persuade him out of retirement. 'Dalí wanted to record a sequence destined to be the end of a film that he wanted to shoot with Buñuel', Revenga recalled. 'A film that he more or less sang to me, inspired by *Babaouo*,[55] and that recalled a scene that seemed exciting to me: a snowfall inside the metro station.'[56] Revenga arrived with two photographers, Gerardo Moschioni and Antonio Marcos, and the team filmed Dalí wildly singing 'La filla del marxant' (The Merchant's Daughter), a Catalan folksong that his 'beloved little demon' – a combination between a devil and a dwarf – would sing throughout the picture. Dalí got through the better part of the song's 134 verses before exhaustion overcame him and his friend, the painter Antoni Pitxot, stopped the filming. The footage was not sent, and Buñuel died only a few months later, on 29 July 1983.

It is revealing that after years of collaborating with such notables as Walt Disney, Fritz Lang and Alfred Hitchcock, struggling to galvanise interest in star-studded paranoiac films like *La Carretilla de carne* and continually pushing the boundaries of every medium and technological advance that was afforded to him, Dalí's final motion-picture proposal returned to the period 1929–32 – a collaboration with Buñuel on what was essentially a Surrealist script. Dawn Ades has suggested that many of Dalí's cinema projects may have been left unfinished because he came to see film as a '"secondary form", involving the intervention of too many people in its creation'.[57] It is indeed paradoxical that the artist conceived increasingly elaborate cinematic spectacles requiring more and more professionals, when the films that materialised to his satisfaction came when he was working alone with a director, brainstorming ideas for a film that could be shot in less than two weeks. With *The Little Demon*, he returned to these roots; unfortunately, it was too late.

Notes

1

'Explosion of the Swan', *Sparrow 35*, Aug. 1975.

2

Author's interview with Robert Descharnes, 4 Oct. 2006, in Elliott H. King, *Dalí, Surrealism and Cinema*, London 2007. There is, however, a scene in Jean-Christophe Averty's *L'Autoportrait mou de Salvador Dalí avec du bacon* 1967 in which Dalí pounds a piano with cats meowing from inside. See also 'My Cinematographic Secrets', republished in this volume.

3

See Dawn Ades, 'Why Film?' in this volume.

4

Robert Descharnes and Gilles Néret, *Salvador Dalí, 1904–1989: L'Oeuvre peint* (1993), trans. in Michael Hulse, as *Salvador Dalí, 1904–1989: The Paintings*, Cologne 1997, pp.472–3.

5

Amanda Lear, *Le Dalí d'Amanda*, Paris 1984, trans. as *My Life with Dalí*, London 1985, p.170.

6

Author's interview with Amanda Lear, in King 2007.

7

Conversation with Denise Sandell, 24 Sept. 2006, London.

8

Felipe Jacinto [Salvador Dalí], 'The Last Scandal of Salvador Dalí', Julien Levy Gallery, New York 1941.

9

Among the works shown that might be considered classical were *The Golden Age* (whereabaouts unknown), *Family of Marsupial Centaurs* (private collection), and *Original Sin* (private collection).

10

See 'My Cinematographic Secrets', republished in this volume.

11

Ibid.; Salvador Dalí, *The Secret Life of Salvador Dalí*, trans. Haakon M. Chevalier, New York 1942 and London 1948, p.332.

12

These include: *Diurnal Illusion: The Shadow of a Grand Piano Approaching* 1931 (as this work is now known, though it was exhibited only as *Diurnal Illusions* prior to the 1964 exhibition in Tokyo), and *Partial Hallucination. Six Apparitions of Lenin on a Grand Piano* 1931 (fig.81), as well as *Babaouo, Giraffes on Horseback Salad*, the discarded ballroom scene in *Spellbound*, *Chaos and Creation* and *Autoportrait mou de Salvador Dalí* 1967. Dalí often associated pianos with sexual organs, a link formed in his childhood by a book on venereal diseases that his father left open on the family piano to teach his son the perils of sexual promiscuity; Lluis Permanyer, 'El pincel erótico de Dalí', *Playboy*, no.3, Jan. 1979, p.161, cited in Michael R. Taylor, 'Salvador Dalí's *Temptation of Saint Anthony* and the Exorcism of Surrealism', in Hank Hine, William Jeffett and Kelly Reynolds (eds.), *Persistence and Memory: New Critical Perspectives on Dalí at the Centennial*, St Petersburg (Fl.) and Milan 2004, p.180.

13

'I had just finished doing *Dalí's Moustache* [New York 1954] with Philippe Halsman. I was in New York for the retrospective exhibit of my two hundred *Divine Comedy* watercolours, when, going through Paris, I had happened on Vermeer of Delft's *Lacemaker*, and discovered the importance of the rhinoceros horn.' Salvador Dalí with André Parinaud, *Comment on devient Dalí*, Paris 1973, p.283. Dalí refers to his exhibition at New York's Carstairs Gallery, which ran 7 Dec. 1954 – 31 Jan. 1955 – thus after his November 1954 visit to the Louvre. See note 15.

14

Salvador Dalí, 'Aspects phénoménologiques de la métode paranoïaque-critique' (1955), in *La Vie publique de Salvador Dalí*, exh. cat., Centre Georges Pompidou, Paris 1980, p.144. See also Fèlix Fanés, 'Film as Metaphor' in this volume.

15

Dalí's visit to the Louvre has also been dated December 1954 (see Robert Descharnes, *L'Héritage infernal*, Paris 2002, p.85, and V.E. Barnett, *Handbook: The Guggenheim Museum Collection 1900–1980*, New York 1980, p.313), and Dalí himself said that the visit occurred in May 1955 (Dalí with Parinaud, p.284). The November 1954 date comes directly from the photographs of the visit in Descharnes's archive.

16

Robert and Nicolas Descharnes, *Dalí, The Hard and the Soft, Sculptures and Objects*, Azay-le-Rideau 2004, p.60.

17

I am grateful to Matthew Gale for this comparison.

18

Fleur Cowles recounts these events as leading to a precise copy of *The Lacemaker* (*The Case of Salvador Dalí*, London 1959, p.253), referring to the painting that Dalí executed c.1955 and subsequently sold to collector Robert Lehman, now in the collection of the Metropolitan Museum of Art, New York (fig.143). Although A. Reynolds Morse corroborates this (*Dalí, A Study of his Life and Work*, Greenwich 1958, p.77), the film makes clear that Dalí began the *Paranoiac-Critical Study of Vermeer's Lacemaker* – not the Lehman painting – at the Louvre in 1954. Dalí painted three versions, all close in size to the original (24 x 21cm): *The Paranoiac-Critical Study*, the Lehman painting, and an unfinished version that he bequeathed to the Spanish State. According to Descharnes, he copied *The Lacemaker* from life only once.

19

'One morning I went to the Louvre; I was also very interested, at that time, in rhinocerous horns, but I went to the Louvre without knowing how my copy would turn out.' Dalí, 'Aspects phénoménologiques de la métode paranoïaque-critique', p.144; my trans.

20

In *Dalí's Optical Illusions*, exh. cat., Wadsworth Atheneum, Hartford 2000, p.164, Dawn Ades notes four books by Matila Ghyka still in Dalí's library: *Esthetiques des proportions dans la nature et dans les arts*, Paris 1927, *Essai sur le rhythme*, Paris 1938, *The Geometry of Art and Life*, New York 1946, and *A Practical Handbook of Geometrical Composition and Design*, London 1952.

21

Descharnes and Descharnes 2004, p.60. This passage is an adaptation of Descharnes's *Dalí de Gala*, Lausanne 1962, p.52, though they differ slightly. Whereas the 2004 publication implies that the artist's links surrounding rhinoceros horns and *The Lacemaker* were conceived *en masse* during the summer of 1954, the earlier book insinuates more correctly that their development was gradual. This passage, as well as others related to *L'Histoire prodigieuse…*, was curiously omitted in *Dalí de Gala*'s English translation, *The World of Salvador Dalí*, New York 1962.

22

See also Helen Sainsbury, 'Chaos and Creation' in this volume for 'performance'.

23

Puignau recounts his filming experience in Emilio Puignau, *Vivències amb Salvador Dalí*, Barcelona 1995, pp.91–2.

24

See Agustín Sánchez Vidal, 'La Carretilla de carne', in this volume.

25

'Interview with Robert Descharnes', in King 2007.

26

Letter from Albert Field to Luis Buñuel with commentary by Dalí, 18 Feb. 1959, repr. in *Salvador Dalí, La Gare de Perpignan, Pop, Op, Yes-yes, Pompier*, exh. cat., Museum Ludwig, Cologne 2006, p.171.

27
Like *Un Chien andalou*, both *La Carretilla de carne* and *L'Histoire prodigieuse …* were independently described by Dalí as 'exactly the opposite of an experimental *avant-garde* film, and especially of what is nowadays called "creative", which means nothing but a servile subordination to all the commonplaces of our wretched modern art'. Salvador Dalí, 'Mes Secrets cinématographiques', 1954, republished in this volume. See also Fèlix Fánes, 'Film as Metaphor', in this volume.

28
Amanda Lear recalls that Dalí's dream sequence was also intended to include a sewing machine that would drive a needle into the eye of Ingrid Bergman. This episode does not appear in any known sketches for *Spellbound*; this appears to be a confusion with *Moontide*. See Ilene Susan Fort, 'Moontide' and Sara Cochran, 'Spellbound', in this volume. The rhinocerous head survives in the Summer Dining Room at Port Lligat.

29
Cowles 1953, pp.155–6.

30
See Helen Sainsbury, 'Chaos and Creation' in this volume.

31
King 2007.

32
Lear 1985, p.269. She adds that Dalí asked her 'to help him by peeing a couple of times on the pens, so that I would contribute to the rusting process.'

33
Christopher Jones in conversation with José Montes Baque, partly extracted in *Tate etc*, Spring 2007. I am extremely grateful to Christopher Jones for providing me with excerpts from his hours of conversation with the director.

34
Lear 1985, p.254.

35
Pat Hackett (ed.), *The Andy Warhol Diaries*, New York 1989, p.119.

36
Jones in conversation with Montes Baquer.

37
In 1966, Dalí told Alain Bosquet that of all the books in the world, he would rescue *Locus Solus*, which he revered even more than Cervantes. Alain Bosquet, *Entretiens avec Salvador Dalí*, Paris 1966, Monaco 2000, p.96.

38
On Roussel's influence on *Babaouo*, see Pilar Parcerisas, 'Dalí and Irrationality in Cinema: "Babaouo, c'est un film surréaliste"', in Hine, Jeffett and Reynolds 2004, p.142.

39
Salvador Dalí, 'Raymond Roussel. – "Nouvelles impressions d'Afrique"', *Le Surréalisme au service de la révolution*, no.6, 15 May 1933, p.41, trans. Martin Sorrell in *Raymond Roussel: Life, Death and Works*, London 1987, p.55.

40
Although *Impressions of Africa* is absent in the 1939 Levy catalogue – it is not recorded in any exhibitions prior to the 1941 Dalí retrospective at the Museum of Modern Art, New York – Eric Schaal's photographs of the 1939 Levy Gallery installation reveal that it was exhibited, presumably as a loan from Edward James; see Montse Aguer and Marc Aufraise, *Dalí versus Schaal*, Figueres 2006, pp.44–57. I have discovered that on 8 April 1941, the Virginia newspaper *The Richmond Times Dispatch* reproduced *Impressions of Africa* with the title *Melancholic Eccentricity*, a title that appeared as number thirteen in the 1939 catalogue. *The Richmond Times Dispatch* may well have published the incorrect title and/or image, though no painting titled *Melancholic Eccentricity* is listed in the catalogue for the 1941 Levy Gallery show on which the article was reporting, and no reference to it appears in any of Dalí's subsequent exhibitions. *Melancholic Eccentricity* was thus either purchased and disappeared, or, like many of his other canvases from the 1930s, is now known by another title. In its online catalogue raisonné, the Fundació Gala-Salvador Dalí hypothesises that *Melancholic Eccentricity* might alternatively have been the title for the painting now known as *Mountain Lake* (fig.12).

41
Pierre Janet, 'The Psychological Characteristics of Ecstasy', *De l'angoise à l'extase* (1926), trans. John Harman in *Raymond Roussel: Life, Death and Works*, p.39.

42
André Breton, 'Têtes d'orgage: Raymond Roussel', *Minotaure*, no.10, 1937, p.6, trans. Sorrell 1987, p.59. The quotation from Roussel is taken from this translation. Têtes d'orage were to become Breton's *Anthologie de l'Humour Noir*, Paris 1939.

43
Raymond Roussel, *Comment j'ai écrit certains de mes livres* (1933), Paris 1985, p.27. Cited in Michel Leiris, 'Conception et Realité chez Raymond Roussel', *Critique*, 89, 1954; trans. John Ashbery in *Raymond Roussel: Life, Death and Works*, p.73.

44
Breton 1937 in Sorrell 1987, p.59.

45
'[A]lready he could see the two of us standing on the Great Wall, brandishing his photo-montage of Mao-Marilyn' (Lear 1985, p.248). Lear refers to the photograph of Marilyn Monroe that Dalí had asked Philippe Halsman to graft onto the head of Chairman Mao in c.1967 and which later graced the cover of the 1971 *Vogue*.

46
Fèlix Fanés (ed.), *Dalí: Mass Culture*, Barcelona 2004, p.95.

47
Ibid. See also Michael R. Taylor, 'Giraffes on Horseback Salad', in this volume.

48
Salvador Dalí, 'L'Ane pourri', *La Femme visible*, Paris 1930.

49
Ian Monk, introduction to Raymond Roussel, *New Impressions of Africa*, London 2004, p.12.

50
Salvador Dalí, 'Le "Vogué" de Salvador Dalí', *Vogue*, Dec. 1971 – Jan. 1972, p.180. On Dalí's esteem for Chairman Mao, see Elliott H. King, 'Little Black Dress, Little Red Book: Dalí, Mao and monarchy (with special attention to Trajan's glorious testicles)', in Michael R. Taylor (ed.), *The Dalí Renaissance*, forthcoming 2007.

51
Dalí, 'Le "Vogué" de Salvador Dalí', p.161.

52
Published in Dawn Ades (ed.), *Dalí: The Centenary*, exh. cat., Palazzo Crassi, Venice and Philadelphia Museum of Art 2004, p.539.

53
Details are provided in Ian Gibson, *The Shameful Life of Salvador Dalí*, London 1997, pp.394–5.

54
Ibid., p.597.

55
Among the strange episodes in this 1932 script is Babaouo's arrival at the Métro platform, where he discovers an orchestra set to play the overture from Wagner's *Tannhäuser*. Chaos ensues each time a train stops and floods the platform with people. Salvador Dalí, *Babaouo: Scenario inédit précedé d'un Abrégé d'une histoire critique du cinema et suivi de Guillaume Tell ballet portugais*, Paris 1932, extract trans. in Finkelstein 1998, pp.141–5.

56
Màrius Carol, Juan José Navarro Arisa and Jordi Busquets, *El último Dalí*, Madrid 1985, p.14.

57
Dawn Ades, *Dalí*, London 1982, 1995, p.206.

Filmography
and Further Reading

Filmography
Compiled by Elliott H. King

Films written by Salvador Dalí or including his (proposed) participation
Scripts are by Dalí unless otherwise stated. Most are held at the Fundació Gala-Salvador Dalí, Figueres (abbreviated as FGSD)

Un Chien andalou, 1929, dir. Luis Buñuel; script by Buñuel and Dalí; prod. Buñuel.

L'Age d'or, 1930, dir. Buñuel; script by Buñuel and Dalí; prod. the Vicomte Charles de Noailles

La Chèvre sanitaire, c.1930, unrealised script, FGSD

Babaouo: scénario inédit précedé d'un abrégé d'une histoire critique du cinéma et suivi de Guillaume Tell, ballet portugais, 1932, unrealised script pub. Paris 1932, Barcelona 1978

Contre la famille, 1932, unrealised script, FGSD.

Cinq Minutes à propos du surréalisme, 1931–4, unrealised script, Scottish National Gallery of Modern Art, Edinburgh

Les Mystères surréalistes de New York, 1935, unrealised script, FGSD

Giraffes on Horseback Salad 1936–7, unrealised scripts, FGSD and Bibliothèque Kandinsky, Centre Georges Pompidou, Paris

Destino, 1946, unfinished script and animation by Dalí; prod. Walt Disney. Completed 2003 (dir. Dominic Manfrey; prod. Baker Bloodworth and Roy Disney)

Moontide, 1941, dir. Archie Mayo; prod. Mark Hellinger. Unrealised script for dream sequence, FGSD

Spellbound, 1946. dir. Alfred Hitchcock; prod. David O. Selznick. Dream sequence based on 1945 designs by Dalí

El Cid, 1948, unrealised project proposed to Errol Flynn

Une vie de Goya, undated (after 1948?), unrealised project with list of credits, FGSD

Fifty Secrets of Magic Craftsmanship, 1948, unrealised project proposed to Jack Warner

La Carretilla de Carne / La brouette de chair / The Wheelbarrow of Flesh (The Story of the Wheelbarrow), 1948–52, unrealised script, FGSD

L'Ame, L'Alma, 1948–52, unrealised script, Luis Marquina Archive.

Le Sang catalan, 1950, unrealised script, FGSD.

Father of the Bride, 1950, dir. Vincente Minnelli; prod. Loew's International Corporation, New York. Dream sequence based on designs by Dalí.

L'Histoire prodigieuse de la Dentellière et du rhinocéros, 1954–62, unfinished script and footage by Dalí and Robert Descharnes, Archives Descharnes, Azay-le-Rideau

Chaos and Creation, 1960, prod. Dalí and Philippe Halsman.

Dalí's Fantastic Dream, 1965, dir. and prod. unknown

Fantastic Voyage, 1966, dir. Richard Fleischer; prod. Saul David. Poster by Dalí, 1965

L'Autoportrait mou de Salvador Dalí, 1967, dir. Jean-Christophe Averty and Robert Descharnes; prod. Coty Television and Seven Arts Ltd. Script, FGSD

Live and Let Die, 1973, dir. Guy Hamilton; prod. Albert Broccoli. Tarot deck commissioned from Dalí, not used.

Dune, 1974, unrealised project by Alejandro Jodorowsky starring Dalí

Impressions de la Haute Mongolie – Hommage à Raymond Roussel, 1975, dir. José Montes-Baquer; prod. Westdeutsches Fernsehen

The Little Demon, 1982, unrealised project proposed to Buñuel, fragment dir. Luis Revenga

Films about Salvador Dalí
Dalí, 1954, dir. Tullio Bruschi; prod. Este Film

In Between, 1964–6, dir. Jonas Mekas

Qui est Dalí? 1965, dir. Henri Champetier; prod. Société Nouvelle Pathé Cinéma

Salvador Dalí in Museum Boymans, 1970, prod. Polygoon

Dalí, toiles inédites, 1973, prod. Ministère des Affaires Étrangers, Magazine France Panorama

Television Programmes Made in Dalí's Lifetime
Produced by ORTF (Office de Radiodiffusion-Télévision Française) unless otherwise indicated.
Key to symbols for other television production companies:
* Produced by A2 (Antenne 2, Télévision France 2)
**Produced by BBC (British Broadcasting Corporation)
† Produced by TF1 (Télévision Francaise 1)
†† Produced by TVE (Televisión Española)

Dalí interviewed by Malcolm Muggeridge, 4 May 1955 **

Interview de Salvador Dalí, 1956

À Paris avec un éléphant, interview, 1958

Premier ballet folklorique soviétique, 1958

Bal des Petits Lits Blancs, 1959

Salvador Dalí fait écalter une bombe au Vel'd'Hiv (en demolition), 1959

Salvador Dalí présente l'ovocipède, 1959

Exposition de bijoux à Londres, 1960

Remise d'une médaille d'or à Salvador Dalí, 1960

Salvador Dalí présente son 'Christophe Colomb', 1960

Couverture Apocalypse, 1961

Conférence Dalí au Polytechnique, 1961†

Salvador Dalí interviewé à propos du livre que lui a consacré Descharnes, 1962

Salvador Dalí inaugure la residence Élysée, 1962

Salvador Dalí à l'X, 1962

Salvador Dalí interviewé à propos de la soirée Tchérina, 1962

Exposition Dalí en Espagne, 1963

Exposition, 1963

Concours de peinture sur le theme de la Joconde, 1963

Dalí à New York, 1964

Première au Lido, 1964

Salvador Dalí dédicace Salvador Dalí, 1964

Interview Salvador Dalí, 1964

Salvador, 1964

Édition spéciale Salvador Dalí, 1964

Gala de l'École de l'Air, 1964

Salvador Dalí, 1964

Inauguration exposition Dalí à Fontainebleau, 1964

Panorama: un genie par lui-même, 1965

Salvador Dalí, 1965

Interview Dalí, 1965

Les voeux (avec sa femme), 1965

Viva Dalí (avec Gala), 1965

Exposition de peinture à Saint-Denis, 1965

Dalí à New York (Galerie Lucas), 1966

Dalí à New York, 1966

Dalí in New York, 1966. Presented by Jane Arden; dir. Jack Bond **

Salvador Dalí, exposition Jules Verne, 1966

Vitrine du libraire, 1966

Dernier fiacre parisien, 1966

Picasso et son temps, 1966

Paris brûle-t-il?, 1966

Conférence Dalí, 1966

Salvador Dalí devant le bronze de John Kennedy, 1966

Dalí, 1967, dir. Adam Saulnier

Soirée Touthankamon, 1967

Dalí à Paris, 1967

Dalí dans les Pyrénées, 1967

Salvador Dalí (interview), 1967

Salvador Dalí au Salon de l'Enfance (il dessine une feuille), 1967

La première d'Hugues Auffray à Bobino, 1967

Salvador Dalí, 1967

Vol de tableaux à Grenoble, 1968

Interview, 1968

Musée des Arts Décoratifs, 1968

Illustration de livre, 1969

Les Airs du temps Dalí, 7 Feb. 1969

Brève apparition au Prix de Cinéma, 1969

Exposition, 1969

Page spectacle, 1969

Salvador Dalí a Gala, 1969

Interview de Joseph Foret (Apocalypse), 1969

Exposition Dalí, 1969

Conférence de presse Dalí, 1970

Conférence de presse Dalí, 1970

Dalí à Lyon (S.N.C.F.), 1970

Affiches S.N.C.F, 1970

Perspectives Surréalistes I et II, 1971, dir. Daniel Le Comte, series *Ombres et Lumières*

Interview de Salvador Dalí, 1971

Exposition (34") aux USA, 1971

Dalí à New York (jeu d'echecs), 1971

Salvador Dalí chez lui, 1972

Les peintres surréalistes, 1972

Exposition de tableaux surréalistes, 1972

Les livres de la semaine, 1973

Hello Dalí!, 1973. Edited by Humphrey Burton, dir. Bruce Gowers, prod. London Weekend Television

Salvador Dalí parle de ses livres, 1973

Salvador Dalí, 1973, dir. N. Risi

Interview à propos du mauvais temps et de la tempête, 1974

Personnage en cire au Musée Grevin, 1974

Salvador Dalí à Figueres, 1974

Salvador Dalí, Moïse et le monothéisme, 1975

Salvador Dalí, gravure: La Conquête du cosmos, 1975

Un jour futur: Message pour l'an 2000, 1975*

Dalí, June 1975†

Dalí, Oct. 1975†

Salvador Dalí, 1975†

Livre Dalí, 1975†

Salvador Dalí, 1977*

149
Dalí painting *Large Head of Greek God*, design for the Walt Disney film *Destino*, 1946
Fundació Gala-Salvador Dalí, Figueres

150
Dalí with Alfred Hitchcock on the set of *Spellbound*, 1945
Harry Ransom Humanities Research Center, University of Texas at Austin

Un sur cinq. Qui étiez vous à dix huit ans, Salvador Dalí, 1978*
Voir, Le Magazine de l'image: Dalí hors cadre, 1978. Prod. FR3 (France 3)
1001 visions de Salvador Dalí, 9 Feb. 1978, dir. Alain Ferrari*
Dalí, 30 May 1979. *Imagênes*. Written, dir. and presented by Paloma Chamorro; prod. Jesús González[††]
Dalí, 6 June 1979. *Imagênes*. Written, directed and presented by Paloma Chamorro; prod. by Jesús González[††]
Dalí, 13 June 1979. *Imagênes*. Written, dir. and presented by Paloma Chamorr; prod. Jesús González.[††]
'Leda Atomica' de Salvador Dalí, 5 Jan. 1979, dir. Charles Paolini[†]
Enigma Dalí, 1983, dir. Luis Revenga[††]
La mascara se transluce. 30 June 1984[††]
Todos los hombres de Dalí, 16 Sept 1984[††]
Dalí, 1986. Prod. Adam Low in association with Demart**
Pintar depués de morir, 25 Sept. 1989[††]

Further Reading
Compiled by Matthew Gale

For an extensive recent bibliography see Dawn Ades (ed.), *Salvador Dalí: The Centenary Exhibition*, 2004

Writings by Dalí
Babaouo, Scenario inédit, precede d'un abrégé d'un histoire critique du cinéma, et suivi de Guillaume Tell ballet portugais, Paris 1932, bilingual French and Spanish ed., ed. Esteban Riambau Saurí, Barcelona 1978
The Secret Life of Salvador Dalí, trans. Haakon M. Chevalier, New York 1942 and London 1948
50 Secrets of Magic Craftsmanship, trans. Haakon M. Chevalier, New York 1948, 1992
Journal d'un Gènie, ed. Michel Déon, Paris 1964, trans. Richard Howard, as *The Diary of a Genius*, London 1966, 1990
Comment on devient Dalí, Paris 1973; trans. as *The Unspeakable Confessions of Salvador Dalí*, London 1977
Christopher Maurer (ed.), *Sebastian's Arrows: Letters and Mementos of Salvador Dalí and Federico García Lorca*, Chicago 2004
Obra Completa: vol.II, Textos autobiográficos 2, ed. Montse Aguer; *vol.III: Poesía, Prosa, Teatro y Cine*, ed. Agustín Sánchez Vidal; *vol.VIII: Album*, Barcelona 2004, trans. as *Dalí: An Illustrated Life*, London 2007

Studies on Dalí
A. Reynolds Morse, *Dalí: A Study of his Life and Work*, Greenwich (Conn.) 1958
Daniel Abadie (ed.), *Salvador Dalí: Rétrospective 1920–1980*, exh. cat., Musée d'art national moderne, Centre Georges Pompidou, Paris 1979, including James Bigwood, 'Cinquante ans de cinéma dalinien', pp.342–53
La Vie publique de Salvador Dalí, Paris 1980

Salvador Dalí, exh. cat., Tate Gallery, London 1980
Dawn Ades, *Dalí*, London 1982, 1990
Robert Descharnes, *Salvador Dalí: The Work, The Man*, New York 1984
Agustín Sánchez Vidal, *Buñuel, Lorca, Dalí: el enigma sin fin*, Barcelona 1988
Karin von Maur, *Salvador Dalí 1904–1989*, exh. cat., Staatsgalerie Stuttgart and Kunsthaus Zurich 1989
Paul Moorhouse, *Dalí*, London 1992
Meredith Etherington-Smith, *Dalí*, London 1992
Salvador Dalí: The Early Years, exh. cat., Centro de Arte Reina Sofía, Madrid and South Bank Centre, London 1994
Rafael Santos Toroella, *Dalí: Epoca de Madrid: Catálogo rasonado*, Madrid 1994
Haim Finkelstein, *Salvador Dalí's Art and Writings 1927–1942: The Metamorphoses of Narcissus*, Cambridge 1996
Ian Gibson, *The Shameful Life of Salvador Dalí*, London 1997
Robert Radford, *Dalí*, London 1997
Dawn Ades and Fiona Bradley, *Salvador Dalí: A Mythology*, exh. cat., Tate Gallery, Liverpool and Salvador Dalí Museum, St Petersburg, Florida 1998
Haim Finkelstein (ed.), *The Collected Writings of Salvador Dalí*, Cambridge 1998
Robert Descharnes and Gilles Néret, *Salvador Dalí, 1904–1989: The Paintings*, 2 vols. Cologne, London, Los Angeles, Madrid, Paris, Tokyo 1993, 2001
Rafael Santos Torroella, *Dalí: Epoca de Madrid: Catálogo rasonado*, Madrid 1994
Fèlix Fanés, *Salvador Dalí: La Costrucción de la imagen 1925–1930*, Madrid 1999, revised as *Salvador Dalí: The Construction of the Image 1925–1930*, New Haven and London 2007
Dawn Ades (ed.), *Dalí's Optical Illusions*, exh. cat., Wadsworth Atheneum Museum of Art, Hartford (Conn.), Hirshhorn Museum and Sculpture Garden, Washington D.C., and Scottish National Gallery of Modern Art, Edinburgh 2000
Joan M. Minguet Ballori, *Salvador Dalí, cine y surrealismo(s)*, Barcelona 2003
Dawn Ades (ed.), *Salvador Dalí: The Centenary Exhibition*, exh. cat., Palazzo Grassi, Venice and Philadelphia Museum of Art 2004
Hank Hine, William Jeffett and Kelly Reynolds (eds.), *Persistence and Memory: New Critical Perspectives on Dalí at the Centennial*, St Petersburg and Milan 2004
Fèlix Fanés, *Dalí: cultura de masas*, exh. cat., CaixaForum, Barcelona, Museo Nacional Centro de Arte Reina Sofía, Madrid, and Salvador Dalí Museum, St Petersburg (Flo.) and (as *It's All Dalí*), Museum Boijmans Van Beuningen, Rotterdam 2004–5

Salvador Dalí, La Gare de Perpignan: Pop, Op, Yes-yes, Pompier, exh. cat., Museum Ludwig, Cologne 2006
Elliott King, *Dalí, Surrealism and Cinema*, London 2007

Film and beyond
Ado Kyrou, *Le Surréalisme au cinéma*, Paris 1953, revised 1963, 1985
Gianni Rondolino, *L'occhio tagliato: Documenti del cinema dadaista e surrealista*, Turin 1972
Alain Virmaux and Odette Virmaux, *Les Surréalistes et le cinéma*, Paris 1976
Paul Hammond, *The Shadow and its Shadow: Surrealist Writings on Cinema*, London 1978 and San Francisco 2000
Linda Williams, *Figures of Desire: A Theory and Analysis of Surrealist Film*, Urbana 1981
Luis Buñuel, *Mon Dernier soupir*, Paris 1982, trans. Abigail Israel as *My Last Breath*, London 1984
Rudolf E. Kuenzli (ed.), *Dada and Surrealist Film*, New York 1987, Cambridge (Mass.) and London 1996
Agnès Angliviel de la Beaumelle and Isabelle Monod-Fontaine (eds.), *André Breton: La beauté convulsive*, exh. cat., Musée national d'art moderne, Centre Georges Pompidou, Paris 1991
Jean-Michel Bouhours and Nathalie Schoeller, 'L'Age d'or: Correspondance, Luis Buñuel – Charles de Noailles, Lettres et documents (1929–1976)', *Les Cahiers du Musée national d'art moderne*, hors-série, 1993
Luis Buñuel and Salvador Dalí, *Un Chien andalou*, ed. Phillip Drummond, London 1994
Yasha David (ed.), *¡Buñuel! La Mirada del siglo*, exh. cat., Museo Nacional Centro de Arte Reina Sofía, Madrid and Museo de Palacio de Bellas Artes de México 1996
Paul Hammond, *L'Age d'or*, London 1997
'Surrealism and Cinema Issue', *Screen*, vol.39, no.2, Summer 1998
Hitchcock and Art: Fatal Coincidences, Montreal Museum of Fine Arts 2000, including Nathalie Bondil-Poupard, 'Such Stuff as Dreams Are Made on: Hitchcock and Dalí, Surrealism and Oneiricism', pp.155–71
Emmanuel Guigon (ed.), *Luis Buñuel y el surrealismo*, exh. cat., Museo de Teruel 2000
Robert Short, *The Age of Gold: Surrealist Cinema*, London 2003
Paul Hammond, 'Lost and Found: Buñuel, *L'Age d'or* and Surrealism', in Peter William Evans and Isabel Santaolalla (eds.), *Luis Buñuel: New Readings*, London 2004
Jordana Mendelson, *Documenting Spain: Artists, Exhibition Culture, and the Modern Nation, 1929–1939*, Pennsylvania 2006
Michael Richardson, *Surrealism and Cinema*, Oxford and New York 2006

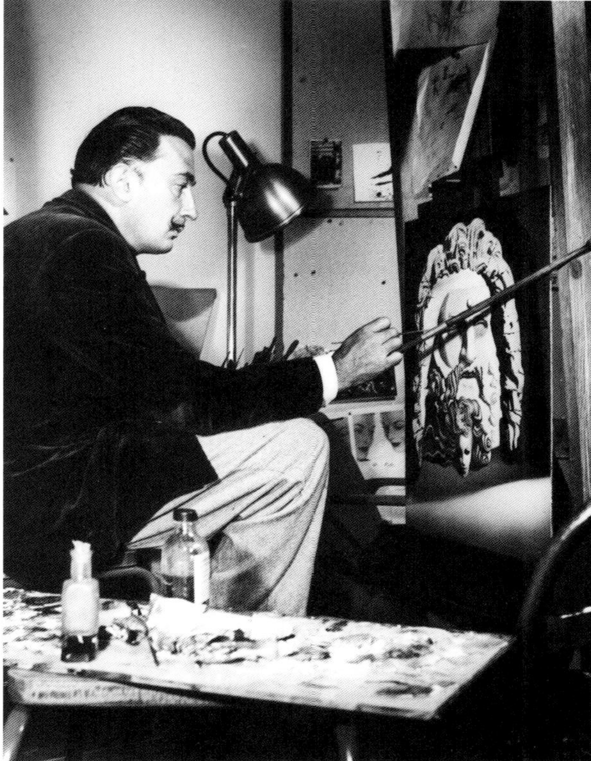

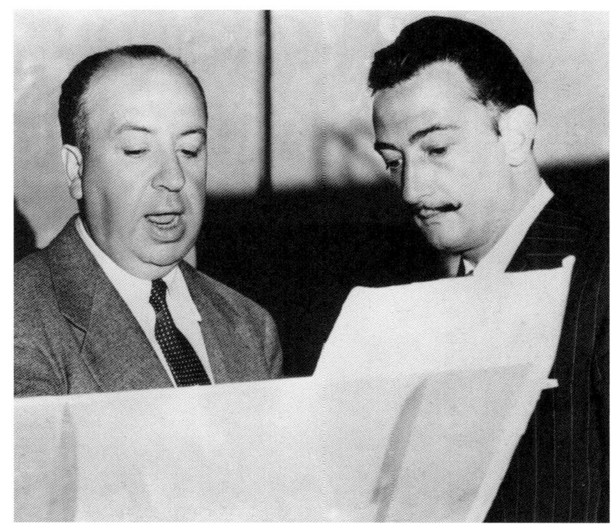

List of Exhibited Works

Works illustrated in this publication but not shown in the exhibition are excluded from this list. Not all works may be exhibited at each venue.

Measurements are given in centimetres, height before width.

**Salvador Dalí
1904–1989**

Brothel 1922
Ink wash on paper 20.8 x 15
Fundació Gala-Salvador Dalí, Figueres
[fig.30]

The Drunkard 1922
Ink wash on paper 20.8 x 15
Fundació Gala-Salvador Dalí, Figueres
[fig.32]

Madrid Night Scene 1922
Ink wash and watercolour on paper
21 x 15.2
Fundació Gala-Salvador Dalí, Figueres

Summer Night 1922
Ink wash on paper 20.8 x 15
Fundació Gala-Salvador Dalí, Figueres
[fig.31]

Madrid Suburb c.1922–3
Wash on paper 20.8 x 15
Fundació Gala-Salvador Dalí, Figueres
[fig.13]

Portrait of Luis Buñuel 1924
Oil on canvas 68.5 x 58.5
Museo Nacional Centro de Arte
Reina Sofía, Madrid
[fig.14]

*Don Salvador and Ana María Dalí
(Portrait of the Artist's Father and Sister)*
1925
Pencil on paper 50 x 33
Juan Abelló Collection, Madrid
[fig.68]

The Marriage of Buster Keaton 1925
Collage and ink on paper, 2 sheets,
each 21.2 x 16.8
Fundación Federico García Lorca,
Madrid
[fig.33]

Portrait of my Father 1925
Oil on canvas 104.5 x 104.5
Museu Nacional d'Art de Catalunya,
Barcelona
[fig.66]

Book of Varicose Veins 1926
Collage on paper 17.7 x 25.6
Fundación Federico García
Lorca, Madrid

Departure (Homage to Fox News) 1926
Oil on panel 43 x 31.5
Private collection
[fig.15]

Penya segats 1926
Oil on panel 27 x 41
Private collection
[fig.44]

Letter to Lorca with collage
of shoes 1926
Ink and collage on paper 21 x 16.1
Fundación Federico García
Lorca, Madrid

Apparatus and Hand 1927
Oil on panel 62.2 x 47.6
Salvador Dalí Museum, Inc.,
St Petersburg, Florida
[fig.18]

Birth of the Child Jesus 1927
Collage on paper 8.7 x 13.5
Fundación Federico García
Lorca, Madrid

The Hand 1927
Indian ink on paper 19 x 21
Private collection

Poem of Little Things October 1927
Ink on paper 23 x 16
Fundación Federico García
Lorca, Madrid

Letter to Lorca dated
18/20 January 1927
Ink and collage on paper 21.1 x 16.5
Fundación Federico García
Lorca, Madrid
[fig.17]

Abstract Composition 1928
Oil on canvas 148 x 198
Museo Nacional Centro de Arte
Reina Sofía, Madrid
[fig.4]

Feminine Nude (final state) 1928
Oil, cork and strings on canvas
70.5 x 60
Private collection
[fig.20]

Inaugural Goose Flesh 1928
Oil on cardboard 76 x 63.2
Fundació Gala-Salvador Dalí, Figueres
[fig.33]

Symbiotic Woman-Animal 1928
Oil and sand on canvas 50.2 x 65.5
Fundació Gala-Salvador Dalí, Figueres
[fig.19]

Unsatisfied Desires 1928
Oil, sand and sea-shells on cardboard
76.2 x 62.2
San Francisco Museum of Modern
Art. Fractional Gift of Jan and
Mitsuko Shrem, Clos Pegase
Winery Collection
[fig.6]

Untitled 1928
Oil on canvas with collage 148 x 198
Museo Nacional Centro de Arte
Reina Sofía, Madrid
[fig.5]

The Accommodations of Desire 1929
Oil and cut and pasted printed
paper on cardboard 22.2 x 34.9
Metropolitan Museum of Art,
New York. The Jacques and Natasha
Gelman Collection, 1998
[fig.35]

Ants 1929
Gouache, ink and collage 11.5 x 16.4
H. Amigorena Collection, Paris
[fig.52]

The First Days of Spring 1929
Oil and collage on panel 50.2 x 65.1
Salvador Dalí Museum, Inc.,
St Petersburg, Florida
[fig.7]

Illumined Pleasures 1929
Oil and collage on board 23.8 x 34.7
The Museum of Modern Art,
New York. The Sidney and
Harriet Janis Collection
[fig.36]

The Average Bureaucrat 1930
Oil on canvas 81.9 x 65.8
Salvador Dalí Museum, Inc.,
St Petersburg, Florida
[fig.67]

The Bleeding Roses 1930
Oil on canvas 61 x 50
Colección Caixa Galicia, La Coruña
[fig.9]

The Font 1930
Oil and collage on panel 66 x 41.3
Salvador Dalí Museum, Inc.,
St Petersburg, Florida
[fig.75]

*La Main (Les Remords
de conscience)* 1930
Oil and collage on canvas 41.3 x 66
Salvador Dalí Museum, Inc.,
St Petersburg, Florida
[fig.45]

The Invisible Man 1930
Oil on canvas 140 x 81
Museo Nacional Centro de Arte
Reina Sofía, Madrid
[fig.21]

Letter to Luis Buñuel detailing
ideas for the film *L'Age d'or* 1930
Ink on paper 26.5 x 21
Filmoteca Española, Madrid.
Fondo Buñuel
[fig.54 a, b]

Script for *L'Age d'or* 1930
Ink on paper 20.6 x 26.6
Fundació Gala-Salvador Dalí, Figueres

*Partial Hallucination. Six Apparitions
of Lenin on a Grand Piano* 1931
Oil on canvas 114 x 146
Centre Pompidou, Paris.
Musée national d'art moderne/
Centre de création industrielle
[fig.81]

The Persistence of Memory 1931
Oil on canvas 24.1 x 33
The Museum of Modern Art,
New York. Given anonymously
[fig.74]

Remorse or *Sphinx Embedded
in the Sand* 1931
Oil on canvas 19.1 x 26.7
Kresge Art Museum, Michigan
State University, East Lansing.
Gift of John F. Wolfram
[fig.84]

The Sense of Speed 1931
Oil on canvas 33 x 24
Fundació Gala-Salvador Dalí, Figueres
[fig.159]

Solitude 1931
Oil on canvas 35.5 x 27
Wadsworth Atheneum Museum
of Art, Hartford, Connecticut.
Purchased through the gift of
Henry and Walter Keney
[fig.40]

*Untitled (Woman Sleeping in
a Landscape)* 1931
Oil on canvas 27.2 x 35
Peggy Guggenheim Collection,
Venice (Solomon R. Guggenheim
Foundation, NY)
[fig.42]

*Frontispiece for L'amour
et la memoire* 1931
Photomontage
Fundació Gala-Salvador Dalí, Figueres
[fig.59]

*Cinq minutes à propos du
surréalisme* c.1931–2
Ink on paper
Film scenario, 15pp
Scottish National Gallery of Modern
Art Archive, Edinburgh.
[figs.61. 63a,b]

Babaouo 1932
Wood and painted glass
25.8 x 26.4 x 30.5
Fundació Gala-Salvador Dalí, Figueres
[fig.72]

Shades of Night Descending 1932
Oil on canvas 61 x 50.2
Salvador Dalí Museum, Inc.,
St Petersburg, Florida
[fig.58]

*Design for a poster for Babaouo,
c'est un film surréaliste* 1932
Mixed media on cardboard 27 x 37.1
Fundació Gala-Salvador Dalí, Figueres
[fig.70]

Script for Babaouo 1932
Facsimile of 2 pages of manuscript
(original ink on paper)
Fundació Gala-Salvador Dalí, Figueres

*Gala and the Angelus of Millet Preceding
the Imminent Arrival of the Conical
Anamorphoses* 1933
Oil on wood 24.2 x 19.2
National Gallery of Canada, Ottawa.
Purchased 1975
[fig.132]

Retrospective Bust of a Woman 1933
Porcelain display bust with ears of
corn, strip of cardboard used as a
necklace, gilded sponge, and couple
from Millet's *Angelus* with
wheelbarrow and two calamai
with quills 54 x 45 x 35
Private collection.
Courtesy Galerie Natalie Seroussi
[fig.97]

Moment of Transition 1934
Oil on canvas 54 x 65
Collection Viktor and
Marianne Langen
[fig.24]

Morning Ossification of the Cypress 1934
Oil on canvas 82 x 66
Collection Mr and Mrs Gilbert
Kaplan, New York
[fig.43]

The Spectre of Sex Appeal 1934
Oil on panel 17.9 x 13.9
Fundació Gala-Salvador Dalí, Figueres
[fig.134]

*Study for 'Singularities'. Surrealist
Furniture* c.1934–5
Pencil on paper 25.3 x 37.3
Fundació Gala-Salvador Dalí, Figueres
[fig.88]

Morphological Echo 1934–6
Oil on canvas 64.8 x 54
Salvador Dalí Museum, Inc.,
St Petersburg, Florida
[fig.59 on p.00]

*Gangsterism and Goofy Visions
of New York* 1935
Graphite pencil and ink on paper
54.6 x 40
Courtesy of Menil Collection, Houston
[fig.80]

The Surrealist Mysteries of New York 1935
Oil on canvas 40 x 30
Private collection
[fig.78]

Script for *Moontide* 1935
Ink on paper 31.7 x 20.2
Fundació Gala-Salvador Dalí, Figueres

Manuscript for *The Surrealist Mysteries
of New York* 1935
Ink on paper, 2pp: p.1 (including
support), 32.2 x 22.8; p.2, 11 x.22.6
Fundació Gala-Salvador Dalí, Figueres

Studies for the Scenario for *Les
Mystères surréalistes de New York* 1935
Pencil, charcoal and Indian ink
on paper 55 x 41
Fundació Suñol, Barcelona
[fig.79]

Paranonia c.1935
Oil on canvas 38 x 46
Salvador Dalí Museum, Inc.,
St Petersburg, Florida
[fig.99]

Singularities c.1935
Oil and collage on board 40.5 x 50
Fundació Gala-Salvador Dalí, Figueres
[fig.89]

Autumnal Cannibalism 1936
Oil on canvas 65.1 x 65.1
Tate. Purchased 1975
[fig.1]

Forgotten Horizon 1936
Oil on wood 22.2 x 26.7
Tate. Bequeathed by the Hon.
Mrs A.E. Pleydell-Bouverie through
the Friends of the Tate Gallery 1968
[fig.77]

Lobster Telephone 1936
Plastic, painted plaster and mixed
media 17.8 x 33 x 17.8
Tate. Purchased 1981
[fig.82]

*Messenger in a Palladian
Landscape* 1936
Indian ink on paper 44.5 x 60
Private collection

Anthropomorphic Echo 1937
Oil on panel 14.3 x 51.7
Salvador Dalí Museum, Inc.,
St Petersburg, Florida
[fig.61]

Chair Garden 1937
Pencil and ink on paper 26.7 x 22.9
Private collection

Death's Cycling Tour 1937
Pencil and ink on paper 30.2 x 20
Private collection

Groucho-Shiva 1937
Pencil and ink on paper 29.2 x 22.9
Private collection

Harpo Marx 1937
Pencil and ink on card 45.5 x 35.6
Philadelphia Museum of Art
[fig.83]

Metamorphosis of Narcissus 1937
Oil on canvas 51.1 x 78.1
Tate. Purchased 1979
[fig.95]

Sleep 1937
Oil on canvas 51 x 78
Private collection
[fig.45]

The Surrealist Piano 1937
Charcoal, watercolour and pastel
on paper 59.9 x 42.9
Mugrabi Collection
[fig.94]

Theatre: Scene of Saliva Sofa 1937
Pencil and ink on paper 25.7 x 17.5
Private collection

Design for the film with the
Marx Brothers (verso of 'La Vie
erotique') 1937
Pencil on paper 28.3 x 20.3
Salvador Dalí Museum, Inc.,
St Petersburg, Florida
[fig.93]

Design for the film with the Marx
Brother (*Dîner dans le désert éclaire par
les giraffes en feu*) 1937
Charcoal and gouache on paper
60 x 46
Salvador Dalí Museum, Inc.,
St Petersburg, Florida
[fig.91]

Film scenario for *Giraffes on
Horseback Salad* 1937
Ink on paper 24 x 16.6
Bibliothèque Kandinsky/Centre
de recherche et de documentation
Musée national d'art moderne, Paris
[fig.87 a–c]

Set design for the film with
the Marx Brothers 1937
Pencil, sienna ink and Indian ink
on paper 26.8 x 20.4
Fundació Gala-Salvador Dalí,
Figueres
[fig.92]

Mountain Lake 1938
Oil on canvas 73 x 92.1
Tate. Purchased 1975
[fig.12]

*The Transparent Simulacrum
of the Feigned Image* 1938
Oil on canvas 73.5 x 92
Albright-Knox Art Gallery, Buffalo,
New York. Bequest of A. Conger
Goodyear, 1966
[fig.11]

*Freud's Perverse Polymorph (Bulgarian
Child Eating a Rat)* 1939
Mixed media on paper 48.7 x 36.3
Fundació Gala-Salvador Dalí, Figueres
[fig.67]

*Shirley Temple, the Youngest, Most Sacred
Monster of the Cinema in her Time* 1939
Wash, pastel and collage
on cardboard 75 x 100
Museum Boijmans Van Beuningen,
Rotterdam
[fig.98]

*Book Transforming itself into
a Nude Woman* 1940
Oil on canvas 41.3 x 51
Private collection, USA
[fig.104]

Café Scene. Drawing for the
film *Moontide* 1941
Pencil, wash and Indian ink
on paper 13.6 x 12.6
Fundació Gala-Salvador Dalí, Figueres
[fig.102]

Face of War. Drawing for the
film *Moontide* 1941
Pencil, wash and Indian ink
on paper 17.5 x 13.2
Fundació Gala-Salvador Dalí, Figueres
[fig.103]

*Ruin with Head of Medusa
and Landscape (Dedicated to
Mrs Chase)* 1941
Oil on canvas 36 x 25.4
Juan Abelló Collection, Madrid
[fig.26]

Sewing Machine and Umbrellas.
Drawing for the film *Moontide* c.1941
Ink on canvas 20.3 x 25.8
Fundació Gala-Salvador Dalí, Figueres
[fig.100]

*Window Display with Umbrella and
Sewing Machine*. Drawing for the
film *Moontide* c.1941
Pencil and Indian ink on paper
8.8 x 12.8
Fundació Gala-Salvador Dalí, Figueres
[fig.101]

*Dream Caused by the Flight of a Bee
around a Pomegranate, a Second before
Awakening* 1944
Oil on panel 51 x 41
Museo Thyssen-Bornemisza, Madrid
[fig.115]

Melancholy, Atomic Uranic Idyll 1945
Oil on canvas 66.5 x 86.5
Museo Nacional Centro de Arte
Reina Sofía, Madrid
[fig.130]

Set design for the film
Spellbound c.1945
Oil on Masonite 88.8 x 113.1
Fundació Gala-Salvador Dalí, Figueres
[fig.105]

Set design for the film
Spellbound c.1945
Oil on Masonite 88.9 x 113.2
Fundació Gala-Salvador Dalí, Figueres
[fig.109]

Set design for the film
Spellbound c.1945
Oil on Masonite 88.9 x 113.2
Fundació Gala-Salvador Dalí, Figueres
[fig.110]

Study for the Dream Sequence
in *Spellbound* 1945
Mixed media on paper 15.8 x 20 cm
Private collection
[fig.108]

Study for the Dream Sequence
in *Spellbound* 1945
Oil on panel 58.7 x 84
Private collection
[fig.106]

Dream Sequence for the
film *Spellbound* directed by
Alfred Hitchcock 1945
Film, 35mm, 2 min. 40 sec.
Buena Vista Television
[fig.113]

Anthropomorphic Tower. Study for
the Walt Disney film *Destino* 1946
Conté crayon on paper 29.8 x 21.3
Fundació Gala-Salvador Dalí, Figueres

Large Head of Greek God. Study for
the Walt Disney film *Destino* 1946
Oil on Masonite 63.5 x 50.5
Walt Disney Feature Animation and
the Animation Research Library,
Burbank, California
[fig.128]

Nude Torso on Building on Checkerboard.
Study for the Walt Disney
film *Destino* 1946
Oil and collage on Masonite
45.5 x 60.3
Walt Disney Feature Animation and
the Animation Research Library,
Burbank, California
[fig.123]

*Open Field with Ball in Centre and
Mountains in Rear*. Study for the
Walt Disney film *Destino* 1946
Oil on Masonite 50.5 x 63.5
Walt Disney Feature Animation and
the Animation Research Library,
Burbank, California
[fig.131]

Study for the Walt Disney
film *Destino* c.1946
Mixed media on paper
on Masonite 50.5 x 63.5
Fundació Gala-Salvador Dalí, Figueres
[fig.128]

Study for the Walt Disney Film
Destino 1946
Pen and ink on paper 23.6 x 28.8
Walt Disney Feature Animation and
the Animation Research Library,
Burbank, California
[fig.121]

Study for the Walt Disney Film
Destino 1946
Pen and ink on paper 23.6 x 28.8
Walt Disney Feature Animation and
the Animation Research Library,
Burbank, California

Study for the Walt Disney film
Destino 1946
Pen and ink on paper mounted
on cardboard 34.9 x 42.5
Walt Disney Feature Animation and
the Animation Research Library,
Burbank, California

Study for the Walt Disney film
Destino 1946
Pen, ink and watercolour
on paper 30.6 x 25.5
Walt Disney Feature Animation and
the Animation Research Library,
Burbank, California
[fig.126]

Study for the Walt Disney film
Destino 1946
Pen, ink and watercolour
on paper 36.9 x 30.4
Walt Disney Feature Animation and
the Animation Research Library,
Burbank, California
[fig.120]

Study for the Walt Disney film
Destino 1946
Pencil on tracing paper 39.4 x 35.5
Fundació Gala-Salvador Dalí, Figueres
[fig.117]

Study for the Walt Disney film
Destino 1946
Pencil on tracing paper 35.4 x 43
Fundació Gala-Salvador Dalí, Figueres

Study for the Walt Disney film
Destino 1946
Pencil and ink on paper 35 x 42.3
Fundació Gala-Salvador Dalí, Figueres
[fig.118]

Study for the Walt Disney film
Destino 1946
Watercolour on paper 29.2 x 37.3
Walt Disney Feature Animation and
the Animation Research Library,
Burbank, California
[fig.127]

Study for the Walt Disney film
Destino 1946
Watercolour on paper 29.7 x 37
Walt Disney Feature Animation and
the Animation Research Library,
Burbank, California
[fig.124]

Study for the Walt Disney film
Destino 1946
Watercolour on paper
on cardboard 28.5 x 38
Walt Disney Feature Animation and
the Animation Research Library,
Burbank, California

26 storyboard drawings for the
Walt Disney film *Destino* 1946
Pen and ink on paper 20.3 x 22.8
Walt Disney Feature Animation and
the Animation Research Library,
Burbank, California
[fig.122 a–b, 125a–c]

Destino 1946 (completed 2003)
Animated film 7 min.
Disney Enterprises, Inc., Burbank

*Portrait of Pablo Picasso in the
Twenty-first Century* 1947
Oil on canvas 65.5 x 56
Fundació Gala-Salvador Dalí, Figueres
[fig.119]

Sentimental Colloquy 1948
Oil on canvas 26 x 47
Salvador Dalí Museum, Inc.,
St Petersburg, Florida
[fig.71]

Script for *The Wheelbarrow of Flesh* 1948
Typescript on paper 28 x 21.3
Fundació Gala-Salvador Dalí, Figueres

Portrait of Colonel Jack Warner 1951
Oil on canvas 106.2 x 126.2
Courtesy of the Syracuse University
Art Galleries
[fig.139]

*Portrait of Laurence Olivier in the Role
of Richard III* 1955
Oil on canvas 73.5 x 63
Fundació Gala-Salvador Dalí, Figueres
[fig.140]

*Study for Rhinocerontic Portrait of
Vermeer's 'Lacemaker'* 1955
Oil on canvas 25.1 x 22.3
Fundació Gala-Salvador Dalí, Figueres
[fig.145]

*Young Virgin Auto-Sodomized
by her own Chastity* 1954
Oil on canvas 40.5 x 30.5
Private collection
[fig.146]

*Paranoiac-Critical Painting of Vermeer's
'Lacemaker'* 1954–5
Oil on canvas on panel 27.1 x 22.1
The Solomon R. Guggenheim
Museum, New York. Anonymous Gift
[fig.142]

Rhapsodie Moderne (Les Sept Arts) 1957
Oil on canvas 84 x 114
From the collection of Jake Shafran,
London
[fig.96]

Chaos and Creation 1960
Video recordings transferred
to 16mm film, 16 min. 54 sec.
Fundació Gala-Salvador Dalí,
Figueres / Filmoteca de Catalunya,
Barcelona

*Impressions de la Haute Mongolie –
Hommage à Raymond Roussel* 1975
Film, 70 min.
Polyphon Film- und
Fernsehgesellschaft mbH

SALVADOR DALÍ 1904–1989
LUIS BUÑUEL 1900–1983

Un Chien andalou 1929
Film, 16 min.
Contemporary Films, London
[figs.47, 48, 50]

L'Age d'or 1930
Film, 63 min.
British Film Institute
[figs.55, 56]

LUIS BUÑUEL 1900–1983
Eating Sea Urchins 1930
Film
Filmoteca de Catalunya, Barcelona

Letter to Dalí with ideas for *Un Chien
andalou*, 22 March 1929
Typescript on paper 30 x 21
Pere Vehí Archive, Cadaqués

ANDY WARHOL 1928–1987
Screen Tests 1966
Two films, each 4 min.
Collection of The Andy Warhol
Museum, Pittsburgh. Contribution
The Andy Warhol Foundation for the
Visual Arts, Inc.
[fig.148]

Barcelona, Filmoteca de Catalunya
Barcelona, Fundació Suñol
Barcelona, Museu Nacional d'Art
   de Catalunya
Buffalo, Albright-Knox Art Gallery
Burbank, Buena Vista Television
Burbank, Disney Enterprises, Inc.
Burbank, Walt Disney Feature
   Animation and the Animation
   Research Library
La Coruña, Fundación Caixa Galicia
East Lansing, Kresge Art Museum,
   Michigan State University
Edinburgh, Scottish National Gallery
   of Modern Art
Figueres, Fundació Gala-Salvador Dalí
Hamburg, Polyphon Film- und
   Fernsehgesellschaft
Hartford, Wadsworth Atheneum
   Museum of Art
Houston, Menil Collection
London, British Film Institute
London, Contemporary Films
London, Tate
Madrid, Filmoteca Española.
   Fondo Buñuel
Madrid, Fundación Federico
   García Lorca
Madrid, Museo Nacional Centro
   de Arte Reina Sofía
Madrid, Museo Thyssen-Bornemisza
New York, Metropolitan Museum
   of Art
New York, The Museum of Modern Art
New York, The Solomon R.
   Guggenheim Museum
Ottawa, National Gallery of Canada
Paris, Bibliothèque Kandinsky/
   Centre de recherche et
   de documentation. Musée national
   d'art moderne
Paris, Centre Pompidou.
   Musée national d'art moderne/
   Centre de création industrielle
Philadelphia Museum of Art
Pittsburgh, The Andy Warhol Museum
Rotterdam, Museum Boijmans
   Van Beuningen
San Francisco Museum of Modern Art
St Petersburg, Florida, Salvador Dalí
   Museum, Inc.
Syracuse, Syracuse University
   Art Galleries
Venice, Peggy Guggenheim Collection

Private collections
Juan Abelló Collection, Madrid
H. Amigorena Collection, Paris
Collection Mr and Mrs Gilbert
   Kaplan, New York
Collection Viktor and
   Marianne Langen
Mugrabi Collection
Private collection. Courtesy Galerie
   Natalie Seroussi
Jake Shafran, London
Pere Vehí Archive, Cadaqués

Lenders and
Copyright credits

Index

Page numbers in **bold** type
refer to main entries.

Supporting Tate

Tate relies on a large number of supporters – individuals, foundations, companies and public sector sources – to enable it to deliver its programmes of activities, both on and off its gallery sites. This support is essential in order to acquire works of art for the Collection, run education, outreach and exhibition programmes, care for the Collection in storage and enable art to be displayed, both digitally and physically, inside and outside Tate. Your donation will make a real difference and enable others to enjoy Tate and its Collection both now and in the future. There are a variety of ways in which you can help support Tate and also benefit as a UK or US taxpayer.

Please contact us at:
The Development Office
Tate
Millbank
London SWIP 4RG
Tel: 020 7887 3937
Fax: 020 7887 8098

American Patrons of Tate
1285 6th Avenue (35th fl)
New York, NY 10019
USA
Tel: 001 212 713 8497
Fax: 001 212 713 8655

Donations
Donations, of whatever size, from individuals, companies and trusts are welcome, either to support particular areas of interest, or to contribute to general running costs.

Gifts of Shares
Since April 2000, we can accept gifts of quoted share and securities. These are not subject to capital gains tax. For higher rate taxpayers, a gift of shares saves income tax as well as capital gains tax. For further information please contact the Development Office.

Gift Aid
Through Gift Aid, you can provide significant additional revenue to Tate. Gift Aid applies to gifts of any size, whether regular or one-off, since we can claim back the tax on your charitable donation. Higher rate taxpayers are also able to claim additional personal tax relief. Contact us for further information and a Gift-Aid Declaration form.

Legacies
A legacy to Tate may take the form of a residual share of an estate, a specific cash sum or item of property such as a work of art. Legacies to Tate are free of Inheritance Tax, and help to secure a strong future for the Collection and galleries.

Offers in lieu of tax
Inheritance Tax can be satisfied by transferring to the Government a work of art of outstanding importance. In this case the amount of tax is reduced, and it can be made a condition of the offer that the work of art is allocated to Tate. Please contact us for details.

American Patrons of Tate
American Patrons of Tate is an independent charity based in New York that supports the work of Tate in the United Kingdom. It receives full tax exempt status from the IRS under section 501(c)(3) allowing United States taxpayers to receive tax deductions on gifts towards annual membership programmes, exhibitions, scholarship and capital projects. For more information contact the American Patrons of Tate office.

Charity Details
The Tate Gallery is an exempt charity; the Museums & Galleries Act 1992 added the Tate Gallery to the list of exempt charities defined in the 1960 Charities Act. Tate Members is a registered charity (number 313021). Tate Foundation is a registered charity (number 1085314).

The Jack Steinberg Charitable Trust
Hugh and Catherine Stevenson
John Studzinski
David and Linda Supino
The Government of Switzerland
Tate Friends
Carter and Mary Thacher
Insinger Townsley
The 29th May 1961 Charitable Trust
David and Emma Verey
Dinah Verey
The Vintners' Company
Clodagh and Leslie Waddington
Robert and Felicity Waley-Cohen
Gordon D. Watson
The Weston Family
Mr and Mrs Stephen Wilberding
Michael S. Wilson
Poju and Anita Zabludowicz
*and those donors who wish to
remain anonymous*

**TATE MODERN BENEFACTORS
AND MAJOR DONORS**
Abstract Select Limited
Howard and Roberta Ahmanson
The American Fund for the
    Tate Gallery
The Annenberg Foundation
The Art Fund
Arts Council England
Arts and Culture Foundation
    of North Rhine Westfalia
Lord and Lady Attenborough
The Estate of Arline Bage
The Estate of Tom Bendhem
Big Lottery Fund
The Charlotte Bonham-Carter
    Charitable Trust
Bettina Bonnefoy
Mr and Mrs Pontus Bonnier
Louise Bourgeois
Pierre Brahm
The Deborah Loeb Brice Foundation
Donald L. Bryant Jr Family
Melva Bucksbaum and
    Raymond Learsy
Canada House Arts Trust
Charities Advisory Trust
Ella Cisneros
Edwin C. Cohen
Sir Ronald and Lady Cohen
Alastair Cookson
The Dr V.J. Daniel Bequest
Dimitris Daskalopoulos
Julia W. Dayton
Gilbert and Janet de Botton
Ziba and Pierre de Weck
The Estate of Andre Deutsch
Sir Harry Djanogly
Mr and Mrs Doumar
Brooke Hayward Duchin
The Clore Duffield Foundation
Yelena Duncan
The Estate of Richard B. Fisher
Mimi Floback
Lynn Forester de Rothschild
Mr and Mrs Koenraad Foulon
Glenn R. Fuhrman
Kathy and Richard S. Fuld Jr
Gabo Trust for Sculpture Conservation
The Gapper Charitable Trust
Nanette Gehrig
Liz Gerring and Kirk Radke
Zak and Candida Gertler
The Getty Foundation
The Horace W. Goldsmith Foundation
Marian Goodman
Antony Gormley
Noam and Geraldine Gottesman
Mr and Mrs Jonathan Green

Calouste Gulbenkian Foundation
Mimi and Peter Haas
The Paul Hamlyn Foundation
Heritage Lottery Fund
Stanley and Gail Hollander
Leili and Johannes Huth
The Idlewild Trust
Institute for Foreign Cultural
    Relations Stuttgart
Angeliki Intzides
IPAC plc
The Italian Ministry of Foreign Affairs
    and the Italian Cultural Institute
    in London
Lord and Lady Jacobs
Stanley Thomas Johnson Foundation
Maurice S. Kanbar and the Murray
    and Isabella Rayburn Foundation
Stephen and Anna-Marie Kellen
Peter and Maria Kellner
Ellsworth Kelly Foundation
Ellen Kern
James and Clare Kirkman
C. Richard and Pamela Kramlich,
    The Kramlich Gallery
Henry R. Kravis Foundation, Inc.
The Kreitman Foundation
The Samuel H Kress Foundation
Leche Trust
Robert Lehman Foundation
The Leverhulme Trust
London Arts
Richard Long
Robert and Mary Looker
William Louis-Dreyfus
The Henry Luce Foundation
John Lyon's Charity
Sir Edwin and Lady Manton
Ministry of the Flemish Community
Solita and Steven Mishaan
Lucy Mitchell-Innes
Mondriaan Foundation, Amsterdam
The Henry Moore Foundation
Mary Moore
The Father John Munton Legacy
Guy and Marion Naggar
National Heritage Memorial Fund
Hartley Neel
Richard Neel
The Nomura Securities Co Ltd
Eileen Harris Norton
Ophiuchus SA
Outset Contemporary Art Fund
William Palmer
Yana and Stephen Peel
The Honorable Leon B
    and Mrs Cynthia Polsky
Presence Switzerland
Pro Helvetia
Karen and Eric Pulaski
Mr and Mrs John Rafter
Ramzy and Maya Rasamny
The Rayne Foundation
Julie and Don Reid
Barrie and Emmanuel Roman
The Judith Rothschild Foundation
Ken and Helen Rowe
Debra and Dennis Scholl
Michael and Melanie Sherwood
    Charitable Foundation
Harvey S. Shipley Miller
Peter Simon
John A. Smith and Vicky Hughes
Paul Smith and Pauline Denyer-Smith
Mr and Mrs Ramez Sousou
The Foundation for Sports
    and the Arts
The Freda Mary Snadow Bequest
Kimberly and Tord Stallvik
Tate International Council
Tate Members

Tate Patrons
Mr and Mrs A Alfred Taubman
David Teiger
Thames and Hudson
The Mary Joy Thomson Bequest
The Vandervell Foundation
Mr and Mrs Pyrros N Vardinoyannis
Andreas Waldburg-Wolfegg
Angela Westwater and David Meitus
Poju and Anita Zabludowicz
Shirly and Yigal Zilkha
*and those donors who wish to
remain anonymous*

Platinum Patrons
Beecroft Charitable Trust
John and Susan Burns
Melanie Clore
Pieter and Olga Dreesmann
Mr and Mrs Charles M. Hale
John A. Smith and Vicky Hughes
Peter and Maria Kellner
Mary Moore
Paul Myners
Catherine and Franck Petitgas
Mr and Mrs James Reed
Simon and Virginia Robertson
Mr and Mrs Harry Woolf
Anita Zabludowicz
and those who wish to remain anonymous

Gold Patrons
Paul-René Albertini
Pierre Brahm
Arpad Busson
Sir Trevor and Lady Chinn CVO
Alastair Cookson
Wendy Fisher
Nanette Gehrig
Sarah Griffin
Deborah Goldman
Birgid Hanson
Fiona Mactaggart
Pilar Ordovás
Mathew Prichard
Mr and Mrs David M. Shalit
Michael Wilson
Barbara Yerolemou
and those who wish to remain anonymous

Silver Patrons
Julian Agnew
Shane Akeroyd
Helen Alexander
Ryan Allen
Kate Anstruther
Zeev Aram
Giorgio Armani
Kiran Arora
The Lord Ashburton KG KCVO DL
Edgar Astaire
Daphne Astor
Christopher Baer
Jane Barker
Oliver Barker
Victoria Barnsley
Stephen Barry
Louise Barton
James M Bartos
Pamela Morgan Bell
Lord and Lady Bernstein
Madeleine, Countess of Bessborough
David and Janice Blackburn
Anthony Blee
George Bloch
Sir Alan Bowness CBE
Lena Boyle
Floyd Bradley
Ivor Braka
The Viscountess Bridgeman
Cornelis Broere

Dan Brooke
Benjamin Brown
John Burke
Michael Burrell
Marlene Burston
Dan Burt
Charles Butter
Elizabeth Capon
Peter Carew
Sir Richard Carew Pole OBE
Francis Carnwath
Lord Charles Cecil
Christina Chandris
Denise Cohen
Frank Cohen
Paul Collins
Terrence Collis
The Hon. Mrs Cynthia Colman
Sir Timothy Colman
Carole and Neville Conrad
Sonia Coode-Adams
Paul Cooke
Cynthia Corbett
Elizabeth Corob
Pilar Corrias
Tommaso Corvi-Mora
Bertrand Coste
Michael Cumming
James Curtis
Isobel Dalziel
Virginia Damtsa
Sir Howard Davies
Sir Simon J Day
John Deckoff
Chantal Defay Sheridan
Mollie Dent-Brocklehurst
Damon de Laszlo
Simon Dickinson
John Dorrance
Joanna Drew
Michelle D'Souza
Joan Edlis
Vangel Efthimiadou
Lord Egremont
John Erle-Drax
Stuart Evans
Gerard Faggionato
Tawna Farmer
Heather Farrar
Margaret Fenwick
Bryan Ferry
Ruth Finch
Sir Harry Fitzgibbons
Joscelyn Fox
Eric Franck
Robert Freeman
Stephen Friedman
Daniel Friel
Julia Fuller
Albert Fuss
Richard Gapper
Daniela Gareh
Candida Gertler
Lady Gibson of Penns
The Hon. Mr William Gibson
David Gill
Mark Glatman
Josefa Gonzalez
Sir Nicholas and Lady Goodison
Noam Gottesman
Penelope Govett
Andrew Graham
Gavin Graham
Martyn Gregory
Sir Ronald Grierson
Kate Grimond
Odile Grogan
Mr Haegy
Louise Hallett
Mrs Sue Hammerson OBE
Samantha Hampshire

Susan Hayden
Richard Hazlewood
Morven Heller
Ian Henderson-Russell
Lady Heseltine
Patsy Hickman
Robert Holden
Jonathan Horwich
John Huntingford
Rachel Hutson
Robin Philip Hyman
Michael Johnson
Peter Johnson
Henry Chester Jones
Jay Jopling
Brenda Josephs
Tracey Josephs
Gabrielle Jungels-Winkler
Isabella Kairis
Andrew Kalman
Dr Martin Kenig
David Ker
Simon Keswick
David Killick
Paolo Kind
James and Clare Kirkman
Brian Knox
Angeliki Koulakoglou
Sarah Kowitz
David Landau
Patricia Lankester
Simon Lee
Zachary Leonard
Gerald Levin
Leonard R. Lewis
Judith Licht
Ina Lindemann
Laura Lindsay
Claire Livingstone
Anders Ljungh
Barbara Lloyd
Gilbert Lloyd
George Loudon
Mark Loveday
Thomas Loyd
Marillyn Maklouf
Eskander and Fatima Maleki
Robert A. Mandell
Marcus Margulies
Lord Jonathan Marland
Brian Marsh
Janet E. Martin
Yaser Martini
Penny Mason
Barbara Meaker
Dr Robert Melville
Peter Meyer
Alfred Mignano
Victoria Miro
Jan Mol
Donald Moore
David Moore-Gwyn
Diana Morgenthau
Houston Morris
William Morrison
Stamatis Moskey
The Hon Marion Naggar
Richard Nagy
Warren Neidich
John Nickson and Simon Rew
Michael Nyman
Julian Opie
Desmond Page
Maureen Paley
Dominic Palfreyman
Michael Palin
Clare Pardy
Ingrid Persaud
Godfrey Pilkington
Oliver Prenn
Susan Prevezer QC